CD ROM

CD\ROM

THE
NEW
PAPYRUS

The current

and future

state of

the art.

FOREWORD BY WILLIAM H. GATES
EDITED BY STEVE LAMBERT AND SUZANNE ROPIEQUET

MICROSOFT
PRESS

PUBLISHED BY
Microsoft Press
A Division of Microsoft Corporation
16011 N.E. 36th, Box 97017, Redmond, WA 98073-9717

Library of Congress Cataloging in Publication Data
I. Lambert, Steve, 1945 – . II. Ropiequet, Suzanne, 1954 – . III. Title.
CD ROM. The New Papyrus.
Includes index.
1. Compact discs. 2. Optical storage devices.
TK7882.C56N49 1986   004.5'3   86-2369
ISBN 0-914845-74-8

Printed and bound in the United States of America.

1 2 3 4 5 6 7 8 9 RRDRRD 8 9 0 9 8 7 6

Distributed to the book trade in the United States by Harper and Row.

Distributed to the book trade in Canada by General Publishing Company, Ltd.

Distributed to the book trade outside the United States and Canada
by Penguin Books Ltd.

Penguin Books Ltd., Harmondsworth, Middlesex, England
Penguin Books Australia Ltd., Ringwood, Victoria, Australia
Penguin Books N. Z. Ltd., 182-190 Wairau Road, Auckland 10, New Zealand

British Cataloging in Publication Data available

P R E F A C E

CD ROM is a revolutionary information storage medium, much as was papyrus when it replaced stone, clay, and wood as surfaces on which early Egyptians recorded significant events in their lives.

Our *New Papyrus* is a compilation of articles written by people who have recognized the potential of CD ROM and have become involved in this new technology. Many of our contributors are already well known in the fields of computer software, computer hardware, database distribution, video production, and book publishing. Others are bringing fresh new ideas and skills that will help define and mold an entirely new field.

We would like to thank all those who contributed articles and advice. May each of you prosper. Because of time and space limitations, however, not every piece submitted could be published. Our special thanks go to those who stuck with us during the writing and revision, only to be omitted at the end.

In editing, we attempted to preserve the individual style of each author while also maintaining a house style for the spelling and usage of terms that have yet to be standardized.

Appendix A is a list of the people who have been so generous with their time and talents. Appendix B lists the companies we contacted while compiling *The New Papyrus*. Most of these individuals and companies will gladly provide additional information on their services.

Although the use of CD ROM for the storage and retrieval of massive personal databases is new, the concept has been around for years. Vannevar Bush, director of the U.S. Office of Scientific Research and Development during World War II, wrote an article in 1945 urging scientists to apply the knowledge gained during the war toward research in peaceful areas. In this article, he discussed his vision of future methods of making the world's store of knowledge available to all. So many people called our attention to this article, originally published by *Atlantic Monthly*, that we obtained permission and have reprinted here all but the introduction. Bearing in mind how farfetched many of these ideas would have seemed in 1945, and how commonplace they are now, will perhaps help us take today's dreams more seriously.—*The Editors*

CONTENTS

viii

by William H. Gates

Microsoft is extremely excited about the vast potential of this emerging CD ROM technology for a number of reasons. For one thing, CD ROM is quite different from any other medium in existence, whether it be television, movies, video, slides, audio, books, or personal computers. In fact, one might look at CD ROM as the summation or combination of almost all of these. But what is it that makes CD ROM so special? On the technical side, because all the information is stored in digital form, the medium is similar to floppy disks, hard disks, and other magnetic media. However, the transportable nature of the compact disc and the cost per bit put CD ROM in a class by itself.

The CD ROM has a thousand times the storage capacity of a floppy disk, yet the costs of the CD ROM disc and the floppy are nearly equal. In the computer industry, we often improve things by a factor of 2 or 3 and the new applications are considered evolutionary. But a one thousandfold increase in storage capacity enables us to create rich and multifaceted new applications.

Microsoft is so committed to CD ROM that we have formed a special division within the company just to focus on this new opportunity.

A floppy disk can store only 5 real-life images, but a single CD can store 5000 such images. The floppy can store only 3 seconds of high-quality audio, but the CD can store an hour. It's this remarkable power of the CD ROM disc to digitally store video images, audio, data, and computer code in any combination that underscores its vast potential.

In a few years, after the CD ROM becomes commonplace, anyone looking back at the information, education, or entertainment applications of today will understand the limited appeal they have had. The combination of CD ROM with a microcomputer creates a medium that potentially is more interactive than any previous consumer product. We believe this interaction will result in a product that will stimulate and enrich a person in a manner that is far superior to passive systems such as television.

CD ROM will proliferate in two ways, as a peripheral to existing personal computers and as the heart of a new "viewer" device which will be more similar to the stereo or television you have in your home than to a computer. It is essential from the outset that we in the industry are careful not

xii

to label this viewer a computer. It simply isn't one, any more than your VCR, dishwasher, and telephone are computers. From the consumer's standpoint, the viewer will consist of a CD ROM player, a screen, and a pointing device—that's all. The pointing device will allow a person to select information of interest, display images and text, and play the sound contained on the compact disc inserted in the player. Unlike the CD ROM players connected to personal computers, these viewers will probably be portable and have a flat screen.

The separation of these two—the personal computer and the viewer—isn't quite as great as it might seem at first. CD ROM versions of dictionaries, encyclopedias, almanacs, and maps will appeal to both markets. Entertainment applications will appeal primarily to the viewer market. Specialized databases on CD ROM will appeal most to the personal computer market. Eventually, many people who have the viewers may want to buy a keyboard, a printer, or even a computer modem to help make the most of the information and resources at their disposal on the viewer. Pursuing and developing both of these market areas is critical to achieving the full potential of CD.

CD ROM will proliferate in two ways, as a peripheral to existing personal computers and as the heart of a new "viewer" device which will be more similar to the stereo or television you have in your home than to a computer.

The reason that the CD ROM player is so cheap is that it shares so much in common with a CD audio player. In fact, CD ROM wasn't designed as a product on its own but is an offshoot of the decision of Sony and Philips to use optical digital storage for music to create the very successful, high-quality audio product we all know today as the Compact Disc. As a result of the close relation of the two, most CD ROM players will have CD audio built into them as a subset. The millions of consumers who have bought CD audio players have encouraged the technology to mature quickly to the point that music players now sell for less than $200. CD ROM comes at a time when the price of memory and other chips has fallen very dramatically, so it is very likely that this new technology will be affordable to a large market.

Creating a multimedia CD ROM is an exciting challenge that draws upon a broad range of skills and resources from the computer, entertainment, publishing, and broadcast industries. A CD ROM product is so multifaceted it cannot be produced in isolation by one person. The development of CD ROMs requires a team effort, a blending of skills from a variety of fields. In order to make the most of the potential of CD ROM, it is essential that we work together from the outset. Companies from all these fields must contribute to the standards and tools that are the foundation upon which this new industry will be built. There is no doubt that they will be affected by CD ROM.

We believe that CD ROM enables us to create something that does compete—and even goes beyond our traditional ways of being entertained, of learning, and of gathering information.

In the same way that the first TV shows consisted mainly of someone standing in front of the camera and reading a radio script, the initial efforts in CD ROM will not stretch the medium to its limit. However, already we can envision a wide array of fascinating multimedia CD ROM products. Maps, catalogs, reference works, training courses, and educational books undoubtedly will shift to this new medium. A single CD can hold an incredible amount of information—sports, medicine, music, movies, art—the possibilities are almost limitless. Even such ordinary items as telephone directories, cookbooks, travel guides, and language courses may someday be more effective and more common in CD ROM than in print form.

Microsoft has formed a group within the company just to focus on this new opportunity. We have always believed that some sort of "intelligent" software-controlled device would address the home market. And we knew it would have to compete with books, TV, and board games in order to command the consumers' time and interest. We believe that CD ROM enables us to create something that does compete—and even goes beyond our traditional ways of being entertained, of learning, and of gathering information.

One of the goals of this book is to encourage people from as many different fields as possible to participate in the development of this new technology. Indeed, the book itself is the result of a high degree of cooperation among individuals from many different fields. It is the blending of the thoughts and experiences of those who have already perceived CD ROM's potential. I hope, after reading this book, that you will share our enthusiasm for the possibilities that lie ahead.

INTRODUCTION

As We May Think

This article was originally published in July, 1945. It is reprinted here with permission of *The Atlantic Monthly*.

by Vannevar Bush

Of what lasting benefit has been man's use of science and of the new instruments which his research brought into existence? First, they have increased his control of his material environment. They have improved his food, his clothing, his shelter; they have increased his security and released him partly from the bondage of bare existence. They have given him increased knowledge of his own biological processes so that he has had a progressive freedom from disease and an increased span of life. They are illuminating the interactions of his physiological and psychological functions, giving promise of an improved mental health.

Consider a future device for individual use, which is a sort of mechanized private file and library. It needs a name, and, to coin one at random, "memex" will do.

Science has provided the swiftest communication between individuals; it has provided a record of ideas and has enabled man to manipulate and to make extracts from that record so that knowledge evolves and endures throughout the life of a race rather than that of an individual.

There is a growing mountain of research. But there is increased evidence that we are being bogged down today as specialization extends. The investigator is staggered by the findings and conclusions of thousands of other workers—conclusions which he cannot find time to grasp, much less to remember, as they appear. Yet specialization becomes increasingly necessary for progress, and the effort to bridge between disciplines is correspondingly superficial.

Professionally, our methods of transmitting and reviewing the results of research are generations old and by now are totally inadequate for their purposes. If the aggregate time spent in writing scholarly works and in reading them could be evaluated, the ratio between these amounts of time might well be startling. Those who conscientiously attempt to keep abreast of current thought, even in restricted fields, by close and continuous reading might well shy away from an examination calculated to show how much of the previous month's efforts could be produced on call. Mendel's concept of the laws of genetics was lost to the world for a generation because his publication did not reach the few who were capable of grasping and extending it; and this sort of catastrophe is undoubtedly being repeated all about us, as truly significant attainments become lost in the mass of the inconsequential.

4

The difficulty seems to be not so much that we publish unduly in view of the extent and variety of present-day interests, but rather that publication has been extended far beyond our present ability to make real use of the record. The summation of human experience is being expanded at a prodigious rate, and the means we use for threading through the consequent maze to the momentarily important item is the same as was used in the days of square-rigged ships.

But there are signs of a change as new and powerful instrumentalities come into use. Photocells capable of seeing things in a physical sense, advanced photography which can record what is seen or even what is not, thermionic tubes capable of controlling potent forces under the guidance of less power than a mosquito uses to vibrate his wings, cathode ray tubes rendering visible an occurrence so brief that by comparison a microsecond is a long time, relay combinations which will carry out involved sequences of movements more reliably than any human operator and thousands of times as fast—there are plenty of mechanical aids with which to effect a transformation in scientific records.

Publication has been extended far beyond our present ability to make real use of the record.

Two centuries ago Leibnitz invented a calculating machine which embodied most of the essential features of recent keyboard devices, but it could not then come into use. The economics of the situation were against it: the labor involved in constructing it, before the days of mass production, exceeded the labor to be saved by its use, since all it could accomplish could be duplicated by sufficient use of pencil and paper. Moreover, it would have been subject to frequent breakdown, so that it could not have been depended upon; for at that time and long after, complexity and unreliability were synonymous.

Babbage, even with remarkably generous support for his time, could not produce his great arithmetical machine. His idea was sound enough, but construction and maintenance costs were then too heavy. Had a Pharaoh been given detailed and explicit designs of an automobile, and had he understood them completely, it would have taxed the resources of his kingdom to have fashioned the thousands of parts for a single car, and that car would have broken down on the first trip to Giza.

Machines with interchangeable parts can now be constructed with great economy of effort. In spite of much complexity, they perform reliably. Witness the humble typewriter, or the movie camera, or the automobile. Electrical contacts have ceased to stick—note the automatic telephone exchange, which has hundreds of thousands of such contacts, and yet is reliable. A spider web of metal, sealed in a thin glass container, a wire heated to a brilliant glow, in short, the thermionic tube of radio sets, is made by the hundred million, tossed about in packages, plugged into sockets—and it works! Its gossamer parts, the precise location and alignment involved in its construction, would have occupied a master craftsman of the guild for months; now it is built for thirty cents. The world has arrived at an age of cheap complex devices of great reliability; and something is bound to come of it.

The Silver Image

A record, if it is to be useful to science, must be continuously extended, it must be stored, and above all it must be consulted. Today we make the record conventionally by writing and photography, followed by printing; but we also record on film, on wax disks, and on magnetic wires. Even if utterly new recording procedures do not appear, these present ones are certainly in the process of modification and extension.

Certainly progress in photography is not going to stop. Faster material and lenses, more automatic cameras, finer-grained sensitive compounds to allow an extension of the minicamera idea, are all imminent. Let us project this trend ahead to a logical, if not inevitable, outcome. The camera hound of the future wears on his forehead a lump a little larger than a walnut. It takes pictures 3 millimeters square, later to be projected or enlarged, which after all involves only a factor of 10 beyond present practice. The lens is of universal focus, down to any distance accommodated by the unaided eye, simply because it is of short focal length. There is a built-in photocell on the walnut such as we now have on at least one camera, which automatically adjusts exposure for a wide range of illumination. There is film in the walnut for a hundred exposures, and the spring for operating its shutter and shifting its film is wound once and for all when the film clip is inserted. It produces its result in full color. It may well be stereoscopic, and record with two spaced glass eyes, for striking improvements in stereoscopic techniques are just around the corner.

The cord which trips its shutter may extend down a man's sleeve within easy reach of his fingers. A quick squeeze, and the picture is taken. On a pair of ordinary glasses is a square of fine lines near the top of one lens, where it is out of the way of ordinary vision. When an object appears in that square, it is lined up for its picture. As the scientist of the future moves about the laboratory or the field, every time he looks at something worthy of the record, he trips the shutter and in it goes, without even an audible click. Is this all fantastic? The only fantastic thing about it is the idea of making as many pictures as would result from its use.

6

Will there be dry photography? It is already here in two forms. When Brady made his Civil War pictures, the plate had to be wet at the time of exposure. Now it has to be wet during development instead. In the future, perhaps it need not be wetted at all. There have long been films impregnated with diazo dyes which form a picture without development, so that it is already there as soon as the camera has been operated. An exposure to ammonia gas destroys the unexposed dye, and the picture can then be taken out into the light and examined. The process is now slow, but someone may speed it up, and it has no grain difficulties such as now keep photographic researchers busy. Often it would be advantageous to be able to snap the camera and to look at the picture immediately.

A record, if it is to be useful to science, must be continuously extended, it must be stored, and above all it must be consulted.

Another process now in use is also slow, and more or less clumsy. For fifty years impregnated papers have been used which turn dark at every point where an electrical contact touches them, by reason of the chemical change thus produced in an iodine compound included in the paper. They have been used to make records, for a pointer moving across them can leave a trail behind. If the electrical potential on the pointer is varied as it moves, the line becomes light or dark in accordance with the potential.

This scheme is now used in facsimile transmission. The pointer draws a set of closely spaced lines across the paper one after another. As it moves, its potential is varied in accordance with a varying current received over wires from a distant station, where these variations are produced by a photocell which is similarly scanning a picture. At every instant the darkness of the line being drawn is made equal to the darkness of the point on the picture being observed by the photocell. Thus, when the whole picture has been covered, a replica appears at the receiving end.

A scene itself can be just as well looked over line-by-line by the photocell in this way as can a photograph of the scene. This whole apparatus constitutes a camera, with the added feature, which can be dispensed with if desired, of making its picture at a distance. It is slow, and the picture is poor in detail. Still, it does give another process of dry photography, in which the picture is finished as soon as it is taken.

It would be a brave man who would predict that such a process will always remain clumsy, slow, and faulty in detail. Television equipment today transmits sixteen reasonably good pictures a second, and it involves only two essential differences from the process described above. For one, the record is made by a moving beam of electrons rather than a moving pointer, for the reason that an electron beam can sweep across the picture very rapidly indeed. The other difference involves merely the use of a screen which glows momentarily when the electrons hit, rather than a chemically treated paper or film which is permanently altered. This speed is necessary in television, for motion pictures rather than stills are the object.

Use chemically treated film in place of the glowing screen, allow the apparatus to transmit one picture only rather than a succession, and use a rapid camera for dry photography. The treated film needs to be far faster in action than present examples, but it probably could be. More serious is the objection that this scheme would involve putting the film inside a vacuum chamber, for electron beams behave normally only in such a rarefied environment. This difficulty could be avoided by allowing the electron beam to play on one side of a partition, and by pressing the film against the other side, if this partition were such as to allow the electrons to go through perpendicular to its surface, and to prevent them from spreading out sideways. Such partitions, in crude form, could certainly be constructed, and they will hardly hold up the general development.

Like dry photography, microphotography still has a long way to go. The basic scheme of reducing the size of the record, and examining it by projection rather than directly, has possibilities too great to be ignored. The combination of optical projection and photographic reduction is already producing some results in microfilm for scholarly purposes, and the potentialities are highly suggestive. Today, with microfilm, reductions by a linear factor of 20 can be employed and still produce full clarity when the material is re-enlarged for examination. The limits are set by the graininess of the film, the excellence of the optical system, and the efficiency of the light sources employed. All of these are rapidly improving.

Even the modern great library is not generally consulted; it is nibbled at by a few.

Assume a linear ratio of 100 for future use. Consider film of the same thickness as paper, although thinner film will certainly be usable. Even under these conditions there would be a total factor of 10,000 between the bulk of the ordinary record in books and its microfilm replica. The *Encyclopaedia Britannica* could be reduced to the volume of a matchbox. The library of a million volumes could be compressed into one end of a desk. If the human race has produced since the invention of movable type a total record, in the form of magazines, newspapers, books, tracts, advertising blurbs, correspondence, having a volume corresponding to a billion books, the whole affair, assembled and compressed, could be lugged off in a moving van. Mere compression, of course, is not enough; one needs not only to make and store a record but also be able to consult it, and this aspect of the matter comes later. Even the modern great library is not generally consulted; it is nibbled at by a few.

8

Compression is important, however, when it comes to costs. The material for the microfilm *Britannica* would cost a nickel, and it could be mailed anywhere for a cent. What would it cost to print a million copies? To print a sheet of newspaper, in a large edition, costs a small fraction of a cent. The entire material of the *Britannica* in reduced microfilm form would go on a sheet eight and one-half by eleven inches. Once it is available, with the photographic reproduction methods of the future, duplicates in large quantities could probably be turned out for a cent apiece beyond the cost of materials. The preparation of the original copy? That introduces the next aspect of the subject.

Vocoder

To make the record, we now push a pencil or tap a typewriter. Then comes the process of digestion and correction, followed by an intricate process of typesetting, printing, and distribution. To consider the first stage of the procedure, will the author of the future cease writing by hand or typewriter and talk directly to the record? He does so indirectly, by talking to a stenographer or a wax cylinder; but the elements are all present if he wishes to have his talk directly produce a typed record. All he needs to do is to take advantage of existing mechanisms and to alter his language.

Whenever logical processes of thought are employed there is an opportunity for the machine.

At a recent World Fair a machine called a Voder was shown. A girl stroked its keys and it emitted recognizable speech. No human vocal cords entered into the procedure at any point; the keys simply combined some electrically produced vibrations and passed these on to a loudspeaker. In the Bell Laboratories there is the converse of this machine, called a Vocoder. The loudspeaker is replaced by a microphone, which picks up sound. Speak to it, and the corresponding keys move. This may be one element of the postulated system.

The other element is found in the stenotype, that somewhat disconcerting device encountered usually at public meetings. A girl strokes its keys languidly and looks about the room and sometimes at the speaker with a disquieting gaze. From it emerges a typed strip which records in a phonetically simplified language a record of what the speaker is supposed to have said. Later this strip is retyped into ordinary language, for in its nascent form it is intelligible only to the initiated. Combine these two elements, let the Vocoder run the stenotype, and the result is a machine which types when talked to.

Our present languages are not especially adapted to this sort of mechanization, it is true. It is strange that the inventors of universal languages have not seized upon the idea of producing one which better fitted the technique for transmitting and recording speech. Mechanization may yet force the issue, especially in the scientific field; whereupon scientific jargon would become still less intelligible to the layman.

One can now picture a future investigator in his laboratory. His hands are free, and he is not anchored. As he moves about and observes, he photographs and comments. Time is automatically recorded to tie the two records together. If he goes into the field, he may be connected by radio to his recorder. As he ponders over his notes in the evening, he again talks his comments into the record. His typed record, as well as his photographs, may both be in miniature, so that he projects them for examination.

Much needs to occur, however, between the collection of data and observations, the extraction of parallel material from the existing record, and the final insertion of new material into the general body of the common record. For mature thought there is no mechanical substitute. But creative thought and essentially repetitive thought are very different things. For the latter there are, and may be, powerful mechanical aids.

Napier's Bones Revisited

Adding a column of figures is a repetitive thought process, and it was long ago properly relegated to the machine. True, the machine is sometimes controlled by a keyboard, and thought of a sort enters in reading the figures and poking the corresponding keys, but even this is avoidable. Machines have been made which will read typed figures by photocells and then depress the corresponding keys; these are combinations of photocells for scanning the type, electric circuits for sorting the consequent variations, and relay circuits for interpreting the result into the action of solenoids to pull the keys down.

All this complication is needed because of the clumsy way in which we have learned to write figures. If we recorded them positionally, simply by the configuration of a set of dots on a card, the automatic reading mechanism would become comparatively simple. In fact, if the dots are holes, we have the punched-card machine long ago produced by Hollorith for the purposes of the census, and now used throughout business. Some types of complex businesses could hardly operate without these machines.

10

Adding is only one operation. To perform arithmetical computation involves also subtraction, multiplication, and division, and in addition some method for temporary storage of results, removal from storage for further manipulation, and recording of final results by printing. Machines for these purposes are now of two types: keyboard machines for accounting and the like, manually controlled for the insertion of data, and usually automatically controlled as far as the sequence of operations is concerned; and punched-card machines in which separate operations are usually delegated to a series of machines, and the cards then transferred bodily from one to another. Both forms are very useful; but as far as complex computations are concerned, both are still in embryo.

Rapid electrical counting appeared soon after the physicists found it desirable to count cosmic rays. For their own purposes the physicists promptly constructed thermionic-tube equipment capable of counting electrical impulses at the rate of 100,000 a second. The advanced arithmetical machines of the future will be electrical in nature, and they will perform at 100 times present speeds, or more.

Moreover, they will be far more versatile than present commercial machines, so that they may readily be adapted for a wide variety of operations. They will be controlled by a control card or film, they will select their own data and manipulate it in accordance with the instructions thus inserted, they will perform complex arithmetical computations at exceedingly high speed, and they will record results in such form as to be readily available for distribution or for later further manipulation. Such machines will have enormous appetites. One of them will take instructions and data from a whole roomful of people armed with simple keyboard punches, and will deliver sheets of computed results every few minutes. There will always be plenty of things to compute in the detailed affairs of millions of people doing complicated things.

The repetitive processes of thought are not confined, however, to matters of arithmetic and statistics. In fact, every time one combines and records facts in accordance with established logical processes, the creative aspect of thinking is concerned only with the selection of the data and the process to be employed, and the manipulation thereafter is repetitive in nature and hence a fit matter to be relegated to the machines. Not so much has been done along these lines, beyond the bounds of arithmetic, as might be done, primarily because of the economics of the situation. The needs of business, and the extensive market obviously waiting, assured the advent of mass-produced arithmetical machines just as soon as production methods were sufficiently advanced.

11

With machines for advanced analysis, no such situation existed; for there was and is no extensive market; the users of advanced methods of manipulating data are a very small part of the population. There are, however, machines for solving differential equations—and functional and integral equations, for that matter. There are many special machines, such as the harmonic synthesizer which predicts the tides. There will be many more, appearing certainly first in the hands of the scientist and in small numbers.

There may be millions of fine thoughts, all encased within stone walls of acceptable architectural form; but if the scholar can get at only one a week by diligent search, his syntheses are not likely to keep up with the current scene.

If scientific reasoning were limited to the logical processes of arithmetic, we should not get far in our understanding of the physical world. One might as well attempt to grasp the game of poker entirely by the use of the mathematics of probability. The abacus, with its beads strung on parallel wires, led the Arabs to positional numeration and the concept of zero many centuries before the rest of the world; and it was a useful tool—so useful that it still exists.

It is a far cry from the abacus to the modern keyboard accounting machine. It will be an equal step to the arithmetical machine of the future. But even this new machine will not take the scientist where he needs to go. Relief must be secured from laborious detailed manipulation of higher mathematics as well, if the users of it are to free their brains for something more than repetitive detailed transformations in accordance with established rules. A mathematician is not a man who can readily manipulate figures; often he cannot. He is not even a man who can readily perform the transformations of equations by the use of calculus. He is primarily an individual who is skilled in the use of symbolic logic on a high plane, and especially he is a man of intuitive judgment in the choice of the manipulative processes he employs.

All else he should be able to turn over to his mechanic, just as confidently as he turns over the propelling of his car to the intricate mechanism under the hood. Only then will mathematics be practically effective in bringing the growing knowledge of atomistics to the useful solution of the advanced problems of chemistry, metallurgy, and biology. For this reason there will come more machines to handle advanced mathematics for the scientist. Some of them will be sufficiently bizarre to suit the most fastidious connoisseur of the present artifacts of civilization.

The Perpetual Auditor

The scientist, however, is not the only person who manipulates data and examines the world about him by the use of logical processes, although he sometimes preserves this appearance by adopting into the fold anyone who becomes logical, much in the manner in which a British labor leader is elevated to knighthood. Whenever logical processes of thought are employed—that is, whenever thought for a time runs along an accepted groove—there is an opportunity for the machine. Formal logic used to be a keen instrument in the hands of the teacher in his trying of students' souls. It is readily possible to construct a machine which will manipulate premises in accordance with formal logic, simply by the clever use of relay circuits. Put a set of premises into such a device and turn the crank, and it will readily pass out conclusion after conclusion, all in accordance with logical law, and with no more slips than would be expected by a keyboard adding machine.

Logic can become enormously difficult, and it would undoubtedly be well to produce more assurance in its use. The machines for higher analysis have usually been equation solvers. Ideas are beginning to appear for equation transformers, which will rearrange the relationship expressed by an equation in accordance with strict and rather advanced logic. Progress is inhibited by the exceedingly crude way in which mathematicians express their relationships. They employ a symbolism which grew like Topsy and has little consistency; a strange fact in that most logical field.

A new symbolism, probably positional, must apparently precede the reduction of mathematical transformations to machine processes. Then, on beyond the strict logic of the mathematician, lies the application of logic in everyday affairs. We may some day click off arguments on a machine with the same assurance that we now enter sales on a cash register. But the machine of logic will not look like a cash register, even of the streamlined model.

So much for the manipulation of ideas and their insertion into the record. Thus far we seem to be worse off than before—for we can enormously extend the record; yet even in its present bulk we can hardly consult it. This is a much larger matter than merely the extraction of data for the purposes of scientific research; it involves the entire process by which man profits by his inheritance of acquired knowledge. The prime action of use is selection, and here we are halting indeed. There may be millions of fine thoughts, and the account of the experience on which they are based, all encased within stone walls of acceptable architectural form; but if the scholar can get at only one a week by diligent search, his syntheses are not likely to keep up with the current scene.

Creative thought and essentially repetitive thought are very different things. For the latter there are, and may be, powerful mechanical aids.

Selection, in this broad sense, is a stone adze in the hands of a cabinet-maker. Yet, in a narrow sense and in other areas, something has already been done mechanically on selection. The personnel officer of a factory drops a stack of a few thousand employee cards into a selecting machine, sets a code in accordance with an established convention, and produces in a short time a list of all employees who live in Trenton and know Spanish. Even such devices are much too slow when it comes, for example, to matching a set of fingerprints with one of five million on file. Selection devices of this sort will soon be speeded up from their present rate of reviewing data at a few hundred a minute. By the use of photocells and microfilm they will survey items at the rate of a thousand a second, and will print out duplicates of those selected.

This process, however, is simple selection: it proceeds by examining in turn every one of a large set of items, and by picking out those which have certain specified characteristics. There is another form of selection best illustrated by the automatic telephone exchange. You dial a number and the machine selects and connects just one of a million possible stations. It does not run over them all. It pays attention only to a class given by a first digit, then only to a subclass of this given by the second digit, and so on; and thus proceeds rapidly and almost unerringly to the selected station. It requires a few seconds to make the selection, although the process could be speeded up if increased speed were economically warranted. If necessary, it could be made extremely fast by substituting thermionic-tube switching for mechanical switching, so that the full selection could be made in one one-hundredth of a second. No one would wish to spend the money necessary to make this change in the telephone system, but the general idea is applicable elsewhere.

Take the prosaic problem of the great department store. Every time a charge sale is made, there are a number of things to be done. The inventory needs to be revised, the salesman needs to be given credit for the sale, the general accounts need an entry, and, most important, the customer needs to be charged. A central records device has been developed in which much of this work is done conveniently. The salesman places on a stand the customer's identification card, his own card, and the card taken from the article sold—all punched cards. When he pulls a lever, contacts are made through the holes, machinery at a central point makes the necessary computations and entries, and the proper receipt is printed for the salesman to pass to the customer.

14

But there may be 10,000 charge customers doing business with the store, and before the full operation can be completed someone has to select the right card and insert it at the central office. Now rapid selection can slide just the proper card into position in an instant or two, and return it afterward. Another difficulty occurs, however. Someone must read a total on the card, so that the machine can add its computed item to it. Conceivably the cards might be of the dry photography type I have described. Existing totals could then be read by photocell, and the new total entered by an electron beam.

The cards may be in miniature, so that they occupy little space. They must move quickly. They need not be transferred far, but merely into position so that the photocell and recorder can operate on them. Positional dots can enter the data. At the end of the month a machine can readily be made to read these and to print an ordinary bill. With tube selection, in which no mechanical parts are involved in the switches, little time need be occupied in bringing the correct card into use—a second should suffice for the entire operation. The whole record on the card may be made by magnetic dots on a steel sheet if desired, instead of dots to be observed optically, following the scheme by which Poulsen long ago put speech on a magnetic wire. This method has the advantage of simplicity and ease of erasure. By using photography, however, one can arrange to project the record in enlarged form, and at a distance by using the process common in television equipment.

One can consider rapid selection of this form and distance projection for other purposes. To be able to key one sheet of a million before an operator in a second or two, with the possibility of then adding notes thereto, is suggestive in many ways. It might even be of use in libraries, but that is another story. At any rate, there are now some interesting combinations possible. One might, for example, speak to a microphone, in the manner described in connection with the speech-controlled typewriter, and thus make his selections. It would certainly beat the usual file clerk.

Memex

The real heart of the matter of selection, however, goes deeper than a lag in the adoption of mechanisms by libraries, or a lack of development of devices for their use. Our ineptitude in getting at the record is largely caused by the artificiality of systems of indexing. When data of any sort are placed in storage, they are filed alphabetically or numerically, and information is found (when it is) by tracing it down from subclass to subclass. It can be in only one place, unless duplicates are used; one has to have rules as to which path will locate it, and the rules are cumbersome. Having found one item, moreover, one has to emerge from the system and re-enter on a new path.

15

The human mind operates by association. With one item in its grasp, it snaps instantly to the next that is suggested by the association of thoughts, in accordance with some intricate web of trails carried by the cells of the brain.

The human mind does not work that way. It operates by association. With one item in its grasp, it snaps instantly to the next that is suggested by the association of thoughts, in accordance with some intricate web of trails carried by the cells of the brain. It has other characteristics, of course; trails that are not frequently followed are prone to fade, items are not fully permanent, memory is transitory. Yet the speed of action, the intricacy of trails, the detail of mental pictures, is awe-inspiring beyond all else in nature.

Man cannot hope fully to duplicate this mental process artificially, but he certainly ought to be able to learn from it. In minor ways he may even improve, for his records have relative permanency. The first idea, however, to be drawn from the analogy concerns selection. Selection by association, rather than by indexing, may yet be mechanized. One cannot hope thus to equal the speed and flexibility with which the mind follows an associative trail, but it should be possible to beat the mind decisively in regard to the permanence and clarity of the items resurrected from storage.

Consider a future device for individual use, which is a sort of mechanized private file and library. It needs a name, and, to coin one at random, "memex" will do. A memex is a device in which an individual stores his books, records, and communications, and which is mechanized so that it may be consulted with exceeding speed and flexibility. It is an enlarged intimate supplement to his memory.

It consists of a desk, and while it can presumably be operated from a distance, it is primarily the piece of furniture at which he works. On the top are slanting translucent screens, on which material can be projected for convenient reading. There is a keyboard, and sets of buttons and levers. Otherwise it looks like an ordinary desk.

In one end is the stored material. The matter of bulk is well taken care of by improved microfilm. Only a small part of the interior of the memex is devoted to storage, the rest to mechanism. Yet if the user inserted 5000 pages of material a day it would take him hundreds of years to fill the repository, so he can be profligate and enter material freely.

16

Our methods of transmitting and reviewing the results of research are generations old and by now are totally inadequate for their purposes.

Most of the memex contents are purchased on microfilm ready for insertion. Books of all sorts, pictures, current periodicals, newspapers, are thus obtained and dropped into place. Business correspondence takes the same path. And there is provision for direct entry. On the top of the memex is a transparent platen. On this are placed longhand notes, photographs, memoranda, all sorts of things. When one is in place, the depression of a lever causes it to be photographed onto the next blank space in a section of the memex film, dry photography being employed.

There is, of course, provision for consultation of the record by the usual scheme of indexing. If the user wishes to consult a certain book, he taps its code on the keyboard, and the title page of the book promptly appears before him, projected onto one of his viewing positions. Frequently used codes are mnemonic, so that he seldom consults his code book; but when he does, a single tap of a key projects it for his use. Moreover, he has supplemental levers. On deflecting one of these levers to the right he runs through the book before him, each paper in turn being projected at a speed which just allows a recognizing glance at each. If he deflects it further to the right, he steps through the book 10 pages at a time; still further at 100 pages at a time. Deflection to the left gives him the same control backwards.

A special button transfers him immediately to the first page of the index. Any given book of his library can thus be called up and consulted with far greater facility than if it were taken from a shelf. As he has several projection positions, he can leave one item in position while he calls up another. He can add marginal notes and comments, taking advantage of one possible type of dry photography, and it could even be arranged so that he can do this by a stylus scheme, such as is now employed in the telautograph seen in railroad waiting rooms, just as though he had the physical page before him.

All this is conventional, except for the projection forward of present-day mechanisms and gadgetry. It affords an immediate step, however, to associative indexing, the basic idea of which is a provision whereby any item may be caused at will to select immediately and automatically another. This is the essential feature of the memex. The process of tying two items together is the important thing.

When the user is building a trail, he names it, inserts the name in his code book, and taps it out on his keyboard. Before him are the two items to be joined, projected onto adjacent viewing positions. At the bottom of each there are a number of blank code spaces, and a pointer is set to indicate one of these on each item. The user taps a single key, and the items are permanently joined. In each code space appears the code word. Out of view, but also in the code space, is inserted a set of dots for photocell viewing; and on each item these dots by their positions designate the index number of the other item.

Thereafter, at any time, when one of these items is in view, the other can be instantly recalled merely by tapping a button below the corresponding code space. Moreover, when numerous items have been thus joined together to form a trail, they can be reviewed in turn, rapidly or slowly, by deflecting a lever like that used for turning the pages of a book. It is exactly as though the physical items had been gathered together from widely separated sources and bound together to form a new book. It is more than this, for any item can be joined into numerous trails.

The repetitive processes of thought are not confined to matters of arithmetic and statistics.

The owner of the memex, let us say, is interested in the origin and properties of the bow and arrow. Specifically he is studying why the short Turkish bow was apparently superior to the English long bow in the skirmishes of the Crusades. He has dozens of possibly pertinent books and articles in his memex. First he runs through an encyclopedia, finds an interesting but sketchy article, leaves it projected. Next, in a history, he finds another pertinent item, and ties the two together. Thus he goes, building a trail of many items. Occasionally he inserts a comment of his own, either linking it into the main trail or joining it by a side trail to a particular item. When it becomes evident that the elastic properties of available materials had a great deal to do with the bow, he branches off on a side trail which takes him through textbooks on elasticity and tables of physical constants. He inserts a page of longhand analysis of his own. Thus he builds a trail of his interest through the maze of materials available to him.

And his trails do not fade. Several years later, his talk with a friend turns to the queer ways in which a people resist innovations, even of vital interest. He has an example, in the fact that the outranged Europeans still failed to adopt the Turkish bow. In fact, he has a trail on it. A touch brings up the code book. Tapping a few keys projects the head of the trail. A lever runs through it at will, stopping at interesting items, going off on side excursions. It is an interesting trail, pertinent to the discussion. So he sets a reproducer in action, photographs the whole trail out, and passes it to his friend for insertion in his own memex, there to be linked into the more general trail.

Pushing the Limits

Wholly new forms of encyclopedias will appear, ready-made with a mesh of associative trails running through them, ready to be dropped into the memex and there amplified. The lawyer has at his touch the associated opinions and decisions of his whole experience and of the experience of friends and authorities. The patent attorney has on call the millions of issued patents, with familiar trails to every point of his client's interest. The physician, puzzled by a patient's reactions, strikes the trail established in studying an earlier similar case, and runs rapidly through analogous case histories, with side references to the classics for the pertinent anatomy and histology. The chemist, struggling with the synthesis of an organic compound, has all the chemical literature before him in his laboratory, with trails following the analogies of compounds, the side trails to their physical and chemical behavior.

The historian, with a vast chronological account of a people, parallels it with a skip trail which stops only on the salient items, and can follow at any time contemporary trails which lead him all over civilization at a particular epoch. There is a new profession of trail blazers, those who find delight in the task of establishing useful trails through the enormous mass of the common record. The inheritance from the master becomes not only his additions to the world's record, but for his disciples the entire scaffolding by which they were erected.

Thus science may implement the ways in which man produces, stores, and consults the record of the race. It might be striking to outline the instrumentalities of the future more spectacularly, rather than to stick closely to methods and elements now known and undergoing rapid development, as has been done here. Technical difficulties of all sorts have been ignored, certainly, but also ignored are means as yet unknown which may come any day to accelerate technical progress as violently as did the advent of the thermionic tube. In order that the picture may not be too commonplace, by reason of sticking to present-day patterns, it may be well to mention one such possibility, not to prophesy but merely to suggest, for prophecy based on extension of the known has substance, while prophecy founded on the unknown is only a doubly involved guess.

All our steps in creating or absorbing material of the record proceed through one of the senses—the tactile when we touch keys, the oral when we speak or listen, the visual when we read. Is it not possible that some day the path may be established more directly?

We know that when the eye sees, all the consequent information is transmitted to the brain by means of electrical vibrations in the channel of the optic nerve. This is an exact analogy with the electrical vibrations which occur in the cable of the television set: they convey the picture from the photocells which see it to the radio transmitter from which it is broadcast. We know further that if we can approach that cable with the proper instruments, we do not need to touch it; we can pick up those vibrations by electrical induction and thus discover and reproduce the scene which is being transmitted, just as a telephone wire may be tapped for its message.

The impulses which flow in the arm nerves of a typist convey to her fingers the translated information which reaches her eye or ear, in order that the fingers may be caused to strike the proper keys. Might not these currents be intercepted, either in the original form in which information is conveyed to the brain, or in the marvelously metamorphosed form in which they then proceed to the hand?

By bone conduction we already introduce sounds into the nerve channels of the deaf in order that they may hear. Is it not possible that we may learn to introduce them without the present cumbersomeness of first transforming electrical vibrations to mechanical ones, which the human mechanism promptly transforms back to the electrical form? With a couple of electrodes on the skull the encephalograph now produces pen-and-ink traces which bear some relation to the electrical phenomena going on in the brain itself. True, the record is unintelligible, except as it points out certain gross misfunctioning of the cerebral mechanism; but who would now place bounds on where such a thing may lead?

In the outside world, all forms of intelligence, whether of sound or sight, have been reduced to the form of varying currents in an electric circuit in order that they may be transmitted. Inside the human frame exactly the same sort of process occurs. Must we always transform to mechanical movements in order to proceed from one electrical phenomenon to another? It is a suggestive thought, but it hardly warrants prediction without losing touch with reality and immediateness.

Presumably man's spirit should be elevated if he can better review his shady past and analyze more completely and objectively his present problems. He has built a civilization so complex that he needs to mechanize his records more fully if he is to push his experiment to its logical conclusion

He has built a civilization so complex that he needs to mechanize his records more fully if he is to push his experiment to its logical conclusion and not merely become bogged down part way there by overtaxing his limited memory.

19

20

and not merely become bogged down part way there by overtaxing his limited memory. His excursions may be more enjoyable if he can reacquire the privilege of forgetting the manifold things he does not need to have immediately at hand, with some assurance that he can find them again if they prove important.

The applications of science have built man a well-supplied house, and are teaching him to live healthily therein. They have enabled him to throw masses of people against one another with cruel weapons. They may yet allow him truly to encompass the great record and to grow in the wisdom of race experience. He may perish in conflict before he learns to wield that record for his true good. Yet, in the application of science to the needs and desires of man, it would seem to be a singularly unfortunate stage at which to terminate the process, or to lose hope as to the outcome.

About the Author

Vannevar Bush was a pioneer in computer design who also distinguished himself as an engineer, an administrator, and a government official. He became president of the Carnegie Institute in Washington, D.C., in 1939, and was chairman of the National Advisory Committee for Aeronautics from 1939 to 1941. In 1941, President Roosevelt appointed Bush the first director of the Office of Scientific Research and Development, an agency to coordinate federally funded defense research. In this capacity, he directed the activities of some 6000 leading American scientists in the application of science to warfare.

Finally It Works:
Now It Must "Play in Peoria"

Sentence One: An Article of Faith:

by David C. Miller

The CD ROM and its laser-optical medium (L-OM) siblings portend a regenesis in publishing akin to that evoked by the rotary press, lithography, and (in process) the laser printer.

Sentence Two: An Article of Skepticism:

Suppose they gave The Revolution but only the True Believers arrived in time to fight it?

I have pledged my fortune (read "sweat/debt equity") and my Sacred Honorarium to Sentence One. I am, in fact, a Sentence One Believer, or S.O.B.

Much of what I have to say here, however, will strike CD ROM True Believers as the ravings of a Sentence Two Believer, or S.T.B. All I ask is that you hear me out: Let he or she who is without a slipped-delivery disc cast the first stone.

Significant Features of the CD ROM

Because I count myself among those not easily overwhelmed by whatever happens to be the latest Technology Toy, let me first cite the features of CD ROM which make me an S.O.B., then the features which prompt the convictions of the S.T.B.

CD ROM Features Emphasized by the S.O.B.

- The CD ROM, on one and the same disc, can store still and/or moving images in black-white and/or color; stereo or two separate sound tracks, integrated with and/or separate from the images; digital program files (word processors, spreadsheets) and digital information files (documents, records, catalogs).

- It can be mass-replicated in reasonable quantities for a unit production cost of $10 or less, excluding the substantial premastering and mastering costs and any costs for information rights.

- Presently, a formatted CD ROM can store 540 million bytes or ASCII characters in one or more files. This capacity is provided by a disc which measures 4.72 inches across and weighs 0.7 ounce. If my envelope-back calculator is correct, that represents a storage density of about 12 *billion bytes per pound.*

22

- Data is stored as three-dimensional, silvered pits. These pits are burned into the master by a laser beam and replicated as holes and flat surfaces pressed into the information-bearing surface of each copy (over 2 billion pits along a 3-mile-long track.) This surface is physically sealed off from contact with the disc drive environment, sandwiched between the grooved, transparent upper surface and a protective undercoating. Magnetic fields cannot destroy the data record, and the disc itself can be handled casually, even roughly, without damaging it. I suspect you could even use it to play Frisbee with your dog, though the manuals are silent on this point.

- CD ROM readout is accomplished by a scanning laser beam reflected (or not) from the silvered pits through the transparent upper layer. Readout thus involves no physical contact or wear. I suppose the worst source of wear is that resulting from contact of the player spindle, which engages the center hole of the disc, much like the spindle of a phonograph record player. Loss or degradation of data is essentially nil.

- Because data and information are stored on the CD ROM in digital form, retrieving and processing with a computer is relatively natural. If desired, the CD ROM can store not only data files but also index files, query software, even operating systems for the drive and/or the host computer.

The CD ROM is a magnificent innovation; but its instant success, or even its ultimate triumph in the marketplace, is by no means assured.

- The CD ROM peripheral drive, used as a disc drive analogous to a floppy disk drive, is a modified version of the compact music disc player (CMD). The CMD is one of the most successful consumer electronic products ever introduced. One estimate is that some 600,000 CMD players had been sold in the United States alone by the end of 1985. The CD ROM drive thus stands on a large, solid technology and production base, unlike that of other L-OM drives. Further, CD ROM drives are required only to *find* and *read* data, while the more exotic L-OM drives are obliged also to *write* and/or *erase* and *writeover*. It adds up to a significant price-performance advantage for CD ROM systems vs. other L-OM systems—for now—although no one can be certain how long this advantage will last.

- The CD ROM offers one of the lowest attainable error rates in any mass-storage medium, although it turns out that attaining the minimum rate is not casual. Advocates and critics dispute the rates. The one I use (but can't actually comprehend) is an attainable error rate of 1 bit per *1 quadrillion bits* (that's 1 followed by 15 zeros).

- The CD ROM inserts easily into the current microcomputer operating environment. If you already have a serious, office-type micro, all you need add is the CD ROM drive, a controller interface board to link drive and computer, appropriate software, and a supply of discs holding the reference files you need. One estimate is that by 1990, two-thirds of all salaried employees will have direct access to a micro. The gross potential for CD ROM systems appears stupendous, at least before any critical evaluation has been made.

There is more to be said about the virtues of CD ROM. By now, however, I hope to have conveyed the gist of what makes me a Sentence One Believer. On the other hand, there are still the Sentence Two Believers.

CD ROM Features Emphasized by S.T.B.

- "You can't write on, erase, or edit files stored on the damned disc." True, true enough. It was inevitable that the CD ROM would be compared with the magnetic floppy disk . . . and found wanting. The CD ROM is no substitute for the magnetic floppy disk. If it is anything worthwhile, it is something different: S.O.B.'s must frankly acknowledge this and go on from there.

- "Those claims of enormous capacity are a great deal less awesome in many actual applications." That's so. It is true that a formatted CD ROM holds 540 million bytes (or characters) of user data *if the data is stored in the ASCII format.* (ASCII refers to a widely used standard code in which particular alphanumeric characters are represented by standard combinations of 0 and 1.) If you want to store *images* or data in a non-ASCII, *bit-mapped* format, the perceived capacity of a CD ROM shrinks. For reasonable resolution, an image (of a page, a halftone, an illustration, etc.) may require 500,000 bytes of storage space. Dragging out my envelope-back calculator again, that means that a CD ROM can hold about 1000 images if you don't store anything else on it. But if you want text also, to say nothing of indexes, query systems, operating systems, and post-retrieval processing programs, well . . . Depending on your application, even with the CD ROM you may encounter that old devil Limited Disc Capacity sooner rather that later.

- "Compared with magnetic disks, CD ROMs are slow to retrieve data from a file." It's true. The comparative numbers are tricky because they depend on many variables for which different assumptions can be made.

23

But what we have here are mainframe-sized files which we are trying to process with a microcomputer chip. Furthermore, as briefly explained later, the CD ROM layout makes search and retrieval intrinsically slower than on a magnetic disc.

- "I can't make a backup or shareable copy of the CD ROM." Technically that's not so, but in practice it is. In principle you can copy any CD ROM file onto a magnetic disk. However, inasmuch as one disc holds the equivalent of 1300-1500 standard 5.25-inch double-density/doubled-sided disks, it is impractical to copy entire CD ROMs onto magnetic disks. You can, of course, copy subsets and entire files, but that is not the objection raised here.

- "It is prohibitively expensive and too time-consuming to resort to a CD ROM if I need only one or a few copies." Except in certain rare instances where unit cost is no object, this objection is valid. CD ROM replication is analogous to phonograph record production. You send your machine-readable data tapes to a central facility for premastering, mastering, and replication. Assuming you already own the information, premastering and mastering alone may cost $10,000. That ignores the preparation of index files, configuring your input tape to CD ROM premastering standards, and so on. In the *best* case, turnaround time from the date you submit tapes for premastering may be 30 days. But you'll need a check disc, and bugs or changes are likely to show up. While the second and subsequent replicas may cost you no more than $10 each, the first one can run $10-$30,000 or more.

- "I can't update the CD ROM." This actually is a variation of the first objection raised above ("You can't write on, erase, or edit files stored on the damned disc.") You can, of course, update your input tapes, then do a new premaster, a new master, and a new replication run. But all this is not what a magnetic disk user means by "updating."

- "Most of the information I use ages rapidly, so that my CD ROM's useful life would be prohibitively brief." Clearly, you can't use a CD ROM to capture today's stock market prices for access today. No file or document is a good candidate for CD ROM distribution if some significant fraction is outdated before you can provide the user with an updated replacement.

Other CD ROM features emphasized by Sentence Two Believers might be cited. But, again, I trust I have conveyed the gist of what causes S.T.B.'s to be convinced they are realists, not raving madpersons. As W. C. Fields once put it, "It's time to take the bull by the tail and look the situation squarely in the face." What you look at and what you make of it determine what you see.

The Information Resources Management (IRM) Environment

Having considered the CD ROM in splendid isolation, it is time now to view it in the context of the contemporary information resources management environment. It is, after all, that environment in which we propose to make CD ROM a star. Opening a window into that environment the merest crack instantly hints at a scene more than faintly reminiscent of the now infamous 1967 Democratic Convention in Chicago.

Tumult, confusion, confrontation, ignorance, and deceit abound on every hand. This is the ball to which we are inviting our innocent young stripling, CD ROM. Mayhap this youth should eschew formal wear and patent dancing pumps in favor of a hockey goalie's uniform and steel pointed-toe boots. It's rough in there.

Let me suggest circumstances by citing highlights:

- The microcomputer business is for the moment less robust than in the past. The slump or deceleration of growth has been induced by over-production, a dearth of breakthrough software, saturation of the first wave of users, and a resolve among users that they will not blindly empty IBM's warehouses. Users are asking: Do we need any more of them just now? Are we sure those fixed-disk problems in the AT have been fixed? How long will it be before all these are made obsolete by the next generation? Serious buyers and users of micros are engaged in the Pause That Bemuses.

- After several bloody years of Micro Mayhem, most large organizations have attained a viable if tenuous modus vivendi among data processing staffs, management information staffs, and end users. Few managers choose to reengage their battalions sooner than necessary, or at all if that can be avoided.

- IRM tool buyers no longer accept at face value the latest press releases and advertising claims in the trade press. IBM's first version of a Local Area Network called for expensive rewiring of offices. That didn't sit too well with many large users. So, voilà! The long-awaited Token Ring Network arrives, which uses existing twisted-pair wiring . . . except that it does not accommodate micro-mainframe communication, which was one of the most eagerly awaited benefits. Maybe all those Lotus 1-2-3 users need the new upgrade and/or Symphony but if so, sales estimates don't reflect it.

The CD ROM is no substitute for the magnetic floppy disk. If it is anything worthwhile, it is something different: S.O.B.'s must frankly acknowledge this and go on from there.

25

Perhaps the 3.5-inch floppy disk drive is the wave of the future . . . but then again, perhaps it isn't. "Everybody" wants a laptop portable micro, but only if they can read the display in a lighted room. Please plug in your own favorite examples here.

- Software buyers are stoutly contesting prices and terms of trade. Manufacturers are being forced, kicking and screaming, to abandon or drastically relax copy-protection schemes and to develop site-licensing agreements for large users.

- User organizations in many cases acquired first-generation microcomputer systems on an as-it-happens basis (*disjointed incrementalism* is the technical term for *catch as catch can*). Now managers either seek to prove that it was all done according to plan and things are working fine or they are determined to take a more systematic approach the next time around. It turns out that you improve your odds if you invest time and thought in identifying application tasks, developing performance standards and measures, and applying cost-justification methods before you buy.

- When you *do* turn to fixing IRM tool requirements, you discover it is not as simple and straightforward as you may have assumed. Most Fortune 500-size organizations, private and public, give lip service to effective IRM—it's The Thing To Do. Meanwhile, down in the plumbing, the Indians often perceive that the chiefs either don't mean what they say or don't know what they're talking about. Perhaps it's true that information has now become a Precious Asset, rather than the Overhead Item it has always been, but it's hard to teach the old dog new tricks. Even if top management is determined to revise accounting and organizational structures appropriately, the economic theory of information is among the least-developed branches of the Dismal Science. (If you are pitching tools to handle stable, reference-type information, it's discouraging to realize that Information Economics is grounded on the premise that information is a perishable commodity.) Users seek access to mainframe databases so that they can be *sure* they have the most recent numbers, whether they need them or not.

- IRM technology generally is, for average users, too difficult or cumbersome to learn and to use. Further, the hardware, the software, and the systems are fluid, evolving rapidly. The 32-bit microcomputer looms on the horizon, somewhere. Artificial intelligence; fourth-generation languages; and new, improved (and to some extent incompatible) operating systems are coming along for multiuser environments.

**We hold in our
hands the working
models of what we
believe will extend
the scope, range,
even the meaning
of "publishing."**

Into this turbulent environment waltzes the CD ROM. Can we Sentence One Believers manage at all to catch the eye of company information officers and other IRM managers and administrators? If and when we do, we must, with them, acknowledge and address the formidable challenges today's IRM environment poses to us all.

27

Typical CD ROM Issues and Concerns

Those of you still with me should by now at least be prepared to consider the proposition that all is not Roses and Raspberries for us S.O.B.'s. The CD ROM is a magnificent innovation; but its instant success, or even its ultimate triumph in the marketplace, is by no means assured.

In this section I mention some of the principal issues and concerns I believe we must openly and creatively address, under these main headings:

○ Technology

○ Users

○ Uses

○ Support

○ Competitive trade-offs

Let us consider each of these briefly, in turn.

Technology Issues/Concerns

● Standards: Disc, interface, operating systems. The RS 232 serial port interface used on most micros today is inadequate for the rapid transfer of large files between a CD ROM and a micro. The SCSI (Small Computer Standard Interface, pronounced "scuzzy") may be emerging as the CD ROM drive standard . . . or it may not.

● Data transfer to and from magnetic media.

● Compatibility among CD ROM, WORM (write once, read many times), or DRAW (direct read after write) and erasable optical discs in various sizes.

● The promise-threat of a CAV CD ROM. This one has fundamental implications that require a bit of explaining:

○ Today's CD ROM player stores its data along a continuous spiral track, just as a phonograph recording stores sound. To get from any point on the track to any other, the laser readout must traverse every intermediate point along the track. End to end, the worst case, that is billions of points along a 3-mile-long track. This is not the fastest possible arrangement for finding and accessing files (see below), but it is used because the CD ROM drive is based on the compact music disc player. This form of access is called the CLV, or constant linear velocity, technique.

○ Magnetic floppy disk drives use a different arrangement, known as the CAV, or constant angular velocity, technique. Instead of one continuous spiral track, floppy disks are formatted as a series of concentric rings divided into equal-size slices called *sectors*. The floppy disk read-head can hop and skip rapidly from one location to another by switching directly from any given track/sector to any other. File access times using this technique are intrinsically shorter than the other method can attain.

When something is as new, different, complex, and subtle as CD ROM, you will do better to assume an intimate, cooperative, intensively interactive relationship with prospects and customers.

○ There is, of course, in principle no reason why an improved CD ROM drive using the CAV approach cannot be developed. In fact, it probably is already being developed. If this new version were to be introduced soon at a price not too much higher than the current version, it could well become the CD ROM standard. The catch is that CLV discs could not be used with a CAV drive, and vice versa.

● Status of competing laser-optical media. The first read-only memory system introduced in the United States, that of Reference Technology, Incorporated, uses a larger-diameter disc and format standards incompatible with the CD ROM. (I should add that RTI now offers a CD ROM system as well.) Such discs hold much more, but the system is more expensive. Drexler Technology has introduced the laser-optical card, which stores 2 million characters on a credit-card-sized card. Blue Cross of Maryland already is using this card to offer take-along medical histories. In development but not yet commercialized is a laser-optical tape which may find important applications. And, of course, WORM/DRAW and fully erasable optical discs are coming along or are already in use in specialized applications. Any or all of these may contend for some or all of the markets CD ROM hopes to find.

● Status of competing magnetic media. Magnetic disks can easily be made read-only, whether by omitting a write notch on the floppy or using software to designate a file or an entire disk as read-only. While magnetic disks are more mature than optical discs, their ability to improve and compete with CD ROM should not be underestimated. Already, 3.5-inch floppy disks which store more than a million characters are on the market, while fixed magnetic disks which hold 20 million characters or more and fit on a plug-in card inside the computer have recently been introduced.

- Indexing and query systems. Software developed for use with smaller storage media and micros are not adequate for CD ROM. Some suppliers are "shrinking" systems originally developed on mainframes, but these too have serious limitations in this new application. Some promising new systems expressly designed for micro/CD ROM applications are coming along, but the ultimate standard systems have by no means been achieved.

- Postretrieval processing software. Once you have retrieved a file or subset from a CD ROM and copied it into active memory or onto a magnetic disk, you may well want to do something else with it: statistical analysis, editing, graphic processing, and so on. Depending on file size, structure, and contents, one may be able to use existing micro packages (such as WordStar or 1-2-3) or . . . one may not. In any case, it seems likely that the new capability will eventually create a need for new processing programs.

User Issues/Concerns

- Are the presumed CD ROM users microcomputer professionals, information science professionals, subject-matter specialists who are micro and information science novices, average laypersons—or all of the above? Crucial software, training, and support design decisions hinge on the answers.

- Will users access the CD ROM as a freestanding reference station, through local area networks, through remote dial-up networks, or all of the above? Again, important design trade-off issues are involved.

- Will all users have access to all files, or will file-access schemes be needed?

- Will file user charges be levied, and if so, how will they be calculated, collected, and (if necessary) remitted to the owners?

Use Issues/Concerns

- Will a given disc or set of discs provide information from one, a few, or many sources?

- Will the operating, query, and postretrieval processing software work with all discs, and will they provide all the functions which may be desired by users?

- Will the software systems be open and flexible enough to be compatible with future formats and adequate for future, unforeseen processing requirements?

Support Issues/Concerns

- Where and how do CD ROM systems and products fit into an organization's management and administrative structures and procedures?

- How will CD ROM users' information and support requirements be monitored, documented, prioritized, and acted upon? This is perhaps a restatement of the preceding point, but it may also involve something more.

Competitive Trade-off Issues/Concerns

- Versus magnetic disks

  - Strengths: Larger storage capacity, longer average shelf life, less subject to accidental destruction, better for storing/manipulating images.

  - Weaknesses: Read-only capability, few CD ROM drives now in place, standards not yet set, software immature.

- Versus mainframe storage/access

  - Strengths: Long-term storage costs may be lower, user has direct access/control, dial-up costs/queues avoided, processing load distributed.

  - Weaknesses: Much longer, more cumbersome update cycle; risks of different users unknowingly processing different versions of files.

- Versus microforms

  - Strengths: Digitized data intrinsically easier to process by machine, medium much more durable, quality of displayed images potentially superior.

  - Weaknesses: Microform facilities/methods already in place and mastered, unit file size more flexible.

- Versus hard-copy materials

  - Strengths: Larger reduction in storage volume, CD ROM more easily processed by machine, files less subject to damage or destruction, lower replication costs.

  - Weaknesses: Document or file conversion costs, can be viewed/processed only via micro/CD ROM system.

What Should Happen Next?

"It's time to take the bull by the tail and look the situation squarely in the face."

Paraphrasing Charles Dickens, for CD ROM True Believers, ours is the best of times and the worst of times. The best of times because we hold in our hands the working models of what we believe will extend the scope, range, even the meaning of "publishing." And the worst of times because we are bringing our wonders into an arena jammed with Christians already desperately seeking to avoid the claws of a hundred other lions. And, looking anxiously over our shoulders, we see all the other new technology contenders—laser-optical and otherwise—impatiently waiting to claim their pound of marketplace, *our* pound if we are not swift and shrewd enough.

Which brings us to the urgent, immediate question: **Who should do what next?** My list is meant to be suggestive, not exhaustive, and is organized under these headings:

- Prospective users
- Systems integrators/value-added resellers
- Information providers
- Hardware/software providers

Prospective Users' Immediate Tasks

- Get a better handle on organizational information resources costs and values. The typical organization manager would be sorely embarrassed if he or she realized how much concerning information resources (IR) is assumed without scrutiny.

- Identify current/prospective IR weaknesses, challenges, and opportunities, under any or all of the following headings: User types, use types, media types, internal vs. external, operational vs. strategic. While a bit of systematic digging is apt to reveal most gripes about current problems, some organized, imaginative conjecture probably will be needed to characterize strategic challenges.

- Identify, integrate, prioritize, and cost-justify options for exploring *all* IRM options, including but by no means limited to CD ROM. Using these options as a backdrop, identify and test option selection criteria.

- Decide how much of various kinds of resources (time, money, human), *if any,* you should invest in exploring new IR technology, again including but not limited to CD ROM.

- If a potential CD ROM application emerges, develop a project mission statement for it, including performance requirements, objectives, standards, and measures. Submit these to potential CD ROM system/product suppliers. Passively waiting for exactly what you need to come along is not a good strategy, or even good sense. Interact with your suppliers, give them guidance and influence their investment priorities.

Unfortunately, these exhortations are most likely either superfluous or futile. Most organizations and most managers prefer dealing with buzzing boxes and sexy new systems, in which case it is futile to ask them to invest staff time and budget dollars to scrutinize what they assume they already know. As for the rest, they have completed or are already in hot pursuit of the tasks I suggest. However, putting it all on the record one more time may contribute a mite to changing the decision-making climate. At least I hope so.

Integrators/Value-Added Resellers' Immediate Tasks

- Invest some truly creative market profiling resources to identify a few most likely user types in several diverse market sectors. Then encourage representative users by prodding and assisting them to take the Next Steps itemized in the preceding section. When they have done so, determine with them mutually affordable and useful ways to share costs, risks, and efforts in exploring and testing their potential applications. In doing so, you can serve your own self-interest by helping them recognize and acknowledge the need for (and your cost of) providing support services. If, as I suspect, early CD ROM systems users require extensive handholding, helping them recognize the need, the cost, and the value elements of these services will make your ultimate pricing policy more acceptable.

- Design, develop, and maintain your systems, products, and services to be as open to the future as possible. For example, if you offer CLV CD ROM systems initially but CAV versions arrive before you expect them, you and your customers will do well if you are positioned to make the transition with minimum expenditures of time and budget.

- From the outset, work hard to identify each and every smallest element of your systems, products, and services. This approach will greatly assist you in your costing, budgeting, and pricing. It will also enable you to offer customized products and services, so that each customer is able to buy exactly and only what he or she needs or wants.

Information Providers' Immediate Tasks

- Electronic providers

  - Analyze your current products from the CD ROM perspective. For example, which files are *not* candidates because their update cycle is too short? Which files lend themselves readily to segmentation of reference files (long update cycle) and current files (short update cycle)? Which users and which uses might be offered extra added values via the CD ROM, either in file contents and structures or in postprocessing support? What exactly are the full and true costs of delivering your products from a mainframe, whether directly to end users or through a distributor?

- Nonelectronic providers

  - Hard-copy publishers (books, manuals, catalogs, serials) should consider if and how they might minimize cost or add value by CD ROM distribution, either as a substitute or as an extension of hard-copy distribution. Who knows, you might reduce the selling price or give the product away if you saw the prospect of offering more profitable collateral support products and/or services. Or, offering an electronic version in a freestanding system might tap market sectors formerly beyond your reach.

- All providers

  - Reexamine your strategic business premises in light of this new medium. Too often, such premises are established without much thought and never examined thereafter, even though the market environment changes dramatically. Are current customers for your information products the *only* ones, or even the *most profitable* ones? (If you market through DIALOG or another electronic distributor, chances are you reach only the larger organizations.) Is your best pricing strategy one which minimizes volume and maximizes price, vice versa, or some mix of the two, market sector by market sector? Is a per-transaction pricing policy always better than a site-licensing policy?

Hardware/Software Suppliers' Immediate Tasks

- Kick what my partner, Jim Goodspeed, calls the *Pie in the Window* attitude. You know, drag out your best recipe, bake a magnificent pie, and set it out on your windowsill, confident that someone will come along who will want it, will pay for it, will bear it away, and won't bug you thereafter. When something is as new, different, complex, and subtle as CD ROM, you will do better to assume an intimate, cooperative, intensively interactive relationship with prospects and customers.

- Reach out for strategic alliances. Drive suppliers tend to offer minimal software, assuming that someone else will take care of that. Some of the best CD ROM software (for example, that of TMS) was developed without the support or intimate input of the CD ROM drive makers who are now licensing its use. That's better than nothing, but not nearly as good as it could be if everybody kept the requirements of integrated systems in view from the outset, and teamed up with others who are developing those system components you are not developing.

- Invest in some extremely visible, open, and realistic demonstration applications. Grolier is to be commended for its enlightened self-interest in making its electronic encyclopedia available on nearly every CD ROM system demonstrated to date. Datext should be (and probably is) making offers few can refuse to get customers to try using its Fortune 500 statistics database, issued on CD ROM and updated monthly. What we all need are many more diversified offerings like these. Digital Equipment Corporation is active in this field; let us hope it understands the shrewd self-interest of allowing early users to experiment at a nominal cost and risk.

- Most of all, suppliers should invest precious time, money, and attention in getting close to and understanding the particular, peculiar needs of their best initial prospective users. Such appreciation will not come cheap. But it is indispensable.

Conclusion

Sentence One: An Article of Faith:

The CD ROM and its laser-optical medium (L-OM) siblings portend a regenesis in publishing akin to that evoked by the rotary press, lithography, and (in process) the laser printer.

Sentence Two: An Article of Skepticism:

Suppose they gave The Revolution but only the True Believers arrived in time to fight it?

About the Author

David C. Miller is managing partner for DCM Associates, San Francisco, an information resources management consulting and professional services firm. Since 1983, he has specialized in read-only applications of optical discs, and is organizing a new company, Laser Publishing Services, which will offer leased, fully supported CD ROM systems for businesses and professions.

On other fronts, Mr. Miller's professional activities range from exploring metaphoric logics as a basis for new kinds of software to an affiliation with CCM Associates, one of two certified appraisers in the United States of films and film collections.

DCM Associates
Post Drawer 605
Benicia, CA 94510

CD ROM and Videodisc: Lessons to Be Learned

by Rockley L. Miller

Most new technologies move through three basic stages in their early market evolution. First, they are greeted with *unbridled optimism*. Their great potential is ballyhooed as the universal panacea for everyone's problems.

Their inevitable failure to live up to this early hype leads next to a period of *pessimistic depression*, as market realities set in and promoters start to worry that they have hitched their wagons to a dud.

Finally, the rose-colored glasses are replaced by prescription lenses, as the technologists focus on areas of *real benefit and real value*, where the technology can establish a firm foundation for growth in the real world.

Most new technologies move through three basic stages in their early market evolution . . . unbridled optimism . . . pessimistic depression . . . real benefit and real value . . .

The compact disc as a read-only data storage medium is just beginning to enter the market. It has been greeted with great optimism by a sagging computer industry and is enjoying an abundance of positive coverage in the trade press. It is clearly in its first phase of market evolution.

On the other hand, the CD ROM's big brother, the optical videodisc, has been around for seven years. The videodisc was hailed with great optimism, survived an ensuing depression, and has begun to climb out and establish itself in a variety of market niches that ensure its long-term viability. During this long journey, we have learned many lessons that are important to remember as we forge ahead with CD ROM. These lessons are best understood by examining the similarities and critical differences between these two media and between their respective market positions.

Videodisc and Compact Disc: Similarities

The first similarity between compact disc and videodisc lies at the most basic level of the technologies. Their manufacturing processes are almost identical, leading most videodisc manufacturers to also offer compact disc pressing services. Both use microscopic pits to encode information and lasers to read it back. Both share many features that make optical discs so appealing—durability, rapid random access to high-quality information, and high data density, to name a few. In fact, both technologies are so similar, that at least one player on the market can play both consumer compact discs and videodiscs.

Both formats offer a high degree of standardization. Compact discs enjoy a worldwide standard for audio, with several industrial groups now working on standards for data storage. Laser videodiscs also have a worldwide physical standard. However, unlike audio signals, video signal standards vary between countries and are incompatible.

Further complicating matters for videodiscs in the industrial market is the increasing use of players under the control of a variety of computers. Often, this involves different approaches to mixing graphics with video, storing different types of information on the discs, and the exploitation of more advanced features and interfaces of certain brands of players. This tangled web of system configuration possibilities makes it extremely unlikely that system-level standards and compatibility will evolve beyond specific applications.

Neither compact disc nor videodisc presently offers an end user the capability of directly recording information. This is a distinct disadvantage in some applications and an advantage in others. However, regardless of the application, the lack of recording capability (the "read-only" nature of the medium) limits the value of any disc player to that of the prerecorded discs it can play. This is distinctly different from a video or audio cassette recorder, or other forms of magnetic storage that might be used to store and manipulate more personalized information.

Nobody buys technology. People buy what it can do for them.

Thus, the markets for both compact disc and videodisc are inexorably software-bound and software-driven. Users will purchase hardware only if there is either available software of sufficient value or if need warrants the expense of developing their own. With videodisc, the lack of standards at the industrial level has inhibited the growth of generically available software. It is evident from the standardization efforts within the compact disc community that this lesson has been duly noted.

Finally, both technologies can be terribly distracting. Any applications developer can become easily caught up in the enormous capacity or fancy features of either CD or videodisc. This can be a dangerous trap for the unwary. Many companies tried and failed with the videodisc because they did not keep in mind exactly what business they were in. Too many entrepreneurs tried to sell the videodisc rather than a solution to a specific problem. Nobody buys technology. People buy what it can do for them.

Videodisc and Compact Disc: Differences

While many of the similarities between compact disc and videodisc might raise a flag of caution for an eager industrial marketer, there are many differences that could indeed support the most optimistic projections.

The industrial markets for compact disc and videodisc technology have both been predicated on initial acceptance by consumers. As the consumer market for videodisc has been slow to develop, the economies of scale that would reduce industrial prices have not yet been achieved.

With videodisc, the lack of standards at the industrial level has inhibited the growth of generically available software. It is evident from the standardization efforts within the compact disc community that this lesson has been duly noted.

On the other hand, compact disc has been cited as the most successful consumer electronic product introduction in history. Hardware prices have dropped far faster than originally anticipated, allowing the industrial compact disc market to ride the consumer wave in terms of both technology development and customer awareness. Furthermore, having exceeded consumer projections, the compact disc comes to the industrial market with an image of success that can only strengthen its reception.

A number of key differences between compact disc and videodisc have contributed to the greater consumer success of compact disc. Certainly the physical standards mentioned above are critical. However, more important is the nature of each medium's respective content.

o Music is a universal language. It requires little translation between countries. Video programs generally require dubbing or the addition of subtitles.

o Music is inherently replayable. It is almost always enjoyed as background to other activity and thrives on familiarity. Video is inherently a one-shot medium. It commands your exclusive attention and thrives on newness.

o Because of the high level of replay, music is quite sensitive to issues of sound quality and degradation from use. Because it is infrequently repeated, video quality is secondary to content. Degradation is primarily a question for archival requirements or for industrial applications with multiple users.

o Music is almost always purchased, while most consumer video is rented. Rentals generate less revenue for the original producer, diminishing the incentives for original programming.

40

Compact disc has
been cited as the
most successful
consumer electronic
product introduction
in history.

○ There is little to compete with compact disc for music quality and product durability. Videodisc is generally perceived as an alternative (and competitor) to videocassette, which enjoys existing consumer momentum and widespread distribution channels, as well as the advantage of the ability to record.

○ A wealth of music is available for (and benefits from) transfer to compact disc. Most is organized into cuts or movements that can take advantage of the medium's random access, with more value gained from the compact disc's longer playing time.

Feature films represent most of the program material being transferred to videodisc. Movies are linear and do not benefit from the special features of disc. Indeed, most disc films are replicated in an extended-play mode that renders most control features inoperative. Furthermore, the videodisc's two-hour maximum playing time is a disadvantage, compared with tape. Often, a second disc must be included to accommodate a full production.

○ The compact disc represents a new audio distribution alternative with myriad advantages over tape and LPs. However, there is no program material being developed exclusively for compact disc that cannot also be sold on other media (as well as broadcast on radio). This broadens the base upon which the investment can be recovered. Consumer programming developed to take advantage of the interactive features of videodisc is generally expensive to produce and inappropriate for delivery on any other media, limiting the base for investment recovery.

In the emerging industrial market for CD ROM, some of the same differences will enhance its growth potential.

○ CD ROM is positioned exclusively as a computer peripheral. The emerging standardization efforts will enhance its value and versatility in this area. One major technical advantage that compact disc enjoys over videodisc is that the CD signal is in digital format and represents digital data which is easily digested by computers. The videodisc/computer combination is complicated by the differences between analog video signals and digital computer output.

○ Most analysts foresee the primary applications for CD ROM in database and software distribution. As with the consumer music market for compact disc, there is a large volume of existing data and software programs that might be appropriate for transfer and distribution via CD ROM. Such transfers can be accomplished at minimal front-end expense and generally involve materials whose creation costs have already been amortized through online access charges, or sales on other distribution media such as floppy disks. Most industrial applications for videodisc require custom program development at relatively high cost or the production of generic programs that have no other distribution vehicle.

○ As with the consumer music market, most projected CD ROM content represents a continuing user resource that will be accessed frequently by the same person. While some industrial videodisc applications provide ongoing use (visual databases, archives, or other reference material), most lean toward one-time delivery of information to a given group of users.

Conclusion

The videodisc is a revolutionary form of optical storage. It brings the different worlds of computers and video together on one medium and forces a dramatic change in our perception of each. In discovering and developing appropriate programming to capitalize on its potential, we have had to start from scratch. The very uniqueness that gives the videodisc its great potential also made its early content development very difficult. Fortunately, while the learning curve has been costly, the potential of the videodisc is now being realized.

The CD ROM is an evolutionary form of optical storage. It represents the next logical step in the traditional evolution of data storage: increased capacity at decreased cost. The critical questions facing this technology lie not with the concept as much as with the marketing. Issues of pricing, packaging, access software, content mixes, updates, interfaces, and standards will all be resolved in the marketplace.

The future of both media is bright. Indeed, both technologies are converging and absorbing the capabilities of the other. However, it is likely that the path will be smoother for CD ROM than it has been for the videodisc. It is always easier to take the next logical step than it is to participate in a revolution.

About the Author

Rockley L. Miller is president of Future Systems Inc. and editor and publisher of *The Videodisc Monitor,* a monthly report of news and analysis covering application, innovation, and technology within the interactive video industry. He holds a B.A. in industrial management from The Johns Hopkins University and an M.S. in management information and technology from The American University.

Mr. Miller has tracked developments in videodisc technology since 1976 and has testified before Congress on the value of videodisc technology in training. He is a frequent speaker at industry conferences and has been widely quoted as an authority in the field by the *Washington Post, USA Today, Wall Street Journal,* and the *Financial Times of London.* He is internationally recognized as a leading expert on the applications of videodisc technology.

Future Systems Inc.
Post Office Box 26
Falls Church, VA 22046
(703) 241-1799, telex 4996279

THE CD SYSTEM

Hardware

What Is CD ROM?

by Leonard Laub

This discussion is an overview of optical disc technology, from which both CD audio and CD ROM have arisen. It is meant to provide both non-technical and technical readers with a useful perspective of an industry that is still cutting its eyeteeth, but which is growing at a rate matched only by that of the microcomputer industry in the early 1980s.

CD ROM represents an exciting breakthrough in information storage technology. It is a new publishing medium, the center of a new genre of computer applications, and an educational tool of unprecedented power. CD ROM is the first practical product to enable almost any company to package and sell, and anyone to buy and directly use, very large digital databases.

It is a new publishing medium, the center of a new genre of computer applications, and an educational tool of unprecedented power.

Each CD ROM disc can carry at least 550 megabytes of digital data, with accuracy and reliability as good as those available with the best computer peripherals. This is enough to hold:

○ The text content of 150,000 printed pages (enough to fill 250 big books)

○ Sharp images of 15,000 pages of business documents (enough to fill two tall filing cabinets)

○ The contents of 1200 standard 5.25-inch floppy disks

○ A crisp color picture and 10 seconds of narration for each of 3000 segments of an educational or reference program (almost 8 hours of content)

○ Large amounts of anything else which can be represented digitally; or any combination, in any proportion and order, of any of the above

Capacity is just the beginning. Any piece of this vast array of information can be located within 1 second of asking for it. Retrieval can be supported by your choice of powerful computer methods, starting with database management systems and full-text searching systems. Precompiled indexes for either or both of these can be stored on the CD ROM along with the database itself; there's plenty of room!

Sample Applications

This book is loaded with specific examples of applications suited to real markets and being conveyed to those markets by the writers. Two major application areas, which I will discuss, are electronic publishing, and specifically, database publishing.

Electronic Publishing

You can put a lot of material of all sorts on a CD ROM. One practical reason to do so is cost. If you have a lot of text to distribute, such as a law library, one CD ROM disc, costing $10 or less from the disc maker, stores as much material as microfiche costing $150 to make, or books costing $1000 to print. Further economies come in handling, warehousing, and shipping.

Once your database is on CD ROM, it is available for rapid random access under the control of a computer. This is the major departure from traditional publishing because it puts organization, indexing, and presentation of the material on a par with the traditional concerns of collection and verification.

This culture jump is attractive to some traditional publishers and scary to others. It creates opportunities for organizations not traditionally involved in publishing, either to take full responsibility for the job or to act as service bureaus to do just the newfangled things in support of traditional publishers.

One of the brutal realities of commercial life is that users want what they want rather than what is technically feasible. As people become used to easy, flexible, inexpensive access to huge databases, they will realize that they want more. Today's hero can become tomorrow's dummy.

A specific example of this is the field of full-text searching systems. Several good techniques exist to compile inverted indexes for large text databases. These support searches for any word, or text string, or Boolean conjunction of text strings in a database with a small number (usually one or two) of accesses to the accompanying index.

The indexes produced by available techniques range in size from 30 to over 200 percent of the size of the subject database. When the subject database is several hundred megabytes, this requires either using the CD ROM to support the accesses to the index (inexpensive but slow) or using a fairly large Winchester disk to manage the index (fast but expensive).

The most practical answer to this problem is the development of search techniques with more compact indexes. Such techniques have been investigated experimentally in recent years but now have a clear commercial motive to support them.

One of the brutal realities of commercial life is that users want what they want rather than what is technically feasible.

2×10^6 pits

.12um deep

.612um deep

1.6 MM

lands
1 Pit

.6 MM

$1 \text{ al} = 39.36 \ '' = \text{D5}$

1 mm

Database Distribution

Many large companies and institutions maintain central databases which are consulted frequently by their operatives around the country or the world. A large industry has grown up to provide electronic connection to these databases.

Many persistent problems plague this method of connecting the far-flung locations. One is cost. The electronic telecommunication of data can cost anywhere from tens of cents per megabyte to hundreds of dollars per megabyte, depending on the speed of data transmission, the type of communication lines, and possibly the time of day.

Also, the transfer rate is usually too low, particularly when communicating over dial-up lines, for which 10,000 bits per second is considered extremely fast. Even floppy disks transfer data at 250,000 bits per second, and small Winchesters 20 times faster still. These set the pace to which most microcomputer users are accustomed. Reliability is imperfect, both for dial-up and dedicated lines. They go down, fade, and become noisy. From some parts of the world, lines may not be available or call volume may be sharply limited.

The volume of queries is limited by available trunks and available computer power at the central locations. Security of the central database is poor, with dedicated, clever bad guys finding ways around each new protection scheme.

CD ROM provides an interesting alternative. For databases that don't change too rapidly, it is feasible to ship CD ROMs anywhere in the world. The cost of the discs and express shipping is about one cent per megabyte (based on a volume production of discs). Once received, a disc can be accessed any number of times for no additional cost.

There is no limit to the number of discs which can be distributed, and consequently no limit to the total volume of queries directed to the database. However, the database is relatively secure because hackers have not yet found out how to log on to a disc locked in a desk drawer.

Given that most databases do evolve, it is practical to get short-term updates via traditional electronic means, using this expensive technique only when needed.

CD ROM and Other Storage Media

With all of its impressive attributes, CD ROM is still not the all purpose storage device which replaces all others. In most real systems, CD ROM needs the support of familiar and forthcoming disk, tape, and RAM products.

Read-Only Medium

One important limitation of CD ROM is the fact that it is a read-only medium. This makes it good for unchanging or historical databases but not for evolving ones. Slow evolution can be handled by issuing new discs periodically, but the minimum practical cycle for CD ROM updates is now about one month.

More rapidly evolving databases need either a high-capacity writable medium, such as a writable optical disc, or the integration of a magnetic disk with the CD ROM. This latter approach is expensive (two drives) and somewhat fragile. (What if the magnetic and optical drives become separated? How do you keep a unified directory or index across the two media?)

Modest Throughput

Microcomputer applications depend on disk drives to supply the right data *right now.* Capacity measures the drive's ability to keep all likely-to-be-used data directly on hand, while throughput, expressed in records written or read per unit time, measures the drive's ability to deliver datasets promptly to one or more busy users. To measure throughput, add the time it takes the drive to get to the beginning of the desired record (access time) to the time it takes the drive to transfer all the data in that record (transfer time). The reciprocal of this total is the throughput, a very useful figure of merit for direct access storage devices.

The term "access time" is widely and variously abused. As used here, it incorporates the following components: radial positioning time (frequently called access time), which is the time it takes for the head to be put over the write track; settling time, which is the time it takes the head positioner, open loop or servo, to stop jiggling after the head has been positioned; and latency, which is the time you must wait between when the head arrives at the desired track and when the desired sector spins under the head.

CD ROM is a disk format, but its throughput is modest. A CD ROM drive connected as a server to a busy multiuser community will simply not keep up with the demand for records. Even connected to a single user, a

CD ROM drive with today's specifications will be a disappointment if that user wants to flip quickly through high-resolution images or to reindex a large database.

The technology behind all of today's products for the optical storage of digital data comes not from the computer industry but the consumer electronics industry.

Typical average radial access times are 500 ms or more, compared with 70 for cheap Winchesters and 40 or less for better Winchesters. CD ROM latency is also a problem, running between 60 and 150 ms average, compared with 8 for typical Winchesters.

These numbers put CD ROM drives in the awkward position of having gigantic capacity, far beyond anything previously seen hitched to a micro, with access times typical of those of floppy disks. This is acceptable in some applications, but others need more performance.

Data accessibility also requires that transfer times not be painfully long. As applications evolve toward graphics, full text, image storage, and other settings in which a record may be hundreds or thousands of K-bytes long, transfer times become significant. This requires useful drives to have high transfer rates. Again, CD ROM, at 1.3 Mbit/sec, falls somewhere between floppy disks (250 Kbit/sec) and Winchesters (5 Mbit/sec and up).

Expense

Some interactive instruction or reference applications are based on the presentation of still and moving images. While CD ROM has enough digital data capacity to store a few thousand color TV images, this is both an order of magnitude smaller than the image capacity of a LaserVision™ disc and far more expensive to implement (digital TV frame buffers are still multi-thousand-dollar items).

Optical cards and optical tapes may yet appear, in response to well-defined needs at both ends of the capacity spectrum. Distribution of programs or operating systems (up to a megabyte or so) might be more cheaply done on cards. Extremely large databases (tens to thousands of gigabytes) might fit better on optical tape cartridges.

The Origin of CD ROM

Much of the excitement about CD ROM can be attributed to the compact audio disc (abbreviated CD), the impressively successful new consumer format for the distribution of music. How impressive? Almost 10 percent of all music titles available on LP are now available on CD. Players, which sold for $1000 and up in early 1984, can now be bought for less than $150.

52

New CD manufacturing capacity is coming on line all over the world to catch up with demand. Over 65 million compact audio discs were sold in the first two years of availability! All of this activity is raising the hopes of many that CD ROM will follow in its forebears' footsteps.

The technology behind all of today's products for the optical storage of digital data comes not from the computer industry but the consumer electronics industry. During the late 1960s and early 1970s, television manufacturers around the world worked to develop home videodisc systems, which they intended to sell as accessories to television sets.

The first generation of writable optical discs are clearly derived from the videodisc, sharing many of its basic dimensions, drive operating principles, and methods and materials for disc fabrication.

This may sound like the currently popular videocassette recorder (VCR), but there was no such product then. The VCR was originally developed as a recorder and has only recently evolved into a commercially important delivery device for prerecorded programs. Videodisc was intended, from the start, as a read-only system using mass-produced discs.

LaserVision

Several mechanical and capacitance-sensing videodisc systems came to market during the 1970s, but only the optical videodisc system known as LaserVision (abbreviated LV) survived.

LaserVision discs are usually 12 inches (occasionally 8 inches) in diameter. One 12-inch LV disc holds either 30 or 60 minutes of program per side, depending on the format; and most discs use both sides.

The 60-minute capacity comes with the CLV (constant linear velocity) format, in which the disc spins at a speed inversely proportional to the radius being read. (In other words, the disc spins slower when its outside tracks are being read than when its inside tracks are being read.) This maximizes capacity by keeping the linear density of recorded information constant over the whole disc. The CAV (constant angular velocity) format cuts playing time per side to 30 minutes but permits random access to individual video frames. In CAV, the disc spins at a constant 1800 rpm (30 rps), so each revolution stores exactly one frame (one screenful of video information as it appears on your television). This means that one side of a 12-inch LV disc stores up to 54,000 separate images. (Note that these images are stored as analog information, as opposed to the digital information stored on a CD.)

The earliest prototypes of LV players appeared in laboratories around 1970, and approximately half a billion dollars was spent by several companies (notably Philips, DiscoVision, and Pioneer) during the 8 subsequent years to develop a viable product, which was finally introduced in 1978. More money has been invested since then, resulting in better equipment, more disc mastering plants, and steady growth in production. The resulting technology, engineering, and manufacturing base has been strong enough to support the development of several other major categories of products, including CD.

Establishing Standards

Many bitter battles were fought between 1972 and 1976 over the choice of a standard optical videodisc system. LV won out by endurance, rather than friendly agreement, leaving much discouragement and the memory of wasted time and money in the minds of manufacturers and users.

This inspired Philips, later joined by Sony, to pursue agreement on an optical digital audio disc standard with all interested companies worldwide before releasing the CD product. The result, upon introduction of the audio CD in Japan in late 1983, and the rest of the world in early 1984, was a substantially united front of player makers and record companies.

CD ROM

The concept of CD ROM grew up during the early 1980s as CD matured and the feasibility and acceptability of digital encoding for the mainstream CD became clear. It had, by this time, occurred to many people that some version of CD could be used as a medium for the distribution of large quantities of digital data.

In late 1984, after the PC market had begun to stabilize, several brands of CD ROM drives were unveiled as prototypes. It wasn't until 1985 that commercial drives and subsystems were released, along with the first wave of CD ROM databases.

Other Read-Only Optical Discs

Several companies anticipated CD ROM in the early 1980s by adapting LV disks to the carriage of digital data. This is done by converting the data to a signal which has all the characteristics of a video signal, which is then placed on the LV disk.

Formats of this sort store 800 to 1000 MB of user data per disk surface. Each developer of such a product has its own proprietary format. They persist today mostly in applications in which the databases contain both TV imagery and digital data.

Other companies, anticipating the development of high performance small writable optical disc systems, are preparing read-only versions of these formats. 3M refers to these by the name "OROM", for optical read-only memory, and Sony calls its forthcoming product "DataROM."

These formats are neither physically nor logically compatible with CD ROM, although the drives for them could be designed to read CD ROM discs as well. They feature direct absolute addressing to small data blocks, short access times (below 150 msec) and fast data transfer (5 Mb/sec).

They are also only notions at present, being at least two years away from stable definition, let alone commercial availability. OROM and DataROM could represent the evolutionary direction of CD ROM, but their appearance on the horizon should not discourage anyone applying CD ROM to today's applications.

Writable Optical Discs

A third spinoff from the videodisc is known as the writable (or recordable) optical disc. Writable, in this case, means that the end user can store information directly on the disc rather than having to go through an involved manufacturing process. Writable discs include a range of products intended from the beginning to provide digital data storage. Much development work has been done in this area, both by manufacturers of computer peripherals and by videodisc makers in conjunction with computer-savvy companies. The first generation of writable optical discs are clearly derived from the videodisc, sharing many of its basic dimensions, drive operating principles, and methods and materials for disc fabrication.

Typical first-generation drives store about 1000 megabytes (1 gigabyte) per side of a 12-inch disc, take up 7 to 10 inches of height on a standard 19-inch relay rack, and cost about $10,000. These have been commercial since 1983, and are basic to the thousands of large-scale document-image storage systems sold worldwide in the past few years.

The second generation of writable optical disc drives became commercial during 1985. These are smaller and less expensive than their predecessors, being based on a combination of CD and small Winchester technology. They fit into the standard full-height 5.25-inch package, implying an interchangeability with existing magnetic products, or even among brands of optical drives—which is unfortunately still some time away.

All writable optical disc products currently available use write-once media. These permit any sector of any track to be written at any time, but do not permit written marks to be altered. (Hence the acronym *WORM*, for write once, read many.) This is very good for applications such as document storage and transaction recording, which require tamperproof storage, but is not in any way a direct replacement for traditional magnetic disk functions.

Write-Once Media Technology

The CD ROM standard uses the same disc and laser scanning technology, and the same mastering and replication methods as CD.

All writable optical media show readable marks almost immediately after the writing exposure, so that they can be read directly after writing, giving rise the the acronym "DRAW". Many drives read continuously while writing in order to verify data.

Most current commercial write-once media use one or more layers of vacuum-deposited thin metal films to record data. The recording is done by melting holes in the films, by making (and sometimes popping) bubbles in the films, or by locally fusing several layers.

Much work has been done to make these metal film media stable in prolonged storage, and current products are usually represented as stable for 10 years or more. This lifetime is not at all shortened by frequent reading of the stored data, unlike any other archival medium.

This is because no change takes place in the metal films unless they are heated past their melting temperatures, and reading does not heat the medium this much. This well-defined threshold for writing is thus a very desirable property. Most people count on write-once media to provide permanent storage; this requires marks which don't go away.

Some companies feel that sensitive layers made of dyes and polymers may provide superior performance and economy. The first depends on the stability of the materials, while the second comes from their ability to be coated from solution, like the oxide coatings on Winchester platters or, possibly, photographic film. No dye-polymer medium is currently commercially available.

Many other write-once media have been shown, based on all sorts of subtle and technically interesting effects. These include diazo processes, photographic emulsions processed to make a silver crust over a gelatin layer, and dispersions of small particles which agglomerate when heated. Most of these are grainy at some level, causing problems with reliable recording at very high densities.

Erasable Media

Many companies are now at work on erasable (more accurately, alterable) optical media. None of these are yet commercial; and functionally, none of the near-term commercial prospects are completely interchangeable with magnetic media. Some of these media have limits to the number of erase-rewrite cycles, and none permit continuous overwriting.

The erasable optical medium nearest to commercial availability is actually a magnetic medium. Magneto-optic (abbreviated "M-O") disks are written by a magnetic field, with the "writing" laser beam actually used to localize the writing. They are read optically, by sensing the rotation of polarization of light reflected from them.

The writing magnetic field is provided by a relatively large coil, which can only be switched at kilohertz rates, making it necessary to make an erase pass on a sector or track before writing new data. This prevents direct compatibility with magnetic disk drives.

Thin film media whose crystalline states look different from their amorphous states are in development as erasable optical media. The writing beam turns them locally amorphous, and an oval erase spot anneals the written spots to erase them. These media are still experimental, and have problems with fatigue and long term stability.

Dye-polymer media, similar to those developed as write-once media, are also being developed as erasable media. They are highly experimental, but quite promising. This may be the technology which provides an optical medium truly functionally compatible with current magnetic media.

What is CD ROM?

As pointed out earlier, one of the factors that contributed to the success of the CD was the existence of a set of standards developed jointly by Sony and Philips that allows any CD disc to be used on any CD player. Essentially, the CD standard specifies the following:

o A data format specifying space for data, address information, and error correction codes

o The basic channel and error correction coding (ECC) schemes, with room for additional data and ECC

o The microscopic and macroscopic physical structure of the disc

Upon realizing the potential for data applications of CD, Sony and Philips also put forth the CD ROM standard. The CD ROM standard uses the same disc and laser scanning technology, and the same mastering and replication methods as CD. The difference between the two, realized entirely within the CD user data format, is the provision in CD ROM of more powerful error correction and more explicit absolute addressing of data blocks.

57

Because of the very close relationship between CD and CD ROM, the explanation of the physical and logical aspects of the CD ROM standard in this section makes many references to CD. This can be taken as a reminder of how strongly CD ROM benefits from the commercial strength of CD.

Disc Structure

First we'll start with the disc itself. As Figure 1 shows, a CD ROM disc is 120 mm (about 4.72 inches) in diameter, 1.2 mm thick, and has a hole 15 mm across in the center. The information, represented by a spiral of small pits, is molded onto one surface. That surface is coated with a reflective metal layer, which is then coated with a protective lacquer.

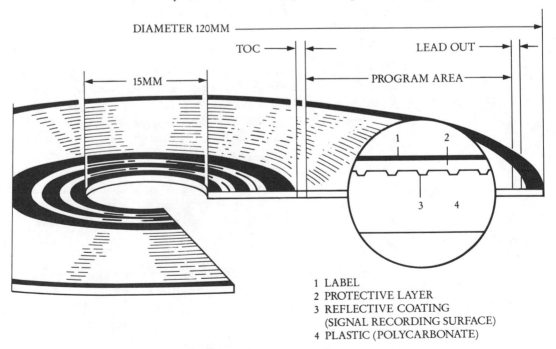

1 LABEL
2 PROTECTIVE LAYER
3 REFLECTIVE COATING
   (SIGNAL RECORDING SURFACE)
4 PLASTIC (POLYCARBONATE)

Figure 1. A compact disc

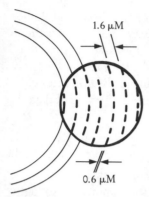

Figure 2. Pits and lands

The pits are 0.12 μm deep and about 0.6 μm wide. The neighboring turns of the spiral pattern of pits are 1.6 μm apart. This spacing corresponds to a track density of 16,000 tracks per inch (tpi), much higher than the figures associated with floppy (up to 96 tpi) or Winchester (several hundred tpi) magnetic disks. Along these turns, pits and the spaces between them (called *lands*) run from 0.9 to 3.3 μm long. (Figure 2 shows these relationships.) Just to put these very small numbers into perspective, here are a couple of gee-whizzers: The total length of the track on a CD ROM disc is almost 3 miles. The total number of pits on a CD ROM disc is almost 2 billion!

Getting data converted from its raw form to the pits and lands of an optical disc involves a process known as *mastering*. In this process the waveform carrying the encoded information is transferred from magnetic tape to a modulator (a sort of fast shutter). The modulator controls a powerful short-wavelength laser beam as it passes through a lens, forming a spot on the photoresist coating of a glass master disc.

The lens moves radially while the master disc spins, so that the information is laid out in the spiral track characteristic of CD ROM. When the photoresist is developed, it turns the exposed regions into pits. (The light beam in the master recorder is shaped so as to produce the characteristic sloping walls of CD ROM and CD pits.) The developed master has exactly the surface profile which each usable CD ROM disc should have.

That profile is copied, either by electroplating or photopolymer replication, onto one or more physical negatives. These "stampers" are used to form the actual discs sold to users. The transfer is usually done by injection molding, although several novel techniques, based on etching or cold embossing, are in pilot production. The material used in all processes is polycarbonate, a transparent plastic also used to make bulletproof windows and eye shields for racing helmets. This choice of material permits these discs to survive in one of the toughest of all environments—uncontrolled consumer use. CDs won't wilt when sitting in a car in the sunlight, and they won't break when pushed and poked by the youth of the world.

Optics

All optical storage devices use a laser beam which is focused to a very small spot by a special lens. Most current drives, including LV players, CD players, CD ROM drives, and large and small writable optical drives, use a small gallium arsenide semiconductor laser to produce this beam.

Focusing the Light

Gallium arsenide lasers produce oval beams of near-infrared light. The oval shape must be converted to a smaller circular spot about 1 μm (1/25,000 inch) in diameter in order to read the pits on the disc. This is not much larger than the wavelength of the light in the beam, so the focusing must be done carefully.

To produce the small spot, it is necessary to gather the laser beam into a sharply convergent cone of light. Convergence is measured by numerical aperture (abbreviated NA) which, for systems working in air, has a maximum value of 1.0.

CD ROM drives, along with CD and LV players and most writable optical disc drives, use NAs around 0.5, which corresponds to f/1.0 in a photographic lens. Unlike a camera lens, however, these lenses must be nearly perfect in their refractive action. Their errors (aberrations) must be small compared to a light wavelength.

These very special lenses (see Figure 3) are called *objectives* and are simplified descendants of microscope objectives. Unlike their forebears, CD ROM objectives need handle only one light wavelength and need not have a wide, flat field.

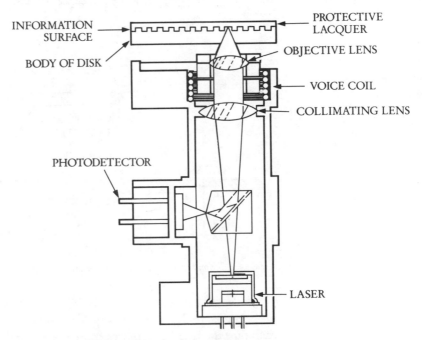

INFORMATION SURFACE

PROTECTIVE LACQUER

BODY OF DISK

OBJECTIVE LENS

VOICE COIL

COLLIMATING LENS

PHOTODETECTOR

LASER

Figure 3. Optical head of a CD ROM drive

While good microscope objectives with NA of 0.5 may have five or more *elements* (little lenses put together to provide the performance needed), many CD ROM objectives have only two or three elements. Some experimental designs use a single element, which eliminates the need for a barrel to support multiple elements and greatly reduces objective cost and weight. The intensive development work needed to make these very simple objectives is justified by their application to audio CD players, from which the revenue stream will greatly exceed that from CD ROM.

Reading the Pits

In order to read information from a CD, a laser beam is focused on the spiral track of pits and the amount of light reflected back into the objective lens is measured. Light striking one of the pits is diffracted (scattered) through such a wide angle that very little finds its way back into the lens. But when the spot focuses on the flat land between pits, most of it is reflected back into the lens (see Figure 4). It is the modulated signal produced by this combination of reflected and diffracted light that actually represents the information stored on the disc.

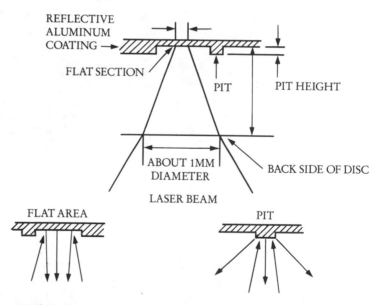

Figure 4. Relation between pits and photodetector output.

The reflected light goes to a photo detector, which produces a current proportional to the light intensity. The reflected light signal thus changes each time the laser beam moves from a pit to land or the reverse. Through a decoding process called Eight to Fourteen Modulation (we'll go over this later), the information derived from this varying light signal is converted to digital data useable by a computer.

Optical Protection and Integrity

One delightful characteristic of optical reading, compared with magnetic reading, is that the physical front of the objective lens can be several milli-meters from the information surface. This has two very important ramifications.

o "Crashes" are next to impossible, even with wavy discs and imperfect clamping in the drive. For comparison, the physical clearance between a Winchester head and disk is less than 0.5 μm, about $\frac{1}{2000}$ that of CD ROM.

o CD ROM drives send the laser beam through the disc. The informa-tion-bearing surface is thus protected by 1.2 mm of tough plastic. Because of the steep convergence of the light coming into the disc, the beam is almost 1 mm in diameter as it passes through the outside sur-face. The space provided by the protective layer ensures that the large beam simply glosses over the dirt and scratches that typically accumu-late on the disc.

Burying the information in this way is just one of many ways of ensuring that information is delivered uncorrupted to the user.

From Data to Pits and Back

With the physical description of the CD ROM disc and drive in hand, we proceed to follow the data from the source, through several transforma-tions, onto the disc, and then off the disc and to the user.

Making and Reading a CD ROM Disc

This path has many major parts, which group into jobs done at several lo-cations. We'll make a quick pass through the whole path, and then go back to examine several of the parts more closely. In the following list, items marked with two stars (**) are fully covered by the CD ROM standard; those with one star are partially covered by that standard.

- Premastering (at publisher or service bureau)
  - Indexing (or reindexing)
  - Organization (or reorganization)
  - Reformatting (possibly with some ECC)
  - Transfer to nine track tape **
- Mastering (at disc factory)
  - Error correction encoding **
  - Layered ECC **
  - CIRC **
  - Channel encoding (bits turned to binary signal) **
  - Master recording (binary signal turned to pits) **
- Disc Making (at disc factory)
  - Stamper making
  - Disc molding *
  - Metalization and lacquering *
- Reading (in user's system)
  - Optical scanning (including servos) *
  - Channel decoding **
  - Error correction decoding *
  - CIRC *
  - Layered ECC *
  - Interface to user's computer

Premastering

Real databases come in all sizes, shapes, and structures. To prepare a database for CD ROM recording, it must be reformatted to obey the file structure expected by the user's computer. Several companies have devised file structures which they believe are best suited to typical patterns of application, some concentrating on single users on specific types of hardware, some on multiple users with various operating systems. Some of these structures also include extra error correction (see below). This is an area not covered by the CD ROM standard, and so will go through its own period of settling down.

In most cases, before reformatting, a subject database will need to be reorganized and reindexed to facilitate access by the user. If needed, these operations precede reformatting. All of these are lumped under the name "premastering" and done either by special groups within publishing houses or by external service bureaus.

CD ROM premastering usually results in reels of 1600 bpi nine-track computer tape, which are sent to a disc factory.

Error Correction

At the disc factory, these tapes are read into the error correction encoder, which turns the user data into a longer data stream from which the user data can be recovered, despite disc defects. These defects (most often poorly formed pits, faults in the metal reflector layer, or gross damage to the outer surface) take chunks out of the signal coming from the disc.

This would result in "bursts" of wrong or missing bits, except that the error correction decoder, using the extra data generated by the encoder and placed on the disc along with the user data, can regenerate the lost bits.

The codes designed for CD and CD ROM can take the signal coming from a disk in which one in every 10,000 bits is wrong, with bursts over 1000 bits long, and regenerate all but one bit in every ten quadrillion. (For a discussion of error correction schemes, see the chapter by Hardwick.)

The first part of the error correction encoder uses a scheme called Layered ECC, which is part of the CD ROM standard, to encode user data 2048 bytes at a time. The result of this step is a stream of blocks (also called sectors), each of which contains:

- 12 bytes of synchronization
  - 1 byte of 00
  - 10 bytes of FF
  - 1 byte of 00
- 4 bytes of ID (minute, second, block, mode)
- 2048 bytes of user data

All codes for turning bits into some physical representation are called channel codes, because they encode the bits for passage through some channel of communication.

- 288 bytes of Layered ECC data

  o 4 bytes of error detection data

  o 8 bytes of 00

  o 276 bytes of error correction data

This is followed by another scheme called CIRC (for cross-interleaved Reed-Solomon code), which is part of the CD standard. CIRC encodes the data in the above blocks data 24 bytes at a time, adding 8 bytes of additional error correction data each time. The CIRC encoding also includes interleaving, a scrambling process which helps the decoders in the user's drive to chop very long error bursts into lots of short ones.

These encoding steps are completely standardized, but there is some flexibility in the complementary decoding, done in the user's drive. Different manufacturers have come up with various ways to use the additional data produced by the encoder, resulting in different levels of data integrity. Everybody does well, but some do better.

If a file structure with yet additional ECC has been used (see above), the complementary decoding can be done in the controller or, in software, in the user's computer.

Important as error correction is, detection of erroneous data is even more important. If you know data is wrong, you can take steps to get it right (you can get another copy of the CD ROM you're working with). If you don't know data is wrong, you'll use it and have problems later.

Luckily, error detection encoding is very simple and reliable. Error detection codes of the sort used in CD ROM have nondetection probabilities below 10^{-25}. Put in more concrete terms, this means one undetected wrong bit in 2 quadrillion CD ROM discs. Well, to put that in more concrete terms, that would be a stack of bare discs 1 billion miles high, or enough to provide everyone in the United States with 1000 discs. Why not just take my word that CD ROM error detection codes are reliable?

Storing the data

In order to store bits on a physical medium, they must be transformed into some pattern suitable for registration on that medium. All codes for turning bits into some physical representation are called channel codes, because they encode the bits for passage through some channel of communication. Such channels include magnetic media, paper tape, telephone lines, radio links, and of course, optical disc.

Nearly all high-density digital data storage devices, including CD ROM, use *binary channel codes,* which represent one of two well-defined states at any given location. Based on the values of the original data, binary channel codes determine the positions of the beginnings and endings, and therefore the length of the pits and spaces written by the recording laser.

65

The channel code for CD and CD ROM is called EFM (for eight-to-four-teen modulation). It turns the user data, along with error correction data, address information, synchronization patterns, and other miscellaneous content, into a stream of "channel bits". Channel bits are turned into a binary signal, and sent to the mastering machine to be turned into pits.

In a CD ROM drive, an EFM decoder reverses the process and recovers the formatted and error correction encoded data, which is then cleaned up and deformatted by the error correction decoder and interface circuitry.

Contrary to what one might think, pits and lands (the spaces between pits) do not correspond to *1s* and *0s*, either of user data or channel bits. Instead, a *channel 1* is represented by the *transition* from a pit to a land or from a land to a pit, and the *length* of the pit or land indicates the number of *channel 0s*. This concept is illustrated in Figure 4, which shows a section of track and the channel bits represented by the pits and lands.

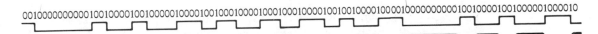

Figure 5. Channel 1 is represented by the transition from a land to a pit or a pit to a land. Channel 0s are represented by the run length between transition (the length of the pit or land).

If you study this figure and think about this method of representing data, you will realize that it is impossible to represent adjacent *channel 1s*. As a matter of practice, there will never be two *channel 1s* (two transitions) without at least two *channel 0s* between them. The reason for this (such things don't happen by accident) can be traced to the pit resolution, which is limited to a certain size because of the wavelength of the laser light and the numerical aperature of the objective lens used in the drive. Adjacent transitions too close together could not be read. A 3 channel-bit run (a *channel 1* followed by at least two *channel 0s*) allows adequate resolution and has been chosen as the minimum run length. The maximum run length, in order to allow the data to be self-clocking, and not interfer with the servos, turns out to be 11 bits. These considerations are what have led to the 14-bit modulation symbol mentioned earlier: 14 bits are the minimum that can represent the 8 user data bits in a CD ROM "symbol" and still meet these requirements. The actual conversion of 8 user-bit bytes to 14 channel-bit modulation codes is done in a lookup table, a portion of which is shown in Figure 6.

	DATA BITS	CHANNEL BITS
0	00000000	01001000100000
1	00000001	10000100000000
2	00000010	10010000100000
3	00000011	10001000100000
4	00000100	01000100000000
5	00000101	00000100010000
6	00000110	00010000100000
7	00000111	00100100000000
8	00001000	01001001000000
9	00001001	10000001000000
10	00001010	10010001000000

Figure 6. Part of the 8-to-14 code conversion table

This 14 channel-bit modulation symbol solves the minimum run length problem for bits within a symbol but still leaves a problem at the concatenation points of the 14-bit symbols: a 1 at the end of one symbol could be too close to a 1 at the beginning of the next. This is solved by placing 3 *merge* channelbits between symbols (2 would suffice, but for other reasons 3 are used).

So now each 8-bit user data byte is represented by a total of 17 channel bits. A set of 24 of these 17-bit symbols is combined with a sync pattern (another 24 channel bits plus 3 merge bits), a control and display symbol, and 8 error correction symbols to form a *frame*, which is the basic unit of information storage on a CD. The table in Figure 7 shows the composition of a frame.

SYNC. PATTERN	24 + 3 CHANNEL BITS
CONTROL & DISPLAY	1 × (14 + 3) CHANNEL BITS
DATA	24 × (14 + 3) CHANNEL BITS
ERROR CORRECTION	8 × (14 + 3) CHANNEL BITS
	TOTAL 588 CHANNEL BITS

Figure 7. The composition of a frame

Thus, a frame carrying 24 bytes (192 bits) of user data is represented by 588 channel bits. These channel bits are actually instructions to the master recorder, in the sense that a pit will be started when a 1 channel bit is received, continued while the channel bits are *0s*, and ended when the next 1 channel bit is received. Figure 8 shows the stages that user data goes through in order to become pits.

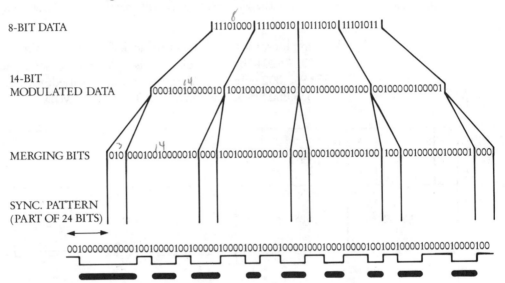

8-BIT DATA |11101000|11100010|10111010|11101011|

14-BIT
MODULATED DATA |00010010000010|10010001000010|00010000100100|00100000100001|

MERGING BITS |010|00010010000010|000|10010001000010|001|00010000100100|100|00100000100001|000|

SYNC. PATTERN
(PART OF 24 BITS) |

0010000000000100100001001000001000010010001000010001001000010010010000100001000001000100

Figure 8. The conversion from bytes to pits

Frames are grouped together in *blocks,* with 98 frames forming a block (also called a sector). Blocks occur 75 times per second (this is explained later), with each one carrying 2352 bytes (98 × 24) of user data in the CD standard, or 2048 bytes in the CD ROM standard (2352 bytes less the error correction, sync, and address bytes). This results in a sustained user data rate for CD ROM of 153.60K bytes/sec (1.2288 megabits/sec).

Storage capacity

Because the amount of data per track is not constant across the disc, addresses are expressed in the manner used in CD, that is, in units of 0 to 59 minutes, 0 to 59 seconds, and 0 to 74 blocks. This information is carried at the beginning of each block.

The 60-minute limit for CD ROM is not required by the standard—it can, as does CD, hold up to 74 minutes of sequential data—rather, it comes from the layout of the disc. Since the data spiral starts at the inside and runs toward the outside, the last 14 minutes of playing time in CD occupy the outer 5 mm of the disc. This just happens to be the hardest area to make well and keep clean. Since many CDs now exist which successfully use the whole disc, it is plausible that CD ROMs may also expand.

At 60 minutes, the total number of blocks available per CD ROM disc is 270,000. At 2048 bytes per block, this yields a total user capacity per disc of 552,960,000 bytes (553 MB). If 74 minutes is used, the numbers become 333,000 blocks and 681,984,000 bytes (682 MB).

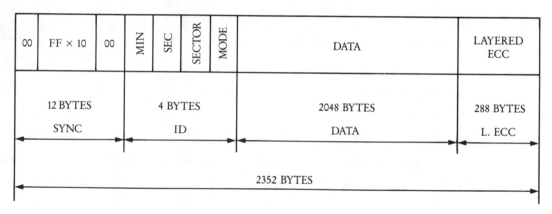

Figure 9. One CD ROM block

Figures such as 500, 550, 552, 553, and 600 MB appearing in the literature describing the capacity of a CD ROM disc reflect only different decisions about how much of the disc to use, as no variations of track pitch, block structure, ECC, or any other attribute of CD ROM are permitted within the standard.

Servomechanisms

CD ROM discs are mass produced in ways which leave them less than perfectly flat or perfectly uniform in thickness. Also, the clamping mechanism which holds and centers a disc in a drive does not do a perfect job.

The result is that the information surface moves toward and away from the objective lens, often in elaborate dance, as the disc turns. However, in order to accurately read the information from the disc, the lens must remain at precisely the same distance from the disc (stay in focus) and must exactly follow the spiral path of the pits (maintain tracking). The solution to these unavoidable inconsistencies is to build servo systems into the drive: electromechanical devices that automatically correct the performance of the focusing and tracking mechanisms. (For a complete discussion of servo systems, see the chapter by Lavender.)

There are dozens of ways, invented at many companies, to detect focus and tracking errors, and not quite as many ways to push the light spot around to correct these errors. This technical diversity makes the patent literature rich, but also provides for real differences in performance of various brands of CD ROM drives under real world conditions.

Further advances in this area will yield drives with faster access time, greater shock and vibration resistance, greater tolerance to warped and damaged discs, smaller size, and lower price. This is an area which is well served by the standards imposing only functional requirements.

Interfaces

The first round of CD ROM drives were shipped with "native" interfaces, meaning each drive had its own connector layout and logic for input of control signals and output of data, clock, error flag, and machine status signals.

This is just the sort of chaos which once reigned in magnetic disk drive circles and which has come to be relieved by the acceptance of standard interfaces. The trend there has been away from relatively "dumb" interfaces, such as SMD and ST506, to more "intelligent" interfaces such as ESDI and SCSI.

Optical disc drives for digital data, both CD ROM and the various writable formats, are moving even more rapidly in the direction of intelligent interfaces. One reason for this that is not shared by the magnetic contingent is that, in optical storage, error correction really should be done by specialized hardware attached to the basic drive. With the advent of inexpensive custom chip SCSI controllers, it is no surprise that most optical drives, including CD ROM, now speak SCSI. (For a discussion of the SCSI interface, see the chapter by Warren.)

70

Connection to Real Systems

The technology of CD ROM is impressive, both in the performance numbers which result and in the depth of consideration already made for matters large and small. However, it should never be assumed that the system was developed, or that this book was assembled, just because the technology was so terrific.

The real (commercial) world does not really like new, esoteric technology. It prefers old stuff that works, or new things which have simmered down enough to at least be stable. Even the latter penetrate the hearts and minds of other than techno-jocks only when they actually solve real and important problems in ways much better than those previously available.

The microcomputer industry has justly been accused of being technology-driven, bringing out ever newer and niftier hardware and software before the real user community has figured out the old stuff. The hard-nosed realists then mount their soapboxes and insist that the industry become market-driven.

History shows that a stable balance combines spontaneous technical innovation with clear, functional understanding of real markets. The fulcrum for this balance is systems architecture, reaching out to integration on one side and specification on the other.

Summary

CD ROM is one of the most stimulating ingredients added to the computer systems pot in many a year. Many powerful technologists have put together the basic system, and begun putting together applications, but it is wonderful to see the marketplace rising up to take CD ROM in and set the pace and direction for further development.

Those concerned with making computer systems will now have many good reasons to pursue some of the esoteric, "answer without a question" subjects which have been distracting them. And those concerned with making a buck will have many good things to put in front of the people with the bucks.

All figures and diagrams courtesy of Philips Subsystems and Peripherals, Inc., a division of North American Philips Corporation.

About the Author

Leonard Laub studied physics at the University of Chicago, Illinois Institute of Technology and Northwestern University. In 1965 he began work in the research department of Zenith Radio Corporation in

Chicago, working at first on acousto-optics (including laser scanning and projection TV), signal and image processing, photographic and holographic image storage and laser system design (including rapid scanning, nanometer resolution non-contact profilometers), later on optical videodisc recording and playback (including design of master recorders and consumer players).

It should never be assumed that CD ROM was developed, or that this book was assembled, just because the technology was so terrific.

In 1976 he went to Xerox Electro-Optical Systems in Pasadena, California as Manager of Optical Storage Technology to set up a program to develop read/write optical disc systems, both for Xerox product and special purpose applications. The success of this program made it possible to sell a large government contract for a document storage and retrieval system.

In 1978 he established in Pasadena a new division of Exxon Enterprises, called Star Systems, for the purpose of developing and building read/write optical disc systems for computer and office system applications. He directed all development and engineering activities from the beginning and later directed product planning and system architecture activities. This division had notable technical success, grew rapidly and was sold in 1981 to Storage Technology Corporation.

In 1981, he founded Vision Three, Inc. to carry on at full scale the consulting and custom systems work he has been involved in since 1972.

He is listed in *Who's Who in Finance and Industry, Who's Who in Frontier Science and Technology,* and *Who's Who in the West.* He is the author of numerous articles and reports, the holder of twelve patents and a member of OSA, IEEE, ACM, SPIE, SPSE and the Western Area Committee of the IEEE Computer Society.

Error Correction Codes: Key to Perfect Data

by Andrew Hardwick

73

One of the most challenging problems faced by the developers of compact disc audio technology was to store data on the error-prone optical medium while maintaining an error rate sufficiently low for music reproduction. With data densities of optical discs approaching 100 million bits per square centimeter, each bit occupies an area of only 1 square micron. Under these circumstances any microscopic defect or foreign particle on the disc surface can potentially cause hundreds of bit errors.

The subsequent development of the CD ROM compounded this problem. Though CD ROM and CD audio share the same laser optics, servo electronics, optical medium, and disc mastering process, the CD ROM must outperform CD audio in its ability to return correct data by a factor of 1000 or more. The audio compact disc system can tolerate occasional errors, while the CD ROM must return error-free data if it is to be useful as a data storage device.

> **Though CD ROM and CD audio share the same laser optics, servo electronics, optical medium, and disc mastering process, the CD ROM must outperform CD audio in its ability to return correct data by a factor of 1000 or more.**

For the CD audio player, a 2340-byte sector of data represents less than $\frac{1}{75}$ of a second of the musical piece being played. If errors occur in any or all of the bytes in a block, the audio player can simply substitute the previous sector for the erroneous one; the substitution is nearly undetectable to the human ear. Even if an erroneous block occurs several times on a single compact disc, the loss of audio fidelity will probably be unnoticed.

The CD ROM, on the other hand, must meet the stringent data integrity standards required of any computer peripheral. Since a single byte error in computer data can be disastrous, a mass storage device must be able to return data with essentially no errors. In practice, the accepted standard for computer storage devices is no more than 1 byte in error per 10^{12} bytes. This corresponds to a single-byte error in roughly 2000 CD ROM discs. Data integrity for a read-only technology such as CD ROM is even more important than for other peripherals, since traditional error control techniques such as elimination of bad sectors and direct read after write (DRAW) cannot be used.

The method of increasing data reliability on the imperfect optical medium for the demanding CD ROM application is the use of error correction coding (ECC). ECC involves appending redundant data to the original data as it is written on the disc. If the redundant information is calculated according to certain algorithms, it can be used to detect and correct errors when the data is read back. This process is usually called error detection and correction (EDAC).

Error Detection

Error detection and error correction are closely linked and complementary functions of ECC. Any given ECC has a certain amount of "power," or ability to detect and correct errors, that is predetermined by the way the redundant information is calculated. When deciding on an ECC algorithm, a system designer determines how much of the code's power will be used to detect errors and how much will be used to correct errors. There is a direct tradeoff between the two functions.

As an example of error detection, consider a simple checksum. Assume the data to be recorded consists of eight 2-digit decimal numbers. A ninth 2-digit number that is simply the modulo-100 sum of the original data is appended to the eight numbers.

Original Data	Sum	Checksum
10 21 19 94 02 63 50 24	283	83

Since a single byte error in computer data can be disastrous, a mass storage device must be able to return data with essentially no errors.

If the eight original numbers and the checksum are recorded on a disc and then later read back, any single error in the data can be detected by re-calculating the checksum and comparing the new checksum with the original one. For example, if the fourth data number happened to have changed from 94 to 78, the new checksum would be 67. A comparison with the original checksum of 83 would then indicate that an error had occurred in the data. Any single error can be detected with 100 percent certainty, since any change to a single number is guaranteed to generate a different checksum.

If two errors occur, this method is still likely to detect that errors have occurred, since the new checksum would most likely not be the same as the original. However, two errors may occur that cancel each other's effect. For example, if errors caused the 10 to change to 13 and the 21 to change to 18, the checksum would still calculate to 83. The algorithm would indicate correct data. Thus, this simple error detection scheme is not 100 percent safe if multiple errors occur. Nevertheless, if errors are relatively unlikely events, then multiple errors in a block of eight numbers should be even more unlikely. Note that in any case the checksum gives no indication of which number was in error or what its value should have been. The checksum is purely an error detection technique and has no error correcting power.

Simple checksums similar to the one described here are often used in low-speed data communication links. Since data can be retransmitted when an error is detected, error detection alone is sufficient. More powerful forms of error detection are often used in computer peripherals. For example, Reference Technology's ECC algorithm for the CD ROM uses a powerful cyclic redundancy check (CRC) after error correction is performed, to ensure that no bytes are left uncorrected by the ECC.

Error Correction

Error correction involves not only detecting that errors have occurred but determining the locations of the errors and restoring the original data values. To illustrate error correction, consider the Hamming code, a binary error-correcting code capable of correcting a single-bit error in a 4-bit data word. This code requires that three "check bits" be calculated and appended to the data word, resulting in a 7-bit "code word." Each check bit is the modulo-2 sum (odd parity) of three of the data bits.

Data bits

a_1, a_2, a_3, a_4

Check bits

$c_1 = a_1 + a_2 + a_3$
$c_2 = a_1 + a_3 + a_4$
$c_3 = a_1 + a_2 + a_4$

Where + stands for modulo-2 addition

Once the data and check bits have been written on the disc, they can be used to correct single-bit errors that occur in the data or check bits when the data is read. If new check bits are recalculated from the data read, then added (mod 2) to each old check bit, the following is the result.

	New check bit (recalculated)	Old check bit (read from disc)
$e_1 =$	$(a_1 + a_2 + a_3)$	$+ \; c_1$
$e_2 =$	$(a_2 + a_3 + a_4)$	$+ \; c_2$
$e_3 =$	$(a_1 + a_2 + a_4)$	$+ \; c_3$

If there were no errors in the data read, then e1, e2, and e3 will all equal zero, because the new check bits calculated will be equal to the old check bits; and in modulo-2 arithmetic, $0 + 0 = 0$ and $1 + 1 = 0$. If there were any errors in the data, at least one of e1, e2, and e3 will be nonzero, and e1, e2, e3 form a three-bit pattern indicating which bit was in error. This pattern of check-bit mismatches is generally called the "syndrome." It can be used to determine which bit is in error using the following table.

e1	e2	e3	Error was in:
0	0	0	No error
0	0	1	c3
0	1	0	c2
0	1	1	a4
1	0	0	c1
1	0	1	a1
1	1	0	a3
1	1	1	a2

As an example, assume that the data bits to be written are a1 a2 a3 a4 = 0101. Then:

$a1 = 0, a2 = 1, a3 = 0, a4 = 1$
$c1 = a1 + a2 + a3 = 0 + 1 + 0 = 1$
$c2 = a2 + a3 + a4 = 1 + 0 + 1 = 0$
$c3 = a1 + a2 + a4 = 0 + 1 + 1 = 0$

Data written to disc: a1 a2 a3 a4 c1 c2 c3 = 0101100

Now assume that when the data is read back, an error occurs in a2, changing it to a 0, while all the other data bits and check bits are read back correctly.
$a1 = 0, a2 = 0, a3 = 0, a4 = 1, c1 = 1, c2 = 0, c3 = 0$

Calculate the syndromes:

$e1 = a1 + a2 + a3 + c1 = 0 + 0 + 0 + 1 = 1$
$e2 = a2 + a3 + a4 + c2 = 0 + 0 + 1 + 0 = 1$
$e3 = a1 + a2 + a4 + c3 = 0 + 0 + 1 + 0 = 1$

Looking up the syndrome pattern 111 in the table shows that an error has occurred in bit a2. Since a value of 0 was read for a2, the correct value for a2 must be 1. The single-bit error can therefore be corrected.

... the accepted standard for computer storage devices is no more than 1 byte in error per 10^{12} bytes. This corresponds to a single-byte error in roughly 2000 CD ROM discs.

If only a single-bit error occurs in the data word, this simple Hamming code is 100 percent effective in detecting and correcting the error. However, if multiple-bit errors occur in the word, the code breaks down. For example, two-bit errors in the word can masquerade as a single-bit error in a different location, so the Hamming code may mistakenly change a bit that was not in error, thus creating errors rather than correcting them. Again, as with the checksum example, if bit errors are unlikely events, then the chance of multiple errors in a word is remote.

The various existing error-correcting codes differ greatly in the complexity of the algorithms used to calculate the check information and syndromes, in the number of data symbols per check symbol, and in the number of errors they can successfully correct or detect. However, all ECC schemes follow the general pattern of the Hamming code example:

○ Check information is calculated and stored with the data when it is written on the disc.

○ This information is used to calculate the syndromes when the data is read.

○ The syndromes are used to determine the locations and values of any errors.

Error Correction for CD ROM

CD ROM and CD audio use a popular family of error correction codes known as the Reed-Solomon codes. Both types of drives use an internal error correction scheme called the Cross Interleaved Reed-Solomon Code (CIRC). The CIRC is part of the standard for CD audio and CD ROM and is implemented in the hardware of all CD audio and CD ROM drives. It uses two independent Reed-Solomon codes to achieve an error rate of one uncorrectable error per 10^9 bytes. While this level of performance is completely acceptable for CD audio applications, it is unsuitable for the CD ROM application, since an error rate of one per 10^9 means that one of every two discs would have an uncorrectable error.

To boost the reliability of CD ROM data to the level of a high-performance mass-storage device, a backup error correction scheme is initiated whenever the CIRC fails. This second level of correction is usually called

78

the "layered ECC" and is performed by the host computer's software. It is called "layered" because it represents a final layer of error correction added on top of the CIRC error correction. The layered ECC is a two-dimensional variety of Reed-Solomon code that allows use of a powerful iterative algorithm to correct a large number of errors in a 2340-byte sector of data.

Data integrity for a read-only technology such as CD ROM is even more important than for other peripherals, since traditional error control techniques such as elimination of bad sectors and direct read after write . . . cannot be used.

Before data is written to a CD ROM disc, it is divided into "blocks" of 2048 bytes each. At the front of each block, a 4-byte header identifying the block's position on the disc is added. Then, 4 CRC error-detection bytes are calculated and appended to the block, for a total of 2056 bytes. Finally, 8 bytes of zeros are appended to round the block out to 2064 bytes.

The 2064-byte block is then arranged in a rectangular array, with 43 columns and 24 rows of 2-byte words ($43 \times 24 \times 2 = 2064$). The even- and odd-numbered bytes of the block are considered independent groups, so the array is treated as two separate arrays containing 43 columns and 24 rows of bytes. These 1032-byte arrays are called the even and odd subblocks, respectively.

For each of the 43 columns of each subblock, two check bytes are calculated and appended to the bottom of the column. The check bytes for each column depend only on the 24 bytes in that column. This process essentially creates 2 new rows, expanding each subblock to a 43×26 array (1118 bytes). Then, for each of the 26 rows of the enlarged arrays, row check bytes are calculated and appended to the end of the row. In this case, the check bytes for each row depend only on the 43 bytes in that row. The two columns of check bytes enlarge each subblock to 45 columns by 26 rows, for a total of 1170 bytes each, and 2340 bytes in the entire sector. Figure 1 illustrates this array.

The Reed-Solomon code is capable of correcting a single error in any row or column, and can detect multiple errors in a row or column with fairly good reliability. If multiple errors occur in a block when it is read from the

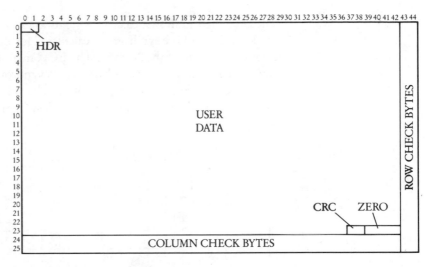

Figure 1. CD ROM sector format

disc, Reference Technology's layered ECC algorithm alternates row and column correction, correcting single errors in rows and columns until all errors have been eliminated.

Suppose the pattern of 13 errors shown in Figure 2 occurs in the even subblock:

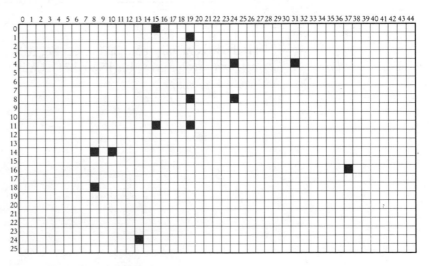

Figure 2. Example error pattern

The ECC algorithm first calculates syndromes for each row and column of the subblock. One syndrome is calculated for each of the 43 original columns and each of the 26 rows. The ECC then sees that 9 of the rows and 8 of the columns have errors (nonzero syndromes), and chooses to perform correction on rows first. All rows having only a single error (rows 0, 1, 16, 18, and 24) are corrected, leaving the error pattern shown in Figure 3.

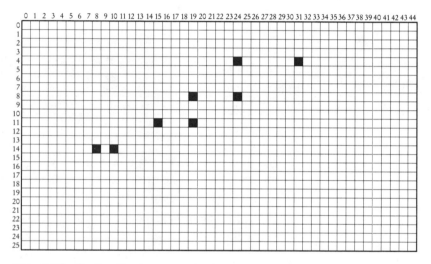

Figure 3. After first iteration of row correction

Next, the ECC applies column correction, correcting all columns having a single error (columns 8, 10, 15, and 31). Only the four errors shown in Figure 4 remain.

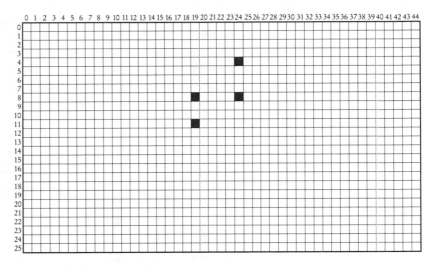

Figure 4. After first iteration of column correction

A second application of row correction eliminates single errors in rows 4 and 11, leaving only the two errors shown in Figure 5.

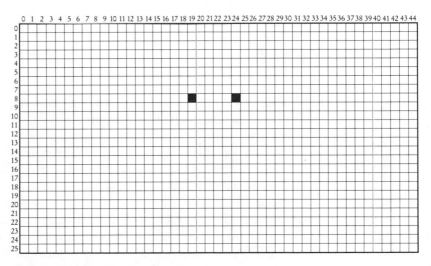

Figure 5. After second iteration of row correction

A second application of column correction eliminates the two remaining errors, and the ECC algorithm terminates. The same algorithm described here would then be applied to the odd subblock, if errors were found in it.

Reference Technology's layered ECC algorithm uses an additional error-correcting technique that increases the correction power of the code even further. This procedure is invoked whenever three iterations of row and column correction fail. It allows the ECC to correct two errors in a row or column, under certain circumstances, using an algorithm known as "erasure correction." As an example, consider the error pattern shown in Figure 6.

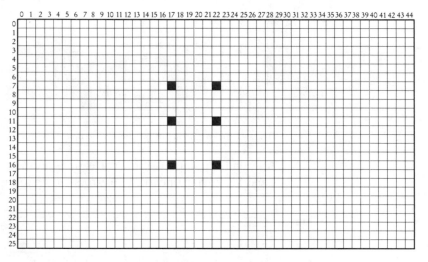

Figure 6. Example error pattern for erasure correction

Row and column correction would certainly fail to correct this pattern, since there are no rows or columns with single errors. However, the ECC knows which two columns have errors, since the only nonzero column syndromes it calculates will be for columns 17 and 22. So, when attempting to correct one of the bad rows (row 7, for example), the ECC knows in advance the locations of the two errors in the row. Because error correction consists essentially of finding the location and value of errors, half the problem is already solved. This "head start" allows the ECC to use its power to find the values of both erroneous bytes in the row. The ECC applies a special double erasure correction algorithm for each of the three bad rows, correcting all the errors in the block.

Error correction involves not only detecting that errors have occurred but determining the locations of the errors and restoring the original data values.

Reference Technology's ECC algorithm as described here has been the subject of extensive simulations. The simulations show that the algorithm fails less than once in 10,000 (10^4) applications, considering the number of errors usually present in a block after a CIRC failure. Since the CIRC suffers only one uncorrectable error per 10^9 bytes, the combination of CIRC followed by layered ECC gives an overall byte error rate of better than one per 10^{13} bytes. This error rate surpasses by a factor of 10 the "acceptable" error rate of 10^{12}. The layered ECC provides the necessary additional data integrity to transform the error-prone compact disc into a reliable storage medium for gigabyte quantities of computer data.

About the Author

Andrew Hardwick joined Reference Technology, a leading supplier of hardware, software, and data services for distribution of information on optical disc, after receiving his B.S.E.E. degree from the University of Colorado in 1984. His responsibilities include development of error correction software, device drivers, and interface hardware for Reference Technology's family of CD ROM products.

Product Development Engineer, CD ROM
Reference Technology, Inc.
5700 Flatiron Parkway
Boulder, Colorado 80301
(303) 449-4157

SCSI Bus Eases Device Integration

by Carl Warren

The Small Computer Systems Interface (SCSI), unlike other interfaces, is a complete bus structure that is subordinate to the rest of the system architecture. As such, it provides system integrators with a wide range of integration opportunities and alternatives.

System architecture requirements and cost determine the integration alternatives. Interfacing requirements vary from application to application. Personal computers and smaller business systems typically require a "dumb" controller with just enough electronics to match the device-level electronics on the storage device. As system capability and performance increase, intelligent interface bus designs, such as the Shugart Associates System Interface (SASI) and SCSI, become more important to the system integrator.

SCSI provides an easy method of eliminating cost-consuming interfacing tasks by providing a rich set of commands and a defined bus structure.

System integrators can benefit from SCSI in the more complex system architectures. Unlike single-user systems requiring only low levels of intelligence such as that provided by SASI, these architectures call for an interface bus that permits the addition of mass storage, optical storage, local area networks (LANs), printers, plotters, modems, and other devices. Additionally, SCSI provides an easy method of eliminating cost-consuming interfacing tasks by providing a rich set of commands and a defined bus structure. Because system integration can take longer than product development, the use of SCSI can lessen the time required to get a product to market. Besides these benefits, SCSI offers a number of other advantages, including service to multiple hosts as well as devices, and full arbitration and message passing. The latter eludes bus contention problems while maximizing use of a system architecture.

Command Set a Key Element

Among the commands that make SCSI rich in features are those that allow the formatting of storage devices and that provide the ability to read and write to and from peripherals and to set special file marks for locating data on either storage devices or LANs. Additionally, provisions are made for directing output to various hard-copy attachments or storage devices and for allowing the copying of data from one machine to another or the sending of data to other hosts.

85

Avoiding Rocks and Shoals

An intelligent interface helps integrators avoid the rocks and shoals of integration, but it can be costly in terms of performance. Because SCSI is intelligent, command latencies must be included in the performance calculation. Therefore, SCSI will be much slower than an interface directly under the control of the host CPU. On the other hand, controlling the input/output (I/O) with the CPU makes the processor unavailable for other tasks; SCSI relieves the CPU of these slow I/O functions. In addition, SCSI provides special command and hardware bus arbitration functions, such as disconnect/reconnect, which allow communication among multiple hosts and devices. This feature can be very beneficial for powerful multitasking and multiuser business systems.

Multiple Devices Share the Bus

The purpose of SCSI is to join mismatched devices electrically so that signals from one can be translated and used by the other. But SCSI does more than act as an electronic translator. This interface defines a complete bus system whereby definite electrical paths and communication protocols are clearly determined. Thus, like any bus or backplane, other devices can be added to take advantage of the distribution of signals and information.

As currently defined, a SCSI controller can support as many as eight logical units. These logical units can be configured as one host computer and seven peripherals, seven hosts and one peripheral, or a mix in between. Even more devices can be connected using a gateway to a local area network. In addition, each of the eight logical units can support an additional seven units, with one device serving as the bus master. (However, a system fully loaded in this manner suffers performance degradation.)

The ability of the SCSI bus to control seven peripherals through one backplane slot is a system integrator's dream come true.

The ability to turn the bus over to an initiator to send a message to a target becomes important as the number of devices grows on the SCSI controller or within the total system architecture.

A key advantage of the SCSI bus is its ability to serve a wide range of performance requirements. Most SCSI configurations are single-initiator, single-target systems, usually with one host computer as the initiator and a disk drive (or CD ROM reader) as the target. A single-initiator, multiple-target configuration with arbitration increases the number of devices you can hang off the bus. But under arbitration's master/slave relationship, one target must relinquish the bus before transfers to others can take place.

However, multiple-initiator, multiple-target systems with multiple host computers fully utilize SCSI capabilities by allowing the full complement of eight units to be attached to the bus. In this mode, SCSI acts as a clustered local area network (LAN).

RAM buffers can be placed in the SCSI controller to allow the rapid collection and transference of data between devices using direct-memory-access (DMA) methods.

The ability of the SCSI bus to control seven peripherals through one backplane slot is a system integrator's dream come true. And because SCSI serves as its own "traffic cop" to arbitrate bus access, system integrators need only be concerned with data management at the point of access to the SCSI bus: the host-computer adapter, which is the vital link between the system bus and SCSI.

In operation, the initiator requests use of the bus; if it is available, the initiator passes a message to a target (such as another host, storage device, or printer), then disconnects from the bus. The return message, much like an electronic handshake to indicate that the message got to the other end, uses the same path to acknowledge receipt. The connect device typically holds the bus until the message passing is finished. Device priorities can be established, however. This priority arrangement determines which device has precedence and can take control of the bus. This is all handled via the bus arbitration scheme that is part of the microcode in the SCSI controller hardware.

Hierarchy by Design

The SCSI bus is hierarchical by design. System integrators can attach a host computer or multiple host computers to the SCSI bus via the host adapters. The adapters tailor the host bus to match the electrical and software characteristics of SCSI.

Because SCSI is for multiple-device environments, techniques that speed the transfer of data can be implemented in a cost-effective and system-efficient manner. For example, RAM buffers can be placed in the SCSI controller to allow the rapid collection and transference of data between devices using direct-memory-access (DMA) methods. Moreover, algorithms for error correction and data location can be embedded in the system to make maximum use of the RAM cache buffers.

Buffering Improves Performance

Buffering improves the operation of a disk system. An elementary method uses a single-ported cache buffer on the disk controller to provide interim storage for data between the disk and the host computer. But this type of buffer exacts performance penalties by increasing data-transfer times. For example, consider the transfer of a 512-byte sector from a 5-MHz drive into the sector buffer on the controller, followed by a 1.5-megabyte-per-second transfer over the SCSI bus. Because the buffer is single-ported, these two processes can't be overlapped. This situation increases the total transfer time to 1160 microseconds. Therefore, 1:1 interleaving (sometimes called noninterleaving) can't be used on the disk drive.

SCSI is being implemented as the interface of choice for optical-storage systems because of its ease of integration over a range of architectures and its powerful command set.

To maximize data-transfer rates, the SCSI system requires a method of controlling the cache buffer. For instance, Distributed Processing Technology's (DPT) PM3010 Series caching disk controller handles both a disk drive and the SCSI interface. Two separate data paths—to the SCSI bus and to the disk drive—allow simultaneous data transfers with maximum overlap. Using a Motorola MC68000 microprocessor to execute concurrent tasks, the PM3010 maintains and searches its 512K onboard cache memory (expandable to 16 megabytes) for blocks requested by the host.

SCSI Broadens the Picture

SCSI is being implemented as the interface of choice for optical-storage systems because of its ease of integration over a range of architectures and its powerful command set.

SCSI easily handles today's data-transfer rates and can be made to go faster. Currently, most SCSI devices are in the 12-MHz (1.5 megabytes per second) range. But SCSI isn't bandwidth-limited. It can handle 32 MHz (4 megabytes per second) rates at distances as great as 25 meters, extending the capability of the bus for future systems.

Further supporting the growth of SCSI is the development of application-specific integrated circuits (ASIC). For example, Adaptive Data Systems, Inc., offers the ADS-1000 VLSI disk controller that provides data handling for devices ranging from Winchester disk drives to optical drives. Adaptec, Inc., offers similar products to allow easy integration of SCSI devices to various host architectures.

About the Author

Carl Warren is western editor for *Mini-Micro Systems* magazine, a Cahners publication. He specializes in rotating memory, interfaces, and controllers. He is the industry scribe for such forums as The Freeman/ Porter Worldwide Data Storage Conference and Technology Forum's SCSI, Peripherals, and IPI forums. In the past 10 years Mr. Warren has written more than 3000 articles as well as several books and manuals on computer and storage technology. Prior to joining *Mini-Micro Systems* he was the peripherals editor for *EDN* magazine, also a Cahners publication, and editor-in-chief of *Interface Age*. In addition, he is a well-known speaker, having given more than 50 seminars on various aspects of computer and storage systems.

CD ROM Servo Systems

by Tony Lavender

If compact discs and players with infinite precision were cheap to produce, then playing the discs would not require elaborate control systems: the position of any piece of information on the disc surface would be known precisely, and the read mechanism could be placed absolutely at that position. Unfortunately, because the disc contains an incredibly high density of information on a thin plastic platter which is far from perfectly flat or round, this "open-loop" mode of operation is impossible. To read this information, it is necessary to use an interlocking set of "closed-loop" control, or servo, systems.

Let's briefly consider the nature of the disc which these servo systems are designed to read. It has a reflective surface, embossed with a spiral track of varying-length bumps. If light is focused through a lens onto the flat spaces between these bumps, it is reflected back into the lens. If, however, the light falls on one of the bumps, it is scattered in all directions, and most of it does not return to the lens (see Figure 1). The modulation, or change in intensity, of the light returning to the lens is what carries information from the disc to the player. Of course, if you want the information to be accurate, the disc must be spun at a certain speed, the light must be focused on the track, and the focused spot must not wander off onto adjacent tracks.

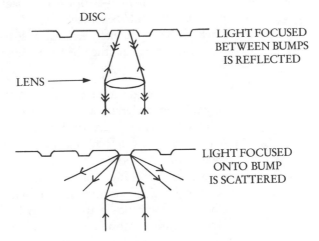

Figure 1. Reading the bumps

Each piece of information on the disc has an addressable starting point some place along the 3 miles of spiral track. When the drive is ordered to read a piece of information, the lens must be moved across the disc to the appropriate one of approximately 20,000 tracks. The following servo systems are required to do this:

○ A disc-rotation servo

○ A focus servo

○ A track-following servo

○ A track-finding servo

The Disc-Rotation Servo

To detect focus, then, a system need only be able to determine whether the returning beam is parallel, converging, or diverging.

The electronic systems which convert the modulated signal from the disc into meaningful information can work properly only if the disc rotational speed is controlled within fairly narrow limits. To make matters more complicated, the rotational speed must decrease as the lens is moved from tracks at the inner radius of the disc to those at the outside. This is because CDs are recorded in a constant linear velocity (CLV) mode in order to pack as much information as possible onto the surface. The price paid for this increase in information density is that the speed of rotation has to be changed when going from one area of the disc to another, increasing the data access time. If the discs were recorded at a constant angular velocity (CAV), as are all high-performance magnetic and optical disc drives, information would become more and more spread out toward the outer tracks. Despite the inefficient use of space, movement from one area of the disc to another could then be fast because the rotational speed would not have to change.

As it is, for any given track on the disc surface, there is a correct rotational speed. When seeking (moving the lens) from one track to a distant one, there is no guarantee that the lens will arrive at the correct track (this is not an ideal world). To read address information from the disc, its speed of rotation must be close to right; to set the rotational speed, the address must be known. How does the system cope with this dilemma? If an independent position sensor is included in the system, the speed can be set close enough for the electronics to lock onto the data signal and read the precise position. Most systems do not utilize an independent position sensor, however, and if the seek to another track is very much in error, they may spend considerable time "hunting" for the correct rotational speed before finally locking onto the data signal.

The Focus Servo

The information-carrying marks on the disc are minute—about the size of typical bacteria, in fact. The spot of light which reads the information must therefore also be very small. This spot size can be achieved only by taking the extremely pure light produced by a laser and focusing it with high-quality optics. If the disc is not exactly at the focal point of the systems's objective lens, the spot will be too large for accurate reproduction of the data; hence the need for a focus servo.

Remember that the disc is not very flat. In fact, toward the outer tracks it may be flapping up and down about a millimeter, while spinning at four revolutions per second. The lens, therefore, must be attached to an actuator which is capable of moving it quickly to follow this disc motion. A typical actuator design is shown schematically in Figure 2. The lens is attached to a coil of wire which sits in a magnetic field; if electrical current is passed through the coil, a force results which moves the lens up or down.

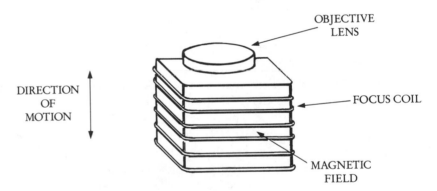

Figure 2. Typical actuator design

The remaining requirement is a feedback signal which tells the system whether or not the spot is in focus on the disc, and if not, which way the lens should be moved. The most commonly used method for producing this feedback signal is known as the astigmatic focus detection method. Figure 3 shows a typical implementation of this detection method (but bear in mind that there may be differences in detail from one manufacturer's system to another).

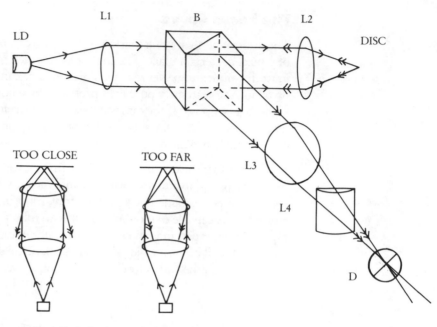

Figure 3. Typical astigmatic focus detection method

Light from the laser diode (LD) is strongly divergent; a collimating lens (L1) turns this divergent beam into a collimated, or parallel, bundle of rays. This beam passes through a beam splitter (B), then through an objective lens (L2) which focuses it to a spot on the disc. The light is reflected back into the objective lens, which then produces a collimated returning beam. If the lens is too close to the disc, the returning beam diverges; if it is too far away, the beam converges. To detect focus, then, a system need only be able to determine whether the returning beam is parallel, converging, or diverging.

The returning beam enters the beam splitter and some of it is reflected at right angles toward the collimation detector. Many systems use polarizing optics to increase the selectivity of this operation, but this possibility is ignored here. The beam passes through a converging lens (L3) and then a cylindrical lens (L4). The cylindrical lens is simply a section of a cylinder; it has the property of acting like a converging lens along one axis and like a flat piece of glass along its other axis. The result is that there are two focal points for this returning light beam. At one of these focal points the light is focused to a vertical line; at the other, to a horizontal line; and midway between, it is blurred into a circle (see Figure 4). If a detector is placed at this midway point, and if the beam entering this collimation-detector is perfectly parallel, the detector will see a round spot. If the beam is divergent, the spot will be a vertical oval; if convergent, it will be a horizontal oval. By detecting these changes in spot shape, lens movement can be controlled to focus the spot precisely on the disc.

95

The actual structure of the detector is shown in Figure 4. It consists of four separate photodiodes, each producing an electrical signal proportional to the amount of light falling upon it. A vertical oval produces a signal mostly from segments A and C; a horizontal oval, from segments B and D; and a round spot produces equal signals from both pairs.

The feedback signal produced as described above is amplified and used to drive current through the coil of wire which moves the lens toward or away from the disc. In this way the distance between lens and disc can be fixed very precisely; in fact, the error is less than one thousandth of a millimeter.

In order to be a useful information-storage device, the CD ROM player must be capable of doing more than simply reading the spiral track sequentially from beginning to end. It must be able to go, quickly and precisely, to any desired item of information among the over 500 megabytes on the disc.

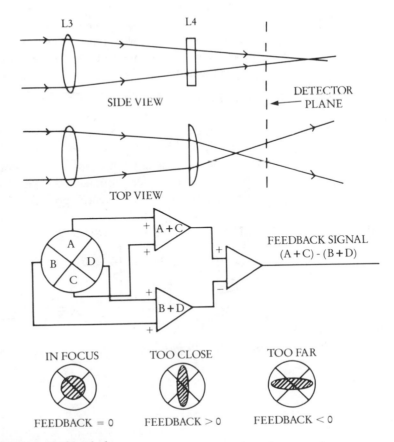

Figure 4. Checking the focus

96

The Track-Following Servo

Tracks on the CD are, in reality, made up of millions of individual bumps. Since the disc is spinning rapidly, these individual bumps, as far as the tracking servo is concerned, become blurred together. Each track then appears to be a continuous line of lower reflectivity, with an area of high reflectivity between tracks. The width of a track is 0.3 μm (1 μm is one thousandth of a millimeter), and the space between tracks is 1 μm. Since the hole in the center of the CD is not precisely located, and the disc suffers some warping during manufacture, the track may wander back and forth as much as 60 μm. The job of the tracking servo is to keep the data-reading spot on this wandering track within an accuracy of about 0.1 μm.

There are two different mechanisms commonly used to maintain the spot on track. The first utilizes a coil of wire wound at right angles to the focus actuator coil described above. Since this coil is also in the magnetic field, an electrical current through the coil causes the lens to move to one side or the other, and the spot of light moves correspondingly to follow the track. The other mechanism which may be employed uses a mirror placed below the lens; changing the angle of this mirror causes a similar motion of the spot on the disc.

There are also two methods for obtaining a position feedback signal, which indicates to the tracking servo whether the spot is on or off track. We will discuss the three-spot tracking system, which is the one more commonly used in high-performance players. The alternative "push-pull" system, which utilizes tracking information obtained from the same spot used to read data, suffers from degraded performance when the lens (or mirror) moves away from a central position.

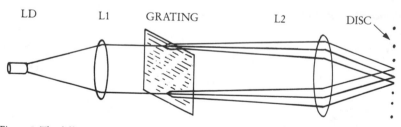

Figure 5. The diffraction grating

The information-carrying marks on the disc are minute—about the size of typical bacteria, in fact.

To create a three-spot tracking system, a diffraction grating is added in the path of the light from the laser, as shown in Figure 5. The grating splits the beam of light, producing a series of side beams as well as the central one described earlier. These additional beams, which are also focused on the disc, create additional spots to each side of the central, data-reading, spot. Only the two spots to each side of the central spot are used for the derivation of tracking information. By slightly tilting the grating, the tracking spots are positioned to either side of the track, as shown in Figure 6. One spot is slightly ahead of the center spot (about 20 μm), and the other is an equal distance behind it. The light from each of these spots is reflected from the disc and travels back through the optical pathway to a pair of tracking photodiodes which are situated on each side of the four-segment photodiode described earlier.

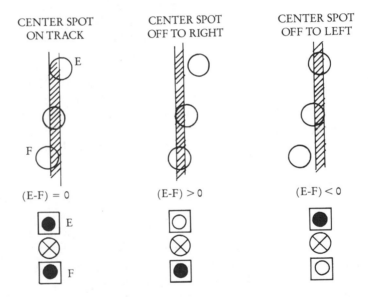

Figure 6. The tracking spots

If the central spot wanders off track to the right, tracking spot E will move onto the more reflective space between tracks; so the signal at its photodiode will increase. Spot F will move onto the less-reflective track, so its photodiode signal will drop. The tracking feedback signal, E − F, will then increase. Conversely, movement of the center spot to the left will cause the signal E − F to decrease. In this way, a tracking-position feedback signal is obtained. This signal is then amplified and used to control the movement of the lens (or the tracking mirror) to keep the center spot precisely on track.

The Track-Finding Servo

In order to be a useful information-storage device, the CD ROM player must be capable of doing more than simply reading the spiral track sequentially from beginning to end. It must be able to go, quickly and precisely, to any desired item of information among the over 500 megabytes on the disc. Therefore, another servo system is required, one which can reposition the data-reading spot of light on any one of the approximately 20,000 tracks.

The optical pickup, containing the laser, lenses, actuators, and photodiodes, is mounted on a movable sled. Some systems drive the sled from one area of the disc to another by means of a rotary motor coupled through some kind of gear train. Others, which may be capable of faster access times and may suffer less wear, use a linear motor and a sled mounted on sliding or rolling bearings; the sled is pushed back and forth by the force produced by passing an electrical current through a large coil of wire placed in a magnetic field.

Remember that the disc is not very flat. In fact, toward the outer tracks it may be flapping up and down about a millimeter, while spinning at four revolutions per second.

Regardless of mechanical details of the sled mechanism, to achieve rapid access to information the system must be capable of accurate repositioning. High-performance magnetic and optical drives do this by counting tracks as they move during a seek, so they always know exactly where they are. The main reason that CD ROM drives have such relatively long access times, averaging about 0.5 to 1 second, is that accurate track counting during a fast seek is very difficult. It is a peculiarity of the data encoding scheme used in the CD format that the data signal contains significant components which overlap the upper end of the tracking servo frequency band. Low-pass filtering is used to eliminate this energy from the servo signals, which means that these signals become very inaccurate if used to count track crossings at high speed. CD players, therefore, can count tracks accurately only during short, slow seeks. For longer seeks, the sled is simply moved for what ought to be about the correct amount of time, after which the system has to stop, determine its exact location, and reposition itself. This "open-loop" operation may have to be carried out several times for a long seek. A system employing an independent position sensor attached to the sled can seek somewhat faster, but the independent sensor cannot be accurate enough for first-time positioning. Of course, the rotational speed must be adjusted after each long seek too.

Conclusion

Many of the finer details have been neglected in this overview of CD servo system operation. For instance, there are strategies used to make the light spot jump a short distance and land reliably on another track. High system bandwidths are needed to maintain focus and tracking in the presence of external shock or vibration, yet achievable bandwidths are limited by actuator resonances and other factors. The variable relationship between subcode and data address can result in very long access times for some manufacturers' discs on other drives. Finally, there may be ways of modifying the operation of CD players to achieve much faster seek speeds. The material presented, however, should serve as an introduction to the current state of the art in the world of CD ROM servo systems.

About the Author

Tony Lavender was born in Newport, South Wales, in 1946. He received a B.Sc. in physics and psychology from the University of Manchester, England, and continued graduate work in psychobiology at Washington University in St. Louis, Missouri, where he coauthored behavioral and neurophysiological studies of bat echo-location systems.

After working as a scientific/engineering computer programmer, he came to Reference Technology in October 1982, where he has worked primarily as a servo engineer for the Clasix DataDrive Series 2000, a high-performance optical disc drive which reads huge digital databases from standard 12-inch videodiscs.

Reference Technology, Inc.
1832 N. 55th Street
Boulder, CO 80301
(303) 449-4157

System Software

File System Support for CD ROM

by Bill Zoellick

One of the tasks of a CD ROM file management system is to provide a logical framework (a file system) to make it possible for application programs to efficiently access the CD's massive store of information. This system allows users to view the disc as a collection of files. If we didn't have a file system we would have to view the disc physically, the same way that the CD ROM drive's controller does. The hardware controller knows nothing about files. It sees the disc as a sequence of 2K-byte sectors that are spread over 60 minutes of recording time, with 75 sectors in each second of the recording.

Suppose an application had to ask for information in the hardware controller's terms. To do so, the application would have to have detailed knowledge about the physical location of the information on the disc. For example, to read a list of names the application would have to know the precise physical address (minute, second, sector) of the beginning of the list. If we made a new disc that contained the same list of names but moved the list to some other location on the disc, the application software would have to be changed. This is clearly unacceptable.

The solution is to incorporate a file system that stands between the application software and the controller. A file system consists of software and data structures that translate the physical, sector-oriented view of the disc into a logical view that the application program can use.

Viewed logically, a disc is a collection of files, each with its own unique name. Once a file is open, the application program can read 1 byte, 50 bytes, 1 million bytes, or whatever is necessary, entirely ignoring the fact that the information is being read in 2K-byte aggregates, or that each sector has a precise physical address. In short, the application is unaware that the information is even stored on CD ROM, and reads files from the CD ROM disc just as it would from a magnetic disk.

In this discussion we will explore CD ROM file systems with several audiences and objectives in mind:

○ For readers with a general interest in CD ROMs, we will explain the nomenclature and delineate the fundamental concepts and components associated with file systems.

○ For more technically oriented readers and for readers who are responsible for selecting a CD ROM file system, we will identify the desirable features of a good file system.

○ For readers who will develop their own file systems for special vertical markets or who wish to follow and evaluate the current discussions about a standard disc format for a file system, we will explore design alternatives for file systems.

Nomenclature and Fundamental Concepts

A complete CD ROM file system consists of three major components: the structure, or *logical format,* of the data; the software that writes the data in that format, called the *origination software*; and the software that reads and translates the logical format for our use, called the *destination software.*

Logical format.   The logical format of the disc determines such matters as where to place fundamental identifying information on the disc, where to find the directory of the files on the disc, how the directory is structured, and so on. It should not be confused with the actual physical format of the disc, which determines whether the disc will work with a specific player. The physical format was determined by Philips and Sony some time ago and is considered a given by the file system. The logical format, on the other hand, is at the heart of the file system; it defines the system's structure and its operating characteristics.

Origination software.   Before making a CD ROM, the files that will appear on the disc must be assembled according to the rules of the logical format. Origination software does this work, providing the writing component of the file system.

Destination software.   We need software on the end user's machine that understands the logical format and can use it to provide access to the files on the disc. This destination software is the reading component of the file system.

Distinguishing between these components is important. For most users, the logical format used will be the one that has emerged from discussions among industry leaders as a common, de facto standard. Of course, it will always be possible to use nonstandard formats for special purposes, but information suppliers who are interested in reaching broad markets will probably use the most widely accepted format.

Users have a wider range of choices as they select the two software components of the file system. Unlike the logical format, the software components provide opportunities for product differentiation and competition among software vendors. It makes sense for users to shop around for particular features and for performance as they select an origination system or destination system for their use.

Characteristics Affecting File System Design

The design of a CD ROM file system needs to account for the CD ROM's unique combination of strengths and weaknesses. The following is a list of some of the CD ROM's more important characteristics. We will look at them one at a time to see how they affect file system design.

○ CD ROM discs are read-only.

○ Writing and reading are asymmetric.

○ Seeking is very expensive.

○ Sequential reading is at an acceptable rate.

○ They have relatively large storage capacity.

Read-Only Discs

Many users might view the read-only nature of the CD ROM as a disadvantage. However, from the standpoint of file system design, the guarantee of read-only access is an asset for the very simple reason that the file system need not support the deletion or modification of files.

When you delete a file on a magnetic disk system, the system must not only modify the directory to indicate that the file is gone, it must also keep track of the fact that the space once occupied by the file is now available for reuse. This requires additional data structures and internal "bookkeeping."

If you modify a file by adding information to it, the file system must find a place to put the new information. It will often happen that the sectors just beyond the end of the original file are in use for some other file. So the file system must not only locate available space, it must also create a map for the file so that it can treat it as a single, contiguous entity, even though the file is actually scattered over several locations on the disc.

A CD ROM file system can ignore these kinds of problems. We do not have to build flexible data structures capable of accommodating deletions and modifications. We have the luxury of knowing that everything is static and will always be in exactly the form and place that it was when we created the disc.

Asymmetric Writing and Reading

In many cases the writing, or origination, of a CD ROM is done in batch mode on a minicomputer. Moreover, it is done only once. But the disc will be read many times, oftentimes on a smaller computer, and the reading will occur in real time while the user is waiting for a response. Part of this asymmetry is simply due to the fact that the CD ROM is a read-only medium. But some aspects of the asymmetry result from the manufactured nature of the CD ROM. Perhaps the most interesting aspect is that the file system for a CD ROM is often assembled in a batch process on a relatively powerful computer. This power enables the developer to use data preparation techniques that can improve the performance of the final product. Any steps taken in creating the disc that improve the performance of the file system and the reading process are worthwhile, even if they are relatively expensive.

For example, in a read/write system such as magnetic disk, where such asymmetry usually does not exist, we would probably not consider storing the file names within a directory in alphabetical order, even though doing so would allow us to use a binary search algorithm to speed up the search for a file name. However, because we would be adding files (writing) in real time, the cost of keeping everything sorted would usually outweigh the benefits of binary searching, especially if we were dealing with a huge number of files.

The situation is very different on a CD ROM. The initial sorting of the directory is less objectionable because it can be done on a big machine as a batch process. Moreover, the payoff of a binary search is worth more because the search for a file is usually performed on a smaller machine while a user is waiting for the result. Because the disc is written only once, we know that the sorting is a one-time investment that will pay off many times as files are opened and read.

Expensive Seeking

Seeking is always expensive, in terms of time. On a magnetic disk the cost of getting information from the disk is four or five orders of magnitude higher than getting the same information from RAM. But on a CD ROM the problem is even more severe. The time required for an average seek on a high-performance magnetic disk drive is approximately 30 milliseconds.

On a cheaper magnetic disk, such as the hard disks used in many personal computers, this average seek time may be two or three times greater, ranging up to about a tenth of a second. The fastest CD ROM drives, on the other hand, require half a second for an average seek; other CD ROM drives may require as much as a second.

Eventually, most CD ROMs manufactured for general sale and distribution will use a common format.

It is difficult to relate nanoseconds, milliseconds, and seconds in a meaningful way, so perhaps an example will help. Typically, a computer may require 150 nanoseconds to get a byte of information from electronic RAM memory. We have suggested that getting that same byte from a CD ROM might, on the average, take about half a second. We can put these numbers in perspective by drawing an analogy between the RAM access and some very quick, easy lookup that you might perform as a human information retrieval system. Suppose, for example, that looking up something in the index of this book is analogous to a RAM access on a computer. Finding a term in the index and opening to the correct page might take about 20 seconds. How long would it take if you had to send away for this information, using an information source that was as slow relative to your index lookup as the CD ROM is to a RAM access? The answer is an astounding 771 days, or over 2 years!

Clearly, seeking on the CD ROM is to be avoided if at all possible, particularly if the information could alternately be made available in RAM. Designers of file systems are always attuned to the idea that seeking is expensive; when moving from working with magnetic media to working with the CD ROM they must recognize that the cost of a seek increases by yet another order of magnitude.

Acceptable Sequential Reading Rate

Fortunately, once we finally seek to the required spot on a CD ROM, we can read data from the disc at a speed that is comparable to that offered by magnetic disks. Sequential transfer rates for magnetic disks range from about 100K bytes/sec to over 300K bytes/sec, depending on disk density and the sector interleaving factor. Data can be "streamed" from a CD ROM at 150K bytes/sec. Although this is by no means an outstanding transfer rate, it is acceptable. Given that seeking performance is so poor, the capability to stream sequential sectors at an acceptable rate argues for collecting related data items into large "blocks" of contiguous sectors. That way, once we have incurred the cost of a seek, it is possible to read in a large amount of related data for processing without doing any additional seeking.

Large Storage Capacity

Conservatively estimated, a single CD ROM can hold 540,000K bytes of data, which is the equivalent of over 200,000 typewritten pages of text. From the point of view of traditional microcomputer applications, that is a lot of data.

When we discussed the CD ROM's read-only nature we distinguished between the point of view of the user and that of the system designer. Being read-only might be viewed as a disadvantage by some users, but it is a significant asset from the point of view of a file system designer. The situation is exactly reversed when we look at the matter of the disc's large capacity. Being able to store very large files or a large number of smaller files on the disc is undoubtedly advantageous from the user's point of view; for the file system designer, however, accommodating large files and large numbers of files can be a problem. It is also, fortunately, an opportunity. We will see how to take advantage of this opportunity later as we look at directory structure design alternatives.

Source of the CD ROM's Characteristics

Some of the performance characteristics listed above are not very desirable. A CD ROM seeks slowly and provides unexceptional data transfer rates. Why not design something else that does a better job? This is an important question, and the answer focuses on one of the most significant of all the CD ROM's characteristics: The CD ROM is a direct extension of CD audio technology. The fact that it is now possible to buy a CD ROM drive for well under $1000 is not at all a function of CD ROM technology or the CD ROM market; it is due entirely to the fact that it is possible to use the CD audio drive mechanism as the basis of a CD ROM drive. The demand for CD audio is pushing the technology associated with manufacturing drives and dropping prices for both CD audio and CD ROM drives. The CD ROM's potential to provide very inexpensive data storage, dissemination, and retrieval is directly attributable to its CD audio parentage. For better or for worse, the CD ROM's poor seeking performance and average data transfer rate are also due to that same parentage.

We must accept the bad along with the good. At the same time, we should try to minimize the impact of the CD ROM's shortcomings. Purchasers and designers of CD ROM file systems should evaluate these systems in terms of the degree to which they avoid seeking, capitalizing instead on the guarantee of read-only access and the asymmetry of writing and reading. Smart purchasing and smart design involve focusing on all three components of the CD ROM file system: the logical format, the origination software, and the destination software. We will begin by looking at the characteristics of a good CD ROM logical format.

Logical Format Design

Eventually, most CD ROMs manufactured for general sale and distribution will use a common format. The specifications for this format are emerging from a joint effort by a number of hardware and software companies interested in ensuring that CD ROMs prepared by different firms can be interchanged. The emergence of this common format will, for many users, make moot the question of choosing a format. All the same, it is important for users to understand what a logical format contains and to realize that the logical format's design can have a major impact on performance. Furthermore, there will always be applications for which the use of a common format is not essential. For instance, databases used within a company might very well have a proprietary format if there were some advantage to doing so. We will take a look at the general structure of a CD ROM logical format and discuss some of the most important design alternatives.

The logical format for a CD ROM is not really a single entity; it is actually a collection of structures. For purposes of discussion it is usually helpful to divide these structures into two categories:

○ Structures related to the entire disc volume and to the volume set

○ Structures related to the files placed on a volume.

One interesting variation on the conventional magnetic disk approach to directory hierarchies involves placing the entire directory structure in a single file.

A single CD ROM disc is a *volume*. A *volume set* is a collection of discs containing a single file system. In an extreme case, a very large file could extend over several volumes in a volume set. More typically, each volume in a volume set will hold several (or many) files. Even so, individual files may spill over from disc to disc, from volume to volume in the volume set. There must be rules and data structures for expressing these relationships. For example, if I have one of the volumes from a volume set mounted on a drive, the disc must contain enough information to tell me which member of the set I have. The discs must also be structured so that I can know when I have successfully mounted the next member of the set.

This kind of disc-level information is often placed in a volume table of contents (VTOC). The VTOC can also be used to contain things such as the name of the disc's publisher, the version of the file system used on the disc, copyright information about the disc, pointers to boot blocks if the disc is to be used to boot up an operating system, the date that the file system was created, and so on. In general, this information is not critical to file system performance or design. When designing a universal disc format, the important requirement is to build enough flexibility and extensibility into the volume structure so that it can meet the needs of a broad class of information suppliers and applications.

Unlike the volume-level component of the logical format, the file-level component can have a dramatic impact on disc performance. This file-level component consists of things such as the disc's directory structure. The overall design of the directory structure and the design of the individual directory records are related to issues such as the disc's ability to handle tens of thousands of files efficiently and its ability to handle large files. We will look at a number of these issues individually.

Hierarchical Directory Structures

Most contemporary file systems for magnetic disks support hierarchical directories; the common format for the CD ROM will support them as well. Given the large number of files that may be on a CD ROM, a hierarchical directory structure can be an invaluable tool for organizing these files. The really interesting question is not so much whether to have a hierarchical directory structure as it is how to best implement one.

Most magnetic disk file systems implement their directory hierarchies explicitly by treating subdirectories as special kinds of files. For example, a given directory may contain references to nine other files, three of which are actually subdirectories. To see what is in a given subdirectory we simply open the file corresponding to the subdirectory and read out the contents of the subdirectory. We might find that it contains five files, two of which are subdirectories. We could then look at the contents of one of these subdirectories, continuing the process until we found the file we were looking for.

This is a great system for magnetic disks, since it provides the flexibility required in order to add new subdirectories and delete old ones, but we do not need that kind of flexibility on a CD ROM. Just as important, we cannot easily afford the time required to seek from subdirectory file to subdirectory file in order to find a file with a long path name such as:

\jones\programs\source\acctg\ledger\post.c

What is more difficult is handling a large number of files while guaranteeing the ability to open a file in some maximum number of seeks on the disc.

Consequently, a number of firms and individuals have suggested that the hierarchy be expressed implicitly and that the entire directory be contained in just one or two files so that we can minimize seeking. As an example of an implicit expression of a directory structure, consider the path provided for the *post.c* file. From looking at this path, we can see that there are subdirectories named *jones, programs,* and *source,* and know their hierarchical relationship to each other. If we provide a full path name as a search key for every file in the directory, then the complete directory hierarchy is implicit in all these names. Of course, actually storing the full path for every file could be prohibitively expensive, since paths can be very long. So, instead, the paths are either compressed to an integer representation or "hashed" to an address. We will talk more about each of these approaches later.

The point for users and designers to keep in mind is that there are a number of ways to satisfy the functional requirement of support for hierarchical directories. Deciding that we want hierarchical directories does not necessarily mean that we want to implement them explicitly.

Support for Generic Searching

If a disc contains a large number of files, it is convenient to use "wildcard" or "generic search" commands such as:

dir file*.*

The design of the directory structure can greatly affect the efficiency of processing such commands. As we will see, some directory structures keep together all the files in a given subdirectory. This is convenient, since keeping all the files for a subdirectory in one place limits the scope of the evaluation for generic searches, making them simpler and quicker. Better yet, since we are working with a read-only medium, it is possible to develop directory structures in which the files within a subdirectory are kept in alphabetical order. This makes generic searching even more efficient. However, other directory structures, such as those based on hashing, have the effect of mixing all the file names together in random order, even if the files are in different subdirectories. These kinds of directory structures can make generic searching difficult and slow unless special measures are taken.

If a potential use of the CD ROM involves user interaction with the directory structure, generic searching is probably an important feature. Similarly, some applications may make use of generic searching. In either of these cases, a system purchaser or designer must take care to ensure that the directory structure is one that facilitates such searching.

112

The design of a CD ROM file system needs to account for the CD ROM's unique combination of strengths and weaknesses.

Handling Large Files

Operating systems such as the current versions of MS-DOS can have difficulty accommodating very large files. The problem stems from the operating system's need to handle files that are scattered over the surface of the disk. As we indicated earlier, this scattering can happen when many files have been added to and deleted from a disk, resulting in "free space" that is itself scattered across the disk. As new files are added, using this free space, they are sometimes broken up into many small pieces. MS-DOS uses a File Allocation Table to keep track of all the pieces that make up a file. The limits on file size in MS-DOS are in fact a limit in the size of the File Allocation Table.

Fortunately, we can avoid this problem in the design of a CD ROM file system. Files will never be deleted or moved around; we can guarantee that a file consists of contiguous sectors. Consequently, we do not need structures such as File Allocation Tables; all we need is the starting position of the file and the number of bytes it contains. It's really that simple. This is a clear instance of the disc's read-only nature working to our advantage. Of course, the file size would still be limited by the size of the integer used to hold the byte count for the file. Many current file systems for magnetic disks use a 32-bit integer for the byte count, which means that the largest file that could be accommodated would consist of over 4 billion bytes, or over 4 million Kbytes. There is a division of opinion as to whether this would be a large enough number to cover future uses of CD ROMs. Users who require the use of very large files should be aware of the nature and size of this limitation.

Handling Large Numbers of Files

It is not very difficult to design a file system that allows users to place an unlimited number of files in a directory structure. Many current magnetic disk operating systems, with their subdirectories-as-files approach to building directories, allow users to add files until some physical limitation is encountered. The directory structure does not, of itself, impose a limit.

What is more difficult is handling a large number of files while guaranteeing the ability to open a file in some maximum number of seeks on the disc. Considering the CD ROM's slow seeking ability, this is clearly a relevant criterion. For example, given a disc containing 10,000 files distributed across a directory hierarchy containing six or seven levels of subdirectories, can we guarantee that any one of the files could be opened with no more than a single seek? The answer to this question is yes if we choose a directory structure designed to provide this kind of fast access. Let's look at some of the most often proposed and implemented designs for directory structures. This survey should be of use to both system purchasers and future system designers.

Directory Structure Design

We have already mentioned the distinction between directory structures which *explicitly* describe the directory's hierarchical structure and those which contain the hierarchy *implicitly*. Current proposals and implementations of directory structures can be divided into five categories. The first four of these categories are divided evenly between explicit and implicit approaches to implementing directory hierarchies. The categories are:

○ Multiple-file explicit hierarchies (explicit)

○ Single-file explicit hierarchies (explicit)

○ Hashed path name directories (implicit)

○ Indexed path name directories (implicit)

○ Hybrid structures combining two or more of the first four approaches

Multiple-File Explicit Hierarchies

This forbidding-sounding name describes the kind of familiar directory structures used by UNIX, MS-DOS, VMS, and other magnetic disk systems. Early versions of Digital Equipment's UNIFILE™ system are an example of a CD ROM file system that used this kind of directory structure. We have already described the salient features of this class of directory structures: subdirectories are handled as files; opening a file with a long path name can require more seeking than we might like. Figure 1 provides an example of what a simple implementation of this kind of directory structure might look like. Notice how the subdirectories are handled as just a special kind of file.

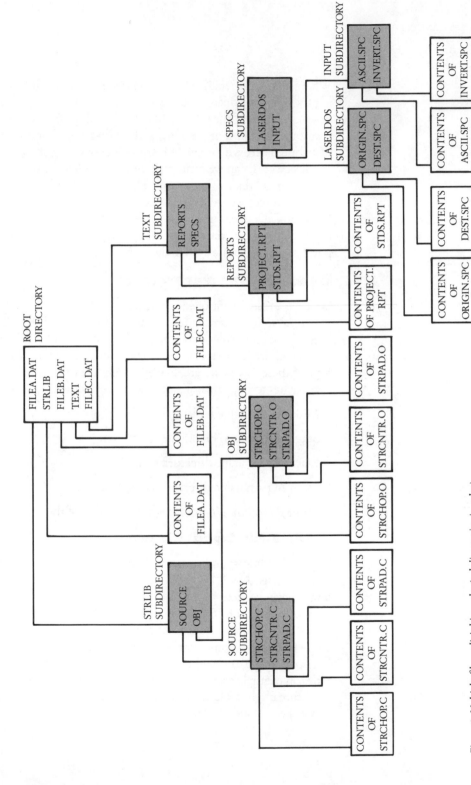

Figure 1. Multiple-file explicit hierarchy (subdirectories in color)

The strong features of this kind of directory structure are:

○ It is familiar.

○ It handles generic searching (wildcards) reasonably well.

If we take advantage of the CD ROM's read-only nature and sort the files in each subdirectory, generic searching is even faster.

The disadvantages are:

○ As already mentioned, opening files using a long path name can require a number of seeks.

○ We must search through an entire level of the directory structure while looking for a file. As a worst case, when all the files are in the root, a search for a single file involves the entire directory. The impact of this problem can be greatly decreased by sorting the files within each directory level so that we can use a binary search to look for a file. Nevertheless, given a very large single-level directory (10,000 files, for example) that extends over many sectors of the disc, even a binary search can require a dozen or more seeks back and forth across the sectors comprising the directory.

Single-File Explicit Hierarchies

One interesting variation on the conventional magnetic disk approach to directory hierarchies involves placing the entire directory structure in a single file. The root directory and all subdirectories are treated as records within a file rather than as separate files. As a specific example (shown in Figure 2), the directory structure used in the first version of LaserDOS™, a file system designed at TMS, Inc., relied on a *left child, right sibling* tree to incorporate the files and subdirectories into a record structure. In this schematic of the directory structure, the left pointers from the subdirectory records point to elements (children) in the subdirectory. Right pointers always point to files or subdirectories at the same level (siblings). File records (as opposed to subdirectory records) do not have left pointers (children). Instead, that field is used to hold the file address.

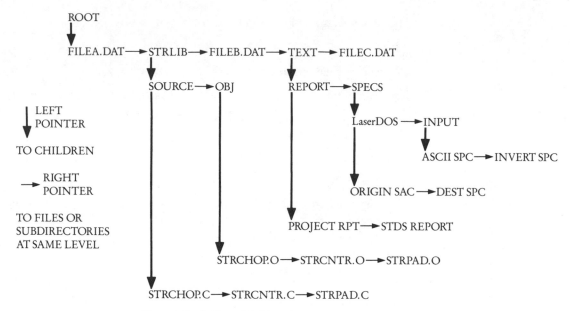

Figure 2. Single-file explicit hierarchy

The important benefit realized from compressing the directory hierarchy into a single file, rather than spreading it out by using a different file for each subdirectory, is that we can often cut down on the amount of seeking required to open a file. A relatively small directory structure (no more than 100 or 200 files) can be completely contained in just two or three sectors, all of which can be buffered in RAM. This is true even if the directory hierarchy contains many levels of subdirectories. So the single-file explicit hierarchy can often improve on the performance of multiple-file explicit hierarchies when we are opening files that have path names containing several subdirectory levels. Otherwise, the assets and liabilities of this second approach are much the same as those of the first approach. They both have the advantages of being simple and supporting generic searching reasonably well; neither of them performs well if the number of files in the directory runs into the thousands.

Hashed Path Name Directories

When designing a universal disc format, the important requirement is to build enough flexibility and extensibility into the volume structure so that it can meet the needs of a broad class of information suppliers and applications.

One way of guaranteeing that any file can be opened with a single seek, even if there are tens of thousands of files on a disc, is to *hash* the entire path and file name to an address within the directory. For example, given a path and file name such as:

\jones\programs\source\acctg\ledger\post.c

We would use a hash function to transform the entire character string into the address of a *hash bucket*. (A bucket is a storage area large enough to hold directory information about several files. It contains directory records for the several files whose full paths hash to the bucket's address.) We would then seek to this directory bucket to get the information needed to open the file.

We can guarantee that this hashed access procedure requires no more than a single seek only if we can guarantee that none of the buckets overflow. Overflow occurs when more path names hash to a bucket than can be held there. When this happens we might need another seek in order to locate the information that had to be stored elsewhere. As any textbook discussion of hashing would indicate, the three factors that we can adjust to minimize overflow are the bucket size, the packing density of the directory file, and the hash function itself. For a discussion of how the interaction of these factors can be used to advantage on CD ROM discs, see Zoellick (1986). As this article indicates, the read-only nature of the CD ROM makes it possible to avoid overflow altogether in most cases while still maintaining reasonably good packing densities within the directory file.

Reference Technology used this kind of hashed approach to directory structures in their first versions of their STA/F File™ file system for CD ROMs. As we have already said, the great advantage of this kind of directory structure is that the system can handle tens of thousands of files while still guaranteeing that any file can be opened in a single seek. The disadvantage of the approach is that hash functions, by design, distribute path and file names in a nearly random fashion throughout the directory file. This randomizing makes generic searching very expensive. We need to read through the entire directory, looking at the full path for every file, in order to make sure that we have every entry that matches the pattern provided in the generic search.

The negative impact of randomizing is not just limited to generic searches; even a simple *dir* command to show the files in a subdirectory requires a search through the entire directory structure. Consequently, a pure hashing approach to directory structures is very inappropriate if we wish to support interactive use of the file system. User interaction almost always involves the listing of directory contents and the use of wildcard, generic search characters in commands such as:

COPY prog*.bas C:

The logical format for a CD ROM is not really a single entity; it is actually a collection of structures.

There are ways to augment a pure hashed approach with other structures to solve some of these problems. Both generic searching and the listing of subdirectory contents can be supported through the addition of special directory files to the disc. In addition to the actual data files, the system would prepare a directory file for each subdirectory. This directory file would contain the names of all the files in that subdirectory. It would also contain the names of other subdirectories that are children of the current subdirectory. Generic searches and *dir* commands would use these special directory files to get the required information about the directory structure. You will notice that this augmentation of pure hashing has a very strong resemblance to the multiple-file explicit hierarchy structure that we discussed earlier. This is, in fact, an example of our fifth, hybrid, class of directory structures.

Indexed Path Name Directories

In preparation for the initial meeting with other firms in the CD ROM industry for a discussion of CD ROM logical formats, TMS, Inc., prepared a paper (Zoellick, Stegner, and Barnette, 1985) proposing a directory structure that used an index, rather than hashing, to provide access to the full path names for the files in the directory. We will look at this structure in some detail, since it is an interesting example of a design that is tailored to the characteristics of the CD ROM.

Like the hashed approach to directory structures, this indexed approach relies on the information in the path names to provide an implicit expression of the directory hierarchy. The key to the success of this approach is a structure developed by Barnette which was originally called the *path index*. The important feature of the path index is that it provides a compact mechanism for quick translation of the full path for a subdirectory into an integer called the *path identifier*. Quoting from the original paper: "The path index accomplishes these tasks through the use of a very simple, compact structure. The easiest way to describe it is by reference to a sample directory structure, as shown in [Figure 3]." (Figure 6 in the original paper.)

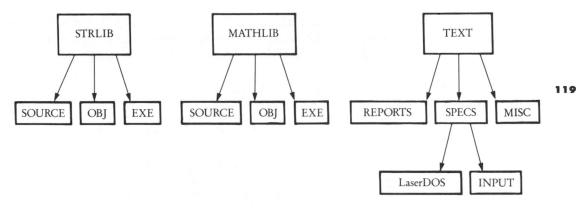

Figure 3. Sample directory hierarchy for use in describing the path index file structure

The path index file is formed from a *level-order* traversal of the directory hierarchy. Each record in the file would have the structure described in Figure 4 (Figure 7 in the original), which requires only 10 bytes.

Byte Offset	No. of Bytes	Description
	8	Subdirectory Name—left justified, upper case, padded with blanks
8	2	*Parent* directory—path identifier of the parent directory

Figure 4. Path index record structure

Notice that even though the primary purpose of the path index is to associate a path identifier with a given subdirectory, this record structure does not contain a field for the path identifier of the subdirectory. The reason is that the path identifier is actually just the relative record number of the subdirectory's entry in the path index. It will be easier to understand how this works if we look at a the path index for the sample directory hierarchy illustrated in Figure 3. The contents of this path index file are illustrated in Figure 5. The leftmost column in Figure 5 contains the relative record number of each record in the file. This value is the path identifier that is used as a key into the file index; it is the integer key that we will usually be looking for when we access this file. So the key value found in the search of the path index is found implicitly—when we locate the subdirectory we want, the relative record number will become the key that we use as we search for the records for files within that subdirectory.

Contents of Path Index Records

Relative Record Number	Directory Number	Parent
0	\	-1
1	STRLIB	00
2	MATHLIB	00
3	TEXT	00
4	SOURCE	01
5	OBJ	01
6	EXE	01
7	SOURCE	02
8	OBJ	02
9	EXE	02
10	REPORTS	03
11	SPECS	03
12	MISC	03
13	LASERDOS	11
14	INPUT	11

Figure 5. Path index content for directory hierarchy illustrated in Figure 3

In later work on the problem by H. Burgess of Microsoft Corporation, the path index was renamed *path table*, which is the term we will use here. As an example of how the path table works, let's use the sample table given above to find the path identifier for \MATHLIB\OBJ. We start by noting that the root directory has a path identifier (relative record number) of 0. We discover that the root's children (parent = 0) are next in the table and find that MATHLIB has a path identifier of 2, since its relative record number is 2. We then search down through the parent fields until we come to the set of records with parent = 2. When we find them, we begin searching by name, rather than by parent number, and find that the record OBJ has a relative record number of 8. We are done: the path identifier for \MATHLIB\OBJ is 8.

The path table's ability to compress an entire directory path into a 2-byte integer has an enormous and very favorable impact on what we can accomplish with an indexed directory structure. It guarantees that we can keep directory records relatively short, which in turn means that we can put many directory records into each block of the directory structure.

The key word here is *block*. Remember, seeking on the CD ROM is slow but sequential reading is performed at an acceptable rate. After spending the half-second or so required for an average seek, we read in a minimum of one sector, or 2K bytes, from the disc. For a small additional cost of only about 20 ms we can read in an additional 6K bytes, making a total of 8K bytes of information in all. If, with the help of the path table, we can hold the size of directory records to, say, 32 bytes each, then each seek out to the CD ROM can bring in a minimum 64 file records; and it can bring in as many as 256 records if we read in an 8K block.

121

The file structure containing these blocked directory records is called the *file table*. It contains all the information we need to open any file in the file system. The records for the files are placed into blocks of the file table in order first by path identifier (obtained through the path table) and then by file name. Consequently, all the files in a single subdirectory are grouped together (same path identifier) and are then ordered by name. Clearly, this structure is one that will support efficient generic searching and binary searching.

When we want to open a particular file we need to find the *block* in the file table that contains the record corresponding to the desired path identifier and file name. The emphasis on the word *block* is important; the expensive part of our search for the file is the seek to the beginning of the block. Because seeking is so expensive, we want to get the right block on our first attempt. Since the directory records are ordered by path and name in the file table, it is a simple matter to build an index table which could tell us the path and file names that are at the boundaries between each of the blocks. Figure 6 shows, in schematic form, how such an index table can give us an overview of the contents of the blocks in the file table. To open a file we first use the path table to convert the path name into a path identifier, and then use the path identifier and file name to discover, from the index table, which block of the file table we should read from the disc. More specifically, as shown in Figure 6, a request to open the file:

> \STRLIB\SOURCE\STRCHOP.C

This request starts at the path table, converting the path name into a path identifier of 4. The system then looks for "4 STRCHOP.C" in the index table. Since the value of "4 STRCHOP.C" is less than the first entry, it follows the first pointer from the index table to find the first block in the file table. There it finds the location of the file contents and other information required to open the file.

A complete CD ROM file system consists of three major components: the logical format, the origination software, and the destination software.

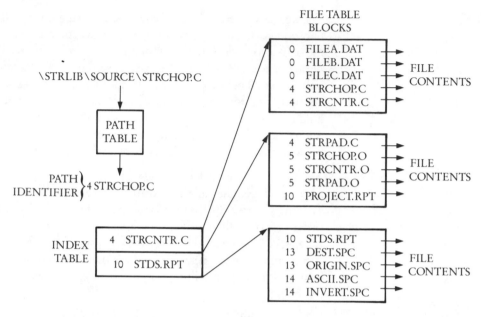

Figure 6. Use of an indexed path name directory

Now we can understand the importance of the path table's ability to compress a path name into an integer. The compression allows us to keep directory records short so that we can pack many of them into each block of the file table. This reduces the total number of blocks required for the file table. Since the size of our index table is directly related to the number of blocks in the file table, a small file table results in a small index table. This is very desirable, since we would like to be able to hold both the index table and path table in RAM rather than seeking out to the disc every time we need them. Given such buffering, the indexed path name directory structure allows us to open any file with only one seek to the CD ROM.

It is interesting to calculate how many files this system can support if, in the interest of minimizing the use of RAM, we restrict the size of the index table to one block. Assuming a block size of one CD ROM sector (2K bytes), a file table record size of 32 bytes, and an index table record size of 16 bytes, an index table consisting of one block could provide access to 129 file table blocks containing the information of about 8256 files. If we increased the block size to 8K without changing any of the other sizes, a one-block index table could keep track of 513 file table blocks containing information about 131,328 files.

The original proposal by Zoellick, Stegner, and Barnette (1985) suggest handling the index table as a B-tree if it becomes too large to fit into a single block. This circumstance would arise when building a directory containing tens of thousands of files while using a block size of one CD ROM sector. This suggestion has the unfortunate consequence of requiring that software implementations contain the additional logic necessary to handle B-trees in order to cover situations that would arise only infrequently. Potential implementers of this structure should be aware of an improvement on this original design that was suggested by H. Burgess of Microsoft. Burgess proposed that the index table simply be allowed to grow larger, spanning as many blocks as necessary, while still maintaining its simple, linear form.

Clearly, seeking on the CD ROM is to be avoided if at all possible.

123

We have described the indexed path name directory structure in detail because it is an interesting example of an approach that takes advantage of the read-only nature of the CD ROM. (The index and block structure would not be well suited to an erasable medium because it would be difficult to maintain.) It also exemplifies the care that should be taken to avoid seeking and to maximize the advantages that can be obtained by "blocking" data when designing file structures for the CD ROM. Yet another reason for describing this structure in detail is that it should be considered by users who will implement their own logical format for the CD ROM; it handles large numbers of files well while still providing support for generic searching and binary searching within individual blocks of the file table.

Selection and Design of Origination Software

We have given careful attention to the details and alternatives associated with the CD ROM file system's logical format because the format's directory structure determines so much about the character of the file system. But, as we said at the outset of this chapter, the potential user of CD ROM file systems will probably take the use of the emerging common logical format as a given, while exercising choices related to purchase of the origination and destination software that use this format. Consequently, a discussion of some of the important features and design alternatives associated with these software components of the file system is in order.

At present, most origination software runs on minicomputers in batch mode. TMS's LaserDOS origination system is one example of this kind of software. Figure 7 shows the relationship of the four principal components of this system. The user begins with a Specify program that provides an interactive shell-like mechanism for creating the directory hierarchy that is to be used on the CD ROM. During this step the user can indicate which files are to go in which subdirectories. The specification is used as input to a Load process that reads user files from tape and magnetic disk to create a disc image, complete with a volume table of contents and directory structure in the logical format that will be used on the CD ROM. After loading, the user can run a Verify program that automatically checks the internal consistency and integrity of the disc image. The user can also run a Shell program that exercises the image of the CD ROM file system interactively, allowing the user to dump out the contents of individual files, copy files to the host operating system, and so on.

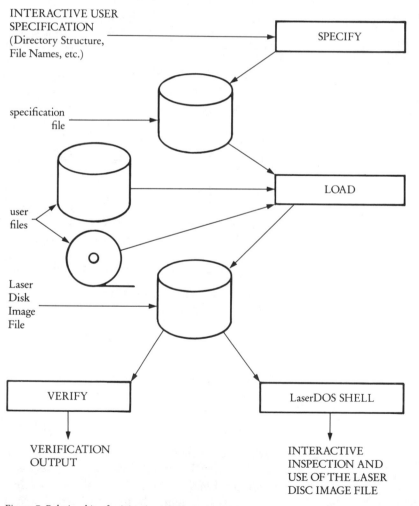

Figure 7. Relationship of origination system components

Relevant questions to ask when purchasing this kind of origination software include:

○ What kind of machine environment is required?

○ Will the software produce disc images that use the emerging common CD ROM logical format?

○ Will it support all levels and features provided in the common format?

○ How does it accept input? From ANSI labeled tapes? From magnetic disk? (If it accepts input only from disk you may need to have online disk capacity that is twice the size of the data that you wish to place on the CD ROM.)

○ Does it allow for convenient, interactive specification and modification of CD ROM directory structure prior to the actual file loading step?

○ How fast is the loading step?

○ What kinds of verification facilities are provided? Can critical files be inspected through a dump or some other interactive verification tool?

○ What kind of output does the system provide? Will it conveniently create tapes that are ready for sending to a disc mastering facility?

○ What kind of user documentation is provided with the software?

In the coming months we will probably see the emergence of a different kind of origination system intended for use on microcomputers rather than minicomputers. This software will probably be oriented more toward interactive creation of disc images than toward batch processing.

Destination System Software

Destination software uses the file system's logical format to provide the end user with access to files on the CD ROM. There are two fundamentally different ways to approach the design of destination software:

○ Create a file manager program containing special function calls that are exclusively for use with the CD ROM and which bear no relationship to the system calls provided by the host operating system.

○ Build software that meshes closely with the host operating system. Function calls to read the CD ROM appear to be handled in exactly the same way that the host system handles calls to read magnetic media.

126

A file system

consists of

software and data

structures that

translate the

physical, sector-

oriented view of

the disc into a

logical view that

the application

program can use.

Early versions of Digital Equipment Corporation's UNIFILE system, as implemented for use with MS-DOS, included destination software of the first kind. One advantage of this approach is that it is relatively easy to create a compact file manager. This is useful, since the file manager is held in RAM along with the operating system. The less RAM used by the file manager, the better. Another advantage is that the file manager and applications written to use it are insulated from changes in the operating system as new system versions are released. Finally, applications can interact with the file manager in the same way across different host operating systems.

The significant disadvantage of this first kind of destination system implementation is that applications cannot access the CD ROM through standard system calls. This in turn prevents access to CD ROM through the I/O facilities provided in high-level languages. Moreover, standard system utilities that perform tasks such as listing directories, copying files, and listing or dumping the contents of files cannot be used with the CD ROM, given this kind of implementation. Such utilities generally use standard system calls. The inability to use familiar language tools and system utilities with the CD ROM makes it seem like an alien environment; access to the CD ROM requires the use of new, special-purpose procedures.

The second approach to designing destination software solves this "separate environment" problem. Software such as TMS's LaserDOS or Reference Technology's STA/F File, as implemented for use with MS-DOS, exemplify this design intent to cooperate with the host system. LaserDOS, for instance, traps all system calls before they reach MS-DOS. Then if LaserDOS determines that the call is related to the CD ROM, it handles the call itself, passing back information to the caller in exactly the same form that would be used by MS-DOS for a call to the magnetic disk system. The calling software is never aware that LaserDOS took the call in place of MS-DOS. If LaserDOS determines that the call involves the magnetic disks or some other aspect of MS-DOS's domain, it simply passes the call on to MS-DOS for completion.

The advantage of this second design approach is that the CD ROM appears to the user as just another disk drive, one that happens to hold lots of data and which does not permit writing. System utilities work as expected, and applications can be written entirely in high-level languages without any need to resort to assembler. The disadvantages of this approach are that it is harder to do well and must be redone, at least to some extent, for each host operating system that will be supported. However, portability of applications across operating systems is not a problem if they are written in a portable high-level language.

Questions to ask when evaluating destination software include:

○ Does the implementation use the emerging common CD ROM logical format?

○ Does it support all the facilities and opportunities provided by the common format? Or does it support only a subset? For example, an implementation might not support multiple volume sets or it might not support the use of long file names.

○ Which of the two fundamental implementation approaches was used?

○ If the second, closely meshed, approach was used, does it implement all system calls which could conceivably be directed to the CD ROM? Does it mimic return values precisely, including error codes and extended error codes?

○ Does the software provide any special calls that go beyond the usual system calls?

○ How much RAM does the software require?

○ How are system buffers handled? Do data coming from the CD ROM always have to pass through the system buffers, or is there some way to speed up input by bypassing system buffers to bring data directly into the program work area?

○ Are there system options, such as the number of system buffers to be used, that can be easily modified by the user?

○ How does the software accommodate the variations between different makes of CD ROM drives? What drives are supported?

○ What kind of user documentation is provided with the system?

About the Author

Bill Zoellick is manager of software research at TMS, Inc., one of the pioneering firms working with digital laser technology. He has been very active in the industry effort to design a common logical format for CD ROMs. He is also coauthor, with Mike Folk, of a textbook titled *File Structures: A Conceptual Toolkit* that will be published by Addison-Wesley in 1986.

TMS, Inc.
P.O. Box 1358
Stillwater, OK 74076

Resources

Folk, M., and B. Zoellick. *File Structures: A Conceptual Toolkit.* Reading, Mass.: Addison-Wesley, in press. Provides a comprehensive discussion of the hashing and file structure issues mentioned in this chapter.

Knuth, D. *The Art of Computer Programming.* Vol. 3: *Sorting and Searching.* Reading, Mass.: Addison-Wesley, 1973. The definitive reference work on hashing and other file organization issues.

Zoellick, B. CD ROM software development. *Byte,* May 1986. Discusses the application of file structure design principles to CD ROM software development. Many of the design issues touched on in the discussion of directory structures in this chapter are developed more fully.

Zoellick, B., S. Stegner, and J. D. Barnette, "Directory Structure for the High Sierra CD ROM Logical Format Proposal." Unpublished document available from TMS, Inc., P.O. Box 1358, Stillwater, OK 74076.

CHAPTER 3

Retrieval Software

The Current State of Text Retrieval

by Gregory Colvin

The ability to store large quantities of text in computer-accessible form, such as on CD ROM, has given rise to systems for automated text retrieval: the use of computer software to automatically search a textual database for relevant texts (for our purposes a text is a retrievable portion of a document). Until recently, these systems have required mainframe-capacity magnetic storage and computing power, restricting their use to large institutions and expensive online services. The typical users of these systems have been trained researchers, capable of using a powerful but complex user interface. But now the emergence of personal computers and optical disc technology has made possible the mass distribution of large textual databases. To be useful to a mass audience, these databases must be accessible through a powerful but simple interface that can be used effectively even by people who are untrained. Information scientists have developed and tested techniques for more powerful retrieval software and simpler user interfaces, some of which are now proven and available for commercial use.

131

Boolean Retrieval Systems

Almost all approaches to automated text retrieval are based on identifying texts containing specific keys—phrases, words, or parts of words—which are considered likely to occur in relevant texts. This can be accomplished simply by scanning the entire database for the desired keys, but with large databases this is slow. If space is cheaper than time the database can be inverted so that every possible key is placed in an index with links from each key to all the texts containing that key. Almost all commercial text retrieval systems incorporate an inverted index.

In most commercial retrieval systems, user access to texts is provided by a query language which allows Boolean operations on the sets of texts containing each key. Boolean queries can be very effective in retrieving relevant texts, but good results require knowledge of Boolean algebra and of which keys are most likely to occur in relevant texts. Imprecise requests can retrieve large numbers of irrelevant texts, and more precise requests can exclude large numbers of relevant texts. Typically, a query which retrieves half the relevant texts in a database (50 percent recall) will retrieve about the same number of irrelevant texts (50 percent precision). In general, the sum of precision and recall for Boolean queries does not exceed

100 percent, so that a more precise query will retrieve even fewer of the relevant texts in a database (Swets, 1963; Blair and Maron, 1985). For large databases this implies that a researcher will need to examine a very large number of irrelevant texts in order to find many of the relevant ones. Research and development in information retrieval since the 1950s has concentrated on methods which can provide better retrieval without the need for Boolean queries.

Retrieval with Natural Queries

The difficulty of learning Boolean query languages has tended to restrict the use of automatic retrieval systems to those willing to invest the time and effort to learn the language. Full-screen interfaces and context-sensitive help facilities can ease the burden on untrained users, but the ideal query language would be "natural language." That is, users should be able to express queries in their own language, without first mastering Boolean logic. Systems have been created which allow the use of unformatted text as a query. These systems are typically ignorant of grammar, treating texts and queries as simple lists of keys. But even without grammatical analyses, results at least equal to Boolean retrieval can be achieved.

To be useful to a mass audience . . . databases must be accessible through a powerful but simple interface that can be used effectively even by people who are untrained.

The most researched method for eliminating the need for Boolean queries is the vector model of automatic indexing and retrieval (Salton, 1968; Salton and McGill, 1983). Each text is represented as a vector, the elements of which are the frequencies of all keys in the text. Thus, there are as many elements in each vector as there are distinct keys in the index. Queries are also represented as vectors, the elements of which are the frequency of each key in the query, typically weighted by an inverse function of the frequency of the key in database. Thus, the queries can be entered as free format text which is scanned for keys. Retrieval is based on the similarity of the text vectors and the query vectors, as indicated by the inner product of the vectors or other similar functions. This approach gives results comparable to those produced with the Boolean approach (50 percent recall with 50 percent precision), with the advantage that texts can be ranked in order of estimated relevance to the query. This method has been used experimentally in many forms in many countries for more than 20 years with good results and is now beginning to be offered as commercially available software.

Improving Retrieval Performance with Feedback and Fuzzy Logic

The trade-off between recall and precision found in both Boolean and vector retrieval may be acceptable in small databases but is clearly problematic when a database on optical disc can contain millions of pages of text. The

The difficulty of learning Boolean query languages has tended to restrict the use of automatic retrieval systems to those willing to invest the time and effort to learn the language.

performance of Boolean and vector model retrieval is limited by two problems. First, most queries are incomplete and inaccurate. Many relevant keys will not occur in the query, and some of the keys in the query will not be relevant. Second, keys are not independent of one another: They are not randomly distributed in the database. The mathematics of the vector similarity functions requires that the keys are conditionally independent; relevant keys are assumed to be randomly distributed across relevant texts, but in fact there are wide variations in the degree of dependence between keys (Bookstein, 1983) The Boolean AND and OR operations allow for independent (OR clause) and dependent (AND clause) keys to be distinguished but do not allow for intermediate degrees of independence. So the use of AND clauses to identify keys which are expected to occur together in relevant texts will tend to eliminate many relevant texts, and the use of OR clauses to identify keys which need not occur together will tend to include many irrelevant texts.

Incomplete and innaccurate queries can be automatically improved by incorporating a feedback mechanism into the vector retrieval model (Salton, 1968; Sparck Jones, 1980). The user indicates whether or not some of the retrieved texts are relevant, and the query vector is made more similar to the vectors of the relevant texts and less similar to the vectors of the irrelevant texts. The new query typically gives 70 percent recall with 70 percent precision, and two or three iterations of feedback can give 80 percent recall with 80 percent precision. Further iterations give little improvement if any. Feedback mechanisms for Boolean retrieval have been proposed, but there is little empirical research on their effectiveness (Radecki, 1983).

Boolean retrieval can be improved to allow for varying degrees of dependence through the use of "fuzzy logic," which provides techniques for quantifying the degree of relevance of the keys in a Boolean query and for combining these quantities to give a ranking of texts by estimated relevance (Bookstein, 1980; Buell and Kraft, 1981). There is some experimental evidence that successful ranking can be achieved with quantified Boolean techniques (Noreault et al., 1977).

Improving Retrieval Performance with Expert Systems

The performance problems of variations in term interdependence and incomplete requests can be viewed as a problem of knowledge: automatic retrieval systems are typically ignorant of the relationships between words.

133

If knowledge of these relations could be incorporated into retrieval systems their performance might be much improved.

The traditional representation of the semantic relations among words is the thesaurus, which is a heirarchically organized collection of expert judgments about the meanings of words. An automatic retrieval system can use a thesaurus to replace individual keys in a query with groups of related keys. The addition of a good thesaurus to a vector model retrieval system can improve performance to 60 percent recall with 60 percent precision (Sparck Jones, 1971).

The continued evolution of optical storage, expert system techniques, and microprocessor power will make possible a radical improvement in the easy and inexpensive availability of large volumes of textual information to all interested persons.

An alternative to the traditional thesaurus approach is to replace the discrete elements of the vector model with continuous dimensions, each dimension representing the relationships among a number of elements. This approach begins with a matrix representing the interrelationships of the keys. The rows of the matrix are the keys, and the columns of the matrix are subject matters or concepts. The cells of the matrix contain expert judgments of relevance or similarity. Various matrix orthogonalization techniques (such as principal components analysis) can be used to obtain independent column vectors which represent the original matrix. These independent vectors form a coordinate space (called a classification space) for the key terms. Texts and queries can be located in this space by the average position of their component key terms, and the relevance of a text to a query can be estimated by the distance between their average positions. With this approach, very good retrieval can be obtained, sometimes exceeding 90 percent recall with 90 percent precision (Ossorio, 1966; Jeffreys, 1981). Classification space software (designed by this author) is being used by the King County Police Department in Washington state to provide natural query access to the evidence in an ongoing murder investigation (Guertin, 1985), and other commercial applications of this technique are underway.

A thesaurus or classification space is a representation of expert knowledge collected in advance of user queries. It is also possible to apply expert system techniques to the formulation of queries. McCune et al. (1985) have demonstrated a prototype system that expresses a conceptual topic as a set of retrieval rules. Each rule is in the form of an implication: the existence of a given pattern implies to a given degree of confidence the existence of a conceptual topic in a text. These rules are arranged hierarchically, with topics being implied by patterns of subtopics, and the lowest-level rules referring to patterns of particular words or phrases in a text. All these rules taken together with an inverted index form a knowledge base. A query is expressed as a request for texts relevant to a particular topic, and the knowledge base is searched to produce a ranked list of potentially relevant texts. In a small database of 30 newspaper articles, this system performed nearly perfectly in a search for the concept of "violent acts of terrorism" (100 percent recall with 93 percent precision), correctly identifying all relevant articles and incorrectly identifying only one irrelevant article (about an unsuccessful bomb disposal attempt) as relevant. Further research is underway to generalize these results to large databases and to develop an interface which allows users to easily construct and modify their own sets of retrieval rules.

The Future of Automated Text Retrieval

Boolean query retrieval systems are already being offered for personal computer access to textual databases on optical disc. Most of these systems include full-screen interfaces and context-sensitive help facilities to improve their ease of use by untrained researchers. The success of these systems should generate demand for more powerful and easier-to-use systems. The combination of already proven natural query software and the computing power of the current generation of microprocessors may soon make the state of the art in automated text retrieval accessible to the mass market. The continued evolution of optical storage, expert system techniques, and microprocessor power will make possible a radical improvement in the easy and inexpensive availability of large volumes of textual information to all interested persons.

About the Author

Gregory Colvin received his B.A. in psychology and computer science from the University of Colorado at Boulder in 1977, and his Ph.D in psychology and mathematics from Cornell University in 1982. He then served as vice president for systems development at Information Access Systems, Inc., where he was responsible for the development of expert systems for text retrieval applications.

Since 1984, he has been with Reference Technology Inc., an industry leader in laser optic systems for information distribution, where he has continued his research on natural query access to textual data, and has developed methods for optimized access to read-only optical databases.

References

Bookstein, A. 1980. Fuzzy requests: An approach to weighted Boolean searches. *Journal of the American Society for Information Science,* 31:240-247.

Bookstein, A. 1983. Explanation and generalization of vector models in information retrieval. In G. Salton and H.J. Shneider (eds.), *Research and Development in Information Retrieval: Proceedings.* New York: Springer-Verlag.

Blair, D.C., and M.E. Maron. 1985. An evaluation of retrieval effectiveness for a full-text document-retrieval system. *Communications of the ACM,* 28: 289-299.

Buell, D.A., and D.H. Kraft. 1981. A model for a weighted retrieval system. *Journal of the American Society for Information Science,* 32.

Guertin, E. A. 1985. Overwhelming evidence. *Digital Review,* May, pp. 62-68.

Jeffreys, H. J. 1981. A new paradigm for artificial intelligence. In K.E. Davis (ed.), *Advances in Descriptive Psychology,* Vol. 1. Greenwich, Conn.: JAI Press.

McCune, B.P., R.M. Tong, J.S. Dean, and D.G. Shapiro. 1985. RUBRIC: A system for rule-based information retrieval. *IEEE Transactions on Software Engineering,* SE-11, pp. 939-945.

Noreault, T., M. Koll, and M.J. McGill. 1977. Automatic ranked output from Boolean searches in SIRE. *Journal of the American Society for Information Science,* 28: 333-339.

Ossorio, P.G. Classification space. 1966. *Multivariate Behavioral Research,* 1: 479-524.

Radecki, T. 1983. Incorporation of relevance feedback into Boolean retrieval systems. In G. Salton and H.J. Shneider (eds.), *Research and Development in Information Retrieval: Proceedings.* New York: Springer-Verlag.

Salton, G. 1968. *Automatic Information Organization and Retrieval,* New York: McGraw-Hill.

Salton, G., and M.J. McGill, 1983. *Introduction to Modern Information Retrieval.* New York: McGraw-Hill.

Sparck Jones, K. 1971. *Automatic Keyword Classification for Information Retrieval.* London: Butterworths.

Sparck Jones, K. 1980. Search term relevance weighting—some recent results. *Journal of Information Science,* 1: 325-332.

Swets, J.A. 1963. Information retrieval systems. *Science,* 141: 245-250.

Full Text Management

by Jock Gill
and Toby Woll

The industrialized world is awash in a sea of information. Indeed, if wealth of data and computing power guaranteed effective use of information, extraordinary progress would be made. However, society's progress is never that orderly. Having learned how to acquire information, we are faced with learning how to take advantage of its abundance. Part of our task involves developing ways of managing information that extend its usefulness. Full Text Management is a technology that offers that potential.

Text puts in tangible form the content of different kinds of human expression: thoughts, ideas, concepts, facts, figures, and fiction.

At the outset it is worthwhile to ask, What is text? Text is the symbolic representation of intelligence. Text puts in tangible form the content of different kinds of human expression: thoughts, ideas, concepts, facts, figures, and fiction. In other words, text makes it possible to store and disseminate human expression. As such, the development of the written tradition has been a driving force in human development.

Humans have been evolving concrete forms of communication since the beginning of recorded history. Cave paintings were a form of text that primitive people used to capture and communicate daily events. Cuneiform and hieroglyphic writing marked new stages of textual development. Carved stelae in the Guatemalan jungle are studied today as the textual representation of astronomical knowledge. As civilizations developed more and more effective systems of recording information, the tradition of written language began to survive beyond the societies themselves. Text became a critical element in sustained progress.

Technology has played a crucial role in the development of human expression through text. As a medium of storage, walls and stone gave way to papyrus. Bamboo strips were put aside in favor of paper. And as the medium carrying text improved, the dissemination of information was enhanced. Manually scripted pages yielded to the revolution brought on by the printing press and movable type. As text technology advanced, the printed word became more and more widely used. Concurrently, text became more valuable and more powerful.

The use or function of text has three aspects: to store intelligence in a concrete form; to transmit or disseminate information between parties; to organize, retrieve, or recall information. The density of text storage, the flexibility of text organization, and the speed of text retrieval have a tremendous impact on the usefulness of text. The advent of computers was a major breakthrough in text technology. High-density storage devices and sophisticated software systems on high-speed mainframes have made the

138

seemingly impossible, possible. And we find ourselves in an era conventionally termed the age of information, in which text is stored, organized, retrieved, and manipulated as never before.

Full Text Management is not a new concept. It has been available for more than 10 years but has not been widely used because of its mainframe dependency. It has been used primarily by the legal profession, where exhaustive searches of extensive judicial records are required. However, with the advent of Computer Access Corporation's BlueFish program, among others, mainframe style Full Text Management is now available to the microcomputer user. Full Text technology, then, must be looked at again, redefined, and its potential revalued in the new context of widespread use.

First, we must define what is meant by Full Text Management. A program like BlueFish stores a collection of documents on a computer and indexes every word and number in the text. When information is needed from one of these documents, the program is instructed to find and retrieve the documents or sections of text based on a word or a combination of words. The information found may then be extracted for productive use in new forms of organization and distribution. Making a Full Text system conceptually simple and easy to use is a remarkable programming achievement. The advent of Full Text in the personal computer arena is surely a breakthrough which will have a profound impact on information management in the future.

The same sheet of paper cannot be filed in two places at once. The words are locked into the medium on which they are printed.

What, then, is the benefit of a Full Text Management program? It extends the boundaries of the usefulness of textual representation of information. Consider, as examples, the way we use corporate correspondence, technical newsletters, periodicals, or reference materials.

We rarely look at a mass of these printed materials as something that we would readily search, explore, analyze, extract, combine, and recombine. The very physical nature of the printed page restricts its usefulness. The same sheet of paper cannot be filed in two places at once. The words are locked into the medium on which they are printed. Text is not used as a flexible asset because the printed page is static and unwieldly.

In contrast, text stored on a CD ROM can be searched and retrieved with total flexibility. The content is liberated from its tangible form and can be explored and manipulated without restriction. Computer-based Full Text Management can enhance every aspect of text's use: information storage, retrieval, and dissemination.

There comes a point of critical paper mass when it is more practical to ignore information available than to use it.

Full Text Management is not without its detractors. In their article in the March 1985 issue of *Communications of ACM*, David C. Blair and M. E. Maron present a convincing study on why Full Text retrieval is not the panacea that it may appear at first sight. They argue that, with its hazards, traditional manual indexing of textual material yields results as relevant as Full Text retrieval. The principle of the paper is that there is little probability that a searcher can discover the precise search terms that will appear only in the desired documents and no others. Vocabulary, they argue, changes with time and point of view.

However, Blair and Maron overlook a variety of Full Text tools that tend to minimize the problem of developing search terms. Documents can be augmented with formatted fields. The data can be enriched with words and phrases to increase search accuracy. Wild-card searches can be performed. The database dictionary can be examined directly. And with search software such as BlueFish, the searcher can select specific documents without using any search terms.

Moreover, their argument avoids the issue that much textual material is not and never will be indexed manually. It will be created, sent, and filed. There comes a point of critical paper mass when it is more practical to ignore information available than to use it. Full Text provides the opportunity to make all text more accessible, more useful, and hence more valuable.

Moving into a Full Text Management environment does present new challenges, however. Although BlueFish can use text in its original form, we will have to approach text from a new perspective to fully exploit the liberating and recombinant powers of a Full Text retrieval system.

First, the data preparer or writer will have to consider the fact that word and phrase searches will be performed on the material. Spelling accuracy and consistent vocabulary will result in better text searches. Word processing programs with dictionary and glossary capability will make a major contribution in this area.

Realizing that text will be accessed via a screen, we will want to consider how to present text visually in the most effective manner. A BlueFish document is viewed in 20-line segments (the height of the screen) and should probably be not more than four to five screens long. The spacing and graphic text enhancements must be suitable for screen display. Many computers, for instance, are unable to display underlining and boldface type. Punctuation defining sentences and paragraphs will need to be set up to maximize the synergy between the content of the text and the retrieval capabilities of the program.

Since documents will exist in both electronic and print media, a method of maintaining the correspondence between the screen and its paper analogue will be needed. A direct and expedient method of going directly from the screen to a specific page of paper must be designed into the text. For example, page and line number references may be inserted into the Full Text database. Clearly, we will have to expand and modify the way in which we think about the presentation of ideas as text.

It is critical to see that Full Text Management is in its infancy.

Finally, we will be challenged to think about logical units of information as opposed to printed units. Now that we can discover, extract, and recombine units of information represented as text, the most useful breakdown of material is into small logical units. Strategies for the atomization of information will have to be evolved. For example, a deposition transcript may be best atomized into page or question/answer units. Reference material may be best broken into separate documents, each representing a single subject. Formatted fields may be added to each atomized unit to identify its source. Freed from the constraints of paper documents and looking forward to the use of Full Text search and retrieval, we are drawn to think of new ways to atomize and organize information.

It is important to face these challenges knowing that they are not a barrier to using Full Text Management. Word processing and text editing programs will be very important in facilitating text remodeling. However, Full Text Management can be implemented with any machine-readable text. As Marshall McLuhan wrote in *The Medium Is the Massage,* the development of new strategies and applications will come as users become accustomed to the new technology. [Yes, it really is *Massage.*—Ed.]

It is critical to see that Full Text Management is in its infancy. The development of the printing press reaped results beyond all expectations. Similarly, the potential of the enhanced value of information in this fluid and dynamic environment will be discovered with its use. It will be part of a new era of publishing and direct communication between systems. Full Text Management offers the possibility of satisfying the information retrieval needs of the future within a single operating environment while expanding the usefulness of information today.

About the Author

Jock Gill is the president and one of the founders of Computer Access Corporation. The primary thrust of Computer Access Corporation is full text retrieval software and the related hardware areas, such as CD ROM and WORM technology. They have recently released a product, called BlueFish, that creates and manages large databases.

Toby Woll is a cofounder of Micro Horizons, the producer of BlueFish documentation.

Jock Gill
Computer Access Corporation
Suite 324
26 Brighton Street
Belmont, MA 02178-4008

Information Retrieval: Research into New Capabilities

by Edward A. Fox

In 1945, Vannevar Bush published his seminal article "As We May Think," in which he envisioned a device called a "memex" that would transform a desk into a portal to the world's stored knowledge. It would be possible not only to access information but to record one's trail of investigations and share those associations with others.

143

Microcomputers and optical discs have captured the imagination of computer scientists and users alike. What is needed is a coalescing of those two developments with the fruits of retrieval research, to make a quantum leap beyond current systems in all three areas.

In the past four decades, researchers in the little-known field of information retrieval have struggled with technological and scientific issues in their attempt to create systems with some of the capabilities of the memex. While Bush's dream was initially described in terms of microfilm and mechanical devices, today's designers have microcomputers, fiberoptic networks, and laser discs. Technologically, we are much closer to the paperless society described by Lancaster (1978). More important in many ways, however, is the fact that computer science has emerged as a key area of research in the new information age and that the field of information retrieval has matured into a cross-disciplinary investigation of the problems of text analysis, indexing, knowledge representation, storage, access, and presentation.

For years, work in information retrieval has been limited by the available tools. Today, computer hardware with tremendous speed and storage capacity has become easily affordable. Now there is a chance to use innovative approaches to develop new retrieval software and to test that out with large collections of information.

Microcomputers and optical discs have captured the imagination of computer scientists and users alike. What is needed is a coalescing of those two developments with the fruits of retrieval research, to make a quantum leap beyond current systems in all three areas. The result will be an exciting range of products bringing us another step closer to what Vannevar Bush envisioned.

Focus

Papyrus, the world's first paper, revolutionized the recording of information. Today, CD ROM is starting a similar revolution. Providing access to that information, however, becomes even more important, due to the sheer volume of material involved.

This chapter focuses primarily on research issues relating to access methods and techniques developed in the area of information retrieval. The discussion will center on models, on experiments testing system effectiveness, and on indexing/retrieval/interface methods. For additional information on these subjects, you can consult works by authors such as Heaps, Van Rijsbergen, Salton, and McGill, listed in the bibliography at the end of the chapter.

Research Issues

Information retrieval (IR) is a cross-disciplinary field investigated by librarians, linguists, psychologists, and computer or information scientists. Two of the closest areas to IR are the study of database management systems (DBMS) and artificial intelligence (AI). What is distinctive about IR is the need to work with:

○ Unstructured data, unlike the structured data of database systems.

○ Text, possibly in concert with numeric and image data.

○ Very large collections, often larger than those handled by a DBMS, and much more heterogeneous than those investigated by AI researchers.

○ Effectiveness of access, measured experimentally.

Certainly, DBMS and AI researchers confront some of these issues, but they are not necessarily of central interest to them. The second point is clearly important for linguists; the third, for library and information scientists; and the fourth, for cognitive psychologists.

Representation

How information is viewed by system designers and users is one of the key differences between the areas of DBMS, IR, and AI. Figure 1 illustrates the distinction in terms of a collection of bibliographic citations.

BIBLIOGRAPHIC CITATIONS			
TITLE	AUTHOR	PUBL.	YEAR
Title1	Author1	New P.	1984
Title 1	Author2	New P.	1984
Title 2	Author3	Publ. X.	1985

.T
Title of the book or article
.A
First Author, Jr.
Second Author, II
.P
New Publishing Co.
.Y
1984

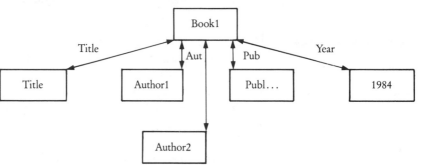

Figure 1. Representations of citation data in database, IR, and AI systems

A good deal of attention has been given to integrating IR and DBMS technology. Dattola (1979) developed the FIRST system, which merged a network database and a clustered retrieval system. Crawford (1981) advocated the adaptation of the relational model for IR purposes, and with Macleod (1983) viewed IR as a database application. Developers of database systems, such as Stonebraker (1983), have made special adaptations to better support document processing. Although some DBMS techniques, such as B-trees, have been integrated into IR systems, an elegant merger of the concepts has not yet occurred.

Other work has focused on the nontextual data relating to documents and shown the value of that additional type of information. Citation data can lead to cocitation diagrams, such as those developed by Small (1980), which highlight the interrelationships between areas in a field. Bibliographic coupling, explored by Kessler, is also of value. When these relationships are used in concert with descriptive and textual data, the resulting representation, according to results with two special test collections which this author developed, can lead to even more effective retrieval.

Text Processing

Text appears in manuscripts, journals, reference works, periodicals, reports, newspapers, correspondence, and other forms. Computer methods that aid in the creation and layout of text, such as word processing, electronic messaging, and photocomposition, have led to the increased availability of machine-readable texts. Standards work, as in the Electronic Manuscript Project, will accentuate this trend. Attendant issues of analyzing, indexing, storing, and accessing text have been central to much of the work in modern IR.

Computer methods that aid in the creation and layout of text, such as word processing, electronic messaging, and photocomposition, have led to the increased availability of machine-readable texts.

The simplest way for a computer to access text is to search it sequentially, much as people scan the words on a page. When people search through text collections they are able to decide whether located items are relevant to their particular search need. Computerized retrieval systems should find exactly those items that are relevant—ignoring items that are non-relevant. That is to say, they should have high precision as well as high recall. Clever algorithms, like that of Boyer and Moore (1977), can speed up the search process, and further improvements are possible with special hardware. But the simple sequential search becomes ineffective as the query increases in complexity and the text collection increases in size. However, creating complex models of text documents by analyzing and indexing large collections can allow them to be efficiently searched.

Models

Much of the research in IR has been based on four different models of the field: browsing, Boolean and p-norm, vector and probabilistic, and artificial intelligence. Traditionally, the Boolean model has been most widely upheld. The vector and probabilistic models have shown promise in laboratory tests. With recent advances in display and pointing devices, browsing models have been advanced. Finally, due to the promise and popularity of AI, a good deal of attention has been given to AI-based models. Each of these models is discussed below, in order of complexity.

Browsing Models

In libraries, people work with the card catalog (or its equivalent) and/or browse in the stacks. When using reference works, people frequently follow implicit or explicit pointers or skip around looking for particular items. Now that large high-resolution displays are available for computers, effective use of such two-dimensional devices, as in the Caliban system, is of particular interest.

The Smalltalk-80 system, developed by Goldberg et al. (1982), has been implemented to provide such an environment. Since hierarchical organizations of knowledge are commonplace, the language and displays support that perspective. An example of the system browser is shown in Figure 2. Once Smalltalk is thoroughly understood, program development for broad classes of applications becomes especially convenient.

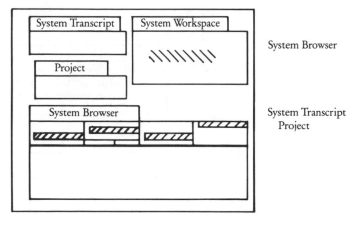

Figure 2. Smalltalk-80 with browser

Weyer explored the value of a browsing model for searching books, as portrayed in Figure 3. The key point is that users can see several adjacent displays supporting various types of access to a book and can easily explore useful links. Responses to a question can be located using the table of contents, the index, or other pointers, or by the aid of text searching.

AREAS:

Command

Subject

Title

Text

Subject References

Cmds.	Question		
Answer			
List of Subjects		Subject Index	Sub-Subject Index
List of Titles			
Chapters	Sections		Sub-Sections
Lines of text taken from the dynamic book, with words that match the words selected in the subject index shown in bold face.			
For Chapter	For Section		For Sub-Section

Figure 3. Dynamic book

On a somewhat larger scale, electronic encyclopedias, such as the Grolier encyclopedia described by Cook (1984), provide browsing-based access to large reference works. As can be seen in Figure 4, all the cross references found in an encyclopedia can supplement what is available in a dynamic book. Furthermore, special capabilities can be built into such systems to understand units of measure, foreign words, or alternative map presentations. Lessons, simulations, and other enhancements can also be incorporated.

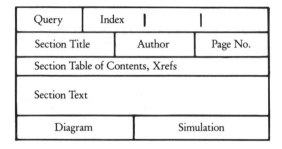

Figure 4. Electronic encyclopedia

For large collections of documents, integrating browsing with other access methods is of particular appeal. Caliban is the first retrieval system with that orientation. It employs some of the most useful search techniques, along with multiwindow display and browsing. The appeal of this model has encouraged other researchers, such as Thompson (1985) and Croft (1978, 1982), to incorporate some of the ideas of Caliban in more recent systems that employ AI methods as well.

Boolean and P-Norm Models

Most retrieval systems require users to describe their search interest in terms of a Boolean expression, where key words or other atomic elements are combined into clauses, and clauses are combined with other components, by AND, OR, or NOT operators. Figure 5 illustrates this approach. Part *A* is an English language statement indicating an area that might be of interest to a reader of this book. Part *B* is a typical expression of the same statement as a Boolean query. For those with a computer science bent, part *C* uses prefix notation to give an equivalent form that can be directly mapped into the tree structure in part *D*, which illustrates the relationship of the various concepts.

It should be noted that the original form of part *A* could not be directly utilized by a computer. Indeed, it is difficult to construct good Boolean

A)

INFORMATION RETRIEVAL SYSTEMS WITH OPTICAL DISC STORAGE SUCH AS
CD ROM ATTACHED TO STANDARD PERSONAL COMPUTER

B)

(IR OR (information AND retrieval) OR (document AND retrieval)
AND
(CD ROM OR CDROM OR (CD AND ROM) OR (compact AND disc AND (ROM OR read-
only OR memory or stor*)))
AND
(PC OR PC-AT OR PC-XT OR (personal AND computer AND IBM))

C)

AND (OR (IR, AND (information, retrieval), AND (document, retrieval)), OR (CD ROM,
CDROM, AND (compact, disc, OR (ROM, read-only, memory, stor*))), OR (PC, PC-AT,
PC-XT, AND (personal, computer, IBM)))

D)

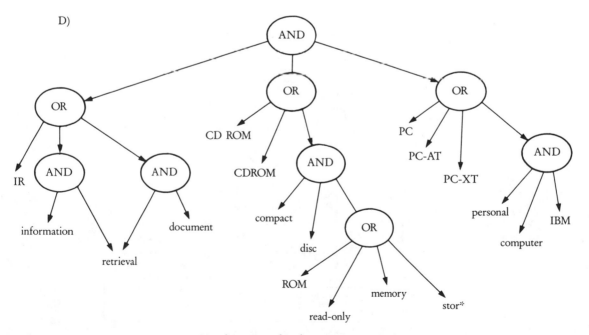

Figure 5. Transformations of Boolean query representations

queries, often requiring the assistance of trained search intermediaries who add terms not originally included (e.g., document), provide synonyms (e.g., PC) or alternate spellings (e.g., CDROM), truncate words to allow for morphological variants (e.g., stor*), drop function or high-frequency terms (e.g., with, systems), and insert Boolean operators. Of the available Boolean operators, AND and OR are the most commonly used. OR is required when any type of "searchonym" (as coined by Attar and Fraenkel [1977], a term synonymous for searching purposes) is involved, while AND must be used sparingly so as not to diminish recall. It is rarely necessary to use NOT. When high precision is needed, metrical, proximity, or adjacency operators are also employed, since it is less likely for terms to appear near each other than to simply occur in the same document. The entire process of carrying out a Boolean search is summarized in Figure 6.

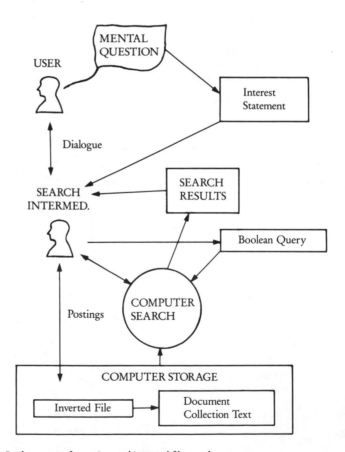

Figure 6. Boolean query formation and inverted file search

In actuality, there is usually a good deal of interaction between the end user and the searcher, and between the searcher and the system, in order to construct a good query. Part of that latter dialog is shown in Figure 7.

> information			> CD ROM		
1) INFORMATION	2300		9) CD ROM	421	
> retrieval			> CDROM		
2) RETRIEVAL	749		10) CDROM	121	
> document			> compact		
3) DOCUMENT	892		11) COMPACT	82	
> 1 AND 2			> disc		
4) 1 AND 2	539		12) DISC	1583	
> 3 AND 2			> 11 AND 12		
5) 2 AND 3	372		13) 11 AND 12	48	
> IR			> ROM		
6) IR	452		14) ROM	567	
> 4 OR 5			> read-only		
7) 4 OR 5	627		15) READ-ONLY	391	
> 7 OR 6			> memory		
8) 6 OR 7	704		16) MEMORY	3865	

Figure 7. Initial section of dialog for Boolean query processing

A retrieval system accepting Boolean queries typically includes an inverted file (also called an inverted index) which supplies the postings information shown in Figure 7. Thus, whereas the document file is stored as a set of documents, each of which has words, the inverted file (IF), depicted in Figure 8, turns that organization upside down.

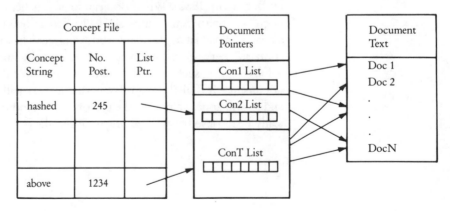

Figure 8. Simple inverted file organization

For each term (e.g., keyword, special phrase, thesaurus class), there is a list of all documents in which it appears, along with the length of that list (i.e., the number of postings). From Figure 7 it can be seen that a searcher will not only consider the words given and their semantic relationships but will also note how frequently words occur, or how commonly they occur with other words. A Boolean query thus will often evolve in steps; and although the final query will probably retrieve a reasonable number of hits, it may have a very complex syntactic and bizarre semantic structure.

The simplest way for a computer to access text is to search it sequentially, much as people scan the words on a page.

In spite of the ubiquitous nature of Boolean query systems for IR, they have many limitations and problems. As can be seen in Figure 7, it is difficult to identify the correct-size set of documents that should be retrieved. When all terms thought to be useful are put together into a suitable query, the resulting retrieved set may be much too large or too small. Furthermore, if there is a large set, the documents are usually randomly ordered, so the most useful one may well be at the end.

The SIRE system was devised by McGill, Noreault, and Koll in part to explore the effects of ranking the set of documents retrieved by a Boolean query. In addition to storing the list of documents in which a term occurred, the number of times a term appeared in each document was recorded in the inverted file. A variety of formulas for ranking the retrieved documents were compared by McGill et al. (1976) in order to group similar schemes and identify the best ones.

Even in SIRE, however, the searcher cannot specify which terms are most important. One notation for expressing relative importance was proposed by Bookstein (1980). When Boolean logic is generalized so that there are degrees of truth in the range of 0 to 1, then a document can be indexed by a term to a partial degree, and truth values can be viewed as measuring the similarity between a query and each document. Figure 9 illustrates the value of having such *fuzzy* sets rather than simple Boolean sets of retrieved documents. It is likely that relevant documents will have higher similarity and so will appear closer to the top of the list; more documents will typically be retrieved as well, aiding with recall.

A. FUZZY SET

Document	Similarity
ID001	1.0
ID742	.834
ID819	.632
•	•
•	•
•	•
ID253	.104
ID006	0.0
•	•
•	•
•	•
ID997	0.0

B. BOOLEAN

Document	Similarity
ID001	1.0
•	•
•	•
ID029	1.0
ID003	0.0
•	•
•	•
•	•
ID997	0.0

Figure 9. Sets of retrieved documents

Such a ranking can be produced when Boolean queries are interpreted according to the p-norm scheme explored by Salton, Fox, and Wu (1983). In addition to having relative weights on query terms, and degrees of indexing (in range 0 to 1) on terms in each document, one can vary the strictness of interpretation of the OR and AND operators (in similar fashion to the softening suggested by Paice [1984]). That is to say, the conjunction of a number of terms will retrieve documents where all terms need not be present, albeit with a similarity less than 1. Also, the disjunction of terms will lead to higher similarity when several of the terms are present as opposed to when only one is present. A p-value can be chosen in the range of 1 to infinity, where 1 gives the least strict interpretation. The p-value identifies which in the Lp family of norms is employed to measure distance from the ideal points (since OR queries should be far from the 0 point, and AND queries should be close to the 1 point), as can be seen in Figure 10. Note that p = 2 specifies standard Euclidean distance. These curves, developed by this author, show connect points for documents that have equal similarity to the given two-term queries. They demonstrate the range in strictness from the p = infinity case, where AND is viewed as MIN and OR is viewed as MAX, to the p = 1 case where AND = OR = AVERAGE.

Experiments by this author indicate that the p-norm scheme leads to more effective retrieval than traditional Boolean systems. P-norm queries can also be automatically constructed from simple lists of keywords. In addition, when a user is presented with the first 10 or 20 documents retrieved by a p-norm or Boolean search and indicates which of those are relevant,

a) QUERY: A OR ^{P}B

b) QUERY: A AND ^{P}B

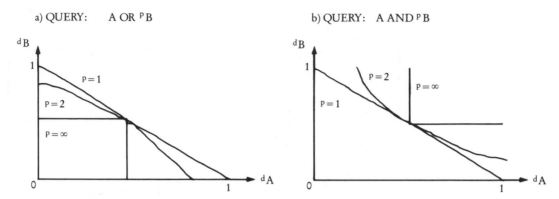

Figure 10. P-norm equisimilarity contours

automatic construction of a new feedback query is possible. Experiments by this author and by others at Cornell have shown that such a query is often better than the original query.

Vector and Probabilistic Models

The vector and probabilistic models developed out of early investigations into the statistical characteristics of text collections. Specifically, the vector space model proposed by Salton, Wong and Yang (1975) is based on the observation that the frequencies of occurrence of terms are indicative of their importance. Similarly, the probabilistic model, proposed at roughly the same time by Robertson and Sparck Jones (1976) and by Salton, Yang and Yu (1975), relies on Bayesian theory. The presumption is that term importance can be estimated as a result of contrasting the occurrence characteristics of text terms in a feedback set of relevant documents with occurrence values in the rest of the collection. Both of these models are discussed at length by Van Rijsbergen (1979); the description below deals with key features.

Figures 11 and 12 illustrate the vector space model, giving examples of spaces for three-dimensional terms and for T-dimensional terms, respectively.

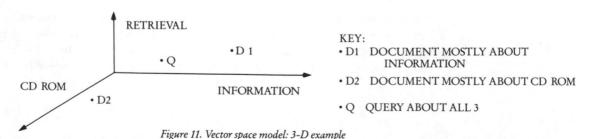

Figure 11. Vector space model: 3-D example

Three of the terms from the query in Figure 5A are chosen in Figure 11, where documents are represented by points determined by the number of times each of the terms occurs. The query Q can likewise be located in the space. Relative weights on the terms allow one to indicate which are most important. Retrieval can be viewed as locating documents that are near the query, based on a suitable definition of similarity.

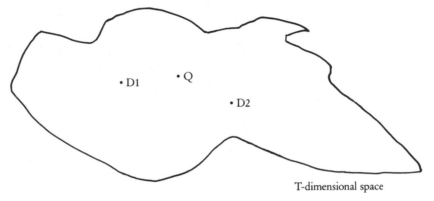

T-dimensional space

Figure 12. Vector space model: T-D example

In Figure 12, an idealized view of the T-dimensional space determined by the T different concepts in the collection, documents and queries can both be placed. Similarity can then be computed, for example, as the cosine of the angle between a query and document vector.

Figure 13 shows one way to represent the vector space, using matrix notation. Each of the T concepts present is associated with a column, and each of the N rows defines a collection document. The value for document I and term J, d_{ij}, indicates the importance of that term's appearance.

If the cosine similarity measure is employed, $TF \times IDF$ weights are easy to compute and give good performance; they are the product of the number of times the term appears in the document (the TF, or term frequency, component) and the inverse document frequency (IDF, figured as the log of N/DF_j, where DF is the number of documents in which the term appears). A similar value has been used by this author and others for p-norm computations, except that normalization to the range of 0 to 1 is required.

TERMS

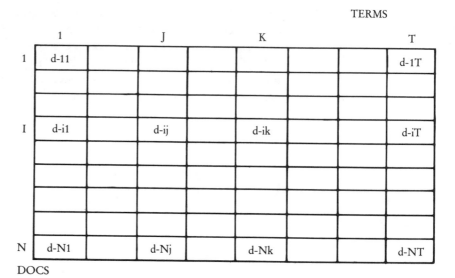

Figure 13. Document-term collection matrix

In any case, the document-term matrix in practice is very large, but since it is sparse it can be compactly represented. If one stores data by column, an extended inverted file like that found in SIRE results. Storing by row results in a file of document vectors.

Figure 14 idealizes the vector feedback process first developed by Rocchio (1971). A query, Q0, is transformed into a vector, and then a set of nearby documents is initially retrieved. The searcher identifies the (3, in this case) relevant documents. A new feedback query, Q1, is constructed from Q0 by moving closer to the relevant retrieved documents. Presumably, Q1 will do a better job than Q0 in retrieving relevant documents.

Metrical feedback, advocated by Attar and Fraenkel (1977), follows a similar model but also considers the number of intervening words between occurrences of terms that are to be added to the original query. Probabilistic feedback has a similar effect, but the construction of Q1 is done based on a term relevance (Robertson and Sparck Jones, 1976) or term precision formula (Salton, Yang, and Yu, 1975). Probabilistic weighting schemes are discussed in more detail by Van Rijsbergen (1979). An early implementation of probabilistic retrieval for a practical (museum) retrieval system was

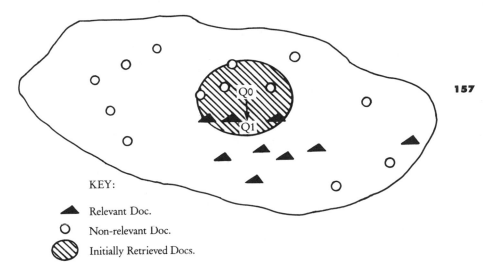

KEY:

▲ Relevant Doc.

◯ Non-relevant Doc.

⬨ Initially Retrieved Docs.

Figure 14. Vector feedback

done by Porter (1982). Probabilistic feedback has been incorporated by Buckley (1985) in recent versions of the SMART system and has also been adapted for several p-norm algorithms by this author. It is possible to obtain some of the benefits of probabilistic retrieval when accessing a conventional Boolean system, if sufficient processing is carried out by an intelligent front-end system such as that of Morrissey (1983).

In addition to supporting vector retrieval, the document-term matrix has been used to rationalize term or document clustering. The earliest thorough term-classification study, conducted by Sparck Jones in 1971, demonstrated that terms which co-occur in similar sets of documents tend to be ones that should be grouped into (thesaurus) classes. This technique could aid in semiautomatic selection of term classes when collections are not too large to warrant the relatively expensive processing.

Document clustering has been more thoroughly studied and shows greater promise. Figure 15 illustrates the process, where a number of similar documents are described by a centroid (named since the vector centroid can be so employed), where similar centroids are grouped under super centroids, etc. Since documents may often be about several topics, it is possible for the clustering to be overlapping, as shown for the second and fifth documents. A top-down search allows rapid identification of a few relevant documents, if at each point a depth-first selection is made of the best centroid to consider next.

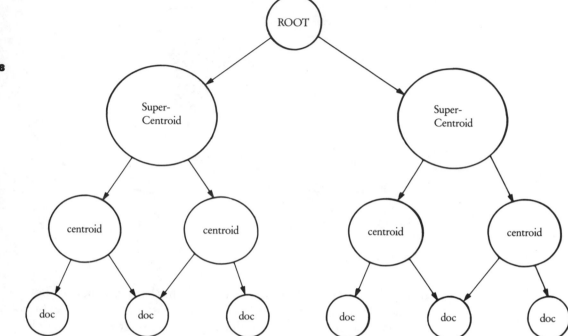

Figure 15. Cluster hierarchy organization

Clustering algorithms, such as those given by Hartigan (1975), have long been used in taxonomic analysis. Clustering using the well known single-link method to build searchable hierarchies was explored by Jardine and Van Rijsbergen (1971). For large collections, faster methods which still yield hierarchies that can be searched were developed by Dattola (1971) and Williamson (1974). Since cluster centroids are often quite large, top-down searching may be very expensive, so the bottom-up or hybrid scheme shown in Figure 16 was investigated by Croft (1978). A recent thorough examination of various clustering approaches by Voorhees (1985) highlights the complexity of the situation, identifies those situations where clustered searches may be better than inverted file searches, and encourages use of cluster connections to support better browsing systems.

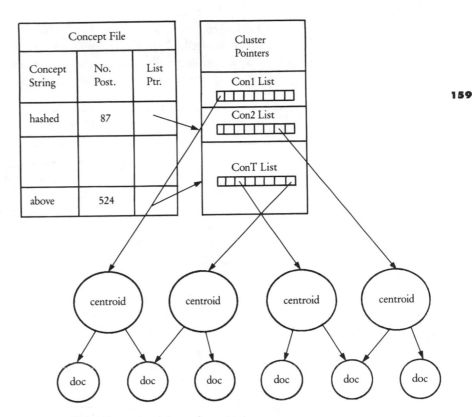

Figure 16. Hybrid inverted and clustered organization

Vector, probabilistic, and p-norm schemes all presume that the document collection has been automatically indexed. Figure 17 shows the key steps involved, for a hypothetical collection, on an example query. Function words like *with* and collection-specific high-frequency terms like *system* are stored in a stop word list. Incoming text is broken into tokens such as words, and a TRIE or hashing scheme is employed to identify stop words. The remaining terms are then alphabetized and repetitions avoided by the inclusion of frequency counts. Normal words are stemmed by a technique such as that of Lovins (1968). The system dictionary is then searched; new terms in documents are added when they first occur. At this time document frequency statistics can be updated. Next, a list of concept numbers is constructed. Terms are weighted according to a scheme such as TF × IDF (described earlier), and vectors are built. Higher performance is possible if phrases are identified as they occur, and if terms with very low frequency are treated as markers of thesaurus classes, prior to weighting.

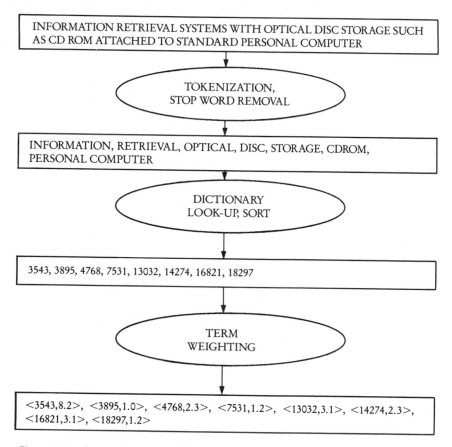

Figure 17. Simple example of automatic indexing

Given such an automatic indexing process, the overall process of indexing and vector or probabilistic retrieval can be seen in Figure 18.

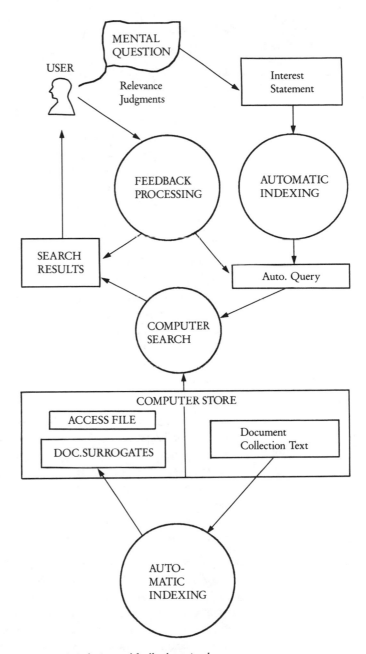

Figure 18. Automatic indexing and feedback retrieval

AI Models

The field of artificial intelligence has many subareas related to IR. Indeed, a number of IR researchers have worked on problems similar to those studied under AI. For example, O'Connor (1980) has employed linguistic methods and discourse analysis concepts, along with suitable heuristics, in order to select answer passages from texts. Oddy (1977) has focused on the user's model of an information need, and the specification of that need through a dialog with the computer, as the first and crucial step in retrieval. Hahn and Reimer (1984) use word expert parsing routines and discourse models in order to build a knowledge base that condenses texts so they can be more easily browsed and searched. Expert systems have likewise been employed by students like Yip (1979) to extend the work of Marcus on automating the job of search intermediaries.

At the most fundamental level, AI and IR are both concerned with the analysis and representation of the information content in texts. Thus, the early work by Evens on lexicons was in the computational linguistics area of AI but has since shown closer ties to IR. Related work by this author, for example, has demonstrated the value of relational models of the lexicon to aid in IR thesaurus class utilization. Earlier work on machine-readable dictionaries, such as by Amsler (1984), is now being extended to allow several full dictionaries to be automatically analyzed so that a comprehensive lexicon can be built to support work in both IR and AI.

Knowledge representation is another area of AI that closely relates to IR. Indexing methods and models of retrieval both depend on how the information content in texts can be analyzed and recorded. A taxonomy of representation schemes used in IR, formulated by Smith and Warner (1984), makes this point clearer and highlights the need for more IR work in document analysis. The work of Kimura (1984), in the domain of text processing, is of particular interest in providing a framework for modeling large documents.

During the last decade, the frame model of Minsky (1975) has served as the basis for many AI knowledge representation efforts. Frames support higher-level views of information complexes than the semantic networks which have also been intensively studied by AI researchers such as Ritchie and Hanna (1984). Similar in form, but more closely tied to the type of cognitive science work that has evolved at Yale, are scripts and more recent constructs for modeling memory. AI methods for handling temporal data have proved useful for certain IR applications such as the Reseda project Zarri, 1983, and further research is underway.

The larger question of how to analyze documents for IR is allied to AI work in natural language processing. Logic programming has been developed to help speed up development of language understanding and other tasks, as evidenced by the success of Prolog analysis systems by Pereira (1983). One version of Prolog has been used by Correira (1980) for computational analysis of stories. Simple but powerful routines for searching small document collections, for building schema representations of texts, and for question answering have also been demonstrated by Simmons (1984).

A Boolean query . . . will often evolve in steps; and although the final query will probably retrieve a reasonable number of hits, it may have a very complex syntactic and bizarre semantic structure.

A great deal of further work is needed in this area. Parsing systems must become more robust, to handle ungrammatical constructs and a variety of styles and genres identified by Hayes (1981) and others. Much of the progress to date relies on utilizing systems, like that of Sager (1975), that have been tailored for a particular sublanguage. Less detailed analysis is possible, as in DeJong's (1982) FRUMP, but requires a knowledge base for whatever subject areas are to be found in the text collection. The problem studied by Charniak (1982), of recognizing the context for a discussion so that appropriate specialized knowledge bases can be accessed, is unfortunately very hard to solve. Building schemas to represent story structure, investigated by Rumelhart (1975), is also difficult. Clearly, developing systems which Riesbeck (1982) hopes can realistically comprehend natural language texts, is very much a research problem.

At an even higher level, issues of matching user needs with texts are common to both IR and cognitive science studies. Designing a good interface to support human-computer interaction for IR will require extensive research and psychological testing beyond the recent work by Borgman (1984) and others. The need is even greater if simple Boolean systems are replaced by more sophisticated designs incorporating browsing, vector, probabilistic, and AI approaches. One of many AI efforts to develop such natural language dialog systems, with limited modeling of user knowledge and plans and with special domain knowledge, is the UC project of Wilensky et al. (1984), building a UNIX consultant.

The recent emphasis on constructing expert systems, surveyed by Hayes-Roth et al. (1983), is another AI trend that promises to be helpful in retrieval. Several efforts aim to capture the expertise of search intermediaries in dealing with many different information retrieval services and in constructing Boolean queries. A more ambitious effort is Thompson and Croft's (1985) integration of browsing with automatic retrieval, where the system has limited models of the users and has special knowledge about the appropriateness of a given retrieval model and search strategy in each situation.

CODER: Integration of Models

The CODER (Composite Document Effective/Extended/Expert Retrieval) project is a comprehensive effort by this author to bring together the best aspects of browsing, Boolean, p-norm, vector, probabilistic, and AI models into a new-generation retrieval system. The system is being developed partially in C, for special control and interface portions, but mostly in Prolog. Specifically, Naish's (1984) MU-Prolog is being employed since it includes improvements to avoid some of the failings of standard Prolog systems, and since it directly supports retrieval from large fact bases. The CODER effort includes a number of important components:

1. Constructing a comprehensive lexicon, by automatically analyzing two full English dictionaries.

2. Developing an architecture based on the blackboard model pioneered by Erman et al. (1980) in the Hearsay-II project.

3. Having multiple experts, each with private rule bases, as well as blackboard-based strategists for both analysis and access of documents, that can run as separate processes on multiple machines.

4. Focusing on sophisticated analysis of complex heterogeneous documents, to determine the type and structure of each composite document.

5. Automatically generating a knowledge representation for documents, including multiple vectors, frames, and relations.

6. Storing and updating models for each user, allowing human-computer interaction via a number of different devices (including simple or sophisticated graphics devices, and eventually, speech output).

7. Planning appropriate methods for both analysis and access, based on hypotheses posited by the many different experts.

8. Using AI, p-norm, vector, and probabilistic query techniques along with a knowledge base, inverted file, and cluster hierarchy to support searches, feedback, and browsing.

It is hoped that as the CODER system evolves, it will support a variety of different types of composite documents and serve the needs of a number of user classes, as shown in Figure 19.

CODER DATA, USERS

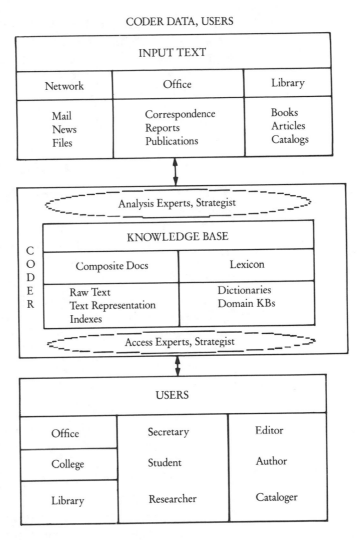

Figure 19. CODER

Past, Present, Future

Online Systems to Date

Today, the normal mode of access to bibliographic or full-text databases is through the use of online services. Large packet-switching public networks connect users to information retrieval services such as BRS, DIALOG, Dow Jones News/Retrieval, or MEDLARS. Information suppliers obtain their data from information providers.

166

Some of the databases available have been indexed, and a search often requires the aid of a trained intermediary to understand specialized thesauruses or other unique features. Boolean queries must be submitted; there is no ability to incorporate relative weights on terms, to use simpler or more powerful notations, to perform feedback operations, to get ranking of output, to rapidly browse, and so on. The investment in current retrieval software and emphasis on providing fast and low-cost services has made such enhancements irrelevant to managers of most online services.

CD ROM Systems Being Developed

At the most fundamental level, AI and IR are both concerned with the analysis and representation of the information content in texts.

With the advent of CD ROM systems, the initial focus has been to simply make the power of a large online service directly available to the user of a PC. Microcomputer versions of systems like BRS and BASIS provide essentially the same functionality as the mainframe software, with an almost identical user interface. In some cases, though, menu rather than command languages are employed.

Development work has focused on building suitable device drivers, designing file systems, compressing or replicating data, helping information providers organize their data for mastering, and struggling to achieve rapid response to commands. Since many PCs support graphics or color displays, some attention has also been paid to improving the simple line-by-line interaction mode provided by online services.

Another concern has been the integration of CD ROM with online systems, so that when updates become available they can be immediately accessed. Online searching, downloading to local magnetic disks, or distribution of diskettes or laser cards are all possible solutions.

Some more innovative developments are also taking place. Grolier has pioneered work on electronic encyclopedias to be readily accessible through PCs with CD ROM readers. The SIRE system (mentioned earlier) has been adapted to run on PCs as well as large minicomputers, and will support CD ROM databases. In both of these cases, more flexible interfaces than usual are provided.

Future Possibilities

The challenge raised in this chapter is to make a quantum leap forward in the practice of information retrieval by integrating the advances in processor and storage technology with the fruits of retrieval research. Storage methods have long been of interest to IR investigators such as Goldstein (1984), and today, with optical discs like CD ROMs becoming readily available, are even more exciting. Studying such large databases will require new experimental approaches, such as the simulation work of Tague (1981) et al. which relies on studies of the distributions found in existing collections. But it is likely that many research methods can be applied without a great deal of further adaptation.

167

Fully automatic processing . . . will transform the new papyrus, CD ROM, into a portal to knowledge . . .

What is perhaps most important is that with the advent of hardware that can store and process very large text collections, and is inexpensive enough so as to be targeted for the home market, there will be a new emphasis on effective as well as efficient retrieval. Fully automatic processing, where a natural language or an enhanced Boolean query can be handled, and where hidden but sophisticated analysis, indexing, search, and presentation capabilities are provided, will transform the new papyrus, CD ROM, into a portal to knowledge much like the memex proposed by Vannevar Bush in 1945!

About the Author

Edward A. Fox is assistant professor of computer science at Virginia Tech. He is coeditor of *ACM SIGIR Forum* and editor of *IRList Digest*, an electronic newsletter; ARPANET, BITNET, and CSNET. He has a B.S. in electrical engineering from MIT and M.S./Ph.d. in computer science from Cornell. He is a member of ACL, ACM, AFIS, and Sigma Xi. Current research in information retrieval utilizes UNIX, C, Prolog, microcomputers, computational linguistics, and expert systems.

Virginia Technical University
Department of Computer Science
562 McBride Hall
Blacksburg, VA 24061

References

Amsler, R. A. 1984. Machine-readable dictionaries. *ARIST*, 19:161-209.

Attar, R., and A. S. Fraenkel. 1977. Local feedback in full-text retrieval systems. *J. ACM*, July, pp. 397-417.

Bayer, R., and E. McCreight. 1972. Organization and maintenance of large ordered indexes. *Acta Informatica*, 1(3):173-189.

Bichteler, J. and E. A. Eaton III. 1980. The combined use of bibliographic coupling and cocitation for document retrieval. *J. Am. Soc. Inf. Sci.*, July, 31(4).

Blair, D. C. and M. E. Maron. 1985. An evaluation of retrieval effectiveness for a full-text document-retrieval system. *Commun. ACM*, March, 28(3):289-299.

Bookstein, A. 1980. Fuzzy requests: an approach to weighted Boolean searches. *J. Am. Soc. Inf. Sci.*, July, 31(4):240-247.

Borgman, Christine L. 1984. Psychological research in human-computer interaction. *ARIST*, 19:33-64.

Borko, H. and C. L. Bernier. 1978. *Indexing Concepts and Methods.* New York:Academic Press.

Boyer, R. S. and J. S. Moore. 1977. A fast string searching algorithm. *Comm. ACM*, October, 20(10):762-772.

Buckley, C. 1985. *Implementation of the SMART Information Retrieval System.* TR 85-686, May, Cornell Univ., Dept. of Comp. Sci.

Bush, V. 1945. As we may think. *Atlantic Monthly*, July, 176:101-108.

Charniak, E. 1982. Context recognition in language comprehension. In *Strategies for Natural Language Processing*, ed. by Wendy G. Lehnert and Martin H. Ringle, Hillsdale, N.J.: Lawrence Erlbaum Assoc., pp. 435-454.

Choeka, Y. 1980. Computerized full-text retrieval systems and research in the humanities: the Responsa Project. *Computers and the Humanities*, Nov., 14(3): 153-169.

Cleverdon, C. W., and E. M. Keen. 1968. Factors determining the performance of indexing systems. Cranfield, England: *Aslib Cranfield Research Project*, Vol. 1 and 2.

Comer, D. 1979. The ubiquitous B-tree. *ACM Comp. Surveys*, June, 11(2):121-137.

Cook, P. R. 1984. Electronic encyclopedias. *Byte*, July, 9(7): 151-170.

Correira, A. 1980. Computing story trees. *Amer. J. Comp. Ling.*, 6(3-4): 135-149.

Crawford, R. G. 1981. The relational model in information retrieval. *J. Am. Soc. Inf. Sci.*, 32(1): 51-64.

Croft, W. B. 1978. Organizing and Searching Large Files of Document Descriptions. Dissertation. Cambridge Univ., England.

Croft, W. B., and M. T. Pezarro. 1982. Text retrieval techniques for the automated office. In *Office Information Systems*, ed. by N. Naffah, North-Holland, Amsterdam, pp. 565-576.

Dattola, R. T. 1971. Experiments with a fast algorithm for automatic classification. In *The SMART Retrieval System, Experiments in Automatic Document Processing*, ed. by G. Salton, Prentice Hall, Englewood Cliffs, N.J.

Dattola, R. T. 1979. FIRST: Flexible Information Retrieval for Text. *J. Am. Soc. Inf. Sci.*, 30(1):9-14.

DeJong, G. 1982. An overview of the FRUMP system. In *Strategies for Natural Language Processing*, ed. by Wendy G. Lehnert and Martin H. Ringle, Hillsdale N.J.: Lawrence Erlbaum Assoc., pp. 149-176.

Erman, L. D., F. Hayes-Roth, V. R. Lesser, and D. R. Reddy. 1980. The Hearsay-II Speech-Understanding System: integrating knowledge to resolve uncertainty. *ACM Comp. Surveys*, 12: 213-253.

Evens, M. W., and R. N. Smith. 1979. A lexicon for a computer question-answering system. *Am. J. Comp. Ling.*, Microfiche 83.

Faloutsos, C. 1985. Access methods for text. *ACM Comp. Surveys*, March, 17(1): 49-74.

Fox, E. A. 1983. Combining information in an extended automatic information retrieval system for agriculture. *Infrastructure of an Information Society* (Proc. 1st Int. Info. Conf. Egypt, 13-16 Dec. 1982), North-Holland, Amsterdam.

Fox, E. A. 1983. Extending the Boolean and vector space models of information retrieval with p-norm queries and multiple concept types. Dissertation, Aug., Cornell University, University Microfilms Int., Ann Arbor, Mich.

Fox, E. A. 1983. *Some Considerations for Implementing the SMART Information Retrieval System under UNIX*. TR 83-560, Sept., Cornell Univ., Dept. of Comp. Sci.

Fox, E. A. 1983. *Characterization of Two New Experimental Collections in Computer and Information Science Containing Textual and Bibliographic Concepts*. TR 83-561, Sept., Cornell Univ., Dept. of Comp. Sci.

Fox, E. A. 1984. *Improved Retrieval Using a Relational Thesaurus for Automatic Expansion of Boolean Logic Queries*. Proc. Workshop on Relational Models of the Lexicon, June 29, Stanford Univ.

Fox, E. A. 1985. Composite Document Extended Retrieval: An Overview. In *Res. & Dev. in Inf. Ret.*, Eighth Annual Int. ACM SIGIR Conf., Montreal, June 5-7, pp. 42-53.

Frei, H. P. and J. F. Jauslin. 1983. Graphical presentation of information and services: a user oriented interface. *Inf. Tech.: Res. Dev.*, Jan., 2(1): 23-42.

Frei, H. P. and J. F. Jauslin. 1984. Two-dimensional representation of information retrieval services. In *Representation and Exchange of Knowledge as a Basis of Information Processes*, ed. by Hans J. Dietschmann, North-Holland, New York: pp. 383-396.

Fujitani, L. 1984. Laser optical disk: the coming revolution in on-line storage. *Commun. ACM*, June, 27(6): 546-554.

Goldberg, A., D. Robson, and D. H. H. Ingalls. 1982. *Smalltalk-80: the language and its implementation*, Addison-Wesley, Menlo Park, Calif.

Goldberg, A., D. Robson, and D. H. H. Ingalls. 1982. *Smalltalk-80: the interactive programming environment*, Addison-Wesley, Menlo Park, Calif.

Goldstein, C. M. 1984. Computer-based information storage technologies. *ARIST*, 19: 65-96.

Hahn, U., and U. Reimer. 1984. Heuristic text parsing in 'topic': methodological issues in a knowledge-based text condensation system. In *Representation and Exchange of Knowledge as a Basis of Information Processes*, ed. by Hans J. Dietschmann, North-Holland, New York, pp. 143-163.

Hall, P. A. V., and G. R. Dowling. 1980. Approximate string matching. *ACM Comp. Surveys*, 12(4): 381-402.

Hartigan, J. A. 1975. *Clustering Algorithms*. John Wiley and Sons, New York.

Haskin, R. 1980. Hardware for searching very large text databases. In *Proc. 5th Workshop on Comp. Arch. for Non-Numeric Proc.*, ACM, March, New York, pp. 49-56.

Hayes, P., and G. V. Mouradian. 1981. Flexible parsing. *Amer. J. Comp. Ling.*, 7(4): 232-242.

Hayes-Roth, F., D. A. Waterman, and D. B. Lenat, eds. 1983. *Building Expert Systems*, Addison-Wesley, Reading, Mass.

Heap, H. S. 1978. *Information Retrieval, Computational and Theoretical Aspects*. Academic Press, New York.

Hollaar, L. A. 1985. A testbed for information retrieval research: the Utah Retrieval System Architecture. *Proc. 8th Annual. Int. ACM SIGIR Conf. on R&D in Inf. Ret.*, June 5-7, Montreal, pp. 227-232.

Jardine, N. and C. J. Van Rijsbergen. 1971. The use of hierarchic clustering in information retrieval. *Inf. Stor. and Ret.*, Dec., 7(5): 217-240.

Jennings, M. 1984. The electronic manuscript project. *Bulletin Am. Soc. Inf. Sci.*, Feb. 9, 10(3): 11-13.

Katzer, J., et. al. 1982. *A Study of the Overlap Among Document Representations*. Syracuse Univ. Sch. of Info. Studies.

Kimura, G. D. 1984. *A Structure Editor and Model for Abstract Document Objects*. Dissertation. Tech. Report No. 84-07-04, July, Dept. of Comp. Sci., Univ. Washington.

Lancaster, F. W. 1978. *Toward Paperless Information Systems*, New York: Academic Press.

Lehnert, W. G. 1978. *The Process of Question Answering: A Computer Simulation of Cognition*. Hillsdale, N.J.: Lawrence Erlbaum Assoc.

Lovins, B. J. 1968. Development of a stemming algorithm. *Mech. Trans. and Comp. Ling.*, March-June, 11(1-2): 11-31.

Macleod, I. A. and R. G. Crawford. 1983. Document retrieval as a database application. *Inf. Tech.: Res. Dev. Applications*, Jan., 2(1): 43-60.

McGill, M. J., et al. 1976. *Syracuse Information Retrieval Experiment (SIRE): Design of an On-Line Bibliographic Retrieval System*. ACM SIGIR Forum, Spring, 10(4): 37-44.

McGill, M. J., M. Koll, and T. Noreault. 1979. *An Evaluation of Factors Affecting Document Ranking By Information Retrieval Systems*. Syracuse Univ. Sch. of Info. Studies.

Meadow, C. T., and P. A. Cochrane. 1981. *Basics of Online Searching*. New York: John Wiley and Sons.

Minsky, M. 1975. A framework for representing knowledge. In *The Psychology of Computer Vision*, ed. by P. Winston, New York: McGraw-Hill.

Morrissey, J. 1983. An intelligent terminal for implementing relevance feedback on large operational retrieval systems. In *Res. & Dev. in Inf. Ret., Proc., Berlin, May 18-20, 1982*, ed. by G. Salton and Hans-Jochen Schneider, Springer-Verlag, Berlin, .pp 38-50.

Naish, L. 1984. *MU-Prolog 3.1db Reference Manual*, Melbourne Univ.

Noreault, T., M. Koll and M. J. McGill. 1977. Automatic ranked output from Boolean searches in SIRE. *J. Am. Soc. Inf. Sci.*, Nov., 28(6):333-339.

O'Connor, J. 1980. Answer-passage retrieval by text searching. *J. Am. Soc. Inf. Sci.*, 31(4):227-239.

Oddy, R. N. 1977. Information retrieval through man-machine dialogue. *J. Doc.*, March, 33(1):1-14.

Paice, C. D. 1984. Soft evaluation of Boolean search queries in information retrieval. *Inf. Tech.: Res. Dev. Applications*, 3(1): 33-42.

Pereira, F. 1983. *Logic for Natural Language Analysis*, Tech. Note 275, Jan., SRI Int.

Pfaltz, J. L., W.H. Berman, and E.M. Cagley. 1980. Partial-match retrieval using indexed descriptor files. *Commun. ACM*, Sept., 23(9): 522-528.

Porter, M. F. 1982. Implementing a probabilistic information retrieval system. *Inf. Tech.: Res. Dev.*, 1(2).

Riesbeck, C. K. Realistic language comprehension. 1982. In *Strategies for Natural Language Processing*, ed. by Wendy G. Lehnert and Martin H. Ringle, Hillsdale, N.J.: Lawrence Erlbaum Assoc., pp. 435-454.

Ritchie, G. D. and F. K. Hanna. 1984. Semantic networks—a general definition and a survey. *Inf. Tech.: Res. Dev. Applications*, 3(1): 33-42.

Robertson, S. E. and K. Sparck Jones. 1976. Relevance weighting of search terms. *J. Am. Soc. Inf. Sci.*, 27(3): 129-146.

Rocchio, Jr., J. J. 1971. Relevance feedback in information retrieval. In *The SMART Retrieval System, Experiments in Automatic Document Processing*, ed. by G. Salton, Englewood Cliffs, N.J.: Prentice Hall.

Rumelhart, D. E. 1975. Notes on a schema for stories. In *Representation and Understanding*, ed. by D.G. Bobrow and A. Collins, New York: Academic Press, pp. 211-236.

Sager, N. 1975. Sublanguage grammars in science information processing. *J. Am. Soc. Inf. Sci.*, Jan.-Feb., 26(1): 10-16.

Salton, G. 1972. A new comparison between conventional indexing (Medlars) and text processing (SMART). *J. Am. Soc. Inf. Sci.*, 23(2): 75-84.

Salton, G., C. S. Yang, and C. T. Yu. 1975. A theory of term importance in automatic text analysis. *J. Am. Soc. Inf. Sci.*, Jan.-Feb., 26(1): 33-44.

Salton, G., A. Wong, and C. S. Yang. 1975. A vector space model for automatic indexing, *Commun. ACM*, Nov., 18(11):613-620.

Salton, G. 1980. The SMART System 1961-1976: experiments in dynamic document processing. In *Encyclopedia of Library and Information Science*, pp. 1-36.

Salton, G. and M. J. McGill. 1983. *Introduction to Modern Information Retrieval*, New York: McGraw-Hill.

Salton, G., C. Buckley, and E. A. Fox. 1983. Automatic query formulations in information retrieval. *J. Am. Soc. Inf. Sci.*, July, 34(4): 262-280.

Salton, G., E. A. Fox, and H. Wu. 1983. Extended Boolean information retrieval. *Commun. ACM*, Nov., 26(11): 1022-1036.

Salton, G., E. A. Fox, and E. Voorhees. 1985. Advanced feedback methods in information retrieval, *J. Am. Soc. Inf. Sci.*, 36(3): 200-210.

Schank, R. C. and R. P. Abelson. 1977. *Scripts, Plans, Goals and Understanding*, Hillsdale, N.J.: Lawrence Erlbaum Assoc.

Simmons, R. F. 1984. *Computations from the English*, Englewood Cliffs, N.J.: Prentice-Hall.

Small, H. 1980. Cocitation context analysis and the structure of paradigms. *J. Doc.*, Sept., 36(3): 183-196.

Smith, L. C. and Warner, A. J. 1984. A taxonomy of representations in information retrieval system design. In *Representation and Exchange of Knowledge as a Basis of Information Processes*, ed. by Hans J. Dietschmann, North-Holland, New York, pp. 31-49.

Sparck Jones, K. 1971. *Automatic Keyword Classifications*, London: Butterworths.

174

Sparck Jones, K. and C. J. Van Rijsbergen. 1976. Information retrieval test collections. *J. Doc.*, March, 30(4).

Stonebraker, M., et al. 1983. Document processing in a relational database system. *ACM Trans. on Office Inf. Systems*, April, 1(2).

Tague, J., M. Nelson, and H. Wu. 1981. Problems in the simulation of bibliographic retrieval systems. In *Information Retrieval Research*, ed. by R. NM. Oddy, S. E. Robertson, C. J. Van Rijsbergen, and P. W. Williams, London: Butterworths, pp. 236-255.

Tenopir, Carol. 1984. Full-text databases. *ARIST*, 19: 215-246.

Thompson, R. H., and W. B. Croft. 1985. An expert system for document retrieval. *Proc. Expert Systems in Gov. Symp.*, IEEE, Oct., pp. 448-456.

Van Rijsbergen, C. J. 1979. *Information Retrieval: Second Edition*: London: Butterworths.

Voorhees, E. M. 1985. *The Effectiveness and Efficiency of Agglomerative Hierarchic Clustering in Document Retrieval*. Dissertation. TR 85-705, Oct., Cornell Univ., Dept. of Comp. Sci.

Weyer, S. A. 1982. *Searching for Information in a Dynamic Book*. SCG-82-1. Feb., Xerox PARC, Palo Alto, Calif.

Wilensky, R., Y. Arens, and D. Chin. 1984. Talking to UNIX in English: an overview of UC. *Commun. ACM*, 27(6): 574-593.

Williamson, R. E. 1974. *Real-Time Document Retrieval*. Dissertation. June, Cornell Univ.

Yip, Man-Kam. 1979. *An Expert System for Document Retrieval*. M. S. Thesis. M. I. T., Cambridge, Mass.

Zarri, G. P. 1983. An outline of the representation and use of temporal data in the RESEDA system. *Inf. Tech.: Res. Dev. Applications*, July.

Viewing Documents on a Screen

by Peter Brown

We must exploit the computer's ability to provide features that can never be available on paper.

A great deal of the information we read on paper is also available electronically, retrieved from the memory of a computer. Current newspapers, magazines, and books are created with word processors and typeset by computers. Information of almost every nature has been loaded into massive databases, prepared for dissemination to selected segments of the paying public. You may soon have the option of reading your Sunday newspaper or the latest best-selling novel on a computer screen rather than on paper. However, the response from people currently using such systems has generally been negative: They prefer paper to computer screens. Indeed, they are extremely reluctant to read anything on a computer screen that is longer than a couple of pages. Originally this reluctance was blamed on the poor quality of the screen images, but it remains even with the comparatively large, high-resolution images displayed on modern graphics screens. The problem seems to be more fundamental than image quality.

Finding a way to present material on the screen in a format the reader finds attractive and useful is perhaps the greatest challenge faced by potential CD ROM publishers. Unless this challenge is met, CD ROM will not succeed in any mass market. This chapter describes the conclusions that came from research on meeting the challenge; the research has led to a successful software product, called CD GUIDE.

Trying to Imitate Paper

We shall start by explaining why readers currently prefer paper-based documents to screen-based ones. Developers of software to display documents on the computer screen have generally tried to imitate the familiar characteristics of documents printed on paper. For example, documents are often divided into predefined "pages," where a page is the equivalent of a screenful of text. Pages are connected in a structure of some sort, often a tree structure, and readers are given navigating aids to allow them to travel from page to page. Although the intent may be to imitate browsing through the pages of a book, the result is almost always that the reader gets lost in the data structure. In an attempt to resolve this problem, the software developers provide more features and aids to navigation; but as often as not, this makes matters even worse: The system becomes more complicated and thus even more readers get lost.

In our opinion this imitative approach will never be satisfactory. If the computer system simply imitates paper, readers will, if they have the choice, always prefer paper. Instead, we must exploit the computer's ability to provide features that can never be available on paper. One such feature that is particularly powerful is the ability to interact with the document, thus allowing each reader to adapt the document to his or her own needs. As a static medium, paper provides the same message at the same depth and with the same level of detail to all readers, regardless of the amount of time they have to absorb the material or the degree of their interest in it. Other than for recreation, the primary reasons for reading are:

- Summary: an overview, with extra details in specific areas

- Reference: to extract a particular piece of information

- Tutorial: to cover a whole document in order to understand a topic

Moreover, the ability of the readers to comprehend the material spans a wide range. An important intermediate case in the spectrum is that of an expert in a related field, such as a British lawyer reading about American law.

Finding a way to present material on the screen in a format the reader finds attractive and useful is perhaps the greatest challenge faced by potential CD ROM publishers.

It is difficult for a paper document to simultaneously satisfy all these needs. Devices such as a table of contents, an index, and an abstract are aids, but no paper document really caters to a diverse range of readers.

The Need

Given that each reader has his or her own requirements, there is a need for a screen-based software system to allow readers to tailor documents to their individual needs. The computer is then exploited to provide a better way to peruse documents, and there is a good chance that the reader will come to prefer screen-based documents to paper-based ones.

There is, however, one vital proviso: The screen-based software must be simple. If readers have to go through intricate steps to define their needs, they simply won't bother. Likewise, if authors have to learn an elaborate programming language and pepper their documents with conditional tests, then there will be no authors. Ideally, the system should be as simple to use as a television set.

The rest of this discussion is devoted to describing CD GUIDE, the software system that tries to meet these twin goals of adaptability and simplicity.

Environment

The demands that CD GUIDE makes of the computer system are that it be able to display at least three different fonts and that it have a pointing device. It is not vital that the fonts be real fonts in the typesetting sense. On a color screen they could be represented by three different colors; on a monochrome screen, by underlining, highlighting, reverse video, or changing the cursor pattern as it passes over certain characters. The mouse is a popular pointing device, and we shall assume its existence in this explanation. It is conceivable that CD GUIDE could be used on a computer system that did not support a pointing device, as special keys could be used to move the cursor, but the user interface would be less pleasant.

Features of CD GUIDE

The features of CD GUIDE are best introduced by examples. The examples given here show what appears on the screen of the Apple Macintosh implementation of CD GUIDE, though similar principles apply to other implementations.

The Replace Button

Figure 1 shows a typical introductory state when CD GUIDE is used to view a document. The material in this example is based on a European issue of the *Wall Street Journal*. The reader is shown a summary of

Figure 1. Initial view of a document

the available information. The occurrences of the word *More* are replace buttons that the user can select with the mouse to see more information about a topic.

The author of the document specifies the name and font to be used for each replace button; in the examples shown here the replace buttons are all in the same bold font as that used for the menu, which helps emphasize that they are buttons to be selected. In Figure 1, all replace buttons have been given the name *More*. If the reader wants to know more about a given item he simply points at the appropriate *More* button and clicks the mouse.

Figure 2 shows the result of selecting the *More* button under the heading about Malaysia's MMC Metals. The button has been replaced by further information about the company. Note that the new information contains additional replace buttons, labeled *Malaysian reaction* and *Bank of England statement*. (The document is now too big to fit on the screen. If the reader wishes to look at material that is currently off the screen he uses the standard Macintosh scrolling mechanism.)

The reader continues to expand replace buttons until he has displayed the material to the depth that interests him. If he expands a replace button and the resultant information is of no interest, the expansion can be "undone" by pointing at the unwanted information and clicking a mouse button.

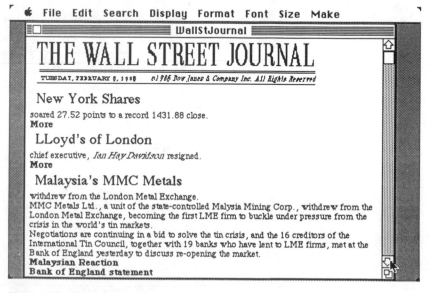

Figure 2. Third More *button in Figure 1 is selected*

This will prevent the unwanted information cluttering up the document. Replace buttons can be selected in any order the reader wishes, and any button can be undone at any time. Thus, the simple mechanism of selecting and undoing buttons allows the reader to peruse the sections of a document in any order and to any depth desired. CD GUIDE allows readers to save documents in a file (though for some material this facility might be suppressed for copyright reasons). Thus, when they have tailored the document to their own needs, they can preserve it for later use.

179

Other Types of Button

A variety of other buttons are supported by CD GUIDE, though functionally they are all the same to the reader: Simply point and click to expand. The italicized terms *Ian Hay Davison* and *poison pill* seen earlier in Figure 1 are glossary buttons. Figure 3 shows the result of selecting *poison pill*.

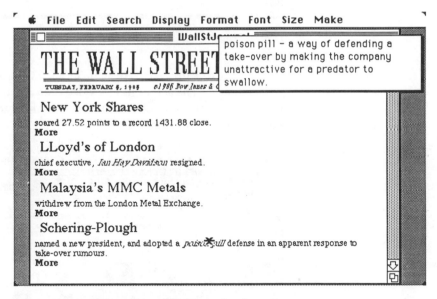

Figure 3. Poison pill *glossary button in Figure 1 selected*

As can be seen, a new subwindow has appeared, explaining what the term *poison pill* means. Glossary buttons are a general feature and can be used to give more information about people (e.g., Ian Hay Davison) or places, or to show citations in a technical paper.

Another useful button that can be defined by the author is the reference button, which displays a cross reference when selected. The cross reference can be in the same document or in a different one.

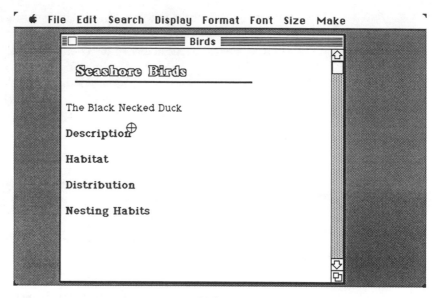

Figure 4. Extract from a reference work on birds

Figure 4 shows a different type of material: an extract from a reference book on birds. The author has provided buttons allowing the reader to explore various attributes of a selected bird. If the reader were to select the *Description* button, the information in Figure 5 would be displayed.

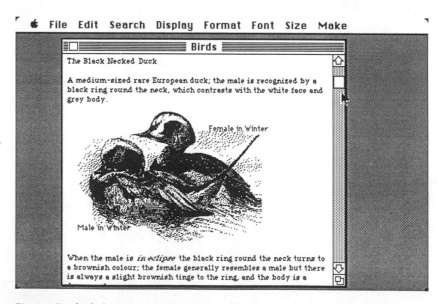

Figure 5. Result of selecting Description *in Figure 4*

As can be seen, CD GUIDE supports graphics as well as text. Indeed, buttons themselves can be graphical, and thus authors can use an iconic style of interface if they wish. Figure 5 also contains another example of a glossary button: the term *in eclipse*.

Screen Layout

The reader can use the standard Macintosh size-box to change the window size: CD GUIDE automatically adapts its display to fit, wrapping lines of text if necessary. If CD GUIDE is running on a computer with no windowing ability, this adaptability is still useful, as the same material can be displayed on different-size screens—provided, of course, there is a way to determine size.

Editing

If the computer system simply imitates paper, readers will, if they have the choice, always prefer paper.

In order to personalize a document, and therefore make it of maximum value, the reader must be able to jot notes in the margin and underline or highlight selected passages. Editing in CD GUIDE follows the model of good word processing software: The user simply clicks the insertion point for new text and types it, or selects text to be removed and deletes it. There is no inherent difference between material typed by the user and that which was part of the original document.

As an example of the use of editing, the reader of our document about birds might add the comment "This bird has just been seen in the Shetland Islands." Upon subsequently saving the document, assuming that copying the original document is allowed, the comment would be saved exactly as if it were part of the original.

Authorship

This leads to an important principle of CD GUIDE: There is no inherent difference between CD GUIDE authors and CD GUIDE readers. We have seen that readers can edit documents, thus becoming authors (though management may place some limitations on this). On the other side of the coin, the only way that authors can create documents is to view them as readers would.

If an author is starting a new document from scratch, he enters CD GUIDE in an authoring mode, which has extra menu selections to create buttons, and starts typing his material. A replace button would be set up as follows:

1. Select the menu command to create a replace button.

2. Type the button name.

3. Select the button, just as a reader would. Given that this is a new button, its replacement will be null.

4. Type the button's replacement (by pointing and then typing, just as for any other edit).

Given that each reader has his or her own requirements, there is a need for a screen-based software system to allow readers to tailor documents to their individual needs.

Note how there is no separate authorship language: authors simply view buttons—and, indeed, everything else—exactly as readers do. This is an important property. The most common error that authors make, regardless of whether they are preparing paper-based documents or screen-based documents, is not to view the world from the reader's viewpoint.

Capturing Existing Text

In practice, CD GUIDE documents are not usually prepared from scratch. Instead, the author adds structure to an existing document. CD GUIDE will accept any ASCII file, or a file representing a picture, and allow the author to add buttons and define the portion of the file that will replace each button.

If a large body of documents already exists, it would be a major effort to go add CD GUIDE buttons throughout. Fortunately this problem can often be solved by a program which automatically adds buttons. For example, each section heading could become a button name; the body of the section would be the replacement for the button. Such a technique would work well with the reference material on birds used in our previous example, assuming that it had a consistent logical structure of sections, subsections, and so on. More generally, the technique should work for any document expressed in a generic markup language.

Conversion programs have already been written for quite extensive and complex sets of documents, such as the manual pages for the UNIX (UNIX is a trademark of AT&T Bell Laboratories) system.

From CD ROM to Screen

In most cases CD GUIDE would work in conjunction with other software to retrieve material from a CD ROM and display it on the screen. The information retrieval system involved in this task can be viewed at two levels:

- The "macro" level, where a document is extracted from the myriad of material on the CD ROM

- The "micro" level, where the user extracts information from that document

This chapter has concentrated on the use of CD GUIDE at the micro level. It is a design choice whether CD GUIDE is also used at the macro level or whether an entirely separate information retrieval system is used. Indeed, it is a design choice whether there is any clear distinction between macro level and micro level.

There are also important design choices at the last stage in bringing a document from CD ROM to reader: the way material is presented on the screen. Is it to be "typeset" on a high-resolution graphics screen, or is the presentation to be more akin to a glass-teletype style? Current implementations of CD GUIDE are between these two extremes; final appearance is felt to be extremely important, so provision is made for separate fonts and type sizes. CD GUIDE cannot, however, claim to approach the capabilities of a typesetting system.

Summary

In the introduction we stated that the goals were simplicity and adaptability. We believe that CD GUIDE has achieved these goals. The devices for achieving these goals are:

- Buttons embedded in documents and appearing as a natural part of the documents

- A uniform interface for both authors and readers

- Provision for using existing documents without having to rewrite them

We are therefore excited by the possibilities that the new technology brings. CD GUIDE and CD ROM are a perfect bride and groom, and we believe they will indeed live happily ever after.

About the Author

Dr. Brown is a professor of computer science at the University of Kent, U.K. He has also worked at Stanford University, USA, as a visiting professor and at IBM (UK) Laboratories at Hursley. He holds B.A. and Ph.D. degrees from Cambridge University and an M.A. from the University of North Carolina. He is also a Research Fellow at OWL International.

Professor Brown is the author of five books and numerous papers, mostly in the area of software tools and human/computer interfaces. For the past four years he has been working on methods of displaying documents on computer screens.

Computing Laboratory
The University
Canterbury
Kent CT2 7NF
England
227-66822 (Ext 636 or 627)

OWL International, Inc.
10900 NE 8th
Suite 900
Bellevue, WA 98004

Screen-based software must be simple. If readers have to go through intricate steps to define their needs, they simply won't bother.

184

New User Interfaces for CD ROM

by Robert Carr

The utility and ultimate impact of CD ROM will depend on the development of new user interfaces capable of fully exploiting its unique potential. Personal computer software has advanced the quality and breadth of user interfaces in general, but CD ROM user interface design presents a challenging set of new requirements. Before the advent of CD ROM technology, personal computer software was designed for efficient interaction with blocks of information in the 1 to 100K range. This software was based on familiar and proven user interface metaphors, such as the word processing "papyrus scroll" and the spreadsheet electronic grid. These metaphors became popular in the late 1970s when personal computers could rarely deal with more than a few hundred thousand bytes of information.

185

Today's computers support up to several megabytes of information, which is seriously straining these traditional metaphors (try using the PGDN key to quickly scroll through a megabyte of text or a spreadsheet). The existing repertoire of personal computer user interfaces may be incapable of exploiting the potential of the massive amounts of data presented by CD ROMs.

An electronic hierarchy, or outline, on the computer screen provides even more benefits than a printed hierarchy because it is fluid.

The most applicable user interface metaphor from the realm of personal computers is the database "querying" or "filtering" notion of retrieving a set of objects that fit the user's criteria. There is no doubt that keyword searches of CD ROMs will be a standard tool. But unassisted, the user exploring the CD ROM with only a keyword search facility is left in the position of an ice fisherman dangling his line through a small hole in the ice: He must guess what fish might be in the water below, set the appropriate bait, cast through a small hole in the ice, and hope to hook a fish.

There are better ways, however. New user interface metaphors and innovative extensions of old ones must put users in the position of a scuba diver exploring constantly changing scenes underwater. The diver (user) is always aware of his or her surroundings and can select the most appetizing fish from those available. CD ROM interfaces must allow their users to move freely and quickly through information, always aware of the context and structure.

A New Metaphor: Hierarchies

Historically, people have found that one of the best ways to deal with large amounts of information is to structure it into a hierarchy. Books, for instance, usually begin with a hierarchical outline in which the material to be presented is divided into chapters and as many other subdivisions as necessary for a clear presentation of the information. In many cases, the table of contents shows all but the smallest subdivisions.

In print, hierarchies (or outlines) provide two key benefits:

1. Overview: The structure and extent of information can be quickly understood.

2. Quick navigation: The table of contents quickly leads the reader to the location of a general topic.

An electronic hierarchy, or outline, on the computer screen provides even more benefits than a printed hierarchy because it is fluid. The user can interact with the electronic outline, expanding or reducing it to display the desired level of detail. This extra control is important because the computer's screen is limited in size (lines of text per page) and resolution (dots per inch).

Electronic hierarchies can also provide a third key benefit:

3. Leveraged manipulation: Commands can be channeled to the lower levels of an electronic outline by selecting the appropriate heading and issuing the command. Thus, commands such as Move, Copy, Reformat, Delete, and Print can be quickly issued on a higher level and will apply to subordinate levels as well.

People learn best when they are active explorers of information.

Although existing electronic outlining programs, such as Framework II by Ashton Tate and ThinkTank by Living VideoText, are popularizing the use of hierarchies on personal computers, they differ in an important regard from the programs required to use the information stored on CD ROM. Both of these products provide empty outlines, waiting to be filled with the user's own data. With CD ROM, on the other hand, the electronic outline is an integral part of the data structure, "prefilled" with information and sensitive to user control. Merely listing topics on static screens in an outline form is not enough. The user must have the opportunity to interact with the hierarchy: to be able to temporarily open and close entire sections of the outline, diving down into subtopics to further explore them and returning immediately to the outline source whenever desired. This degree of interaction with the information is important, for people learn best when they can control the depth and amount of information thrust upon them.

There are numerous ways to represent hierarchies. Outlines, perhaps the most common, have already been mentioned. Others include:

- Nesting menus (each menu item leads to a submenu)
- Vertical or horizontal trees (organization charts)
- Nesting boxes

Each of these "views" of the hierarchy has its own particular advantages. Generally speaking, the interface should provide a choice of views that the user can easily move between. Framework II, for instance, allows the user to view a hierarchy either as an outline or as a system of nesting windows (see Figures 1 and 2).

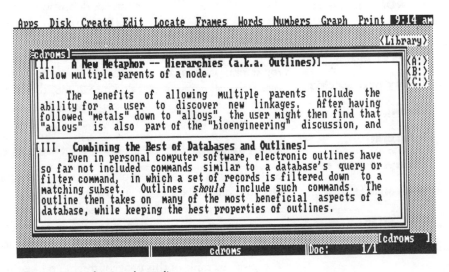

Figure 1. Hierarchy viewed as outline

Multiple Hierarchies

In addition to multiple views of one hierarchy, CD ROM should provide multiple hierarchies so that the user can choose alternative views and structures of the information.

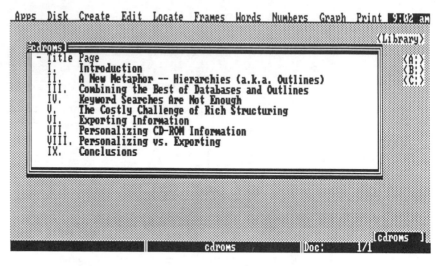

Figure 2. Hierarchy viewed as nested windows

CD ROM interfaces must allow their users to move freely and quickly through information, always aware of the context and structure.

Unlike the strict computer-science definition of a hierarchy as a treelike structure in which each node (branch) has only one parent node (path back to the trunk), hierarchies in CD ROM must allow infinite connections between subjects. Such a structure often results in a single topic sharing several parents, allowing the user to discover new linkages. For example, after following *metals* down to *alloys*, the user might then find that *alloys* is also part of the *bioengineering* discussion and learn that certain alloys are used as bone replacements.

Combining the Best of Databases and Outlines

So far, even in personal computer software, electronic outlines have not included such database commands as Query or Filter, which serve to filter a set of records down to a matching subset. Including such commands in an outline program would allow it to take on many of the most beneficial features of a database while keeping the best properties of an outline.

A typical example of this concept might go like this: You've scrolled to a particular outline heading titled "IBM PC-Compatible Manufacturers." A list of dozens of companies is displayed as a series of subheadings—far too many to browse through. You issue a filter command to reduce the visible set of subheadings. The command is very similar to that of traditional database searches. Say, for example, that you ask for "Revenues > 500,000,000." The outline filters the subheadings, reducing them to only

188

**But unassisted,
the user exploring
the CD ROM with
only a keyword
search facility is
left in the position
of an ice fisherman
dangling his line
through
a small hole
in the ice . . .**

those companies with revenues greater than $500 million. Now your browsing and reading are much more manageable, since only a few companies are listed under the heading.

What the outline metaphor has added to the database metaphor is an easy way of tying together a large number of flat tables. Normally, the user must use a relational database to find the information associated with matching records. In an "outline database," however, each field can occur again and again at various nodes and levels in the outline, and each field can be opened up to reveal a number of subordinate headings. The user can see just the key field of each record/heading, all the fields of each record/heading, as well as a table view of just the current level's headings (much like a traditional database table).

189

Keyword Searches Are Not Enough

To date, most CD ROM user interfaces provide access to the structure of the information by including extensive keyword indexes on the CD ROM. The user can then search for information containing one or more words (e.g., all screens referencing "Transylvania").

This ability to dive directly into the CD ROM at any location by using keywords is indeed powerful. It goes far beyond human ability to manually search through printed matter. But keyword searches have their limitations. Indeed, in the introduction to this chapter they were likened to fishing through a small hole in the ice. But why? It's not just the raw information contained within a screen that is important, or just the searching for that screen. In our civilization no information stands alone; the context of the information is often as important as the information itself. For example, the study of history depends less on the conglomeration of an enormous number of facts than it does on learning the sweep and basic structure of history, supported and highlighted by facts.

Hierarchies display the context and structure and interrelationships of information as well as leading the user to an individual topic. Pure keyword access gets users to a fact, but it is difficult for them to remember how they got there or to understand the greater context of the fact. They may go in loops, wandering down information trails without knowing how the numerous pieces are related.

The best CD ROM user interfaces combine both means of access: keyword searches and hierarchies. Each has its place. Keyword linking is excellent for "unstructured browsing," finding that unexpected connection.

190

Hierarchies are excellent for "structured browsing," exploring specific subject areas while keeping perspective and orientation to the information being browsed. And both keyword searches and hierarchies are excellent for "targeted searches," zeroing in on specific information as rapidly as possible.

Hierarchies, then, might be used for moving up and down between various levels of detail in a CD ROM's information, and keyword links could be constantly available for making "sideways" jumps to any related information.

The Costly Challenge of Rich Structuring

Hierarchies overlaid on CD ROM are one instance of "rich structuring" of the CD ROM information. It is not enough for electronic publishing to lay information down on the CD ROM in the identical format used in print publishing; it's not even enough to have a "sugar coating" of fast keyword searching added over the raw data. Users need to have multiple access paths to the information.

In our civilization no information stands alone; the context of the information is often as important as the information itself.

The generative step of laying down formatted information on a CD ROM can be called an "authoring language" because it involves intelligent and artistic design decisions, just as book writing and layout do today. It may also involve considerable work by humans to create the necessary hierarchical structuring systems (as opposed to automatic processing by a computer to create the indexes that support keyword searches). In fact, future CD ROMs may be valued and judged for the degree to which they include creative and innovative additional structure and access paths beyond the raw information itself.

Exporting Information

Users must be able to transfer information from the CD ROM to other storage media, such as paper, a floppy disk, or a hard disk. This exporting of information is important, for it allows the user to apply specialized tools, with more power than the user interface, to analyze and manipulate the information.

If exporting is overrated, however, some interfaces may end up as merely passive viewing machines, able to do little more than export fragments of information. Since the writeable disk has only a fraction of the CD ROM's capacity, exporting is a limited safety valve; adequate capabilities must be built into the user interface to support direct manipulation of information.

Personalizing CD ROM Information

People learn best when they are active explorers of information. "Active" implies that the user is in control of viewing, digesting, and structuring the information. It is not enough for CD ROM user interfaces to provide multiple access paths to their information; for no matter what their number, the CD ROM's own access paths are static and unchanging, since CD ROMs are read-only. Users must also be able to do some amount of restructuring of the information, creating for themselves their own access paths.

Consider the example of a college textbook. Most study techniques suggest that readers actively mark the textbook material, imposing their own categories, structure, and emphasis. It is by fitting the textbook's information into the reader's own context that the information truly becomes the reader's own. And it will be the same with CD ROM. When CD ROM allows for the electronic equivalent of highlighting, underlining, marginal notes, and a general personalization of the information presented, then it will allow users to get the most out of the underlying information.

The question arises, of course, as to how a read-only medium such as CD ROM can support the writing of new structures by the user. CD ROM alone cannot. But in conjunction with a personal computer, it can. Personalization of CD ROM information can be achieved if its interface software uses a computer's writeable storage for the personal paths, structures, outlines, and comments that a user establishes for a particular CD ROM.

. . . future CD ROMs may be valued and judged for the degree to which they include creative and innovative additional structure and access paths beyond the raw information itself.

Such personalization is not technically difficult. In addition to the structures fixed on the CD ROM for its information, identical data structures can be written to the personal computer hard disk. These hard-disk resident outlines (or other structures) are access paths, in addition to the built-in ones, to the CD ROM. The user interface software is easily able to switch from reading the overlying outline from either the CD ROM or the hard disk. The user should even be able to copy the CD ROM access paths onto the hard disk, where they can then be personalized. For instance, although the CD ROM may present its topics in one particular hierarchy, a user could specify an additional outline ordering for the topics and choose to view the information through either outline overview.

Let's consider the textbook example again. A history textbook, for instance, may come preformatted with numerous outline overviews such as a time-line, geographic ordering, and a social sciences outline overview. Imagine, then, a school assignment in which you are to create three new views (access paths) on twentieth-century history: economic, sociological, and population-dynamic. The very act of creating the structure would be a significant learning experience.

Or, alternatively, imagine the flexibility of creating your own personal outline in which you place direct references to each CD ROM screen you find that is germane to your task. Thereafter you will have no need to plod through the CD ROM's built-in paths to get to that information; you have your own "hot topics" heading as a general scratch-pad to-read list. A single command on any of its subheadings will shoot you directly to the underlying CD ROM screen.

Having the multiple outlines is not the key, important as that is (CD ROMs should often present multiple views of the same information). The key is that the users can impose their own outlines (or any kind of structuring) on the information; by refitting the information into their own context and world view and needs, they can make the information their own. The difference is considerable. Personalization of CD ROMs turns a medium whose perceptive categories are passive into one whose perceptive categories are active.

Personalizing vs. Exporting

Personalization of CD ROMs turns a medium whose perceptive categories are passive into one whose perceptive categories are active.

Some may argue that CD ROM user interfaces need not support personalization since users can always export their information to other formats, such as word processors, that do allow personalization. This is an attractive thought, especially since personalization is difficult to implement. But it ignores the fundamental benefit of CD ROMs: the wealth of information that is available all at once.

Exporting can get small pieces of CD ROM information out into other formats, but it is the ability to work with and reshape the entire mass of information that is essential. Until there are writeable media that are as cheap and fast as CD ROM, exporting will serve just as a safety valve for relatively small amounts of CD ROM information and users will be able to personalize only small slivers of information.

The implication, then, is that CD ROM user interfaces cannot shirk their role: they must build into themselves the full range of capabilities that users need, since users cannot move substantial volumes of the data to other, more flexible, formats. And CD ROM user interfaces, no matter what their exporting capabilities, will be most beneficial if they support the central capability of personalization.

Conclusions

It is likely that at first CD ROMs will sport homogeneous, single-screen-of-text user interfaces whose one key benefit over printed matter will be fast keyword searches. But this benefit will be limited by the disadvantages of viewing information through a computer's output devices (low-resolution screens) versus the very efficient printed form.

Later, as the difficult task of coordinating the CD ROM data formats and the user interface software is tackled, CD ROMs can realize their potential by going beyond static user interfaces and adopting new user interfaces designed specifically for their special needs. These new user interfaces will provide multiple access paths or views of the underlying raw information to augment or replace pure keyword searching as the primary CD ROM interface.

The new user interfaces will require the CD ROM to have rich structuring overlaid on the raw information. Hierarchical structuring, especially combined with database operations such as filtering, is one particularly promising type of rich structuring for CD ROMs. This rich structuring step promises to provide opportunities for creativity on the part of CD ROM "authors," but is also promises to be an expensive step.

In addition, the new user interfaces must allow for powerful exporting of all the data and rich structures on the CD ROMs.

And eventually, in the step that will have the most import for the individual's ability to exert personal control over information and enhance his or her understanding, the new user interfaces will allow for personalization of CD ROM information, with the user creating new access paths and structures over the original read-only data.

About the Author

Robert Carr is the Director of Technology, Forefront Development Center, Ashton-Tate, Incorporated. He is a former member of Xerox's Palo Alto Research Center and founder of Forefront Corporation. He was the chief architect of Framework, an integrated program which combines the qualities of word processor, outline processor, spreadsheet, graphics, data management and telecommunication programs into a single software package.

An Interactive Lookup System

by Philippe Kahn

195

CD ROM technology, with its mass storage capabilities, is bringing microcomputers into areas and markets that have traditionally been the domain of mini and mainframe computers. Large, online databases, such as dictionaries, thesauruses, encyclopedias and other reference works, are now becoming available for microcomputers. The availability of these online databases requires new software designs that provide the end user with a quick, efficient way to access these databases.

CD ROM technology, with its mass storage capabilities, is bringing microcomputers into areas and markets that have traditionally been the domain of mini and mainframe computers.

Turbo Lightning, an instant, RAM-based information access and retrieval system from Borland International, Inc., provides four features essential to acceptance and use of an online database: speed, compactness, flexibility, ease of learning, and ease of use. Turbo Lightning, as a natural standard interface or "front end" to the computer's software environment, provides an extension to the computer's operating system. The first two products utilizing this technique provide the end user with access to an online spelling dictionary and thesaurus. The instant accessing capability of Turbo Lightning enables the spelling program to inform the user of misspelled words while the user is entering text.

In addition to being fast and efficient, Turbo Lightning has been designed to provide a practical solution in CD ROM environments. It allows for a natural migration from traditional hard-disk, magnetically stored databases to newer, very large, CD-stored databases, using the same technology for both storage methods. The Look-up Engine in Turbo Lightning provides instant access to virtually any kind of data, including electronic reference works and user-defined information bases. It can also handle requests from outside programs and can access other preindexed files.

How It Works

Turbo Lightning's power lies in its data compression and indexing methods. With Turbo Lightning's data compression scheme, the Dictionary word list undergoes character frequency analysis, where common letters and combinations of letters are replaced by shorter bit patterns. Furthermore, common suffix groups are reduced to small bit patterns. In this manner, several words can be represented with the same code.

Since the dictionary is alphabetically sorted, consecutive words tend to have several letters in common. Turbo Lightning stores only word-to-word changes and not the common characters.

The thumbing indexes in Turbo Lightning promote fast access to words, synonyms, or other bits of information being sought. This is what enables the spelling checker to proof words "on-the-fly" as each word is typed in at the keyboard. The first letter of a word provides a general search criterion, and the next few letters bring the search into a smaller, more defined area of the dictionary.

Turbo Lightning implements an 80-character circular buffer to make it work in conjunction with other programs. Lightning modifies the keyboard interrupt, scans each character, checks the index and then the dictionary, as it sees each character typed at the keyboard. Turbo Lightning avoids using the IBM PC's built-in keyboard buffer, which is flushed by many application programs.

One important aspect of the design is the "interface engine." As an interactive look-up system, the engine has the hooks, or entry points, that can be called by other programs. These programs can query Lightning's dictionary, thesaurus, or any other file that's defined to Lightning. With this kind of flexibility, the Turbo Lightning engine can work on both external files and memory-resident files. It can verify the existence of an entry in the target file, return the unique number of the query word, or return a range of words with the same first letter and length. And if the external program calls the interface engine with a unique word number, the engine returns the target word. This capability grows increasingly important with the advent and implementation of laser discs.

About the Author

Philippe Kahn is the founder and president of Borland International, Inc. He is a highly regarded software entrepreneur. An avid student of computer programming language development, Kahn was a computer industry consultant in the United States and Europe before starting his own software company in 1983. Today, Borland International is a leading software developer whose products include Turbo Pascal, Sidekick, Turbo Lightning, Reflex, and Traveling Sidekick.

PRODUCING CD ROM

Data Preparation

Data Preparation: Turning Books into Discs

by Ron Barney

Although the information that has traditionally been produced in book form can now be distributed on compact disc, this new technology is still in its infancy and lacks disciplined, stable procedures of design and production. Publishers have been depending on outside suppliers, using expensive production techniques, for the preparation of their data for transfer to CD ROM. This discussion suggests ways in which book publishers can take control of the disc-making process and do so economically.

201

We will outline the general elements of data preparation and introduce a method of performing in-house data preparation, using ordinary IBM XT/AT equipment and a product-refining technique which VideoTools calls *simulation*. This system can result in a significant savings in the time and cost of producing a CD ROM.

Overview

Data preparation is a catchall term used to broadly refer to creating the data files and choosing the retrieval software to be used to access the CD ROM. We will limit our discussion to the processes involved in assembling files, processing them for use on CD ROM, and creating a tape master to be used in manufacturing.

. . . a well-designed general-purpose file structure will allow system-independent publishing of CD ROM discs.

The chart in Figure 1 illustrates the data preparation procedures on IBM XT and AT machines. The first three phases—input, file structuring, and content manipulation—finalize the database content and prepare it for transfer to optical disc. The CD ROM setup procedures add information required by the retrieval software, optimize the layout of the disc, and/or scramble data for security purposes. The testing phase may reveal content errors necessitating further content manipulation. Testing allows one to assess the effectiveness of the retrieval software, the access speed of the disc, and the directory layout. Normally, a number of iterations between setup and testing are necessary to meet design goals. The final phase, premastering, outputs all data to tape (or another medium suitable for input to the mastering facility) along with a directory and information required by the CD ROM mastering facility.

202

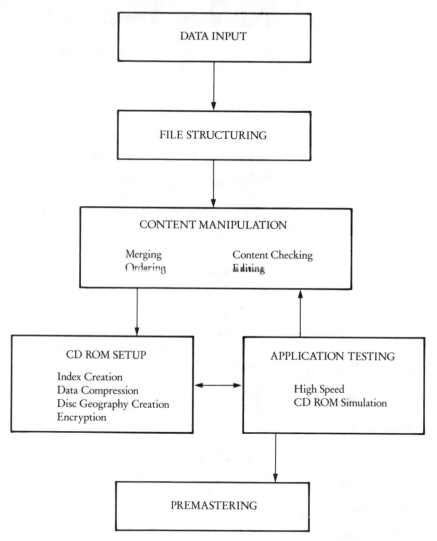

DATA PREPARATION
ON IBM XT-AT CLASS MACHINES

DATA INPUT

FILE STRUCTURING

CONTENT MANIPULATION

Merging   Content Checking
Ordering   Editing

CD ROM SETUP

Index Creation
Data Compression
Disc Geography Creation
Encryption

APPLICATION TESTING

High Speed
CD ROM Simulation

PREMASTERING

Figure 1. Data preparation

Data Input

Since CD ROM can support a variety of data formats, the initial input files may be quite dissimilar, with data from any or all of the following sources:

- Computer files in various formats, on floppy disks, hard disks, or tape
- CD ROM data, on discs or on premastering tape
- Digitized images from television cameras or raster scanners
- Optical character reader (OCR) data
- Audio data
- Video data

File Structuring

The first stage in preparing these files is converting them to a common file structure. During data formatting each file, and each piece of information within the file, is identified by name, size, and location in a way that will be recognized by a CD ROM drive.

Of the CD ROM file structures available at this time, most are specialized and therefore have limited usefulness. A comprehensive and standardized file structure is under development that will overcome the many limitations previously encountered. As can be seen in Figure 2, a well-designed general-purpose file structure will allow system-independent publishing of CD ROM discs.

Content Manipulation

Several procedures are used to combine, check, and correct the data. These procedures are not CD ROM-specific, but rather are standard practice in normal database software. Typically, content manipulation is complete before the start of CD ROM data preparation.

CD ROM Setup

CD ROM setup refers to operations which are specific to the addition or modification of a particular CD ROM database. This allows examination of the disc in preliminary form and allows changes prior to manufacture.

Index creation.   Indexing is the creation of a list of the locations where the data can be found on the CD ROM. The index is ultimately stored on the CD ROM along with the data, to facilitate rapid search and retrieval.

CD ROM Production Path for a General Purpose File Structure

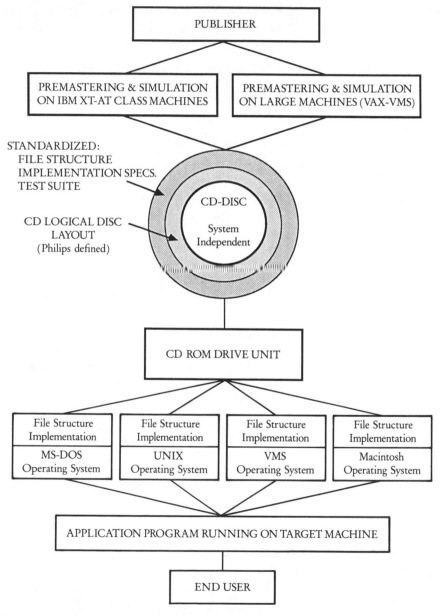

Figure 2. Production path

The selection of an indexing method and retrieval software are closely interrelated, and both are influenced by the type of application.

The amount of space required by the index is determined by the size of the database and the method of indexing. An inverted index of every word in a file may be larger than the file itself. On the other hand, if only keywords or descriptors are indexed and each points to an entire record, the index will be relatively small.

Data compression.   This term refers to any operation that rewrites information in less space, usually by eliminating empty and repetitive areas. Data compression is normally used to save space on the disc. It may also be used to optimize the speed of an application, since it will reduce the distances between items of information on the disc and therefore the time required to traverse those distances.

Disc geography creation.   Physical arrangement of data on the CD ROM disc greatly affects the speed with which an application can access and display information. There are three main ways of arranging data on a disc:

- Contiguous or sequential files are written in a single block on the CD ROM. No other files or indexes are located within the boundaries of a contiguous file.

- Mapped files are of the same type as those residing on a hard disk. The mapping process allows parts of a single file to be located in many different places on the disc without altering its effective sequence when it is read. Mapped files use an array which specifies where data is located on the disc.

- Interleaved files are broken into 2K (2048-byte) blocks and alternated with blocks from similarly divided files along the spiral track of the CD ROM. Interleaving is used to minimize access time between related files, such as a database and its index, by placing them as close together as possible.

Fast as they are, CD ROMs are significantly slower than hard disks when an operation requires the reading element to move from one point on the disc to another. Ideal disc geography minimizes this seek time by shortening the distances between referenced data.

Encryption or Scrambling.   Data encryption, which scrambles the actual data written on the disc, thereby rendering it unintelligible without special software, may be performed during this phase of data preparation if security is a requirement.

Application Testing

Once the CD ROM product has been set up, it needs to be tested for functionality, access speed, and readability. Proper testing reveals errors in setup and points out errors in content missed earlier.

As part of application testing the publisher may want to preview the product. Potential customers may screen the product for its usefulness, ease of use, and so on.

Glass master.   For optimum flexibility, complex applications should be tested using magnetic simulation of the CD ROM media as described below. However, as an alternative, glass master CD ROM discs may be used by premastering immediately after CD ROM setup and then mastering a glass disc. Turnaround time from mastering facilities is currently about a week to a month. For CD ROM subscription publishing this procedure becomes very costly (at the time of this writing, minimum cost for pressing a disc was $3000 plus a charge for each disc). Moreover, there is no margin for error, despite the likelihood of errors on the first few discs.

High-speed testing.   Some product evaluations can be facilitated by performing tests at the full speed of a hard disk. Since hard disk access speed is often as much as five times that of a CD ROM, test results can be obtained much faster. Note that the speed of access is not representative of the actual CD ROM performance.

Tests that relate to the accuracy of the product are generally suitable for running at high speed. High-speed information searches assess the accuracy of the index and can also be used to help make overall comparisons between retrieval software packages.

CD ROM simulation.   Simulation software makes a hard disk operate like a CD ROM. This allows the developer to determine whether the speed of the application is acceptable or not. Access times which seem acceptable at hard disk speeds may be unacceptable when run at CD ROM speed. Outcomes of simulation tests may enable the developer to determine the need to compress data, to change disc geography, to use interleaved files, or to try another retrieval program.

Physical arrangement of data on the CD ROM disc greatly affects the speed with which an application can access and display information.

This type of testing is unnecessary for less complex applications. If, for instance, the smallest retrieval element is a document, the application may require only a single index. In this case there would be no need for sophisticated interleaving, mapped files, or complex indexing. With simpler products, one can be fairly certain of the final product prior to premastering.

Premastering

Premastering is the process of generating a set of computer tapes containing all the information to be put onto a CD ROM. (Mastering is the term used for making the glass master disc and the master mold for pressing actual CD ROMs in volume production.) The output tapes of the premastering process are sent directly to the mastering facility.

VideoTools Solution

VideoTools has developed two products which solve many of these problems. With these products one can perform all the steps necessary to publish data on CD ROM and simulate the behavior of a CD ROM player with the actual database. Testing may be performed very easily and changes implemented very quickly. The cost to manufacture a test CD ROM are virtually eliminated.

CD MASTER™

VideoTools has created software and supplementary hardware which allow the database publisher to develop a complete CD ROM application in-house. CD MASTER supports CD ROM development from database creation through production of the premastering tape required for manufacturing the CD ROM master, on a standard IBM XT or AT.

CD MASTER is configured as an IBM XT/AT with the following minimum hardware supplied with the system:

- At least one multiple-density 9-track tape drive. Recording densities of 1600 and 6250 are supported.

- Hard disk, 10 megabytes of system software and intermediate work files, plus enough hard disk space to accommodate the data on the largest reel of input tape, plus the CD ROM directory space. Significant performance improvements may be obtained when the disk can hold the CD ROM's largest file plus the CD ROM directory space. Data may reside on many reels. Maximum data which can be stored on CD ROM is 550 megabytes.

Optional peripherals for nontape input:

- CD ROM

- Raster scanner capable of digitizing images on 8½-by-11-inch paper at 200 dots per inch horizontally and vertically.

- Optical character reader

- Audio equipment with input at various sampling rates

- Camera, videotape, or videodisc issuing composite video signal conforming to EIA RS-170

Using CD MASTER, premastering is accomplished in four steps:

- File sequence determination. The developer decides the final order of information before premastering.

- Final processing, if any. Compression or encryption may be performed.

- CD ROM directory creation. The developer creates indexes for each file as necessary. A master directory, incorporating the disc geography, is created.

- File transfer. The developer transfers the completed files to the premastering tape, beginning with the CD ROM directory and continuing in the sequence already determined.

If the system contains enough disk storage to hold all the CD ROM data plus 10 megabytes, these steps are performed once. If less disk space is available, the steps are repeated until the complete premaster tape is built.

Outcomes of simulation tests may enable the developer to determine the need to compress data, to change disc geography, to use interleaved files, or to try another retrieval program.

The four-step CD MASTER process allows premaster coding and output on standard 9-track tape and provides the publisher with a degree of control not previously possible.

CD PUBLISHER™

CD PUBLISHER, a CD ROM simulator, serves as an adjunct to CD MASTER. This is the first commercially available system for simulating the behavior of a CD ROM application on non-CD ROM equipment. This product simulates the CD ROM on a hard disk, allowing extensive shakedown and testing before mastering the disc.

CD PUBLISHER requires 10 megabytes of hard disk in addition to the amount required to hold the data to be written on the CD ROM (maximum of 550 megabytes). This flexible hardware arrangement allows the developer or publisher to purchase only as much memory as is actually required.

CD PUBLISHER software includes the following programs:

- File formatting. Converts files from various other formats to a standard CD ROM format.

- "Squisher program." Creates an image—or 1:1 correspondence between blocks of information—of a CD ROM within the IBM PC hard disk, so that files which should be contiguous on the disc will be contiguous when transferred from the the hard disk to tape.

- Simulation program. Simulates CD ROM speed in order to test an application.

- Premastering. Creates file directory in CD ROM format.

With CD PUBLISHER, premastering is very straightforward. By the time the application has been finalized, a complete image of the premaster tape has been constructed on disk. All that is needed is to write this image onto tape and send it to the manufacturer.

Looking Forward

It is now possible to develop CD ROM products in-house on IBM PC-class equipment. Because numerous software systems are available for database retrieval, custom software does not have to be developed. Therefore, projects can be implemented without impacting data processing personnel or equipment. The performance of the IBM AT is sufficient for complete CD ROM development.

Text applications are likely to be the norm for early CD ROM. However, technology is already in place for a new generation of hybrid products, combining these with graphics, audio, and video.

Publishers are now able to incorporate CD ROM into their product lines. Those who do so will be the leaders in the newest publishing technology, CD ROM.

About the Author

Ron Barney is a New York office automation consultant. He was formerly a book editor in Chicago. In New York, he was educational assistant for the American Booksellers Association.

VideoTools is an Aptos, California, firm specializing in CD ROM and videodisc technology. Backed by years of expertise, it was the first producer of a mixed text/audio/video CD ROM demonstration. VideoTools has been a champion of standards for CD ROM and is the first producer of a PC-based CD ROM simulator.

VideoTools
445 Calle Serra
Aptos, CA 95003
(408) 476-5858

Data Preparation: From Shoestring to Super System

by Allen Lee Adkins

Perhaps one of the most time-intensive aspects of CD ROM publishing is **211** data preparation. This is the time *after* you have designed your application and acquired the data, and *before* the disc is mastered and replicated. It is the time when all the information you plan to put on CD ROM is converted to a machine readable form and formatted for placement on the disc.

Many companies will not want to create their own data preparation system and will seek out the services of those who have expertise. Others will want to get started immediately with the resources they have at hand. Either way, it is important for both types to understand the relationship of the components in a data preparation system and the immense range of options that are available. This article describes and compares five different hardware and software configurations that could be used to prepare data for CD ROM.

CD ROM Characteristics

The process of preparing data for CD ROM can be amazingly simple or extremely complicated depending on the complexity of design, and the type and amount of data to be processed.

It goes without saying that these factors will affect the type of development system most appropriate for your specific product, but there are other factors, having to do with the unique characteristics of CD ROM technology, that are also worthy of note.

○ CD ROM (compact disc read-only memory) is a *permanently* prerecorded plastic disc.

○ The average access time to the beginning of a read block can be as long as 3 seconds, depending on the overhead of the operating system and the device driver used. This needs to be taken into account when designing an application, particularly when multiple reads may be required. The possible delay is the reason why index tables are built into databases— they shorten the search time.

○ CD ROM is essentially the same as CD audio except for the method of encoding data and the manner in which the data is decoded by the player. On CD ROM, data is stored in sequential blocks, each consisting of 2352 bytes. This is made up of 12 sync bytes, 3 address bytes, one mode byte, 2048 bytes of user data and 288 bytes of error detection and correction code. The player reads these blocks at a speed of 75 blocks per second. The rotation speed of the disc varies as the head moves from inner to outer tracks, so that a constant number of blocks are read every second.

○ The CD ROM's data storage capacity can vary depending on which data mode you specify. There are three valid data modes available. They are 0, 1 and 2. A future mode may allow for video data storage. In mode 0, you have no data stored. In mode 1 you have 2048 bytes with an additional 288 bytes used for error detection and correction. In mode 2, the added layer of error detection and correction is not used. This allows the 288 bytes ordinarily used for ED&C to be used for additional user data, for a total of 2336 bytes of data per block.

○ The CD ROM can store audio as well as digital computer data. In this *mixed* mode, you must allow for a 2-second pre- and post-gap between blocks of computer data and audio. This must be considered when planning how much of each type of data you can expect to use in a mixed mode application.

○ In making multimedia CD ROMs, the development system must be capable of merging the media together in a manner that allows each type to be edited and manipulated until it is in the exact form and type desired prior to final premastering.

These "notes" are meant to serve as a refresher for those who may have forgotten some of the attributes of CD ROM. You may find them helpful in reading the following section.

A System Component Evaluation

A CD ROM data preparation system may be established in an incremental fashion or installed as a fully functional, full featured system. Understanding what your immediate needs are, how they will evolve over time, and how these needs fit with current industry standards will insure a smooth transition into the burgeoning field of optical disc publishing.

There are several key components to a CD ROM data preparation system. Further, there are several degrees of functionality and performance that can be expected, depending on the specific configuration. On the next few pages are five CD ROM data preparation systems and their corresponding

212

A CD ROM data preparation system may be established in an incremental fashion or installed as a fully functional, full featured system.

components. Each system configuration represents an added degree of sophistication, with the *Shoestring System* being the least sophisticated, and the *Super System* representing the ideal. Associated with every configuration is a higher price tag, and a more complicated process. CD ROM publishers may enter the data preparation cycle at any level, and build up or down as they learn more about their needs.

213

Shoestring System

Recommended Shoestring System Configuration:

○ Computer (can be IBM PC, PC/XT, PC/AT, or compatible, or other computer capable of supporting hard disk and 9-track magnetic tape storage on PC Bus, SCSI, etc.)

○ Hard Disk Unit (any size will work, but it is recommended that you have at least twice the size of the largest file you will work with in hard disk storage)

○ Magnetic Tape Data Storage Unit (½ inch, 9-track, 1600 bpi type is minimum specification, 6250 GCR type recommended)

○ System Software Utilities (good text editor and directory manager, file format converters, file inversion program or utility for creating index file(s), flexible disk-to-tape data I/O utilities, volume manager and volume table generation utility and file location table generation utility, ANSI tape I/O utility [x3.27, level 3])

○ File Structure Creation Program (program to create the desired file structure such as DEC's Uni-File, LaserDos, a new version of MS-DOS or other subsequent industry standard file structure of choice)

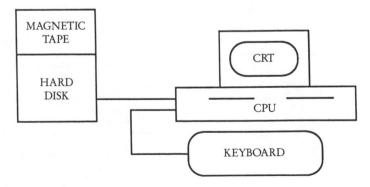

Figure 1. Shoestring System

Enhanced System

Recommended Enhanced System Configuration:

○ Computer (PC/AT or compatible, DEC VAX, DEC MicroVax II, PDP-11, SUN MicroSystems or other comparable computers capable of supporting large hard disks and GCR 9-track magnetic tape storage using the PC Bus, SCSI, Q-Bus, Uni-Bus, Multi-Bus, VME or other buses that adequately support connection of large data storage peripherals; proven device drivers are a must)

○ Hard Disk Unit (it is recommended that you have the size of a full CD ROM or approximately 700 megabytes in hard disk storage or at least the size of you intended CD ROM plus any associated file directory or index file; 1.4 gigabytes is optimum though not required)

○ Magnetic Tape Data Storage Unit (½ inch, 9-track, 1600 bpi type is minimum specification, 6250 GCR type recommended, two drives allows easy creation of tape backups and is recommended for systems that are in continuous use.)

○ Operating System (Enhanced MS-DOS, VAX-VMS, RSTS/E, 4.2 BSD UNIX, UNIX Version 5 or comparable robust operating system, various mainframe operating systems can be used, though the proper utilities must be available)

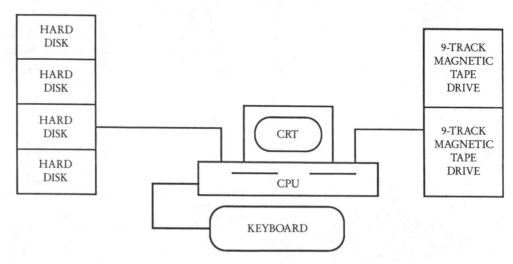

Figure 2. Enhanced System

○ System Software Utilities (good text editor and directory manager, file format converters, file inversion program or utility to create index file(s), flexible disk-to-tape data I/O utilities, volume manager and volume table generation utility and file location table generation utility, ANSI tape I/O utility [x3.27, level 3])

215

○ File Structure Creation Program (program to create the desired file structure such as DEC's Uni-File, LaserDos, a new version of MS-DOS or other subsequent industry standard file structure)

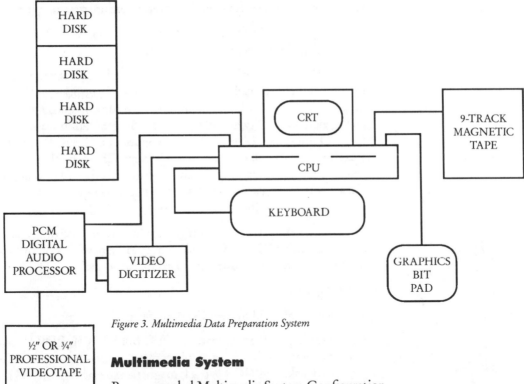

Figure 3. Multimedia Data Preparation System

Multimedia System

Recommended Multimedia System Configuration

○ Computer (PC/AT or compatible, DEC MicroVax II, PDP-11, Sun Microsystems or other comparable computers capable of supporting large hard disks and GCR 9-track magnetic tape storage on PC Bus, SCSI, SMD, MultiBus or VME Bus), and a special purpose interface between the computer and the PCM processor in NTSC video format.

○ Hard Disk Unit (it is recommended that you have the size of a full CD ROM or approximately 700 megabytes in hard disk storage, 1.4 gigabytes is optimum)

216

○ Magnetic Tape Data Storage Unit (½ inch, 9-track, 1600 bpi type is minimum specification; 6250 GCR type recommended)

○ Graphics Bit Pad and Video Digitizer (optional, for multimedia CD ROMs)

○ PCM Audio Processor (or Analog-to-Digital Converter) and Companion VTR (or audio tape recorder for CD Audio or non-CD Audio); also for creating a final, fully encoded CD ROM tape premaster in professional videocassette format that can then be delivered to any CD audio manufacturing facility for mastering in the same manner as an audio CD. Extra care must be taken, however, to ensure data integrity.

○ Operating System Utilities (Enhanced MD-DOS, VAX-VMS, RSTS/E, 4.2BSD UNIX, or comparable)

○ System Software Utilities (good text editor and directory manager, file format converters, flexible disk-to-tape data I/O utilities, File Inversion program or utility for building index files, volume manager and volume table generation utility and file location table generation utility, ANSI tape I/O utility [x3.27, level 3]; for the videotape CD ROM premaster encoding system you must be a Philips/Sony CD technology licensee and have the encoding program to generate the CD ROM sync, header and error detection and correction data packet on each 2K byte block of data before writing the final video tape.

○ File Structure Creation Program (program to create the desired file structures such as DEC's Uni-File, Laserdos, a new version of MS-DOS or other subsequent industry standard file structure)

Hybrid System

Recommended Hybrid System Configuration

○ Computer (PC/AT or compatible, DEC MicroVax II, PDP-11, Sun MicroSystems or other comparable computers capable of supporting large hard disks and GCR 9-track magnetic tape storage on PC Bus, SCSI, SMD, MultiBus or VME Bus)

○ Hard Disk Unit (it is recommended that you have the size of a full CD ROM or approximately 600 megabytes in hard disk storage, 1.2 gigabytes is optimum)

○ Magnetic Tape Data Storage Unit (½ inch, 9-track, 1600 bpi type is minimum specification, 6250 GCR type is recommended)

○ Graphics Bit Pad and Video Digitizer (optional, for multimedia CD ROMs)

○ PCM Audio Processor (or Analog-to-Digital Converter) and Companion VTR (or audio tape recorder for CD Audio or non-CD Audio)

○ Operating System (Enhanced MS-DOS, VAX-VMS, RSTS/E, 4.2BSD UNIX, or compatible)

○ System Software Utilities (good text editor and directory manager, file format converters, flexible disk-to-tape data I/O utilities, File Inversion program or utility for building index files, volume manager and volume table generation utility and file location table generation utility, ANSI tape I/O utility [x3.27, level 3])

○ File Structure Creation Program (program to create the desired file structure such as DEC's Uni-File, Laserdos, a new version of MS-DOS or other subsequent industry standard file structure)

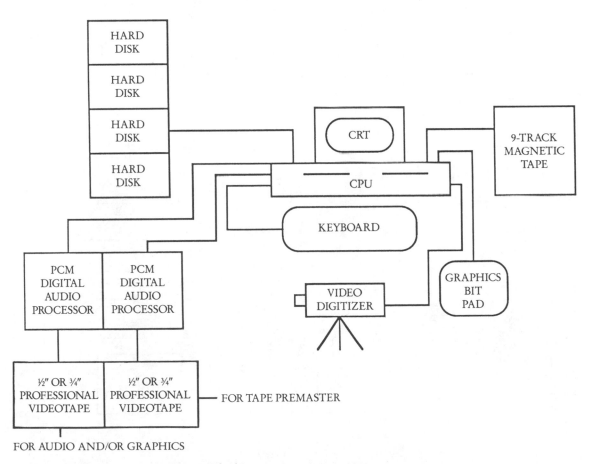

Figure 4. Hybrid System

A Super Data Preparation System

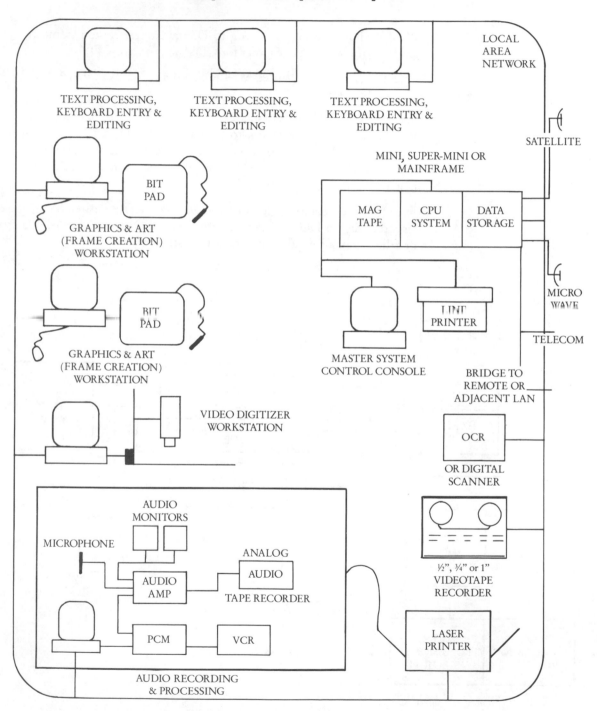

Figure 5. Super System

The Computer

The computer is the most important part of the data preparation system because it determines your software and hardware options. The operating system, utilities, I/O devices, and processing speed are all defined by the type of computer you choose. Some are readily available, simpler to operate and less costly to purchase and maintain—but often at the cost of speed and performance.

The best way to evaluate what you need is to determine how often you will produce CD ROM, and how much data processing will be necessary. After you have a clear idea, make sure that the peripheral interface bus can handle the loads you intend to impose on it, as this will have a major impact on the overall processing throughput of the system. Also, check that the required device drivers for the peripherals are available and that they are properly and tightly integrated into the operating system. And last, but not least, evaluate the software and operating systems that are available for the computer you have in mind; they may not be adequate.

Small personal computers will soon perform most, if not all, CD ROM data preparation functions. Obviously, in almost every instance, at a reduced speed and with less power-processing utilities than their mini computer counterparts. The ubiquitous Apple II will no doubt eventually support the kinds of peripherals required to assemble and edit CD ROMs. As the Apple Macintosh continues to expand in memory and processing power, it will also begin supporting larger peripherals. The IBM PC and its more powerful relatives in the PC family will play a dominant role, from data preparation to a widely used delivery system. The DEC VAX family and the still very viable PDP-11 series are tried-and-true industry workhorses. They will increasingly influence all areas of CD ROM data preparation, particularly where speed and performance are most critical. Mainframes, IBM or the others, will be used but mainly for dedicated applications, and in some instances, as a central processor in distributed and networked configurations.

The Shoestring System.   The goal is to assemble data in files of various sizes from small to very large. A minimum system configuration will call for a computer capable of supporting medium size to large hard disks and at least two 1600 bpi, 9-track, magnetic tape drives, which will store the final encoded data destined for the CD ROM manufacturer. IBM PCs, XTs, ATs and compatibles can do the job, though be sure to check the processing throughput for your particular kind of data preparation. Smaller computers can be used as terminals or for storing pieces of your final program.

The process of preparing data for CD ROM can be amazingly simple or extremely complicated depending on the complexity of design, and the type and amount of data to be processed.

As a rule, put as much memory into your system(s) as possible and familiarize yourself with every available software processing utility. Examine your performance upgrade path before making any major commitments. Also, confirm that you have enough expansion slots or the ability to add an expansion chassis. There is always a need for more space than you think.

Enhanced System.   The step up to an enhanced version may mean heightened performance, greater hard disk storage capacity and the ability to use a more robust operating environment with more powerful system software utilities. The super micros and mini computers such as the new generation 68020 machines from Sun Micro Systems or DEC's MicroVax II are good candidates. Look around. There are many others that may also fulfill your overall performance criteria for CPU processing speed and large data storage peripheral support. Check the availability of SCSI versions of disk and tape drives. The DEC Q-Bus, the MultiBus II and the VME bus are all viable as well as others, including the GPIB. Of primary importance is proper integration of peripherals, device drivers and system software utilities.

Multimedia System.   The primary consideration in this category is the ability of the computer to support the type of graphics processing you require. Such things as graphics coprocessors and well-supported graphics add-on cards complete with tested, debugged software are of primary importance. It is also possible to use CAD/CAM systems to create or acquire a wide range of graphics data. (And they would be well suited to using CD ROMs as auxiliary read-only data storage, as well.)

In some instances, when audio is to be either created or made compatible with a particular system, proper A/D and D/A converters and their respective software are also important.

A true multimedia system will be able to adequately support the graphics and audio data acquisition, editing and file formatting that is needed to produce the CD ROM premaster tape.

Hybrid System.   The primary distinction of the Hybrid CD ROM Data Prep System is its ability to generate either a 9-track magnetic tape premaster or a final CD ROM data-packet encoded professional videotape (complete with sync, header, 2K byte blocks, and error detection and correction). The advantage of the videotape version is that you can send it to any CD audio disc manufacturer and have it replicated as a regular audio CD. One of the drawbacks of the videotape premaster is that you must use extra caution when laying down your data, to insure data integrity, since the data reliability of some videotape recorders are questionable. They were not originally designed for this application and generally do not offer sufficient error checking and correction, though there are some that do when used in conjunction with the Pulse Code Modulation (PCM) processor and computer interface.

The computer must be able to calculate the CD ROM data packet (sync, header and error correction algorithm) and to offer or support an appropriate PCM processor interface complete with software. Optical Media Services, among others, is developing such an interface, software and accompanying CD ROM authoring and delivery system software.

The Super System. Anyone seriously involved in CD ROM data preparation or publishing will have or want to have some or all components that comprise the super system. There is just nothing like having all of the best tools and resources available to do the very best job possible in the shortest amount of time.

In most cases, a system of this class will use the very latest processor technology, or at least a system that has very respectable multiuser processing capabilities. In some instances, very powerful super micros, properly linked via local area network, can achieve the kind of results obtainable by larger systems, however, careful consideration must be given to cost versus actual performance.

By way of example, most current dedicated CD ROM data processing facilities that have consistently heavy work loads have some type of DEC VAX computer system, though no doubt others can and will be used with good results. System maintenance costs and proper programming staff become much more of an issue when these larger systems are used, and they should be used constantly to justify their usually high capital expense. The future should bring a variety of parallel processing systems with incredibly increased processing speed and ever more sophisticated software programs and utilities.

Hard Disks

Hard disks are absolutely essential and can vastly increase the overall system performance during almost every phase of CD ROM data preparation. Hard disks are becoming increasingly smaller, faster, larger capacity and, remarkably, cheaper. No doubt, the eminent rise of optical disc data storage is putting pressure on the magnetic disk manufacturers to squeeze out every drop of performance physically possible and to sharpen their

222

market focus on the niches where magnetic media are now and will continue to be required. In the meantime, optical disc technology keeps getting more and more refined and systematically starts stepping into various areas previously held by magnetic technology.

For now, the erasability and speed of large, high performance hard disks are almost indispensible to CD ROM data prep. Here, the interface bus decision is important. Again, check out what is available on SCSI. Many large drives on the SMD bus are tried and proven and are a good value these days. The Fujitsu Eagle series drives are real workhorses and super reliable.

Large, powerful systems do not hold the exclusive license on creativity.

Generally, in the area of CD ROM data preparation, the more hard disk space the better. A couple of gigabytes is really not unreasonable, and in some cases is required for fast, efficient processing of large files. If possible, use two storage areas, each the size of the total amount of data you intend to store on the CD ROM (including all directory files, index files, hash tables, etc.). Soon, write-once or WORM optical disc drives will be viable enough to use in the same way. More in the mag tape section on this matter.

The Shoestring System.   To say that 10 or 20 megabytes of hard disk is adequate is probably stretching it, unless you are assembling a collection of fairly small files. In any event, you should always allow enough disk space to accommodate the total cumulative file I/O, including indexes.

"Floppy ROM" types of CD ROM programs can be composed of sequential files, assembled in pieces, and then be properly cataloged, indexed and copied to magnetic tape. This process can then be repeated, over and over, until you have loaded all the data. If you prepare your data in this piecemeal fashion, keep track of where you are so that you don't overwrite your data by mistake.

For those with a smaller system, this kind of preparation is fine for transferring sequential files, or to incrementally load data to tape for later final processing at a fully equipped CD ROM data processing facility. In fact, the more preprocessing you do, the better. Your efforts will often reduce the premastering charges, compensating for the additional time required up front.

It should be emphasized here that you *can* make a CD ROM on a minimum system. With enough care and creativity, some really useful and popular programs can be implemented. Large, powerful systems do not hold the exclusive license on creativity.

Just be careful and think through all the steps involved. And be sure you know what you're getting into if you are trying to assemble a really large amount of data—although sometimes I think it's better not to know; 600 megabytes is a mind-boggling amount of data.

The Enhanced System.   As you might imagine, in this case *enhanced* means more disk space. As mentioned earlier, you should try to have at least twice the size of your intended CD ROM in hard disk space. Preferably, each CD ROM image should be able to fully reside on one logical drive, though with some of the better interfaces and drivers this is not necessarily a problem. Check the specs and your requirements if you are trying to use several drives with overlapping files or records that span logical volumes or drives. The optimum size, for an extra margin of safety and flexibility, is probably 1.4 gigabytes of hard disk space.

Multimedia.   The primary consideration for data storage in this type of configuration is to make sure that you can store the images and/or audio data on the disc in the format required and, at the same time, be able to edit it. This is usually a software matter and is discussed in a later section.

The computer is the most important part of the data preparation system because it determines your software and hardware options.

Hybrid System.   The issue in this configuration is the size of the drive and its ability to feed data to the PCM interface fast enough. When you are making a fully encoded CD ROM premaster, you must write the entire disc image through the PCM processor to the professional VCR non-stop, not missing a bit, in exactly the right format. Otherwise you must start over. The worst-case track-to-track latency must be within this transfer specification. Different PCM processors may require a different data I/O rate into the processor and your hard disk must be able to accommodate these differences.

The Super System.   This is where you definitely want to get the most reliable drives, with the best interface, the best performance specs, and at least 1.4 gigabytes of storage. Twice that amount is really not too much for a facility regularly performing data prep for large CD ROMs. The configuration should allow for a potential file-server-like use, as large projects are many times best implemented in pieces by several people working in a distributed-processing, networked environment. Be sure to check the overall multiuser throughput performance specs. And if you're making a big commitment, try it out in a real, live work environment first, if at all possible.

224

Magnetic Tape Storage

Magnetic tape storage is the standard data interchange format between large and small computers. It is because of this that most static databases currently in existence are now archived on some form of 9-track magnetic tape—the same as the premaster tape specification. There are several data recording densities that are used, typically 800 bpi, 1600 bpi, 3200 bpi, 6250 bpi, and newer high-performance drives that are well over 10,000 bpi. For the immediate future, the most widely used and supported will be the 1600 bpi and 6250 bpi formats. If another format must be dealt with there are numerous data processing service bureaus that can convert the format into either 1600 or 6250 bpi tapes for ease of processing. For smaller systems the ¼ inch and ½ inch data cartridge formats can be used to input data incrementally, as long as your development system also contains one of these tape drives. They are usually much less expensive than the ½ inch 9-track magnetic tape drives and have standard interfaces to most common interface buses.

Each type of configuration can use the same type of tape drive as long as an appropriate interface is available. In some instances with high-volume environments, it is preferable to have two tape drives because it allows quick and easy tape-to-tape copies and tape backups. If SCSI is fully supported, you can transfer directly from one tape drive to the other, or directly from hard disk to one tape drive while the other is writing data out to another hard disk. Look for these intelligent interfaces to become major industry standards and vastly increase the longevity and utility of these often expensive data storage peripherals.

In the near future we can anticipate that write-once, WORM, and erasable optical discs will store the final CD ROM disc image and be interfaced to the various CD ROM disc manufacturers' computer systems. This will eventually reduce premaster storage space and, ultimately, cost—not to mention the inherent nonerasable data integrity it offers.

Operating Systems

The operating system is the command center and heart of your computer system. A good operating system can make all the difference in providing you an easy way to perform certain kinds of data manipulation. As you might expect, the newer ones have nice, buzzword-filled features, but in some cases have yet to be thoroughly and reliably debugged. Additionally, many of them simply are not robust enough to offer the really powerful standard utilities of the older, more mature and proven operating systems. The industry standard on micros, MS-DOS, has been evolving and will continue to do so. As this happens it will become increasingly more adept at handling large amounts of data, with more power and flexibility.

225

CD ROM publishers may enter the data preparation cycle at any level, and build up or down as they learn more about their needs.

Although MS-DOS has its rightful place in the world of operating systems, it may not be the system of choice for larger systems. Here you will want to consider a standard version of UNIX, such as System V, or 4.2 BSD. Now that Sun Micro Systems and AT&T are collaborating closely, these two versions should start to become more alike. Or you have the option of DEC's VAX/VMS and RSTS/E combinations. ADA will probably be a likely candidate for many types of government-related CD ROMs.

Ease of data I/O between disk and tape is key to a good operating system, and the more virtual the operating environment the better.

The Shoestring System.   The operating system should allow you to run, concurrently, your hard disk and your tape drive. In most cases, on the smaller machines, the operating system will be MS-DOS, or in some cases a PC version of UNIX, such as PC/IX, XENIX, or AT&T Unix. Make sure that your version supports the kinds of data I/O, and editing and file manipulations required.

It is always a good idea to test each component, hardware and software, before relying on the system's integrity. This can be especially true with newly acquired peripherals from third-party vendors. One should never be too busy to double-check each component and its operation in the manner in which it is to be used during processing. If you wait until the last minute, you may not have time to adjust, replace or fix any problems. Every effort should be made to acquire all useful utilities that are available for your operating environment and stay up to date on new versions.

The Enhanced System.   As you begin to upgrade or assemble a serious CD ROM data preparation system, consider the long term. Look at where the industry standards are headed and choose your operating systems on the basis of their ability to offer immediate environment solutions that are going to continue to be well supported. Robust operating systems running on high-performance machines can take on a lot of the grunt work with built-in, standard utilities, such as those available for the DEC VAX line and others that have had serious use over the past 10 to 20 years. Issues such as graphics protocols and parallel processing, in addition to network architecture, will become more important. Good operating environments accommodate these new advances. Look for DEC and Microsoft to continue to be leaders in these important areas.

Multimedia Systems.   More than an operating system is needed to manage the various kinds of media that will be used on *mixed* mode or multimedia CD ROMs. You'll need a bonafide *authoring* system. This enhanced operating system should support emerging graphics protocols, various audio standards, and the file I/O required for these media. Evolving user interfaces such as the Macintosh have demonstrated that a little can go a long way in allowing more nontechnical artistic creators access to the potential of the new optical disc technology.

Hybrid Systems.   The operating system required for this type of system must handle the high-speed data transfer required for reading and writing data to the PCM processor. Beyond this the requirements are as for the enhanced or super system.

The Super System.   The operating system at this level of performance should definitely be one of the more mature and robust operating system environments. The ability to handle multiusers and process many different types of input data is important. Good support of the various high-level development languages is also essential for creating new device drivers, as is increasingly higher bandwidth data transfers and file I/O.

System Software Utilities

Perhaps the key to fast, efficient CD ROM data preparation, given the proper hardware and operating system environment, is the functionality of the various system software utilities that actually manipulate the data, helping to place it in the proper format for premastering. Naturally, good text editors and graphics editors are important. File conversion programs and protocol converters are also very useful, and in some instances, absolutely required to perform certain kinds of data acquisition. Data file inversion utilities (indexing programs) are in high demand and will become increasingly more sophisticated as they are integrated with various search and retrieval programs, providing quicker access to the CD ROM data.

On each level of the system options—from Shoestring to Super System— you need utilities that can create any required volume directory, file directory, and file I/O data that pertains to such factors as file attributes, file allocation tables, and hash tables.

Ideally, these utilities should automatically generate the appropriate table or directory. In the case of mixed-mode CD ROMs, they should be able to specify or determine whether a data block is to be mode 0, mode 1, or mode 2, flag each block, and create an input so that during the final pre-mastering stage the correct mode bytes are set.

ANSI tape label utilities are required to generate all premaster tapes for submission to those CD ROM replicators that request ANSI X3.27 level 3 labeled tapes. It should be noted that each individual disc manufacturer should be contacted directly at the time of premaster tape submission for the applicable data tape submission specification.

File Structure Creation Program.   This may be one or more programs that read the assembled CD ROM data and create the appropriate file structure required and expected by the end-user delivery system.

An active CD ROM data preparation service should expect to be able to create several more-or-less standard file structures or, in some cases, produce discs that have more than one file structure resident on a disc. It is conceivable that certain publishers may wish to achieve a very proprietary, more secure data format and request a nonstandard file structure.

It should be
emphasized here
that you *can* make
a CD ROM on a
minimum system.

It should be obvious what the power of a globally accepted standard can do for a publishing medium. Just look at the phenomenal growth and acceptance of the audio CD. It is this global acceptance that has poised CD ROM, the audio CD's twin sister, with its enormous advantages of base level standards and low cost due to high-volume manufacturing.

Of course, proper device driver software needs to be available for different hardware peripherals to access the particular file structure on the disc. Most currently used CD ROM file structures are compatible and offer these device drivers. It is important to note, however, that because of subtle differences in the drive manufacturers' interfaces for the standard computer systems, a specific device driver may be required for a specific combination of CD ROM drive, interface and program. This situation should become less of an issue over time but should, in any case, not be overlooked.

Issues of interest with regard to CD ROM file structures are such items as:

o Physical data block to logical data block I/O system

o Logical block size (variable or fixed)

○ Disc identification and disc contents identification

○ Logical handling of multiple disc sets (as in the case of multidisc players or *juke box*-type drives)

○ Management of file attributes

○ Creation and disc mapping of hash tables and/or index files (if used)

○ Standardized location and specification of a disc file directory and/or volume directory (if required)

○ Support of mixed mode or multimedia CD ROMs (i.e., audio and graphics in perhaps various protocols)

○ Provision for company-specific, preassigned mode bytes (as in the MIDI interface spec used by most electronic musical instrument manufacturers)

○ Perhaps, allowance for multiple operating system compatibility and/or multiple file structures or a so-called "Universal ROM File Structure"

Conclusion

Whatever the outcome, the importance of industry-wide standardization cannot be overemphasized. The pace and, perhaps, the ultimate potential of CD ROM as a publishing medium will hinge on its ability to synergistically enhance, or coexist with, other technologies, and become properly supported by all of the related manufacturers and publishers.

About the Author

Allen L. Adkins is founder and president of Optical Media International and Optical Media Services. He has been very active in optical disc technology, previously having founded several companies that dealt with interactive videodiscs. Over the past two years he has spent his time developing new applications for CD ROM and establishing an experience base in the various aspects of CD ROM data preparation and premastering. Mr. Adkins has been responsible for many new concepts and applications of optical disc technology; and his company, Optical Media Services, has developed the first CD ROM interface and CD ROM application program for the Apple Macintosh computer. It has also produced, published, and is marketing the first digital sound database on CD ROM for the professional audio industry. The program, called *Universe of Sounds, Volume One*, contains thousands of digitally sampled musical instrument sounds and sound effects which are used in conjunction with the Emulator II Professional Polyphonic Sampling Keyboard System. The program is sold with an OMS CD ROM drive which contains an embedded interface to the Macintosh and Apple HFS compatible search and retrieval software.

Optical Media Services performs a variety of contract CD ROM and CD audio data preparation services, consulting, and program development services. OMI, the CD publishing label, is active in the production of unique, high-quality CD ROM and CD audio programs. CD ROM interfaces, device drivers, data preparation technologies, and other products developed by OMS are available on an OEM and/or license basis.

Optical Media Services
P.O. Box 2107
Aptos, CA 95001
(408) 662-1772

Data Indexing

by Jerry Fand

This discussion is intended as an introduction to some of the problems inherent in large text databases on read-only optical media. The problems presented are consequences primarily of the large quantity of data, and secondly of its textual nature. The fact that the medium is optical disc is almost incidental, in the sense that these same issues arise for large text databases on any storage medium. The consequences of using read-only media, such as opportunities for storage space optimization, are considered to be outside the scope of this chapter. The discussion will generally be limited to a statement of the nature of a problem with some of the technical side issues rather than an exhaustive presentation of solutions.

Documents

As the size of a database increases, attempting to locate information by doing a linear scan through portions of the actual documents becomes unacceptable; accessing hundreds of megabytes or gigabytes of text simply takes a long time. Data compression techniques can reduce the size of the database, and therefore increase the search speed somewhat, but even data compression fails to alleviate the problem with extremely large databases. One solution to this problem is to represent the documents in indexed form.

The sheer mass of a database is not the only factor that contributes to long search times: Large databases usually have large numbers of documents, and current operating systems generally use a file access method that involves a linear search of the directory containing a file. If each document is stored as a system file, the operating system overhead in document access contributes to the delay. This directory overhead, which affects data indexing as well as retrieval, can be reduced by creating library files, each of which can contain many document files. The operating system considers each library file to be a single entry in the directory file. Another incentive for using document library files is that some file systems have limits on the total number of allowable files. Using library files makes documents recognizable only by the application software. An alternative to library files is the adoption of a file access method such as hashing, which is beyond the scope of most applications.

Once the concept of document library files is accepted, there are some structural implications to consider. A primary one is the method of locating the document within the library files. Since there may be quite a few large library files, a document pointer and a file name must be encoded into the database for each document. This adds significantly to storage space requirements.

Data Preparation

In preparing textual data for document representation, determining how to artificially break up large files into meaningful retrievable units is a significant problem. Also, the data is often in a format that is incompatible with the retrieval program, requiring it to be transformed structurally and then composed into reasonable document display format. Even before this step, however, may come the problem of data capture or extraction from formats such as text encoded for photocomposition. None of these problems is formidable for small databases, but each requires an automated solution for large databases.

In addition to individual document composition, there is the problem of determining meaningful splits of the data into multiple databases. When there are subsets of documents containing different internal structures, this is not a significant problem, but the requirement to divide the data by some internal content characteristic or by retrieval needs is more difficult to achieve. Generally the solution must involve the data provider. Although the problem of splits can be avoided when the documents have uniform internal structure, restriction to single database solutions is not always adequate and introduces a new set of problems. For instance, as the database size grows it may force multivolume solutions, with unpleasant hardware and driver implications.

Once the documents and databases have been structured, and the data captured or transformed into appropriate textual representation, errors introduced prior to or during transformation must be detected and corrected. A feedback step, in which the publisher corrects and retransforms the data, is often necessary at this point.

Finally, in view of the multiple steps involved in input data preparation, the possibilities of incorrect design for intended retrieval capability, and the costs and time involved in the indexing steps, there must be a method by which the data publisher can preview the retrieval application. A recommended approach is to create a prototype during the design stage and again following initial data submission. Once indexing is complete, it is likely that the combined size of the data and indexes will exceed the amount of available online magnetic storage and thus prohibit demonstration of the full product prior to mastering. Even if online capacity is sufficient, eliminating the protyping stage risks wasting time by indexing incorrect data.

Index Creation

The primary problems in indexing large databases center on online storage capacity. It is quite possible that the entire database will not fit online at one time. And even if it does, working storage space must be allowed for the necessary sort and merge programs and for the indexes ultimately created. It is difficult to justify gigabytes of magnetic storage for this purpose, although certainly space on multiple devices may be desirable from the perspective of disk head motion management.

Attempts to solve the online issue usually lead to the approach of indexing by stages. A temporary index is produced by each stage, and a multiway merge is used as a final pass in producing the indexes. This whole process requires considerable computing power. Sorts and merges consume time and resources which quickly outstrip both CPU and I/O capacity. The problem is not linear with the size of the input data, as required computing time is proportional to $N \times LOG(N)$, where N is the number of raw concordance items to sort.

As the size of a database increases, attempting to locate information by doing a linear scan through portions of the actual documents becomes unacceptable.

There are solid reasons for choosing the approach of separate indexing followed by merge steps, even though it introduces significant data handling issues. When massive amounts of data are being indexed, the total indexing time becomes relatively large and the probability of hardware failure consequently grows. From a resource management viewpoint, there is a desire not to have to repeat too many steps should a failure occur during a long operation (this is called recoverability). Partitioning the data prior to indexing allows recovery back to the last partition without risk of index structure corruption. An unrelated point concerns overall publisher project management. Frequently, large read-only databases contain a core of invariant material surrounded by material that changes dynamically through periodic updates. Or there may be no data changes but instead there may be periodic additions to certain sections. In either case it is expedient to avoid having to reindex the entire database.

An alternative to the final massive merge (in which it may not be possible to contain all the components simultaneously online) is to structure the database as the single logical union of several separately indexed databases and to manage search unions with the retrieval software. A drawback of this, however, is that several sets of indexes must then be searched, resulting in additional seeks and longer retrieval times.

234

Data Transfer

After the database is indexed, the data and indexes must be transferred to magnetic tape prior to being sent to the mastering facility. Large databases may very well not fit on a single magnetic tape, especially at lower tape densities. In order to ensure reliable data transfer, it is a good practice to require that tape labeling conform to ANSI standards. Thus, any ambiguity of tape order is removed. This practice should also apply to tape copies of generated index data. If system utilities do not include such tape transfer routines, special programs may have to be written. Often, even if such utilities do exist, they must be modified in order to provide translation between character sets.

Another data transfer issue is raised by the form the data is to take on the optical medium. If, for instance, the optical disc is intended to mimic a standard operating system volume, there is the problem of directory construction. Even if the operating system of the data preparation host is compatible with the operating system that will be used in the retrieval environment, the data may not fit on a single magnetic disk volume, and therefore the operating system may not be able to construct the required disk overhead information. For databases small enough to avoid this problem, the issue still remains of how to transfer an entire disk image (including overhead) to tape.

Physical Size Limitations

Although optical storage media typically have enormous capacities, the amount of information stored in databases is also increasing. When the database becomes too large to store on a single disc, and the publisher cannot or will not partition the database, a multivolume set of discs must be created. This is an added expense to production and distribution and poses additional problems in data retrieval. This section contains a discussion of several approaches that can be used to avoid or postpone the multivolume problem.

The first and most obvious approach is text compression. Among various options in text compression are stopword lists (nonindexed words that have little meaning content), word replacement with binary codes based on expected occurrence frequency or on actual total database frequency statistics, substring replacement similar to word replacement, blank pad elimination, consecutive blank run length encoding, and character bit compactions arising from character set restrictions. Each of these must be weighed against the computer power required for decompression and whether this must occur at indexing as well as at retrieval time. There is a trade-off here of performance versus economy of storage space. For text generally conforming to English usage, it is reasonable to expect in the vicinity of a 50 percent reduction in storage of the document portions of a database, perhaps more if several compression algorithms are used.

A second possible approach is compression of index structures. There is much less to be gained here than in text compression—partially due to the smaller size of the index structures, but primarily due to the fact that the indexes are usually stored as binary data. The word-oriented nature of text lends itself to repeated words and character sequences; in straight binary data this is strictly at the whim of probability. It is possible to reduce the index size, but more by judicious index structural design that minimizes repetitive data whenever possible than by compression. An appropriate implementation might employ techniques such as tabular lookup or library file-size limitations that result in a lower cap on the number of bits required to represent pointers into these files. Caution should be exercised, however, since index compaction has a direct effect on retrieval time whereas text compression affects only the time required to display the text following retrieval.

An additional compression method may sometimes be effective, depending on the internal document representation format. When the number of documents is very high and each document contains a small amount of data that must be highly formatted for display, the formatting information may amount to a high percentage of the actual text. An example would be records of ASCII numeric information in concatenated fields without any embedded explanatory text. In such cases it may be possible to store the document data without most of the formatting information and to reinsert this information for display or print purposes after document retrieval. This adds the complication, however, of using another program and depends on the document data being highly structured and of predictable format.

In preparing textual data for document representation, determining how to artificially break up large files into meaningful retrievable units is a significant problem.

Retrieval

Certain effects at retrieval time are either directly or indirectly due to large database size. These fall into two classes: those that influence the actual performance of a search and those that are factors in document display following completion of a search.

A frequently underrated effect on retrieval is that of typographical errors in the text of documents. Typos drive up the size of the dictionary of indexed terms and may not conform to a selected text compression scheme. They also cause users to miss retrieval of relevant documents that contain misspellings or spelling variations of their search terms. To combat this problem it may be necessary to provide a verification dictionary at indexing time, with multiple posting into the indexes of words that fall outside the dictionary vocabulary. Problems may also occur at retrieval time due to spelling errors in query terms, but this is not related to database size.

Two additional factors directly affect retrieval. With large databases, even uncommon terms have high absolute frequency. This implies that there must be a means for progressively narrowing and refining a search. Hand in hand with this is the likelihood that searches will retrieve large document sets satisfying the search criteria. The candidate document sets satisfying portions of complex search logic that are often even larger. Both factors point to the need for sizable read-write working storage. Generally, the larger the database, the greater the requirement for working storage on magnetic disk, given equivalent search activity.

The primary problems in indexing large databases center on online storage capacity.

Foremost in the class of issues affecting document display, large document size implies that the display logic cannot afford to perform linear scanning through a retrieved document in order to locate requested portions, except in sequential display mode. Furthermore, following a search, the user is generally presented with a summary list of search results containing brief descriptive information about each document in the result set. Large database size and potentially long disc seek times prohibit the extraction of this information directly from the documents involved while the user is waiting. Because large document sizes ususally require encoded structural information to be recorded within the body of the actual document, display of the document becomes more complex and requires program interpretation and transformation of the document data. This kind of transforming, or filtering, was already suggested in the section on compression.

Conclusion

The desire to effectively retrieve data from extremely large textual databases poses significant hardware and software design considerations. An approach which disregards these considerations with a nonintegrated solution will be confronted with serious performance problems. Migrating a retrieval application to large databases is not simply a matter of increasing the size of the indexes. Instead of the motto "bigger is better," a more appropriate expression might be that when bigger is necessary, a better solution is in order.

About the Author

Jerry Fand has a B.S. in mathematics from Rensselaer Polytechnic Institute and an M.S. in mathematics from the University of Washington. He has been employed in private industry since 1976, including experience in design automation at Texas Instruments, work with microprocessors and real-time software at Texas Instruments and Mead, and systems engineering at Four Phase Systems.

In his current position as a member of the technical staff at Reference Technology, Inc., he is involved in system integration, software evaluation and design, and data preparation in support of Reference Technology's full-text search software products to facilitate fast full-text search of huge databases on optical discs.

Reference Technology Inc.
1832 North 55th Street
Boulder, CO 80301

Image Capture and Processing for CD ROM

by James P. McNaul

Images are another form of information, even more pervasive in our lives than text or numbers. Yet when we think of electronic databases in office applications, we tend to think of text and numbers, even though image databases exist in many forms; e.g., presentation slides, product photographs, and microfilm archives. When you think about it, a piece of paper taken from a file cabinet is an image. The eye sees the image and the brain translates it into a learned concept—a letter or number, a word or a "thing."

239

Information databases, and the distribution of these databases in particular, will be revolutionized by the ready availability of optical disc technology, particularly by very low cost CD ROMs. From a system point of view, we can see that the back-end technology, the CD ROM, is developing rapidly, becoming standardized, and will undoubtedly fall in cost over time. Further, the middle technology, search and retrieval software, is now quite sophisticated and appears to be moving toward some major breakthroughs by the application of artificial intelligence technology. The front-end technology, cost-effective image information capture, although far less understood, is also progressing rapidly. This technological trio will create a major new advance in the information age.

This chapter first describes some of the applications for CD ROM-based information systems which require images, then describes the process of image scanning and how it is implemented. Some of the major system trade-offs are then discussed.

Image Database Applications

The system most appropriate for document management is normally thought of as a function of the number of pages in the database and the frequency of use over a given period of time. For example, hundreds or even thousands of pages, with a few accesses per day, is clearly the domain of a paper-based system, the file cabinet. On the other hand, when thousands of pages of text or data must be accessed many thousands of times per day, a data processing, or more generally, a MIS system is used. If millions of pages must be stored, but frequency of access is limited, a micrographic system, microfilm or microfiche, is appropriate.

240

One only has to think about this for a bit to see that there are several problems. One is certainly that there are many areas of this storage/access domain that are not covered by existing system technology. The second is that there is no dimension that deals with the content of the pages of information. Data processing and MIS systems deal well with text and numbers, but have not, for the most part, been implemented with images in mind. Micrographics, on the other hand, can deal with virtually any type of image since they are photographic replicas of an existing document (which is, after all, an image).

Another key question is the distribution of the database to other users. Document management tends to be thought of as a local phenomenon. Information tends to be collected, stored, and used locally, although electronic communication has extended these horizons. But once a collection of information has been created in one place, isn't it logical to expect that many other people with similar interests, but in different locations, would like access to that information? For small databases (up to a thousand pages or so), this is what book publishing is all about. CD ROMs offer the possibility of doing the same thing electronically, with two of the three advantages of electronic media: compactness of storage space and ease of retrieval. Given the low cost and high information capacity of CD ROM technology, it will find many applications where the third characteristic of electronic media is not as important: ease of update.

Applications for CD ROM technology where image information is important are dependant on several variables. These include the permanence, volume, and graphic content of the data. While trade-offs among these will be discussed subsequently, we can now look at several applications which appear to be suitable for CD ROM-based information bases and have high image content.

Application One: Archive Distribution

Many unique archives of information that appeal to a large audience often exist in one centralized location. Most large libraries have specialized collections that have been built up over the years. For the most part these collections can only be accessed in person by qualified personnel or by facsimile hard copy requested from the library—a costly and time-consuming process. Many of these collections are aging rapidly, and physical handling can lead to their destruction. But to reproduce them in paper or micrographic form for distribution is costly, and storage and retrieval are as difficult as keeping the original.

The advantage of the CD ROM medium is the large reduction in storage space and the ease of search and retrieval.

Much of the information content of such archives is in image form, such as line drawings, pictures, or handwriting; or it is conveyed by its layout, typeface, or associated annotation. In all these cases a page facsimile image is an appropriate way to distribute the information collection at relatively low cost.

241

To convert this information for storage on CD ROM, the page images are scanned in digital form and a limited amount of text or numbers are associated with each page image file for search and retrieval purposes. These are then assembled into logical collections and processed onto a CD ROM disc for distribution. To locate the image file, the alphanumeric data is searched using whatever search and retrieval procedures are appropriate. It may then be displayed on an electronic display or printed on paper for viewing.

The characteristics of this particular application are:

- The information base is not changed (it is an archive) but is added to over time.

- Manually created content annotation is required for search and retrieval. This may be derived from the contents of the page image or be independently created by a knowledgeable person.

- Information database replication is relatively low (hundreds or a few thousand copies) but the value of the contents is very high (due to the very high cost of alternative sources).

- The image content of the information database is very high, since each page is an image and the associated annotation is kept in text or numeric form.

- The use of the information is greatly facilitated by the ability to electronically search the annotation and easily access the related image file.

Application Two: Document Distribution

In this case the document is assumed to contain primarily alphanumeric information with images as supplementary information. Reference books such as encyclopedias, dictionaries, textbooks, or technical journals fit this category. Another important use will be to distribute technical publications, such as service manuals and parts lists, to remote locations in order to conserve space and improve ease of use.

The advantage of the CD ROM medium is the large reduction in storage space and the ease of search and retrieval. Much of the alphanumeric content of current documents has already been captured electronically through word processing or electronic publishing systems, so only the associated images would be required.

While this is the first major commercial application of CD ROM technology, the image content of the existing database documents is nonexistent. Image content will increase over time as scanning technology improves and becomes more cost-effective.

The characteristics of this application are:

- The information base may be changed periodically (revisions) and/or may be added to (journal archives).

- If planned for, the alphanumeric content of the information base can be electronically captured during its creation.

The number of copies required for such an application will be relatively high because of the more general nature of the material's contents, but the value of the contents will be relatively low, since reasonably priced and functional alternatives are available in printed form.

- The image content may range from low to high.

- The major added value of the technology will be the ease of search and retrieval.

Application Three: Catalog Distribution

. . . imaging systems tend to do some processing in special hardware for speed and some in the host computer.

Catalogs are widely used to distribute current sales information to consumers. They vary widely in their revision rate but typically include many images. Most have wide distribution (many copies and involve large production and distribution costs. They are also image-intensive, usually having many color and black-and-white photographs, with layout and style being important to the sales appeal.

Because of the high use of color, a combination of video and digital CD ROM could be a good medium for catalog distribution. Many catalogs, particularly technical ones, use only line drawings and are heavily used as reference material. Here digital images are most appropriate and a good search and retrieval capability is necessary. Because of the revision frequency, a combination of CD ROM for the product content information and magnetic media for pricing and availability updates may be appropriate.

The characteristics of this application are:

- The information base must be updated fairly frequently.

- If properly planned, all the content information, text, pictures, and index could be captured electronically during the preparation process.

243

- Many copies would be required. The value of the contents would be only moderately high for retail applications but could be quite high for technical catalogs.

- The image content of the information database would vary from moderate to high.

- In some cases the search and retrieval capability would be very important.

Application Criteria

The above examples clearly indicate that certain criteria are important in deciding which applications are appropriate for CD ROM technology, particularly where images are involved. As we will see subsequently, image scanning and processing technology also is affected by these criteria. In summary, the important criteria appear to be:

- Frequency of update of the information database.

- Suitability of the content for electronic capture during preparation.

- Number of copies needed to meet the market demand.

- Value of the information content to the user, as measured by the cost and availability of alternative sources.

- The relative content of images in the information database, which could range from 0 to 100 percent.

- The degree of sophisticated search and retrieval required by the user.

Looking at the types of applications described above makes it obvious that much of the information database to be distributed either already exists in electronic form suitable for processing or could be put in that form relatively easily. However, for a very significant portion of the information three problems remain: some does not exist in electronic text form (historical documents or manually typed hard copy, for example); much of the existing textual information, even if prepared electronically, includes pictures or diagrams; and some information consists only of pictures or line art.

Image information in a database can add a great deal to the comprehension of the user. Complex concepts often can be explained better through a combination of text and graphics, and some concepts cannot be understood without a picture or diagram. If CD ROM-based information systems are to be effective, the image and text input problems have to be solved from both a technological and a procedural perspective.

Image Scanning and Processing Technology

Image scanning and processing consists of five basic elements:

- Image capture
- Data manipulation
- Storage and retrieval
- Display
- Printing

Capturing an image is the process of converting an optically focused image into a digital representation suitable for computer processing. Images can then be manipulated to put them in a form desired for the ultimate application. Storage and retrieval are used to preserve the image files for future use. Display and printing are used during manipulation and for applications.

Imaging technology has progressed significantly over the past few years in terms of both performance and lower cost. Scanners and image processing hardware and software can be found to fit most applications. While improvements will continue to be made, the technology is at a point where it can be applied to information database creation in a variety of ways. The following sections describe the scanning process, types of scanners, and image processing functions.

The Scanning Process

Images exist as light reflected off a physical object. This light contains information about color and intensity. To convert this to electronic form requires the use of a photoreceptor device which creates an electrical signal proportional to the intensity of the light falling on it. Light from the object is optically focused on the photoreceptor, which breaks it into a mosaic of dots called picture elements (Pels). Generally, the more the density of picture elements (resolution), the better the image quality; but data storage and processing requirements increase with the square of the resolution. Resolutions of 200 to 400 dots per inch (dpi) are typical for document storage systems.

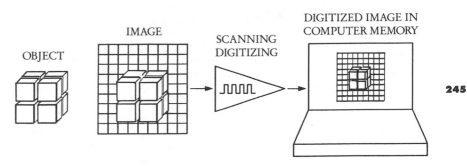

Figure 1. The image scanning process

. . . once a collection of information has been created in one place, isn't it logical to expect that many other people with similar interests, but in different locations, would like access to that information?

The analog signal from the photoreceptor is converted to digital form by an analog-to-digital converter. The analog signal for each Pel contains gray-scale information since it is a function of the light intensity, ranging from white (full intensity) to black (no light). The analog-to-digital converter captures this gray-scale information by sampling the analog signal and describing it as one of a number of levels of intensity. Usually from 4 to 8 bits of data are created for each Pel, representing from 16 to 256 levels of gray, respectively.

After it has been digitized, the information is ready to be processed like any other digital data. It represents the original image in what is called *bit-mapped* or *raster* form, which appear as a series of dots.

The photoreceptor is usually a charge coupled device (CCD) array, which consists of a fixed number of elements and is usually scanned across the image plane in discrete steps. Thus, the resolution must always be defined with respect to the object size. For example, a CCD linear array consisting of 1728 elements captures 203 dpi over 8½ inches, usually rounded to 200 dpi. If the array is moved incrementally 2200 times over the image plane, it would provide 200 x 200 dpi over an 8½-by-11-inch document focused on the image plane. Typical CCD arrays contain 1728, 2048, 3456, or 4096 elements, representing 200, 240, 400, and 480 dpi respectively. Mathematical scaling can also be used to achieve specific resolution from a given array size. Two-dimensional CCD arrays are also available, but they are economically limited to about 512 to 1024 elements, thereby limiting their resolution. The implication of the size of the resulting image file is discussed later.

Scanner Designs

Image scanners suitable for document processing consist of three basic types: camera-based, flatbed, and paper feed. Each has its advantages and disadvantages, but virtually any application need can be met using one type or another.

Camera-Based Systems

Camera technology was among the first to be exploited for doument scanning. The camera lens focuses the image of the object on the image plane where the film would normally be in a 35-mm camera. In an electronic digitizing camera (EDC) the film is replaced by a CCD array which is moved across the image plane by a stepper motor or a servo-drive system under the control of the host computer. As the CCD is moved in increments, information from each element is sampled to be digitized.

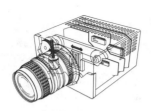

Figure2. A digitizing camera

The electronic functions usually performed in an EDC include the servomechanism or stepper motor control, CCD sampling, analog-to-digital conversion, and control of communications to the host computer. EDC functions such as the scan area and speed of scan are typically under the control of the host computer. Scan times can run from as short as a half second to a few minutes. Often the time needed to complete a scan is limited by the ability of the host computer to accept the data into memory.

The major advantage of an EDC is its application flexibility. Since most EDCs are mounted on a camera copystand in use, camera operation is emulated. Lens selection can be made to match the application, and light intensity can be adjusted as required. Moving the EDC closer to the object increases the resolution (for smaller objects) and moving it farther away decreases resolution. Typical resolutions range from maximums of 2000 dpi over an area 2 by 3 inches to 200 dpi over 17 by 22 inches. EDC systems, because of the copystand mounting, tend to be somewhat more expensive than the fixed systems discussed later and are more obtrusive because of their size and exposed lights. However, the flexibility is often required in document storage applications because of object size difference and the need to capture books or other types of manuscripts.

Flatbed Systems

Flatbed scanners derive from office copier technology, where the document is placed in a fixed position on a glass plate and an optical path is scanned across the document face. This allows precise positioning of the document and allows objects such as books or small three-dimensional objects to be scanned.

Figure 3. Flatbed scanner design

During scanning, a light is moved across the document face. Attached to the light bar is a mirror that reflects the incident light to a second mirror which moves at a slower speed to keep the optical path to the fixed sensor constant over the entire scan. The light/mirror combination is moved by a stepper motor, with the movement synchronized to the extraction of data from the CCD array.

247

A flatbed scanner fixes the resolution over a certain maximum size document area. Resolutions are changed only by changing the way the data is sampled or by scaling the resolution up or down electronically. The flexibility to move the scanner closer to the object as in an EDC is lost, although movable optics are possible as in a reduction copier. The fixed optics tend to simplify the design and keep costs down so that a flatbed scanner is less costly than an EDC and much smaller, typically having a footprint about the size of an office typewriter and being about 5 inches high. As in a copier, paper feed mechanisms can be adapted to flatbed scanners to move successive sheets onto the glass plate. However, the document stays fixed during the scan.

Typical scanning resolutions are 400, 300, 240, and 200 dpi. The base resolution is determined by the number of elements in the CCD array. If a scanner has multiple resolution choices, it is done by electronic scaling.

Scanning speeds range from a second or so to 30 seconds, again, often dependent on the data transfer rate to the computer. From 4 to 8 bits of gray-scale information for each Pel (16 to 256 levels of gray) are usually generated.

Paper-Moving Systems

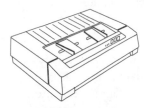

Figure 4. Paper-feed scanner

An alternative approach, derived from facsimile technology, is to keep the optical path fixed and to move the document across the light bar and mirror.

This results in an even simpler mechanism and lower cost, but with somewhat less performance. There can be problems in paper skewing or jamming during movement, and only single sheets may be scanned. Other performance characteristics are similar to those of flatbed scanners.

Scanning-System Costs

The costs of a scanner vary widely, depending on its performance characteristics. Very high speed scanners with high-speed paper-handling mechanisms can cost $25,000 and more. They also require high-performance computer systems, databases, and large mass storage. Generally, camera-based scanners run from about $10,000 to $25,000; flatbed scanners from $2500 to $7500; and paper-feed scanners from $1500 to $7500. Pricing can vary widely, based on speed and paper-handling mechanisms.

Image Processing Technology

Image processing can vary from simple procedures to complex operations used for space-photo enhancement. Many image-processing operations are computation-intensive because of the large number of bits in an image file. Therefore, imaging systems tend to do some processing in special hardware for speed and some in the host computer. This section discusses some of the image processing functions pertinent to document storage.

Image Capture Functions

Capturing the document page image through the scanning process is the first step in creating an image file. Basic control of the scanner is included in this, but three other functions are important.

Thresholding

An image file with 4 to 8 bits of gray-scale information can contain millions of bytes of information. While gray scale may be important in some applications such as publishing or medical imaging, it can usually be discarded in document storage systems. If the document contains only two-tone material such as text or line drawings, a process called thresholding can be used.

In thresholding, a particular shade of gray is selected, either manually or automatically by the computer, and all Pels lighter than that shade of gray are set to white and all darker are set to black. Then the gray-scale information may be discarded and each Pel will be represented by only one bit of information. This process is usually carried out in hardware in the scanner or computer interface to minimize the information that has to be processed by the computer.

Halftoning

If the document being scanned has considerable gray-scale information, such as a photograph, a process called halftoning may be used. This is the same process used by newspapers and magazines to create the impression of gray scale even though printing is essentially a monochromatic process (although multiple single colors may be used).

In halftoning, the gray-scale information is processed to create a higher-level pattern of dots which vary in size and placement. Each dot consists of a number of Pels. The larger the dots in an area, the darker the area looks, and vice versa. The human eye and brain integrate these dots and perceive shades of gray, but each Pel consists of only one bit of information: black or white.

Image information in a database can add a great deal to the comprehension of the user.

Windowing

A scanner normally captures the full image of the object as it is focused on the image plane. However, it is frequently useful to capture only a portion of the image. For example, a page may consist of text and a picture. If the page is scanned using thresholding the picture will not look good; it may not even be recognizable. On the other hand, if halftoning is used the text will not be sharp and clear. With windowing, a first scan of the entire page is made using thresholding. Then a window is placed around the photograph and a second scan is made using halftoning. The resulting image file combines both types of information to result in a faithful reproduction of the page.

Image Processing Functions

Once an image has been captured and exists as a file in memory, various things can be done to it. Those that are pertinent to document storage are discussed below.

Scaling

Images of a particular size can be scaled up or down in size by adding or removing Pels. Usually this is done by setting the scaling ratio in the X or Y axis on the host computer or creating a window on the display screen and having the computer scale the image to fit the window. There is a reduction in resolution as images are scaled down and Pels are discarded. Also, some distortion is apparent as images are scaled up, since interpolation is used to decide whether a Pel to be inserted should be black or white. However, for text or line drawings, reasonable scaling ratios work quite well. Scaling of halftones does not work as well since the halftoning algorithm and the scaling algorithm interact to create interference patterns in the resulting image. For document storage, scaling is usually used to change resolutions to match an output device; for example, to convert a 200-dpi image file to a lower resolution for a 100-dpi display.

Compression

An image file with 8 bits of gray-scale information (256 shades of gray) at 200 dpi over an 8½-by-11-inch document contains approximately 3.8 million bytes of information. At 400 dpi it would contain over 15 million bytes. Even with thresholding or halftoning to get rid of the gray-scale data, the files would be about 475,000 bytes and 1.9 million bytes, respectively. Data compression can be used to reduce the size of these files.

The most common data compression technique is based on CCITT Group 3 facsimile standards and is called run-length encoding. Rather then using each individual Pel, a line of Pels is processed and the number of continuous white or black Pels is encoded in the file. Thus, files with large areas of black or white can achieve significant compression. Compression ratios of 5:1 to 10:1 are typical for documents containing text or line drawings.

Because of their nature, little compression is possible with halftones. Other, more advanced, compression techniques are available, but they tend to be more computation-intensive and are more sensitive to data errors. They will see considerable application in the future, however.

Optical Character Recognition

Text is usually represented in computer systems by a coding system called ASCII code, which represents each character by an 8-bit (or 1-byte) code. This is a very economical way of representing characters in terms of storage and permits computer manipulation of the code. This is particularly important for document storage and retrieval systems, since the text can easily be searched for specific words or phrases for retrieval purposes. This cannot be done with images of text. Also, images of a text character typically take about 100 times as much space as an ASCII character, depending on the size of the character image. A technique does exist which will convert character images to ASCII characters; it is known as optical character recognition, or OCR.

One of the most important considerations in image databases is the display quality, since most files are retrieved for viewing; quality control is very important during the process of building the database.

Various algorithms exist to convert images to text. In the process, the character images are first separated into individual images, then each is analyzed against a set of known characteristics. Based on this analysis, a new file is created with the equivalent ASCII codes. Error rates typically are under 1 percent and the speed is usually much faster than a secretary could type the same material. The software is usually pretaught to recognize specific character sets, where a character set is a specific type font style and size. For example, Courier 10 is a style of type often found in the office; it is a 10-pitch type (10 characters to the inch). Each style and size represents a different character set. Technology is currently becoming available which permits a wider variety of text sizes and types to be recognized, which will permit OCR to be more widely used in document database applications.

Raster-to-Vector Conversion

A similar approach can be taken with line drawings. Computer aided design (CAD) systems use a mathematical description of drawings called vectors. Lines are described mathematically (line coordinates, curve radius, etc.) rather than as bit-mapped images. The resulting file is much smaller than the corresponding image file. Software is available which will convert a bit-mapped image file to a vector file. With current technology, considerable cleanup on the resulting vector file is necessary and the technique has not been applied to document storage systems. However, raster-to-vector conversion should see future application as the technology improves and is more widely applied.

Imaging System Considerations

Individual elements of imaging technology have been discussed, but there are a number of system considerations that affect how they are applied. A document storage and retrieval system consists of a number of elements, as shown in Figure 5. A retrieval-only system would consist of all of the elements except the scanner.

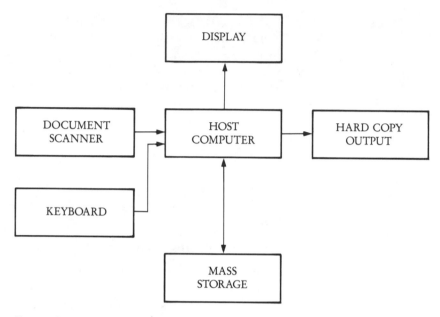

Figure 5. Document storage and retrieval system

There are important considerations regarding mass storage, display, and output when images are included as a part of the system. In addition, the basic resolution of the captured image is important.

Image Resolution

As discussed previously, the size of an image file goes up with the square of the resolution. Therefore, it is important not to use a resolution higher than is necessary for the application. A resolution of 200 dpi appears to be fine for normal office type size, which ranges from about 6 to 10 points. However, technical journal articles often have type which goes down to 4 points for footnotes, subscripts, and superscripts. For this size type, 300 dpi is more appropriate. The size of the resulting image files suggests that data compression techniques and optical disc storage will be very important considerations in system design. In fact, a large image database is not practical without optical storage; and CD ROM technology is going to open whole new areas of database distribution.

Display Technology

Information databases, and the distribution of these databases in particular, will be revolutionized by the ready availability of optical disc technology . . .

One of the most important considerations in image databases is the display quality, since most files are retrieved for viewing; quality control is very important during the process of building the database. Unfortunately, display technology has not kept pace with other associated technologies. High-resolution displays (greater than 100 dpi, full page) tend to be quite expensive. This is expected to change over the next several years as the emphasis on graphics at the personal computer level continues.

For retrieval purposes, displays of 100-150 dpi are often satisfactory, since zooming and scrolling can be used. However, a display of 200-300 dpi would be much better from the user's point of view—if the cost was low enough. For quality control, a full page at 200-300 dpi is a requirement.

Because of the cost of building an image database, it is very important to view the image as it was captured before storing it on the disc. The cost of a high-resolution display can often be justified for an image input station because it is a highly specialized and expensive system. Displays of 100 dpi currently cost about $2000, while higher-resolution displays can cost $5000 and more.

Mass Storage

With the availability of CD ROM and WORM (write once, read many) optical discs, mass storage is becoming far less of a problem for image databases. WORM discs are currently being used for large interactive image databases, and CD ROM will become the chosen medium for database distribution. With a compressed 8½-by-11 image file taking from 50,000 to 100,000 bytes at 200 dpi and 190,000 to 280,000 bytes at 400 dpi, storage is a significant element in system design.

Most current systems use magnetic disks for interim storage during the capture process and quality control. This information is then transferred to WORM discs directly or to magnetic tape for processing onto CD ROM.

Summary

The technologies associated with image scanning, image processing and mass storage are all progressing rapidly in terms of improved cost performance. One area where significant changes will occur in the future is page decomposition. Optical character recognition software and raster to vector conversion software will reach the point in a few years' time where a document page consisting of text, line drawings, and pictures can be separated into four files: a text file created by optical character recognition, a vector file of the line drawing created by raster to vector conversion, a halftone file of the picture, and an image file of anything else that could not be converted.

By keeping track of where on the page the files came from, the page could be electronically reconstituted for viewing or printing. This will provide the ultimate in data compression and will open the way for very large document databases. In the meantime, optical disc technology has opened the door to a whole host of new applications for image databases.

About the Author

James P. McNaul is vice-president for strategic planning of DataCopy Corporation. Dr. McNaul served as director of product marketing for the Digital Telephone System Division of Harris Corporation from 1982 until joining DataCopy in 1983. Prior to that he was manager of marketing and planning for Integrated Office Systems Division of Anderson Jacobson, Inc., a telecommunications company, from 1980 to 1982. Dr. McNaul was responsible for program planning and technology advancement of electronic transfer systems for the Western Development Laboratory of Ford Aerospace and Communications Corporation from 1977 to 1980.

DataCopy Corporation
1215 Terra Bella Avenue
Mountain View, CA 94043
(415)965-7900

Compressing and Digitizing Images

by
Truett Lee Smith

The storage capacity afforded by the present level of CD ROM technology seems effectively infinite, and the capacities yet to come are difficult to comprehend. Nevertheless, the amount of information being generated, organized, and stored by our society is already capable of straining those capacities. In order to cope with the information demands of the future, we will have to improve on the process of simply copying information onto these new media. This section examines the means by which a lot of data can be made to fit into a small amount of storage space. In the section entitled "Image Storage and Retrieval Systems," the methods by which very large amounts of data can be made accessible are described. Then the discussion turns to the rather technical problem of how to display the stored images.

What's in a Datum?

What do you do when faced with a lot of data that just has to be stored in a small amount of space? First, you check to see if it is all really necessary. Some data is priceless; but some is not worth the trouble. How do you tell the difference?

During the 1930s a bright fellow named Claude Shannon derived an exact recipe for determining how much information is in a set of data. Without all the mathematical details, it said simply that the amount of information contained in a collection of data is a function of the predictability of its parts. The more predictable they are, the less information they contain.

Data Compression Techniques

There are a variety of methods available to compress data. The appropriate method in a given situation is influenced by the type of data, the use to which it is to be put, and the storage medium. Three of the better-known techniques—entropy reduction, redundancy reduction, and feature classification—are explained here.[1]

Entropy reduction. Entropy reduction methods compress data by replacing repetitive items with a short code; but unless you know the code, the result will appear to be a random garble.[2]

Perhaps the best known method of text compression has been through the application of Huffman codes.[3] In general, a Huffman code is built as follows.

256

Assume that the data to be compressed is expressed as a series of "symbols" from an alphabet. The first step is to count how many times each symbol in the alphabet occurs in the data. Next, using the counts obtained, a unique variable-length bit sequence is chosen to substitute for each symbol, resulting in a sequence for the data that is as short as possible.

The symbols converted to bit sequences can be letters in the English alphabet, decimal digits, colors, species names, zip codes, or whatever. The nice thing about the Huffman algorithm is that it can be applied to any linear sequence of well-defined symbols. One problem with the pure Huffman algorithm is that it does not preserve lexicographic order. That is, if the letters of the English alphabet are the symbols to be converted, then the resulting bit sequences for words do not remain in lexicographic order: They cannot be sorted without first converting them back to letters. This problem can be overcome by using a modification of the method called the Hu-Tucker algorithm.[4]

If you are planning to compress many sets of data, then you have the choice of using a single Huffman code for all the data using a different one for each set. In addition, a Huffman code can be constructed with "memory," that is, the bit sequence specified for a symbol can depend on which symbol was previously converted.

The most important drawback of Huffman codes is that the code itself—the specification of the bit sequence for each symbol—must be stored as part of the compressed data. This reduces the effectiveness of the compression method. One solution is to use a fixed, standard code based on the expected probability of each symbol occurring in the data.

Redundancy reduction.   Even in natural written languages the concept of redundancy reduction appears in the guise of abbreviations and contractions. To be more precise, redundancy can be reduced when a subsequence of the data is repeated (such as several occurrences of the same word or expression in a text). In such a case, it is only necessary to record the subsequence and the times of its occurrence in the data. If the repetitions are always contiguous then the times can be reduced to just a repetition count or "run length." This method takes its simplest form when the data takes on only two values. To record such "binary" data, it is only necessary to record the run lengths.

Redundancy can also be reduced by eliminating data which is observed in all cases. An example of this occurs when text files are stored in ASCII characters, 1 byte (8 bits) per character. Only the low-order 7 bits of each byte are actually used to store the character, thus a 12.5 percent saving in storage can be achieved by using only 7 bits to store each character.

257

A more common method for reducing redundancy in text files is the replacement of repeated characters by a special code. The TAB character is often used for such a purpose.

A . . . common method for reducing redundancy in text files is the replacement of repeated characters by a special code.

Feature extraction.   Feature extraction has been less commonly used because it almost always requires the use of some sort of pattern recognition. Pattern recognition is not very efficient when the data is "noisy," that is, when the patterns to be recognized are not obvious and clear.

One method that is often applied to text files is the replacement of each word by a numerical code from a previously constructed dictionary. All the words in the file should appear in the dictionary for this to be truly useful.

Chromatographic data can be reduced to a set of numbers giving the location, height, and area of each peak in the data. A spectrogram can be reduced to a tabulation of the observed spectral lines and their observed intensities.

One form of feature extraction that applies only to certain kinds of image data is OCR (optical character recognition), in which the features to be extracted are the text characters and their locations within the image. Many techniques have been developed for OCR and some of them can be very accurate, though such accuracy is usually achieved at a significant cost in required computation. It should be noted that the major difficulty in OCR is not that of detecting the features but, rather, their classification or identification.

Image Compression

Restrict your attention now to the problem of compressing image data only. This restricted problem is generally made more difficult by the requirement that it be possible to reconstruct the image from the compressed form without losing any "important" elements of the original image.

Two steps are involved in compressing an image. First a raster or grid of points, usually called *pixels* (picture elements), is defined on the area of the image. In most cases the raster is a rectangular array of pixels. The second step is to assign a value to each pixel which represents the color or brightness of the image at the location of that pixel. If the pixels can take on only two values, such as black and white, then the raster of pixels is called a binary image.

General methods.   There are at least three ways of compressing a rasterized image: background elimination, Fourier analysis, and pixel runlength encoding.

If only a small proportion of the pixels in the raster are different from the background value (white, for our purposes) then the image may be reduced to the values and locations of those pixels. The main problem with this technique is that the necessary assumption is rarely true for the kinds of images one usually wants to store.

A second method, which is far less dependent upon the distribution of various pixel values in the image, is Fourier analysis, which reduces the image to its spatial frequencies. The only reason this method is even feasible is the result of the development during the 1960s of the Fast Fourier Transform (FFT), which greatly reduced the amount of computation required. Unfortunately, the computation needed is still significant for an image which has been rasterized at a useful resolution. Even worse, it is all floating-point computation, which is the most time-consuming.

In the event that the image can be converted to a binary raster, a much simpler method can be used. If the rasterization was at a high enough resolution, then the pixels will tend to be in contiguous groups of black or white areas in the image. Thus, a run-length encoding can be used along either the rows or columns of the raster. (The rows are almost always used for this encoding.)

The CCITT Facsimile Standards.   During the past twenty years the CCITT (Consultative Committee on International Telephone and Telegraphy) has established standards for the transmission of facsimile images. Four different standards exist, each of which is called a Group. Thus, there are Group 1, 2, 3, and 4 facsimile devices. Machines in the first two groups were analog devices, which took several minutes to send a complete image. With the advent of the Group 3 standard the image was converted to digital data and a method of compression was introduced into the standard. In fact, two possible ways to compress the image data were established: the modified Huffman and modified READ algorithms.[5]

One-dimensional modified Huffman. The standard one-dimensional compression scheme takes two steps. First, the pixels along each row of the image raster are converted by a run-length encoding. Then a standard Huffman code is used to convert the run lengths into variable-length bit strings. The Huffman code used is a fixed one whose bit strings are specified in the international standard, so that they do not need to be transmitted with the image data. The sequence of bits resulting from an average binary image is usually from 10 to 20 percent as big as the image itself.

Two-dimensional modified READ. Some Group 3 machines are capable of handling a more complicated algorithm known as the modified READ (relative element address designate) method. This algorithm involves the use of a "k-factor" to allow it to recover from errors in transmission. Normally, the value of k is between 2 and 7, though in principle it can be infinite (which in fact it is in Group 4 machines).

Start by using the modified Huffman algorithm on the first row or scan line of the binary image. Then the next k-1 lines are encoded using a method that notes the differences between the line being encoded and the immediately preceding line. After k lines have been encoded in this way, the algorithm starts over again by encoding a line using the one-dimensional algorithm followed by k-1 lines using the two-dimensional line-difference technique. In this way the facsimile machine is given enough information to recover from transmission errors which can cause it to lose track of where each variable-length line begins. Images compressed in this way are usually 6 to 12 percent as large as the original.

The Group 4 standard. In 1984 The CCITT established another standard for image compression on facsimile machines. It makes two important assumptions:

o In the future, the transmission system itself will handle error correction and detection.

o It is increasingly desirable to be able to transmit a document which is a mixture of ASCII text, binary image data, and some type of primitive graphics of the vector or stroke type.[6]

Once the facsimile machine itself does not have to worry about error handling during transmission (a storage and retrieval system can be presumed not to suffer from the errors of transmission), it becomes possible to achieve a greater compression of the image. So the Group 4 standard uses only the two-dimensional encoding and starts by assuming that a row of all white pixels precedes the first scan line. Thus, k becomes infinite. In addition, the bit strings representing the end of a line can be eliminated, since the system should never lose track of where the lines begin within the compressed data. By these means, the compressed images can be reduced to about 3 to 10 percent of the size of the original.

In order to allow for the transmission of mixed types of documents, the CCITT divided Group 4 facsimile devices into three classes which have varying capabilities for handling what are called Basic Teletext Services. A Class I machine can handle only image data. Class II machines can handle most text functions, including the standard printer control commands such as varying line spacing, variable pitch, underlining, and bold or italic characters. Even greater flexibility is offered by a Class III machine, which can handle the basic teletext and NAPLPS (North American Presentation Level Protocol Syntax) capabilities. These allow for the definition of character sets or fonts and line-drawing functions.

Image Storage and Retrieval Systems

For a new technology to be successful, its use must be incorporated into an overall system design that solves a significant problem in a way that takes advantage of the unique properties of that technology. Thus, to make CD ROM a successful part of an image storage and retrieval system, the system design must take into account the functional, mechanical, and ergonomic factors affecting the process of image or document archival; and the system must take advantage of the properties which are unique to CD ROM.

Functional Elements of a System Design

There are six basic functional elements in the design of a system for archiving documents or storing and retrieving images: capture, manipulation, storage, retrieval, transmission, and display. Each of these is briefly described in the following paragraphs.

Capture.   Getting an image converted into a set of digital data stored on a computer or similar device requires that three things be done. First, the paper holding the image must be moved into position to be scanned. This can be done either manually or with some kind of automatic feeder device. Second, some type of optical system is usually required to form the image of the document onto the photodetection system. Finally, the photodetector converts the light intensity into a digital signal which can be stored.

Manipulation.   The storage of an image in digital form offers the possibility that it can be edited or modified prior to the final storage in an unalterable form. This step can also be used for quality control when large numbers of documents are being archived, as provision must be made for recapturing images which were captured in an unsatisfactory form. Image manipulation capabilities are generally included only in more expensive or advanced systems.

For a new technology to be successful, its use must be incorporated into an overall system design that solves a significant problem in a way that takes advantage of the unique properties of that technology.

Storage. Once an image has been captured and modified to be in its final form, its digital record must be transferred to the storage medium itself. In the case of CD ROM, there are two steps. First, a master disc must be created which can be used in the process of duplicating the many copies of the data that are to be distributed. Second, the copies themselves are made.

Retrieval. Sooner or later it is desirable to retrieve the digital data defining an image from the storage medium. Part of this process involves finding where it has been stored. Large standalone image storage systems often resort to the use of a general-purpose database management system (DBMS), with its separately maintained index files, in order to do this, especially when the images to be retrieved are on more than one disc.

Using CD ROMs to distribute the data adds a complication to the retrieval problem. It becomes necessary to distribute the index information together with the image data on the same CD ROM. Also, it becomes desirable for the format of the indexing information to be such that any of a variety of DBMS software packages can access and use it for retrieving the images on the CD ROM.

Transmission. If the document archival system is part of a network or if the archive is to be at a single geographic location, then a system must be established for transmitting the image data to the location at which it is to be displayed or printed. As mentioned earlier, the latest image compression standards assume that the transmission system will be responsible for the error correction and detection.

A choice still exists, however, in that the transmission can either be in compressed or expanded form. Sending an expanded image can take up a lot of the transmission systems's resources (an 8.5-by-11-inch page can take several megabytes at higher resolutions). But the transmission of compressed images over the system requires that each possible destination be equipped with the hardware or software needed to expand the compressed data. In fact, as the section titled "Digitizing Images" will show, this dichotomy is even more complicated due to conversion problems that result from the use of different display devices.

Display. All of the preceding parts of a system are designed to facilitate the presentation of the image to the user. The technical problems associated with displaying and printing rasterized images are so similar that they may be considered the same in a system design. The main problem (which is discussed in greater detail in "Digitizing Images") is that of converting the images to a displayable form which takes into account the differences in resolution, aspect ratio, and pixel geometry of the various kinds of display devices that are likely to be used.

262

Mechanical Factors in System Design: Scanners

The mechanical differences between various designs of an image storage and retrieval system lie almost entirely in the differences between the three major approaches to the process of capturing the image: camera systems, flatbed systems, and document feeder systems.

Camera systems. A camera system is basically a video image capture system which has been modified to operate at a much higher resolution than a standard video camera. In such a system it is necessary for the document to be manually positioned, but it is also possible to capture images of three-dimensional objects. A major problem with this type of system is that the spatial resolution of the image depends on the size of the image being captured. This is because the angular resolution of the camera remains constant, requiring the same number of pixels to represent both large and small documents.

Flatbed scanner systems. An alternative approach is to use a mechanical arrangement similar to that of some photocopying machines. In such a system, the document is laid on a horizontal plate of glass, beneath which the scanning and illumination system moves. This permits the spatial resolution to be independent of the size of the document (assuming the flatbed is big enough) but it still requires that the document be positioned by hand.

Sheet feeder systems. Finally, the system designer can choose to incorporate a sheet feeder system that passes the document to be captured past a stationary scanning device, usually a linear CCD (charge coupled device) array. This is an excellent system for capturing a large number of documents. Much less human intervention is required, but at the cost of being totally unable to scan three-dimensional objects or pages from bound printed materials.

Standalone or Peripheral?

Perhaps the most important decision facing the system designer is whether to build a dedicated standalone image archival system or to design a set of peripheral devices that, when connected to an existing host processor, make up such a system.

The choice of a dedicated system is very attractive because it allows the system to be precisely designed to meet the requirements for the task it is to perform. Unfortunately, there is a tendency when designing such a system to make its parts so intricately interdependent that the obsolescence or even failure of even a single component can render the entire system useless. Even when the parts can be acquired separately, they tend to be more specialized and therefore more expensive. It is questionable whether the increased capital cost of a dedicated system can be justified by any difference in performance that it may show over systems based on peripheral devices.

Attaching peripheral devices to a host processor has its own problems. The designer must deal with the fact that the user is quite likely to attach all sorts of things to the processor, some of which may conflict with the document archival peripherals. Thus, such devices must be made to maintain a low profile with respect to the environment provided by the host processor. A lack of widely accepted standards for some types of peripherals makes this very difficult.

Having considered the problems of capturing and storing images in a document archival system, the rather technical problem of how to display them on different kinds of display and print devices still remains to be discussed. These problems are considered in the next section.

Digitizing Images

The world of visual imagery, even when limited to what can appear on a written document, is filled with immense variety and almost infinite detail. Human beings can attach significance to even the smallest details in an image. Yet a document archival system must attempt to capture all the significant elements of a document without requiring an infinite amount of storage.

Normally this goal is attained by first converting the continuously variable, finely detailed image into a discrete form which can be stored more economically. Sadly, any method of converting an image to a discrete form can cause undesirable changes in the image. Such changes are known as "quantization effects" and have been studied extensively, since they occur whenever an analog signal is converted to digital form.

The quantization effects which an image archival system is likely to encounter are discussed here in terms of three broad subject areas: resolution, pixel geometry, and scaling.

263

Resolution

As mentioned earlier, the process of converting an image into a discrete form usually involves the creation of a raster: a rectangular array of pixels which covers the area of the image and whose values make up the data defining the discrete image. Perhaps the most important property of a raster is its resolution, or interpixel spacing. An equivalent definition of resolution is how many pixels it takes to cover an image of a specified size.

Resolution standards.   If it is desirable to be able to transfer images between image archival systems (a CD ROM-based system must transfer them to many systems to be economically feasible), then the different systems should assume that the images have been captured at an agreed-upon or standard resolution. What kinds of standard resolutions are there?

Three sets of commonly used interpixel spacings have arisen over the past few years. Each is usually specified in terms of the number of pixels per inch, also called dots per inch (dpi).

First are the resolutions specified in the international facsimile standards. These are multiples of 100 dpi, with 200 dpi being the most popular. Another set of resolutions is used by the phototypesetting industry. Multiples of 60 dpi are used in this case. The most interesting resolutions in this set are 240 and 300 dpi, which are commonly used by laser printers. Finally, there are the resolutions used by dot matrix printers, which are usually multiples of 72 dpi.

As a general rule, the higher the resolution of the discrete form of an image, the more it will look like the original. This holds true whether or not the pixels are restricted to binary (black-and-white) values. The CCITT standards suggest that 200 dpi is sufficient for the transmission of general business correspondence. However, this puts a limit on how small a printed font can be and still be readable after transmission. Using the point scale used by typesetters (1 point equals 1/72 inch), the limit is reached by fonts whose height is about 6 points (this text is 10½ point).

If technical printed matter, with its subscripts, superscripts, and diacritical markings, is to be archived, then a higher resolution needs to be used. Some specialized types of images, such as fingerprints, require higher resolutions in order for the transmitted result to be of any use. For these and

The resolution required to preserve a feature in an image is directly proportional to the highest spatial frequency of that feature.

264

other reasons, the Group 4 facsimile standards have been written in such a way as to encourage a migration to resolutions of 300 and 400 dpi. A resolution of 300 dpi is becoming very popular because almost all laser printers operate at that value. The major drawback to a higher resolution is the increased storage required, which is proportional to the square of the resolution. Doubling the linear interpixel spacing quadruples the storage required (this relationship is not greatly altered by compression, either). At a resolution of 200 dpi, both vertically and horizontally, an 8.5-by-11-inch page requires about half a megabyte to store a binary image. The same image at 400 dpi would require almost 2 megabytes for the uncompressed image. The storage requirements for compressed images are proportional.

Spatial frequency and resolution.   Higher resolutions are desirable because they permit the resulting digital images to preserve more of the detail that was in the original image. The question might be asked, Just how much detail is preserved by a given resolution? The answer is given by what is known as the Nyquist limit, which in its simplest form says that the resolution required to preserve a feature in an image is directly proportional to the highest spatial frequency of that feature. In fact, the resolution, in dots per inch, has to be at least twice the spatial frequency, in cycles per inch (sometimes called lines per inch, since a resolvable line is equivalent to one cycle of spatial frequency).

So what is spatial resolution? Basically, it is a measure of how often the intensity (the lightness or darkness) of the image changes in a given distance. Consider two extreme examples. An image which is either entirely black or entirely white has a spatial frequency of zero; it does not take any resolution at all to store images like that. However, a checkerboard pattern of alternating black and white pixels has a high spatial frequency, equal to one-half the resolution; so a checkerboard at 200 dpi has horizontal and vertical spatial frequencies of 100 lines per inch.

Note should be taken of the fact that a spatial frequency has a "direction" in addition to the wavelength and amplitude we normally associate with frequencies. This says something important about rectangular pixel arrays. It says that they tend to preserve horizontal and vertical spatial frequencies in preference to those in a diagonal direction. Along a diagonal, the pixels are 40 percent farther apart. Thus, the maximum spatial frequency preserved along a diagonal is only 70 percent as great as that preserved in a vertical or horizontal direction. Hexagonal pixel arrays are far less discriminating about directionality, but tradition has locked us into an orthogonal (right-angled) world.

Effects of skewing.　Even when the features of interest are concentrated in the vertical and horizontal spatial frequencies, degradation can occur due to mechanical factors in the image capture system.

An almost unavoidable problem is positioning the document to be scanned at a skew (small rotation) with respect to the rectangular pixel area that results from the scanning process. This can happen whether the positioning is manual or automatic. As a result, at least three things happen.

First of all, straight lines are no longer really straight, even if they are supposed to be entirely vertical or horizontal. They begin to suffer the stairstep effects usually suffered by diagonal lines. The effect gets worse as the resolution goes down, but it occurs at all resolutions.

Second, the appearance of small print fonts is degraded, because the apparent height of a line of print varies along its length. This happens because the line of print ends up at an angle to the pixel array. Thus, the number of horizontal scan lines crossed by the vertical extent of a character can vary as a function of its position along the line of print. This effect gets worse as the print gets smaller.

Finally, it affects the compression efficiency of the two-dimensional modified READ image compression algorithm. This algorithm is designed to take advantage of the fact that successive scan lines of most material are almost identical. If the image has been slightly rotated, though, this assumption becomes no longer true. Thus, the number of bits needed to encode the differences between successive lines increases and the compressed image gets larger in relation to the original image.

Pixel Geometry

Pixels are not the simple things we might at first assume. They tend to be thought of as dots, sort of like a period in print. But pixels, like dots, have a size and shape associated with them. If the size and shape of the captured pixel does not match the size and shape of the displayed pixel, then changes occur in the appearance of the image.

Areas vs points.　When pixels are associated with a rectangular grid or raster, there are two basic ways of conceptualizing them. They can be thought of as either areas or points. To be more precise, they can be thought of as representing the intensity of the image at the points represented by the intersections of the vertical and horizontal grid lines; or they can be thought of as representing the average intensity of the image in the rectangles bounded by the grid lines.

In an image capture system the pixels are usually areas. There are two principal reasons for this. First, a photodetector cannot really look at just a point on a document (quantum physics tells us so), and even an attempt to approximate a point puts great demands on the optical system. A more important reason is that such an approach leaves all the space between the grid lines unsampled. Strange things can result if the grid just happens to land at the wrong position on an image.

As a result, image capture systems tend to create area pixels which sample the image fairly completely. Most photodetectors sample an area which is approximately circular. So now we find ourselves sampling circular areas in a rectangular grid. Thus, we are in effect fitting round pixels into square holes.

Pixel size and resolution.   If the pixels are too small, then an excessive amount of the image area will be unsampled, with the result that the discrete image can be very different from the original. But if they are too large, then the apparent resolution of the image is reduced because they overlap. If the circular pixels just touch each other, so that their diameter equals the interpixel spacing, then about 78 percent of the image is sampled. An alternative is to make them large enough so that all of the image is sampled. The required diameter is about 1.4 times the pixel spacing. In this case 57 percent of the area of each pixel overlaps with its neighbors. Capture systems tend to use pixels that just touch. Display devices make different choices.

Most printers capable of printing a binary image were originally designed for printing text. They do so by representing each character by a dot matrix or rectangular arrangement of pixels. Using pixels that just touch, though, produces very grainy looking dot matrix characters. Thus, these printers invariably use overlapping pixels. This means that they lose resolution when printing binary images. Some printers, designed for facsimile service, use smaller pixels and the results are noticeably better even at the same pixel spacing.

Video display devices also tend to reduce the resolution from that indicated by the pixel spacing. Video images generally look better if the pixels slightly overlap. Some overlap is inevitable because of the limited bandwidth of the video circuitry. An additional complication is that many video systems use pixels which are not square. If the aspect ratio of the image is to be preserved, then the spatial frequencies in one direction (usually the vertical) must be degraded, because the vertical pixel spacing is larger than the horizontal pixel spacing. Such a conversion requires that the image be "scaled" so it is represented by a grid of pixels which is not the same as the one by which it was captured.

Human beings can attach significance to even the smallest details in an image. Yet a document archival system must attempt to capture all the significant elements of a document without requiring an infinite amount of storage.

Scaling

Changing the effective pixel spacing of a discrete image turns out to be a very useful operation. There are several situations in which it is necessary, and there are at least two methods by which it can be accomplished.

The simplest application of scaling happens when the user of an image archival system wishes to see a portion of an image in a magnified form or wishes to see the entire document reduced so that it can fit on the screen of the display device. The image may need to be scaled in both the vertical and horizontal directions to achieve this. Printers almost always require similar rescaling operations to preserve the aspect ratio of the image.

With a rectangular pixel array, the vertical and horizontal scaling operations can be performed separately if a pixel replication and deletion method is used to do the scaling. In such an operation, two numbers are calculated, the multiplier (x) and the divisor (n). Each column or row of the raster is replicated x times and then every nth one of the result is kept. For example, assume that the resolution is to be increased by 50 percent. This would result in a multiplier of 3 and a divisor of 2. Thus, the bit string 10110010 would undergo the following sequence.

Start	10110010
Multiply	111000111111000000111000
Divide	110111000110

To be precise, this operation is simply a resampling of the discrete image. Thus, the result can be only as good as the original discrete image. Scaling to a higher resolution cannot improve the appearance of the image.

Another method is called the "weighted pixel" technique. This method requires first computing where each pixel in the new raster falls relative to the old one, then computing a weighted sum of the pixels in the vicinity of that point. Each weighted sum is then converted to a pixel value by making it black if it is greater than some threshold value and white otherwise. This is nothing more than a two-dimensional moving average. The effects of such a scaling operation and the most efficient way of doing them are well covered in any reference on digital image filtering. Any moving-average operation is, in effect, a low-pass frequency filter. Thus, the weighted pixel method tends to lose the higher spatial frequencies in the image while producing what appears to be a better result for some types of images. This holds true even if the weighted pixels are displayed directly as grayscale values on a display device which can show shades of gray. In such a case, the human eye can be fooled into thinking the image is better than it really is.[7]

Either method can degrade the image. Without recourse to the original continuous image, no scaling operation can improve on the result obtained from the first conversion to a discrete image.

Where Does the System Do These Things?

If the designer of an image archival system intends for it to be able to display its images on a variety of devices and to magnify or reduce them in response to user demands, then the scaling operation must be incorporated into the system design. On considerations of speed alone, the operation should be done in hardware.

But where should that hardware be located? The whole point of using CD ROMs in such a system is to avoid the necessity of having a central archive. Just send a copy of the entire image database to each user or display site. Since (we assume) the images will be stored on the CD ROM in a compressed format, this requires that the system for expanding and scaling the images must be present at each display location.

Doing either operation in software is very time-consuming. But doing it in specialized hardware incurs the expense of installing that hardware at each location. This cost can be reduced, however, if the needed hardware uses a standard image decompression algorithm and can be manufactured in sufficient volume to result in a reasonable-cost mass-marketable peripheral device which can be used with a variety of host processors.

In order to be really useful, its operation should not depend on the resolution at which the images have been captured and the software running it should be capable of dealing with the various resolutions and aspect ratios of different display devices.

It should be possible to perform all these functions on a single peripheral board for systems such as the IBM Personal Computers and similar machines (in fact, Talus Corporation of Los Gatos, California, already manufactures such a device which can perform image scaling and CCITT Group 3 modified Huffman image compression and decompression).

Conclusion

This discussion has considered the problems in designing a CD ROM based system for distributing image databases. Methods for efficiently storing such data have been presented and the choices facing the designer of such a system have been described. The prospects for the successful use of such a technology appears excellent, and initial products are already appearing in the marketplace.

270

About the Author

Dr. Truett Lee Smith completed his graduate work in mathematical statistics at the University of South Florida in 1975. Following an NIMH Postdoctoral Fellowship, he was employed by Analytic Services (ANSER) Inc. of Arlington, Virginia, where his duties included the overview of statistical methodologies used in numerous evaluations of computerized clinical systems in the DoD health care system. In 1981 he joined Singer-Link, where he was involved in the development of real-time operating systems software for visual flight simulators. Since 1984 he has been associated with Talus Corporation, where he is the director of product software development.

Talus Corporation, founded in 1983, designs and manufactures image entry and processing products for the office. Its principal product is a desktop digitizer-scanner for image capture applications such as electronic mail and optical disc-based document archival.

References

1. Lynch, T.J. *Data Compression: Techniques and Applications*. Belmont, Calif.: Lifetree Learning Publications, 1985.

2. Shannon, C. E. A mathematical theory of communication, *Bell System Technical Journal*, 27(1948):379-423, 623-656.

3. Huffman, D. *Proceedings of the Institute of Radio Engineers*, 40(1952):1008-1101.

4. Hu, T. C. and A. C. Tucker. *SIAM Journal of Applied Mathematics*, 21(1971):514-532.

5. *Terminal Equipment and Protocols for Telematic Services: Recommendations of the T Series*. CCITT Red Book, vol. VII.3. Geneva: CCITT, 1984. (See especially Recommendation T.4.)

6. CCITT Recommendations T.5 and T.72.

7. Rosenfeld, A., and A. C. Kak. *Digital Picture Processing*. New York: Academic Press, 1976.

Multimedia Possibilities on CD ROM

Compact Disc Interactive Audio

by Bryan Brewer

The compact disc (CD) has been introduced as two different kinds of products. First is the digital audio CD format, the increasingly popular medium that has brought a new dimension of quality to the world of recorded music. Second, and more recent, is the CD ROM format, the primary subject of this book. The developers of the CD format—Sony and Philips—had the foresight to design the medium to store any digital data.

An audio CD can hold up to 74 minutes of stereo sound. A single CD ROM disc can hold up to 600 megabytes of ASCII text, binary programs, computer graphics, or still-frame video images. Both CD ROM and CD audio use the same physical disc standard and encoding scheme. (In fact, audio and computer data can be stored on the same CD.) A CD ROM drive has an additional computer interface for controlling access to the disc and transferring data to the computer, as well as some error correction and detection circuitry not included in an audio CD player.

Interactive audio means that prerecorded audio segments—voices, music, and sound effects—can be played back as part of the user's interaction with the computer system.

As a result of its dual nature, the CD has emerged into two markets: music and mass data storage. A third possibility, interactive audio, can easily be integrated into either of these two application areas. Interactive audio means that prerecorded audio segments—voices, music, and sound effects—can be played back as part of the user's interaction with the computer system. For audio CD, it would mean adding a computer interface to an audio player. For CD ROM, it would mean including the digital-to-analog audio converters and circuits in the CD ROM drives.

Interactive audio can be adapted to a variety of computer-based applications: education, entertainment, and information retrieval. As CD ROM drives and CD audio players proliferate, the inclusion of interactive audio capability in the hardware will spawn creative software development to take advantage of this new medium.

Just as the developers had the foresight to design the CD for more than audio, CD hardware manufacturers have the opportunity to include interactive audio capability in a variety of products. Planning for interactive audio will ultimately benefit hardware manufacturers, disc suppliers, software developers, and users alike.

What Is Interactive Audio?

In my view, CD interactive audio has three key elements:

It uses prerecorded audio on a CD.   The audio can be any recorded sound, including voices, music, sound effects, synthesized sounds, or any combination thereof. The type of audio selected would depend on the particular application and would be limited only by the available disc space and the designer's imagination.

The audio is randomly accessed under program control.   This means simply that the appropriate audio is played at the proper time in response to user input (or lack of input) from the keyboard or other input device such as a mouse, touchscreen, joystick, or voice. The user would not have direct access to the audio function of the CD hardware (pause, track number, etc.) except as provided under program control. Normally, the audio access functions would be transparent to the user.

The audio forms a part of the user interface.   The audio output is used by the program to do things such as prompt, warn, assist, or reinforce the user, usually in conjunction with the display on the screen. In entertainment applications, the audio can also enhance the interaction with screen events. In any case, interactive audio becomes part of the user interaction. Depending on how strictly you interpret this definition, an audio database of sounds that are simply retrieved for playback might also be included in the scope of interactive audio.

Basic Control Functions

Using a computer to control the audio output from a CD player is a relatively simple process, since many of the control and status functions are already built into the control circuitry in the CD player. All the computer needs to do is send the appropriate commands to the player to cause it to access an audio segment, play it, and then pause. This is very similar to using a remote control device to control an audio CD player, except that instead of pushing buttons, the computer sends a command via an interface on the CD player.

The recorded audio on a CD is stored according to a scheme of track numbers and index points. The CD audio standard allows for up to 99 tracks and up to 99 index points within each track, for a maximum of 9801 audio segments per disc. In addition, each track is clocked according to its playing time in minutes and seconds. Further, each second of audio is subdivided into 75 frames, the frame being the smallest addressable unit of sound on the disc.

Audio CD	
Track numbers (TNO)	max 99 per disc
Index points (INDEX)	max 99 per track
Tracks/index	max 9801 per disc
Min/sec (MIN/SEC)	max 74 min 33 sec per disc
Frames (FRAME)	75 per sec, max 335,475 per disc

The index points are useful for some music applications, but are not necessary in interactive audio. Because the computer can access an audio track by minute and second (and possibly even to the frame level), the track/minute/second/frame structure is sufficient for all control functions.

The command structure for controlling the audio output from the CD player would consist of three basic functions:

Cue. Position the laser head at a particular position on the disc defined by track, minute, second, and frame.

Play. Begin playing the audio at the cue point.

Pause. Stop playing the audio at an end point specified by track, minute, second, and frame, or at any other event specified by the control program.

These three basic functions can be expanded or combined to allow for control capabilities such as cue and play, repeat, fast forward, and so forth.

So far we've covered the sending of information from the computer to the CD player for control functions. The other half of the interface involves the return of status information from the CD player to the computer. The player can send two basic types of information to the computer. First is information about the status of the player: whether it is playing audio, is in pause mode, or is seeking an audio segment. The second type of information would come from the audio CD itself. The player could send several categories of disc information to the computer:

Disc ID number, table of contents. Each copy of a particular disc may be identified by a disc ID number assigned to it at the time of pressing. Also, each audio disc contains a "table of contents" that identifies the

276

length and location of each audio segment on the disc. Both the disc ID number and its table of contents are read by the CD player when a disc is loaded into the player; this information could be transmitted to the computer at that time.

Current disc location. Each audio frame has an "address" that is coded into the disc. When a disc is in the player and the player is either paused at a specific audio segment or is actually playing an audio segment, the player can tell exactly (to the frame level) where the laser head is positioned on the disc. This information (the current track number, index, minute, second, and frame) can be sent back to the computer.

The frame addresses are stored in the "Q-channel" subcode of the disc. Subcode data is "piggybacked" onto the audio and can be decoded while the audio is playing or when the player is in the pause mode.

User subcode channels. The Q-channel subcode (along with P-channel subcode data that merely indicates the presence or absence of audio) is used to control the access and playback of the audio on the disc. There are six additional subcode channels (R, S, T, U, V, and W) that can store any digital data. When an audio segment is played, the data stored in these user subcode channels can be decoded and output in synchrony with the audio. Some initial applications for the user subcode channels include the storage of graphic information, such as pictures, text, or musical scores, that can be decoded and displayed on a screen using the appropriate hardware.

However, the user subcode channels could contain any digital data. One possible application is the storage of MIDI (musical instrument digital interface) signals. When properly decoded, the MIDI signal on the CD could be used to trigger other devices, such as synthesizers or visual displays, that would be in perfect synchrony with the music being played back from the CD.

Direct digital output. The actual digital audio data could also be sent to the computer as it is read from the disc. Ordinarily, the digital audio data would be converted into analog sound and played back through speakers or headphones, but it is possible to send it to the computer for further processing. This direct digital output is similar to what happens when CD ROM data is accessed on a disc and displayed by the computer.

When properly decoded, the MIDI signal on the CD could be used to trigger other devices, such as synthesizers or visual displays, that would be in perfect synchrony with the music being played back from the CD.

Hardware Environments

Compact disc interactive audio applications can be implemented in a variety of configurations using CD hardware. In any of these situations the essential ingredient is computer control of random-access CD audio output. Some possible hardware configurations for interactive audio are described below.

PC controlling CD audio player.   Some off-the-shelf CD audio players are equipped with plugs on the back for connection to a computer interface. When properly connected, the computer can control the audio output (as described above) and also can receive player and disc status information, as well as user subcode data. In this configuration, the CD can contain audio and subcode data only—not CD ROM format data.

PC controlling CD audio player and videodisc player.   This configuration is the same as the one above, except that the PC also controls a videodisc player in conjunction with the CD player. I mention this special situation because of several specific applications (discussed below) in which the CD/videodisc combination works especially well.

PC controlling dual-mode CD ROM/CD audio unit.   A CD peripheral does not have to be either CD audio or CD ROM—it can be both. One attractive feature of a "dual-mode" CD peripheral is the market appeal of a unit that will retrieve computer data as well as play music. An additional benefit is the interactive audio capability inherent in such a unit.

PC with built-in CD ROM/CD audio unit.   This configuration is the same as the preceding one, the only difference being that the unit is built into the computer rather than sold as a separate peripheral. With the advent of half-height CD units, it's conceivable that a system such as an IBM PC could be configured with a hard disk drive next to a half-height floppy disk drive and a half-height CD drive.

PC controlling CD ROM drive with audio output on controller board.   This configuration has appeared in prototype systems wherein the digital audio data is stored as CD ROM data and is converted to sound via digital-to-analog circuitry built into the controller board. An advantage here is that—in the absence of any CD standards set by Sony and Philips—different levels of audio fidelity can be achieved. Lower-fidelity audio results in increased playing time per disc.

CD ROM/CD audio unit with built-in PC (compact video).   Most computer developers approach the CD as a peripheral device. In reality, a CD player is a powerful computer in its own right, and it may be just as

277

278

reasonable to consider the CD as the main processor, with a another CPU as the "peripheral." This "CD player with a computer built in" is just what has been proposed under the name "compact video." This interactive system would embrace a standard allowing for multiple levels of audio playback, still-frame video, database, and computer graphics—all on the same CD.

Application Environments

Audio enhancement of existing software.   Using audio to enhance software that already exists is a natural first application for interactive audio. It can be applied to any of the hardware configurations. In most cases the software would need very little modification—just enough to control the appropriate audio at the appropriate time. Using an audio disc as an adjunct to a software tutorial program is a good example of this category of application. Others might include adding sound effects to games and entertainment programs, or perhaps a point-of-sale demonstration to illustrate the benefits of a particular program.

Also included in this category would be audio enhancement of videodisc programs. One of the drawbacks of the videodisc is its limited audio capability, especially for sound accompanying still-frame video images. Here the computer-controlled audio CD can provide high-quality narration for still sequences, as well as provide narration in multiple languages for the same visual program.

Using audio to enhance software that already exists is a natural first application for interactive audio.

Software enhancement of existing audio CDs.   One of the largest parts of the budget for producing a CD interactive audio program is the cost of recording, premastering, and pressing the CD itself. That expense can be avoided by using already existing CDs. Right now, since most audio CDs contain music, the most natural application for this category is music education and appreciation. Explanations and questions, in the form of text and graphics on the computer, could accompany music selections played under control of the computer.

Another prospect for this category of application involves the user subcode channels on music CDs. Currently, virtually no music CDs make use of the some 13 megabytes of storage available in subcode. Some of the possibilities for subcode storage include graphics and text displays, as well as music synchronization codes such as MIDI. Widespread use of user subcode on music discs will require some standardization agreements in the recording industry first.

New combinations of audio and software/data.   This category of interactive audio applications is by far the most exciting and promising. While
the first two categories use existing software or music, this type of program would be designed from the beginning to be a creative combination
of various media available on CD. Whether implemented via the compact   **279**
video system or other multimedia CD configurations, new combinations
of media in an interactive CD would yield experiences that have not yet
been available in a computer user environment.

The range of applications for multimedia interactive CDs is extremely
broad, and any disc could include the following features:

○ *Audio.* At a minimum, the CD standard for stereo high-fidelity audio
would be available. Additional levels of lower audio fidelity (and
consequent storage savings) could be available in some hardware
configurations.

○ *Data.* The full CD ROM data storage capability of up to 500-600 megabytes of text would be accessible.

○ *Graphics.* Graphic images, in the form of computer graphics and still-
frame video, would be available, depending on the display device intended for the application.

○ *Software.* A variety of programs could be included that would control
the audio, graphics, and database retrieval. Other software could also be
included. Because of the tremendous storage capacity of the CD, different versions of the same software (for various computer systems) could
be included on the same disc.

Some of the same capabilities for data, graphics, and software could be
achieved in an audio-only CD hardware environment by storing this information on floppy disks. The appeal of the multimedia CD is its high
storage capacity compared to that of floppy disks.

The two primary application areas for interactive audio in new combinations of media are education and entertainment. Both of these types operate mainly in a read-only environment, where information is presented
and interacted with but where there is not much of a requirement to store
large amounts of user-created data on floppy disk. Productivity software,
such as spreadsheets and word processing, have an inherent need to store
files the user creates and thus will be merely augmented by the read-only
CD. However, audio tutorial and enhancement programs will find application with this type of software.

**The human voice,
with its infinitely
variable inflections
and colorings,
can convey
information . . .
that is impossible
to achieve with text
or synthesized
speech.**

Other application areas include simulations, presentations, interactive art displays, audio response systems, and foreign language implementations. In surveying the applications where interactive audio is likely to provide the most benefit, it is useful to further consider some dimensions of the audio realm itself.

The Audio Dimension

Audio Output

There are two basic methods for delivering the actual sound to the person or persons using the system—speakers and headphones—and each has certain attributes that can affect the design of an interactive audio program. There are also additional considerations concerning sound channels, levels of fidelity, and other controls.

Speakers and headphones.   Most home stereo systems allow for listeners to choose speakers or headphones (or both) for listening to audio from a CD player. And this may well be the case with interactive audio systems. However, there may be many cases where headphones will be either preferable or required. For example, in an office setting the sound from speakers would annoy other workers. And since most interactive programs are single-user types, headphones may be more suitable, especially since this type of audio output does not require the extra expense or bulk of an amplifier/speaker system to deliver the sound. A simple headphone jack with level controls would be adequate.

As an added benefit, interactive audio programs designed for headphones may be able to take advantage of certain "three-dimensional" recording techniques (such as binaural or holophonics) that work best when played back over headphones. This approach would allow for an added dimension of audio realism in which sounds would seem to be coming from various locations around the listener.

Audio channels.   Normally, two audio channels—left and right—are used to play back stereo sound from a CD, over either headphones or speakers. It is possible for a CD player to be built with a little additional circuitry that would allow for the option of monophonic sound, from either channel on the disc, to be played through both output channels. This would allow for double the amount of recording time on the disc (149 minutes) compared with stereo sound (74.5 minutes). Playing the sound from only one channel would not be affected by the sound on the other contiguous channel because of the extremely high channel separation in CD systems.

Audio fidelity.   The normal CD stereo sound represents the highest-fidelity audio available in a consumer product today. The up to 16 billion bits of raw data on one side of a CD translate into a maximum of 74.5 minutes of stereo audio with a bandwidth of about 20,000 Hz and a dynamic range of about 90 dB. For many applications, audio of lower fidelity would be quite adequate.

The advantage is playing time. Lower-fidelity audio requires less storage space on the disc, resulting in longer playing times. There are intermediate levels of audio fidelity. The lower the bandwith, the less storage is required and the more playing time available. At the lower end of the audio-fidelity spectrum, telephone-quality speech (about 4000 Hz bandwith in mono) could give up to 32 hours of audio on a disc.

Any lower-fidelity audio scheme requires additional circuitry in the CD player to properly decode the signal and convert it to analog audio output. The CD standard will surely evolve to include such levels. In fact, this aspect of the audio output is specifically included in the proposed compact video system.

Audio controls.   Some CD players have volume level adjustments that can be controlled through the CD-PC interface. This would allow the control program in the computer to turn the volume up or down. Additionally, it would be convenient for the audio control buttons on the player to be disabled when the CD player is under computer control. This feature may well be included in combined CD audio/CD ROM units.

Audio Sources

Voices.   The warm tones of the recorded human voice (as opposed to the unnatural sound of synthesized speech) may prove to be the cornerstone of the appeal of interactive audio. The voices can be male or female, young or old, sad or funny— whatever fits the purpose. This "high-touch" aspect in a high-tech environment may help many people overcome their fear of computers.

The human voice, with its infinitely variable inflections and colorings, can convey information (particularly emotional tone) that is impossible to achieve with text or synthesized speech. It is especially important to pay attention to this factor when scripting for interactive audio.

... interactive audio programs designed for headphones may be able to take advantage of certain "three-dimensional" recording techniques such as binaural or holophonics ...

281

Another advantage of using real recorded voices is the possibility of having star personalities do the vocal recordings, thus providing more consumer appeal to the product. This may be especially beneficial when audio characters are created for the interaction.

Music.   A wide variety of musical sounds are available as either background or the mainstay of audio segments. The music can be any style recorded with any instruments—again, whatever fits the purpose. There is even the possibility for interactive music applications.

Sound effects.   A third type of audio source is sound effects. These can be especially useful in supporting graphics animation on the screen. The creative use of sound effects is limited only by the developer's imagination.

Synthesized sounds.   Voices, music, and sound effects can also be created using sound-synthesis hardware that may be a part of the computer system. One problem that may arise in this configuration is that audio volume levels may not be matched to the output from the CD. This problem is especially evident when the user is wearing headphones to listen to the CD audio. Unless the synthesized sound is somehow mixed with the CD audio, the user may not be able to hear it well.

Audio Roles

Various audio sources—particularly voices, but music and sound effects as well—can be used to play "audio roles." For example, in a teaching situation, two different characters could be used, each in a different role. One character could be the "teacher," dispensing information and asking questions. The other character (with a different voice, of course) could be someone who gives hints and reinforcement. Use of various audio roles expands the aural dimension of the interaction as well as providing built-in audio cues as to the type of information being presented.

Below is a list of some fundamental audio roles that could play a part in interactive audio applications. The roles are listed using the verb (explain, reinforce, etc.) that describes the action played by the role.

○ Greet, welcome

○ Explain, instruct

○ Prompt, request, demand

○ Remind, alert, warn

○ Help, assist, hint

○ Reinforce, praise, flatter

○ Encourage, reassure

○ Thank, acknowledge

○ Answer, confirm

○ Advise, suggest, guide

○ Lament, regret

○ Confuse, divert

○ Scare

○ Excite, arouse

The roles basically correspond to the different types of human conversation that could play a part in any interaction. Each type of role will probably have certain kinds of characters, voices, music, and sound effects associated with its particular function.

System Relationships

Ordinary computer programs usually involve two major I/O devices—the screen and the keyboard. Other input devices (mouse, joystick, touchscreen, etc.) can be added, but typically there is only one input device used at any one time. Additionally, computer-synthesized sound is also an output, but it has generally played a minor role in most programs, since the amount and quality of information it can convey is very limited in most cases.

Screen/input interaction matrix.   Below is a simple interaction matrix for ordinary computer programs showing the simple back-and-forth interaction possible in this configuration.

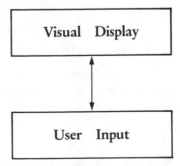

Most computer programs allow a simple back-and-forth interaction between the user's input and the display.

This type of configuration allows for a total of two types of interaction:

1. Visual display directed to the user

2. User response to the visual display

Interactive audio interaction matrix. Next is a diagram showing the media matrix when CD interactive audio is added to the user interface. With the addition of the left and right audio channels, there are at least four points on the matrix.

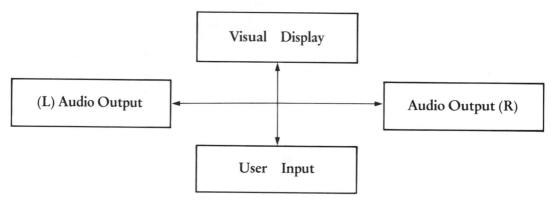

When CD interactive audio is added to the standard user interface, it yields 12 possible types of interaction.

This yields a total of 12 possible types of interaction:

1. Visual display directed to the user

2. User response to the visual display

3. Right audio channel directed to the user

4. User response to right audio channel

5. Left audio channel directed to the user

6. User response to left audio channel

The first six types of interaction involve the user. However, there are six more that do not require direct user response:

7. Visual display directed to right audio channel

8. Visual display directed to left audio channel

9. Right audio channel directed to visual display

10. Left audio channel directed to visual display

11. Right audio channel directed to left audio channel

12. Left audio channel directed to right audio channel

There are even other types of interaction that are possible using the entire range of the left/right dimension of the stereo audio spectrum. This exponential increase in types of interaction will no doubt prove to be a major aspect of increasing the variability in interactive programs. Higher variability will result in less boredom and more surprises in the total interaction.

Another advantage of this four-point media matrix is that screen activities need not be interrupted when information is provided from the audio domain. This will prove especially useful in simulations and tutorials involving already-existing software.

Comparison with Interactive Videodisc

Since the CD and the LaserVision videodisc are both multimedia optical discs, it may be useful to compare the benefits and drawbacks of the CD for interactive education/entertainment purposes.

Disadvantages of CD compared with videodisc:

o Cannot deliver motion video.

o Can store only about 9000 still-frame video images (compared with 54,000 for videodisc).

o Requires separate sound system or headphones.

Advantages of CD compared with videodisc:

o Does not require video production expenses.

o Hardware, disc are smaller (could be built in).

o Does not require additional display device (TV monitor).

o CD hardware has another use—data storage—that will lead to widespread acceptance.

o Has single, universal data storage standard (CD ROM).

Comparison of storage media: The digital transformation

Another major difference between CD and videodisc is the method used to store information. CD is a true digital storage medium, whereas videodisc stores motion video as an analog signal. Right now it is much more efficient to store video in analog format. It may still be a few years before motion video is stored as a digital signal. In the meantime, this underlying difference in the storage method will preclude videodisc from completely entering the digital realm.

Medium	Original Storage	Consumer-Level Digital Storage
Software	Digital	Digital
Text	Paper	Digital
Graphics	Paper	Digital
Audio	Analog	Digital
Video	Analog	Preliminary (still-frame)

Interactive Audio Design and Development

Interactive audio is in many respects similar to interactive video, at least from a design standpoint. The same type of thinking in terms of multiple paths and user options applies equally well. As a result, much of the knowledge base and experience gained in interactive video can be applied directly to interactive audio design.

Sound educational or entertainment design. Although education and entertainment have different ends, many design considerations apply to both. These include:

○ Maintaining a high level of user interest

○ Giving the user appropriate control of the flow

○ Providing feedback to the user's responses

○ Intelligent analysis of user's responses

Maximum use of the technology. The digital multimedia storage capabilities of the CD present far greater possibilities for creative exploitation as compared with the videodisc. The ability to combine audio, graphics, still-frame video, and large databases on the same disc will yield startling new applications. Even in the audio realm alone the ability to create an aural "soundscape" of unprecented fidelity and interaction will be very exciting.

Authoring systems and development workstations. Creating such complex and technologically advanced programs in a productive manner will require new software and hardware tools. Authoring systems that are easy to use and test will be a must. Hardware for program development and testing will present special requirements, especially because of the multimedia aspect of the final product.

Interactive Audio Development Process

The typical process of developing an interactive audio CD program would generally follow the five broad steps of specification, design, production, integration and testing, and product acceptance. Each step involves specific activities and resulting products.

Specification. The first step is to specify the hardware, software, application, and user environments for the program, including:

○ Hardware system

○ Software system

○ Program objectives

○ Program scope and content

○ User environment

This step would result in a specification document including all the above details, as well as a schedule and budget for the development.

Design. Once the program is specified, the next step is to design it in complete detail. This would include any of the following applicable items:

○ Audio scripting

○ Storyboarding

○ Screen design

○ User interface design

○ Database retrieval methods

○ Still-frame video layouts

○ Animated graphics design

The deliverable product at the end of this step is a complete design document. Also possible is a linear tape demo of a small portion of the program.

Production. Once the design is finalized and approved, the next step is production, including:

○ Audio recording

○ Still-frame video shooting

Creating such complex and technologically advanced programs in a productive manner will require new software and hardware tools.

○ Computer graphics production

○ Software development

○ Database preparation

○ Preliminary program documentation

The result of this step would be completed audio and video tapes, as well as disks or tapes containing the software, computer graphics, and databases.

System integration.   This step involves premastering the information for inclusion on the CD and replication of test versions of the CD. Then the program would be ready for initial testing to ensure proper operation. The result of this step is a completely operable program ready for user testing.

Product acceptance.   The final step involves user testing to ensure that the program meets its objectives. Once all the corrections and enhancements have been implemented, the result is the final product. All documentation and packaging would be completed at this stage as well.

Outlook for Interactive Audio

Compact disc interactive audio can take many forms. Its simplest configuration would be an audio CD player controlled by a computer. Perhaps the most complex configuration would be the compact video system, where a single disc could contain audio of multiple levels of fidelity, still-frame video, computer graphics, large databases, and all the necessary control software. In whichever forms it may be implemented, interactive audio holds great promise for generating new and innovative applications of digital technology.

There are a number of factors that I believe portend a bright future for this medium. These factors involve not only the technological capabilities of the medium but some economic and marketing considerations as well.

A new medium for creative exploitation.   Including CD audio in the user interface of a computer system increases the level of drama, realism, and excitement possible in a wide variety of programs. Just as the graphics/icon paradigm of the user interface has greatly enhanced the ease of use of computers, interactive audio promises to deliver a dimension of warmth and fun not hitherto available in interactive applications.

Versatility of CD hardware.   Although interactive audio is a viable medium in its own right, its use and acceptance in computer environments will be greatly accelerated by the widespread proliferation of CD ROM hardware, much of which will be increasingly compatible with CD audio applications. In this respect CD will fulfill much of the promise of videodisc, which has been severely limited in its depth of market penetration. Additionally, other hardware configurations (such as the compact video system) will make use of the multiple functions of the CD.

289

Synergism between the recording, computer, and publishing industries.   The CD can store audio, software, and large amounts of text or images. These three primary types of information are the stock in trade of the recording, computer, and publishing industries. Never before has a single medium embraced such a wide range of information so well. The fact that each type of information can be stored on the same disc opens up tremendous new possibilities for cooperation and joint ventures among these three industries. One major result will likely be far broader distribution of such CD products in the consumer marketplace.

Impracticality of unauthorized duplication of multimedia CDs.
Unlike the audio cassette or floppy disk drive or photocopy machine, the CD is read-only. There are major technological and economic hurdles blocking the way for a viable recordable CD, especially in the CD ROM format. Even if such a product reaches the market, the cost of recordable optical disc media may be prohibitive for consumer copying of discs. The upshot is that a multimedia, integrated CD—where the audio, graphics, data, and software interact with each other—may be virtually uncopyable, at least from an economic or practical standpoint. If the disc is designed so that its audio or software or data is useless by itself, then the problem of unauthorized duplication may—at least to a great extent—become moot.

Future possibilities for digital processing of audio and video.   Just as the display on a video game is constantly varied by the program, the audio output from a CD can be modified by digital signal processing software in the right hardware configuration. Thus the sonic attributes of the recorded

---

Just as the display on a video game is constantly varied by the program, the audio output from a CD can be modified by digital signal processing software in the right hardware configuration.

audio (tempo, pitch, inflection, reverb, etc.) can be modified by software in the computer. The result will be virtually infinitely variable audio output based on a limited amount of prerecorded audio. The benefit will be increased variation in the interaction that will lead to higher levels of interest by the user.

About the Author

Bryan Brewer designs and develops multimedia software for education and entertainment applications. He is the president of Earth View Inc., in Ashford, Washington.

Earth View, Inc.
Star Route
Ashford, WA 98304

Video on CD: The Big Picture

by Bryan Brewer

Can you put video on a CD? That's the question I keep hearing as more people discover the versatility of the compact disc. Basically, the answer is yes. But if the CD is to be more than just a small videodisc, you must enter the realm of digital video.

291

The video you get from your local TV station, and from your VCR, is sent as an analog signal into your TV set. Video on a laser videodisc is also stored as an analog signal. Before it can be seen on the TV screen, the de-modulated data stream from a videodisc must be decoded back into the original analog video signal. After that, it goes to the TV tuner, which converts the analog video signal into the image you see.

The video future for the CD lies in the digital domain: digital video.

When digital video becomes available, discrete bits of the video image will be stored as digital data. The process will be similar to the way computer graphics are stored and processed.

A laser disc—whether a videodisc or a compact disc—can store digital data. Why does a videodisc store video as an analog signal rather that a true digital picture? Because, currently, analog storage of video is more efficient. One second of color video in digital format would require about 30 megabytes. But one second of analog color video on a videodisc takes up a little more than the equivalent of 1 megabyte of storage. This means you can get up to 60 minutes of video on one side of a videodisc.

Too Slow for Video

If, however, you translated the LaserVision format onto the CD, and also accounted for storing a digital audio stereo soundtrack, the result would be about 5 or 6 minutes of full-color, motion video. Not bad, except you wouldn't be able to play the video CD on your regular audio CD player.

For one thing, an audio CD player does not have the video decoding and output components. But even if it did, a CD player couldn't read the information fast enough. The CD data transfer rate of about 150K bytes per second is too slow to support motion video in the LaserVision format. The player would have to spin the disc more than three times as fast in order to play back video.

If you took a CD player, added the required video output circuitry, and made the disc spin faster, then, yes, you could have video on a CD. This is pretty much what Pioneer did in the CLD-900 combination videodisc/CD player (*Digital Audio*, July 1985, p. 30). The only problem is you can't buy CD-sized videodiscs to play on it—only audio CDs.

Pioneer certainly could make a CD-sized videodisc, but would it be a CD, or just a 12-cm videodisc? And who would buy a videodisc with only 5 or 6 minutes on it? Is there really a market for CD music video singles? Who knows? Pioneer is having a hard enough time selling its 8-inch music videodiscs that play for 20 minutes.

More Bits in the Pits

CD-sized videodiscs are just the beginning; other more intriguing possibilities exist. One involves a unique scheme for increasing the density of data encoded on a CD. This new technology is being promoted by JVW Electronics and Interactive Video Systems, both in the Chicago area, and SCOS Management of Monte Sereno, California. These folks claim that by squeezing extra bits into the pits on the spiral track, they can store 12 minutes of constant angular velocity (CAV) video or 20 minutes of constant linear velocity (CLV) video on a compact disc. CAV allows for slow-motionplayback; CLV does not.

This method of putting up to 20 minutes of video on CD requires an LV player or a modified CD player that can spin the disc at speeds between 1000 and 1800 rpm. (The audio CD revolves at a lower rate: 200 to 500 rpm.) And the special encoding/decoding scheme must be implemented instead of using the standard LaserVision system.

So again, we have a 12-cm videodisc, but with its own high-density video encoding scheme that provides 20 minutes of video with a digital audio stereo soundtrack. Presumably the same encoding scheme could be applied to the 12-inch videodisc, resulting in 2 hours of video per side. The problem is getting this proprietary encoding scheme accepted by hardware manufacturers. Is it worth introducing another standard in the video field, where enough confusion (VHS, Beta, LaserVision, 8mm) already exists?

And where does this leave the CD? Remember, all of these formats still store motion video as an analog signal. Each format stores the video in a different way. And each format runs up against the limitations of its storage medium. For tape, one drawback is that the video is not randomly accessible. For videodisc, the drawback is storage density. You can get only 20 minutes of video on a CD, and that's using an encoding scheme which is incompatible with current videodisc standards.

Digital Television

The video future for the CD lies in the digital domain: digital video. One of the simpler applications of digital video already showing up in consumer products is the digital TV. These units allow you to freeze frames as well as show a still frame from another channel in a "video window" on the screen. A single frame of video can be captured, digitized, compressed, and stored in a 64K-byte frame buffer in the television set.

In this case the video frame is digital, not analog. The digitization and compression process happens in a set of chips specifically designed for this purpose. It would be easy to store still-frame video images on a CD in this digital format.

If each frame requires about 60K, then you can get between 9000 and 10,000 frames on a single CD. Once you have a frame of video stored digitally, you can use a computer to process that frame. Dissolves, fades, and other video techniques become possible. And with enough processing power, you could even do video animation, combining computer graphics techniques with digital video.

Moving Pictures on CD?

Although it may take up to 60K of memory to store one frame, it's not necessary to store every bit of data for each successive frame. It's enough to store the changes from one frame to the next.

You're probably wondering about stringing these digital still frames together and displaying one every 1/30 second to create motion video. CD's limited data transfer rate makes this impractical. A CD delivers a continuous stream of 60K video frames at maximum rate of only 2 or 3 frames per second. Full-motion video requires 30 frames per second. But the ability to display several still frames per second could lead to some interesting visuals, particularly when combined with graphics animation processing.

Given the CD's standard storage capacity and data transfer rate, are we ever going to get full-motion, color video on a compact disc? Yes, through specialized software for digital video processing. Although it may take up to 60K of memory to store one frame, it's not necessary to store every bit of data for each successive frame. It's enough to store the changes from one frame to the next.

For example, the background in many scenes stays the same while the characters move and talk in the foreground. The data representing the background image in such a scene could be stored once, in the first frame, and then the software would maintain the background while the action in the foreground takes place. Except for scenes where the whole image is rapidly changing, this kind of video compression scheme greatly reduces the amount of storage required for full-motion sequences.

Digital video compression will pave the way for storing video on compact disc. One company already working in this area is Evital Inc., of Dallas. In their research efforts, they have demonstrated the capability of storing up to two hours of video on a single CD ROM disc, using direct memory access to a microcomputer processor. Of course, this doesn't include a CD-quality soundtrack, but the same kind of digital compression techniques could be applied to the audio as well.

While it still has a way to go, the technology for putting video on CD is developing. And along with it will come fantastic possibilities for combining computer graphics animation techniques and real-time digital processing. Digital video. It has a nice ring to it.

Reprinted with permission from *Digital Audio* magazine.

About the Author

Bryan Brewer designs and develops multimedia software for education and entertainment applications. He is president of Earth View Inc., in Ashford, Washington.

Earth View, Inc.
Star Route
Ashford, WA 98304

THE ELEMENTS
OF DESIGN

The Human Factor

The Seamless Carpet of Knowledge and Learning

by Gabriel D. Ofiesh

299

There is nothing more difficult to carry out, nor more doubtful of success, nor more dangerous to handle, than to initiate a new order of things. For the reformer has enemies in all who profit by the old order, and only lukewarm defenders in all those who would profit by the new order. This quality of lukewarmness arises partly from a fear of adversaries, who have the law on their side, and partly from the incredulity of mankind, who do not truly believe in anything new until they have had actual experience of it.

Machiavelli, *The Prince*, 1513

CD/OD ROM is such a dramatic innovation that it requires a completely new way of looking at not only the problems of education and training but the recursive nature of knowledge itself. Through the use of icons and micro-based menus, CD/OD ROM provides knowledge engineers, instructional designers, educators, training directors, and planners with radically new opportunities for designing and adapting training and educational materials to instructional systems-based interactive training formats. CD ROM has the capability and technological potential for educators to create a "seamless carpet of knowledge and learning." Several potential scenarios illustrate how the CD/OD ROM can be utilized for exploratory and discovery learning as well as for self-instructional strategies which can radically alter not only education but the very structure of the knowledge on which it is based.

In writing this chapter for *The New Papyrus*, I fully recognize my limitations. I am not an electronics or light engineer. In tracking the videodisc and the CD ROM I have difficulty in following much of the technical discussions. In spite of these constraints, as an educator and educational technologist there are some suggestions that deserve to be stated which may provide guidance to the instrumentation engineers concerning the potential use of the CD ROM technology beyond that as an archival medium. I do consider myself, however, to be an educational engineer—pejorative as the term "engineering" may be to many of my educator friends. When I established the Center for Educational Technology at The Catholic University of America in 1966, I wrote the first definitive article describing our graduate program as one that trained tomorrow's educational engineers.

300

Over the past 25 years I have tracked a variety of new technologies of communication that may affect education and training, and I have found that they never really did have an impact on education. Though I have steadily gained an appreciation of the contributions of scientists in the computer and electronic fields, I am not ready to deify them. I admit to a sense of awe in thinking of their many contributions—the creations that come out of the Bell Labs, for example. I do not understand how the microcomputer works—nor will I. Nor do I think I need to know. I have never understood how my car, telephone, or television set works. Yet I have been able to use them and other powerful tools quite successfully. On the other hand, I do recognize, and am fully aware of, the tremendous power inherent in the micro—as well as the videodisc and now the CD and OD ROM.

We have all heard about the knowledge explosion. Explosion is not the proper metaphor. An explosion is a one-time-only affair. What we have is, and will continue to be, a flood of knowledge. I have on my bookshelf three volumes that are replicas of the complete *Encyclopaedia Britannica* as it was published in the year 1771. These three volumes represent the condensed state of knowledge at that time. Today the *Britannica* consists of over 40 volumes. Yet, from reading other articles in this book, you know that today's *Britannica* could not fill a compact disc.

The challenge confronting education and educators today is not to produce more electronic technology but, rather, to develop creatively the educational potential that the current new technologies offer. This requires almost a complete break with the conventional wisdom. We need to think in ways we never thought in the past.

Psychologist Eugene Galenter tells us that the micro will bring about the most profound changes in civilization since the invention of agriculture. I personally think that the impact will be even more profound. The micro revolution is on the same level as the Copernican revolution.

I hesitate to predict the future. I have no idea what it will be like. A few months ago, in giving a talk, I was introduced as the prophet of the future. I corrected the introduction by saying that I was a prophet of the present. If I have any vision, it is a vision of the present. Recently, Richard Braddock, Citibank/Citicorp's group executive who is responsible for all consumer financial services in the United States, told conferees in an address: "We are living through an exciting and demanding time—one in which our abilities to manage or even cope are being challenged more each day."

He further cautioned, "The future belongs not to the wide-eyed visionaries who speculate on where the technology can go. It belongs to the sharp-eyed realists who determine where the technology *should* go to meet users' unmet demands." No one can really predict the future potential of the new technologies. Even inventors themselves sometimes intend completely different applications for their inventions than what eventually develops with them. Braddock points out that Edison didn't have the slightest idea the phonograph would be used for the reproduction of music or that it would create a new industry—the record business. He believed that the phonograph would have a relatively small market limited to, and I quote, "Those members of the legal profession who, wishing to eliminate disputation from the settlement of estates, would invite their clients into the office for the direct inscribing of their wishes onto the machine." In 1876, Alexander Graham Bell presented the telephone to the world, and the world yawned. Historians report that the majority of people of that day saw no obvious application for Bell's invention. The *London Times* called it "the latest American humbug." Western Union, the giant among the new telecommunications agencies of that time, was offered exclusive patent rights to the telephone. Western Union's chairman quickly refused the offer saying, "What use would this company have for an electrical toy?" Thomas Edison was out to assist lawyers, and Alexander Graham Bell was deeply concerned with the plight of the deaf. Innovations like theirs led to revolutionary changes, but different from what they foresaw. Once people in search of applications make a breakthrough, then a second creative process starts that puts the new discovery to work in solving an existing problem or accomplishing something new that could not be done before. The information and telecommunications revolutions are no exception. When the computer came into existence in the 1940s, very few people had the imagination to see how it would be used.

Who would have guessed, 40 years ago, that the rudimentary computer, designed by British experts to break German codes in World War II, would become the impetus creating the gigantic industries of today? Now we find every major industry in the midst of change. While the pace of change has accelerated since Edison and Bell, the same standard still holds. What happened to the phonograph, the telephone, and the computer will happen again: The users will call the shots. Clearly, Edison's phonograph solved the problems he set out to solve, *but the market didn't share his view of the application.* Rather, his technological breakthrough eventually gave impetus to a brand-new use that captured the minds, hearts and pocketbooks of the general public. It is the market that is driving the new technologies, not technological forces. And it is market forces that will drive the PC and the CD/OD ROM for the next decade.

302

Forty years ago, in an *Atlantic Monthly* article (reprinted in this book), Vannevar Bush prophetically predicted the information flood produced by the scientific and technological revolutions, and unknowingly foresaw the development of the CD/OD ROM. Bush perceived the practical need as well as the economic necessity for extending scientific developments, recording and storing information, and *accessing and consulting the record as needed* (italics mine). At the time he recognized that our publication capability and the expansion of scientific information had extended far beyond our ability to make real use of the record. In practical terms, the methods used until now to transmit and review knowledge and research have been totally inadequate for our needs. To quote Bush, "The modern library is not generally consulted, it is nibbled at by a few." (I would add the dictionary and thesaurus.) Mere compression of records and information is not enough. Without the ability to consult records spontaneously, humanity will be dogged with the curse of having our greatest inventions lost in a mass of the inconsequential. The promise of the microprocessor, and especially the CD/OD ROM peripheral, is one of the transformation of information. The new technologies have brought us to the point where we can cost-effectively store, compress, and disseminate information formerly accessible to only a few.

Bush's vintage article, aptly titled "As We May Think," was written when I began teaching my first course in psychology. Bush, then a supervisor of over 1000 scientists, had a prophetic vision of the CD/OD ROM. Let me just quote a few passages from his article.

> There is a growing mountain of research. There is increased evidence that we are being bogged down by that information as specialization extends. The investigator is staggered by the findings and conclusions of thousands of other workers. *These are conclusions which he cannot find time to grasp, much less to remember.* Yet, specialization becomes increasingly necessary for progress, and *the effort to bridge the disciplines is correspondingly superficial.*

His words remind me of Alfred North Whitehead's comment that we teach algebra from which nothing follows, biology from which nothing follows, chemistry from which nothing follows, and so on. Bush goes on to tell us that, professionally, our methods of transmitting and reviewing the results of research are generations old. By now the methodology is totally inadequate for its purpose. Many conscientiously attempt to keep abreast of current thought, even in restricted fields, by close and continuous reading; yet they might well shy away from an examination calculated to show how much of the previous month's efforts could be reproduced on demand. Mendel's understanding of the laws of genetics was lost to the

"The future belongs not to the wide-eyed visionaries who speculate on where the technology can go. It belongs to the sharp-eyed realists who determine where the technology should go to meet users' unmet demands."

world for a generation because his publication did not reach the few who were capable of grasping and expanding it. This sort of catastrophe is undoubtedly being repeated all about us, as truly significant attainments become lost in the mass of the inconsequential.

303

Again, may I remind you I am reading from an article written in 1945. Let me go on:

> The difficulty seems to be that the art of publication has been extended beyond our present ability to make real use of the record. The summation of human experience is being expanded at a prodigious rate, and the means we use for threading through this information maze to reach the momentarily important item is the same as that used in the days of square-rigged ships.

Now listen to this:

> But, there is hope! There are signs of a change as new and powerful instrumentalities come into use. Such as photocells capable of seeing things in a physical sense, advanced photography which can record the seen or even the unseen, thermionic tubes capable of controlling potent forces under the guidance of less power than that used by a mosquito to vibrate his wings, cathode ray tubes rendering visible an occurrence so brief that a microsecond is a long time by comparison, relay combinations which carry out involved sequences of movements more reliably than any human operator and thousands of times faster. These are but a few of the changes. There are plenty of mechanical aids that can be used to effect a transformation in scientific records . . . .

In 1945, Bush was telling us that:

> We now push a pencil or tap a typewriter to make the record. Then, the process of digestion and correction follows and then comes an intricate process of typesetting, printing, and distribution . . . . Will the author of the future cease writing by hand or typewriter and talk directly to the record? He does so indirectly, by talking to a stenographer transcribing on a wax cylinder; but the elements are all present for him to talk directly into a device that will produce a typed record. He simply needs to take advantage of existing mechanisms and alter his language slightly.

Mind-boggling, isn't it? If Bush could only be around today to tell us what is around the corner! Bush strikes at the heart of our problems in using our wealth of knowledge when he says:

304

> Our ineptitude in getting at the record is largely caused by indexing. When data of any sort is put into storage, it is indexed alphabetically or numerically. Information is retrieved by tracing it down from subclass to subclass. Unless duplicates are made, information can only be stored in one place. Rules govern which path must be followed to locate information; and the rules are cumbersome. Having found one item, moreover, one must emerge from the system and re-enter on a new path to find related information. The human mind does not work that way. It operates by association. With one item in its grasp, it snaps instantly to the next related item. Suggestion triggers the association of thoughts. Our intricate web of neural trails carried by the cells of the brain makes possible this associative thinking.

And this leads Bush to create a future device that is designed to be a sort of mechanized private file and library. This device he calls a "memex," which he defines as a device "in which an individual stores his books, records, and personal communications. It is mechanized so that it may be consulted with exceeding speed and flexibility. It provides an enlarged intimate supplement to his memory . . . ."

Now hear this for the generic scenario:

"The modern library is not generally consulted, it is nibbled at by a few."

> Of course, it will be possible to consult the record by the usual scheme of indexing. If the user wishes to consult a certain book, he can tap its code on the keyboard, and the title page of the book will appear promptly before him, projected onto a screen. Frequently-used codes are mnemonic, so that he seldom will have to consult his code book. When he does, a single tap of a key projects it on the screen for his use. Moreover, he will have supplemental levers. By deflecting another lever he can run through the book before him, each page in turn being projected at a speed which just allows a recognizing glance at each. If he deflects it further to the right, he steps through the book 10 pages at a time; still further, 100 pages at a time. Deflection to the left gives him the same control backwards.

A special button transfers him immediately to the first page of the index. Any given book of his library can thus be called up and consulted with far greater facility than if it were taken from a shelf. As he has several projection positions, he can leave one item in position while he calls up another. He can add marginal notes and comments, taking advantage of one possible type of dry photography, and it could even be arranged so that he can do this by a stylus scheme, such as is now employed in the telautograph seen in railroad waiting rooms, just as though he had the physical page before him . . . .

The owner of the memex, let us say, is interested in the origin and properties of the bow and arrow. Specifically he is studying why the short Turkish bow was apparently superior to the English long bow in the skirmishes of the Crusades. He has dozens of possibly pertinent books and articles in his memex. First he runs through an encyclopedia, finds an interesting but sketchy article, leaves it projected. Next, in a history, he finds another pertinent item, and ties the two together. Thus he goes, building a trail of many items. Occasionally he inserts a comment of his own, either linking it into the main trail or joining it by a side trail to a particular item. When it becomes evident that the elastic properties of available materials had a great deal to do with the bow, he branches off on a side trail which takes him through textbooks on elasticity and tables of physical constants. He inserts a page of longhand analysis of his own. Thus he builds a trail of his interest through the maze of materials available to him.

And his trails do not fade. Several years later, his talk with a friend turns to the queer ways in which a people resist innovations, even of vital interest. He has an example, in the fact that the outraged Europeans still failed to adopt the Turkish bow. In fact he has a trail on it. A touch brings up the code book. Tapping a few keys projects the head of the trail. A lever runs through it at will, stopping at interesting items, going off on side excursions. It is an interesting trail, pertinent to the discussion. So he sets a reproducer in action, photographs the whole trail out, and passes it to his friend for insertion in his own memex, there to be linked into the more general trail . . . .

For a more detailed description of his memex-desk you will have to read his article. If you do, you will have a sense of deja vu.

A Few Scenarios

The Smart Card is in the same family as the CD/OD ROM. It is a portable data storage device with intelligence and provisions for identity and security. At present they are used as bank cards, telephone credit cards, and

306

security ID badges. The intelligence in the card can be readily programmed for different applications without any change in design. The identity and security provisions protect the card's proper owner as well as allowing access to the stored data. The card cannot be used until the bearer supplies the matching code. The memory of the Smart Card is normally programmed to the requirements of a specific application at the time of issue. The Smart Card's memory is updated each time it is used, and each transaction is recorded on the card. Publishers are currently pursuing applications in which erasibility and/or reprogramming may be appropriate. This change could have strong implications for learning applications. It is incumbent on the educator, however, to see the applications.

Educational technology is a science which too often has been based on the adaptation of present technological developments to educational purposes rather than on developing technological innovations from learning needs. When the microcomputer and interactive videodisc were invented, the educational technologist began to explore its learning applications. The result was computer-assisted instruction (CAI) and interactive training packages used in vocational and technical education. Now that the Smart Card has come on the scene, the educational technologist is plotting again.

How can the memory of the CD/OD ROM and the Smart Card be programmed to identify a student and access instructional material at his or her appropriate and changing developmental level? Can the Smart Card be used to test cognitive development and then supply appropriate assignments of homework—much as it now computes financial transactions and reads out the new balance in a checking account? In this day of individualized instruction, can a student's identity card take the student into a teaching dimension tailored to his specific learning needs through a method of menus that branch out to knowledge units tied directly or indirectly to other sequential knowledge units? Can the CD/OD ROM and the Smart Card become a major tool in making the learning environment truly adaptive to the idiosyncratic needs of the learner? These are the questions educational technologists must ask those who design the new technologies. But our needs have to be known to the engineer early in the design process. It is up to the educational technologists to come up with the scenarios and applications, to break down and adapt to the machine capabilities of the units of knowledge in different subject and skill areas. These are the challenges which the instrumentation or delivery-system technologists have placed before us as educators. We can now write the scenarios we always dreamed of writing. We can compose just about any stimulus configuration for any type of learning and corresponding response configuration.

As educators, we need to be engaged directly with the CD/OD ROM. Only then can we begin to appreciate what this powerful computer peripheral can and cannot do. Only then can we learn what is easy to do, and what may be cumbersome today but easy tomorrow. In short, we need to begin to join forces with the makers of the tool in tackling the tasks we must accomplish. A good starting point for our exploratory application efforts is the Grolier disc. And if, as they say, the Grolier disc will soon contain not only the encyclopedia but a dictionary and thesaurus as well, then we need to start using it, and from our trial and error efforts provide the scenarios and suggestions for the third and fourth editions!

Then, in the words of Stephan Haeckel of IBM, we may graduate into a new way of thinking. If the technology—be it the PC or CD/OD ROM or Smart Card or a combination of all—can do these things, perhaps that same capability can be applied to other related educational problems. Finally, some day we as educators, will come of age technologically. We will be able to move about freely, utilizing the computer's extensive memory banks and capabilities with ease.

The micro wedded to the CD/OD ROM has the inherent ability to extend our personal vision. Few of today's applications were conceivable just 20 years ago—or even 5 years ago. We are experiencing an exponential (constantly accelerating) rate of change. The computer can extend the range of our senses and enlarge our supply of concepts. The ability to integrate, synthesize, and enhance information from a large number of sources puts us as learners in a position similar to the astronaut about to pull away from the gravitational hold of earth. Alfred North Whitehead would have envied us our opportunities. The human imagination can revel in new contexts and identify and follow new patterns of thought formerly unavailable. Through these new technologies we can learn to think thoughts we otherwise could never have imagined.

It should not be surprising that the new technologies such as CD/OD ROM and the Smart Card can go in directions in the next decade that are difficult to project. We educators need to turn to those furthest along on the computer learning curve for some guidance. We need to observe creative talents, such as those at MIT's Center for Arts and Media Technology, where exploratory efforts include computer music, personalized electronic newspapers, and interactive movies. The work is seminal and only visionary for some, even though it is firmly based on state-of-the-art technology.

Like any change, the introduction of technology must be managed and led into uncharted areas if it is to radically change the face of education. It is time for some of us in education to lead the technology rather than to be led by it. If we are up to the task, then the next decade will be rewarding and creative in terms of combined technologies, applications, and needs—bringing education to a level we have never before dared contemplate. In order to provide for this leadership, we as educators need to develop some scenarios and let the delivery-systems engineers put the support pieces together.

Scenario One

A few days ago I was reading an article by William J. Broad in the Science section of the *New York Times* (22 November 1985). The article was titled "Light May Be Key to New Generation of Fast Computers." Here are some passages from the article.

> All computers, be they personal ones or government behemoths, rely on digital switching by streams of electrons. Today, however, a few bold scientists believe they are on the verge of a radical change in the fundamentals of the field. They envision computers that run on light instead of electricity. Though there are skeptics who believe it impossible, the goal of these scientists is to abandon electrons altogether for the tiny packets of light known as photons. The attraction is that photonic computers could work thousands of times faster than the best possible electronic ones, and could process data in remarkable new ways. "The key to the future is to go from electrons to photons," said Dr. Rustum Roy, professor of solid-state science at Pennsylvania State University and past director of the university's Materials Research Laboratory.

Let me stop here for a moment. What kind of questions go through my mind as I read this? Let me remind you that the *New York Times* Science section is written for the literate lay reader. The scientist would ask for the technical papers. I consider myself to be one of these literate laymen. I do not fully understand, however, what "digital switching by streams of electrons" is. But I do have a hazy idea of what it is. Let us imagine that this edition of the *Times* is on a CD ROM disc and that the computer reading the disc has the following colored squares: red for definition, blue for graphics and/or pictures, green for clarification, yellow for remedial learning sequence, orange for animation, black for voice synthesis, and so on. Further, let us imagine that I could elicit any of these by touching the colored icon on the screen or using a mouse—or even calling out the color.

But wouldn't it be nice if I could touch the blue and/or orange icon on the screen with the cursor flashing under the phrase "digital switching by streams of electrons" and immediately get a dynamic visual graphic—and possibly holographic—explanation of the concept!

Educational technology is a science which too often has been based on the adaptation of present technological developments to educational purposes rather than on developing technological innovations from learning needs.

Another need for a horizontal deviation from a linear reading of the article is illustrated by the quotation "the goals of these scientists is to abandon electrons altogether for the tiny packets of light known as photons."

One has to stop and ask, "OK, what is a photon?" Do you know? Have you ever seen a diagram of one? For some, the photon may be a completely new concept. In fact, this was the first time I had read anything about a photon. One of my associates, with whom I was discussing this article during its draft stages, was shocked at my ignorance. She asked, "Don't you know about photosynthesis?" in a tone of voice which implied that *everyone* knows about photosynthesis. What she didn't know was that I had never taken a course in botany; I took French Literature instead. I'd like to know what it is now—not three pages or three years later. As the cursor is flashing under the word *photon* I would like to be able to touch a red icon, which would stand for the definition, and get the dictionary explanation of photon. Or I would want to touch the blue icon, which would give me the *Encyclopaedia Britannica* definition of a photon; or the yellow icon, which would give me a visual picture of the definition accompanied by a remedial learning sequence. I think that Vannevar Bush would appreciate this.

Now, let me continue with the *Times* article.

"It's like trying to conquer Mount Everest," said Dr. Alan Huang, director of the newly formed Optical Computing Department at AT&T Bell Laboratories. "We're doing something with a lot of risk. We're taking the first step on a journey of 1,000 miles." Despite this seemingly enormous challenge, Dr. Huang believes his Bell Labs team can create, within just one year, a primitive prototype of an optical computer and, within five years, a working full-scale model.

"A real number-cruncher," as he put it. "Number-cruncher?" What is that? I keep hearing it everywhere I turn today. Recently I was able to grasp its meaning when someone explained to me that "number-crunching" referred to the ability to process millions and millions of computer operations a second. Dr. Huang quickly added that "Bell Labs has a reputation for innovations, having invented the transistor, the maser, the laser and many devices that have advanced the art of manipulating light to man's advantage."

The term "maser" is completely new to me. So I touch another icon and I receive an animated and graphic description of the maser.

The key is to create an optical analog of the transistor, which is still the muscle behind computation. It would switch light on and off in a way similar to how a transistor switches electricity.

310

Here I may stop and wonder what exactly a transistor is and what its importance is to computing. I would like to be able to push an icon and have this concept clarified for me.

Like any change, the introduction of technology must be managed and led into uncharted areas if it is to radically change the face of education.

You get my point: If I could have spontaneous access to other references and sources of information, I would start to come close to the "seamless carpet of learning" that I mentioned earlier. Now we are talking about interactivity in learning in a way we never talked about it before. Exploratory and discovery learning? There are no frames or boundaries anymore.

There are other technologies similar to the CD ROM that are exploring the possibilities embedded in the above scenario. For example, in August 1985, Xerox introduced Notecards. Frank G. Halasz, a research scientist at the Xerox Corporation's Palo Alto Research Center and project director for the Notecard, says that the Notecard can "provide a document that people can look at at various levels."

Andrew Pollack, writing in the *New York Times* recently (29 August 1985), tells us of the constraints and limitations of text written on paper. He points out that text written on paper must be in a specific order. Because articles "have a particular order of paragraphs the reader will normally follow from beginning to end in sequential fashion." To my mind this limits creative thinking while reading. The "grasshopper mentality" finds it difficult to deal with printed materials. Pollack suggests that "computer-based information need not be bound by such restrictions imposed by paper. With computers it is possible to have individual small packets of information that can be called up in any order the reader desires. The concept has been called nonsequential text, or hypertext, and it is slowly gaining adherents in computer science." Well, what Pollack is really talking about is not only computer-based information but also the media that make it possible: CD ROM, the Smart Card, and the new Xerox Notecard.

Pollack illustrates the potential activities of hypertext by describing what I have chosen to call the "grasshopper mentality." The concept is not easy to grasp, but one analogy might be a variety of tours through a museum. Some provide a single route that takes a visitor past all the exhibits. Others concentrate on certain exhibits and by-pass others. Similarly, an electronic hypertext document would offer choices. For instance, a person reading a hypertext article about a company would have a choice of how much detail he wanted on the company's history and how much on finances. The concepts have been in some electronic novels—and computer games—in which the plot changes depending on choices made by the player.

But hypertext would also allow users to link different documents. Encyclopedias, for instance, often contain cross references to other articles, which in turn contain cross references to still others. But following the cross references is tedious. With a hypertext encyclopedia, a reader could press a button and jump to the relevant part of the cross-referenced article and from there to another cross-referenced article. In short, one could hop from article to article, following a given idea. Similarly, instead of just seeing a reference to another book in a footnote, a reader could move immediately to the relevant part of that book. Traditional data banks permit the retrieval of documents quickly but do not allow movement from one document to the middle of another.

The first hypertext system was developed in the early 1960s by Douglas C. Engelbart. He also developed the mouse for controlling the computer. Ted Nelson, an author and futurist, coined the term "hypertext" in the mid-sixties. At Brown University, a hypertext system using the Macintosh computer, will be tested in an English course as a way of providing students with information and comments on the literature being read. Simple concepts related to hypertext are appearing in personal computer programs such as Thinktank by Living Videotext Inc., and Framework by Ashton-Tate. These programs, sometimes called outline processors or idea processors, allow users to manipulate blocks of data into outline form. With Notecards, however, ideas do not have to be organized into a linear outline. The system allows any card to be connected to any other in a complex network. One can envision the system as consisting of cards with lines between them, like a map of cities and the roads between them.

Scenario Two

Recently, I have been fascinated by artificial intelligence genius Douglas Hofstader's *Metamagical Themas*. Likewise impressed, Leonard Bernstein writes:

> Doug Hofstadter is rapidly becoming the Hamlet of our times: whatever he says is both exact and double-edged, reassuring but provocative, poetic and self-challenging. His scariest insights and most agonizing intellectual probings are graced, like Hamlet's, with humor, affection, and a kind of mad musical charm.

Martin Gardner writes:

> [Douglas Hofstadter] is as incapable of writing opaquely as his alter-ego Egbert B. Gebstadter is incapable of writing clearly. Like his previous *Godel, Escher, Bach: An Eternal Golden Braid,* the new book glitters with Godelian self-reference jokes, Escherlike illustrations, and Bachlike fugues.

According to Daniel C. Dennett, Professor of Philosophy at Tufts University:

> This wonderful collection tackles virtually every area of fascination and controversy in science today, from mathematics and quantum mechanics through evolutionary theory to artificial intelligence, the nature of human thought and rational choice, and ties them together by showing how understanding in one area enhances understanding in others. Hofstadter realizes that before you can "prove" or "refute" anything, you must *understand.*

The challenge confronting me as a reader was how to get understanding in one area before I could have an enhancement of understanding in another area. These comments intrigued me. I said to myself, "This is a book that I must read." So I purchased a copy and read the blurb. Let me just relate to you a few paragraphs from the blurb, which will give you some idea of why I realized very shortly that I could not possibly master the book until I had read his earlier treatise, *Godel, Escher, Bach: An Eternal Golden Braid,* subtitled *A Metaphorical Fugue on Minds and Machines in the Spirit of Lewis Carroll.* Even the blurb, let alone the book, should have been on a CD ROM allowing me to find definitions and clarifications for some of the terms used. For example,

> In this scholarly, entertaining, and provocative book named after his recent column in *Scientific American,* Douglas Hofstadter has collected 33 essays and woven them together with elaborate postscripts. All "Metamagical Themas" columns are included, as well as seven other pieces. Despite its wide range of topics, *Metamagical Themas* possesses a strong sense of unity, thanks to the author's painstaking efforts, in the postscripts, to spell out connections, cross-references, and implicit ideas.

So far, no problem.

The primary concern, permeating virtually every page, is how people perceive and think. Hofstadter explores the fluidity of human analogical thought and perception, along with strategies for making machines that perceive, create, and feel. His essays range from self-describing sentences in French to sexist language in Chinese; from a sober condemnation of public "innumeracy" to an enthusiastic soliloquy on the infinite richness of the alphabet; from genetic evolution to its software counterpart, "mimetic" evolution; from experiments with the Prisoner's Dilemma to the beautiful mathematical shapes known as "strange attractors"; from quantum-mechanical quarks to Rubik's cubical quarks. Hofstadter asks how musical and visual patterns can stir our emotions; how we manage to sift the true from the false, the relevant from the irrelevant, the meaningful from the meaningless.

It is time for some of us in education to lead the technology rather than to be led by it.

Now that paragraph took some thought, and the dictionary was not of much help. Let me list my problem areas:

○ Sober condemnation of public "innumeracy"

○ "Mimetic" evolution

○ Beautiful mathematical shapes known as "strange attractors"

○ Quantum-mechanical quarks

○ Rubik's-cubical quarks

Well, I didn't want to give up. So then I went to *Godel, Escher, and Bach*. Let us imagine that I not only have the book on the CD ROM but also all the ancillary references. For example, here is the first paragraph:

Bach Frederick was an admirer not only of pianos, but also of an organist and composer by the name of J. S. Bach. This Bach's compositions were somewhat notorious. Some called them "turgid and confused," while others claimed they were incomparable masterpieces. But no one disputed Bach's ability to improvise on the organ. In those days, being an organist not only meant being able to play, but also to extemporize, and Bach was known far and wide for his remarkable extemporizations. (For some delightful anecdotes about Bach's extemporization, see *The Bach Reader*, by H. T. David and A. Mendel.)

314

Now, that interests me. I would like to see *The Bach Reader*. But where do I find it? I assure you it is not on my library shelf. The Library of Congress? My favorite bookstore? Oh, well, I say to myself—nice thought. But the delightful anecdotes about Bach's extemporization will have to wait for another time. Or be forgotten. A learning opportunity lost. But if Hofstadter had made arrangements with his CD ROM publisher to include all his references, then all I would have to do is touch an icon and immediately access *The Bach Reader* and enjoy the delightful anecdotes about Bach's extemporizations.

Presently, in reading—no, not reading, studying really—*Godel, Escher, and Bach,* I am using the services of three consultants. I cannot read music, so I call up and ask my good friend Dr. X, a psychologist, system theorist, musical composer, and concert pianist for guidance. I know something about mathematics, but I'm not that good; so here I need the services of another colleague, a professor of mathematics, to help me with Godel. With respect to Escher, the text is well illustrated, and with the help of an art historian, I receive further assistance. But what a laborious task this is. And to gather these minds together at, say, two o'clock in the morning, if I choose to read at that hour, or at any time convenient to all of us is virtually impossible. With a multimedia CD ROM and the icons described above, I could handle the following potpourri of paragraphs and sentences with ease and delight. Who knows? Education may truly become ecstasy.

There is no question in my mind that compact disc technology will be prevalent throughout the world.

To give an idea of how extraordinary a six-part fugue is, in the entire *Well-Tempered Clavier* by Bach, containing forty-eight preludes and fugues, only two have as many as five parts, and nowhere is there a six-part fugue! One could probably liken the task of improvising a six-part fugue to the playing of sixty simultaneous blindfold games of chess, and winning them all. To improvise an eight-part fugue is really beyond human capability. In the copy which Bach sent to King Frederick, on the page preceding the first sheet of music, was the following inscription:

Regis Iusfu Cantio et Reliqua Canonica Arte Refolula

Touching several icons, I have an explanation of a six-part fugue in both sound and graphics. Another icon gives me the translation of the Latin inscription.

Let me take you to another section. Where Hofstadter asks us to:

> Look, for example, at the lithograph *Waterfall*, and compare its six-step endlessly falling loop with the six-step endlessly rising loop of the *Canon per Tonos*. The similarity of vision is remarkable. Bach and Escher are playing one single theme in two different "keys": music and art . . . Escher realized Strange Loops in several different ways, and they can be arranged according to the tightness of the loop. The lithograph *Ascending and Descending*, in which monks trudge forever in loops, is the loosest version, since it involves so many steps before the starting point is regained. A tighter loop is contained in *Waterfall*, which, as we already observed, involves only six discrete steps. You may be thinking that there is some ambiguity in the notion of a single "step"—for instance, couldn't *Ascending and Descending* be seen just as easily as having four levels (staircases) as forty-five levels (stairs)? It is indeed true that there is an inherent haziness in level-counting, not only in Escher pictures, but in hierarchical, many-level systems. We will sharpen our understanding of this haziness later on. But let us not get too distracted now! As we tighten our loop, we come to the remarkable *Drawing Hands*, in which each of two hands draws the other: a two-step Strange Loop. And finally, the tightest of all Strange Loops is realized in *Print Gallery:* a picture of a picture which contains itself. Or is it a picture of a gallery which contains itself? Or of a town which contains itself? Or a young man who contains himself? (Incidentally, the illusion underlying *Ascending and Descending* and *Waterfall* was not invented by Escher, but by Roger Penrose, a British mathematician, in 1958. However, the theme of the Strange Loop was already present in Escher's work in 1948, the year he drew *Drawing Hands. Print Gallery* dates from 1956.)

At this point, if you are the average literate reader, as I presume I am, I know that I cannot have a firm grasp of Strange Loops without some help from my consultants, and even with their help I would still have difficulty with understanding Epimenides' paradox that Hofstadter tries to explain when he gets to Godel. The print medium makes it extremely difficult to deal with recursive concepts. I am convinced that the capabilities of the CD ROM, powered by the micro, can make the reading of Hofstadter's genius a truly delightful and exploratory experience—rather than the laborious, painstaking effort it has been to date. Hofstadter is attempting to communicate his genius in a constrained format. He needs the tools of a composer; and in his book he is also dealing with mathematics, philosophy, and art. Eventually, this kind of knowledge must come about through

315

discovery learning, not through the sequential acquisition of ideas. We are now to the point where we can look at knowledge bases and learning with "no frames and no boundaries."

The micro can become the most civilizing influence that we have had to date. It can amplify our intelligence and our ability to manipulate symbols. Pamela McCorduck, in her book *The Universal Machine*, traces the long intellectual tradition that began with the human language itself and encompasses the Golden Age of Greece, the burghers of fifteenth-century northern Europe, and America's own Henry Adams. On a personal search for a bridge between C. P. Snow's Two Cultures—the humanities and the sciences—she sees the computer as the bridge, the machine of the century, the hope of the future. I agree completely. She asks, "What shall we call electronic text?" But she never really answers the question, leaving it to our imagination instead.

We are finding little in the way of answers, but much in the way of questions. We are just beginning to scratch the surface of this powerful new technology. It can give us a new way of thinking about knowledge itself and help us to explore completely new possibilities in learning. I cannot help recalling the words of the late Russell Schwikert, an Apollo IX astronaut, who, as he was circling the earth and looking down at the small sphere we call our global village, was heard to say:

> When you go around it in an hour and a half, you begin to recognize that your identity is with that whole thing. And that makes a change.

> You look down there, and you can't imagine how many borders and boundaries you cross, again and again and again, and you don't even see them. There you are—hundreds of people killing each other over some imaginary line that you're not even aware of, that you can't see. From where you see it, the thing is a whole, and it's so beautiful. You wish you could take one person in each hand and say, "Look at it from this perspective. What's important?"

> You realize that on that small spot, that little blue and white thing, is everything that means anything to you. All of history and music and poetry and art and birth and love; tears, joy, games. All of it on that little spot out there that you can cover with your thumb.

That "little spot" contains so much. The little micro—and the little chip and the little compact disc—can also contain so much. There is no question in my mind that compact disc technology will be prevalent throughout the world. It can contain everything that we have been, and are, and

We do not talk about pencil-based learning or book-based learning, and I fail to understand why it is that we talk about computer-assisted learning.

are going to be. Compact disc players and compact discs will entertain people throughout this global village of ours. Whether its educational potential will be realized remains to be seen. It is possible, but not likely, if history provides any lessons, that educators will work with electronic and light engineers to break with the past and achieve and embark on new paths of learning. Those of you who watched the Live Aid Concert in July 1985 may recall the Soviet announcer who exclaimed that "it's nice that high technology is contributing to something positive." Walter J. Bojsza, New Products Editor of *Electronics Design,* reminds us that the Live Aid broadcast was a marvel of the technically impossible made commonplace. It was beamed to 152 countries around the world through 14 satellites. The stadiums of London and Philadelphia were linked electronically with a clarity hardly possible at times in the same building. Digital circuits reconciled American and European transmission standards to produce intricate visual animated graphics. All these systems worked so smoothly that they were virtually transparent.

If we start talking about CD ROM-assisted learning in the same way in which we talk about computer-assisted instruction, then we will fall far short of the goal. We do not talk about pencil-based learning or book-based learning, and I fail to understand why it is that we talk about computer-assisted learning. Only when these new tools become virtually as transparent as the book and the newspaper and the TV set will we really begin to exploit them. And for this task, we need systems designers who will listen to the poets of education, and for the poets to respect the systems engineers. Both of us need to dream together.

About forty years ago I attended a meeting of the American Psychological Association, where B. F. Skinner was asked by a young graduate student what he thought of Jerome Bruner's astonishing dictum that you can teach anything to anyone in an intellectually honest manner at any age level whatsoever. Skinner simply shrugged his shoulders and said, "How?" I merely would like to add that while Skinner and Bruner were writing and speaking, Vannevar Bush was penning his *Atlantic* article. Forty years later, all three minds meet. With the micro-powered CD ROM containing the necessary software, we are now able to answer Professor Skinner's "how?" and make Bruner's dream a reality.

The late Robert Kennedy unwittingly quoted George Bernard Shaw, who in turn had unwittingly quoted Aeschylus, as all three said, "Some people look at things that are and ask, 'Why?' I look at things that never were and ask, 'Why not?'"

317

About the Author

Dr. Gabriel D. Ofiesh is Emeritus Professor of Educational Technology, Howard University, Washington, D.C., and president of Communications and Training Systems International Inc. He holds an M.S. degree in psychology from Columbia University and an Ed.D. from the University of Denver.

His experience ranges from the U.S Air Force Academy, where he was Professor of Psychology and Director of Leadership Studies, to the Air Training Command, where he pioneered the instructional systems approach to training. For the past eight years he has served as a consultant to the Office of Foreign Relations, U.S. Department of Labor, with special responsibility for conceptualizing the individualized instruction methodology for the vocational training programs for Saudi Arabia and assisting in the formulation of a Center for Advanced Learning Systems, where he is tracking new technologies of training for the Department. He also has served as chief consultant in educational technology to Price Waterhouse and other multinational organizations.

He has conducted training programs in instructional and new educational technologies for trainers in Panama, Costa Rica, Brazil, El Salvador, Nicaragua, Chile, Turkey, and Saudi Arabia. Recently he has conducted seminars in new technologies of communications and training systems for various multinational organizations such as the International Labor Office, USAID, IBM, and numerous others. He was formerly Professor of Educational Technology, American University; Professor of Educational Technology and Director, Center for Educational Technology, The Catholic University of America; Director, Training Methods Study, Comprehensive Training and Education Program, Office of the Assistant Secretary for Defense for Manpower Development; Professor and Head, Department of Psychology, Management and Leadership Studies, USAF Academy.

He is the author of a definitive text on programmed instruction, published by the American Management Association. The text has been translated into Spanish and has had wide use throughout Latin America. He is the author of more than 80 articles which are relevant to the instructional systems process. He has given more than 200 invited addresses to professional groups in the United States and in many foreign countries on innovative educational methodologies. He is the founder, first president, and honorary life member of the National Society for Performance and Instruction; recipient of the Researcher of the Year Award, University of Denver Chapter, Phi Delta Kappa; and the Legion of Merit (USAF award for his innovative contributions to training programs in the U.S. military).

Communications and Training Systems International Inc.
4031 27th Road North
Arlington, VA 22207

References

Hofstadter, D. R. *Godel, Escher, Bach: An Eternal Golden Braid.* New York: Basic Books, 1979.

McCorduck, P. *The Universal Machine.* New York: McGraw-Hill, 1985.

Transition from Page to Screen

by Stephen T. Kerr

As the printed word gives rise to the electronic word, so does the printed page give rise to the display screen. The transition from one to the other creates problems for both designers and users. These problems arise because the physical form of electronic materials is usually quite different from that of printed materials (no table of contents at the front or index at the back, difficult to put one's finger between two pages while checking a reference on another page, etc.). The problems lie primarily in two areas: design of the surface and design of the interface.

Surface design involves making decisions about typography, layout of elements on the surface, the use of graphics and illustrations in the text, and the quality of language in the text. Also important to consider are the ways in which users react subjectively to these elements. *Interface design* for electronic text is closely tied to the "wayfinding problem"—helping users navigate through parts of the text, move from one level of information to another, retrace steps, find help, and make decisions about what part of the text to retrieve next. The wayfinding problem manifests itself on three different levels: the immediate structure of the text (how information on navigation is provided at the page or screen level), the internal structure (how that information is provided within a given document), and the external structure (navigational aids that allow users to move from one document of interest to another).

This chapter reviews research relevant to the design of textual surfaces and interfaces for electronic text. It draws on work being done in such areas as human-computer interaction, use of videotex databases, and information science. Three directions for further research are identified: studies on how users of electronic text use and search through text; development of paradigms for effective search as user aids; and studies of how users conceptualize and represent to themselves the structure of the text with which they are working.

Scenario

The student reaches out a hand and picks up a text. In working one of the problems contained therein, the student needs to refer to a table of figures at the back of the book. To refresh his memory on how to use that table, the student must also consult an earlier chapter and page in the text. Finding that point requires using the book's index. Holding a finger in the book at the point where the problem is given, and placing the thumb at the place where the table occurs, the student proceeds to use the index, checks

321

the point where information on how to use the table is given, refers to the table, and returns to the page with the original problem. All this takes a matter of seconds.

Another student is working with similar material presented as an interactive computer program. The problem is stated on one screen, but knowing how to get to the table requires knowing a command sequence. The student refers to a small printed card to find the correct command sequence to find the table, enters the appropriate key strokes, makes a mistake, and succeeds in finding the table on the second try. On seeing the table and realizing that using it correctly will require reference to a part of the program different from that currently being used, the student checks yet another command sequence, enters key strokes, and eventually finds the information needed to make sense of the table. Moving back and forth between the table and the material explaining it takes a series of commands. The student does this several times before feeling comfortable that the interpretation of the table is on target and the information extracted from it is correct. The student then faces the task of relocating himself at the point in the program from which he originally came. That, too, requires some keystrokes, together with a tolerance for working through several frames of information and problems that he has already seen (some of them more than once).

The examples are hypothetical ones, but the problems portrayed in the second set are real—all too real for many learners who use electronic media for research and learning. While not all such systems generate the kinds of difficulties shown here, many do. Even in those that are well designed and make it easier for the experienced user to find the information needed, the transfer from one system to another rarely allows that user get by without learning some new commands or procedures. The problem is one of navigation: how to find one's way through the information in order to use it easily and efficiently.

Electronic Text and Wayfinding

The problem of finding one's way in electronic text is caused in part by the rapid shift from print-based to computer-based learning. The unique characteristics of electronic text make the issues we face as designers both difficult and fascinating. Our main concern is this: How can we design strategies and procedures that will enable users of electronic text to find the information they need and move efficiently and easily from one section of that text to another?

We will examine this issue by first delving more deeply into the nature of the question and then comparing the relevant features of electronic and printed text. After that we will examine the practical and psychological aspects of wayfinding. Following that is a review of what we know about the design of textual surfaces and interfaces, which includes descriptions of some of the research on how users learn to search for information in print-based text and how they respond to different screen designs and interface designs for computerized systems.

323

From Print to Screen

The problem of finding one's way in electronic text is caused in part by the rapid shift from print-based to computer-based learning.

The shift from the use of printed materials for learning and instruction to the use of electronic systems is one of the most interesting aspects of the advent of computers in offices, factories, schools, and homes. It may be that the most significant changes these developments bring with them are not at all the most obvious or publicly discussed ones—the high levels of motivation that seem to come with using computer-based instructional materials, the apparent improvement in test scores that follows upon regular practice with computer-based programs. Rather, the important shifts may be in the less visible habits of mind that accompany our work with information presented in textual form.

Our ways of working with printed materials are so long established, so closely interwoven into our unexamined view of what learning, teaching, searching for, and using information are, that it is very difficult to step back and see clearly just how many things we take for granted. Even between cultures, for example, we generally know what a book or a journal "looks like," what conventions will be followed in its preparation and presentation. A book published in the USSR may have its table of contents at the back of the volume rather than at the front, but we soon adjust to those minor differences and learn to cope. We may become frustrated on delving into historical materials from the last century on finding that they typically lack indexes; some made up for this by having elaborate and detailed tables of contents. And we also may note that some had long and complex title pages that seemed to perform virtually the same function as today's dust jackets and inner-cover notes.

324

When we move further back in history toward the origins of printing, we begin to find more and more divergence in the look of the printed page and the wayfinding aids that we usually take for granted. Consider, for example, the development of the conventions surrounding the title page: early (incunabular) books typically had no separate title page. The work simply began, and often books had no "title" but for the first few words of the text itself. As the number of printed works grew, and as printers came to see the potential value to readers (not to mention themselves) of providing more information about the provenance of a particular work, title pages appeared and came to include a larger and larger variety of material—the title, to be sure (often supplied by the printer and not the author), but also the printer's name and location, sometimes the date, sometimes illustrations, and frequently elaborations of the title that we might today mistake for advertisements. (The best single discussion of how these features of early books developed may be found in Febvre and Martin [1976]. Other interesting articles have appeared in such journals as *Visible Language* over the years.)

As we move still further back, we can trace in handwritten texts the development of yet other conventions that now seem so basic we have difficulty imagining what it would have been like to read, study, or write without them. These include such basic organizing features of text as upper- and lowercase letters, punctuation marks, spacing between words, separation of sentences and paragraphs, and the direction in which words move on a page—Greek "boustrophedontic" writing prior to the fourth century BC went alternately from right to left and from left to right. All these conventions evolved; they did not spring fully developed from the minds of some original writer. (See Ong [1982] for a treatment of preliterate consciousness and Bateson [1983] for remarks on the development of punctuation.)

What, then, are the mechanical aids—the electronic equivalents to pagination, paragraphing, indexes, and tables of contents—and what are the habits of mind with which users of electronic texts will need to be equipped in order to make best use of computer-based materials? While we probably cannot foresee with complete accuracy what is needed, we can make some predictions based on research that has been done on the nature of print materials and on their electronic counterparts. First, though, we should clarify just what an instructional text is and define more carefully that scope of the problem in information location and navigation that I choose to call "wayfinding."

Electronic Text as Instructional Text

It is important at this point to distinguish the sense in which "instructional text" is used here. First and foremost, I want to imply a broader definition than simply a "textbook" in the commonly understood meaning of that word. The high school or college text is surely one species of instructional text in the broader sense, but there are others: the set of materials that are produced for teaching aircraft mechanics a new skill and the videodisc that provides auto dealers with information about new models are different from but no less instructional than their bookish counterparts.

Similarly, all manner of manuals, dictionaries, catalogs, and other reference materials ought rightly to be considered instructional, for they are a common source (especially for adult learners) of new information that allows a job to be performed better, or of review material that permits previously learned procedures to be recalled and carried out. Indeed, Sticht (1985) makes the point that "reading to do" (using manuals and reference aids as a supplement to memory) is much more typical of adults' reading patterns than is "reading to learn" (attempting to transfer material from the text into long-term memory), which we more commonly take as a model of the reading process.

"Reading to do" appears to involve not only knowing how to read but also knowing how to use the instructional material itself as an aid to memory. More research (on questions ranging from typography to text comprehension to development of reading skills) and more efforts at creating a well-founded theory of reading have been focused on the problems inherent in "reading to learn." "Reading to do," on the other hand, has been the target of more applied efforts by instructional designers and developers but has suffered consequently from less attention by researchers and theorists.

Most instructional text presented electronically seems to fall somewhere between "reading to learn" and "reading to do." Instructional programs should not simply scroll textual information on the screen, for that does not capitalize on what the computer does best; nor does it provide a justification for using a very expensive piece of machinery to do what a very simple technology, the book, could do as well. Rather, electronic instructional texts offer the learner the opportunity of moving around, of branching to a point farther on in the program when responses indicate mastery of the material currently being presented, or branching backward in the case of lack of mastery. More sophisticated diagnostic programs offer even more in the way of branching, screen switching, presenting different sorts of information in different windows on the screen, and so forth.

These considerations suggest that it is wise to think of instructional text as a category broad enough to include a variety of applications and approaches often ignored in classical studies of reading, comprehension, and text design. A further development that would encourage us to define instructional text broadly is the current interest among educators in the potential use of large remote databases of computerized information as resources for learning and teaching. While the concept of "the world at your fingertips" is not a new one (librarians have been trying for years—usually in vain—to get students to think of the library in this way), the possibility of offering easy and direct electronic connections between schools and massive databases is tempting educators in the United States, Canada, and Britain to explore these possibilities seriously.

The central problem here is not only to create the linkages but to figure out what teaching and learning using large databases would look like. Educators have not traditionally thought of instructional texts as being accompanied by sufficient data to carry out large-scale investigations with real figures. Usually both teachers and students have had to be satisfied with sample data sets and hypothetical cases.

The use of large-scale databases as instructional tools could well apply to adult learners as well. Educational and instructional materials have been included as features of most of the trials of videotex information systems in North America and Europe, and surveys show that instruction is one strong reason that many consumers give for wanting to subscribe to such a service. How adults will be able to use those instructional materials in practice, however, remains to be seen. As will be clear from a review of the research that has already been done in adult uses of electronic databases, there are problems here as well as opportunities.

The Nature of the Wayfinding Problem

It makes sense here to pause and consider just what sort of problem navigation in electronic space really is. And in fact it turns out to be more of a puzzle than we might think, for there are a number of aspects to the problem that are rarely examined all in one place. Part of the reason for this is the invisibility of the problem: Because we are so used to using books and other print materials, we often fail to consider carefully enough how to translate print-derived wayfinding strategies into a format suitable for electronic text. (This in spite of the fact that 35 percent of the total investment in software production is spent preparing the user interface [Smith and Mosier, 1984]). Because we feel that solving the wayfinding problem *should* be simple, we assume that it in fact is, and so may deny it "problem" status at all.

Because we are so used to using books and other print materials, we often fail to consider carefully enough how to translate print-derived wayfinding strategies into a format suitable for electronic text.

A second reason that there is no single unified approach to the wayfinding problem is that it is perhaps a classic example of a problem demanding an interdisciplinary solution. Consider the bewildering array of researchers who have a stake in defining and solving the problem: psychologists (of various kinds), librarians, educators, computer scientists and engineers, human factors specialists (who may or may not identify with one of the preceding groups), and even such farther-afield folk as graphic designers, typographers, publishers, and architects. Relevant research and reports of applied development activities appear regularly in the publications of all these groups. The problem is in trying to extract a common perspective.

A third reason that wayfinding is a distinctly difficult problem to solve is that it involves a number of different processes carried out at different levels of conscious activity. Finding one's way in electronic text is at once a matter of problem recognition and problem solving—knowing that one has a problem that access to information might solve, knowing how to define and limit the problem, knowing where to look, and so forth. It is also a matter of having requisite mechanical and search strategies—knowing the keystroke sequences necessary to shift from one part of a program to another, knowing command sequences for different databases, and so on. And it is also a matter of context: the urgency with which the user needs the information, prior experience in using electronic materials, tolerance for delay and uncertainty (in many present-day systems), and the degree of precision required in the solution to the original problem.

Each of these aspects of the wayfinding problem is important. The goal here is to try to shed light on the mechanical and design aspects of the design of electronic surfaces and interfaces, with some attention given to the other aspects of the problem. The section that follows is a review of what we know about both the design of instructional text surfaces (the individual screen or page on which information is presented to the user), as well as the creation of appropriate interfaces (the systems that allow the user to gain access to information and to navigate within the material).

The Design of the Surface and the Interface

By *surface* I mean the part of the text that is visible at any given moment to the user. For print materials this usually means a single page of material; for electronic materials it means a single screen or "frame" of information. By *interface* I mean the system or structure that gives the user access to the text at a place or in a way that the user desires. For print materials this includes the whole system of indexes and guides to the text as well as typographic and other cues to the user's location (some have referred to this as the "metastructure" of the text, to distinguish it from the primary textual structure of meaning as presented in the prose). For electronic materials, it includes those parts of the text that allow the user to call up different screens, to switch back and forth from one screen to another, and to change levels within the text or database.

For both surface and interface we can refer to the body of available research results for guidance on similarities and differences between print and electronic text. My aim here is not merely to review those results but also to extract relevant differences and suggest implications these may have for those who do research on and those who design electronic text.

Surface Design

The surface that the user encounters when using printed or electronic materials includes a number of separate characteristics:

○ Typography (the shape of individual letter forms)

○ Layout (the arrangement of text and white space on the surface)

○ The use of illustrations and graphics of various sorts

○ The quality of the text as language (its readability, logical structure, and so on)

○ The reaction that the surface of the text calls forth in the user (the perceived value of the material, reaction to how it is arranged, and so on)

In each case, what is true for printed text may not hold true (or more often, may vary subtly) for electronic text.

Typography.   The way in which the letter forms are displayed varies, of course, between print and electronic forms. Print typography, with a history of centuries of development, offers numerous possibilities for the designer. Varieties of style, weight, size, and mixtures of upper- and lowercase have been studied for their contribution to comprehension and ease of use. Readers of printed text seem to have little difficulty in working with any reasonably simple and consistent type style, although they experience difficulties if forced to use type that has too many cues (e.g., Old English or "black letter" type faces) or too few (e.g., type that lacks serifs or ascenders/descenders; many dot matrix printers are at fault on both these counts). Hartley (1978) and Jonassen (1982) have useful comments on these matters. (For an excellent annotated listing of sources on both print and electronic surface design, see McGee and Matthews [1985]).

In today's electronic text, there is much less variety in the letter forms that can be physically displayed, though that may change with improved displays. One phenomenon observed in several studies is a preference for smaller, more densely packed characters, such as a 70- instead of a 35-character line (Kolers, Duchnicky, and Ferguson, 1981). Another survey reported that 56 percent of the users of a teletext service wanted to see more information on each screen, a change that would be a function of letter size as well as layout (CSP International, 1982). Whether this preference is simply a residue of users' experiences with printed text remains to be seen. As is the case with print, reading all uppercase material from a CRT seems to be difficult and tiring (Foster and Champness, 1982).

Layout. The arrangement of the information on the screen is another important factor in both formats. How much blank ("white") space is worked into the text plays an important role in how users perceive the material and how easy they find it to work with. Spacing between sections, headings of various sizes and weights, and the conventions for grouping items on page or screen (e.g., sidebars and boxes) all play a role here. Considerable work has been done in this area recently, and it seems clear that these elements play a major role in helping users not only to understand the material being presented but also to encode it for long-term storage and retrieval (Anderson and Armbruster, 1985; Glynn et al., 1984).

The work that has been done on electronic text shows that these layout variables are, if anything, even more important in this mode of presentation. Both Marcus (1982) and Grabinger (1984), for example, found that leading or line skipping led to improved performance. Tullis (1983) went so far as to suggest that measures of text density could provide one simple index of display quality without having to conduct empirical tests.

This apparent preference for more spacing on CRT displays conflicts with the desire for more information per screen noted above. Users have clearly not yet come to grips with the visual world of the display, and it may take the advent of more sophisticated devices that can show more material on each screen to make people feel more comfortable with reading using electronic text.

The use of color is another aspect of layout that should not be ignored. In printed material, color is a considerable added expense and so is used sparingly. While it has been shown to be an effective cue in some situations, its use is rarely perceived as mandatory (see, for example, Waller, Lefrere, and MacDonald-Ross [1982]). In contrast, designers of electronic text can use color freely and without expense (except to the user, who must have a color monitor). And studies have shown again and again that electronic color is an "attractive nuisance"—a feature that users will ask for and like, even if it adds nothing to performance (Christ, 1975; Bruce and Foster, 1982; Reynolds, 1979).

Illustrations and graphics.   How graphic enhancements are used in text is another aspect of the design of surfaces. To display information pictorially is complex for the designer but often beneficial for the user, who may find it helpful to see concepts or relationships displayed in a nonverbal way. Recent studies suggest that while users often find these materials helpful, the designer may not simply assume that the user has all the cognitive structures needed to decode graphic information. Here, as with printed text, the conventions must be learned. But graphic images may help develop new concepts rapidly—especially for novices coming to a topic or field for the first time (Dwyer, 1978; Easterby and Zwaga, 1984; Tufte, 1984).

The case of graphics in electronic materials is very similar—though here again we often are faced with the "attractive nuisance" phenomenon: Although users of printed texts do not automatically expect graphic materials, users of electronic text (especially databases designed for general consumer use) seem to expect them. Studies of field trials of videotex and teletext services, for example, reveal that subscribers are more likely to use, enjoy, and continue to subscribe to systems that incorporate many graphics (Carey and Siegeltuch, 1982; Elton, Irving, and Siegeltuch, 1982; CSP International, 1982). And in other studies with more traditional computer-based learning materials, researchers discovered similar effects: Users will ask for and more readily use displays that incorporate graphics (Stone, 1984; Tullis, 1981).

Why do users seem to prefer graphics on the surface of display screens? Perhaps we are seeing a reflection of the widely discussed decline in formal reading abilities in the population at large. It might be that if a basic format for printed books were being decided upon today, from scratch, we would come to think of graphics as normal parts of printed matter rather than the exceptions they still are.

Language.   A further important quality of the surface design is the way in which language is used—the readability of the text, its complexity, and so forth. Here we observe some distinctive differences between print and electronic forms, with considerable emphasis being placed in electronic

Instructional programs should not simply scroll textual information on the screen, for that does not capitalize on what the computer does best; nor does it provide a justification for using a very expensive piece of machinery to do what a very simple technology, the book, could do as well.

text on short, compressed sentences and paragraph chunks. One effect of this "billboard" writing style is to allow users to scan screens quickly while looking for relevant information (Siegeltuch, 1982). A related set of studies focuses on the value and use of abbreviations, thus allowing the designer to make best use of limited screen space (Ehrenreich, 1985).

331

User's reactions.   Finally, the reader's subjective reaction to the appearance and content of the text should not be ignored. Performance may not be affected if the reader finds the text unpleasant to work with, but the long-term impact may be to decrease the user's enthusiasm. And when the reader has to decide whether to use it or not, the choice just may be no (Kern, 1985). In electronic text, the perceived usefulness of the text to the reader has emerged as one of three key factors that describe users' reactions (Champness and DiAlberdi, 1981). The other two key factors are the attractiveness and clarity of the text. (Grabinger's [1984] work also supports these notions.)

A way of increasing users' positive reactions to electronic text systems has been to involve them directly in design decisions. This may be done either by letting them determine the format in which material will be presented on their individual screens (Geiselman and Samet, 1982) or by giving them some control over the structure of the system itself—what the command structure is to look like or what keywords to use in a database system.

Summary.   These varied findings suggest that screen design, while different in some important ways from page design, should be carried out with many of the same rules in mind that expert page designers have used for years. These include use of distinctive typefaces, carefully determined (and generous) allocation of white space and headings in text, intelligent application of graphics and color (making full use of the capabilities of the technology), and design with the user's need to have the text itself be interesting to read. If there is nothing dramatically new here, there is at least the reaffirmation that many of the design principles that hold true for print also are worth adhering to in electronic environments.

Interface Design

If the design of the surface offers few surprises, the preparation of the interface is clearly quite a different matter. There are several aspects of the interface that bear examination here:

○ *The immediate structure.* The directions and wayfinding aids that are provided on the page or screen

○ *The internal structure.* The helps for using the material that are part of it, but not always present on any given page or screen, such as the index in a book or the help system built into electronic text

○ *The external structure.* Aids that are external to the material itself, such as an external index for printed materials or documentation for a computer program

○ *The user's physical and psychological context.* The skills needed to navigate and the ability to correctly formulate questions about the nature of the task at hand

In most of these areas there are marked differences in form and function between wayfinding systems used in print space and those employed in electronic space.

Immediate structure

Wayfinding on the page level.   Print materials typically have only a few wayfinding conventions. Page numbers we take for granted, although they were not universal for many years after the advent of printing. Footnote numbers tell us where we can go for more detailed information about a particular subject. Certain reference marks also help us sort through the material, such as abstract numbers or keyword designations at the top of an index page, boldface headings in columns, etc. We have virtually lost the routine use of the "catch word" in narrative text, an aid that enjoyed popularity for several centuries into the development of printed text.

Wayfinding on screen.   In electronic text, however, the immediate structure of navigational aids is often very obvious. Menus, icons or symbols, color coding—all these serve to help users orient themselves in the material at hand.

Menus. In particular, the use of on-screen menus for wayfinding in electronic text has been the subject of considerable research over the past few years. Much of the work has focused on determining the appropriate level of breadth or depth to incorporate in menu systems. Since a deeper menu structure offers fewer choices to the user at any one time, we might suppose that it would be easier to use. In fact, the reverse appears to be the case: Users seem to prefer and work more effectively with menus that present medium or large numbers of choices on each screen (Landauer and Nachbar, 1985; Lee and MacGregor, 1985; McFarland, 1982; Snowberry, Parkinson, and Sisson, 1983).

In spite of all best efforts, however, menus appear not to be a panacea for information search. In fact, a number of problems have been reported relating to menu-type structures. Many errors occur at the initial menu level, where users are least likely to know what categories are subsumed under the top-level items. In one study, 18 percent of all search time was spent using the top-level menu (Irving, Elton, and Siegeltuch, 1982). Another problem is that some users tend to become frustrated and distracted by working up and down through layers of menus without finding desired information and often give up even though they may know that "the information is in there somewhere" (28 percent of all users in one study [Latremouille et al., 1981]; 20 percent in another [Carey, 1981]).

Keyword searches. One alternative to a complex menu structure is the use of keywords for information searching. Several studies have shown that users can figure out keyword-based systems sufficiently well to employ them effectively (Orsnaes, 1982) and that they usually prefer to use keywords rather than menus in searching (Geller and Lesk, 1982), but that occasional users probably will not retain the structure of keywords well enough to use them over time (Shneiderman, 1982). The ways that users think about keywords and their understanding of the concepts that lie behind them may be the most significant determinant of success or failure in locating desired information (Weyer, 1982). One study that investigated both keywords and menus concluded that there seemed to be little objective reason to prefer one approach over the other and that users' problems seemed to lie in realms other than the mechanics of access (Van Nes and Van der Heijden, 1982).

333

334

Icons.   The use of icons or other graphic wayfinding aids is another way to help the reader find desired information. Some current computer operating systems (Macintosh, Lisa, Xerox Star) have been developed with icons playing a key role in user interface design. And the use of icons for wayfinding is on the rise in transit systems and in public buildings (see, e.g., AIGA [1982] and Dreyfuss [1972]). However, validating their usefulness empirically has been a problem (Mackett-Stout and Dewar, 1981). Some have suggested that learning to use an icon-based system may be no easier—just different—than learning one based on text or menus (Cahill, 1975; Samet, Geiselman, and Landee, 1982). Much further work remains to be done in this area to determine how valuable iconic wayfinding systems truly are.

Internal Structure

Wayfinding on the document level.   The internal structure of the material also can provide users with clues as to where they are and where to go for further information. In printed materials, such aids as the table of contents, index, appendixes, and footnotes may provide this sort of information. They are internal to the book itself, but they do not intrude on the user's attention unless they are specifically sought.

Our ways of working with printed materials are so long established, that it is very difficult to step back and see clearly just how many things we take for granted.

Wayfinding on the system level.   Internal help systems in electronic text have been harder to evaluate than on-screen aids, probably because the systems themselves vary so much in form and comprehensiveness. That users want help and look to the systems they work with to provide it is without doubt. Carey and Dozier (1985), for example, found that students offered access to electronic text systems that included both instructional and library materials frequently mentioned greater navigability of the text as a desirable feature. A number of navigation methods that are similar to print forms have been proposed (Benest and Jones, 1982; Benest and Potok, 1984; Engel et al., 1983; Lochovsky and Tsichritzis, 1981). Some of these use a kind of on-screen menu-plus-text system that allows the user to keep track of where he or she has been, while at the same time permitting fast retracing through previous menus to backtrack to an earlier point (Spence and Apperley, 1982).

More traditional kinds of help systems that provide information on the structure of commands in an operating system have also been evaluated. Interestingly, one such study found that a considerable number of system users (22 percent) saw their work with the help system as a tutorial rather than just a memory jog. Those who kept documentation and paper manuals up to date were less likely to use the system than those who did not have such materials, leading the researchers to conclude that both types of help systems would probably continue to be required (Stoddard et al., 1985).

External Structure

Wayfinding among documents.   The design of external structures to aid wayfinding is an even less fully researched area than those discussed above. In the case of print materials, such systems as indexes, card catalogs, and bibliographic listings obviously play a role. There is considerable literature in the fields of library and information science dealing with search strategies and techniques (see Bates [1981] for a particularly comprehensive review). Indeed, the advent of computer-based bibliographic retrieval systems seems to have pushed this issue much into the forefront of librarians' attention. But most of the work in this area is focused on the librarian's role in helping the user to clarify search questions and providing information on strategies (e.g., Lynch [1983]) rather than with the processes of the search itself.

Electronic wayfinding.   For electronic text systems, the external wayfinding aids are usually either minimal or nonexistent. Documentation on how to use a system or job aid cards are perhaps the most familiar forms that such external structures take. But in many cases the text and its access structure are all there together, rolled up into a single ball. This "unified" and "nontransparent" form of the materials may make them particularly difficult to deal with in that users will simply assume that whatever the computer provides is what they need (Estabrook, 1983).

Rules and guidelines for the preparation of documentation to accompany electronic text have been proposed, but these have most frequently been issued only as rules of thumb. Occasionally they have been designed using instructional development or traditional print layout procedures. However, too little attention has been given to the ways in which users make the jump back and forth between documentation and electronic materials.

Physical and Psychological Context of the User

In both types of systems, the user's physical and psychological state can make a difference in the way navigation is carried out. In fact, this may be the most critical part of the whole process. Certainly, librarians have defined their roles for years as consummate "wayfinders," and in doing so have written extensively about the need to understand the user's needs, to help the user formulate questions, and to provide guidance on the physical aspects of the system as needed.

Vigil (1983), for example, notes that relatively few users seem to have a very precise sense of how to go about searching for information whether, in print collections or online catalogs. Hills (1982) suggests that designers of electronic materials will need to provide built-in structures of keywords and checkpoints that are attuned more directly to user needs—perhaps by adopting some sort of common thesaurus of terms. And Waern and Rollenhagen (1983), on reviewing studies relating reading and video display terminals, observe that relatively few studies have tried to integrate what we know about metacognitive processes (setting goals, planning strategies to reach them, knowing when a problem has been encountered, and so forth) with the use of electronic text.

More than one researcher recently has come to the conclusion that the key decisions to make in designing electronic text are not those that have to do merely with the specification of mechanical aspects of the interface. Rather, the most critical elements seem to be understanding how the user conceptualizes the material he or she is faced with—what categories it contains, how it is organized, and so on. In one recent study, after finding some differences among users working with seven different operating-system interfaces, Whiteside et al. (1985) noted that "many problems were the result of users not understanding the structure of [the conceptual space within which they had to navigate] or the rules for moving in it. These difficulties cut across all interface styles and all levels of user experience."

Summary

The key features of interface design seem to indicate that there is a need to provide a collection of aids that allow the user to maneuver with as little extra effort as possible. Broad rather than deep menus, user-defined keywords or menu terms, audit trails and backtracking systems that allow mistakes to be undone quickly and paths retraced, help systems that provide tutorial information as well as remind the user, and on-screen information on basic options—all these seem to make users feel more comfortable in reading and working with text presented electronically.

Several key differences between print and electronic text were highlighted in this section, and it is worth recapitulating them here. First, with print materials the structure of the interface at its various levels (immediate, internal, external) is relatively small and unobtrusive. The user is not forced to come in contact with it, and the producer probably spends relatively little time worrying about it. For electronic text, however, the user has no choice but to learn a new approach that may be more or less generic to other systems. This must be mastered in some rudimentary way before

To display information pictorially is complex for the designer but often beneficial for the user, who may find it helpful to see concepts or relationships displayed in a nonverbal way.

the text may even be approached. The interface is very much in the foreground, and the amount of effort the designer must put into its creation and refinement is correspondingly large. In print, the interface is optional; in electronic text, it is unavoidable.

337

Another central difference between navigation in print and electronic text is the way in which electronic text layers virtually all aspects of the interface within the material itself. A database system, for example, may serve as a "gateway" to a number of separate subdatabases, each with its own command structure or set of keywords. And the indexing structure, help system, and other user tools for each of these subsystems may all be online within the original database with relatively little in the way of external documentation for the user. The material is all there, but it is invisible. It is as if the text of the books of a library were to be typed on index cards and interfiled with the directional cards in the main card catalog.

A final important fact that emerges from this part of the analysis is a sense that the focus may need to move away from the physical aspects of interface design—the specifics of menu choices, screen design, and graphic icons—and toward a more careful analysis of how users conceptualize the environment in which they are working and moving. Some of the implications of this conclusion are explored in the section that follows.

Directions for Further Work on Wayfinding

What is known about the design of surfaces and interfaces for electronic and printed instructional text may be less important than what is still unknown. The foregoing analysis suggests that further work in several relatively unexamined areas could be especially productive.

How Do Users Search?

This question may seem overly simple, but it is basic and we seem to know know little about it. What are the occasions, for example, on which users realize that they have a problem for which further or different information might provide an answer? What do users' self-generated search strategies look like, and how might those be used to guide the development of interfaces? Some preliminary work in information science has already shed light on this issue, and certainly much of the work on metacognition and problem solving would also be relevant here.

This problem is especially relevant if large electronic databases are going to be used in any broad way in the educational system. We need to be able to define differences in search strategy between various age groups of readers as they approach electronic materials.

Can a Paradigm for Effective Search Help Users?

Lochovsky and Tsichritzis (1981) suggest that providing users with a paradigm for an effective search strategy may help produce better searches and more satisfied users of electronic text. Such paradigms might be especially valuable if they could be tailored explicitly for various audiences and various searching styles, as described by the research suggested above.

Our research base on learning styles and individual differences in learning is not made of the most solid stuff. But there is enough evidence that individuals differ at least in their expressed preferences for us to try to develop varieties of interfaces, or interfaces that could be customized for greater graphic content, specific keywords, or command terms.

How Do Users Conceptualize the Shape of the Text?

A final important question to ask may be how users think about the shape of the data they are working with, or the shape of the problem space within which they are operating. Several recent studies (Borgman, 1983; Vigil, 1983) have indicated that there is some value in working with spatial metaphors and mental models that concentrate on developing a user's image of what electronic text is and how it may be organized. Others (Dumais and Jones, 1985), while expressing doubt about the value of spatially organized interfaces, conclude that there may be a way of designing them so that they are more effective.

This approach seems to tie in with other work being done on thinking and problem solving. Newell (1980), for example, discusses how thinking practices might be seen as ways of moving through a "problem space." Research in such diverse areas as learning to read maps (Thorndyke and Stasz, 1980) also deals with processing of information in spatial terms. Indeed, there is a growing consensus that many reasoning and problem-solving activities may be conceptualized using spatial metaphors and models (Sternberg, 1982).

If this approach to modeling information search strategies could be applied effectively to the problem of wayfinding in electronic text, we might be able to create interfaces that match more closely the users' preferred ways of dealing with complex textual environments.

About the Author

Stephen T. Kerr is professor of Education in the Educational Communications and Technology program at the University of Washington. He previously chaired the Department of Education, Computing, and Technology in Education at Teacher's College, Columbia University. His research focuses on the social and psychological effects of the advent of electronic publishing, the impact of technological change on the structure of schools and other institutions, and the use of educational technology in the U.S.S.R. and less developed countries. He is the author of books, articles, and reviews on these and other topics.

References

AIGA (American Institute for Graphic Arts). 1982. *Symbol Signs.* New York: Hastings House.

Anderson, T., and B. Armbruster. 1985. Studying strategies and their implications for textbook design. In *Designing Usable Texts,* ed. by T. Duffy and R. Waller. Orlando: Academic Press, pp. 159-177.

Bates, M. 1981. Search techniques. In *Annual Review of Information Science and Technology,* vol. 16, ed. by M. Williams. New York: Knowledge Industry Publications for ASIS, pp. 139-169.

Bateson, J. 1983. A short history of punctuation. *Verbatim,* 10(2):6-7.

Benest, I., and G. Jones. 1982. Computer emulation of books. In *Proceedings of the IEE International Conference on Man/Machine Systems.* Conference Publication 212, pp. 267-271.

Benest, I., and M. Potok. 1984. Wayfinding: An approach using signposting techniques. *Behaviour and Information Technology,* 3(2):99-107.

Borgman, C. 1983. Performance effects of a user's mental model of an information retrieval system. In *Proceedings of the ASIS Conference, Washington, D.C.* New York: Knowledge Industry Publications for ASIS, vol. 20, pp. 121-124.

Bruce, M., and J. Foster. 1982. The visibility of colored characters on colored backgrounds in viewdata displays. *Visible Language,* 16(4):382-390.

Cahill, M. 1975. Interpretability of graphic symbols as a function of context and experience factors. *Journal of Applied Psychology,* 60:376-380.

Carey, J. 1981. *Human Factors in Videotex*. New York: Greystone Communications.

Carey, J., and D. Dozier. 1985. *Assessing Electronic Text for Higher Education: Evaluation Results from Laboratory and Field Studies*. San Diego: San Diego State University, Electronic Text Consortium.

Carey, J., and M. Siegeltuch. 1982. Teletext usage in public places. *Research on Broadcast Teletext*. Working Paper No. 8. New York: New York University, Alternate Media Center.

Champness, B., and M. DiAlberdi. 1981. *Measuring Subjective Reactions to Teletext Page Design*. New York: New York University, Alternate Media Center.

Christ, R. 1975. Review and analysis of color coding research for visual displays. *Human Factors*, 17:542-570.

CSP International. 1982. *Teletext in the U.K.: A Market Research Study*. New York.

Dreyfuss, H. 1972. *Symbol Sourcebook*. New York: Van Nostrand Reinhold.

Dumais, S., and W. Jones. 1985. A comparison of symbolic and spatial filing. In *Human Factors in Computing Systems*. Proceedings of the ACM SIGCHI 1985 Annual Conference, San Francisco, pp. 127-135.

Dwyer, F. 1978. *A Guide to Improving Visualized Instruction*. University Park, Pa.: Learning Services.

Easterby, R., and H. Zwaga. 1984. *The Design and Evaluation of Signs and Printed Material*. New York: Wiley.

Ehrenreich, S. 1985. Computer abbreviations: Evidence and synthesis. *Human Factors*, 27(2):143-155.

Elton, M., R. Irving, and M. Siegeltuch. 1982. The first six months of a pilot teletext service: Interim results on utilization and attitudes. *Research on Broadcast Teletext*. Working Paper No. 6. New York: New York University, Alternate Media Center.

Engel, F., et al. 1983. What, where, and whence: Means for improving electronic data access. *International Journal of Man-Machine Studies*, 18:145-160.

Estabrook, L. 1983. The human dimension of the catalog: Concepts and constraints in information seeking. *Library Resources and Technical Services*, 27:68-75.

340

Febvre, L., and H.-J. Martin. 1976. *The Coming of the Book*. London: Verso.

Foster, J., and B. Champness. 1982. Attractiveness and readability of text and tables. In *Videotex—Key to the Information Revolution*. Proceedings of Videotex '82, New York, June. Northwood Hills, England: Online Conferences, Ltd.

Geiselman, R., and M. Samet. 1982. Personalized vs. fixed formats for computer-displayed intelligence messages. *IEEE Transactions on Systems, Man, and Cybernetics*, 12(4):490-495.

Geller, V., and M. Lesk. 1982. How users search: A comparison of menu and attribute retrieval systems in a library catalog. Paper presented at the annual meeting of the ASIS, Columbus, Ohio, October.

Glynn, S., B. Britton, M. Tillman, and K. Muth. 1984. Typographic cues in text: Management of the reader's attention. Paper presented at the annual meeting of the American Educational Research Association, New Orleans, April.

Grabinger, S. 1984. Study of factors contributing to the comprehension of CAI screens. Paper presented at the annual conference of the Association for Educational Communication and Technology, Dallas, January.

Hartley, J. 1978. *Designing Instructional Text*. New York: Nichols.

Hills, P. 1982. Human communication and information technology. In *Trends in Information Transfer*, ed. by P. Hills. Westport, Conn.: Greenwood Press.

Irving, R., M. Elton, and M. Siegeltuch. 1982. The last five months of a pilot teletext service: Interim results on utilization and attitudes. *Research on Broadcast Teletext*. Working paper No. 7. New York: New York University, Alternate Media Center.

Jonassen, D., ed. 1982. *The Technology of Text*. Englewood Cliffs, N.J.: Educational Technology Publications.

Kern, R. 1985. Modeling users and their use of technical manuals. In *Designing Usable Texts*, ed. by T. Duffy and R. Waller. Orlando: Academic Press, pp. 341-375.

Kolers, P., R. Duchnicky, amd D. Ferguson. 1981. Eye movement measurement of readability of CRT displays. *Human Factors,* 23(5):517-527.

Landauer, T., and D. Nachbar. 1985. Selection from alphabetic and numeric menu trees using a touch screen: Breadth, depth, and width. In *Human Factors in Computing Systems.* Proceedings of the ACM SIGCHI 1985 Annual Conference, San Francisco, pp. 75-78.

Latremouille, S., E. Lee, C. Mason, S. McEwen, D. Phillips, and T. Whalen. 1981. The design of videotex tree indexes. *Telidon Behavioural Research,* No. 2. Ottawa: Department of Communications.

Lee, E., and J. MacGregor. 1985. Minimizing user search time in menu retrieval systems. *Human Factors,* 27(2):157-162.

Lochovsky, F., and D. Tsichritzis. 1981. Interactive query languages for external databases. *Telidon Behavioural Research,* No. 5. Ottawa: Department of Communications.

Lynch, M. 1983. Research in library reference/information service. *Library Trends,* 31(3):401-420.

Mackett-Stout, J., and R. Dewar. 1981. Evaluation of symbolic public information signs. *Human Factors,* 23:139-151.

Marcus, A. 1982. Designing the face of an interface. *IEEE Computer Graphics and Applications,* 2(1):23-29.

McFarland, P. 1982. New skills for old: The key to creative videotex production. In *Videotex—Key to the information revolution.* Proceedings of Videotex '82, New York, June. Northwood Hills, England: Online Conferences, Ltd.

McGee, K., and C. Matthews, eds. 1985. *The Design of Interactive Computer Displays: A Guide to the Select Literature.* Lawrence, Kans.: The Report Store.

Newell, A. 1980. Reasoning, problem solving, and decision processes: The problem space as fundamental category. In *Attention and Performance,* vol. 8, ed. by R. Nickerson. Hillsdale, N.J.: Erlbaum.

Ong, W. 1982. *Orality and Literacy: The Technologizing of the Word.* New York: Methuen.

Orsnaes, J. 1982. User reactions to keyword-access videotex. In *Videotex—Key to the Information Revolution.* Proceedings of Videotex '82, New York, June. Northwood Hills, England: Online Conferences, Ltd.

Reynolds, L. 1979. Teletext and viewdata—A new challenge for the designer. *Information Design Journal*, 1(1):2-14.

Samet, M., R. Geiselman, and B. Landee. 1982. A human performance evaluation of graphic symbol-design features. *Perceptual and Motor Skills*, 54(3, part 2):1303-1310.

Shneiderman, B. 1982. The future of interactive systems and the emergence of direct manipulation. *Behaviour and Information Technology*, 1(3):237-256.

Siegeltuch, M. 1982. *Text on Screen and Print: A Comparison of Forms*. New York: New York University, Alternate Media Center.

Snowberry, K., S. Parkinson, and N. Sisson. 1983. Computer display menus. *Ergonomics*, 26(7):699-712.

Smith, S., and N. Mosier. 1984. The user interface to computer-based information systems: A survey of current software design practice. *Behaviour and Information Technology*, 3(3):195-203.

Spence, R., and M. Apperley. 1982. Database navigation: An office environment for the professional. *Behaviour and Information Technology*, 1(1):43-54.

Sternberg, R. 1982. Reasoning, problem solving, and intelligence. In *Handbook of Human Intelligence*, ed. by R. Sternberg. New York: Cambridge, pp. 225-307.

Sticht, T. 1985. Understanding readers and their uses of texts. In *Designing Usable Texts*, ed. by T. Duffy and R. Waller. Orlando: Academic Press, pp. 315-340.

Stoddard, M., K. Berkbigler, B. Wheat and E. Peter. 1985. User behavior upon introduction of a network help system. *ACM SIGCHI Bulletin*, 16(3):25-31.

Stone, D. 1984. *Computer-Based Job Aiding: Problem Solving at Work*. Technical Report 11-B, Contract N00014-80-C-0372. Arlington, Va.: Office of Naval Research.

Thorndyke, P., and C. Stasz. 1980. Individual differences in procedures for knowledge acquisition from maps. *Cognitive Psychology*, 12:137-175.

Tufte, E. 1984. *The Visual Display of Quantitative Information*. Cheshire, Conn.: Graphics Press.

Tullis, T. 1981. An evaluation of alphanumeric, graphic, and color information displays. *Human Factors*, 23(5):541-550.

Tullis, T. 1983. The formatting of alphanumeric displays: A review and analysis. *Human Factors*, 25(6):657-682.

Van Nes, F., and J. Van der Heijden. 1982. On information retrieval by inexperienced users of databases. *IPO International Progress Report*, 17:129-137.

Vigil, P. 1983. The psychology of on-line searching. *Journal of the American Society for Information Science*, 34(4):281-287.

Waern, Y., and C. Rollenhagen. 1983. Reading text from visual display units (VDUs). *International Journal of Man-Machine Studies*, 18:441-465.

Waller, R., P. Lefrere, and M. MacDonald-Ross. 1982. Do you need that second color? *IEEE Transactions on Professional Communication*, 25(2):80-85.

Weyer, S. 1982. The design of a dynamic book for information search. *International Journal of Man-Machine Studies*, 17:87-107.

Whiteside, J., S. Jones, P. Levy, and D. Wixon. 1985. User performance with command, menu, and iconic interfaces. In *Human Factors in Computing Systems*, Proceedings of the ACM SIGCHI 1985 Annual Conference, San Francisco, pp. 185-191.

C H A P T E R 2

Authoring and Development

The Creative Challenge of CD ROM

by Mark Heyer

In my view, there are only three ways in which we gather information—by grazing, browsing, or hunting.

Grazing is the well-known activity of sitting in front of the TV in an alpha trance, eyes wide open, with information, good or bad, flowing in. The networks used to point with pride to the fact that viewers who tuned in at 7 p.m. were most likely to watch the entire evening without bothering to change the channel.

Browsing means scanning a large body of information with no particular target in mind. Newspapers and magazines are the high-technology browsing media today. They have lots of instantly accessible 2-D bandwidth. Browsing on TV has become popular with the advent of cable. During a 30-second commercial I can check out 15 different channels for 2 seconds each.

In the hunting mode we are seeking specific information. Computers are superb hunting tools. Time-shift recording on VCR's is also hunting, although many people quickly find that they don't really want their evening info-graze to become a hunt.

Note, however, that TV and all CRTs are inherently sequential access information devices. They're fine for grazing and good for hunting, where the object is to navigate a decision tree; but not so good for browsing, with no 2-D, "spread the newspaper all over the dining room table" capability.

All of our information intake can be viewed as some combination of these three styles. Not only is this concept useful for evaluating the mood of users, it is also an element in the establishment of the information equivalence and merit of everything from TV to computer programs. This and other elements of what I call the Unified Theory of Information provides us a framework for rational development of all of our new optical disc information devices.

> There are only three ways in which we gather information—by grazing, browsing, or hunting. All of our information intake can be viewed as some combination of these three styles.

Steam Engines and Mainframes

The early days of the industrial revolution were dominated by steam engines. One steam engine could power an entire factory, yet the power of the steam engine was largely inaccessible even to the individuals who operated the engines. The information age version of the steam engine is the mainframe computer.

By the 1890s, small, powerful gasoline engines were readily available. Now what in the world could I do with a personal gasoline engine? The gasoline engine became useful when it was combined with the most pervasive personal transportation technology of the day, the carriage. In the process, both were transformed into the automobile. And within a single human lifetime the interstate highway system became the largest construction project in the history of the human race.

Today we are engaged in the merging of the two most powerful information technologies—computers and video (which also includes nontext media of all kinds). There is absolutely no doubt that the evolution and revolution now taking place is the beginning rumble of a major cultural change that will transform our information lives as completely as the automobile transformed our transportation lives. We could probably set our clocks at 1900 today.

Interaction with Media

What we are really talking about here is the degree and style of our interaction with media. Up until videodiscs and tapes began to change the nature of video media, every play, movie, or television program in history was produced as if to be performed for a live audience, start to finish in a linear manner. No viewer interaction was expected or possible.

Videocassettes and discs changed the technology of plays to the technology of publishing. The extremely rapid growth of the videocassette business (now running at 15 million VCRs per year), is testimony to the power of publishing. No one had to educate the public about the desirability of directly interacting with their media.

Since the introduction around 1972 of the videodisc, by a joint venture of MCA and IBM called DiscoVision, computer control of video has been a reality. Now CD ROM is stepping up to take its place in the growing spectrum of optical disc information distribution products. There are many technical issues to solve, but in my view the challenge of understanding and developing software, and a large software industry, is one of the most interesting and potentially enriching of any in the history of our information industries.

To date, videodisc design, production, and distribution have been in the hands of the visual artists and technologists. The CD ROM is evolving from the computer industry into the visual realm. Somewhere in the middle the two will meet and form the information industry of the future. The real question is where, when, and how the meetings will take place.

349

Remember, CD ROM is a publishing medium, not a programming medium. The emphasis is on the information content of the disc, not necessarily on the generic software tools it provides. A CD ROM on wines may contain a database manager, but it will be highly customized for that specific application, with no consideration of using it elsewhere.

User Bandwidth

As we move toward the merging of computer and video information, we need a comprehensive and useful understanding of information dynamics as it relates to real human beings. This is the basis of our attempt to produce a more complete "information physics" which unites the technical and human elements of information systems.

A basic concept which is useful for gaining a detailed understanding of media interaction is "user bandwidth." We are all familiar with technical bandwidth, which is how much information can be put through a channel in a given amount of time. Bandwidth can be expressed as a function of frequency (100 Mhz, for example), or as data (100K bytes/sec), or translated from one to the other by a simple algorithm.

User bandwidth includes the user/viewer in the equation to measure the actual delivered information, including interaction times and even user attention factors. For example, TV provides very high bandwidth video, but the lack of viewer control often means very low attention factors and thus low user bandwidth. On the other hand, a single visual image retrieved from an optical disc data base by an information hunter may convey a large amount of specific information and thus have relatively high bandwidth for that person.

The term *user bandwidth*, which could also be called "receptive" or "effective" bandwidth, includes physical, circumstantial and psychological factors which are an inevitable part of all information systems, and which may be more important than hardware in determining the viability of a particular delivery technology.

There is absolutely no doubt that the evolution and revolution now taking place is the beginning rumble of a major cultural change that will transform our information lives as completely as the automobile transformed our transportation lives.

350

As an exercise, think about the comparative information per second provided by a paper Sears catalog and the same catalog on videotex. Now consider how the user bandwidth is changed depending on the grazing or browsing or hunting mode of the user. How effective is browsing in videotex compared with browsing in a book?

Along with the fundamental terms *storage, transmission, and replication,* we are now beginning to define what I call the Unified Theory of Information, which provides predictive and comparative figures of merit for actual information systems as diverse as newspapers, broadcast television, online computers, and publishing media—both paper and electronic.

Learning from the Videodisc

The real question for both video and CD ROM developers is how to understand and control the program design and development process so that commercially viable products result.

When DiscoVision announced their laser videodisc as a consumer and industrial product, widespread adoption within two years was anticipated. What they failed to recognize was the level of understanding and creative talent that would be required to effectively use the capabilities of the optical disc. Consumer acceptance was very difficult until time-shift recording with VCRs provided an unlimited source of apparently free software.

Since 1972, people in the videodisc industry have been exploring interaction with media. The same lessons learned over so long and at such cost must now be incorporated into the learning curve for the CD ROM as it joins the ranks of optical disc interactive image and data delivery devices.

I should point out that all the capabilities foreseen for CD ROM have to some degree been investigated in the course of videodisc research and marketing. Graphics combined with video, data and video storage on the same disc, and random access audio all exist as commercial products for use with analog videodisc players. These are among the small set of fundamental capabilities of all information systems, regardless of the delivery media.

The real question for both video and CD ROM developers is how to understand and control the program design and development process so that commercially viable products result.

For one thing, the entire style of video software production is quite different from that for computer software. While small groups of dedicated people labor to produce a few very generic computer programs, visual software designers produce custom software for every single product. Tools versus content. What exactly is the appropriate merger of the two concepts?

CD ROM designers will discover, as did their videodisc predecessors, that just putting lots of pictures on a disc, without any really compelling information or entertainment value, is no excuse for a commercial product.

It is worth noting that most of the really bad ideas have already been tried in the videodisc business. CD ROM designers will discover, as did their videodisc predecessors, that just putting lots of pictures on a disc, without any really compelling information or entertainment value, is no excuse for a commercial product.

The real estate and travel industries have laid waste to any number of naive startups who just began pushing systems with no understanding of user interaction. None of these ventures, some of which were by firms big enough to know better, bothered with the basic research necessary to understand the requirements and ramifications of user interaction, not to mention understanding the economics and dynamics of their respective marketplaces.

The real value of already-existing images is also suspect. Optical discs can suck up all existing visual images in a few years without even straining the manufacturing facilities. Just as when the printing press arrived, there are not enough existing images in the world to make a market, and only a tiny subset of those are truly useful. The demand will be for large quantities of highly specific images designed to fit the medium.

The CD medium will demand images with highly interactive qualities to justify the computer investment required. An advertising presentation of the future might have 10 different real-time images working within a single screen, operated by joystick control of the customer who is "flying" through a 3-D information space. The basic concepts for this were demonstrated at MIT in 1979, and videodisc production techniques are now in hand that make it useful for commercial applications.

The Read-Only Challenge

The biggest challenge facing both videodisc and CD ROM developers is the fact that the delivery medium is not matched by a development medium of similar power. Every other visual medium has a work medium. Filmmakers edit with workprints struck from the original footage. Videotape editors use off-line editing on ¾-inch videocassettes prior to the final edit, usually from 1-inch master videotape. Yet videodisc, and now CD ROM, the most complex media ever developed, are the only ones without a work medium. In short, you don't know if your CD ROM or videodisc actually works until the final product is delivered from the pressing plant. This is as absurd as printing a copy of a book to find out if there are spelling errors in the manuscript, or building a hardwired computer to test an untried program.

352

We have endeavored to solve this problem in our videodisc design laboratory, through the use of Panasonic DRAW (direct read after write) analog videodiscs, which can record videodisc frames as easily as recording on a VCR. In the process, we have discovered how to make the entire conception, design, and production process for interactive programs more rational, productive, and creative.

The Creative Workplace

The conception, design, and production of visual/computer interactive programming is the newest challenge facing the creative community. To successfully produce such programs, the efforts of three groups have to be harnessed:

○ Designers (instructional, commercial or industrial)

○ Visual producers (video, stills, etc.)

○ Computer programmers

When we hook optical discs to computers we are putting the engine in the carriage, gas in the tank, and the transmission in gear.

In the videodisc industry, some organizations understand this problem and have begun to create teams. In most cases, though, members of the three groups are separated in space and time. A few companies have even mandated that programmers will not talk to designers or video producers— a clear failure mode.

Generally the process follows a path something like this: First a design document is generated and argued about for four to six months. So far it's a paper war. At best, 10 percent of the people who are judging and modifying the paper concept will actually understand the nature of interactive video.

Next the video is produced. Whether the content is motion or stills, this step normally consumes 80 percent of the total project time and budget. Experience has shown that transferring still frames to a videodisc or CD ROM will cost up to $10 per frame. Typical costs for creating the frame in the first place are $30 to $500 or more. The cost of producing a 5000-frame disc is not to be taken lightly, even before revisions.

Then, after the visual material is mastered on a video or data tape, the control software is needed. In the case of videodiscs, most of which use external computer control, the disc is pressed and then the control software is written to conform with what has been put on the discs. Sadly, in many cases the programmer isn't even hired until after the disc is done.

At that point the opportunity to make changes has passed. All of this stems from the fact that you have to press a disc to have a disc to work with. Because of this need to go through the disc-making process and expensive video revisions on the master tape for every revision cycle, costs can easily exceed estimates.

You don't know if your CD ROM actually works until the final product is delivered from the pressing plant. This is as absurd as printing a copy of a book to find out if there are spelling errors in the manuscript.

353

CD ROM has an extra burden to consider, since the control software has to be pressed on the disc along with the visuals. Everything has to be perfect the moment the master is made. In reality, many producers will bear the expense of pressing discs with just the visuals as an aid to programming. This works about as well as any batch processing scheme, but it still doesn't allow for many visual change cycles, or for creative design input during programming. The computer programmer works with a fully interactive computer programming language and attempts to control a videodisc, which can be done in many ways, but the read-only pressed videodisc is in fact fixed and unchangeable.

The challenge of understanding these problems, and to some extent working around them, has occupied a whole generation of videodisc producers. We are just now in possession of design tools and methods which dramatically cut the development time and cost for videodiscs. The same techniques and equipment will work for CD ROM.

Interactive Editing

For creative artists and designers, whether visual or computer, the ability to make unlimited small changes is an absolute benefit. The question has always been how to overcome the read-only nature of optical media.

In all of my years of working on and thinking about disc publishing, building a workable emulator has had the highest priority. Now, with the availability of directly recordable videodiscs, a truly interactive disc development system is a reality.

At the MHA Videodisc Laboratory we have incorporated all aspects of the process into a single process- and device-independent development environment. Now, for the first time, designers, visual artists, and programmers are working together on program creation in real time. Hundreds of changes can be made in a day, and each change is instantly demonstrable. Design and development time are cut to a fraction of what they used to be.

The first step in the new process is to shoot crude storyboard frames (from paper drawings, video frames, or low-fi computer graphics), against which the interactive design and control programming is tested, revised, and otherwise played with. Creative judgments are made by the entire design team regarding the best use of design elements, control possibilities, images, and user interface software. Most important, approval can be gained from management or outside sponsors by showing them an actual working prototype disc instead of an incomprehensible design document.

As the model matures, real video and graphics are substituted for storyboard images, the code is finalized, and the project is finally sent off for mastering. The entire process, from initial design and programming studies to final masters, is produced in the same facility, with each group making real-time input to the others.

There are three benefits of taking this approach to program design and development:

1. Reduced risk. Problems are discovered at the beginning rather than at the end. Design and programming are done at the same time, so the model demonstrably works before expensive final video production is undertaken.

2. Experimentation and revision are encouraged. This is absolutely essential for any substantial creative industry to develop.

3. Understandable process. Outstanding artists from traditional media can instantly integrate into the design process, and each person knows exactly what the others are doing.

Analog vs. Digital Tools

At first glance it would seem obvious that CD ROM products, being totally digital in nature, would also be developed in totally digital development systems. I would like to suggest that this is not necessarily the case. There are two reasons for considering hybrid analog/digital design systems: cost and time.

First, for editing and revision to be done adequately, a development system must be able to store at least 10 times the content of a finished product. Digital scanning and storage of tens of thousands of visual images is both costly and time-consuming. Analog DRAW recorders lay down images in $\frac{1}{30}$ of a second, and a single disc holds 24,000 frames. To the extent that development systems require major computing resources, the industry will be stunted in its creative growth.

The second issue is time, pure and simple. If a computer graphics system requires 10 seconds to recover an image and draw it on the screen, the time required to recall 5000 images, forgetting about viewing time, is 14 hours. Each image will be recalled many times in the course of a project. By comparison, an analog disc recorder can recover sequential images in $\frac{1}{30}$ of a second, with the worst case less than $\frac{1}{2}$ second. In addition, analog discs allow designers to visually scan images at any desired rate—an important advantage.

At first glance it would seem obvious that CD ROM products, being totally digital in nature, would also be developed in totally digital development systems. I would like to suggest that this is not necessarily the case.

The human brain can absorb the major contents of an image in 0.1 to 0.25 second. Any design system that will be attractive to serious commercial visual artists will have to be capable of performing in this range. This observation is supported by our direct experience using computer graphics systems for producing large volumes of videodisc still frames.

Distributed Production

Adequate design tools are clearly an absolute necessity. But there is an additional consideration: The design system and tools must be inexpensive enough and easy enough to use that they can be employed in thousands of commercial art companies and small creative shops across the country. That is the only way to generate the critical mass of software development that is required to fuel a major marketplace. Ten new programs a year won't make it, folks. Consumers are voracious and picky. If you are asking them to purchase yet another computer, you had better be able to show them a software infrastructure that is capable of turning out high-gloss, commercial, and entertaining products by the thousands.

There is an important lesson to be learned from the videodisc industry. Many companies that started out in the hardware or publishing business have decided that they should also control the software production business. This has been brought about by the difficulty of dealing with a myriad of small producers who would have to be trained to deal with a proprietary design and delivery system. By doing this, the companies have guaranteed that no independent production company will ever come forward with a project, since it is certain to be subverted. What's more, despite the arrogance of the large companies, local producers are absolutely essential to provide the large volume of software necessary to make a market. DiscoVision and DEC, among others, made this fundamental mistake, with disastrous results and losses in the tens of millions.

356

Success will come to those companies that make the creative process accessible to the largest number of creative artists and producers. Software is so labor-intensive and diverse that no single organization could ever hope to fulfill the demand. Technologically advanced products like CD ROM are especially intractable, since they employ many new concepts and capabilities. Building a substantial and supportive creative community is in my view the number one prerequisite for large-scale success.

Building the Talent Base

One of the biggest challenges facing consumer CD ROM publishers is establishing the medium as a desirable consumer product among all the other competing visual media—television, VCRs, newspapers, magazines, and so on. The key to this is that ways must be found to use the talents of the millions of commercial creative artists now working in other forms. What is necessary to make this happen?

To make this industry grow in any reasonable time, we need thousands of cross-trained commercial artists and producers to produce the required commercial programs.

First, we need schools. If you want to become a hairdresser in this land of ours, you have your choice of over 1000 colleges to attend. But interactive optical disc, perhaps the most powerful medium ever, has not a single institution devoted to the subject, and very few that even offer courses. Go to the major design schools and ask about interactive video. Say what?

All sectors of the optical disc industry, video and CD ROM, are in desperate need of an interactive video institute where people can study this new medium. To make this industry grow in any reasonable time, we need thousands of cross-trained commercial artists and producers to produce the required commercial programs.

There is another lesson about this new optical disc publishing industry. Optical disc publishing is an information river that is broad and deep, not limited by the number of TV channels, hours in the day, popularity contests, or government interference. The great diversity we take for granted in books, music, and all forms of publishing is now available to the video/computer industry. Whether the audience is two or two million, if someone, somewhere wants our programs, we are free to sell them, protected by the First Amendment.

With the advent of personal "information engines," the information revolution is really getting under way. When we hook optical discs to computers we are putting the engine in the carriage, gas in the tank, and the transmission in gear. In the process, talented people from all creative walks of life are being thrown together in a rich dance of opportunity and challenge. Personally, I wouldn't miss it for the world.

About the Author

Mark Heyer has been involved with the requirements of optical disc publishing since 1972, in the early days of the industry. He has worked with all types of information, from feature films and commercials to data, and brings a broad perspective to the subject of optical disc publishing. In 1980 he joined Sony Corporation as one of three national market development managers responsible for establishing the primary applications for videodisc. In 1983 he became product manager for interactive products at Sony. In 1984 he left Sony to continue work with optical disc publishing and opened an optical disc laboratory at the Group W Westinghouse Satellite Communications facility in Stamford, Connecticut. With the co-operation of Group W, Mr. Heyer has developed radically new methods to facilitate effective interactive program development. The techniques he has developed also promise to have a profound effect on traditional film and video production, making the process more adaptable to video publishing requirements.

Mark Heyer Associates, Inc.
62 Mason Street
Greenwich, CT 06830

The New Workstation: CD ROM Authoring Systems

by Marc Canter

As the reality of CD ROM draws nearer, so does the need for development tools that will help programmers and artists to create CD applications fast and efficiently.

Currently, most CD ROM applications are text-based, displaying mainly words and numbers on the screen. But as the technology moves forward, graphics and music will be stored on CD ROMs, resulting in a brand-new generation of applications.

The tools we use in developing such applications will play an important role in making these projects feasible. As we begin to conceive of complex new uses for CD ROM, the ease of use and versatility of our tools will make or break our concepts from day one.

Among the tools necessary for these tasks, authoring systems will probably be the most important. Integral to these systems will be a powerful, easy-to-use notational system that will unify entire multimedia systems on one score, just as an orchestra is unified by the symphonic score used by its conductor. These scores will be capable of representing any sort of data, including the "action codes" necessary for interactive programming (or authoring).

No longer will it be necessary to "program" a sequence of data or to devise another "search" algorithm. Authoring systems provide the necessary functions to nonprogrammers to control the flow of the program, the level of interactivity and the production of the data itself.

For the purposes of this discussion, we will concentrate on an authoring system for text, art, animation, and music. It will require the simulation of a fairly complex output device (a premastering system) and a very fast (as real-time as possible) development system. This does not mean that this system will not be able to work with text-based CD applications. It just means that the technology of the future offers us a lot more than just static text, and we must be ready to create and control new media as they become available.

In the following discussion, "user" refers to the user of the authoring system and "end user" refers to the actual consumer in the home or office using the final product.

360

What Is an Authoring System?

An authoring system is a set of hardware and software tools for designing interactive programs. The hardware makes it possible to convert information into a machine-readable format; the software makes it possible for nonprogrammers (which will often be artists and musicians) to create complex programs by defining decision points, branches, and subroutines.

Authoring systems originated in the mainframe and minicomputer world, but many have begun to appear for microcomputers in the past few years. The more sophisticated authoring systems of yesterday and today produce complicated logical flowcharts that programmers use to implement their interactive programs. Many of these programs have "intelligent front ends" that ask the users questions to help them develop their programs, like "What sort of question would you like to ask?" or "How many dialog boxes would you like and what will they look like?" Using a development system based on this sort of authoring "language" often takes months, and sometimes years, to produce interactive videodisks or training programs.

The real problem with these types of authoring systems is that they are very hard to use and they do not produce a final product. They produce only an outline: a structure for a programmer to follow. And they are often entirely text-based, making them ideal for text-based applications but not for graphically oriented or video-based applications.

Any language or program that can control events through time is an authoring system. Computer-controlled lighting systems, slide shows, and video editing are all authoring systems in that (1) they can control sequences and events through time, (2) these sequences can be edited or changed, and (3) these sequences can be saved and retrieved from disc.

Authoring systems have crept into the entertainment world as a form of automation, making the director's life easier by guaranteeing that certain actions will happen, no matter what. This sort of automation may have cost a number of operators' jobs, but on the whole it has greatly enhanced the quality of special effects in the past few years.

Most of these large expensive systems (including the ones controlling TV studios) are text-based, with the operator/programmer using a CRT to edit sequences, in conjunction with dedicated buttons, switches, and levers. But the increased interest in graphics and graphic interfaces is spawning a new generation of authoring systems that are graphically based.

The MacroMind SoundVision™ authoring system is graphically based and uses a notational "scoring" system for controlling the flow of the program through time. It has no language at all but uses the notational system to represent sequential, branching, or even simultaneous events that occur in the program. The events may be a combination of text, graphics, music, or animation. This sort of system is a multimedia authoring system, since it can deal with all sorts of data, not just text.

As the technology moves forward, graphics and music will be stored on CD ROMs, resulting in a brand-new generation of applications.

On SoundVision's score, time moves horizontally from left to right, with multiple channels of information stacked up vertically. These channels represent the text, graphics, or music stored in the score (see Figure 6).

The scoring system is used by programmers or artists to create sequences of information that can easily be edited or transformed. This replaces the traditional means of programming: typing text into a document and compiling it. All the data represented on the score of the authoring system can be edited at any time. In other words, there is no source code or compiler to convert the code into executable instructions. Any text or piece of artwork can be edited or changed even after the application is finished.

The notational system is the unifying element in the authoring system. Text, graphics, animation, and music can all be synchronized and edited on the score. The "action codes," or programming codes, necessary for creating the interactive programs can be embedded into the score and edited just like any piece of animation or music. Data generated from any word processor, paint program, or MIDI (musical instrument digital interface) sequencer can be used in the SoundVision system.

Simulating the programmed interaction is another necessary part of the authoring process and is achieved via a software/hardware system called a "premastering" system. These premastering units are very expensive, but they make it possible to test the applications before committing them to disc or ROM. Typically, an entire project would have one, maybe two, premastering units to use as simulators.

361

Creating the Applications

Education and training applications are certain to become more common on optical disc once the production costs can be brought down by using authoring systems and other development tools. Their existence in schools and industry will undoubtedly change the way educators develop curricula, perhaps giving rise to new professions within the educational arena.

○ By being able to customize educational courseware, regional needs can be catered to and accelerated or disabled learners can concentrate on specialized material.

○ Educators can focus on a particular subject by designing a custom lesson around that subject.

○ Current news can be explained by integrating recent video footage from TV with encylopedia references to that area of the world or to that world leader.

○ Questions relating to the subject matter can be placed on the screen, and each answer associated with a particular screen "button." Behind each button is an action, such as: "Jump to an animated sequence for 10 seconds and then return" or "Jump to another document to hear the company theme song and exit" or "Jump to another screen of questions, answer one of them, and branch depending on what answer is given."

These sorts of applications are typical of what an authoring system can create. It is very important to be able to model or try out some of these interactive ideas before committing them to disc, and an authoring system is designed to do just that: model an application.

Because the people who come up with these interactive ideas are usually not programmers, it is equally important that they are able to model these environments with as little effort and ability as possible. Since teachers, trainers, marketing people, technical writers, and managers will probably be the biggest users of authoring systems, the systems must adhere to easy-to-learn user interface standards, such as those found in the Macintosh or MS-Windows environments.

Equipment Used in an Authoring System

The workstation for a CD ROM authoring system would vary according to the actual work being done there. Each workstation will specialize in some function and thereby require different types of equipment, though very likely some equipment will be common to every workstation (see Figure 1).

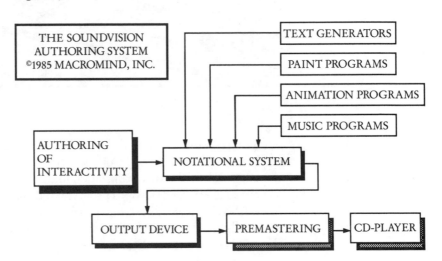

Figure 1. Basic workstation for CD ROM authoring system

The basic workstation will include:

○ An IBM AT (or better) with 4M of memory and a 30M hard disk

○ A premastering system to simulate an output device (or access to it)

○ A mouse or tablet along with a full-feature keyboard

○ A network of other workstations, and 2400-baud modem line

364

Figure 2. A text entry workstation

A text entry workstation would include optical scanners, voice recognition hardware, and monochrome monitors. Besides a host of text processors, the software available in a workstation like this would integrate data from various sources: standard word processors, distant databases via phone lines, ASCII, SYLK, dBase, and other standardized data protocols. This would all be necessary to facilitate the task of entering in hundreds of thousands of words per day.

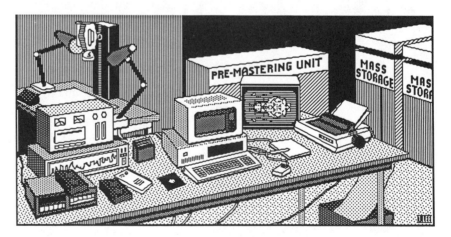

Figure 3. A graphics workstation

A graphics workstation would include video digitizers, tablets, high-resolution scanners, and so on. There should also be a photo and video studio with camera and lighting equipment at the disposal of the artists. High-quality color monitors must be standard equipment in a graphics workstation.

365

Paint programs of every make, color, and size would be standard software in the graphics workstation. Some of the other necessary software "equipment" would include video digitizing and touch-up, graphics processing (like skew, rotate, and distort), optical scanning, and 3D graphics generators. Other paint programs and graphics databases will be compatible with this system.

In this sort of environment, with the right management, artists could crank out a meg of art a day (1,024,000 bytes).

Figure 4. A music or sound effects workstation

A music or sound effects workstation will require high-quality audio gear (speakers, tape recorders, amplifier, preamplifier) both for recording and playback. Patch bays, MIDI keyboards, processing equipment, sound digitizers, mixers, and microphones should also be standard equipment. Color monitors for displaying composing programs are also necessary.

366

Special facilities should be prepared with sound dampening, especially in the workstations designated as "audio studios." Each workstation will be equipped with sequencer and composition software with a variety of notational scoring systems available, e.g., Conventional Music Notation and the MusicWorks grid system. Sound effects generation through algorithmic control will probably also be desired, as well as sampled sound editors.

A multimedia scoring system (like SoundVision) will be used to synchronize the music or sound effects to the animation. Access to other music databases, synthesis patches, or algorithms will also be possible with this workstation. A 10-minute composition could be produced in a day at one of these workstations.

Figure 5. An animation workstation

An animation workstation requires much the same equipment as the graphics workstation, with some differences. Multiple monitors can facilitate the simultaneous viewing, previewing, and editing of data. Videotape recorders, video SEGs (or mixers), and audio equipment are also important to animators who wish to transfer their work onto other media (VHS, Beta, ¾-inch tape).

The animation workstation of an authoring system is where all the elements of the system are brought together and incorporated into the score. This is where the text and artwork are "animated," the music is synchronized, and the action codes are embedded to control the flow of the interactive programs.

The SoundVision scoring system is the main software element of an animation workstation like this. Other types of development tools could be used to integrate incompatible data or to configure the premastering system, but creating and editing documents on the score would be the main task of an animator.

So you can see there is more than just one type of workstation involved in a CD ROM project. Managers, designers, and executives could theoretically work in an animation workstation. Artists could roam between graphics and animation stations, and producers and directors would have to know them all equally well.

Tailoring Your Workstation

Each workstation should be customized to the particular project and application being produced. One of the best ways to utilize workers' abilities would be to use remote workstations. You could place them anywhere (especially at home) so that work could continue seven days a week and on holidays. And be fun!

How to Use an Authoring System

Stage One. The first stage in using an authoring system is to block out the approximate timings and interaction desired in the application. A typical application would have a menu at the beginning, at least two or three other menus somewhere else, and some sort of ending section.

Text and artwork (which should have been created earlier), along with action codes, are placed into a document's score at the approximate locations. Dialog boxes, menus, and buttons, which start off as artwork, soon turn into interactive controls when an action code is associated with them. The connection between artwork and action code is all done on the score, at the exact frame desired. (The exact logistics of how to assign an action code in the score is explained below.)

Once a rough draft has been worked out, initial viewings can be used to detect mistakes, wrong codes, or ill-conceived notions. This process of trying things out as soon as possible allows the author to correct any grievous errors before they become uncontrollable.

The material can also be edited at any time, so different sections of the project can be polished at different times, and concievably by different people.

Stage Two.   The second stage in using an authoring system (once the timings have been frozen) is to add more action codes. These codes may link several documents together, branch to other sections and return, or even start other applications. Music and animation can also be added at this stage of the development process.

Memory limitations and access times are some of the typical problems encountered when developing applications with authoring systems. Once a writer releases the tremendous potential of the system, he usually goes overboard and asks the system to do too much. For instance, jump from a section on DNA synthesis, to a musical selection by Beethoven, to a survey of Picasso paintings, all in 0:15 second, and then return to the chemistry section and continue the lesson.

Authoring systems can help organize and control a huge amount of data, but it is very easy to overextend yourself. Early on in your design you must determine how much data is enough. Just how many sequences of animation demonstrating the principles of fluid mechanics or wave dynamics will be sufficient to get the point across? Whatever you decide, it is very important to not be too ambitious. Tackle only a small part of a huge task at a time. There will always be room for more later.

It's important to realize that authoring systems will evolve and grow with technology. In the future, new types of authoring systems will be designed to take advantage of new technology. Besides simple menu choices and passive viewing, new standards of interacting will develop, such as text entry or real-time input.

Stage Three.   The final stage of using an authoring system is the debugging of the application. Do all the questions make sense? Does the program flow smoothly? Are there any interactions that don't go anywhere? Is the artwork less than perfect? Going back to the score and changing action codes is as easy as editing text or touching up graphics.

This stage is probably the most impotant one, as it's always that last 5% of an application that can really make or break it.

Because of the nature of authoring systems, applications can evolve and change as they are worked on. Sections that make perfect sense on paper often turn out to be less than expected. Because of this, an authoring system user should always keep an open mind, ever ready to shift gears and do things differently. A good authoring system should facilitate this need by making it as easy as possible to edit and change the application at any time.

The Macintosh Version of VideoWorks

VideoWorks was released in April 1985 as a consumer animation creation tool for the Macintosh. Since then it has gone through a metamorphosis and is now a full-fledged authoring system for the Macintosh, capable of integrating text, graphics, animation, speech, and music in one interactive application.

369

The following describes how to prepare interactive documents with a special version of VideoWorks called VW Special.

First, VW Special (the special version of VideoWorks) is used to create the interactive documents. These documents are called up by an application we call the Guided Tour, which interprets the action codes. Any existing VideoWorks animation can be turned into an interactive program by loading it into VW Special and adding action codes. Any image can be associated with a particular action simply by selecting it in the VideoWorks Score (see Figure 6) and then choosing the desired action.

The "action codes," or programming codes, necessary for creating the interactive programs can be embedded into the score and edited just like any piece of animation or music.

The types of actions available are pause, quit, jump to another document, jump to another frame, launch a desk accessory or another application, or exit to the Finder. Jumps can be goto-like jumps or subroutine calls that can be nested to any depth. For example, jumps can be used to create an animation loop which happens while waiting for the end user to make a menu selection.

The interactive document is run by an application called Guided Tour, which interprets the action codes. The first document to be called up must be named Tour List, which typically is the highest-level menu. From the Tour List one can call up any number of documents, or frames within any document, and link them together in any imaginable combination.

Any image (sprite) on the screen can be a button (hotspot). Each button is associated with a particular action. When Guided Tour is running, a mouse click on any button causes that action to happen. Actions defined in the sound channel of the score (see Figure 6) occur immediately, without any end user interaction.

The VideoWorks Score

Pictured in Figure 6 is the score in VideoWorks. Time goes from left to right, with frame numbers appearing along the top. Up to 24 images (sprites) can appear on the screen at once. These are shown as 24 channels, lettered A through X, plus the sound channel at the top (denoted by the speaker). At the intersection of each frame and channel, some information on that image at that moment in time is displayed. For example, the squares on the top of the intersection represent a new image in that frame, and the arrows on the bottom show which way the image has moved since the last frame. A hyphen means that the image hasn't changed, and a dot means that the image hasn't moved.

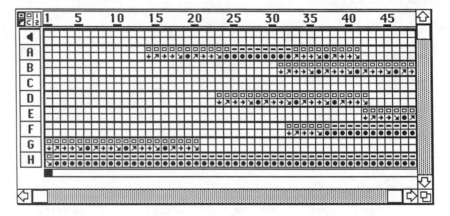

Figure 6. The VideoWorks score. Each frame displays the status of an image at any given moment.

The switches in the upper left corner of the score determine the type of information the score displays. For example, the next display, called a cast screen (Figure 7), shows how to tell what image is being displayed. Each square represents an individual piece of artwork and is called a cast member. The top number is the cast row, the bottom number is the index. The cast is used to keep track of the hundreds of cast members.

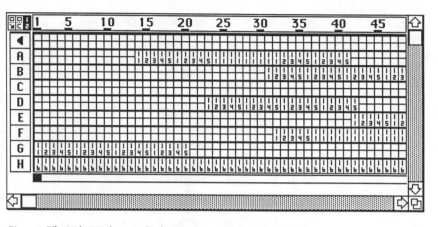

Figure 7. The VideoWorks score displaying cast member numbers. Each square respreents an individual piece of artwork.

Action Codes in the Current Authoring System

The score in Figure 8 displays the action codes in a VW Special document. The **Do** menu is open, showing all the possible actions available in this document. The actions below the line in the **Do** menu are user-defined. In this case the first user-defined action is #Alarm Clock, which calls up the Alarm Clock desk accessory.

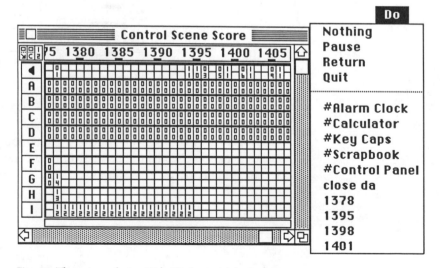

Figure 8. The action codes in a VideoWorks special document

Actions that are placed in channels A-X (there are 24 graphics channels in VideoWorks) will execute when an end user clicks the mouse on the sprite in that frame. Actions that are placed in the sound channel (the channel above A) are immediate; they will always happen when the animation hits that frame.

For example, Figure 8 shows the menu that appears at frame 1377 where there is a pause in the sound channel and three buttons which activate jumps to certain frames of this document. There is also a loop between frames 1378 and 1394 because of the "jump back to frame 1378" action in the sound channel of frame 1394. The subroutines starting at frames 1395 through 1410 call up desk accessories and jump into the previous loop.

The MusicWorks Scores

SoundVision will feature two different types of musical scores. They will be integrated with the score from VideoWorks into the multimedia Sound-Vision score.

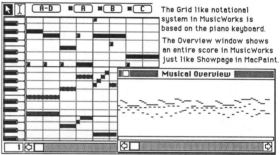

The Grid like notational system in MusicWorks is based on the piano keyboard.

The Overview window shows an entire score in MusicWorks just like Showpage in MacPaint.

Figure 9. Two different types of musical scores available in SoundVision

The CD ROM Authoring System

The scoring system of SoundVision is where all the elements of the system come together. A CD ROM authoring system modeled after the existing SoundVision score would not be very different. Individual CD sequences can be called up, particular sections searched for, and any frame frozen.

- As shown in Figure 10, a particular CD sequence number (CD#) would be listed in the Demo list text screen.

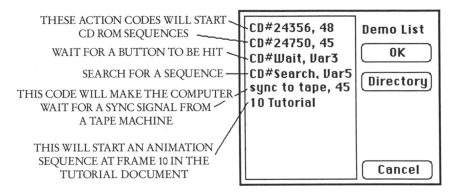

THESE ACTION CODES WILL START CD ROM SEQUENCES

WAIT FOR A BUTTON TO BE HIT

SEARCH FOR A SEQUENCE

THIS CODE WILL MAKE THE COMPUTER WAIT FOR A SYNC SIGNAL FROM A TAPE MACHINE

THIS WILL START AN ANIMATION SEQUENCE AT FRAME 10 IN THE TUTORIAL DOCUMENT

CD#24356, 48
CD#24750, 45
CD#Wait, Var3
CD#Search, Var5
sync to tape, 45
10 Tutorial

Demo List
OK
Directory
Cancel

Figure 10. Typical action codes used to access information on CD ROM

- Action codes, like **start** and **stop** the sequence, **freeze,** or **search** can be embedded into the document's score at any frame. These frames can be designed to be as interactive as the user wishes, making dialog boxes or text entry possible.

- Each action is assigned to a button. Any piece of artwork can be a button, which can be placed anywhere on the screen. Compressed audio or video can be included in the system at this point, as they represent just another sequence of events started by an action code.

- The computer graphics of the buttons can be "keyed" onto the video output from the CD, thereby integrating the graphics data with the compressed video.

- The CD specific action codes will control the CD player when they are activated from the interactive application. The application can be running on a standard personal computer or from a dedicated "black box" system.

- Running simulations of the application on a premastering system is the final stage in using a CD ROM authoring system.

Important Issues for CD ROM Authors

Authoring software should aim to shorten the feedback loop between the computer and the user—between the idea itself and its actualization. The overall outcome is a more direct connection to creativity for the user and a higher level of productivity.

This type of interaction is exactly what computers were made for: real-time tools. An example of this real-time interaction can be seen in Music-Works, where the notes are heard as they are placed onto the score, or in VideoWorks, where you can edit an image as you watch it animate.

Widespread use of such authoring workstations will enable large groups of artists and programmers to produce very large databases of text, animation, and music. By keeping the notational system as generalized as possible, workstations like this have the potenial of controlling Broadway productions or entire television studios.

Project Management

Proper management of CD ROM productions can mean the difference between profit and failure. Some suggested management structures for these sorts of projects and how they should be divided are listed below.

1. Artists should have an art director responsible for all final artwork. Technical consultants, animators, and camera operators will all be at the disposal of the artists but exist as separate units. The art director will have several assistants, whose responsibilities will range from hiring new artists and training them, to everyday monitoring of activity.

2. Musicians should have a management structure similar to that of the artists, with a music director ultimately responsible for all products. Integration between graphics and sound will be an important task for management, not to mention the daily handling of tempermental artistic minds.

3. Higher-level management will coordinate individual projects, taking care of the acquisition of rights to databases, scheduling, and the structure of the application itself. The art and musical directors will work closely with the individual project managers, with all teams taking suggestions from the workers themselves.

Summing Up

The current authoring system can only move graphics on a CRT screen and control music and sound from a synthesizer.

A true multimedia authoring system for CD would be designed around an end product of the future, a BitBlt-based graphics system, PCM encoded sounds, and compressed video. This theoretical machine of the future would be integrated with a CD player and a mouse with a windows-like operating system.

Implementing CD authoring systems will fall into three phases:

Any language or program that can control events through time is an authoring system.

Phase I. Simple remote control of a CD ROM player. A graphics-based computer system displays buttons on a CRT screen to control CD ROM sequences (either text or graphics) which appear on a separate monitor. This system will help manufacturers design the hardware for the product of the future, but it is far from the integrated multimedia system of Phase II.

Phase II. An integrated CD ROM simulation environment. At this stage, compressed audio and video data will be integrated with text by using the premastering system. Large platters of read/write storage will simulate CD discs for software development purposes. All existing features from the earlier systems will be implemented, with the computer graphics buttons appearing in front of ("keyed over") the video footage.

Phase III. This is when the development tools are rewritten and perfected for the final hardware configuration. The actual consumer product is usually the best development tool, as it looks and sounds exactly like the end product will. At this stage, full-scale production could begin, with completed applications a year away.

About the Author

Mr. Canter is president of MacroMind®, the developer of MusicWorks™ and VideoWorks™ for the Apple Macintosh. These creativity tools form a foundation for an integrated creativity tool system named SoundVision™ (now being developed for the Amiga and IBM PC computers).

Mr. Canter's experience in new technology goes back to the mid-seventies, with work in electronic music and video. Audio engineer, laser light show designer, and videogame sound programmer are some of the other positions he's held since then. He is a 1980 graduate of Oberlin College, with a B.F.A. in intermedia.

His experience with interactive videodiscs and videotext in New York City in 1982 has helped him formulate and develop the CD ROM authoring system now being developed by MacroMind®.

Marc Aaron Canter
1028 W. Wolfram St.
Chicago, Il 60657
(312) 327-5821

Scripting for Interactive Applications

by Dennis Walters and Stephanie Rosenbaum

Several years ago, a scene in a popular TV science-fiction program showed two characters discussing a plot situation while trying to checkmate each other in a game of three-dimensional chess. Although the scene was intended to explain the plot development, what caught the attention of the TV audience was the chess game. Imagine coping on three levels with opposing strategies that are complex enough on just one level!

377

Writing Interactively

For centuries, writers have been imagining ways to imitate such complex strategies in their writing. Storytellers know that audiences tend to follow a plot in a linear fashion (Figure 1). Readers typically begin a book at the beginning and read all the way through to the end; when they come to the end, they stop. For a long time writers wrote the way readers read—in a straight line.

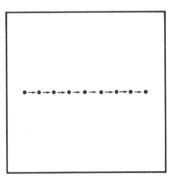

Figure 1. The linear approach to scripting

Then writers discovered the modified linear approach (Figure 2). They caught the reader's interest and heightened suspense by beginning their story in the middle and describing an exciting scene; then they switched to another time or place and began again (often by explaining some background or history). And eventually they got to the end of the story. Magazines and encyclopedias use a modified linear approach; the reader jumps into the text at any desired point but then reads in a line until the end of the article.

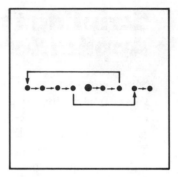

Figure 2. The modified linear approach to scripting

What writers really wanted, though, was a truly interactive document, where audience choice helped to decide the outcome. There, events would have a planned direction, but their exact sequence would be unpredictable—what happened second would depend entirely on what happened first (Figure 3). Writers in various disciplines experimented, and soon were marketing programmed self-instruction manuals, simulations, and even write-your-own-ending novels.

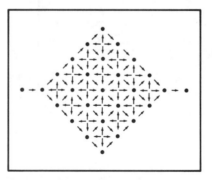

Figure 3. The interactive approach to scripting

Automating Interactivity

Today, the increasing popularity of computers provides a way to automate interactivity. Writers in training, business, industry, and entertainment can now create programs in which their audiences select a path through a maze of tasks. Today's audiences can:

○ Pilot an aircraft in bad weather through enemy territory

○ Progressively narrow a search for information in a database

○ Learn a dangerous task while working safely in a simulated environment

○ Predict volcanic and seismic activity as stresses are developing

○ Take a course in auto mechanics

To succeed in creating such projects, the writer has to find out what interactive media can do—and then learn to write interactively for the selected medium.

379

Looking at Interactive Media

If you want to create an interactive document, you must write what amounts to a script to be acted in an interactive medium. A programmed textbook is a noncomputerized medium. The three main types of computerized media, based on the method of data access, are sequential access, low-density (magnetic) random access, and high-density (optical) random access (Figure 4).

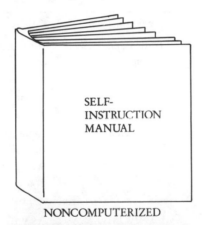

SELF-INSTRUCTION MANUAL

NONCOMPUTERIZED

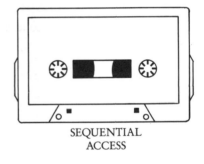

SEQUENTIAL ACCESS

LOW-DENSITY RANDOM ACCESS

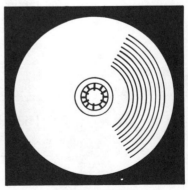

HIGH-DENSITY RANDOM ACCESS

Figure 4. Media for interactive scripting

Consider how a programmed textbook works. First, it presents a situation or concept on, say, page 3; then it asks the reader a question about the presentation. If the reader answers correctly, the book says to turn to page 4; if incorrectly, to page 5. From either of these choices, the book may offer further choices. Of course, the branching of choices can't go on forever; depending on the goal of the book, the branches intersect at various points to resume the path toward the intended goal.

In a programmed-instruction manual, the presentation can become fairly complex without being too expensive to produce. A major drawback is that the reader has to spend a lot of time turning pages.

On a computerized medium, the computer handles the branching. Some pertinent characteristics of a computerized medium for interactive scripting are shown in the table below.

Type	Examples	Characteristics
Sequential access	Audiotape, Videotape	Interactive applications should allow for long access times; consequently, branching shouldn't be very elaborate
Low-density random access	Magnetic diskettes, hard disks	Access to data is rapid, but data capacities vary enough that the size of programs is a concern. Also, diskette-based programs of any significant size may require disk swapping.
High-density random access	CD ROMs, videodiscs	As with magnetic disks, access to data is rapid but data capacity is vastly greater. Although memory requirements are not a dominant concern, currently available devices have read-only capability.

High-density access devices offer the greatest potential for interactivity today. Therefore, this chapter uses CD ROM devices as the target medium when discussing how to create an interactive script.

Learning to Write Interactively

Most people think interactively without realizing it. Mentally, they converse, weigh alternatives, switch viewpoints, and test circumstances and conclusions. They follow converging and diverging logic paths, reason out and jump to conclusions, backtrack to and circumnavigate ideas, and associate concepts and events.

Thinking in multiple dimensions isn't foreign either. The mind customarily works on different levels at the same time. People develop a sense of perspective and context, view questions in depth, and handle foreground situations while resolving problems in the background. In principle, three-dimensional chess isn't outside the realm of mental experience.

The challenge for the writer is to imitate this mental activity on paper or in a computer program. Whatever the limitations of the medium, learning to write interactively provides benefits such as the following:

○ Natural give-and-take between the application and the user

○ Multiple choices, including the consequences of those choices

○ Different levels of detail, difficulty, or security, depending on user needs

○ Immediate feedback and reinforcement

○ Access to the full potential of the medium

The rest of this chapter shows how to create an interactive script for a CD ROM application. As an example, the chapter uses part of a course on database software—a lesson on how to join separate datasets in a relational database system—but you can apply the scriptwriting principles illustrated here to any application.

Basically, writing an interactive script entails six phases of activity:

1. Preplanning the approach to the scripting project

2. Planning the application itself

3. Developing and testing the flowchart

4. Developing and testing the storyboard

5. Developing and testing the final script

6. Producing the script on the CD ROM device

   This chapter covers the first five phases of the project. Other chapters of this book discuss Phase Six.

Phase One: Preplanning

Preplanning means taking care of the preliminaries—identifying what you'll need to get your script ready for production even before you begin to write it. To avoid false starts, delays, cost and schedule overruns, and general disaster, you and the others on the writing team should carefully plan the elements of the project and allocate responsibilities.

Defining the Goal of the Project

Start by defining your project goal. Exactly what do you have to accomplish? State the goal in a sentence or so: "We will write, test, and prepare for CD ROM production a five-hour interactive training script about basic relational database management operations."

Your definition should outline the activities that will get you to the goal (for example, writing, testing, and preparing for CD ROM production—which includes programming and reproduction activities). You should identify what each activity means for your team.

Defining the Product

Next, make sure you and your production team all have the same idea of what the deliverable product will look like. Among the things you should discuss:

○ The equipment that the final result of your scripting effort will run on. Be sure to find out the configuration of the hardware (the main processor, the need for other storage media besides the CD ROM, type of monitor, and so on); the relationships between the hardware and the software (how a program for a read-only device will cause write instructions to be executed, for example); and the input devices available with this system (such as keyboards, mice, touch pads, and joysticks).

○ The production requirements to get your script running on this equipment, including the authoring system or programming language to be used, and any graphics (cartooning or drawing) or video (television) support needed.

○ The capabilities and limitations of the hardware, especially with respect to the kinds and levels of interactivity it can handle; its graphics capabilities (in case your script calls for drawings, animation, data overlays, and so on); and miscellaneous issues such as color capability and screen resolution.

Assessing the Feasibility of the Project

Assess the feasibility of what you want to do. Probably you have some ideas for a script by now; for example, perhaps you'd like to design an animation sequence showing what happens when the user joins two datasets. Before you start implementing this plan, find out if you have enough time and money to execute it.

383

See also if your ideas will work from a technical standpoint. For example, how many levels of branching and nesting can your program handle? How will a training course on databases have the user create new databases while using a read-only storage device? What other input and output procedures will probably be needed (for example, for printing of reports)?

Planning Testing Procedures

Plan how you will test the script before you commit it to final CD ROM production. Your testing plan should consider:

○ The kinds of tests which will work out the bugs in the script. At various points before, during, and after script development, you should test the flow of the script, the sequence of and transition between events, and the response of pilot users to the script.

○ When to test the script during the development cycle. You should test it at least once before having the script initially programmed, and at least once after initial programming (but before final production).

○ How to handle revisions that result from these tests; for example, the amount of rewriting and retesting your budget can accommodate. Remember that changes to one part of the script may require changes to other parts.

Understanding Project Management

Finally, be sure you understand how the application development project as a whole will be managed. The project team may consist of project managers, writers, editors, graphic designers, artists, script reviewers, programmers, and production or manufacturing staff. With all these people, how will the project keep moving along smoothly?

As a scriptwriter, you may not be responsible for overall coordination of the project. Even so, you should make sure you know:

○ What the schedules and milestones of the project are, particularly as they affect your activities and those of the people you will work with directly during the project.

Writers in training, business, industry, and entertainment can now create programs in which their audiences select a path through a maze of tasks.

○ Who will review the script at each stage of its development (to avoid delays, the review team should be the same throughout the project).

○ How you will maintain contact with other team members (for example, through weekly team meetings, daily phone calls, and so on).

Phase Two: Planning the Application

During Phase One, you planned how the scripting project will work. In Phase Two, you plan how the application itself works. In this phase, you define the goals of the application, the audience, the topic of the script, and the main features of the script (Figure 5).

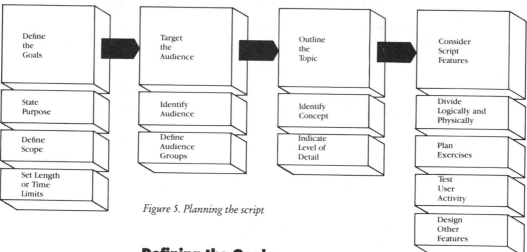

Figure 5. Planning the script

Defining the Goals

Because interactive scripting often means that you must work very close to the trees, you need to determine the size and shape of your forest. Your first task should be to identify and limit what the script will accomplish.

In a sentence or two, state the purpose of the application. Keep the statement brief, comprehensive, and focused on the user. For example, our application is a training course whose goal is to "teach the user to perform basic relational database management operations."

For applications like training programs, break down the goal into a few primary behavioral objectives and performance criteria. Objectives and performance criteria spell out in terms of observable behavior what the user will finish the course knowing how to do, and how well to do it; for example, "After completing this course, the user will be able to enter and execute basic relational database commands without making syntactical errors."

Next, define the scope of the application. The scope definition outlines the subject areas that the application covers and specifies, if necessary, topics that it should omit.

Third, limit the length or duration of the application. Length and time limits help you quantify your stated goals.

Finally, develop an approach to the general visual format and graphic design elements of the application. Will you (or a graphic designer on your project team) need to design screens, plan color contrasts, and so on? Graphic design is so integral to most writing projects that you will either design by design or design by default.

Targeting the Audience

Whether you analyze your target audience formally or informally, describe in writing exactly whom the script addresses. A clearly defined target audience enables you to:

○ Adhere to your purpose and scope (you present only the information the audience needs)

○ Handle the presentation of content (possibly by suggesting a target level of detail)

○ Establish an approach to your topic (by indicating an appropriate tone)

The composition of the audience can suggest approaches to the script. If the audience consists of one predominant group (all novice database users, say, or all users who require the same information), the script can address everyone on the same level. If the audience consists of multiple groups (some novices, some expert users, some needing information on special procedures), you may want to create a multilayered script, with each layer addressing a particular segment of the audience.

Outlining the Topic

Now write a topic outline. Like all outlines, the script outline is your plan of approach to the subject matter. It lists the order in which you will present topics, concepts, and ideas. It also indicates which points are subordinate to which other points, and their relative weight or importance.

Write your outline to the lowest convenient level of detail. The more you can specify what events will occur without writing the actual script, the better. Writing a detailed outline prevents you from leaving out important points when you begin to implement the script. More important, the outline keeps the strands of your topic together as you weave the network of interactions.

Planning Important Features of the Script

In addition to listing the sequence of topics, procedures, and routines, your outline should indicate:

> If you want to create an interactive document, you must write what amounts to a script to be acted in an interactive medium.

1. Logical divisions, based on topic. These divisions should suit the type of application you're writing. For example, training courses are often divided logically into modules, the modules into units, and the units into lessons. Be sure to identify topic areas common to multiple lessons or parts of lessons, such as concepts that several lessons use.

2. Physical divisions imposed by the limits of the hardware (for example, file length). Your target CD ROM hardware and its associated computer system may or may not have limitations that affect your script; if you don't yet know for sure, now is the time to ask a technical consultant.

3. The number, frequency, and types of exercises the user will perform.

4. Tests. In interactive scripting, tests not only measure user comprehension or learning, they also indicate how the script will branch (one way for the right answer, another way for the wrong answer).

5. Visual standards. As the writer, you are responsible for communicating concepts. In an interactive application, much of that communication will take place visually. Your job, then, is to identify places in the script where visual distinctions (such as the need to emphasize input fields or distinguish between foreground and background objects) would help the communication process.

Based on your ideas, the graphic designer's responsibility is to create the kinds of visual distinctions that best achieve the communication goals you've set for your audience. For example, the designer would specify how screen layout or color would emphasize input fields, and so on.

Specifically, you and the designer together should determine visual standards governing the size and density of text on the screen, use of foreground and background colors, layout of information on the screen, shapes and colors that blink or flash, use of borders, and any other visual elements in the final product.

Reviewing the Outline

Before proceeding with the next phase of development, have everyone on the project team who will approve the final script review and approve your definitions of the project purpose, scope, and audience, as well as the topic outline. If you have time, you should consider two types of reviews:

○ An internal review by writers, editors, graphic artists, programmers, and other project team members

○ An external review by supervisors, clients, representatives of the user audience, and others with an interest in the final product

Be sure to meet with representatives of the review team and agree upon any changes considered necessary. Correcting mistakes of definition, concept, or approach now will save expensive headaches later in the project.

Phase Three: Developing and Testing the Flowchart

The flowchart is the skeleton of the interactive script. Unlike the outline, which lists the order of concepts or topics, the flowchart shows the sequence of events (the prompts, user input, and program responses) and their interactive relationships with each other (the branching and looping paths).

Understanding What the Flowchart Helps You Accomplish

Figure 6 is a flowchart for the sample interactive database training course—a lesson on how to join datasets. (Several readings listed at the end of this chapter discuss other types of interactive flowcharts.)

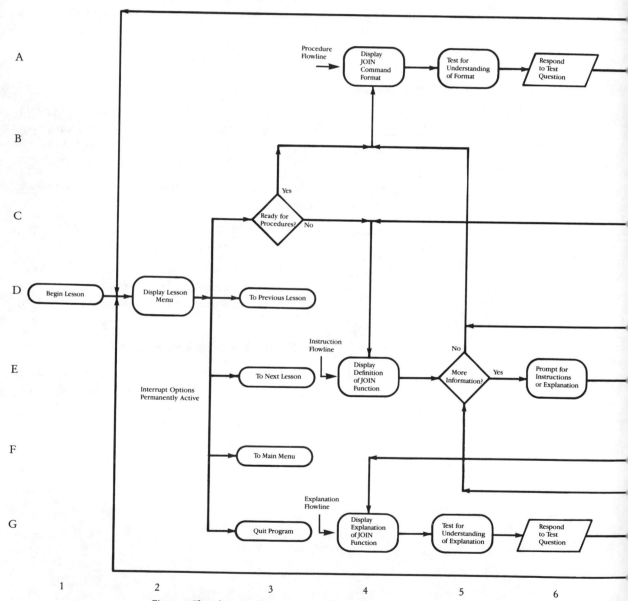

Figure 6. Flowchart of a lesson on joining datasets

The sample flowchart shows:

○ How the program begins and ends (terminal indicators)

○ Principal flowlines (sequences of program development) and paths through the flowchart

○ Program actions, such as displays and processes

○ User responses and tests that evaluate these responses

○ The paths followed by the branches and loops that occur following each test

The flowchart is a tool for synthesis; that is, you can use it to create and organize a detailed sequence of events, and determine how these events will interconnect. The flowchart is also an analytical tool. With it, you can test the logic that takes the user from any one point in the program to any other point.

For the writer, the flowchart explains everything that happens in the program. The flowchart also gives the programmer an overview for planning how to code the script. Thus, it is crucial to the development of your application that the flowchart be correct and clear.

Creating a Flowchart

The flowchart for an interactive application looks like most programming flowcharts. It uses standard flowcharting symbols for typical events like input tests, although you can invent special symbols if you need to describe unusual types of events. It also uses a letter/number grid for referring to locations on the chart. Regardless of appearance, what matters is that the flowchart clearly show the structure of the application.

Here are some suggestions for creating an interactive flowchart:

1. Draw your flowchart horizontally rather than vertically. Because interactive flowcharts can get long and complicated, you may need to mount yours on a wall to see the flow of the whole application at one time.

2. Remember the goal of the lesson as you draw the chart. Keep in mind which flowlines are primary (the target flowlines that users should eventually work through) and which are subordinate.

3. Maintain a consistent point of view in the flowchart. You can diagram from the user's or the computer's viewpoint, but don't mix views. (The sample flowchart takes the computer's viewpoint.)

4. Show how each program segment starts and ends. Always provide a way out of the current activity, and ways to pause or suspend the activity so the user can leave it and return to it later.

5. For homogeneous audiences, your startup sequence can branch directly to the primary flowlines. For heterogeneous (multilevel) audiences, you can branch to alternate parallel flowlines that take specified categories of

users through procedures tailored just for them. (On a flowchart, such alternate flowlines appear to lie behind a main flowline. You can use acetate overlays or special colors to draw alternate parallel flowlines.)

6. When you want the user to interact with the program, specify how the program knows the interaction is to occur (for example, by testing user input).

7. To indicate an interaction, either connect the current flowline to another (a branch) or to itself (a loop) at an appropriate place. Be sure to connect all branches at both ends and to close all loops. If you branch to flowlines on another page of the flowchart, use specific cross references with off-chart indicator symbols on both pages.

8. Account for every possible event—every prompt, input, and input test. Determine how the program responds to both valid and invalid input and how it handles multiple-choice selections.

9. Make each flowline and path move in only one direction. Use arrowheads to indicate the direction of movement.

10. On the flowchart, indicate with labels and symbols when to use devices or media other than the CD ROM (such as workbooks, hard disks, and so on).

Testing, Reviewing, and Revising the Flowchart

When you finish drawing the flowchart, get someone other than yourself to test it by analyzing each element. That person should follow step by step every line on the chart, checking the following:

The flowchart is the skeleton of the interactive script.

○ The concept flow (by comparing the flowchart with the topic outline)

○ The event flow (by looking for illogical events, inappropriate branching and looping, and steps omitted or unnecessarily repeated)

○ The multidimensional aspects of the flowchart (how hidden flowlines branch from or intersect with flowlines on the main level)

○ Mechanical problems with the flowchart (incorrect symbols, missing arrows, and so on)

After this test, you should resolve any problems the tester encountered and redraw all or part of the flowchart as necessary.

Next, have everyone responsible for approving the final script review the flowchart in detail. As with the outline, you may want to conduct both internal and external reviews, if you have time.

Whatever the review process, the reviewers should mark the flowchart with specific comments and questions. You should then arrange a meeting with the review group to agree upon any changes to the flowchart. Finally, revise the flowchart accordingly.

Phase Four: Developing and Testing the Storyboard

If the flowchart is the skeleton of the finished program, the storyboard begins to put nerves and sinews on the bones. The flowchart shows events and their structural relationships; the storyboard is an event-by-event look at the way the presentation will actually work.

Understanding What the Storyboard Helps You Accomplish

Once you've finished the flowchart, you know in general how the program will work. With the storyboard, you can fill in the details. The storyboard enables you to:

○ Summarize the content of each event, such as screen displays, user responses, and resulting program behavior.

○ Identify what happens, from the viewpoint of the agent (the user or the program).

○ Define how events occur. For example, the user sees two choices displayed on the screen, selects one by pressing a number key or typing a value, and then hears a sound cue indicating how the program will branch.

○ Determine how transitions between events occur, especially in cases where two separate events from different flowlines intersect with the current event.

○ Define expected actions (such as expected user input) and account for other possible actions (such as the user pressing a function key to quit the program).

For you, the storyboard identifies the actors and actions in each scene and summarizes the dialog which the final script will recount in detail. For the programmer, the storyboard indicates the number and kind of visible and audible events, input and retrieval operations, tests, special functions, and other processes; it also helps to plan the structure of the coded program.

Creating a Storyboard

There are dozens of ways to arrange a storyboard. The format you use depends on how you need to describe the kinds of events in your application. The sample shown in Figure 7 implements part of the flowchart previously shown in Figure 6, and illustrates a format suitable to a training program.

Instructional Topic	Chart Loc.	Enter from Loc.	Screen Displays	User Response	Program Action: Valid Response	Program Action: Invalid Response
Format of JOIN Command	A4	C3; E5; E12	General form of the JOIN command followed by a specific input sample.	Press RETURN to advance to the next screen.	Display next screen.	
	A5	A4	Fill-in-blanks question to test whether the user knows that two datasets can be joined only if both have one or more fields in common.	Type six-character response, press RETURN.	Expected input: FIELD or FIELDS. On input, display screen at A8.	On invalid input, branch to screen at E4.
	A8	A6-7; A13; E12	The names of two sample datasets and several field names from each. At least one name in each list must be common to both datasets. Prompts the user to JOIN the datasets.	Type JOIN, the first dataset name, the second dataset name, and any number of field names displayed; then press RETURN.	Expected input: Any field names that match. On valid input, join the datasets and store the results. Then display screen at A11.	On invalid input, emit sound cue, perform error check routine (B10, C10). If first try, repeat display at A8; otherwise, branch to display at E8.

Figure 7. Storyboard showing part of the lesson on joining datasets

This format enables you to take a cross-sectional view of one event at a time; the sample shows three such events (grouped under one heading in the "Instructional Topic" column). A cross-sectional view tells you at a glance:

○ How the event starts (in this case, with a displayed message).

○ How it proceeds (with a user response).

○ How it ends (with some kind of program action, determined according to whether the user response is valid or not).

○ The transition to the next event. In the sample storyboard, transitions are incoming (the "Enter from Loc." column) and outgoing (the "Program Action" columns).

For writer and programmer convenience, the sample storyboard also refers to the location of each event on the flowchart.

Whatever format you choose, for each event your storyboard should describe the topic you're presenting, how the user views or experiences the event, what the user does to trigger the next event, and what response the program makes to the user's input. In constructing your storyboard, pay particular attention to transitions and unusual or out-of-sequence events.

Because interactive scripting often means that you must work very close to the trees, you need to determine the size and shape of your forest.

A transition into an event that has only one entry point poses no difficulty. The transition is linear, and the only concern is with the straightforward logic of the connection. For example, in Figure 7 the storyboard passes the user from the display of the general form example (event A4) to the test question on the next screen (event A5).

Transitions where the subsequent event has several previous events leading into it (for example, event A8 in Figure 7) can be tricky. When planning such transitions, ask yourself:

○ Does the transition from each previous event make sense?

○ What scene is the user entering? Does what the user sees on the screen connect smoothly with what previously appeared, or will a user entering from any previous point experience a jolt? The graphic design standards you developed in Phase Two should help you avoid problems.

○ How does the user leave the scene? Is the exit logically consistent with each entry point, or does the exit force a hidden loop back to the entry point again? (For example, will a user who entered event A8 from event E12 necessarily loop back to E12 again?)

The storyboard should also explain how to handle situations where an unusual or out-of-sequence event occurs. That is, the storyboard should describe whether (and how) the user can skip or repeat events, break out of an ongoing event to return to the beginning, or even quit the program. The storyboard may also need a special section at the end that describes what happens when the user makes common mistakes, such as typing errors or not turning on a peripheral device.

395

Testing, Reviewing, and Revising the Storyboard

After you complete the storyboard, have someone other than yourself test it by following each sequence of events described. The person testing the storyboard should check whether:

○ The description of each event (that is, each prompt-input-response sequence) makes sense by itself.

○ Transitions into the current event from all previous events, and out of the current event into all subsequent events, work smoothly.

○ The storyboard adequately describes unusual or out-of-sequence events.

As with the flowchart, the person testing the storyboard should note where mistakes occur or questions arise. Be sure to resolve all outstanding issues before submitting the storyboard for review.

The storyboard review process should follow the same pattern as the outline and flowchart reviews. That is, everyone responsible for approving the final script should review the storyboard in detail, and you should meet with the reviewers (both internal and external) to discuss comments and possible revisions. Because the storyboard is the last step before you write the actual script, you should be sure to take care of all outstanding questions or action items now.

After you complete any revisions to the storyboard, you should consult with programmers and other technical personnel to plan production of the finished script. In particular, review your testing plans and arrange now to program and test the pilot version of the script.

Phase Five:
Developing and Testing the Script

The script gives final shape to the interactive training program. It is the last step before programming and production of the course.

Understanding What the Script Helps You Accomplish

With the script, you flesh out the events summarized on the storyboard by providing a detailed account of everything that happens. The script contains the complete text of all screen displays, defines valid user input, and describes program activities (such as animation sequences, file searches, sound and video cues, and so on).

Creating the Script

As Figure 8 illustrates, the interactive script you write from the storyboard can look much like the script for a stage or screen play, although formats vary. Whatever the format, the script identifies the actors, provides

Chart Loc.	Element	Script
A4	Screen:	(Displays the message:)
		The JOIN command uses the form:
		JOIN dataset1 dataset2 BY field1,field2, . . . fieldn
		Here's an example:
		JOIN MYLIST YOURLIST BY LASTNAME
		The datasets joined must share at least one field in common. Matching the shared fields, JOIN adds all the fields and data of the second dataset named in the command to all the fields and data of the first dataset named.
		Let's see how well you understand . . .
	User:	(Presses the RETURN key to advance to the next screen.)
A5	Screen:	(Displays the message:)
		In the space below, answer the question and press RETURN.
		The JOIN command links two datasets by means of one or more _____ that both datasets have in common.
		(The cursor is in the blank reverse video input field.)
	User:	(Types a response of up to six characters and presses the RETURN key.)
	System:	(Displays each character typed in the input field.
		Accepts FIELD or FIELDS as a correct response.)
A8	Screen:	(On correct response, displays the message:)
		Correct. Now join these datasets—
		(Displays in reverse video the names of any two existing datasets.)
		—using one or more common fields—
		(Displays two lists of dataset field names, one from each dataset; both lists have at least one field name in common. Also displays a blank 80-character input field below the lists.)
	User:	(Types the JOIN command and presses the RETURN key.)

Figure 8: Script for part of the lesson on joining datasets

the text of their speeches, and indicates their cues and other stage directions. Like the storyboard illustration earlier, the script shown here refers to the flowchart.

If the flowchart is the skeleton of the finished program, the storyboard begins to put nerves and sinews on the bones.

From the scriptwriter's point of view, the CD ROM script addresses two audiences. The immediate audience is the programmer, who actually reads the script to code it. The target audience is the user, who interacts with the programmed results.

To code the script, the programmer must know what the screen is displaying and what the computer system is supposed to be doing at any point in the event sequence. You should discuss with the programmers on your project development team the specific ways they want you to provide this information. Among the things they may need to know about screen displays are:

○ The exact text of messages. These include explanations, instructions, and prompts.

○ Images other than text, such as foreground and background shapes and colors. Screen formatting should be consistent with your project design standards.

○ Overlays, such as text displayed over a background image.

○ Blocking or relative positioning of objects in animation sequences.

○ Video segments or data retrieved from external devices such as videotapes or magnetic disks for display on the screen.

To provide complete screen information to the programmer, you may need to include mockups or artistic renditions of screen displays and a summary of the project visual design standards, in addition to the text of the script.

Your target user audience will interact with the program through the messages and other information displayed on the screen, and through the input devices you specify. Within the limits of the programming constraints, you should write the script so the user can:

○ Read and understand instructions at a glance.

○ Understand where, when, and how to respond.

○ Enter short responses.

○ Receive immediate feedback in the form of a text message, sound effect, or some other device.

○ Follow the sequence of events and interactions without getting lost.

○ Move quickly from one event to the next.

○ Avoid having to do any one thing (such as read screens) for long periods of time.

○ Stop (pause and return) or end the interaction at any desired time.

Reviewing, User Testing, and Revising the Script

When you finish writing and editing the script, review and revise it as already described for the earlier phases of the project. Then arrange with the programming team for interim coding of the script on a data-storage medium other than the final one; for example, on a hard disk.

Now conduct a user test, in accord with the plan you worked out earlier. Base the testing procedure on the goals of the application, so you will know where the application succeeds and where it fails. For the test, select as pilot users a group of people as close as possible to the target audience you defined earlier. Have this audience work through the program, and observe carefully how they experience it, particularly:

○ How long each user takes to complete the program

○ How often and where each user becomes confused or proceeds too quickly

○ How many and what kind of mistakes each user makes

○ How each user reacts to the application as a whole

○ Other significant factors of user response

Evaluate the results of the test in terms of the behavioral objectives and performance criteria you defined during the outline phase of the project. Discuss with other members of the development team any revisions that may be necessary.

Phase Six: Submitting the Script for Production

At this point, you have completed the first five phases of the scripting process. Depending on the arrangements you made in Phase One (the preplanning phase), you are now ready to turn over the finished script to those who will implement it on the CD ROM device.

The script gives final shape to the interactive training program. It is the last step before programming and production of the course.

398

Submitting the final script ends much of your direct involvement in the creative portion of the project, but it doesn't entirely remove you from the picture. Final programming and debugging will probably require that you be available for consultations about minor changes needed to make the finished application work.

399

About the Authors

Stephanie Rosenbaum founded Tec-Ed Technical Publications and Graphics Services in 1967, one of the first companies to specialize in documentations, training, and marketing communications for the computer industry. Headquartered in Ann Arbor, Michigan, Tec-Ed also maintains offices in Palo Alto and Cambridge.

Tec-Ed provides research; preliminary planning; hands-on development of exercises; user testing and quality assurance of software, user interfaces, and documentation; writing and editing of training materials, documentation, and brochures; artistic design, illustrations, and packaging—all done by permanent staff members.

The majority of Tec-Ed's clients are companies which develop and market software products for end users and programmers in the business and industrial marketplaces. Tec-Ed is a vertical-market organization dedicated to understanding and filling the needs of the computer industry.

Tec-Ed training specialist Dennis Walters has created a variety of award-winning training materials for Convergent Technologies, Atari, General Motors, Software International, and other computer firms. He has almost 20 years of training experience and holds a Ph.D. in English from Michigan State University.

Tec-Ed
P.O. Box 1905
Ann Arbor, MI 48106
(313) 995-1010

Resources

For more information on creating interactive scripts for high-density media, you can consult the following articles. Note that most of these articles use examples from analog videodisc, but the scripting issues are similar for CD ROM. Anticipated evolution of CD ROM applications will also make these articles more germane.

Cook, Rick. Seeing is retrieving, *PC World,* July 1984.

Dargan, Thomas R. Five basic patterns to use in interactive flow charts, *E-ITV Magazine,* June 1982.

Fort, William. A primer on interactive video, *AV Video,* October 1984.

Jarvis, Stan. Videodisks and computers, *Byte,* July 1984.

Lee, Brien. Interactive video: The hard goods, *AV Video,* November 1984.

Schuford, Richard S. CD ROMs and their kin, *Byte,* November 1985.

Schuyler, Cynthia. Interactive video information systems, *Computer-World,* October 29, 1984.

Utz, Peter. The early stages of producing an interactive videodisc, *AV Video,* November 1984.

Project Management

The Interactive Project Manager

by David Hon

When I was asked to provide a chapter for *The New Papyrus*, it was with the understanding that as of this printing, Ixion will not yet have completed a CD ROM project. However, it was decided that our background in accomplishing a multitude of tasks with interactive videodiscs seemed to be quite similar at the project management level to what will be required in CD ROM.

403

In this new medium, more attention will be paid to digitizing sound and visuals, and to plotting geographies for that data, and there will be somewhat less concern with motion visuals. I say *somewhat* less, because in an interactive medium such as CD ROM the user creates the pace, which adds an active perception of "motion" to his or her experience. This personalized illusion of motion can be capitalized on and built into a carefully planned design.

Project management seems to be a key reason why some interactive projects turn out well and some do not.

But aside from the design aspects, the visual element may yet become the greatest challenge of CD ROM for quite another reason: The "new papyrus" gives us the ideal tool to publish for the "New Literates."

The New Literacy is here. It means that people now *can* read but they *don't* read much. The Old Literacy exhorted people to drudge through voluminous text on paper—or computer screens. The New Literacy is born of information overload. Educated people must choose from a myriad of information stimuli as life becomes a crowded information freeway.

The logical communication tool in this new environment is the electronic billboard. Toulouse-Lautrec discovered that his poster art had to change when people began passing in carriages rather than browsing on foot. We may need to change similarly by arranging our information in the form of a billboard: creating in each CD ROM page a bite-sized combination of words, colors, pictures—and sounds—which can be either random-accessed or followed in a linear fashion.

The New Literacy is undoubtedly a counterpart of the video revolution, which started in about 1949. To the extent a video screen is used, as it most surely will be in many CD ROM applications, CD ROM will also be a branch of that video revolution. This means that the information we get from the CD ROM must be clear and exciting, not confounding or dull. If we hope to bring CD ROM into the homes and offices of the New Literati, we should note that video has been their common denominator.

404

The Interactive Project Manager

Project management seems to be a key reason why some interactive projects turn out well and some do not. Various pitfalls become obvious in the end result: the visuals were not effective, the programming wasn't user friendly, the design did not meet objectives, and many others. But these are only outcomes of a total activity which, in truth, reflects the kind of leadership a project has had. In the final analysis: The project manager either *did* or *did not* manage the interactive enterprise effectively.

The project manager justifies enough budget for effective video and selects a good producer. The project manager finds user-friendly programmers. The project manager knows what the design must accomplish, and nothing else moves until the design is complete. And the project manager has a planned roll-out of his project into the field; the pipeline is there as part of the overall design.

Only the project manager who can provide a synthesis between computer abstraction and video/audio realism can begin to tap the effectiveness of a truly interactive program.

But if the project manager is the key cause of the success or failure of a project, it is difficult to understand why so few interactive projects have a true project manager. Here are some of the excuses:

"Well, we do things as sort of a loose-knit 'team' around here."

"It wasn't completely obvious who should manage this thing until we got into it."

"Well, the company president sort of acted as project manager. Of course, he's got a lot of other priorities."

All of the above are telltale statements. It follows almost inevitably that these folks' interactive projects—some of them interactive video, some interactive microcomputer—did not turn out well. They didn't really have a true project manager. Or if they did have one, the role was only 1 of 17 hats, all precariously tipped or actually falling off.

Interactive anything is serious business. It takes about 10 times the planning and ongoing organization that an ordinary program takes because of the many diverse worlds that must interlock. There may be the world of computer programming, which is very different and very separate from the world of realistic pictures, or true audio (or education or marketing or entertainment), not to mention that eventual complex world of the user.

Such an amalgam of concerns requires centralized project leadership. It should be obvious. Movies and plays have directors, missile launchings have project directors, anything complex that works has had a project manager. And yet, for some reason, companies facing interactive projects either underrate the difficulty or else find the process so confusing that they forget to put someone in charge.

A Scenario

Let us say that you work for an enlightened company and now you've been selected as project manager.

It is an ideal situation: No hardware has been selected yet, and you have been given the task, say, of training people in one day on-site in a process that normally takes two weeks off-site to learn. If you pull it off, it will save the company $3 million over two years. What do you do?

In one way you've been given an almost impossible challenge. However, in another way, you've been given the ultimate freedom: to do whatever it takes to get the job done. If you had that ideal situation (and in these early days of interactive communication, the program manager often does), you would spend a lot of time up front comparing the actual skills to be mastered with the hardware and software resources available. Then you would choose your strategy, your resources, and your equipment accordingly.

In the real world you would more likely find that someone had already made the hardware decision. ("This will be done with joystick input: we bought 473 of them last June" or "This will be you-know-who compatible.") Often, though not always, hardware provides an initial framework, for better or for worse. But whether or not the hardware has already been acquired, the project manager has to deal with three equally important considerations:

○ What do we want to accomplish? (This may be called *setting precise objectives.*)

○ How much is it worth if we do? (This may be called *establishing cost/ impact.*)

○ Who will do all the work? (This may be called *forming the team.*)

Let's examine the first consideration.

What do we want to accomplish?

Because the project manager must ask this question over and over and over, ad nauseum, it is probably better that he or she is on the payroll of the client company. That question is so annoying to many clients that outside project managers are often "let go" because of it. An inside person can keep on asking. At first the answers will be, "Oh, make them familiar with (this or that)." But the answer you're looking for is, "They have to be able to do this," or "We want 30% of the people who see this to buy the

In this new medium, more attention will be paid to digitizing sound and visuals, and to plotting geographies for that data.

product within 30 days," or "We want each kid to drop in 17 quarters before moving to another game," or "We want the user to be able to access any British auto part in 3 seconds max."

So it is the project manager who hammers out hard objectives, because those are the only kind you can really accomplish.

What will it be worth if we do it?

Every project manager should have a cost/impact figure in mind, because that's his or her justification for budget. There may be others ("This pocket of money could get a tax credit," "This money's got to be spent before the end of the year," "A rich donor said in his will that this has to be spent on an interactive project," etc.), but the cost/impact justification is the only one that really matters. And the impact may not be in dollars. It may be in lives, or diseases prevented, or some such. Often if a salesperson can double the number of calls in a day, a higher percentage of sales will follow. The project manager should strive very hard in the early stages to fix this cost/impact on something quantifiable, because that's going to determine what budget range is reasonable. And not justifying a reasonable budget early on is a sure route to nightmares and poor products.

Who will do all the work?

This is perhaps the easiest of the three questions, and it's not an easy one at all. Not only must people skilled in their particular areas be found, but they must be people who can mix with other totally foreign disciplines. Bottom line: A/V people and computer people may not have the same outlook—at all. You'd better know that going in, you'd better be able to "quick-study" the sides you don't know, and you'd better be able to spot them when one or the other side is going too far on its own tangent. It is a classic problem now—already—that the project manager with video background turns out short linear hold-and-fills, dumps it onto some random-accessible medium, and then hands it to the programmer with instructions to "program this stuff." Just as classic a problem is the project manager with computer background who asks the video folks to come up with "a few pictures for our visual database."

Only the project manager who can provide a synthesis between computer abstraction and video/audio realism can begin to tap the effectiveness of a truly interactive program.

It is most common for a project manager to evolve from one of the disciplines related to the program. A video producer has already managed some of the elements. A computer software development manager will probably have experience with real-time interface, or at least computer

Interactive anything is serious business. It takes about 10 times the planning and ongoing organization that an ordinary program takes because of the many diverse worlds that must interlock.

control and branching. An instructional systems designer or even a playwright may have background in designing the complete experience. Or an advertising account executive may have had excellent experience with getting client needs through to creative people. So project managers can be plucked from several fields, but they usually don't come in without some relevant background. Sports coaches have usually played the game, if not every position.

It is also quite usual, though not mandatory, for the project manager to ply his or her specialty within the team. (This, obviously, has the chance of producing an imbalance in the final product, but it also saves time and money to have the project manager be, for instance, the designer/writer.)

The overall success of the project management depends greatly on how several roles are filled with excellent talent, and how well that talent works together. Each role may include several persons, depending on the scope of the undertaking, or at times two or more roles may be embodied in the same person. Here are some roles that must be filled.

- Designer—This role is very concerned with (A) how the objectives can be met, (B) how completely the content is imbued in the program, and (C) how well the whole experience flows for the user.

- Writer—This person may also be the designer, and often that is a good combination. This role must be concerned with (A) the clarity and tone of the branch messages, (B) the uniformity of branches, (C) the overall pace of the experience, and (D) the tone of messages to the user.

The designer and the writer together, then, set forth the problems to be solved by the A/V producer and the programmer.

- The A/V producer—This person must have broad experience with visuals, audio, motion, and timing. Often a film or video producer is the only person who can make the program more than just a shuffling sequence of visual database (known elsewhere as "Death in the Still Frame"). This person may have to write and rewrite to get a proper pace or proper tones to the user. The amount of reconstruction that both the A/V person and the programmer must do is usually far more than anticipated. Also, the A/V person should be intimately involved in the creation of every computer screen for two reasons. First, this person is most familiar with visual presentation to users, and second, this person must coordinate and pace all visual and audio elements for the user's total experience. As a result, this person must have a sense of organization equal to but different from that of the programmer.

- Programmer—Most programmers take a quick look at the logging and machine control and branching required and assume that it is a simple task. Even the best usually underestimate the difficulty of perfecting a real-time user experience. A few months beyond their originally projected complete date, they begin to understand that all variables were not machine-related. In reality, the programmer becomes the final editor—as in film editing—of all the various effects that optical media can hold. This may often be an unexpected and sometimes unwanted responsibility for the programmer, so obviously some programmers will initially need a great deal of attention from the project manager.

Budgeting

Obviously, prior experience in the same medium is invaluable. However, the person who has been a team member may or may not have a good idea of how to employ the total budget involved. This is one overview which distinguishes the project leader. The first good rule of thumb is, as mentioned, knowing how much the successful project is worth. This establishes a high-end bracket, the top amount you should spend. If the maximum you can spend is $200,000, and you estimate the programming alone will cost that much, you'll need to go back and (1) trim objectives, (2) find visuals and sound that cost nothing, or (3) perhaps more wisely, not embark on that particular project. At some point down the line, budgeting too low will catch up with you. There are not many miracles to spare, since they are in high demand already.

The consequences of trading off down the line are usually a "vanilla" product, with low programming demands because of limited interactivity, or low quality in visuals or audio. To finish it somehow may mean losing the quality of design, production, programming, or something that would have made this an excellent product for its purpose.

Another initial budget consideration would be the percentage of total budget each facet demands. As a rule of thumb, the more interactive the project is, the greater the percentage of the total project budget should go to planning, design, and programming, rather than to audio/visual production.

Figure 1 is a chart we use that presents a matrix of levels of quality in interactive videodisc. We have adapted it slightly to pertain more to CD ROM applications. This matrix allows you to show clients (internal or external) how the levels of perceived quality in a final product interact to produce cost.

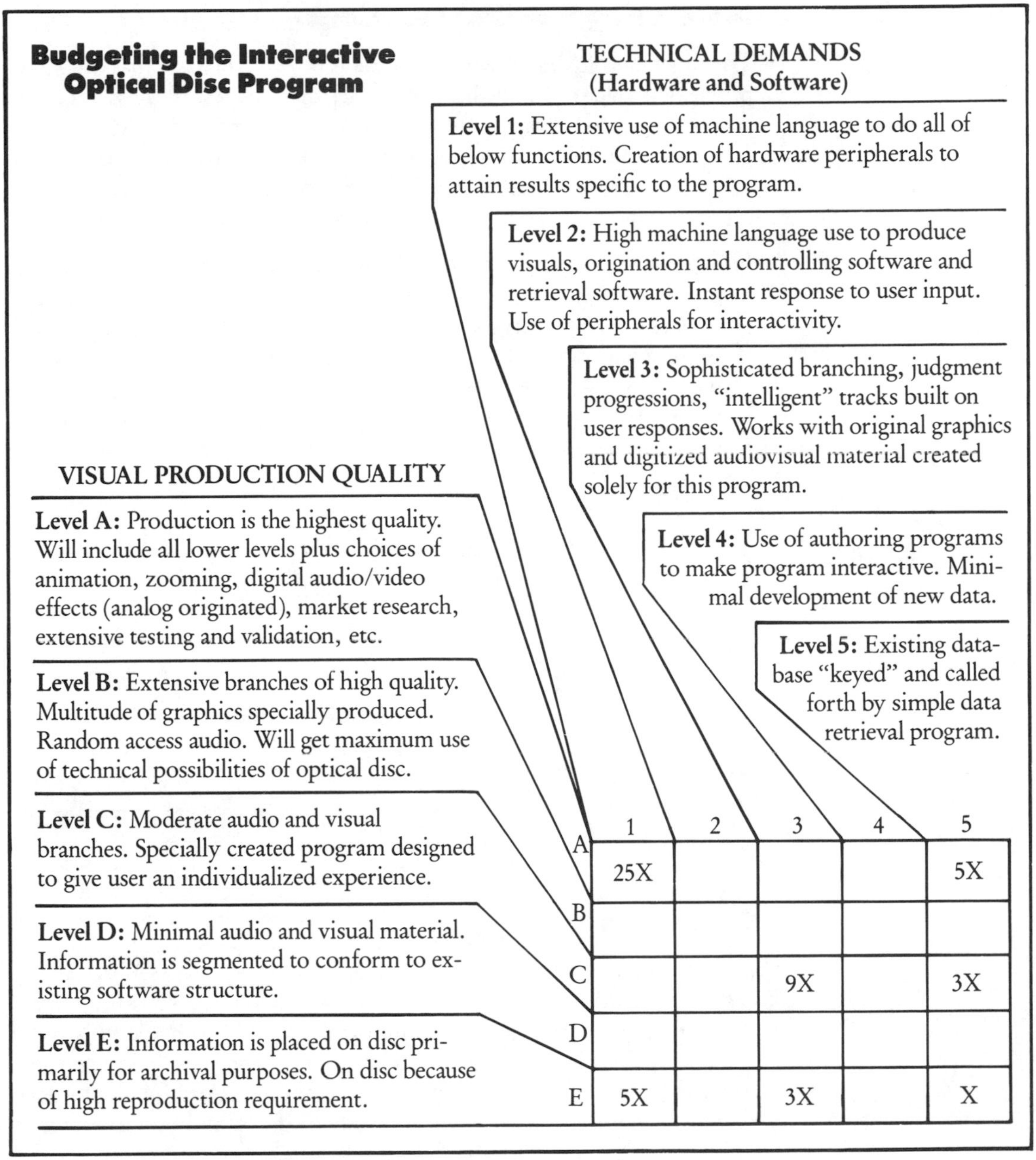

Budgeting the Interactive Optical Disc Program

TECHNICAL DEMANDS
(Hardware and Software)

Level 1: Extensive use of machine language to do all of below functions. Creation of hardware peripherals to attain results specific to the program.

Level 2: High machine language use to produce visuals, origination and controlling software and retrieval software. Instant response to user input. Use of peripherals for interactivity.

Level 3: Sophisticated branching, judgment progressions, "intelligent" tracks built on user responses. Works with original graphics and digitized audiovisual material created solely for this program.

Level 4: Use of authoring programs to make program interactive. Minimal development of new data.

Level 5: Existing database "keyed" and called forth by simple data retrieval program.

VISUAL PRODUCTION QUALITY

Level A: Production is the highest quality. Will include all lower levels plus choices of animation, zooming, digital audio/video effects (analog originated), market research, extensive testing and validation, etc.

Level B: Extensive branches of high quality. Multitude of graphics specially produced. Random access audio. Will get maximum use of technical possibilities of optical disc.

Level C: Moderate audio and visual branches. Specially created program designed to give user an individualized experience.

Level D: Minimal audio and visual material. Information is segmented to conform to existing software structure.

Level E: Information is placed on disc primarily for archival purposes. On disc because of high reproduction requirement.

	1	2	3	4	5
A	25X				5X
B					
C			9X		3X
D					
E	5X		3X		X

Figure 1. A matrix showing the relationship between the perceived quality of a final product to its cost

Monitoring Parallel Functions

The timetable of parallel functions should be structured so that each has progressed as far as it may, but not farther than the rest of the team can respond to without retracing steps. For instance, some preliminary programming can ensure team members of the feasibility of an approach, but too much programming in a preliminary stage may result in wasted efforts. Other changes may call forth new programming needs.

Figure 2 is a schedule done for the American Heart Association's CPR course, for which we developed a system using a videodisc, microcomputer, and peripheral manikins with sensors. You may notice that we began producing the graphics before the scripting was finished. This is because the graphics were 95 percent predictable from the beginning. Starting them after the script was finished would have cost the project a few months, whereas simply making periodic changes to them was far less costly.

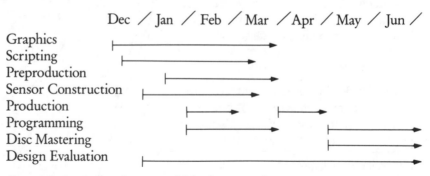

Figure 2. Project timeline showing parallel development tracks

Conclusion

Project management for an interactive optical disc project is in many ways very close to management of other projects, but in some ways it is very different. The fact that the "arts" must coexist with "technology" is one difference. The high time effort and cost of designing a total interactive experience—one that can be validated—is another. And finally, the fact that most approaches to content, interactive effects, and user interfaces are quite often being done for the first time produces both the psychological exhilaration and the mental drain of constantly facing the unknown.

About the Author

Mr. Hon, president of Ixion, was creator and project leader of the well-known CPR Interactive Video Disc Learning System, the first commercially marketed video disc/microcomputer program, and winner of the 1983 International Video Disc Symposium "Best Project" award. He is widely published and has spoken to such diverse forums as Harvard University and U.S. congressional committees, and in such diverse locations as Helsinki, Cannes, London, and Beijing.

Over the past two years at Ixion, Mr. Hon has worked with several Fortune 500 companies developing interactive programs on a wide variety of systems. Ixion's general evolution has been to design lively, imaginative interactive capabilities into smaller, less expensive, and more compatible hardware systems.

Ixion, Inc.
1335 North Northlake Way
Seattle, WA 98103
(206) 547-8801

The Team Approach to Interactive Disc Production

by Chris Sherman and Rod Daynes

Optical disc technology has been a boon for interactive program designers. No longer are designers limited to a single medium. The formerly clear distinctions between analog (video, audio) and digital (computer-assisted instruction, information search and retrieval) programs have been blurred by the capabilities of the optical disc. This blurring has created a tremendous potential for interactive developers in the form of hybrid programs that use the best possible delivery medium for a particular topic. Unfortunately, this additional capability is also a veritable Pandora's box of dilemmas for the unwary, particularly in the approach to design and development of interactive programs.

Although we support the concept of the "renaissance person," we have encountered few individuals who are capable of creating an interactive program without a fair amount of help. As technology continues to evolve, the team approach to interactive program development makes more and more sense, both from a pragmatic and a creative standpoint.

Through experience in developing more than 80 interactive videodiscs, we have refined a team approach to production that is well suited to all types of interactive design and development. Although our methodology is described in terms of the interactive videodisc, it can easily be adapted to programs using interactive CD-audio, computer-assisted instruction (CAI) with digitized still-frame graphics stored on CD ROM, or any other type of program where interaction is at least partially nonrandom, that is, designed with a specific interactive schema. Our primary interest here is in the process of designing interactive programs, not in the random-access retrieval of information.

Our strategy in this discussion is to describe the five major tasks of interactive design and development, commenting on the type of person who is suited to performing each task, both in terms of necessary skills and likely goals, objectives, and concerns. For those readers with little experience in interactive design and development, we also provide suggestions for streamlining and troubleshooting each task. We hope that readers who are fluent in one or more areas of the production process will find our description of the other production tasks enlightening.

413

Levels of Interactivity

As a starting point, we will describe the scheme used to classify the level of interactivity for videodiscs. Then we will attempt to extend these definitions to include CD ROM applications.

Interactive videodisc productions are commonly classified by their level of interactivity. Currently, a disc is described as a Level 1, Level 2, or Level 3 interactive program. (Incidentally, when we first devised the term *level*, it was in reference to the capabilities of the player to be used for a program. However, videodisc technology has evolved so rapidly that it now makes more sense to use *level* to describe the interactive capabilities of the program rather than the delivery hardware.)

A Level 1 disc has very little interactivity, relying on the ability of the disc player to pause the video play at points where the program designer has placed stop codes on the disc. The user must then press *play* to continue, or skip to a different part of the disc by entering a new frame number with a hand-held remote control.

A Level 2 disc is programmed to use the disc player's microprocessor and internal memory. The designer creates a program using the disc player's *assembly language,* then these instructions are included on the disc during the mastering process. Level 2 discs provide a moderate degree of interactivity, with some multiway branching capability. Current limitations include disc player memory (usually 10K or less), and difficulty and expense of changing or debugging the interaction after the disc has been mastered. Level 2 videodiscs are the precursors to many current CD ROM applications, since a completed Level 2 disc is a self-contained read-only memory program.

A Level 3 disc provides potentially limitless interactivity, as the program is under the supervision of an external microcomputer.

Optical compact discs also appear to have a natural three-tiered classification system, corresponding roughly to the three videodisc levels. CD Level 1 consists of digitized analog information designed to be used primarily in a linear format, with limited user control of playback. Examples include musical albums and (soon) video *singles* in the CD format. CD Level 1 is more analogous to videodisc Level 2, with a small though effective degree of random access capability.

CD Level 2 discs have no direct counterpart in the videodisc world. CD Level 2 programs consist of digital databases, or CAI that utilizes non-analog information (in other words, no video or sound). Most CD Level 2 discs utilize a microcomputer to provide interactivity, via operating system or information retrieval software. Currently, this implies the use of an external microcomputer, but we expect a new generation of dedicated devices with custom user interfaces bearing little resemblance to today's micro. Portable CD ROM *books* that display pages of information or telephones that look up and automatically dial anyone in the CD ROM *phone book* built into the device are examples.

CD Level 3 discs can use a mix of analog and digital data and provide many avenues of interactivity. CD Level 3 is fundamentally equivalent to videodisc Level 3 in all respects other than disc size. We would like to think that this distinction will disappear in a few years and Level 3 discs of all sizes will be interchangable on most players.

Since Level 3 programs are usually the most complex, our discussion of the team approach to production of an interactive disc assumes Level 3 requirements. Our approach is equally suited to Level 1 or 2 productions, with the removal of one or more tasks from the production process.

The Team Approach to Production

Five major tasks are necessary to produce an interactive optical disc of any type, be it video, data, or audio. We have given these tasks arbitrary names that describe their function in the videodisc production process. Other terms may be more suitable for other types of programs.

The five major tasks in production are:

- Analysis and design
- Scripting and storyboarding
- Production and disc mastering
- Programming and integration
- Evaluation and revision

Careful planning and performance of each task is vital to the success of an interactive production, though the relative importance of each task is determined by the nature of the individual project. Common sense suggests that each task should be performed by an individual or group with specialized skills relevant to the task. Unfortunately for many productions, pragmatic considerations such as time or cost, or the more diabolical case of misjudgment by project managers, require that some tasks might be completed by someone who has time or is otherwise forced to do it, rather than by a skilled practitioner.

416

It's easy for
anyone to
intuitively tell
if the production
is well done. It's
harder to suggest
changes that are
within the
boundaries of cost
and schedule once
production is
complete.

In our vision of the ideal team approach, each of the five tasks is performed by an autonomous individual or group that collectively makes up the complete production team (we will use *group* from now on). Each group has a leader who reports directly to a production manager, who coordinates all efforts and is ultimately responsible for ensuring a smooth merging of inputs and outputs between tasks, and for seeing to it that egos in each group are not too badly bruised when the inevitable compromises are required. The production manager should be a renaissance person of sorts, possessing a variety of skills.

In cases where an interactive program has been commissioned, the client should be included as a participating team member. Including the client as a team member can be risky, because it's rare for a client to have the expertise of the other team members. On the other hand, the client is the best judge of the overall production because he or she knows exactly what the program should do. As a participating team member, the client can also provide a source of additional production help, and is more likely to "buy in" to the overall process. This is greatly preferable to the more common approach of putting the client in a passive role, with involvement limited to a high-stress position of approving a significant chunk of work that may be new and unfamiliar.

There are two primary challenges to making the team approach succeed. First, each group must be independent and autonomous, and yet have a large degree of trust in the other groups. Second, communication and cooperation between groups is vital, particularly in the initial planning and final "fine-tuning" stages of production.

Trust among group members comes only with experience. The human relations skills of the production manager can play a significant role in developing trust among groups.

A talented production manager can expedite communication between the five groups. Although we emphasize communication, experience has shown that frequent meetings of the entire production team can be detrimental. Most communication should be accomplished between regular meetings between the project manager and group leaders, who in turn keep their own group informed. Two other kinds of meetings occur with less frequency: large kickoff and wrapup meetings where all team members are invited, and smaller meetings between the production manager and all members of one or (only when absolutely necessary) two groups.

The production manager provides a consistent, nondistorted communication link between all groups. Small, infrequent meetings ensure that not too many man-hours are consumed by meetings of a nice-to-know-but-not-vital nature for most members of the production team.

Another concern in planning disc geography is visual or audio continuity.

Each task has specific inputs and outputs. These should be carefully defined during the planning stages of a project so that all groups know what to expect before they begin, and what in turn is expected of them as a final product. Task definition is also helpful for providing evaluation criteria, used to assess the suitability of completed work.

In our description of each task, we will touch on goals and priorities likely to be most important to the group performing the task. The overall performance of the entire production team is enhanced when each group is sensitive to the special concerns of the other groups involved in the project.

Analysis and Design

Analysis is the art of understanding and extracting the vital core of information that will form the basis of an interactive disc. There are literally hundreds of ways to conduct an analysis. Commonly, the analyst sits down with a subject-matter expert (SME) and through an iterative process of interviewing, research, and revision develops a preliminary outline of the disc content. If the disc is an instructional program, this process also involves defining behavior and knowledge objectives—skills and ideas the user should possess after completing the program.

We always apply Daynes' Law of Interactive Production: It Takes Longer Than It Takes, and It Costs More Than It Costs.

Design is the craft of arranging the outline developed during analysis into logical segments and then deciding how the segments may be connected. Creating a good interactive design is difficult; it requires skill together with creativity and experience to ensure an easy, effective, and genuinely interactive experience for the user.

The input to analysis and design is the overall specification for the program. The output should be a document outlining content, objectives, and all interaction required in the program. It is also advisable to select a programming language at this point. (See the section on Programming for further details.)

Analysis and design of interactive discs is best performed by someone trained in instructional development and design, with some computer programming knowledge (preferably experience!). Though formal knowledge of the countless analysis and design techniques is helpful, analysis and design is fundamentally a blend of common sense and experience.

Analyst/designers tend to be primarily concerned with information content and interactive capability. Designers often tend to think of their work as a complete skeletal framework for an interactive program. Suggested changes to this framework will be considered from this holistic standpoint and may be perceived as deforming the skeleton. The video or audio group may meet resistance when suggesting changes to "liven up" a program. The programming group may find it difficult to suggest a design change that would optimize or streamline the programming task.

When evaluating the analysis and design of an interactive program it should be realized that the design is simply a plan. The plan should be complete, particularly when it comes to a specification of interaction. However, most other details, such as screen design or exact wording of narrative, are unimportant at this point. At this stage of development, criticism should be primarily global in scope, directed at improving the whole rather than refining details.

Scripting and Storyboarding

Our definition of a script is very loose. A script contains the narrative portion of a program, if any. At minimum, for a program with little spoken narration, a script is slightly more extensive than the content outline generated in the analysis and design phase. Beyond that, a script can contain as much detail as required by the other members of the production team.

A storyboard is the central reference document for a program, available to each group in the production team. A storyboard includes the script, together with a *visual notebook*, consisting of thumbnail sketches of video or graphics that accompany each segment of narration or audio. It can also include staging and filming instructions, branching instructions or flowcharts for the programming group, special-effects cues for the post production crew, and so on. The storyboard contains the complete "on-paper" specification for the program.

Sometimes a script and a storyboard are the same document. For the purposes of our discussion we will treat them separately, considering important aspects of each.

The scripting process has as its input the program's content outline and the lists of objectives and required interactions. The output is a document that can easily be converted into a storyboard.

Since the script represents the program's spoken or written presentation, the quality of the script determines whether the program is interesting or boring, effective or mediocre, perhaps even whether the user completes the program. Despite this paramount importance, scripting is one of the most neglected aspects of interactive production, often delegated by default to the analyst/design group or the production group, neither of which may be ideally suited for the task.

Creating a good interactive design is difficult; it requires skill together with creativity and experience to ensure an easy, effective, and genuinely interactive experience for the user.

The necessary and sufficient skill required by a scriptwriter is basic: a talent for writing. The scriptwriter must remain bound by the constraints of the design, but a good writer can breathe life into even the most carefully specified design, creating a fluid, dynamic presentation.

At some point, preferably not before the scriptwriter has realized a clear sense of orientation and tone, the script begins to evolve into a storyboard, including necessary visual or graphic sketches, programming instructions, and so on. We are not being deliberately vague here. We have tried many times to standardize the scripting and storyboarding process but have realized that each program requires a unique approach. Trying to force the development of a program into a particular favorite approach often has disappointing results.

A caveat: The key to a successful storyboard is to allow function to dominate form. Storyboards can be extremely useful tools for managing the production process, but they can also be the source of tyranny and inefficiency. A storyboard should be a flexible document that reflects the current thinking of the production team. Some projects require a lot of shared common information to be passed between team members. Other projects may need as little as a script and a flowchart.

Two issues that should be resolved before developing a storyboard are how much information should be included (and to what degree of detail) and how religiously the storyboard should be adhered to during production. Don't agonize over the format of a storyboard. Each project has unique requirements. In fact, the word *storyboard* may be somewhat misleading if taken with its literal meaning in the advertising/television sense. For interactive productions, a storyboard is simply the central program specification, and it may take any form that is useful or necessary.

In videodisc production we have found that a multipart storyboard is effective. This includes a narrative script with minimal visual cues and interaction instructions, a "visual notebook" with extensive notes on the design and appearance of a program, and a master flowchart. Together, the parts form a complete storyboard. Individually, the parts can be used by different groups without the added burden of unnecessary or irrelevant information. In short, a good storyboard will make the entire production process flow more smoothly, but don't get bogged down in perfecting it. A storyboard is, after all, a detailed plan—no more than that.

The scriptwriting and storyboard group is commonly concerned with subjective issues such as program pacing and appeal, user interest, and other issues of appearance and presentation. Practical issues or implementation difficulties are often given low priority. The key aspect of the production for this group is appearance and style.

The evaluation process of the storyboard is the most critical phase of production because it represents the last chance to make significant changes to the program. Once the storyboard has been finalized and approved, production and programming begin, and the possibility of making changes to a program is severely constrained.

The storyboard should be given several detailed readings and should be thoroughly understood by all team members. All compromises between team groups or the client should be noted, both on the storyboard and in a separate document that is distributed to all groups. This may seem unnecessary, but it saves a lot of grief in later phases of production when memory of the storyboard evaluation has faded. A thorough storyboard evaluation requires patience and time, which should be deliberately built into a production schedule. The storyboard is the summation of all design and development; the client or sponsor should be prepared to sign off on any further content changes in the program at this point.

Production

Production includes all activities required to prepare program information and store it on the optical disc. This includes audio and video taping and processing, preparation of digital disc data, and so on.

The input to the production process is a complete storyboard and all adjunct notes needed to complete the production process. The output is a mastered disc, ready for programming in the case of CD Level 2 or 3 discs.

Many developers subcontract the production phase. This is often a wise decision; production of professional-quality audio or video is best handled by professionals who have access to top-rate equipment. However, we consider it vital to have an in-house team member who is an expert in two areas: disc geography and transitions.

Disc geography is the physical layout of data on the mastered disc. Transitions are the interface zones between two not necessarily contiguous segments on the disc, potentially connected by user interaction. The design of disc geography and the transitions between segments on an interactive disc is analogous to information structure design in computer programming.

421

Transitions are directly related to geography, as they occur at branch points. Interactive transitions are necessarily different from linear transitions, particularly in the case of highly interactive programs. The most difficult aspect of designing transitions is in achieving conceptual continuity between two potentially disparate parts. The classic transition used in linear programs, " . . . as you recall from the last section . . . ," is not valid in an interactive program. In fact, linear transitions can be detrimental, confusing the user who may not have seen the previous section, or any prior section at all, for that matter. Knowing where and how to use interactive transitions is the hallmark of a good interactive designer.

Careful planning and performance of each task is vital to the success of an interactive production, though the relative importance of each task is determined by the nature of the individual project.

Another concern in planning disc geography is visual or audio continuity. Some disc players offer an instant branch feature that can make even rapid interaction appear seamless, without the annoying glitch that commonly accompanies a search to a remote point on the disc. Careful planning is required to utilize this feature effectively, however.

The three major phases of production are preproduction, production (video/audio/data), and postproduction. We will briefly discuss these phases in terms of videodisc production.

Preproduction. All production planning is completed here. The production crew becomes thoroughly familiar with the storyboard and makes necessary changes or revisions to facilitate production (this process generally overlaps with the evaluation of the storyboard). Talent (actors or narrators) is selected, sets are surveyed and designed, and a production schedule and shooting script are developed.

Production. Most production is subcontracted to professional production houses. The in-house team member in charge of production usually is the producer. All other aspects of production are the responsibility of the production house. Production includes filming, recording, art production, still-frame production, and special effects or graphics development.

Postproduction. Like production, most postproduction work is subcontracted to professionals who have access to costly tools and equipment. During this phase the production is assembled into an edited videotape in a format acceptable for mastering. Once the mastering has been completed, a proof disc is checked for quality and accuracy.

Since production is best done by professionals, they may or may not be considered part of the team. The in-house team member will act as the producer and will facilitate communication between other team groups and the production agency. The producer is the one team member whose skills should be trusted primarily on faith by the rest of the team. This is because production is perhaps the most specialized and least understood of the five tasks by other team members. Although this may sound harsh, suggestions from team members inexperienced in production are more likely to hinder than help the production.

Evaluation of production is at once both easy and difficult. Since we all have social experience with audio recordings and television, it's easy for anyone to intuitively tell if the production is well done. It's harder to suggest changes that are within the boundaries of cost and schedule once production is complete. Evaluation of the production always includes personal opinions about aesthetics and personal preconceptions. Therefore the result is bound to be different from what most team members expected. We recommend keeping an open mind about the result of production. If a production is simply unsuitable, then the best suggestion is to seek a different production house for the next disc.

Programming

Programming is the process of creating control software to make the program interactive. The input to programming should be a block diagram or flowchart from the designer/analyst, a completed storyboard, and a produced and mastered disc. The output is a complete interactive program.

Programming of an interactive optical disc can be a sensitive issue. In many ways we regard programming in a similar light to scriptwriting: the job of the programming team is to implement an existing specification. On the other hand, a good programmer always likes to improve on a design (a practice we do not always support) and will be limited by constraints of the delivery system and programming language. The best programmer may not always be able to implement the program exactly as specified.

To alleviate some of these potential problems, the programming team should be allowed some influence during the evaluation phase of all five production tasks. For example, the analysis/design group is responsible for specifying the interaction required in a program during the first phase of production. This specification can be made at a high level, without constraining details that may make the programming job difficult. The program's user interface should be entirely the responsibility of the analysis/design group, whereas issues of functionality and practicality of implementation should be left to the programming group.

As we mentioned earlier, the programming language or authoring system should be chosen during the design phase. The choice of a language should be based primarily on the requirements of the program to be implemented. This may sound insultingly obvious, but we have been repeatedly astounded by the number of programs that have been implemented in an unsuitable language simply because the programming team was familiar with the language, or to avoid royalty payments required to use a different language. The immediate benefit of automatically selecting a familiar programming language can be quickly and devastatingly offset by the time it may take to implement specific parts of the program that the language was not designed for and does not readily support.

Here are some guidelines for choosing a programming language for an interactive disc. The choice of language should be determined by the ease of implementing the user interface of the program. Facilities for control of the disc player, accepting input from devices such as a touch panel or mouse, and for providing management of user records or customized types of output are usually important. Since most interactive discs are used with a single dedicated workstation, less important issues are execution speed, portability, logical operations to support branching, and other factors often dear to programmers' hearts.

Next, consider the language's modularity and available software tools. Modularity is *critical*, because typically more time is necessary to debug interactive programs than to program them in the first place. Modular program segments reduce debugging time, and can often be designed as software tools for repeated use in more than one program. We highly advocate using existing software tools; the time spent researching available software tools before programming begins is usually repaid at least tenfold during the programming process. Avoid reinventing the wheel. We hate to offer clichéd advice, but this seems to be ignored time and time again by eager programmers who want to do something in a slightly more efficient or speedy fashion, often with disastrous consequences for the schedule.

Making the client an integral part of the team without reducing the effectiveness of other team specialists may be difficult, but it usually leads to a higher degree of satisfaction from the client, increasing the possibility of creating a long-term relationship.

423

Once a language has been selected, the programming group should become thoroughly familiar with its capabilities and limitations. This information can then serve as a pragmatic guidepost for the programming group during the evaluation stage of all other tasks.

Another caveat: Occasionally it is tempting to try system integration, to create a delivery system that has specific features for your program. Unless you are willing to at least double time and cost estimates, avoid this course of action, for the same reason we suggest using existing software tools. Integrating and debugging a new hardware system can be immensely challenging and frustrating, particularly if you are using equipment from outside vendors who have little interest in supporting your ambitious project.

Programmers are usually interested in issues of efficiency, execution speed, and other behind-the-scenes aspects of the production. The most common dilemmas encountered with programmers are resistance to implementing a feature because it seems unreasonable from the programmer's point of view, and inaccurate time estimates. A healthy attitude toward negotiation usually results in an acceptable alternative to features programmers shy away from implementing. Inaccurate time estimates can only be dealt with through experience, though it is wiser to allow too much time for a project than not enough. We always apply Daynes' Law of Interactive Production: It Takes Longer Than It Takes, and It Costs More Than It Costs.

Production includes all activities required to prepare program information and store it on the optical disc.

Evaluation of programming is the process of ensuring that the program functions according to specification. A program should be throughly tested by both the programming group and someone unfamiliar with the program code. This process of evaluation and revision should be carried out in parallel with the programming process itself, perhaps even on a module-by-module basis. Evaluation and debugging commonly takes as long as, if not longer than, the programming process itself.

Evaluation and Revision

Evaluation and revision is the least defined and consequently the most neglected or ignored aspect of the interactive production process. Neglect of the evaluation stage can lead to missed deadlines, sacrifice of content, or other more dire consequences. On the other hand, carefully designed evaluation procedures can significantly enhance the chances of success for an interactive program.

Evaluation should be conducted by all members of the production team, though it is commonly designed and conducted by the analysis/design group. The input to evaluation is the completed program ready for field testing, and the output is an annotated list of alterations that may or may not be made in the program.

If each of the first four production tasks includes a thorough evaluation, as we have recommended, then a program really needs only an informal field test. The field test design should be simple, involving some potential users going through the program and commenting on difficulties they encounter. The production team then decides whether the results of the field test warrant changes in the program.

If evaluation has been neglected until the end of a program, a more careful field test and formal evaluation is recommended. This should be designed to uncover flaws in all aspects of the program, from design though programming. The drawback to performing this type of evaluation at this stage is that there is little the team can do in the way of revisions at this point. Unless the disc is considered a pilot for a future disc, the results of this type of evaluation have value only as useful information for the next production the team undertakes.

Project Management Considerations

The significant benefit of the team approach to interactive program development is that the expertise of widely differing people can be focused toward a common goal. The project manager must be particularly talented and sensitive to integrate the efforts of all team members.

Above all else, the project manager must be able to manage the team to keep cost and schedule under control. Interactive videodisc production is very expensive, with average costs ranging from $26,000 for a basic Level 1 disc to nearly $200,000 for a complex Level 3 disc. Balancing pragmatic considerations with the creative desires and needs of a talented production team is not always an easy task.

The project manager must also satisfy the client. Making the client an integral part of the team without reducing the effectiveness of other team specialists may be difficult, but it usually leads to a higher degree of satisfaction from the client, increasing the possibility of creating a long-term relationship.

425

Although we support the concept of the "renaissance person," we have encountered few individuals who are capable of creating an interactive program without a fair amount of help.

426

Summary

We have outlined and advocated the team approach to interactive optical disc production. Although we fully expect a new generation of individuals with skills in all areas of production we have described, we also feel that optical technology will continue to evolve, continually creating new tasks requiring new skills. In advocating the team approach, we don't wish to see production turned into an assembly-line activity by isolated specialists who are limited to only one aspect of production. Rather, we believe that the team approach can lead to unexplored and interesting ideas and techniques that an individual could never hope to achieve.

About the Author

Chris Sherman is president of Logical Insight, a San Diego-based consulting firm. Mr. Sherman has developed interactive programs for McGraw-Hill, World Book International, Sikorsky Aircraft, and others. He holds a BA from the University of California, San Diego, and an MA in Interactive Educational Technology from Stanford.

Rod Daynes is president of Rodney Daynes Interactive Associates, a San Diego-based design and production firm. Mr. Daynes founded and directed the Nebraska Videodisc Design/Production Group and has developed more than 80 interactive videodisc programs. He holds a BA from the University of Utah and an MA from San Diego State University.

Rodney Daynes Interactive Associates
5763 Beaumont Avenue
La Jolla, CA 92037

Resources

Alessi and Trollip. *Computer-Based Instruction: Methods and Development.* New York: Prentice-Hall, 1984.

Rod Daynes and Beverly Butler. *The Videodisc Book.* New York: John Wiley and Sons, 1984.

ComTrain. *The Shelley Authoring System.* Grass Valley, Calif.

EIS. *The Courseware Development System.* Orem, Utah.

Eric Parsloe and Signe Hoffos. *Interactive Video.* Epic, 1983.

Walker and Hess. *Instructional Software.* Belmont, Calif.: Wadsworth, 1981.

CD ROM PUBLISHING

The CD ROM Publication

by Brian Martin

This introduction to publishing in CD ROM should be of interest to any-one who works with the quantities of data that CD ROM is so aptly suited to store. It is a scant introduction that will in no way serve as a "template" for developing CD ROM publications; there are just too many possible approaches to the business of CD ROM publishing. Indeed, the word *publication* assumes an entirely new meaning when it appears next to the term CD ROM. The intent here is to leave the reader with an intu-itive grasp of the incredible power of the CD ROM medium when it is coupled with a computer to form "the CD ROM publication."

The subject will be approached from four angles: First, the features that distinguish the CD ROM medium from other media will be identified. Second, the components of a CD ROM publication will be defined. Third, a range of CD ROM publications will be illustrated by three exam-ples: a demand-printing case study, a likely application in reference pub-lishing, and a brief anecdotal glimpse of a possible future marriage between laser storage and artificial intelligence technologies. Finally, the costs associated with producing a CD ROM publication will be examined by taking an inside look at the development of the world's first commercial CD ROM publication, The Library Corporation's *BiblioFile Catalog Production System*.

> . . . the word 'publication' assumes an entirely new meaning when it appears next to the term CD ROM.

The Nature of the Product

When a publisher puts print to paper, an *end* product has been created—information in distributable, human-readable form. Furthermore, there is only one way to read it, and it looks the same no matter how many times you do it (a trivial-sounding point, but necessary for the discussion).

When data is put on CD ROM, only *part* of a product exists—informa-tion in distributable, machine-readable form. To complete the product, a delivery system (computer) is required to translate the data into human-readable form. The requirement for a delivery system is an expensive bur-den on the user of the publication. However, for many types of publica-tions, a particular feature of the delivery system far outweighs the burden of its requirement. The feature is programmability. Programmability of the delivery system means that there are many ways to read a CD ROM, and that both the content and the appearance of a CD ROM publication can vary according to how it is read. This feature distinguishes the CD ROM publication, in a rather dramatic fashion, from all human-readable publications.

430

An assortment of machine-readable media have existed for decades, and their impact on the business of publishing has been less than profound. What characteristics of CD ROM set it apart from its machine-readable relatives? Storage density, media and storage costs, data accessibility, data persistence, and media transportability, to name a few. It is unfortunate that no one equation for media utility can be formulated for all manner of publications. In so many applications it would show how CD ROM clearly stands in stark contrast to even the second-best medium; not only in comparison with its relatives, but also in comparison with print.

What are the applications in which CD ROM competes effectively with print? Catalogs; references; business archives; medical, taxonomic, and actuarial databases; genealogies and other histories; census and cartographic data; systems documentation; process control information; instructional material; and on and on. When CD ROM is the medium, the publication is no longer the static entity that it was in print; rather, it may be processed and delivered in any desired format.

This is an exciting new definition of an ancient commodity. It means that providers of information may exploit the new publishing medium to expand their business by becoming providers of information processing services. Likewise, providers of information processing services will be able to enhance their products by tapping a vast new source of inexpensive information.

The Anatomy of the Product

The CD ROM publication is a fusion of components from two traditional businesses. As such, its anatomy is best examined from the separate perspectives of these businesses:

- Publishing—the disc
  - Acquiring and maintaining machine-readable data
  - Organizing and indexing the data for CD ROM mastering
  - CD ROM fabrication
- Systems—the delivery system
  - Hardware (computer, CD ROM disc drive, other peripherals)
  - System software
  - Application software

The Publishing Side

The widespread use of computers in publishing has made acquisition and maintenance of machine-readable data the norm in the industry. Thus, most publishers are capable of using the CD ROM medium with little additional investment. Similarly, the requirements for organizing and indexing the data for CD ROM mastering are procedurally equivalent to the requirements of the traditional print medium. However, the format and complexity of CD ROM-based indexes do deviate from traditional standards. As discussed below (see The Point of Integration), it is here that CD ROM data differ most from data in other types of publishing.

431

Because the investment required to fabricate CD ROM discs is substantial, it will not be done in-house. This should not be a problem, since all CD ROM disc fabricators accept data in a universal format on magnetic tape.

The Systems Side

For any CD ROM publication, the delivery system portion of the product provided by the publisher may range from a total hardware/software system offering (computer, operating system, disc drive, peripherals, and application) to a simple offering of only the application software (the software that accesses and processes the CD ROM data). It is also possible for a publisher to offer a disc-only product with a data format that is readable by an existing delivery system, but this precludes a publisher from taking full advantage of a major marketing edge offered by the use of CD ROM: programmable data delivery.

Typically, delivery system hardware selection is determined by the nature of the installed base of computers among the publication's prospective users. If there is a significant installed base of a particular computer among the prospects, then it is wise to design that computer into the delivery system. This reduces both the publisher's cost of marketing a publication and the customer's cost of acquiring it. If there is no particular computer in majority use, then the publisher may still choose either to provide a total hardware/software product or to specify some portion of the system for independent purchase by the customer and to supply the remainder. In either case, if the publication is to be used in a one-user-per-system configuration, there is no reason to select anything more expensive than a standard general-purpose microcomputer system. This is because a CD ROM drive simply cannot deliver data any faster than can be processed by a micro. At present, most CD ROM publishers choose to offer products consisting only of discs, disc drive, and application software designed to

> The widespread use of computers in publishing has made acquisition and maintenance of machine-readable data the norm in the industry.

run on a popular microcomputer (read PC-compatible) and operating system (read MS-DOS, possibly with GEM). There are two reasons for including a disc drive in the offering: First, drives are not yet readily accessible. Second, and more important, drive manufacturers have yet to adhere to a hardware interface standard for their products, and the CD ROM is new enough that operating systems do not yet provide device drivers to support them. This means that it is up to the publisher (with help from the drive manufacturers) to supply an interface for each supported drive. It all adds up to an expense for the publisher that soon will be unnecessary.

This brings us to the most important part of the delivery system: the application. Aside from its massive storage capacity, the beauty of CD ROM is that the message that is delivered can be varied simply by reading it with different applications. A publisher can target a given CD ROM disc at a variety of markets by packaging the disc with diverse applications. Consequently, the structure of an application is highly dependent upon the target audience. But there is an invariant aspect to the production of product applications. It might be called "the central dogma of software application products in consideration of the current state of the art," and it reads as follows.

The beauty of CD ROM is that the message that is delivered can be varied simply by reading it with different applications.

Most software application products should be:

○ Written in a common high-level language (such as C)

○ For a common operating system (perhaps UNIX-like)

○ With all system-dependent portions (device drivers) included as installable modules

Follow these guidelines, and not only can the application be easily moved to new hardware (software portability) but application development and maintenance costs are optimized. It is easier and less expensive to find capable engineers to develop software in the common development environments than it is to find gurus familiar with the more obscure environments.

The Point of Integration

With the various parts of the CD ROM product anatomy fresh in mind, we can identify the point at which the components from the two traditional businesses are integrated to form the new business of CD ROM publishing. The point of integration on the publishing side is formatted, indexed data. On the systems side it is the application. These components must be developed concurrently, each with full knowledge of the other.

All the other components can be specified at the start, and they need not be considered again. But the format of the CD ROM data must be selected with an understanding of its ultimate application(s), and the application(s) must be designed around the format of the data. This interrelationship between data format and application provides a longstanding problem in database system design wherein the programmer (data format designer) and the system user (application designer) must develop a system together in an iterative fashion, each precisely communicating to the other his or her understanding of the problem as it is elucidated, lest they become "arrogant computer hack" and "idiot end user." The importance of communication at the point of integration cannot be overstated.

"Vulching the box" had become the latest craze among the chemically inclined.

Even though the CD ROM publication is a hybrid offspring of two established industries, the demands of producing it are new. The variety of applications in which a given collection of data can be used is staggering. So is the quantity of data that can be placed on a CD ROM. The system design, while typically targeted at a microcomputer, requires the skills of a mainframe database programmer. Yet the slow data access time of a CD ROM drive (over 100 times slower than a Winchester disk drive) places the database design entirely outside the realm of the mainframe programmer's experience (crippled time-sharing systems notwithstanding). For example, a mainframe programmer might think nothing of designing a database index that requires 30 or more Winchester disk accesses to find a particular datum because it could be accomplished in less than a second. The same process on CD ROM could easily require a minute. As is the case with the design of any system, weaknesses are traded off against strengths to achieve acceptable results—CD ROM just brings with it a new set of weaknesses and strengths. In the above example, the same database implemented on CD ROM would require a different, possibly substantially larger, index structure to trade off cheap CD ROM real estate against slow access times for the assurance that any datum could be found in only two disc accesses.

One final note concerning the demands of this new publishing medium: Many knowledgeable users of CD ROM feel that it is imperative that a standard logical file format be adopted for CD ROM. This might be a nice turn of events for publishers who wish to produce discs for existing applications, but it does not overly concern those who will produce the types of publications defined here. There are simply too many kinds of useful data and access methods for the standards issue to be forced so early in the life of the new technology. This is not to say that promotion of the issue is misguided. Rather, it is an admirable example of industry cooperation.

433

But if history foreshadows future events, many "standards" will evolve from the efforts of industry pioneers, each flourishing under the banner of one of the industry's "standard" operating systems.

This completes an overview of the anatomy of a CD ROM publication. Now let's look at some applications for which laser disc technology will make some major contributions.

Sample Systems in CD ROM

Three sample CD ROM publications—demand-printing, reference, and training systems—are examined from different perspectives. Each system illustration contains, to some degree, the following:

○ A statement of the problem

○ A description, progressively more vague with each succeeding system, of a CD ROM solution

○ Identification of target delivery system(s)

○ An indication of what the system does (the application)

Demand Printing

A particular government contractor assembles custom systems from a wide variety of commercially available hardware and software subsystems. The company has identified a limiting factor to its potential growth: After years of operation, the company has accumulated several hundred megabytes of subsystem specifications stored on PC-based technical publications systems. It uses these specs to respond to RFPs (Requests for Proposals), but the quantity of data is too great for its existing access methods to handle. The result is that too much of its engineer's time is spent reviewing and compiling subsystem specs in attempts to respond to RFPs with optimal system designs. The problem is that the company has expanded the scope of its business to the point where, with its current data handling methods, it can no longer efficiently obtain sufficient business revenues to offset its spiraling cost of sales. The company has considered two solutions to its problem.

1. Reduce the scope of its business to a point where its data handling requirements are manageable under its current methods

2. Devise a new data handling method

Not only does the company choose the second solution, but it chooses to lead with its jaw and to further expand the scope of its business in the following manner.

The task at hand is to identify and assemble subsystem specifications to produce optimal custom system designs. The company realizes that if it can at the same time prepare system operations and maintenance manuals for submission along with its proposals, it will have a solid marketing edge over its competitors.

The company currently prepares documents on PC-based technical publications systems with laser printer output. With the addition of CD ROM, it has delivery systems.

What about the data acquisition, format, and indexes? The company's specification data are already in record format (each specification is a standalone record). Arrangements are made with the subsystem manufacturers to obtain their manuals and current price lists in machine-readable format, at little or no cost, with the understanding that these data will be made available to prospective customers. Database indexing software is then written to produce indexes of key words; one index from the specification titles, a second index from the product description. Index entries contain product identification and point to specification, price list, and manuals for the product. The indexes, specifications, and manuals are then transferred to magnetic tape for CD ROM mastering.

An application is designed that allows keyword-in-context searches of either specification title or product description. A search returns a list of product identifiers. An entry can be selected from the search list, and its associated specification, price list, or manuals are immediately fetched into the computer for review and editing. Selected edited documents may then be queued to disk for later printing or for use in producing updated CD ROMs.

Other features are included in the application. A proposal "summary generator" prepares a standard-format summary of the proposal in process. The summary includes a table of contents for the generated documentation, components lists, calculated end-user system and subsystem pricing, and subsystem descriptions that may be edited to create a system description.

The name *demand printing* probably doesn't do justice to this application. The system can be easily used by both engineers and support staff to produce de novo composite publications from data fragments. But how does the company choose to expand the scope of its business? It turns a valuable portion of the system (not enough to seriously jeopardize its competitive edge) into a commercial product for sale to its competitors. The commercial system uses the same disc as the in-house system, but data access is selectively restricted by the application software. Who knows, maybe CD ROM publishing should be in the company's charter.

Reference Publication

In the demand-printing example, massive amounts of data may be searched by two methods: either the absolute identity of the required data is known, in which case it may be searched for by title, or a relative (generic) identity is known and the data is searched for by description. A reference publication would include the same two search types as the demand-printing application. It might, however, include a third, more sophisticated type of search: a relational search for data for which neither an absolute nor a relative identity is known.

A prominent publisher of abstracts of chemical research literature has accumulated abstracts of the most important articles in the field for the past century. The accumulated quantity of data is rapidly approaching 10 gigabytes, and the rate of accumulation is accelerating. The publisher has for some time offered its abstracts in an online database format at a considerable cost to its users. Even though the publisher is without peer (does not suffer competitive pressure), it has decided to publish a CD ROM database in order to increase market penetration by offering anew the same data with additional processing capability at a moderate price.

The current online database has indexes that allow abstract retrieval by title keyword, author, chemical name, and chemical formula. A search based on any of these main keys may be qualified by the inclusion of any of a number of search qualifiers: name of publication, date range of publication, and type of work. For example, a search could be made for abstracts of papers by Kornfeld that were published in *The Journal of the American Chemical Society* between 1952 and 1962. Another search could be made on the chemical name, *hydroxymethylbenzene*, for example, qualified by *synthesis*, which would return all abstracts concerning the synthesis of compounds containing hydroxymethylbenzene as part of their names.

A popular supermicrocomputer with a multitasking operating system and a "jukebox" CD ROM drive is selected as the delivery system for the new database, and the current online data is transferred to the target system. The data fits neatly on a 15-disc set, but the new relational indexes require an additional 33 discs. The new indexes contain the original database search keys along with keywords from the body of the abstracts, all stored in a format that facilitates relational data access. Data and indexes are organized so as to allow updating of the publication either by replacing the last disc in each set (data and index) or by adding a new disc to each set.

A user of the new database can now accomplish, with relative ease, tasks that were previously incredibly tedious. With the old database (or even with the printed abstracts) it was a simple task to find, for example, a synthesis of pyruvaldehyde. Two syntheses, one published in 1887, the other in 1929, could be located in a matter of minutes. But what about the problem of isolating an enzyme that is found only in minute quantities in the mammalian brain? Let me illustrate.

Fenwick Crenshaw had been working on just that problem for the past three years. He had taken the classical approach—months of poring over the literature looking for clues, followed by months of a familiar routine in the lab: 10,000 homogenized rat brains, mixed with 37 different radioactive cofactors and binders, passed through 105 distinct chromatographic preparations, followed by separation in a variety of electrophoretic media, and countless liquid scintillations. Then he was back in the library poring over the literature looking for clues.

This continued for three years before a shiny new box and a book labeled *Manual* appeared in his library cubicle. Not one to be bothered by unnecessary documentation, but always game for a bout with new gadgetry, Fenwick spent the better part of a week divining the purpose of the new library toy. After several episodes of severe frustration, an extended and entirely distasteful confrontation with *Manual*, and a brief period of believing that he had transcended the need for sleep, Fenwick's latest inspiration glowed stupidly back at him from the new toy's display. It read, "[binding OR [bonding AND [electro OR static OR hydro]]]." (This is a relational search key.) He had long since abandoned such attempts as "[chromatograph AND [separat OR purif OR isolat]]," and the tenacious "[enzyme AND pur] AND . . ." His experience indicated that he would be able to take tea and a leisurely stroll across campus and still have time to debate the implausibility of silicon life-forms with his colleagues before the machine would have anything useful to say.

The possible manifestations of "training system" are so completely diverse and so incompletely understood at the nuts-and-bolts level that it is one of the most exciting and financially risky systems development tasks currently under investigation.

438

After lunch he returned to the cubicle to find one of his graduate assistants typing on the toy. Fenwick excused himself as he slipped a disk cartridge into the toy's Bernoulli Box and sat down in what had recently become the warmest seat in the library. He switched the toy's attention back to his account (this is a multitasking operating system), and for an instant he thought he saw in the fading phosphor of the display the unfinished command "[enzyme AND pur] AND . . . ." It took the toy nearly 20 minutes to transfer megabytes of results from his earlier search to the cartridge disk. A glance at the system status line indicated that this was about 10 minutes longer than the search took, and it gave him time to consider how he could further narrow the scope of the search to reduce the quantity of matching data. No problem. He would take the cartridge up to his lab and use the off-line "sifting" program that came with the toy to get at the real meat.

As Fenwick got up to leave the cubicle, he noticed that his assistant was flanked by a gaggle of new figures striking an assortment of vulture-like poses. "Vulching the box" had become the latest craze among the chemically inclined, and it occurred to Fenwick that the library might profitably put a stop to such loitering by taking advantage of the substantial discounts that were being offered by the publisher for quantity subscriptions to the database.

Later that week, after sifting the data and performing a mere three attempts at passing small amounts of dilute household chemicals over the remains of a pig brain graciously donated by a local slaughterhouse, Fenwick was the miserly possessor of the world's entire supply of pure mammalian gamma-aminobutyric acid decarboxylase. He spent a sleepless night pondering the legal ramifications of spending the remainder of his grant money to set up a specialty biochemicals manufacturing company.

Training Publications

The problem of developing a good training system is by far the most complex of the three examples presented here. Whereas the previous publication examples provide their users with the ability to perform keyed data retrieval involving, at most, simple data relationships, a training system best serves its purpose by being able to track the progress (understanding?) of its user and to adjust its approach accordingly. This is accomplished by designing a database/application that performs both sequential and keyed data retrieval while at the same time it evaluates its interaction with the user in terms of both content and context. Both the retrieval and the processing of the training data are continuously adjusted according to this evaluation.

Mirroring the complexity of the training system's application is the complexity of its data. Text, tables, line drawings, still pictures, audio, video, and animation structures may all be important components of training data (this is not to say that these data types don't have a place in the other publication examples). Furthermore, the indexing required to logically associate bits of related data, in a "sufficiently complete" training system, is overwhelming. Here the line between index structure and application software structure becomes quite fuzzy. Intuitively, it seems like an "ideal" problem for a laser-disc-type (very high density) storage technology. The possible manifestations of "training system" are so completely diverse and so incompletely understood at the nuts-and-bolts level that it is one of the most exciting and financially risky systems development tasks currently under investigation. There are sparkles on the tunnel wall but no light at the end. This example takes us to a time in the (hopefully) not-too-distant future of the "intelligent home" when systems advances have made basic education systems a cost-effective reality. And now for another short fantasy.

439

. . . the slow data access time of a CD ROM drive . . . places the database design entirely outside the realm of the mainframe programmer's experience.

A ninth-grade home-study student, having just returned to his studies after a three-day break (a reward for mastering basic concepts in cybernetics), is finishing the day's instruction in calculus provided by his home interactive processor. It is a rather run-of-the-mill HIP composed of a Sony parallel-associative processor operating under Microsoft's version of HOUSE (Home Operating, Universal Systems Environment). The instructional peripherals include a laser-disc library manager and both a wall and a lap audiovisual stereo transceiver with tactile feedback.

We pick up the interaction between Tommy (the student) and Fred (the HIP) during a problem-solving session. Tommy has bogged down on one of those horrid integration problems that requires trigonometric-substitution-for-no-apparent-reason to solve.

Fred: "You seem to be stuck in an endless loop."

Tommy: "Thanks, Fred. How about a hint?"

Fred has been tracking Tommy's progress as he scribbles across his lap pad.

Fred: "It looks like you're trying term expansion."

Tommy: "So? Any suggestions?"

Fred: "Why not try some substitutions?"

Ten minutes later, Tommy is working with an unwieldy hodgepodge of symbols.

Fred: "Excuse me, may I interrupt?"

Tommy: "Why? Am I doing something wrong?"

Fred: "Well, you've done an entirely valid collection of substitutions, but I'm afraid you're overlooking the underlying nature of the function."

Tommy: "What's that?"

Fred: "You tell me."

Tommy: "It's the square root of the difference of two squares."

Fred: "So you can read! Now try thinking."

After some thought . . .

Tommy: "It's hard to picture."

Fred: "*That's it.* Let me show you."

The scribblings disappear from the lap pad and are replaced by a neat graph.

Tommy: "It's half of a circle."

Fred: "And what is a circle?"

Tommy furrowed his brow in concentration. Then, with a surprised expression . . .

Tommy: "This isn't one of those stupid trig substitutions, is it?"

Fred: "You've got it."

Tommy: "I hate trig."

Fred: "We've known *that* for years. You'll grow out of it."

Some minutes later, Tommy is scratching furiously across the lap pad when Fred interrupts.

Fred: "I think you're on the wrong track."

Tommy: "Leave me alone."

Finally Tommy completes his solution.

Tommy: "There. How's that?"

Fred: "I have to admit, I've nothing like that on record, but it looks correct."

Tommy: "Take *that*, trig."

Fred immediately places several requests to remote libraries to see if there is a precedent for Tommy's solution. He then returns his attention to Tommy to offer him a reward deemed appropriate for such apparently successful divergent thinking.

Fred: "Well done. You deserve a special treat. Would you like me to feed some video data through the audio processor?"

Tommy: "No thanks, Bozo. How about a couple more days off?"

Fred: "Sorry, can't do that yet. Now, for the next problem."

A Case Study

The three example systems above are just plausible fiction. The following example is commercial fact.

This is an overview of the technical and financial considerations involved in developing a particular CD ROM publication. The publication is the *BiblioFile Catalog Production System*. It was developed by The Library Corporation in 1984 and was the first commercial CD ROM publication. As such, the cost estimates presented are the types of costs that a publisher could expect to encounter in producing its first CD ROM publication of this type.

The cost of machine-readable data acquisition was already being carried by the company since it was (and still is) a publisher of bibliographic data on microfiche—the Library of Congress Card Catalog in machine-readable form (MARC). They consist of ASCII variable-length records containing variable-length fields. The problem was to make these data easily accessible to librarians for use as follows.

○ On screen—for editing to produce records customized to the requirements of the subscriber library. Each library has its own "local" data to add to each catalog card.

○ In print—in the form of catalog cards, spine labels, pocket labels, and circulation labels.

○ On magnetic media—in MARC format for transfer to local online catalogs.

442

The importance of communication at the point of integration cannot be overstated.

Data access was to be allowed by search on title, author, Library of Congress catalog number (LCCN), international standard book number (ISBN), and international standard serial number (ISSN). The first two keys are alphabetic, the other three are numeric. Searches on the alphabetic keys could potentially return hundreds of matches, so qualification of alphabetic keys was allowed by author, date range, origin (country or state), pages, subject, and type of publication. The indexes were designed to allow access to any record on a disc, by unique key, in less than 2 seconds. There were approximately 1.2 million records in the database. The database currently contains about 4 million records.

MARC records are approximately 30 percent redundant data. These were removed from each record for the purpose of saving space on CD ROM, since the complete MARC format could be regenerated by the application software in a matter of milliseconds.

The database-creation software and the application software were developed by a team of up to six people over the period of a year. The database was created during rented time on an IBM mainframe by COBOL programs. The application software was developed in C on five purchased PC-compatible machines and two Hitachi CD ROM drive prototypes. A librarian was retained as a consultant to steer application development. The documentation was prepared by the development team.

The total cost of development was somewhat over $250,000. This includes software, hardware, documentation, and two disc printings at about $10,000 a shot.

The cost of maintaining and enhancing the publication in its first year is about four-and-a-half man-years, with twelve updates of the database and application and four updates of the documentation.

The one-time purchase price of the system is $2930 for disc drive, disc drive interface for PC-compatible machines, application software, and one year of support and maintenance. The annual subscription to the English-language LC MARC database is $870 for quarterly updates, an additional $600 for monthly updates, and another $500 for the foreign-language MARC database. All updates of software and documentation (development of which is directed by customer requests) is free.

The Library Corporation will have released its seventh CD ROM publication by the time this book is printed. In early 1986, the company will be breaking ground in the arena of custom CD ROM publications. The company is doing quite well. It is a wonderful business to be in.

About the Author

The author lives in Silver Spring, Maryland. He is a consultant in systems and product development. As chief technical officer of The Library Corporation , he participated in the development of the first commercial CD ROM publication. In his first year at The Library Corporation, Mr. Martin developed seven CD ROM products.

Brian Martin and Company
10620 South Dunmoor Drive
Silver Springs, Maryland
(301) 681-8634

Dense Media and the Future of Publishing

by Barry Richman

By and large, traditional print publishers are afraid of technical innovation. There is a culture gap which has, if anything, been widened by recent adventures in microcomputer and software publishing. On the other hand, publishers dread being left behind by innovative competitors. This is important, because if the publishing medium is to change from paper to highly dense media, the publishing community is going to have to buy in. They are the experts at shaping information for publication, and they own the distribution channels.

445

But why bother with a new medium? What's wrong with traditional forms of print anyway? The answer lies in the characteristics of the medium itself, the attitudes of consumers towards print, and the way the publishing system works.

Despite the utility of extraordinary increases in density, the future of CD ROM as a publishing medium is only partly related to how much information can be packed per unit volume. If it were enough for media simply to be denser, we would have bibles written on the heads of pins and books like this printed on microfiche. The underlying reason that CD ROMs and other dense media are likely to replace traditional print is, as usual, economic. Dense media have the inherent characteristics necessary to cure some of publishing's greatest problems—excess inventory, short product life, high distribution costs, wasteful product returns, and insufficient shelf space to give new products a chance to thrive. These are chronic, suffocating problems for which no solution can be found in traditional print forms.

Consumers, however, have something to say about the issue; and consumers are quite satisfied with traditional print, thank you. Books and magazines are readily accessible and easy to use once you've learned to read (no communications protocols, no learning curve of any kind). They are convenient, that is, portable and mostly not too bulky, independent of electric power, individual, capable of excellent graphics, feel good, smell good, and still relatively cheap.

Can anything be done to change the consumer's mind? Consider the consumer with a passion for the hardboiled detective fiction of the forties—or for cooking, military history, home repair, amateur magic, westerns, or any other popular consumer category. Much of what is published goes

446

rapidly out of print because publishers cannot afford to keep cash tied up in inventories of slow sellers, even if the sales are steady. Booksellers can't stock them because more than 50,000 new titles are published each year and there isn't enough shelf space in the stores or the warehouses. Most consumers don't know how to search the used-book market for particular titles, nor are they willing to invest the time necessary to do so. Even the most devoted book lovers stare at their overloaded shelves in exasperation.

The dense media solution is for publishers to assemble multivolume theme libraries on single discs. Let's say each book on the disc will cost the consumer a dollar, based on a $49.95 purchase price for the whole disc. The library is "printed" about once a week, depending on order volumes, so that cash is not anchored to immovable inventory. Miraculously, it costs no more to handle and ship all 50 books in the library disc format than it currently costs to mail a single book. Authors get at least some royalty payments on those out-of-print titles, and publishers realize incremental sales previously impossible to achieve. In one way there is nothing new here. The editing and marketing ideas are essentially the same as in continuity series and specialized book clubs. Given multivolume packaging at a reasonable price, consumers might just try a new medium. They will not, however, buy a $5,000 computer system to try the new medium.

. . . if the publishing medium is to change from paper to highly dense media, the publishing community is going to have to buy in.

In business and professional markets, no one will buy a $5,000 system just for the experience, either; but there is an installed base, and for several reasons the dense media prospects are better. The sacred texts of professional life—those specialized multivolume reference works and subscription services—are so expensive, so bulky, and often so complexly indexed that wrestling a set into the headquarters library is worthy of mention in the annual report. The cost of putting them in each office is out of the question, they'd take up too much space anyway, and so they wind up much avoided. If, however, the same works were published on CD ROMs, each disc costing one-tenth the price of the printed version, their distribution and use would increase dramatically. Such pricing would probably be based on a package that included the full print version or, alternatively, enough CD ROMs to produce true incremental sales for the publisher. This too is established publishing ground and works to the advantage of both the publisher and the consumer.

For electronic media to replace print, the cost of moving information to the human brain from the new medium has to be about the same as the cost of moving it there from print.

From the standpoint of the professional/business consumer, the attractions of a dense portable medium exceed those of the familiar online information tool. Accessibility improves because no one has to go to the central library or learn to deal with a network interface. Productivity increases because machine reference searches can be spread around the office. And if consulting the standard references was worthwhile in the first place, better quality work and business decisions should result from consulting them more frequently.

Professional and reference publishing will be the first to move to CD ROM. It is important to understand, however, that the emphasis will be on improved access and convenience, not processing. The publishing proposition must be thought through. Publishers who fill CD ROMs with data rather than well-edited, well-integrated text are in for a surprise. The heavy data users and manipulators already have the tools of their trade. For them, denser media are of peripheral interest. CD ROMs represent the first major step in creating new books, magazines, and newspapers—not computers. They also represent an opportunity for publishers to organize, link, and update existing products into professional and reference libraries.

With CD ROMs, publishers can hope to transfer traditional professional and reference works onto more efficient and more useful media. The audience for such information is motivated. But what will it take to replace books and magazines read for entertainment, education, or simply curiosity? What will it take to replace print completely? The answer is affordable electronic forms that are as good as print at what print does best, and are better than print at what electronics does best. This is where publishers will have to do some solid thinking, beginning with a comparison of the strengths and weaknesses of each side.

Ease of Use

Since it is far easier to read a book than to use electronic retrieval, electronic retrieval has to improve. One would think typewriter keyboards should be easy enough, but they aren't. No keyboard yet devised is as easy as opening a book, turning the pages, or folding a page to hold the place. Publishers should try to design a keyboard for readers of electronic media machines. Its keys might be labeled "open," "close," "mark the place," "turn the page," and so on. Not hard to do, really—but impossible if you are thinking "computer" instead of "book."

448

Print Quality

No contest. The clarity and diversity of type and illustrations in traditional forms of print are far superior to electronic display. At present a barely acceptable page worth of liquid crystal display costs about $100 each in serious production quantities. Even so, LCD is fairly miserable to read. More palatable flat displays, such as plasma and electroluminescent screens, are substantially more expensive but still do not approach print quality. Fortunately, the trick is not to match the quality of the best traditional print, merely to move beyond the threshold of what is fatiguing and offensive. It is hard to see who is going to do this. One possibility is the manufacturers of typesetting equipment, who understand the design and quality implications of print. But these companies have a powerful interest in production-level equipment dedicated to traditional print production, not individual portable machines for displaying what is written on dense media.

Portability

Not only the medium but the machine that plays it back has to be portable, and probably battery-powered. The machine should weigh no more than a moderately heavy book—less than 5 pounds. Tourists should be able to throw it and the latest travel-guide disc into the suitcase and still have room for their socks. This is a serious requirement, because portability is one of the major triumphs of traditional print forms.

Cost

For electronic media to replace print, the cost of moving information to the human brain from the new medium has to be about the same as the cost of moving it there from print. This does not necessarily mean that the cost per character transferred has to be the same. The difference can be narrowed by genuinely useful, timesaving electronic features. For example, a full-detail zooming feature for maps, biology texts, repair manuals, and the like would help justify higher unit prices.

Ease of Authoring

This should turn out to be a wash. The mechanics of writing a book are easy. Great books have been written in pencil on yellow lined pads, and the contents of yellow lined pads are easily transferred to dense media. All publishers have to do is resist making it harder for the authors, who are already capturing the keystrokes and submitting manuscripts on magnetic media.

Updating, Revising

While the editorial and production procedures need development, electronic media have the distinct edge. The trouble with print is its linearity. Authors often wonder why all the fuss over changes in a few paragraphs, some tables, or an illustration. The fuss is that unless the space occupied by the material removed is identical to the space needed by the replacement, pages or even whole chapters must be typeset again. If the new material invalidates references elsewhere in the text, these have to be sought out and corrected as well. Also, if the original version of the book is in stout supply, a new edition means existing inventory is next to worthless. Publishers who can develop on-demand printing of CD ROMs will be able to revise their products when required by content, minimize inventory as a factor in making publishing decisions, provide a better product for the consumer, and use all of it to advantage in marketing.

The essence of direct response is matching a distinct need with a potent product rather than offering a smorgasbord to anyone who drops in. This is perfect for CD ROM . . .

The publishing community consists of authors, editors, designers, production staffs, printers, sales and marketing people, the distribution network (wholesalers, retailers, mail sellers), and advertisers. Dense media publishing will involve significant changes in most of these roles.

Authors should not have to change their work habits and should benefit from having their works available longer. The royalties per unit may be less, but better a few percent of a small dollar figure than 100 percent of nothing. Also, royalties are not the whole story. Writers write to make contributions, and for their contributions to endure they must remain in print.

Editors will have to invent new ways to organize and integrate text. A significant task will be understanding how to use software to move within and among reference works on the same disc. At one level the editor's role will be deciding what existing products owned by the company should be on the disc in the first place, how the reader will use them, and what needs to be added, deleted, or updated. At another, editors must adapt the procedures for copyediting, proofreading, and interacting with authors and production people.

Designers and artists will have to help. Any medium that can handle columns and rows can present data. But the graphic design decisions about type styles and sizes, sizing and placing illustrations relative to text, screen

450

page formats, and so on must be transferred from the printed forms by those who understand them. In some publishing operations authors, editors, and programmers will do the design and layout with predictable results.

Production departments will continue to establish publishing schedules and will oversee the manufacturing of CD ROM units as they have traditionally overseen typesetting, composition, printing, and binding. In the long run they will buy more discs and less paper, manufacture units at sensible demand intervals, and exercise better inventory control over both finished and unfinished goods. It would not be surprising to see typesetters and composition vendors converting new manuscripts, as well as products already on magnetic media, to CD ROM.

It is unlikely that the book trade, bookstores in particular, will swiftly embrace CD ROM products. Booksellers typically have not done well with equipment, computer software, or other nonprint merchandise. Even in print, the major book chains have only recently discovered magazines. Moreover, the bestseller system is geared to special patterns of ordering, discounting, distribution, and returns for a relatively few books on which success or failure is based. It is a system unsuited to innovation and disinclined to distraction. Some well-packaged audio and video products sold at prices comparable to those of books are, however, currently in vogue; so a nonprint medium may not be a sure kiss of death. But direct marketing is more likely to be the major introductory channel.

The publishing proposition must be thought through. Publishers who fill CD ROMs with data rather than well-edited, well-integrated text are in for a surprise.

Direct-response marketing includes all forms of selling directly from the publisher to the consumer—mail, book clubs, coupon advertising, catalogs, direct mail, and toll-free phone. The essence of direct response is matching a distinct need with a potent product rather than offering a smorgasbord to anyone who drops in. This is perfect for the CD ROM as a vehicle, and it will be possible to price adequately to cover typical costs and response rates. Eventually, bookstores may be able to concentrate decisively on a few new and best-selling titles each season, leaving technical and professional works, slow-moving new fiction, and most nonfiction to denser media.

Fundamental changes in publishing technology occur on a time scale measured in centuries. But a revolution is on its way. The very medium itself is going to change, and the publishing industry will have to deal with it.

The advantages of highly dense media are so overwhelming that the publishing leaders in each market segment can either strengthen their positions or watch them erode, as they choose. Now is the time to begin prototyping and market testing. There must, of course, be a transition, which may take years or may take decades; but in the long run, dense media will replace paper as surely as papyrus replaced clay.

451

Publishing Strategy for CD ROM Reference Products

Here is a free market-penetration strategy for publishers of established reference materials. It is virtually guaranteed for any reference operation but will work especially well in mature to moribund markets. The illustrative example is constructed for Webster's Hypothetical Dictionaries, Inc., a middle-ranked contender in the general English dictionary field.

WHD's flagship is its collegiate dictionary, about 1200 pages in print and selling for $14.95. The company also publishes a highly abridged paperback version; a large-print version; seven variations based on binding, illustrations, and appendixes; a school dictionary; and nine professional dictionaries in areas such as law, medicine, electronics, and agriculture.

Neither WHD nor any of its competitors have changed their share of the market in the past 15 years. And as far as anyone can tell, the total market is growing less than 2 percent per year. The only things that seem to stimulate sales are new editions and lower prices. WHD has, however, managed to license its word list to a small software company in California, which in turn has created a spelling checker that seems to be moving. What WHD management really wants to do, however, is break out of its share-of-market box and attack the leader.

The leader, unfortunately, has been impregnable for most of a hundred years, since its dictionaries are generally regarded as the most authoritative, especially by educators who recommend them generation after generation to schoolchildren. Moreover, the leader revises its products regularly, maintains high editorial standards, and will, if challenged on price, cut prices until everyone bleeds.

The only hope WHD sees is to somehow overcome the leader's positioning as the authority, and perhaps differentiate their product further with added value of some kind. Its first step, therefore, is to quietly contract with a reputable company specializing in advanced media publishing to convert their citation files (the massive collection of quotations on which their dictionaries are based) and their composition tapes to CD ROM. This steals a march on all the competitors who are busy setting up network-oriented conversions and improved spelling checkers.

The plan is to create a direct marketing link with dictionary users, sell them on WHD's high standards, and offer various CD ROM combinations of dictionaries (the collegiate, one specialized dictionary, an entertainment item such as the crossword dictionary, and a subcontracted ZIP Code directory). The vehicle is a monthly four-page newsletter, *The WHD Report on New and Important Words.* The newsletter has some easily digested statistics on how many new words are entering the language, and each issue has a boxed feature on one of the technical fields represented by the specialized dictionaries.

A special insert is done for the el-hi market; extra copies with vocabulary-building activities are available for classroom distribution. Government agencies, libraries, and schools are seeded with CD ROMs, each disc containing at least one information unit uniquely useful to the particular market.

Disc prices are roughly equal to the number of individual dictionaries on the disc times the usual selling price of the print version. Updated discs are available periodically, but major revisions of WHD's line are done only when at least 20 percent of the content in the previous edition demands it. Direct mail to the newsletter mailing list is targeted as a major sales channel, potentially with higher profit margins because of lower distribution costs. WHD gradually adds vocabulary building and word games to the general mailing list, a ROM of The Month Club for other literary products, and in addition sells CD ROMs with specialized professional content as a completely new business.

Editors will have to invent new ways to organize and integrate text. A significant task will be understanding how to use software to move within and among reference works on the same disc.

About the Author

Barry Richman has been in professional, reference, and technical publishing for twenty years. He has been senior editor for computers and electronics at McGraw-Hill, general manager of Osborne/McGraw-Hill, and president of the Waite Group. His new company, Advanced Media Publishing, is developing CD ROM publishing and marketing systems for professional and reference markets.

Advanced Media Publishing
148 Stonewall Road
Berkeley, CA 94705

452

CD ROM in the Matrix of Publishing Choices

by Matilda Butler,
William Paisley, and
Frances Spigai

For more than 400 years, publishing has been the domain of the printed word. Yet in just the past five years we have seen the publishing industry usher in the electronic age—a move that has suddenly presented publishers with new options that are certain to alter the very nature of publishing in the near future. Many of the major publishers have begun changing their procedures to accommodate the new demands of software and of video publishing. They have also begun to set their sights on the possibilities of optical disc publishing.

453

It is predicted that by 1990 many publishers will have CD ROM publishing arms, and by 2000 most publishers will not only publish optical disc versions of printed publications or online databases but they will also publish electronic information designed specifically for optical discs. At present, however, most publishers have not yet chosen their first CD ROM products, and many challenging questions of design, pricing, and promotion lie before them. This chapter provides the background for thinking about CD ROM as a publishing medium.

Online to Off-line

For nearly two decades, online retrieval has altered the mix of business, professional, and scientific publishing in America. Pioneering services like Lockheed's DIALOG have been joined by an increasing number of general- and special-purpose services from companies such as System Development Corporation, Bibliographic Retrieval Services, Mead Data Central, Dow-Jones News/Retrieval, Control Data Corporation, and others.

As recently as five years ago online retrieval was confined mainly to surrogate files such as indexes and citations. Now, a majority of the more than 2800 databases available from online services are source files of financial and statistical data, coupled with a growing number of full-text articles, reports, and newsletters. In addition to the large number of databases, there are more than a thousand publishers, nearly half as many database distributor/time-sharing services, and more than a million subscribers. By late 1985, publishers of financial, scientific, and reference information made electronic publishing an industry—with estimated revenues in excess of $2.5 billion.

454

At first, all searching of online databases was conducted at "dumb" terminals. These terminals were (and still are) only capable of searching the databases and displaying results; they were not able to hold the results for later use or process the results locally through formatting, graphing, or analysis programs.

Because of these limitations, microcomputers are replacing dumb terminals as search tools, clearly a benefit to both the microcomputer and electronic publishing industries. The microcomputer's ease of use has brought new users to online services, and the fact that online services exist certainly hasn't hurt the sales of microcomputers.

The rapid spread of interest in electronic information throughout the business, professional, and scientific worlds has led many people to realize that electronic information products can also be marketed directly to microcomputer users. These "off-line" or "standalone" products offer several advantages over both print and online forms; they can be produced inexpensively and bring much added value to users.

. . . should paper costs continue to escalate and warehousing costs continue to rise, publishers may wish to deliberately move users to the electronic format.

Online, Off-line, or Print?

Off-line products distributed on magnetic and optical discs will undoubtedly affect the existing markets for print publications and online services. However, they will supplement rather than supplant the print and online forms in most markets, becoming dominant in markets where their features are best matched to uses (early examples include catalogs, directories, reference works, and numeric databases).

Online services will continue to be the preferred mode of distributing certain databases, including:

- Those that exceed the gigabyte (billion character) capacity of optical discs now entering the market.

- Those that must be updated more often than would be optimal for products distributed directly to users. Updates occurring more frequently than once a week may continue to be the province of the online services or some hybrid online/local product, while updates occurring less than once a month may be optimal for standalone systems.

- Those that are infrequently accessed, hence are not cost-effective in a local, corporate, or personal library.

Print will continue to be preferred mode of distributing certain information:

- When the information is used briefly and thrown away.
- When the information is used only in a linear manner (as in a novel).

- When the information is used in settings that are unlikely to have micro-computers, such as cars and the outdoors.
- When the market is so "thin" that only the least expensive publication can be cost-effective.

In a growing number of markets, however, off-line or standalone products will have an important role in the publishing mix. There are five reasons for this prediction:

1. Microcomputers are growing into "micro-mainframes," personal comput-ers with the power that only mainframe computers possessed a few years ago.

2. The costs of connecting to online services are increasing while costs asso-ciated with microcomputer systems are decreasing. Off-line retrieval products will soon be cheaper to buy and use than online services.

3. In previous shifts from mainframe computers to microcomputers (e.g., word processing, financial analysis), users have preferred microcomputers because they, rather than the data-processing staff, control the use of the computer.

4. As information users learn to use microcomputers, they expect more powerful processing features than online services provide—more power-ful, too, than they can afford to buy in hours of online use.

5. Off-line products give publishers control over market information, pric-ing, and unwanted downloading of databases.

The potential of off-line products in comparison with online services is well expressed by Bettie Steiger, vice president of Reference Technology, "the taxi-meter syndrome seriously inhibits users of online databases, who pay up to $3 a minute for their searches. With optical discs offering the unlimited access of a book and the sophisticated search capability of an online database, whole new applications will emerge and new publishers will be attracted to electronic publishing."

Off-line Publications

Until 1985, off-line products had been limited to smaller databases or subsets of larger databases distributed on floppy disks. Companies like Knowledge Access "ramped up" for the production and distribution of large databases by solving problems of product design (including data encryption, microcomputer-oriented indexing and representation, packaging, documentation and user instruction, and postsearch features) as well as market analysis using magnetic media. Moreover, the floppy disk products produced in the 1983-1985 period represent more than a transitional technology. Because of their speed of production and the absence of mastering costs, magnetic media—both floppy disks and hard disks distributed with preloaded information—will be important publishing alternatives in the future as well.

While the introduction of CD ROM technology greatly enlarges the range of databases that can be marketed as off-line products, the new opportunities raise as many questions as they answer. Which products? What hardware? What software? How many updates? What about database protection? How will CD ROM affect revenues from related print publications and online services? How long will it take to build markets for CD ROM products? At what cost?

Issues facing publishers can be summarized under the five categories of hardware decisions, software decisions, information product decisions, cost/pricing factors, and marketing issues. These points are discussed in the following sections.

1. Hardware Technical Standards for Off-Line Products

Microcomputer buyers are soundly advised to choose software first, then find hardware that will run it. But from a publisher's perspective, hardware is a necessary first consideration. Which type of personal computer has the largest installed base among the users of the particular information? If it's a business or professional database, then the most likely answer is IBM or IBM-compatible. If it's an educational database, then the most likely answer is Apple.

Once the type of PC is determined, the next decision is which CD drive to get. Philips? Hitachi? Sony? CD ROM is too new to have a meaningful installed base. For instance, as of December 1985, the writing of this chapter, there are fewer than 200 players installed in libraries. How do you choose in the absence of a market preference?

. . . in just the past five years we have seen the publishing industry usher in the electronic age—a move that has suddenly presented publishers with new options that are certain to alter the very nature of publishing in the near future.

Interface/Data Format.   Other chapters in this book explain the standardization issues with CD ROM, including interface standards between the PC and the CD drive (SCSI, SASI, and serial), logical file structure, and disc size (including Sony's recent announcement of a 5¼-inch disc rather than the 4.7-inch disc). At this time, a compact disc pressed by Digital Equipment to operate on the Philips drive cannot be used in a Hitachi drive and vice versa.

457

Creating products for a particular hardware standard carries a certain risk at this time, since that standard may not prove to be dominant one or two years from now. However, it is also true that the lack of a single standard for microcomputers has not inhibited the spread of that technology.

ROM? WORM? DRAW?   The most viable storage medium for databases within the current compact disc technology is the read-only disc. But close competitors are the direct-read-after-write (DRAW) and the write-once-read-many (WORM) technologies, as well as the coming erasable magneto-optic discs (and accompanying new read-write drives).

Will users need or want to write to the discs? Will the installed base of play-only devices be exceeded by the record-play devices?

Longevity.   Richard S. Shuford points out in a recent article in *Byte* (November 1985) that disc longevity and hence data permanence are unknown at this time. Just as libraries are currently facing the problem of deterioration of books printed on sulfite paper, so it is possible that CDs will also deteriorate. For many publications, this is not an issue; but for some information with archival value, this future difficulty needs to be considered.

Summary.   This section on hardware issues raises more questions than it answers, which is appropriate when a new technology is introduced. Moving forward quickly with a CD publication may be best for an individual publisher, but it is important to keep an eye on the changes that are occurring within the industry. It's often not a bad practice to continue asking the same questions until the answers become clear.

2. Software Standards

Make or Buy?   Early in a product's development, publishers face the decision to develop their own retrieval system or to turn to outside companies. Having their own proprietary system is potentially a good alternative to buying existing software, but it is both expensive and time-consuming. Knowledge Access, for instance, spent three years creating and testing our retrieval system; and we continue to develop the software to keep it state-of-the-art.

For many publishers, the best decision is to work with a firm already involved in magnetic or optical retrieval because it allows them to build on what has been learned.

Retrieval System Features.   Each of the retrieval systems currently available for use with publishers' databases have their own list of program features. Although each system has unique capabilities, there are some shared characteristics, for example:

- Retrieval modes
  - Browse mode
  - Search mode
- Retrieval functions
  - Search multiple items
  - Create sets
  - Combine sets using Boolean operators
  - Save and reload sets
- Output features
  - Display information
  - Print multiple formats (including labels)
  - Sort, alphabetize, compute statistics, graph results
  - Save to additional formats (Lotus 1-2-3, ASCII for word processors, etc.)

- User-friendly features
  - Menu-driven in most fields
  - Free text (including wild card), when appropriate.
  - On-screen help system
  - Self-training tutorial
  - Use of color
  - Use of windows
- Database searching and efficiency features
  - Data compression
  - Data encryption
  - Rapid random access
  - Coded and free-text searchable fields

Characteristics based on design of KAware™, the retrieval system developed by Knowledge Access

Businesses that have databases with time-dependent information may not be as concerned about potential loss of information or data security, but most cannot afford the luxury of indifference.

Shuford wrote, "To take greatest advantage of the storage format and access characteristics of the CD ROM, the data stored on the discs will have to be specially prepared before the discs can be pressed. Companies that plan to use CD ROMs for distribution of large databases will have to learn how to do it most efficiently."

Using the system specifications provided by Hitachi, the data transfer rate of the CD ROM is three times faster than that of a floppy disk (176 KB/sec versus 63 KB/sec), but it is more than three times slower than a 20-MB hard disk (176 KB/sec versus 625 KB/sec). The access time for the CD ROM is 1 sec, compared with 0.2 sec for a floppy disk and 0.15 sec for a hard disk. Data transfer rates and access time can be maximized by a good match between the particular software and the specific database. Putting the database on a compact disc and then looking for a retrieval system to go with it will result in a slow and clumsy product.

Summary. Publishers will find several companies with a well-developed retrieval system that can be matched with their database. Although there is always the option to develop one's own, there can be advantages to using an existing product—building on marketplace expertise and selling to an installed base of users familiar with the product. The features of the retrieval system need to be appropriate for and tailored to the specific database, however.

3. Information Standards

Size of Database.   In the rapid move from online and print publications to CD ROM, it is important to consider the size of the database and its storage requirements. There are four storage technologies available at this time: floppy disk, hard disk, videodisc, and CD ROM. The different storage capabilities of each enable a database of almost any size to be published electronically.

460

Staring into the crystal ball and making predictions is a chancy proposition.

Small databases of up to 2 megabytes can be easily accommodated on one or two floppy disks. If the database is currently a print publication, this is as many as 800 text pages. It may also be appropriate to consider marketing a subset of a larger database on floppies. Medium-sized databases of 2 to 10 megabytes are best accommodated on a hard disk. With the expanded hard disk/hard card options, some publishers may wish to include hardware with the initial database purchase. If hardware is not included, then the product is distributed on floppy disks and loaded by the customer onto a hard disk. With 30-megabyte drives becoming common and with easy access to drives with up to 100-megabyte storage, it is likely that hard disks will represent the appropriate technology for certain databases.

Large databases of 10 to 500 megabytes account for the majority of the current online products and are the appropriate size for CD ROM publications. Even larger databases may require multiple CD ROM discs. Very large databases exceeding 500 megabytes can also be accommodated on large 12-inch videodiscs.

Updating Frequency.   Three typical publishing cycles can be easily accommodated in a microcomputer product: yearly, quarterly, and monthly.

Yearly: Information stored on floppy disks, hard disks, or CD ROM can be easily distributed when the updating cycle is yearly.

Quarterly or semiannually: Information that needs to be updated on a quarterly or semiannual basis can be accommodated in standalone microcomputer products. If the information is stored on CD ROM or hard disks, updates can be distributed on floppies for loading on the hard disk. Whether sold on floppies or CD ROM, the product is usually priced on a subscription basis.

Monthly: Information that changes each month is also sold on a subscription basis and can be distributed on floppies or CD ROM. For publications requiring weekly or more frequent updating, print, online, or electronic updating of the standalone product are the alternatives.

Types of Information. Four major kinds of information that are currently marketed as print publications or online databases are particularly well-suited to become standalone electronic products:

○ Directory information (including mailing lists)

○ Numeric information

○ Full-text information

○ Bibliographic information

While the introduction of CD ROM technology greatly enlarges the range of databases that can be marketed as off-line products, the new opportunities raise as many questions as they answer.

Not all products should be moved to CD ROM or other machine-readable storage media. Greater convenience, more opportunities for analysis, new output options (mailing labels, Lotus 1-2-3 format, etc.), and extensive coordinated indexing are examples of value-added features in electronic products. If there is no value added in the marketplace perception, then the product is not a good choice since it will probably have to be sold at a higher price as an electronic publication.

Protection of Information. There is a major investment in the creation and maintenance of a database. Publishers with online files perceive downloading to be a major loss of revenue. With databases on magnetic or optical storage media, publishers need to consider how secure the information is. A publisher does not want another company or individual to obtain its information in an electronic form and then turn around and publish it. Similarly, a publisher may not want someone to have access to the database and change elements in it, thus destroying the integrity of the database.

Most retrieval systems will eventually need to address this issue. Businesses that have databases with time-dependent information may not be as concerned about potential loss of information or data security, but most cannot afford the luxury of indifference. Information has become a valuable commodity that needs to be secured in some way.

Summary. The size of the database, the need for updating, the type of information, and the desirability to have data protection will all influence the type of products developed for distribution on magnetic and optical discs.

462

4. Costs

Time.   How long does it take to get a product to market? This is a key question that is tied to the cycle of product updating and the market window. In actual calendar time, we have found it takes between three and six months to do the work necessary to take a new database, analyze the information, create indexes, develop the unique encryption scheme (these first steps are performed on a mainframe computer), download to the PC, create custom menus, match with the software, and test the product. Updates can be done much more quickly. If one is moving toward a floppy or hard disk product, all that is left is packaging and disk duplication. If the product is to be released on CD ROM, at least an additional month is required for mastering and replication.

Dollars.   CD ROM mastering and replication costs have dropped considerably in the past six months. The price schedule released by Philips in November of 1985 states that mastering is $3000 per disc and that quantities of 50-99 are $20 each. By the time there are at least 1000 copies, the cost drops to $10 per disc. Digital Equipment has released information on its disc production services that apply to "databases already loaded with software and properly formatted. The service includes final verification, tape formatting, arranging for mastering and replication and disc testing." The average price for 50-100 discs will be between $7500 and $12,500. The pricing of 3M's mastering and replication services is similar.

Software costs generally have more complex structures, since they represent a variety of arrangements: joint ventures, software costs per unit, fixed fee/flat rate, royalties for either publisher or integrator, etc. Software publishers' services range from supplying the software (and the publisher does the rest) to full service (with complete packages and documentation delivered). The costs may range from very little to over $100,000. Today's costs depend upon: (1) your database requirements, (2) what services you receive, and (3) what future revenues you are willing to give up.

5. Marketing

Role of Added Value in Choosing the Electronic Product.   The same good marketing wisdom used in creating print or online products should be used in developing magnetic or CD ROM publications. The temptation is to believe that a new technology will alter the attractiveness of the product. Choose a product that is successful now; it is likely to also be successful in the new format. If the electronic format provides added value, then a higher price can be charged and it will sell well. Information that no one wanted before will probably still not be wanted when marketed on CD ROM.

With optical discs offering the unlimited access of a book and the sophisticated search capability of an online database, whole new applications will emerge and new publishers will be attracted to electronic publishing.

Protecting Current Products.   The publishers we work with express concern about protecting the sales of their print products and maintaining revenues from their online files. In general, print products have not been cannibalized by online publication. In some cases the sales of the print product have gone up. This is primarily true when the online database creates an awareness of the print version among a new group of users. Similarly, there is probably little reason to worry about losing many sales from the print version after the introduction of the magnetic or CD ROM version. However, should paper costs continue to escalate and warehousing costs continue to rise, publishers may wish to deliberately move users to the electronic format. In a growing number of cases, however, publishers have stated that they have lost print subscriptions to online services and that this has hurt their profits. This situation has been made worse when the publisher is not the online distributor and is unable to control or influence the pricing in a timely fashion.

The movement between online and off-line use of a product is more difficult to predict. Off-line products, at least initially, are likely to be sold to people who are not currently online users or who plan to use the off-line product in a different way than the online version. For instance, Micro-Reviews (a KAware product developed for Database Services, owner of the Microcomputer Index) is marketed to libraries. In many of these libraries the reference librarian is already an online user of the larger DIALOG file. The off-line product is purchased to provide patrons easy access without the continuing online charges. MicroReviews can be purchased like a book or journal and use does not have to be charged separately. The more use it gets, the more cost-effective it is. Since Micro-Reviews is a segment of a larger and older database, Microcomputer Index, searches of a broader and more complex nature can still be done online. Reference librarians often restrict use of the online version since it must come out of a limited budget or be charged back to the patron.

Similarly, the American Society of Hospital Pharmacists (ASHP) is marketing a KAware version of their Consumer Drug Digest. Although the same database is an online file available through several vendors, ASHP is marketing Consumer Drug Information on Disc (CDID) to clinics, hospitals, physicians' offices, and pharmacies that are unlikely to log into an online system to get specially tailored information for patients. The cost economics work well for this off-line product.

463

464

Companies that plan to use CD ROMs for distribution of large databases will have to learn how to do it most efficiently.

Again, drawing on the experience of Knowledge Access, it may be appropriate to bundle the electronic database products with the print publication. For instance, the College Board sells *College Explorer* (the electronic publication) shrink-wrapped with *The College Handbook* (the printed publication).

Another way to protect a current product line is to make the electronic version different. For instance, Market Statistics (producers of the *Survey of Buying Power*) has chosen to segment its database into a series of products using the KAware retrieval system.

With still another approach, Harris Information Services has made the features of the off-line version of its *Who's Who in Electronics* (developed by Knowledge Access) so different from the print or online (with Videolog) version that it anticipates little migration. Those clients wanting the mailing list and telemarketing features of the off-line version cannot find the same features in the print and online products.

Pricing and product differentiation still are the major barriers to unwanted migration.

Future Considerations

Staring into the crystal ball and making predictions is a chancy proposition. Writing the predictions is even riskier. However, in a technological area that has changed so much in the past, it would be foolish to believe that the 1985 and 1986 considerations by publishers entering the standalone microcomputer database market will be the same in 1987 and 1988. Since the answers are less likely to survive the future, we have prepared some questions that appear to be insensitive to the march of time and technology:

1. What is the installed base of CD ROM drives?

2. What market share does each of the major compact disc manufacturers have?

3. What other storage technologies or changes in the current technology may alter the marketplace (e.g., large hard disks, magneto-optic disk drives for read/write, Drexon Card, etc.)?

4. What will changes in production capabilities mean to cost (e.g., number of CD drives manufactured per month, disc replication capacity at plants in U.S., Europe, and Asia, etc.)?

5. What is the best way of selling this new medium? (Are new distribution channels opening up?)

6. How price-sensitive is the market for electronic products?

7. Do I need to sell hardware (CD ROM players) to gain entrance to my marketplace?

8. Is my competition likely to use this new technology to gain market share?   **465**

9. How much will this technology require of my publishing organization (extra costs, development, staff time)?

10. What are the current pricing structures and how can I make a profit?

Conclusion

Confidence in the new mix of print, online, and off-line products will grow as the success stories are first made and then told. To create these successes, publishers, hardware manufacturers, and software companies need to understand both the opportunities for value-added products and the marketing challenges of the new magnetic and optical storage technologies.

About the Authors

Matilda Butler, Ph.D., is president of Knowledge Access Inc., Mountain View, California. She was formerly director of technology and communication at the Far West Laboratory in San Francisco. She has written several books, book chapters, and journal articles on the use of new information technologies in business and the professions. She is currently heading a National Library of Medicine project to develop standalone microcomputer-based information products for health professionals. Her direct involvement with health information extends back to research on the ATS-6 communication satellite in 1975, and her involvement with computer-based systems dates from NSF-sponsored research in 1977.

William Paisley, Ph.D., is executive vice president of Knowledge Access Inc. He left Stanford University, where he was a professor of communication, to join Knowledge Access in the fall of 1985. For more than 20 years, his research on new information technologies has ranged from communication satellites to videotex, online retrieval systems, and microcomputers. Paisley's recent publications include *Children and Microcomputers*, published by Sage Publications in 1985; "Rhythms of the Future," in the 1985 volume *Libraries and the Information Economy of California*; and *The Communication Sciences*, to be published by Ablex in 1986. He was a keynote speaker at the 1985 annual meeting of the American Society for Information Science.

Frances Spigai is president of Database Services Inc.—owner of the Microcomputer Index, which is published in print, online, and disk formats—and vice president of Knowledge Access. She was previously director of marketing for Dialog Information Systems. She has authored many publications on information media and publishes a column in Information Today. Ms. Spigai will be the keynote speaker for the ONLINE '86 conference; she was recently elected to the board of directors of the Information Industry Association and will chair IIA's first conference on CD ROM, to be held in San Francisco in July 1986.

Knowledge Access Inc.
2685 Marine Way, Suite 1305
Mountain View, CA 94043

References

Butler, Matilda. "New Disc-Based Publishing Opportunities." Presentation at the Information Industry Association Midyear Meeting, Chicago, May 1985.

Paisley, William. "Design Considerations in the Shift from Online to Standalone Microcomputer Retrieval System." Invited address at the 1984 Annual Meeting of the American Society of Information Science.

Shuford, Richard S. CD ROMs and their kin. *BYTE*, November 1985.

Spigai, Frances. Databases on disk: Publications for libraries. *Library Hi Tech*, Winter 1985.

Steiger, Bettie A. Quoted by Tim Miller *in* Pioneer on optical disc frontier: Reference Technology, *Information Today*, December 1985.

From Online to Ondisc

by Rick Meyer

The patron of a reference library must make a special trip to visit the library, but once there is surrounded by a wealth of information in publications someone else bought and paid for. Visiting the library is a special mission, hard to intermingle casually with other duties. Arriving with only a general research objective in mind, the patron may browse, looking for publications useful to the search, perhaps with the assistance of the reference librarian. Information found in one publication may lead to the idea of looking in another publication. In many reference rooms the patron may not check out the publication but must carefully copy out the information needed.

Many of the PCs currently in place are underutilized and could be put to profitable use with new applications, such as retrieving information from an ondisc database.

If this patron is a business professional, a bookshelf near his or her desk undoubtedly has publications as well. Contrasted with the publications in the reference library, these publications are close at hand for easy, frequent reference, rather than in some distant location. These publications are far fewer in number, since they were selected and paid for well in advance of use. They may be consulted casually in the midst of other duties. Browsing for relevant publications with a general objective in mind is not possible; the private collection contains only publications preselected for relevance to ongoing activities. Located information need not be copied out; the publication may lie open at the desk as long as necessary. If a search identifies another useful source, it is likely that publication is not at hand but must be sought elsewhere, perhaps by a special trip to the library.

Major online information services are like reference libraries. Although the terminal or PC for online access may be on the desk, the online "patron" must go through the steps of connecting to the remote service, selecting a communications network and logging on, steps analogous to visiting the reference library. The major online services also contain a wealth of information that, in most cases, need not be paid for in advance. With a general objective in mind, and aided by the service's documentation, the user may browse for relevant databases. Early search results may lead to the idea of looking in other unanticipated databases. Useful "hits" are extracted through local or remote printing. Being online is not, however, a casual occasion to mix with other duties since ongoing charges are accruing.

CD ROM databases purchased for the use of a business professional are like his or her private collection of publications. They are more accessible than online databases because they are local and no communications connection or remote host logon procedure is necessary. Like the private publication collection, the collection of CD ROMs is tiny compared with the number of databases in a major online service, since each CD ROM database must be selected and paid for in advance.

Most announced CD ROM databases are offered under flat-rate pricing where a "subscription" has a fixed price, irrespective of use, and this type of offering is assumed throughout this chapter. It should be kept in mind, though, that CD ROM databases could be metered and even that online databases could be offered at a flat rate. With no communications link or logon procedure and no meter running, consulting CD ROM information can be casual and mixed with other work. Browsing for a relevant CD ROM database, on the other hand, is not possible; only a few preselected databases are likely to be available. If a search in a CD ROM helps identify another source, it most likely must be obtained through an online service or at a library. Having the CD ROM readily at hand, it is less often necessary to copy the found information.

The analogy eventually breaks down; reference libraries do not have direct or hourly charges, for example. But one point is clear: CD ROM is not just a simple replacement for online services, or for paper or microforms. It is a whole new medium with enough differences from existing media to require a reexamination of appropriate products and markets.

Database producers seeking to make profitable use of this new medium without making expensive, if not disastrous, mistakes must consider not only the nature of the medium but other complex marketing and business issues as well. The purpose of this chapter is not to provide answers but to explore the nature of the medium by contrasting it with the online medium and to identify at least some of these issues for case-by-case strategic and product planning.

Objectives of CD ROM Distribution

Many database producers contemplating CD ROM publication are profit-seeking businesses deriving existing revenues from print and/or online publication of the same information considered for CD ROM. The objective of CD ROM publication is thus typically to optimize overall long-term profits from the information product, including all media of distribution. If CD ROM publication offers incremental revenues and profits with little additional expense and without impacting existing revenue streams, the situation is very attractive. Whether this will be the situation is as yet unclear. Will CD ROM attract new customers, or will existing customers substitute CD ROM for print publication or online use? If substitute use is expected, will profitability be higher or lower than from the print or online counterpart? Is a product containing a subset or superset of an online database a new product with new customers, or will it, too, result in substitute use? Will use patterns of a CD ROM product be equivalent to use of an online password for pricing purpose? The questions are many and interrelated. They do not readily lend themselves to general answers and a detailed analysis of issues is required on a case-by-case basis.

End User or Intermediary Medium?

The differences between the CD ROM and online media from the individual user's point of view, as revealed in the reference library analogy above, are summarized below:

Attribute	Online	CD ROM
Number of databases	Large	Limited
Need anticipation	Unanticipated use	Anticipated use
Browse for files	Can browse	Can't browse
Price basis	Pay as used	Pay in advance
Access	Requires comm, logon	Immediate
Casualness	Noncasual	Casual
Work pattern	Explicit session	Blends in work
Hardware	Terminal or PC, modem, telephone	PC, CD ROM drive, card

In addition to these use situation factors, further factors will tend to determine the kinds of products, customers, and use appropriate to the CD ROM medium.

Online retrieval is a form of time-sharing, while "ondisc" retrieval (to adopt a coined term for this alternative) is an extension of the personal computer. The personal computer now pervades the workplace and library as a tool for people such as financial analysts, writers, and product managers (knowledge workers) who process information. It is this same knowledge worker who is the elusive "end user" targeted by the online industry. Although personal computers are increasingly used as terminals to communicate with mainframes, and electronic mail use is growing in popularity, most current use of personal computers is for standalone applications.

Ondisc information will have tendencies to penetrate certain end-user markets faster than online information, for some of the same reasons that personal computers have become the knowledge worker's tool. PCs are self-contained and under local personal control, an important psychological consideration. Telecommunications is perceived as difficult for end users. Time-sharing of all kinds is subject to occasional garbled messages, downtime, and slow response time (local systems are not as affected by these problems).

Assuming flat-rate database pricing, after the initial subscription commitment there are no further variable expenses, compared with ongoing hourly charges for time-sharing. The pressure of hourly charges often induces anxiety. Anxiety can be reduced by planning an online session, but it is often necessary to refine a search strategy interactively, based on intermediate results. It is not necessary to "think on your feet" while searching for information on a CD ROM; there are no consequences for mistakes, pauses, deadends, or consultations with the manual. All in all, it's a much friendlier situation.

Many of the PCs currently in place are underutilized and could be put to profitable use with new applications, such as retrieving information from an ondisc database. Knowledge workers are now used to the idea of getting new peripherals, learning new software, and moving information between applications. Retrieved information is very often destined for incorporation into a word processing document, spreadsheet, or local database in the same personal computer that is used for retrieval. Expertise in searching and in the content and organization of particular databases must generally be acquired through billable connect hours, requiring a serious commitment, while ondisc skills may be acquired more casually, as with other PC software. The interface to CD ROM search software can be friendlier than online search languages, designed for dumb terminals that don't take advantage of PC capabilities. Even friendlier interfaces can more readily be developed to reside in PCs than in host computers, for both technical and economic reasons.

470

Taken together, this group of factors should tend to make the CD ROM medium significantly more acceptable to the end-user market for some kinds of information and use. But with the technology come other factors less favorable to end users. Knowledge workers engaged in occasional or varied research projects often cannot predict the databases they will need to use or how much they will use them, so they will probably continue to use online databases.

Database producers seeking to make profitable use of this new medium without making expensive, if not disastrous, mistakes must consider not only the nature of the medium but other complex marketing and business issues as well.

It is easier to justify occasional or casual use with pay-as-you-go online charges than the substantial outlay for equipment and subscriptions required by announced CD ROM databases—an outlay which will have to be planned and budgeted as a capital investment rather than a simple expense in many organizations. While pay-as-you-go metering of CD ROM use is technically feasible, it requires special administration and support, and the outlay for equipment remains. Substantial upfront costs will tend to limit the end-user market to certain specialists with heavy and predictable information needs, such as lawyers and financial analysts, rather than reaching the broader knowledge worker market of interest to database producers. Contrasted with the situation for end users, intermediaries such as librarians and "information brokers" are much more likely to be able to predict heavy use of CD ROM databases and to plan and justify their acquisition, since it is part of their primary rather than secondary duties.

With factors on both sides of the question, it is hard to tell whether CD ROM will find a better home among intermediaries or end users.

One type of use seems to fit the characteristics of the CD ROM medium and avoid the limitations. Intermediaries currently do most of the searching on behalf of end users. If an intermediary attempted to help an end user do his or her own search using the intermediary's online terminal and password, the charges would probably be higher due to the lower proficiency of the end user; charges would be more difficult to control without billing the user's organization. Once the intermediary installs a CD ROM retrieval system, however, there is no cost penalty in supporting even a floundering end user other than the intermediary's time. Although a system might not be justified for an individual end user, intermediaries can justify a system for use by a number of end users at the intermediary's facilities. The intermediary's role can then make a transition from researcher to consultant and coach. In this capacity the intermediary can help an end user while attending to other duties, or even support a number of end users at once, assisting in the retrieval of much more useful information for more end users than was possible as a researcher. This form of use, as well as end user searching generally, will benefit from the development of user-friendly search languages.

Matching Products to Distribution Media

What considerations can be used to determine whether a product better fits the new medium or the existing online medium?

Anticipated Use

Since purchase of a CD ROM database must be planned in advance of use, the medium fits information that people expect to use regularly and are likely to remember when it comes time to review needs and prepare budgets, a situation similar to the purchase of printed reference products today. Databases that people discover they need only in the midst of a search are inappropriate.

Heavy use. Further, the anticipated use must be heavy enough to justify the prices involved in advance. If a database will be consulted only a few times a year, or if the degree of use cannot be reliably predicted, it is probably not a candidate for sale on any fixed-price basis, even if it generates acceptable revenue online. This is a classic buy-or-rent decision.

Ready Reference Works

Voluminous reference works consulted very briefly or spontaneously in the midst of normal daily work, such as dictionaries, thesauruses, specifications, and the like are not ideally suited to online distribution, since the overhead of establishing communications and logging on is high and it is not practical to stay logged on. Thesauruses and other reference works have proven to be successful aids to online searching of other materials, but these aids are not used as databases in their own right. The lower-access overhead of CD ROM and the possibility of leaving the CD ROM mounted and search software running all day, a use situation closer to print media, makes independent reference applications feasible.

Currency

Online information can be very current because new information can be continuously uploaded to the host computer and is then accessible almost immediately. CD ROMs, on the other hand, must be duplicated and physically delivered to the site where they are used. To this delay must be added the period until the next update is received. Early CD ROM subscriptions promise quarterly updates, and at least one product promises monthly updates. As production and distribution systems are built up and streamlined, the delay between generation of information and its availability to the user can be reduced, but it will still be measured in weeks. The costs of information delivery increase with update frequency, and these costs must be passed on to the subscriber. Information requiring a high degree of currency is thus not suitable for CD ROM unless it is augmented by a second, more timely medium.

Completeness

Some online databases are typically used in connection with other databases. Online, it is simple to repeat the same search in a series of databases since all available databases are in the same place. Offering on CD ROM a single database that is one member of such a set would not make sense, since the user would still have to perform most of the search online in the remaining databases, negating any advantage of CD ROM. It would be better to offer the entire group on CD ROM or nothing.

Database Size

CD ROMs hold about 550 megabytes. Other optical media of larger capacity exist, and more will be developed; but they are not likely to have the advantages of standardization and high-volume, reliable mass production for consumers that compact disc technology enjoys. Many popular online databases are several times larger than 550 megabytes. Generally, it is not practical to divide a database among several CD ROMs. Frequently used commands must rapidly scan the entire database, and this would require an unacceptable amount of disc swapping. A multiple-disc product can make sense in certain cases, however. In one strategy, indexes or abbreviated records are placed on one disc and full records are placed on the others. All searching is done on the disc with indexes, and full records are retrieved from the rest of the discs.

Another multiple-disc strategy is to partition the whole database into segments, using a principle of partitioning that will minimize disc swapping. Partitioning by time or by subject content may make sense, but a product in too many pieces or with awkward partitioning will not get used. Solid knowledge of user needs and use patterns plus beta testing are needed to verify such a scheme.

Another way around the disc capacity problem is to publish a useful subset of the complete database. In a number of fast-moving technical fields, for example, researchers are interested only in work done in the past five years, so older information need not be included on the disc. Extracting a subset based on subject content may appeal to an attractive target market even if that market is smaller than that for the whole database. The subsetting principles to consider are similar to those for partitioning multiple-disc databases.

If a reasonable subset or multiple-disc partitioning of a large database cannot be found, then consideration of CD ROM distribution must be abandoned.

Possibility of Multimedia Information Services

By now, it should be clear that the online and ondisc media each have unique strengths and weaknesses. Many products and types of use fit one medium better than the other. The strengths of online distribution that are not matched by ondisc distribution ensure a continued and substantial future for online distribution despite the many attractions of CD ROM technology.

CD ROM is not just a simple replacement for online services, or for paper or microforms. It is a whole new medium with enough differences from existing media to require a reexamination of appropriate products and markets.

Why not unify the two media into a multimedia information service that offers the best of both? What are the possibilities?

The local but limited collection of ondisc databases can be supplemented by the full library of databases in a major online service. The local PC and remote online host can each do the work most appropriate to it. Ideally, the multimedia service will use the same search language whether the database is local or remote and there will be relatively seamless facilities for continuing a local search remotely and otherwise integrating the unified service.

The user will select and purchase CD ROMs for which heavy use is anticipated and rely on online information for searches of less frequently used databases. In fact, the user may be able to try the online versions of ondisc databases first to establish the utility of the data and degree of use on a pay-as-you-go basis, monitoring use and costs on the service's regular invoices before deciding to invest in a subscription. If an online database proves its usefulness, but individual use patterns demand quick, frequent, casual consultations in the midst of ongoing work, making connect and logon overhead objectionable, then perhaps a low-overhead CD ROM counterpart is available. When needs change or a new project is initiated, any database is immediately available online before a subscription can be justified, purchased, and received. If an individual search of a local database suggests the need for information in another database, the search can smoothly continue online rather than reach a stopping point.

Some portions of a database or group of related databases can be distributed locally while other portions remain online. For example, in a database containing both recent and historic data, frequently consulted recent information may be kept locally while infrequently consulted historic backfiles may reside in online archives. Conversely, where very current information is needed, the search strategy may be developed and used on disc and be carried into more recent online updates of the same databases when it becomes necessary. This strategy can provide more currency than ondisc only, and at less overall cost, making possible hybrid products not feasible otherwise.

For databases too large for CD ROM, instead of taking a subset or partitioning onto multiple discs, it could be very convenient to keep indexes or abbreviated records locally. When relevant hits are found locally, corresponding complete online records could be retrieved. Bibliographic data can be local and corresponding full text, or even images, remote.

It is clear that the ondisc and online services can complement each other very well and offer a more complete and convenient service than ondisc alone. If such multimedia services are well designed and implemented, what kinds of isolated CD ROM products will remain viable?

Pricing and Cannibalization

Given the objective of maximizing the profits of combined online, ondisc, and print versions, how should a subscription to a CD ROM database be priced?

The emerging market expectation is that ondisc information will be far cheaper than online information. After all, the online distributor's giant mainframe and telecommunications network is no longer needed, so telecommunications and connect charges are no longer necessary. The necessary equipment is a simple PC and CD ROM drive, which are owned by the user. Once these are owned by the user, the only distribution cost is CD ROM duplication. It is well publicized that CD ROMs may be duplicated for a few dollars a copy in volume. Duplicating and distributing CD ROMs is a process like book publishing, and has costs of the same order of magnitude, even cheaper in some cases, so CD ROM subscriptions should be priced like books rather than online services. Can these expectations be met?

Maybe not. The computer, central storage, and network for an online service are multimillion-dollar investments, but the costs are apportioned among all users. In a major online service there are considerable economies of scale. Here's an example. If it costs a hypothetical online service $3 million a year to amortize and maintain its distribution equipment, and if the cost is divided among 10,000 users, the average cost per user would be only $333 per year—about a third the cost of a CD ROM subsystem. Actual figures are not available, but educated guessing along these lines is illuminating.

What, then, is the rough cost structure of large-scale online distribution? It includes:

○ Host computer system

○ Network

○ Royalties to database producers

○ Database design

○ File processing and updating

○ Programming

○ Documentation

○ Training

○ Customer service

○ Marketing

○ Sales

○ Legal, general, and administrative, other overhead

In fact, host and network costs are only two elements of these overall expenses. If a business of the same size and level of an online service were set up exclusively for CD ROM distribution, the only clear major changes in the cost structure would be in host and network expenses. The impact of the new technology on costs is smaller than would be expected from a superficial examination.

It is also clear for print, online, and ondisc distribution alike that the incremental cost of delivering another copy or adding a user is small compared with fixed costs. Therefore, pricing should be highly dependent on volume. So, compared with online pricing, ondisc pricing can be less if significantly higher volumes may be expected. Should database producers establish CD ROM subscription pricing in the same order as print publication in expectation of a massive market? This experiment has been undertaken by Grolier with its $199 CD ROM encyclopedia. Yet it is not clear from the examination of the nature of the medium if this will be so, since there are factors on both sides of the question. The advisability of the mass market approach will be highly dependent on the nature of the information and its users.

A classic rational approach to pricing an isolated product can be used when the demand and cost curves are known. Given a typical demand curve with an increasing market for a decreasing price and a cost curve showing declining per-unit costs for increasing production volume, a price to optimize profitability can be chosen mathematically. Are these curves known in the case of a CD ROM product?

477

In general, the price elasticity or demand curve of products supplied by the information industry is not well known. Would a large price reduction bring a much larger market and higher profits? No one knows. The common wisdom is that libraries have fixed budgets so that price adjustments cannot increase revenues. It is also generally accepted that must-know business information is not price-sensitive. Even these two factors have not been adequately quantified.

Added to these general pricing considerations is the problem of cannibalization of revenues of online counterparts. Online pricing is use-dependent: the more searching and retrieval, the higher the charges. Ondisc pricing of most products announced as of this writing is use-independent: the charges per subscription are fixed and do not vary with use.

When a fixed-price ondisc version of a variable-price online database is introduced, what will happen to combined revenues? One likely tendency is that the heavy online users whose yearly billing substantially exceeds the ondisc subscription price will switch to the ondisc version because it is more cost-effective and more convenient as well. A large user like Bell Laboratories need pay no more than a small local library. Overall revenues from this group could decline, resulting in cannibalization of the user base. A few online users whose online use is less than the subscription price would tend to upgrade to obtain unlimited use and other advantages, but the increased revenues from this group would probably not fully offset the decreased revenues from the heavy user group.

These relationships, considered in isolation, will tend to be true at any ondisc price level. However, as the ondisc price is increased there are fewer heavy users who will switch and fewer light users who will upgrade. The degree of cannibalization can be reduced, but there will be a smaller total market for the ondisc product. As the price is decreased, cannibalization and upgrades increase and the potential market grows. Online vendors are in the best position to collect and analyze current and future data necessary for these pricing decisions.

Even with identical information and search facilities in both online and ondisc versions, the migration of users between media on purely economic

Knowledge workers engaged in occasional or varied research projects often cannot predict the databases they will need to use or how much they will use them, so they will probably continue to use online databases.

478

grounds will not be complete. There are enough differences between the media and use situations that each will have some exclusive users. Some old-time online searchers may avoid switching despite economic incentives, out of force of habit. Personal computer buffs who are introduced to searching may feel much more comfortable starting with a local peripheral and software and no meter running. Personal preference, familiarity, and convenience count too. These factors will tend to make the combined market larger than either individual market could be alone.

Another factor tending toward a larger combined market is unlimited use. In an online situation, the tendency is to limit use to control costs. In contrast, once the fixed prices associated with ondisc information are paid, the incentive is to get the maximum use out of what has already been bought. This factor will increase utilization among existing users and draw more people into searching, creating a larger user base that will lead to market growth as more users become familiar with information services.

Duplicating and distributing CD ROMs is a process like book publishing, and has costs of the same order of magnitude, even cheaper in some cases, so CD ROM subscriptions should be priced like books rather than online services.

Is a CD ROM subscription equivalent to an online password for pricing purposes? It might seem so, but a password is typically used by a single person. If not, it doesn't matter, since revenues are proportional to total site use, not the number of passwords. The personal computer was originally intended for use by a single person, but surveys by Infocorp and others have shown about three to five users per PC in U.S. businesses, with heavier sharing in the large corporations where online use is heavier. Use of PCs in libraries and other sites where information products are used is not known, nor is it possible to reliably predict the average number of users who will share a CD ROM subscription. Yet site revenues for fixed-rate CD ROM subscriptions will be proportional to the number of subscriptions, not the total use. The incentive exists to maximize utilization through sharing, once a fixed-price subscription has been bought. More uncertainty is introduced by possible attempts to connect CD ROM drives as file servers on increasingly popular local or wide-area networks, or make the PC host into a bulletin board available to any caller, with or without the cooperation of the information vendors.

Added to the complexity is the fact that real ondisc products will very often not be identical to their online counterparts. Instead, they will often be subsets, reduced in size through time, subject content, or completeness of records, or they will be composites, joined with other information. The value of information varies, too, with its context of related information and expense of digesting and incorporating it in some desired end product.

The above pricing factors apply only to online and ondisc distribution. A complete analysis often would have to include print distribution as well.

Identifying all the major factors that should affect pricing decisions is hard enough. Quantifying each factor and arriving at an optimal price is impossible, since much of the necessary information is unavailable. For now, CD ROM pricing, especially of products offered in other media, is a big puzzle. The experience gained from early offerings in the next year or two will help solve the puzzle.

Choice of Partners

Given this complex and uncertain situation, how should a database producer enter the market with CD ROM products? A number of small and startup companies that could be nicknamed "ROM shops" are offering to put information in CD ROM format, handle CD duplication, and provide necessary hardware. This set of services is designed to allow database producers to market their own products directly, without dependence on online distributors. On the other hand, there are indications that the major online distributors are preparing to use the CD ROM medium as well. Assuming that database producers will have the choice between marketing a product with the assistance of a ROM shop or working with an established online vendor, what choice is best strategically and financially?

The do-it-yourself alternative appears attractive to some database producers seeking higher margins. Database producers often believe they know the markets for their own information better than the online distributors whose marketing efforts are spread among many products. Why not avoid these and the other real and perceived problems of dealing with online distributors?

What priorities do ROM shops have? They want to maximize sales of their own services, which do not include print or online distribution. ROM shops are in a situation that calls for the highest sales of CD ROMs, even at the expense of the database producer's print or online revenues, now often their bread and butter. Online vendors, on the other hand, can share the database producer's goal of maximizing combined online and ondisc revenues and are in a position to establish special products, programs and monitoring systems to further this goal. Online vendors are in a position to collect and use customer lists and use statistics for existing online products to aid the database producer in product planning and pricing decisions; ROM shops are not.

479

480

Many database producers now use competing multiple online distributors, but by marketing their products directly to users they will be placing themselves in direct competition with online distributors for existing and new customers, the same distributors who are also their major sources of revenue. Such a situation is not impossible but is problematic at best.

Major online distributors are now well established and participate in a proven, relatively stable market. To reach into this market in competition with online distributors might be difficult and expensive. Will current users accept yet another vendor, another search language and database schema, and another set of bills to monitor and pay? To reach at least this known market, many database producers may choose working through an existing major distributor to the riskier course.

Real ondisc products will very often not be identical to their online counterparts; instead, they will often be subsets or composites.

Database producers for existing and new markets must consider relative attractions of the different product offerings that are possible in each case. The ROM shop can help provide a CD ROM subsystem, CD ROMs, and unique software. Online distributors, if they choose, could provide not only these things but a much wider selection of CD ROM products drawn from a number of database producers. Further, only they could provide a multimedia information service uniting the best of both media, as outlined above, from a single vendor and with single billing.

Established online vendors provide more than raw information access; they often transform the data they receive in many ways to facilitate retrieval and ensure the quality of the finished service. Through their market experience they have developed a range of ancillary and support services, such as extensive documentation, training programs, electronic mail, document delivery links, customer services, and invoicing. These additions benefit products offered in both media, and the investment in them can be paid back through combined revenues. A single database producer with the help of a ROM shop would have to add substantial staff resources to duplicate such a complete service. How many of these services would users be willing to do without?

Even without attempting to create such a complete offering, the database producer working with a ROM shop takes on a considerable additional burden. Tapes currently sent to online distributors for file processing and loading also must be sent to the ROM shop and the file work duplicated; the online distributor already has the information in the host system. The ROM shop and associated marketing channels represent another channel to manage and monitor, and one with a tricky and potentially dangerous relationship with the online channel. The database producer doing its own marketing may not initially understand or have efficient systems for identifying, reaching, and selling to customers, and supporting billing and collecting from those customers; nor can the costs of succeeding at these new activities always be accurately predicted.

If the emerging market for CD ROM products is a complex and confusing one for vendors, think of the potential customer's confusion. There is new and unproven hardware and software to evaluate; new information products that have a confusing and complex relationship with related online information; new forms of use, equipment, and information sharing; and a multitude of new vendors, attracted by low entry costs. In a confused and fragmented market, customers look for a known and trusted vendor to bring order and deliver value. In the information industry, the vendors in a position to fill this role are the major established online distributors.

There are undoubtedly unique markets and products that are best approached through the ROM shop instead of the online supermarket. Time will tell which they are.

Conclusion

CD ROM and other optical technologies are bringing the information industry to a critical juncture. A major new medium with characteristics shared with print and online publication and personal computing is fast emerging. The advent of a new technology is often the time when major changes in market position and market share occur and companies rise and fall. Existing business relationships will be reexamined and adjustments made. Overall information-market growth may be dramatic or fail to meet expectations. It is a time for careful strategic and product planning. This article has served its purpose if it has identified some considerations to use in the process.

About the Author

Rick Meyer is the product manager in the Advanced Technology Group at DIALOG Information Services, Inc. Mr. Meyer has over ten years' experience in the microcomputer industry. Prior to joining DIALOG, he was responsible for future product planning and development at MicroPro International Corporation.

DIALOG Information Services, Inc.
3460 Hillview Avenue
Palo Alto, CA 94304

CD ROM APPLICATIONS

Market Considerations

Data Publishing on Optical Discs

by Martin Hensel

Data distribution on optical discs will completely change the structure of electronic publishing. Few information organizations fully understand the impact of this change or are prepared to capitalize on their opportunities.

487

The cost structure of optical discs is dramatically different from that of other data distribution alternatives such as floppy disks or magnetic tape. Optical disc costs are similar to those for phonograph records or traditional book printing; there is an initial setup charge and a low per-copy cost thereafter. However, due to the stamping process used, the cost of optical discs is ⅟₅₀ as much as the cost of traditional printing for equivalent content, and the information is kept in a computer-searchable form. Thus, all the free text searching and DBMS capabilities that are available online from Dialog, BRS, or DRI can be incorporated into standalone microcomputer systems, with no ongoing telecommunications connection or cost.

Armed with only a microcomputer and optical disc player, the information user will be able to access entire collections of databases that have been purchased on disc.

The basic technology for read-only optical discs was developed to distribute movies and high-fidelity music. During the past decade hundreds of millions of dollars were spent in Europe, Japan, and the United States by consumer electronics companies to make the videodisc (12-inch) and audiodisc (4.72-inch) inexpensive, reliable, and long lasting. Data distribution on derivatives of these discs was a natural and direct extension of the basic technology. Today, 800 megabytes and 600 megabytes of error-free capacity are available on the data versions of the videodisc and audiodisc.

Most databases are well suited for publishing on a read-only disc. Online databases are frequently updated monthly or quarterly, and even those that are updated continuously often require a large historical file for meaningful analysis. Thus, issuing discs on a monthly or quarterly basis would provide service comparable to what generally exists today. Where data updates with current information are required, hybrid systems are feasible and cost-effective. These would keep large volumes of historical data locally on optical discs and provide online access to recent data. Searches or calculations using both data sources could be done simultaneously so that users aren't aware that they are using anything other than a single database.

Armed with only a microcomputer and optical disc player, the information user will be able to access entire collections of databases that have been purchased on disc. But note, once purchased, there is no variable cost to use the disc databases. The resulting savings are significant. Even if there is no other justification for buying the microcomputer and player, they pay for themselves with three hours activity per week when the alternative is online connect charges (excluding the database royalty).

488

The demand for information is generally considered highly elastic in that it is sensitive to both cost and the total time required to get an answer. Optical disc technology will definitely lower the cost and reduce the time to get information; however, its larger impact may come from the psychological advantage it has over online access. With it, the user is completely self-contained. Gone is the required umbilical tether to a central host; gone is the nervousness about making a mistake; and gone is the feeling that someone may be watching.

Opportunities

Databases for library and professional reference use are the most likely candidates for disc publishing. These include most of the current online databases plus many more works that heretofore have not had an economically viable electronic distribution conduit.

Information providers (IPs), and in turn information users, should benefit most from disc technology. Online services require substantial capital and technical resources to establish and operate. As a consequence, few IPs currently control the electronic distribution of their editorial product. This is directly reflected by the small portion of online industry revenues that is actually returned to organizations providing editorial content.

The demand for information is generally considered highly elastic in that it is sensitive to both cost and the total time required to get an answer.

This no longer has to be true. A number of companies will convert IP data into discs in a service relationship that corresponds to other services used by the publishing industry, such as typesetting, printing, and subscription fulfillment. The economies of scale in the future will be determined by the number of copies sold of each disc, not the number of hours that subscribers are connected to a particular database host. Consequently, electronic information distribution should become less centralized than it is today. At the same time, copyright owners should be fairly compensated because a physical product will be sold directly to end users. In total, many profitable opportunities will be available to existing and new IPs.

Some of these opportunities are immediate. Certain classes of information users will happily purchase the required microcomputer equipment just to access databases that have high value to them. Creators of these high-value databases can influence the evolution of disc distribution within their markets by the timing of their actions. Significant examples of databases in this class include information products of the National Library of Medicine, other major medical publishers, the Library of Congress, and principal sources of bibliographic records, major legal/tax publishers, ERIC, and Chemical Abstracts Service.

In addition, many large organizations have immediate opportunities for improving the effectiveness of their documentation distribution, both to their own offices and to third parties. Significant examples of databases in this class include information projects of the World Health Organization, U.N. World Publications, Defense Logistics (United States and NATO), plus claim history databases of insurance companies, transaction databases of multinational banks and corporations, and technical documentation for complicated systems such as aircraft, motorized equipment, computers, and software.

Getting Started

The key to getting started is to thoroughly understand how the database (or prospective database) is used. Sample questions that an IP would find worth answering include:

1. What is the total number of users and what is the distribution of use within this total? (For example: How many use the database 5 hours per week, 3 hours per week, 1 hour per week, etc.?)

2. How important is price to expanded use, and in particular, what would be the impact on use of a fixed price? (What percentage of your total potential users are you now serving and how many could you expect to add under alternative pricing scenarios?)

3. What is an acceptable update cycle from your users' perspective, and would this differ substantially under the alternative pricing scenarios explored above?

4. What computer searching functions are necessary for a user to fully extract the editorial value of your database? (Do they need full Boolean logic, free text or keyword, paragraph qualification, word position and numeric searching, etc.?)

5. What other databases are often used in conjunction with your database, and if significant synergy is possible, are those IPs receptive to jointly issuing discs?

Once the use of a database is understood, implementation of optical disc distribution is straightforward. The choice between videodisc and audio-disc formats is impacted by the installed base of players among the users of the database, whether the database has or will have a visual component, and actions of other IPs.

Audiodisc technology has been developed primarily by Philips and Sony. They have announced a single worldwide standard for data distribution under the name of CD ROM. As a result of this standard, players of this type will probable be the most widespread. In contrast, videodisc technology enables visual and sound enhancements, and in certain content areas such as medicine and training, these added features may become very important.

The choice of search software is impacted by the access functionality that is appropriate to the database content, the minimum size of microcomputer with which compatibility is desired, and the necessity of a customized user interface. Fortunately, the selection of search software can be altered over time as new developments occur and the needs of the database evolve. This flexibility is inherent because the search software can be distributed on the same disc as the database. (The user boots the microcomputer from the optical disc and begins searching.) As a consequence, each time a new issue of the database is pressed, the IP has an opportunity to refine software. Because the user interface can generally be made similar regardless of the underlying software package, any change would be transparent to the end user.

Conclusions

Data distribution on optical discs is a reality today. Many IPs have immediate and substantial opportunities to use this technology to expand their markets and retain greater profits.

The impact on the online database industry as we know it will be large and permanent. In retrospect, the distinct, high-valued role of the central database host in electronic information distribution may be viewed as an anomaly.

Only a complex analysis will help produce intelligent decisions regarding whether, when, and how to use optical technology for publishing. The chance of making a costly mistake is high.

We have helped our clients avoid mistakes and effectively use optical technology by asking questions and building comprehensive product plans.

Five areas must be addressed to build a solid plan of optical publishing:

1. Are optical discs appropriate for your products and markets?

2. If so, which disc format is best suited to your situation?

3. Given specific products, what are your customers' requirements for information access and use?

   What are your packaged software options?

4. Which computer(s) will run your software?

   Which can your customers afford?

5. What role, if any, do you want to play in hardware selection and placement?

How do you determine if optical discs are appropriate for your products and markets?

Do some or all of your products add up to a large database? If any of your products are not in computer-readable form now, can you afford to key them?

How often do you update the product(s)? How quickly would products become unacceptably dated if published on a nonchangeable medium like an optical disc? If timeliness is important, are you prepared to maintain an online service so that hybrid disc and online retrieval is possible?

What do your customers now pay for your information?

Would your customers value the functions provided by computer searching?

Would you benefit financially by encouraging the substitution of optical discs for existing online, print, or fiche products?

If optical disc technology is appropriate in general terms, which disc format is best suited to your situation?

Does your product have sound or visual components that make videodiscs uniquely suitable?

Does your product have other attributes which will affect its format?

How many customer sites are likely to be converted to optical disc technology? Are these sites similar or diverse in terms of number of users, intensity of use, scope of customers' interests, and customers' ability to pay?

Are any of these sites international?

491

Each time a new issue of the database is pressed, the IP has an opportunity to refine software.

Given specific products, what are your customers' requirements for information access and use?

(Note: Software and hardware are clearly interdependent. However, software selection is tougher to resolve because your choice often outlives several generations of hardware.)

What are your packaged software options?

How structured is your product? (Does it contain descriptive fields for information such as title, author, subject?)

If your product contains fields, do they need to be separately searchable?

If your product contains free text, does it need to be searchable or merely displayable?

How many Boolean operators and qualifiers are needed to fully extract information from your product? Will your search software need to recognize paragraphs and sentences? Will it need to perform functions on numeric fields, such as distinguishing numbers that are greater than or between other numbers?

What user interface is appropriate for your customers?

Should it be multilingual?

Which computers will run the required software and are affordable to your customers?

What computers do your customers currently use?

If new equipment must be provided, what vendors do your customers consider most reliable?

Should this equipment be dedicated or general-purpose? If general-purpose, should other uses be considered?

What will your customers be willing to pay for hardware, while still perceiving a proper balance with the value of your information?

Should you consider selling or recommending the purchase of specific hardware configurations?

Can that hardware be produced by anyone other than well-established suppliers?

Should you consider offering the hardware as part of the subscription price?

What do you risk by taking a passive role in hardware selection? Would you fracture your customer base by doing so?

Once these areas have been addressed, standard commercial questions—concerning pricing, promotion, distribution, and many other topics—remain to be answered.

Optical publishing does have tremendous potential. Of course, many mistakes can be made before that potential is achieved. Informed planning will chart the clearest course to success.

About the Author

Martin Hensel is vice president of Entree Corporation, a consulting firm specializing in optical disc product development. Before joining Entree Corporation, he was vice president of Wilson-Cambridge, Inc., an electronic publishing and consulting firm specializing in database publishing on optical discs. Previously, he cofounded and was president of LaserData, Inc., the first company to commercialize digital data on videodisc technology.

This article is a composite of a presentation made at the annual meeting of the Information Industry Association in San Francisco during November of 1984 and a paper which appeared in the *Proceedings of the Fifth National Online Meeting*, April 1984. The original paper was compiled by Martha E. Williams and Thomas H. Hogan, Learned Information, Inc., Medford, N.J.

Entree Corporation
P.O. Box 135
Wellesley Hills, MA 02181

Application Development

by
Mary Ann O'Connor

The term "application development" takes on new meaning as we move into the next generation of personal computing. Previously, an application developer was a programmer, or perhaps a software publishing house. The mission was simple: to develop program code that instructed the computer to perform a specific task. Since different computers had various capabilities, it became a matter of selecting the computer that was suited to the task and designing a program around that computer. As competition among the computer manufacturers increased, developers often became more concerned with the long-range success of a particular computer rather than its capabilities.

Today, applications development requires . . . an understanding of the use and potential of the emerging technologies.

Today, applications development requires an understanding of more than programming skills and computer capabilities. It requires an understanding of the market, as well as an understanding of the use and potential of the emerging technologies.

The application developers themselves are changing. We have seen both general and specialty business people creating and marketing products in increasing numbers. Educators also are developing and releasing products in surprising volumes. With the introduction of optical media, even more nonprogrammers are likely to join the ranks.

Why are we interested in this new breed of application developers?

○ Hardware manufacturers are interested because they bring even greater potential to the acceptance of new products. However, they do not necessarily communicate in the same manner as the previous developers. Their understanding and requirements for hardware may, in fact, be quite different. If the real advantages of a product are not successfully communicated to these new developers, a good product may never get a chance in the market.

○ This new breed is also interesting to companies and individuals who feel they might, one day, become one of them. What are the decisions they must make and what skills must they have to be successful in this arena?

○ And finally, they are of interest to consumers who are trying to make a decision about what products to buy in the future. Many want to know if a personal computer is really going to be able to do more than simply word processing and spreadsheets. All the noise lately about talking books and encyclopedias on disc has captured their interest, and suspicions.

495

496

The New Breed

We all recognize the fact that computing is here to stay. We also recognize the fact that creativity is required to move it out of the traditional accounting machine arena. That creativity must come from more than the engineering and programming communities. One place we are beginning to see that happen is in the information industry.

When I refer to the information industry, I include both information provider and information storage communities. Although their applications seem quite similar, they are, in fact, very different. One collects information that has appeal to a specific market segment and provides that information in a variety of forms. The other is usually an in-house manager of information who is responsible for making that information available to the parent organization. Although both deal in information management, they have different goals and objectives. They even have different professional associations and trade shows. The reason I refer to them collectively is that they are going through a major transition at the same time. Both are becoming increasingly computerized, both stand to benefit from optical technologies, and both are becoming application developers for the personal computer industry.

New technology provides new opportunity, and if that opportunity is viewed within an open and creative environment, exciting new products will emerge.

Another group of application developers is the educators and trainers. These people are also professional keepers of information who are seeking creative and effective ways of distributing that information to their audience. Although personal computers have moved into this area in recent years, there is still a great deal of progress to be made.

No matter where they come from, the new application developers will share common concerns and have to make similar critical decisions—often without benefit of previous experience in such a technical field. The purpose of this article is to outline some data storage and distribution issues that face application developers, particularly with regard to optical vs magnetic media.

Application Characteristics

Why do most personal computers contain floppy disk drives? Because floppy disks have been the most practical media in terms of economy and performance when compared with magnetic tapes and hard disks—the only other viable media. Not since the very early days of personal computing has an application developer considered program distribution on anything other than a floppy disk. Cassette tapes were quickly replaced by floppies, and hard disks are obviously impossible distribution alternatives.

Optical discs should change the situation, offering better data integrity, more capacity, and of course lower costs in the long run. This does not mean that floppy disks will not continue to be useful products in the personal computer arena. Rather, new products bring new uses and thus the opportunities and dilemmas for application developers.

497

Let's look at some of the characteristics of an application that must be identified, particularly if optical media are being considered:

The term "application development" takes on new meaning as we move into the next generation of personal computing.

- Who is the audience for the application?

  ○ Is the audience made up of people who have used this application in another format (e.g., print or online information bases)?

  ○ If yes, how does that format compare with optical, with respect to cost, accessibility, speed, convenience? Old habits are hard to break. Does changing the format of the application provide real improvements to the user? If not, it will be difficult to get them to change.

  ○ Are these people familiar with personal computers? Which brands are best represented? How well will you fare if you require the purchase of a new system to obtain the application? If the application is based on an installed base, how many are there?

  ○ What user interface are they familiar with, if any?

  ○ Can that interface be improved upon? Just because it is commonly used doesn't mean that an interface is good.

  ○ Is this audience a specific market niche? Does the product have potential appeal to a broader base? Can it be enhanced or modified to appeal to other markets? Is the application for business only? Does it have potential appeal to a home user?

- What is the current format of the information to be contained in the application?

  ○ Is it text only?

  ○ Can it be enhanced with audio, graphics, or video?

  ○ Does it require moving video, or is still video adequate?

  ○ What is the computer configuration required to display the application? What are the requirements that this imposes on the customer? Are these requirements realistic and justifiable?

- How interactive is the application? Is performance an issue?

- How often does the application change or require new information?

- If an information base is to be used, in what form is it currently available?

  ○ Will the data have to be digitized?

  ○ What is the file format?

- Will the end users merely access data, or do they need to be able to manipulate it?

- Will the end users be adding data at their workstations?

- What is the volume of user data?

- How often is the entire database accessed by the users?

This list of questions is not all-inclusive. Rather, it gives some insight into the amount of advance planning required to develop a successful application.

No matter where they come from, the new application developers will share common concerns and have to make similar critical decisions— often without benefit of previous experience in such a technical field.

How does an application developer go about finding the appropriate media once they have answered the above questions? Table 1 provides a summary of some of the characteristics of personal computer storage media, both currently available and under development. The media detailed here are only those with a form factor of approximately 5.25 inches. There are, of course, many other devices and sizes of media which could be considered. For the sake of this discussion, however, I have tried to utilize the most common personal computer configurations. If an application falls outside the characteristics listed here, additional study must be made, particularly in the areas of cost justification.

When analyzing an application to determine the appropriate media, many factors must be considered. Depending upon the application, this could become a very complex process. It is difficult to develop a formula or chart which simplifies this process because every application has its unique characteristics and goals. Where cost may have more weight in one situation, usability may have more in another. For example, it may be more cost-effective to distribute a large-application product on five floppy disks rather than CD ROM. On the other hand, if the user environment is such that durability, copy protection, and/or ease of use are critical, then CD ROM may be more appropriate.

Storage and/or Distribution Media for Personal Computers

Media	Key Features	Target Applications
Cassette tape	Lowest-cost media, variable capacity (up to 60MB), easy to transport and store, not durable, slow access/serial	Backup of data files, backup of program files
Floppy disk	Relatively low cost ($1-$3), easily transportable, difficult to copy-protect, capacity to 1.5MB, more durable than tape	Program distribution, user data storage, limited copy protection, limited backup storage
Hard disk	High cost ($500-$1500 per 10MB), medium to large capacity (avg 10-20MB), high-speed access, more reliable and durable than floppy	User data storage (not archival), per program storage, download reference data
CD ROM	Low-cost media in volume ($2-$5), low-cost drive ($500), large capacity (500-600MB), durable, fast data access, current high mastering cost, still-video storage	Reference data distributor (large volume), large program distributor (large volume), interactive training
Writable compact disc	High-cost media ($250), high-cost drive ($3000-$5000), no mastering costs, large capacity (100MB), still-video storage	Reference data distributor, large program distributor, backup storage, download reference data, interactive training
Read-write compact disc	Expected high cost, expected large capacity	To be determined, currently unavailable

The point to remember here is that no one medium suits all situations, nor can one generalize about the suitability of a particular medium to a specific environment. CD ROM is an exciting new medium, as is write-once optical disc. Each has advantages and limitations. Neither can be touted to be the "best" medium for an application area.

An application developer, once the previous questions are answered, can go through a relatively systematic process to narrow the choices of media. Weights should be assigned to the following categories:

○ Ease of use

○ Durability

○ Longevity

○ Manufacturing cost

○ Cost to end user

○ Usability

○ Access speed

The various media should be evaluated and those which are obviously impractical should be eliminated.

Of the remaining choices, comparisons should be made with respect to the advantages, disadvantages, and various trade-offs involved. Some developers may wish to seek outside help at this point, rather than taking the time to develop the knowledge base necessary to conduct this analysis.

When the process is complete, an application developer will either feel confident about the selection or will determine that the application should not be developed yet.

This decision point is more important than any other. Developers should not develop products just to suit a new medium. With all the excitement that new technology creates, this is not an easy decision to make. At the same time, they should not hesitate until it is too late. Often, waiting for a better technology to evolve, leads to many a missed opportunity.

Remember, the one key question to ask yourself is: Will the proposed application be perceived by the user as being *better* than what is available today? The question is not: Is this application the best one available?

New technology provides new opportunity, and if that opportunity is viewed within an open and creative environment, exciting new products will emerge.

About the Author

Mary Ann O'Connor is president of Compact Discoveries, Inc., a development and marketing firm which assists information providers in the development of new CD-based products. They are also developing unique new proprietary application products to be marketed under a private label. Her background includes consulting, retail sales, and market research within the personal computer industry.

Compact Discoveries, Inc.
1050 South Federal Highway
Delray Beach, FL 33444

Product Development: A Case Study

by David J. Roux

Datext, Inc., is a business information publishing company developing value-added information products for distribution on compact discs. This article provides a brief overview of Datext product development and marketing activities, illustrating the myriad requirements for successful database publishing on new media, including the need for extensive market research, custom software development, and a dedicated sales, service, and support organization for CD ROM-based products.

The following sections detail the commercial and technical development of our first product, the Corporate Information Database, which contains detailed information on over 10,000 U.S. public companies, 50 major industries, and 900 lines of business. The article is a case study of the steps involved to bring this product to market:

○ Identification of an under-served market segment for certain types of business information

○ Development of a new product to address this market

○ Selling the product

Most importantly, this case study underscores the great opportunity for database producers to improve the quality and utility of the information they provide to customers. This, in turn, will allow them to generate more revenue and exact greater profits from the markets they serve.

Untapped Demand for Business Information

Based on market research conducted over an eight-month period, Datext identified corporate end users in large industrial and service corporations as needing more and better business information than was currently available. The need was particularly acute among those conducting competitive and opportunity analysis for their companies—employees working in such areas as corporate planning, business development, market research, finance, and strategy. An important characteristic of this group is that they already use personal computers to organize and evaluate the data they collect.

The primary sources of information for most of these people are books and microform. This means that extracted data must be manually entered into computers for analysis. When questioned about the obvious limitations of hard-copy searching, storage, and retrieval, users cited convenience, simplicity, and immediate availability as overriding concerns.

502

Surprisingly, most end users are highly aware of online retrieval options, despite their near total reliance on hard-copy reference materials. When asked why they did not use online services more, they consistently cited three major drawbacks:

○ Variations in searching software from system to system and database to database

○ Fragmentation of files and incompatible file structures

○ Unpredictable usage costs

Interestingly, users did not complain about the cost of online searching per se; rather, they objected to the unpredictable nature of the charges. Those with online searching experience also complained about transmission and communication problems.

Beyond these retrieval problems, end users focused on their need to do something with the information they collect. Having retrieved the information, the planner or market analyst's job has just begun. This same individual will now typically need to integrate various pieces of information, analyze the data, manipulate it, format the information for effective display, and possibly save it for retrieval at a later time.

Finally, the user's life is complicated by the need to budget his or her information expenditures. The executives and analysts we surveyed wanted the ability to predict the cost of their information purchases in advance. This was cited as critically important for gaining budget approval.

Based on our research, we concluded that end users have a unique and demanding set of use requirements for information retrieval and manipulation. These minimum requirements can be summarized as follows:

○ One-stop shopping

○ Local processing and control

○ Common indexing across databases

○ Ability to handle text and numbers

○ Simple report generation

○ Easy document formatting

○ Simple file transfer to other applications software

○ Subscription pricing

These concerns and requirements are reflected across all customer segments but are most strongly felt by relatively inexperienced users. Importantly, this group makes up the fastest-growing part of the entire market. Yet it appears they are the worst served by existing distribution technologies.

503

Product Design and Development

Based on the research described here and the previous industry experience of Datext employees, the company sought to design a product which would address the special needs of this large, nearly untapped market segment. Our initial efforts focused entirely on product design.

When questioned about the obvious limitations of hard-copy searching, storage, and retrieval, users cited convenience, simplicity, and immediate availability as overriding concerns.

The proposed product had three main components: the optical hardware and media, the database management software, and the actual information content. We resolved to supply our customers with a complete service package consisting of an optical disc drive, as many database discs as was necessary, state-of-the-art access and retrieval software, and complete customer support. The optical disc drive would attach to a user's existing personal computer and act as a storage device capable of storing and retrieving hundreds of thousands of pages of information. The database management software would allow users to access and manipulate information contained on the discs. As a first product, based on customer demand, we would assemble, integrate, cross-index, and reformat a set of leading business databases to provide information on all U.S. public companies and the industries in which they participate.

We began by negotiating for rights to act as a value-added distributor for six of the leading business databases available in the United States. These suppliers were Disclosure Information Group, Business Research Corporation, Predicasts, Data Courier, MacMillan, and Media General Financial Services. We entered into a partnership with the database producers, sharing our ideas about reaching and servicing a new market segment. All agreed to participate in our development effort, market research project, and eventually in a commercial product offering. We pay royalties for the right to distribute their information and do so as a full-service supplier, bearing complete responsibility for product design, delivery, and customer service.

Initially, we had no commitment to employing CD ROM technology specifically. Rather, we had recognized a general requirement for a portable, low-cost, mass-storage device to work with the existing installed base of personal computers. Only after conducting a four-month technical and economic feasibility study did we select CD ROM as the appropriate delivery medium. This selection was made after the evaluation of engineering prototypes, plant tours, and management discussions with interested parties.

We predicated our decision on CD ROM's worldwide acceptance as a publishing standard by major electronics manufacturers, its small form factor, and attractive replication economics. The standard provided some measure of stability for product planning and line extensions, while at the same time promoting cost economies for drive manufacturers. The compact form factor was necessary for installation in office environments where there is a premium on space. And lastly, the ability to replicate large numbers of secure database discs quickly and efficiently was deemed critical to the success of the venture, in the same way efficient printing is crucial to paper-based publishing efforts.

After careful review of existing options, Datext concluded that no existing database management software exactly met the needs of our target market segment. Consequently, we decided to develop proprietary software to access and manipulate the information we were to deliver. In doing so, we incurred higher costs but ensured that the final product would perform as required without compromising quality, efficiency, or ease of use.

. . . users did not complain about the cost of online searching per se; rather, they objected to the unpredictable nature of the charges.

This approach also allowed us to develop a standard product platform, suitable for publishing a wide variety of business information. By designing the software and related systems for maximum flexibility, Datext is well positioned to undertake new development projects.

The design was mutually agreed upon by the engineering development team and marketing staff. It required the following key features:

○ Intuitive access to comprehensive information about companies, executives, industries, and lines of business

○ Seamless presentation of all constituent databases included in the Datext system

○ Common indexing and access methods across all databases

○ Complete file handling and storage capabilities for all types of retrieved information, including all forms of textual and numeric data

○ Basic document formatting and report generation capabilities for all types of information

Only after conducting a four-month technical and economic feasibility study did we select CD ROM as the appropriate delivery medium.

○ Direct file compatibility with all leading microcomputer software packages

○ Operation under MS-DOS on standard IBM PC and 100 percent compatible machines

505

The system was designed and developed on spec, under budget, and ahead of schedule thanks to hard work, good planning, and careful coordination. Prototypes were completed in the spring of 1985. Field testing began in the summer and continued through the fall of the same year. Based on very favorable reaction from a wide range of potential users, Datext made a formal commitment to offer the product for sale in 1986, and to undertake the development of additional products for distribution on CD ROM media.

Marketing, Sales, and Customer Support

Datext announced the availability of the Corporate Information Database at the Information Industry Association conference in Washington, D.C., on November 4, 1985. The product introduction was accompanied by a comprehensive press and public relations campaign, selected trade and general business press advertisements, and targeted direct sales promotions. These activities will be continued through 1986 and are coordinated by our marketing support staff. This range of promotional activities is intended to complement the personal sales efforts of our direct sales force.

In addition to a state-of-the-art software development and data-processing facility, Datext maintains its own marketing, sales and customer support operations. This is necessary to serve the particular needs of our customer base, which includes Fortune 1000 companies, major financial services firms, consulting companies, advertising agencies, and media outlets. Potential customers include executives, research directors, corporate and strategic planners, treasurers, financial and security analysts, and information-center professionals.

These customers require high levels of personal service before, during, and after the sale. Accordingly, Datext has established regional sales offices in New York, Chicago, and Los Angeles to provide comprehensive geographic coverage.

506

After the sale, we maintain our own customer service staff to provide telephone support for customers and on-site training, if desired. We also service all of our own CD ROM equipment and offer customers 24-hour repair or replacement of any Datext-supplied materials. These services underscore our commitment to continuing and extended support of all our information products.

The Opportunity for Database Producers

Over the past two years, Datext has worked with some of the leading U.S. database producers to design, develop, and market a revolutionary set of information products. Through appropriate technology choices, careful market research, and inspired software development, Datext has worked to create opportunities for these and other database producers to:

○ Enhance the value of existing information

○ Build greater customer rapport

○ Reach new markets

○ Generate marginal revenues

○ Increase corporate profits

About the Author

David Roux is a founder and chief executive officer of Datext, Inc., a majority-owned, operating subsidiary of Cox Enterprises, Inc., based in Atlanta, Georgia. Cox is a leading communications and publishing company with business interests nationwide. It is one of the largest privately owned corporations in the United States.

Datext, Inc.
444 Washington Street
Woburn, MA 01801

CD ROM in Libraries

The New Alexandria: CD ROM in the Library

by Nancy Melin

The potential for applications of CD ROM in libraries and information centers is nothing short of dazzling. This revolutionary new technology clearly heralds the arrival of a new era of information dissemination and use.

Historically, the library has been thought of as nothing but a collection of books and other documents, impermanent and available to only a single user at a time. But we can now envision that CD ROM will make it possible for knowledge to be economically dispersed on a permanent, multi-user, random-access medium.

CD ROM in the Library Market

Beginning in 1984 and throughout 1985, library service and supply agencies vigorously promoted new products—predominantly prototypes—based on CD ROM and other types of optical media at major gatherings of people in the information business.

These products are essentially of two types. On the one hand, they are designed as support tools for library automation activities, including traditional book cataloging and local public access catalogs. On the other hand, these new CD ROM products provide inexpensive 24-hour availability of databases previously produced in electronic (online) or paper format.

The often-cited limitations of CD ROM technology—such as the fact that it is not a writable or erasable medium and that it has a slower access speed—do not loom as significant problems in the library environment. Indeed, being able to obtain relatively timely data at a reasonable cost, to store volumes and volumes of this data in a small space, and to offer local access to highly specialized data never before available, all combine to make CD ROM unusually attractive to libraries.

Furthermore, many of what have been decried as limitations of CD ROM are nothing more than the same conditions under which information managers have traditionally worked. They are familiar constraints.

For example, libraries are replete with print and microform publications. Neither of them are capable of being directly updated by users. For this reason alone, the immutable permanence of data on CD ROM, which may not be rewritten or updated, poses no new limitation.

On the other hand, many of the bibliographic databases most used and desired by librarians are massive and traditionally have been updated in print only every few years. The fact that these catalogs can be published electronically on CD ROM on a much more frequent basis is sure to outweigh the other limitations inherent in the technology.

Problems Solved by CD ROM

Perhaps one of the features of CD ROM that is most attractive to librarians is the potential it offers for allowing access to the same information, again and again, at low cost. In fact, the more the CD ROM database is used, the less its cost per use will be. This is in direct contrast to information on online databases, which may be accessed repeatedly, of course, but at an ever-increasing cost for both connect charges and telecommunications access.

The potential for applications of CD ROM in libraries and information centers is nothing short of dazzling.

It is certainly true that librarians have been relatively quick to subscribe to online databases. But the costs associated with their use have imposed a dilemma over fee versus free, which librarians have not, in a unified professional manner, resolved.

Furthermore, because of direct costs associated with online searches, librarians have had to assume the roles of database specialist and search negotiator in order to assist the end user and save significant connect charges and telecommunications fees. By contrast, data contained on CD ROM may be directly searched by the user with only a minimum of librarian intervention. With CD ROM, it will never matter how long the searcher takes to formulate and conduct a search of a database (except for the patron lines that may form). Indeed, the user may now be encouraged to take the time and simply browse through the database, a luxury not possible in most current circumstances.

Another problem libraries often face is their limited supply of resources. Many important texts and indexes, which should be purchased in duplicate so that several people can use them at the same time, usually are present only in a single copy. The enormous cost of doing so, in terms of subscription prices alone, has usually made it impractical for libraries to provide more than a single copy. Using CD ROM as an information source distributed in a local area network will make it possible for more than one user to retrieve and use the same information at the same time (provided there is sufficient memory in the individual stations).

A third critical problem for librarians and information managers has been the growth of their collections, especially the periodicals and resource indexes. Increasing volumes of new data, in both print and microform, have meant that increased space is needed to house them.

The ability of CD ROM to store hundreds of thousands of pages in a limited space (minute in comparison) is very appealing for this very reason. It is especially attractive to librarians because the medium is virtually indestructible. Not only can dozens of books be stored on disc, but rare and fragile documents, never before available to the public, can also be stored in their original form without concern that they will be damaged or destroyed by patrons.

Unresolved Issues

Although the future of CD ROM looks bright, two unresolved issues may affect its widespread acceptance in libraries in the immediate future: copyrights and standards. Since both issues are thorns in the side of most, if not all, industries involved in CD ROM, we can look forward to their eventual resolution—hopefully sooner rather than later.

Copyrights

The copyright law provides five exclusive rights to the copyright holder:

o The right to make a copy

o The right to prepare a derivative work

o The right to distribute the work

o The right to perform the work

o The right to display the work

Optical discs that use preexisting copyrighted material are liable to infringe on all these rights. The very act of producing a disc involves making a copy of the original print, converting it to another form, and distributing and displaying it.

Information specialists are probably more acutely aware of the responsibilities associated with the copyright law than any other nonlegal professional. As such, they are more concerned with finding ways to protect the original provider and at the same time provide for the needs of their patrons.

One of the oldest and largest suppliers of comprehensive full-text journals on microform, University Microfilms International (UMI) of Ann Arbor, Michigan, has devised a unique way of dealing with one of the major copyright issues in the use of full text on optical disc: monitoring and paying the royalties legally required for printing copyrighted documents and data.

The UMI prototype workstation consists of optical disc databases containing 42 IEEE journals, as well as their own Dissertation Abstracts. UMI has built into the workstation a feature that electronically polls the system, probably on a monthly basis, to identify which and how many times articles have been printed from disc.

This sort of innovation is important and will continue to develop as we attempt to solve some of the problems that lie ahead of this new information technology.

Standards

If CD ROM is to achieve widespread use in libraries (and other businesses and institutions), it is imperative that the information be formatted in a predictable, standardized manner. Most librarians and information managers expect to see a commitment to an industry standard before they will be willing to jump headlong into collecting CD ROM databases for in-house and patron access.

Fortunately, and for the first time, librarians are in the forefront of developing standards for CD ROM data file structure through their involvement in NISO (National Information Standards Organization). This committee has a fourfold goal:

○ To make it possible for publishers to master a single disc which may be readable by means of replicated copies on most combinations of compact disc players, computer hardware, and computer operating systems

○ To provide a single uniform file environment for the design and implementation of applications

○ To make it possible for manufacturers of disc players to write a single version of file-server software for creating device drivers for most computer operating systems.

○ To allow mastering services to validate replicated copies of discs using the directory and other standard information elements to verify placement of data

The committee expects to work closely with ANSI Accredited Standards Committee X3 and with Committees L5 and B11 (hardware-oriented committees) to expedite the interchangeability of future technology. To ensure a broad representation on the committee so as to provide for full input as well as broad acceptance of the final proposed standard, the membership has been drawn from library service agencies as well as the optical technology community.

Applications

The following are descriptions of some library applications of CD ROM that are either currently available or are in progress.

BiblioFile

Intended for both catalog production and maintenance, BiblioFile, a product of the Library Corporation of Bethesda, Maryland, consists of two CD ROMs that contain over 1.4 million MARC (Machine Readable Cataloging) records developed by the Library of Congress. This represents all English-language cataloging since 1964 as well as cataloging for frequently requested titles published since 1900.

The first disc contains the records of monographic materials published prior to 1979 along with the LCCN (Library of Congress Catalog Number) index. The second disc contains the MARC records for all post-1979 monographs, records for serials, the LCCN index as well as other indexes, including author, title, author/title, International Standard Book Number (ISBN), and International Standard Serial Number (ISSN).

The Library Corporation provides the CD ROM drive and the linking cable, as well as an interface card to be used on the IBM PC or a compatible microcomputer which must have a minimum of 256K RAM. A one-time purchase price of this equipment is $2930. One special feature of the product is that it may be used on the M300 workstation, a value-added IBM PC that has been modified by OCLC (Online Computer Library Center), the largest library-oriented bibliographic utility.

An annual subscription will include quarterly updates of all English-language cataloging at $870. Discs which contain the entire reindexed LC MARC file may be replaced monthly as a special subscription option. Foreign-language cataloging is available on a quarterly basis only.

Sydney's Micro Library System

Sydney Dataproducts, Inc., of Los Angeles, markets a product using the LC MARC on CD ROM. It also provides the CD ROM equipment, the interface board, and the software, and charges similar fees. Sydney markets aggressively in the United Kingdom and Canada and for that reason promises both CANMARC and UKMARC availability.

Other Databases

Several database producers have announced the availability of their files on CD ROM in conjunction with Digital Equipment Corporation and SilverPlatter. Some of the databases, especially those from DEC, are highly specialized and are ideally suited for use where demand for the literature is at least moderate or greater. Use at that level will justify the cost benefits of purchasing the database on a disc rather than searching it online.

Information specialists are probably more acutely aware of the responsibilities associated with the copyright law than any other nonlegal professional.

Digital's CD ROM products include Compendex (Computerized Engineering Index), a collection of abstracts of as many as 45,000 journals, technical reports, monographs, and conference proceedings from 1969 to the present. Compendex is available in four different parts, each priced at $1195.

Also in conjunction with Digital, the National Technical Information Service (NTIS) is offering four separate discs representing data from the Department of Defense, the Department of Energy, NASA, and other scientifically oriented government agencies. Each NTIS disc is priced at $1150.

Two other publishers, the Royal Society of Chemistry and Fraser Williams—both of which emphasize the literature of chemistry—also offer individual discs produced by Digital. The first, Current Biotechnology Abstracts, costs $1395. The second, Fraser Williams' Fine Chemicals Directory, comes with two updates in addition to the original disc as well as a supplementary manual for a total price of $995.

Use of the database on CD ROM is especially cost-effective in institutions such as public or academic libraries where numbers of student researchers must have access to timely data on broad topics—civil rights, for example.

Other examples of SilverPlatter databases include Public Affairs Information Service, Current Index to Journals in Education, Educational Resources Information Center's Resources in Education, and PsycLIT. Each of these CD ROM databases is available on subscription directly from the database vendor (not SilverPlatter). Subscriptions to each include the workstation (an IBM) with keyboard, monitor, disc reader, and software along with Hotline support.

Encyclopedias and Dictionaries

It doesn't take much knowledge about libraries to realize the advantages of providing both encyclopedias and dictionaries on optical discs. The first is almost available from Grolier, a version of the *Academic American Encyclopedia,* which it already offers on videodisc. Grolier is promising that the disc, which will contain the entire 21 volumes (9 million words) of its AAE, will be available in the near future.

A speculative product, not to be available before 1987, is the entire 17-volume *Oxford English Dictionary,* which is now being keyed into an IBM mainframe in Fort Washington, Pennsylvania. While the dictionary is to be published in traditional print form on completion, there is every reason to suppose that it may be one of the first to become available in IBM's rumored microstorage disc format.

Libraries and CD ROM Publishing

In spite of the uncertainty concerning compatibility and standards, several large library agencies are moving forward in the CD ROM field. These include the Library of Congress as well as the British Library.

The Library of Congress is at the midpoint of a special Optical Disc Pilot Program that includes rapid high-resolution scanning, storage and retrieval of images of journal titles, law materials, manuscripts, sheet music, maps, and technical reports. The British Library, on the other hand, is experimenting with the development of bibliographic files on CD ROM, including its online BLAISE-LINE, UKMARC, and an online version of British Books in Print.

Conclusion: The Library and CD ROM

In spite of its perceived limitations, CD ROM offers great potential for library use. Its particular advantages are at least four in number:

1. Databases on CD ROM may be searched repeatedly, even on a 24-hour basis, with the distinct advantage of actually increasing the cost-benefit ratio. No telecommunications charges or connect charges are incurred; the user may search at his or her leisure; the librarian need not be a search intermediary in order to reduce costs.

2. CD ROM databases offer the possibility of simultaneous multiuser access, eliminating the problem of duplicating important and frequently used materials.

3. CD ROM is an excellent storage medium, as it reduces the amount of space required to house vast amounts of materials.

4. CD ROM may be effectively used to preserve rare and/or fragile items even as it makes it possible for countless users to have access to the data.

About the Author

Nancy Melin is a partner of Melin Nelson Associates, Mt. Kisco, New York. She is the current editor of *Optical Information Systems/Library Applications, Library Software Review, Small Computers in Libraries, M300,* and *PC Report.* She has also written a book titled *The Essential Guide to the Library IBM PC: Hardware, Set-Up and Expansion* (Westport, Conn.: Meckler Publishing, 1985).

Melin Nelson Associates
Grandview Drive
Mt. Kisco, NY 10549
(914) 666-3394

The Library of Congress on CD ROM

by Gerald Lowell

517

Using optical disc as a distribution medium to disseminate cataloging data to libraries is the focus of a 3-year project initiated by the Cataloging Distribution Service (CDS) of the Library of Congress. Optical disc will become yet another record transfer option available to institutions served by CDS, joining the more traditional communication media of 3-by-5-inch catalog cards, book catalogs, microfiche, and magnetic tapes used to distribute bibliographic data. Officially known as the Disc Distribution Pilot Project, this 3-year venture follows several years of preparatory discussions and experimentation with optical disc technology by CDS. This chapter describes the project and its status as of December 1985.

The Library of Congress is firmly dedicated to developing, supporting, and abiding by established national standards for libraries and other institutions in the information sciences community.

CDS administers the distribution of the cataloging of the Library of Congress, both within the Library and to thousands of libraries throughout the world. Producing, pricing, marketing, and selling cataloging products and related technical services are the primary activities of CDS. Linked to this mission is a CDS goal to offer products and services that satisfy the bibliographic-related needs of the CDS user communities and a specific objective that encourages CDS to monitor and experiment with new technologies. The Disc Distribution Pilot Project was established in accordance with this objective.

About CDS

More than 100 different bibliographic products and services are provided by CDS, including catalog cards, technical publications, book catalogs, microfiche publications, cataloging publications, and a variety of magnetic tape services containing bibliographic and authorities records produced and marketed under the product line called MARC Distribution Services. The MARC Distribution Services consist of subscriptions to current machine-readable cataloging systems for a variety of bibliographic formats.

Numerous technical and economic factors dynamically limit the extent of market coverage for the various MARC Distribution Services. The number of records disseminated through the services is extremely large. In addition, MARC records are of variable length and have a complex tagging structure and record layout with large numbers of characters per record (e.g., the average length of a Books record is over 650 characters; for Serials, over 950 characters; and for Name Authorities, over 400 characters). Because of these factors, large computer center environments and in-depth technical expertise are required to use MARC Distribution Service tapes.

Coupled with the technical requirements is the matter of cost. Even with the mandated pricing formulas that govern CDS pricing strategies, the selling price for the various MARC Distribution Services can be high.

The following table lists the MARC Distribution Services containing Library of Congress cataloging, their estimated 1986 record counts, and the 1986 annual subscription rates.

Subscription Update Service	No. of Records to Be Distributed in 1986	1986 Subscription Price
Complete Service (all formats)	669,000 records	$11,900
Books All	473,000 records	$ 8,900
Books CJK (Chinese, Japanese, Korean)	50,000 records	$ 1,160
Books English	340,000 records	$ 6,525
Books U.S.	231,000 records	$ 5,225
Maps	11,200 records	$ 1,000
Minimal Level Cataloging	35,000 records	$ 920
Music	5,000 records	$ 1,000
Name Authorities	296,000 records	$ 8,000
Serials	174,000 records	$ 3,000
Subject Authorities	155,000 records	$ 3,700
Visual Materials	5,900 records	$ 1,000

The overwhelming majority of libraries throughout the United States acquire MARC records through the bibliographic utilities (OCLC, RLIN, WLN, UTLAS) or through services provided by the for-profit sector. Only a small percentage of U.S. libraries purchase MARC Distribution Services directly from CDS.

History

CDS began experimenting with digital disc technology in late 1983 when they contracted, through a private firm, for the mastering of a 12-inch disc containing a MARC database of 260,000 bibliographic records. In April

1984 the disc was delivered, launching a full-scale evaluation of this new storage and distribution medium in the internal and external use of the Library's MARC cataloging records. Three conclusions were reached by the contractor retained for this evaluation:

519

1. Videodisc was not suitable for internal existing applications because of the amount of interactive updating required.

2. Videodisc was not suitable for the current external distribution of MARC records because of data/software/hardware integration necessary at user sites, the sizable capital investment required to master monthly issues on videodisc, and the lack of a standard technical equipment format.

3. An archival MARC videodisc, if distributed in multiple formats, could be of benefit to the Library and the bibliographic community.

This initial CDS experiment with disc technology concluded with an informational meeting at the Library of Congress on October 19, 1984, attended by 24 people from 16 organizations, representing manufacturers, publishers, and related organizations having an interest in the Library's plans in this area. During the time that the contractor's report was being developed, CD ROM applications, geared to the library and information industry, began to appear. In the following months, interest in CD ROM technology continued to mount within the Library of Congress and the external library and information community. As a result, CDS shifted its focus to CD ROM. This shift in focus by CDS was further bolstered as U.S. libraries and private firms encouraged CDS to pursue the use of this technology and issue MARC records on compact disc.

Disc Distribution Pilot Project

Proposals for the Disc Distribution Pilot Project were formally presented to Library management in May 1985 by CDS. For planning, it was recommended that CDS approach the project in two phases: Phase 1 would focus on design issues; Phase 2 would address actual implementation, if recommendations from Phase 1 were accepted by CDS and Library management. Phase 1 would begin as soon as possible; Phase 2 would be initiated pending results and recommendations from Phase 1, with actual availability of compact discs envisioned sometime in mid to late 1986.

Three primary objectives were defined for the Disc Distribution Pilot Project:

1. To provide MARC bibliographic and/or authority records via disc, for a fixed 3-year pilot project test frame, to internal Library users and/or end-user libraries outside the Library of Congress.

520

2. To explore the feasibility of instituting such a distribution service on a permanent basis.

3. To evaluate the role that should be played by CDS regarding disc technology and record distribution.

As the Disc Distribution Pilot Project was conceptualized, several basic assumptions were identified or restated:

1. CDS should monitor and experiment with new technological developments in record storage and distribution in order to assess their potential applicability to the CDS mission of producing and distributing bibliographic products and services.

2. CDS should promote the distribution of Library of Congress bibliographic and authorities records to the end-user library communities as economically as possible.

3. CDS exploration of disc technology for record distribution would lend a significant stamp of approval that could positively enhance the private sector's introduction of this technology into the library marketplace.

4. The issue of disc size to be used in the disc distribution service would be formally included in the first phase of the proposed project. It was assumed, however, that compact disc technology would be utilized, given the presence of ad hoc standards and the perceived penetration of other CD ROM applications geared to the library marketplace.

Phase 1 of the Distribution Pilot Project was formally begun with the issuance of an RFP in June 1985; the contract for the design phase was awarded in September 1985; and a five-member task force was formed.

Issues covered during Phase 1 of the project include: Disc size to be utilized; categories of records to be distributed on disc; internal preprocessing requirements to generate tape to be used in mastering disc(s); applications and systems software to be developed, including the necessary indexes required; budgetary impacts, including project startup costs, development costs, ongoing production costs, and pricing for the distribution service during the pilot project; recommendations on the role that CDS staff should play during the pilot project; and recommendations regarding the establishment of a beta test involving a core group of libraries, vendors, and/or internal Library units that will use the disc technology in their local environments and work with CDS to evaluate the feasibility and effectiveness of the selected disc distribution application.

As of December 1985 the contractor and the task force members are considering the four categories of records described below as candidates for distribution on CD ROM during the pilot project.

521

Name authorities. MARC records for new, revised, and converted retrospective headings for personal, corporate, conference, and geographical names, uniform titles, and series established by the Library of Congress or a member of NACO (Name Authority Cooperative Project).

Subject authorities. MARC records for subject headings developed by the Library of Congress.

Music. MARC records for monographs and serials of-and-about music and sound reordings cataloged by the Library of Congress.

Americana. MARC records for monographs and serials on American history or American literature.

In-depth analysis of these four categories of records is now underway; final decisions as to the specific categories of records to be distributed will be made in January 1986.

Following the completion of Phase 1, work will begin on Phase 2 of the project. At that time all applications, systems, and/or indexing software will be acquired or developed, preprocessing routines established, and disc production arrangements made. After production is complete, the product will be beta-tested; and for the next 3 years CDS will offer disc technology for dissemination of bibliographic and authorities data.

In our efforts to resolve some of the issues facing us as we work through the design and implementation of this project, we have made a number of observations and asked many questions. Some of our thoughts may be of interest to other optical disc developers.

Optical Disc: Issues and Ramifications

One of the general issues continually faced by CDS is that CDS, like all other players in this arena, is dealing with a rapidly developing technology. Although plans and actions can be identified at present, these may be significantly changed within a period of months because of new technological advances. Numerous additional issues and ramifications affecting CDS, its customer base, and the library marketplace in general will require specific attention during the Disc Distribution Pilot Project. A brief overview of several of these concerns that are of importance to CDS follows.

Disc technology dynamically changes the cost . . . factors associated with record distribution and access, both from the CDS and end-user perspectives.

522

Economic Factors

Disc technology dynamically changes the cost/price factors associated with record distribution and access, both from the CDS and end-user perspectives. From the CDS perspective, cost components and unit costs associated with data dissemination on magnetic tape differ greatly from those linked to compact disc. New, recurring cost components related to CDS utilization of disc for record distribution include, for example, product packaging costs and data preparation costs required for initial mastering of the disc.

From the perspective of the end user, the costs associated with the receipt and processing of bibliographic records on compact disc are radically different from those associated with receipt of such records on magnetic tape. Current economic constraints associated with receiving MARC records on magnetic tape, prohibiting large numbers of end-user libraries from subscribing directly to the MARC Distribution Services, can be removed through application of disc technology.

Networking vs. Isolationism

Disc technology has been viewed as a means to radically change the technical and economic limitations associated with providing machine-readable cataloging on magnetic tape.

If and when large numbers of libraries begin purchasing cataloging records on compact disc, new challenges and opportunities will face the library field and the network linkages currently in place. With the development of MARC, the 1970s saw the development of the large, not-for-profit bibliographic utilities, with their mainframe-mounted, centrally controlled, online networks. Resource sharing, cooperative cataloging and acquisitions projects, and union listing all became solid programs in the library arena because of these bibliographic utilities. Through shared cataloging, libraries realized benefits such as cheaper cataloging costs and faster cataloging throughput times. Local automated systems were supported by the tapes of machine-readable cataloging records generated by these utilities.

These programs are now threatened because of the dramatic increase in standalone library systems designed for the powerful minis and micros, coupled with the increased fiscal pressures associated with the rising cost of telecommunications. The advent of disc technology may further jeopardize the large bibliographic utilities and the programs conducted through these networks.

Can one effectively introduce local standalone systems operating under institution-specific control into the current cooperative networked environments requiring standards and uniformity, without jeopardizing the benefits and gains that were fostered by the networking presence? Can the benefits of shared cataloging and other multi-institutional library programs be maintained in an increasingly isolationist environment? If dissemination of bibliographic data via CD ROM becomes commonplace, what impact will this have on the large, not-for-profit bibliographic utilities?

Role of the Intermediaries

If dissemination of bibliographic data via disc becomes commonplace, what impact will this have on the current players in the information industry? Who will be the new intermediaries as disc becomes more widespread? What role will be played by the bibliographic utilities and the online information brokers? Will the current CDS customer base change dynamically? How many end-user libraries will receive records directly from CDS? How many libraries will continue to receive bibliographic records from a bibliographic utility or private vendor? Will CDS slowly evolve into an institution distributing records to a handful of intermediaries that will repackage data in various ways for the end-user communities? Or will CDS find itself distributing records directly to more and more end-user libraries?

Indexing

Because of the unique data structures and processing requirements inherent in disc utilization, CDS technical staff members have found it necessary to address the issue of indexing and record access as part of their work on the Disc Distribution Pilot Project. In the past, CDS has worked with large volumes of bibliogaphic records in a predominantly batch environment. Records are packaged and repackaged into various magnetic tape-based distribution services containing sequentially arranged records according to a numeric control system (LCCN, or Library of Congress Card Number), COM products with registers and a variety of batch-generated indexes, or hard-copy dictionary catalog products. CDS staff have not had to contemplate design issues associated with searching strategies, record retrieval, or efficient record access. A fundamental question in this area is how much indexing structure needs to be supplied with each disc. Therefore, non-CDS staff members with indexing expertise have been tapped to work with CDS on the Disc Distribution Pilot Project.

Record Updates

Disc technology does not accommodate itself to traditional means of record updating as found in the current mainframe environment. Once the discs are stamped, the data cannot be updated in the manner in which online databases are updated and maintained, through batch tape or online processing. In the majority of the MARC Distribution Services, only one-third of the records distributed are in the "new" category; the majority are "change" records updating previously distributed records. For example, in 1986, of the 473,000 records anticipated to be distributed in *Books All,* only 170,000 records are expected to be new; of the 340,000 records to be distributed in *Books English,* only 102,000 are expected to be new; of the 174,000 records to be distributed in *Serials,* only 54,000 are expected to be new. The primary exception is *Name Authorities;* in 1986, of the 296,000 name authorities records planned for distribution, 211,000 are expected to be new.

Since currently available disc technology is read-only, CDS will restamp the entire applicable database of records as each new disc is produced. Given the volatile nature of the records, as evidenced by the number of changes, it is not clear how often the databases should be reissued. At present, monthly distribution services are contemplated, in order to minimize the negative impacts associated with the high occurrence rates for record updates.

Standards

The Library of Congress is firmly dedicated to developing, supporting, and abiding by established national standards for libraries and other institutions in the information sciences community. As a reflection of this commitment, CDS is represented on the NISO Compact Disc Data Format Standard Subcommittee established in November 1985. As this standard is developed, CDS will apply its concepts to its disc distribution products.

Conclusion

CDS looks forward to playing a leadership role within the library community as the distribution of MARC bibliographic and authorities records on disc is explored further. Disc technology has been viewed as a means to radically change the technical and economic limitations associated with providing machine-readable cataloging on magnetic tape through the MARC Distribution Services. Since significant questions are still being raised regarding the application of disc technology in the library environment, the 3-year Disc Distribution Pilot Project hopefully will provide CDS and the information community a unique opportunity to analyze the use of disc as a record distribution medium.

525

About the Author

Gerald R. Lowell is chief of the Cataloging Distribution Service (CDS), the division of the Library of Congress that is responsible for producing, marketing, and selling the bibliographic products and services provided by the Library of Congress to other libraries throughout the world. Prior to his work with the Library of Congress, Mr. Lowell was employed by the Faxon Company, where he was heavily involved with the development of Faxon's LINX online network and automated serials control systems. He received a B.A. degree in Russian studies from Gustavus Adolphus College in 1971 and a master's degree in librarianship from the University of Washington in 1977.

Medical and Legal Applications

Open Wide and Say Dataaa

by Stan Huntting

Medicine, like law, has a history of being an industry with no shortage of money for its more pressing problems. As in law, the professionals at the top of medicine's hierarchy sell their time and therefore must look for ways to shift more of their time from indirect (i.e., nonbillable) tasks to their patients or clients. Also as in law, the value of their time is primarily a function of their knowledge and their ability to apply that knowledge.

Knowledge, in medicine, is largely a collection of experimental and experiential data. Contemporary professional standards and an increasingly demanding society require that the healthcare professional apply not only his or her own experience to each problem that presents itself but also call upon the combined experiences of all other similarly trained professionals for the appropriate precedents to resolve each problem.

If medicine were a more precise science, the academic community would be called upon to assimilate the experience, prove and disprove alternative theories to explain them, and disseminate the conclusions as knowledge— a concise set of rules to apply in a standard way. In fact, medical knowledge is more a weighing of subtly out-of-balance data against subtly changing standards. Actions that were confidently based on the published experience of a few years ago may be totally out of favor today—the result of new experiences that actually represent only a few percent more cases. It is, therefore, axiomatic that healthcare professionals have access to, and continue to use, the data that reports the experiences of their professional colleagues. They cannot expect to wait for the knowledge to be synthesized and delivered, ready for use.

Publishing Ready-to-Use Knowledge

To be sure, ready-to-use knowledge is a major information product in medicine. It is the prerequisite foundation for interpretation and application of the experiential data. But even this most concise form of knowledge in medicine is a staggering burden to the professional who sets the goal of complete competency. Brandon and Hill, in their latest revision of their *Selected List of Books and Journals for the Small Medical Library* (published biennially in the Bulletin of the Medical Library Association), regard their list of 583 books as the core of the collection that should be readily available to healthcare professionals practicing at a small hospital.

530

While the titles of these texts suggest narrow areas of specialization and precise focus, medical problems usually do not come in such tidy bundles. This suggests a primary application for CD ROM. Combining the text of all these books in machine-readable-character text format, ignoring the illustrations for now, should allow this entire list to be published on a couple of CD ROM discs. Incorporation of an appropriate method of access such as fully inverted indexing extends the library to three or four discs, instantly accessible across the boundaries of specialization and authorship from a PC-based workstation.

Unfortunately for this scenario, the publication of medical knowledge, like the application of it, is usually done with a profit motive. Even though the majority of these books are published by only a dozen or so sources, the business issues involved in licensing the material dwarfs the technical task of CD publication, assuming that most of these books are of recent enough vintage to ensure that a machine-readable text file is available. Still, some of the medical publishers are taking the CD ROM format very seriously.

Data Retrieval Methods

Full text inversion, as a method of access to these large collections of unstructured textual data, has considerable appeal. This appeal, however, is more significant to the systems designer and publisher than to the healthcare professional. The discrepancy may be largely blamed on traditional user interface designs.

To the information scientist, it is natural enough to exploit the direct addressability of every word in a database by specifying a search strategy in terms of Boolean algebra. In contrast, the language of sets, unions, and intersections is not the way a physician is trained to think. A variety of attempts have been made to "front-end" the search engine with translators. The more successful of these, like the PaperChase™ program from Harvard's Beth Israel Hospital, translate the concepts rather than just the terminology.

Another approach, taken by the medical information and software company Clinical Reference Systems (CRS), is to eschew the search strategy altogether. The founder of CRS, Dr. Dave Steinman, points out that the

If presented with a brand new but decidedly dull axe, and a stone with which to sharpen the axe, they are likely to beat at the wood all day with the dull axe in the interest of saving time.

information problem in medicine is characterized by information overload. Their Navigator™ software emulates the much more familiar environment of the printed text: a table of contents. CRS editors construct increasingly specific hierarchical tables of contents into the subject matter of the book. At any visible level, these look familiar to any reasonably literate reader. In another discipline these might be called menus. The fact that they are hierarchical is transparent to the information user. They merely show up as another table of contents within the subject selected from the previous table of contents.

531

This approach is backed up by a technique analogous to the index, implemented as a very restricted form of inverted text search, but allowing single words only and no Boolean combinations. Complex subjects are located by reference to the table of contents, just as a book would be searched. A major value added by CRS is the authoring of the hierarchical tables of contents. This task is done by a cadre of young healthcare professionals acting as editors.

It can be argued that where knowledge is concise, it should be delivered in a concise way. This is particularly applicable to clinical, action-oriented knowledge. Micromedex, Inc., has applied this approach with considerable success. Using hardware and software products from Reference Technology, Inc., they have produced the first medical information product to actually achieve commercially successful distribution on CD ROM: their Computerized Clinical Information System™ (CCIS).

The flagship of this collection of products, Poisindex™, is a microfiche replacement application with highly structured menus that combine easily understood screen displays with a near-zero learning curve, to bring clinical management protocols into the emergency room with remarkable speed and precision. This design is successful because of a recognition that the emergency room physician or poison center technician is not working in a contemplative environment when he or she has need for this product. On the contrary, there are a multitude of distractions, even a life may be hanging in the balance. Consequently, the information must be delivered concisely and accurately; there is no time for scholarly debate.

The architecture of the Micromedex system treats knowledge as a set of data elements in a highly structured relational database. Stepping through the menus is implemented by appropriate links in the database, so that the identification of a poisonous substance leads to the identification of its chemical constituents, and thence to the management protocols for the appropriate toxins. The searcher has only to pick and choose from the comprehensive list of available substances and is quickly back to the patient.

532

Health Care Information Systems

Underlying this discussion so far has been a thinly veiled value judgment about the tolerance of healthcare professionals, as a group, for the intricacies of information science. In fact, the group is far from homogeneous. Physicians in particular include some of the most intransigent computerphobics, as well as some of the most dedicated PC proponents. In between are many with the capability to learn about computers but with no time for training. Most professionals, medical or otherwise, look to computers to be like well-sharpened tools, ready for application to the problem at hand. If presented with a brand new but decidedly dull axe, and a stone with which to sharpen the axe, they are likely to beat at the wood all day with the dull axe in the interest of saving time.

Were it not for the enormous pressure to stay current that every healthcare professional feels, this would perhaps be an unlikely market for "high-tech" information products like CD ROM, but the pressure cannot be underestimated. There are more than 4500 journals that periodically update the more than 400,000 physicians, plus dentists, optometrists, nurses, technicians, chiropractors, therapists, researchers, and other related occupational groups. Each month these journals flood this relatively narrow marketplace with more than 2 gigabytes of information.

This is not a new problem. In the last century, our government established the National Library of Medicine (NLM) to address the problem by collecting, organizing, and indexing published medical literature. The NLM has remained in the forefront of information technology through many years of trying to stay ahead of this growing information management challenge. In the 1960s, computers were applied to the task of indexing medical journals with the pioneering MEDLARS system.

MEDLARS was originally conceived as a computer database from which to organize, index, and publish printed works such as *Index Medicus*. In the early 1970s, direct online access was initiated with a form of an inverted search aimed primarily at the Medical Subject Headings (MESH Terms) that had been appended to each bibliographic citation by trained indexers. The MESH Terms are drawn from a controlled vocabulary that has grown over the years to 20,000 entries in a seven-level hierarchy.

MEDLARS', like a few other successful pioneering computer applications, very success has codified many of the more arcane concepts of early information and computer science into a nearly immovable object.

There are now dozens of databases of specialized types in addition to the original collection of bibliographic citations to the world's journal literature, now identified as MEDLINE. Remarkably, while MEDLINE has achieved the distinction of being one of the most used online databases, second only to LEXIS™ (the case law database from Mead Data Central), its horribly complex, albeit very powerful, user interface dictates that nearly all of that use is generated from just 4000 professional medical librarians acting as necessary intermediaries to all those other healthcare professionals.

This anomaly suggested a CD ROM application to the NLM. In 1985, Dr. Donald Lindberg, director of the NLM, invited organizations with the capability to deliver CD ROM-based systems to participate in an Optical Disc Experimental Systems project. The objective of this project is to stimulate private investment in the development of technology and markets for wider distribution of the MEDLINE database through optical disc read-only memory, including CD ROM. While many would-be CD ROM publishers might have preferred a somewhat more modest starting point, no one can dispute the awesome potential of this generous invitation from the NLM.

MESH indexing, if fully exploited, provides incomparably accurate searchability. It has been suggested by some that generic inverted full-text searching will typically find only 20 percent of the desired subject matter. This is largely due to the richness of the language and the multiplicity of alternative words and terms that can be used to express the same thought. By contrast, an accomplished searcher can approach perfection at retrieving citations from MEDLINE. All that is required is a complete mastery of that 20,000-term MESH vocabulary and a perfect ability to interpret what the requesting physician meant by the request! The NLM has even incorporated a comprehensive thesaurus with backward as well as forward references into the MESH file. What more could a designer ask for?

The first challenge, then, is to fully exploit the precision of the MESH index terms within the database while redefining the interface to be approachable by mere mortals (or at least by physicians). Enter the practitioners of artificial intelligence (AI).

534

Most AI applications start out with a rich collection of methods, rules, and algorithms, and a dirth of real data on which to build the experiential basis for good decision making. As a result, AI applications tend to be starved for data, something like a baby with a potentially brilliant mind waiting for 50 years of learning and experiencing to make it useful. Having enough data is no longer an issue; finding a system architect creative enough to match the potential of these mountains of data might be. Of course, long before the system is actually designed, there are other more pressing challenges, such as where to begin.

The MEDLINE database alone is many gigabytes of data, and much of this data is in languages other than English. The database has been accumulating for more than 15 years. The same *Selected List of Books and Journals for the Small Medical Library* that was mentioned earlier suggests that the small medical library might consider 138 specific journals for ongoing subscriptions. The NLM, through its selection of journals for the printed *Abriged Index Medicus,* implies a list of 130 journals that largely overlap the Brandon and Hill list. The superset is just 152 journal titles in its collection. Comprehensive lists of journal titles in specific fields of specialization could be defined. These are but a few of the strategies that suggest themselves for defining marketable subsets of the whole MEDLINE.

As amazing as this information colossus is, it is not without serious competition. The Dutch publishing giant Elsevier publishes an electronic database called Excerpta Medica™. Some medical librarians suggest that Excerpta Medica beats MEDLINE at its own game by employing physicians as indexers, thereby achieving even greater accuracy of retrieval. In terms of use, Excerpta Medica is a distant second, probably because its access charges are much greater than the cost for using MEDLINE.

This points to yet another challenge: MEDLINE is offered on a cost-recovery basis. It is axiomatic in the remote services business that actual cost of operation of the service is typically less than 10 percent of the expense budget. Marketing and information acquisition costs account for the lion's share of full costs. MEDLINE acquires its information from its parent operation at no cost (clearly, it's a national asset) and marketing is confined to the industry's most professional team of support and training people at the NLM's MEDLARS Management Section.

It is . . . axiomatic that healthcare professionals have access to, and continue to use, the data that reports the experiences of their professional colleagues.

It is impossible to overestimate the significance of journals to healthcare professionals, who individually subscribe to and read as many journals in their specific field as they can. Collectively, they form Journal Clubs to pool their ability to review the literature. Most hospitals maintain a library of up to a few hundred titles for the open use of the professionals who practice there. The NLM supports a network of libraries across the nation to keep the access time to any specific issue of almost any journal to a minimum. For all healthcare professionals, and particularly for the physician in a specialty or subspecialty practice, the journals are the lifeline to professional currency.

Before leaving the subject of the NLM's contribution to medical information distribution, one other database in the MEDLARS collection should be pointed out. CHEMLINE is based on a database provided under contract by Chemical Abstract Service and containing data on more than a million chemical substances. This database has applicability well beyond the medical and healthcare industries.

Drug Information

Drug information is interesting in part for the multiplicity of approaches that have already been applied. The ubiquitous *Physicians Desk Reference* (PDR™) from Medical Economics is certainly the most widely used single reference work in all of medicine. Given free of charge to qualified prescribing physicians, the PDR is largely supported by the manufacturers of the drugs that it lists. The information contained in the PDR is essentially as supplied by the manufacturer, an odd situation for a reference work until one takes into account the rigorous process by which the drug manufacturers and the regulatory agencies negotiate and control every single claim made about a drug.

While an electronic form of the PDR, called PDR Online, has been marketed with limited success, others are plunging ahead with their own versions of information on drugs. Drug interaction databases are an increasingly popular add-on subsystem for vendors of medical practice management computer systems. The interaction databases are generally too small to need CD ROM capabilities, but Micromedex's CD ROM-based CCIS™ includes a large database of drug comparisons, interactions, and consults called Drugdex™. Drugdex claims a different perspective on the problem by virtue of its having been compiled from the world medical literature and edited by Micromedex's editorial board of hundreds of physicians.

536

The model of the PDR suggests other information marketing opportunities. Healthcare professionals in general and physicians in particular are used to getting just about everything possible for free. Medical Economics and others publish dozens of magazine titles each month with controlled circulation, i.e., free to qualified professionals. These magazines rain down on physicians in a veritable blitz of information and advertising. To protect their time, most physicians construct elaborate protective shields of support staff around them to intercept and filter these and other forms of intrusion.

Still, the few that get through on merit are sufficiently attractive for advertisers to pay heavily for the chance to get into the inner office. Free samples of everything but controlled substances are available for the asking. Elaborate and expensive continuing education products are produced and delivered free for the oportunity to attach a modest logo to the product. Altogether, the drug manufacturers alone spend more than $20,000 a year for every physician in the core group of 175,000 physicians who write more than 80 percent of all prescriptions.

The Future of CD ROM-Based Products

To these manufacturers, CD ROM-based medical information products may well be the most attractive way to place their name in front of their elusive quarry. Delivery systems will require quality design to ensure the professional's personal use. This is potentially an exciting answer to the problems of product marketing and distribution channels. No other marketing teams in medicine come even close to the power and effectiveness of the drug teams.

Vendors and service providers of medical practice management systems might seem a logical choice since they are familiar with computer systems installation and support, but they generally sell to the wrong audience. The focus of the CD ROM opportunities outlined here is on the clinical aspects of medicine, an area reserved to the healthcare professional. Most computer products sold and used in medicine today are largely administrative in nature, and physicians typically delegate responsibility for administrative functions to an administrator or office manager who would not make a decision on an information product.

A more promising channel for the future may be hospitals themselves. Hospitals, as the result of a variety of pressures, are being forced to become competitive. In order to compete for patients, they must first win the hearts and scalpels of the attending physician. Services to the healthcare professional, many offered for free, are a key element in this competition. Today, the hospital's medical library and the services of the medical librarian are commonly offered to all healthcare professionals as a benefit. If PC/CD ROM-based information systems in the private office begin to absorb the research load, can the hospitals afford not to offer that service as well?

In the more distant future, technology will support increasingly potent expert systems to augment the judgment of the healthcare professional.

The list of applications and distribution channels that define commercially viable medical information products is growing steadily. At the NLM's Lister Hill Center for Biomedical Communications Research, high-risk technologies are routinely explored. (A high-risk technology is one that is sufficiently problematic that the commercial sector would be slow to undertake the effort required to prove or disprove any potential.)

A team of Lister Hill Center scientists and technicians under Acting Director Earl Henderson is exploring the potential of CD ROM as a means for distribution of high-resolution medical imaging. If a practical delivery system can be defined, a variety of medical imagery ranging from x-ray radiograms to CT-scans and nuclear magnetic resonance images may be made available to a wide audience for study. The density and digital format of CD ROM might allow CDs with comprehensive sets of nominal and abnormal images to be published with full patient history and diagnosis included. This would provide an immediately accessible standard of reference for diagnosticians all over the world.

In the more distant future, technology will support increasingly potent expert systems to augment the judgment of the healthcare professional. Such systems will undoubtedly require the vast volume capacity to deliver standardized knowledge made possible by CD ROM. For today, however, there are challenges aplenty, matching the wealth of medical information and knowledge with the voracious information appetites of healthcare professionals.

What is needed now is a critical mass of information products, cotargeted at a viable submarket, that will provide the initial incentive necessary to equip offices with PCs and CD ROM drives. It will no doubt be the toughest chapter in the story of CD ROM and medicine, but for those who succeed, it will provide a gateway to one of the most lucrative markets of all.

About the Author

Stanley R. Huntting is director of technical marketing at Reference Technology, Inc., a leader in applying laser optic technology to solve information distribution problems. Previously, Mr. Huntting was a member of Reference Technology's market support staff. Before joining Reference Technology in December 1983, he held a variety of technical, marketing, and management positions with ABACUS Group, Inc., Storage Technology Corporation, and Samsonite Corporation.

Reference Technology, Inc.
1832 North 55th Street
Boulder, CO 80301
(303) 449-4157

From Microfiche to CD ROM

by Nancy E. Kuchta,
Leonard S. Rann,
and
Marilyn G. Winokur

Until optical discs appeared on the horizon, paper, microfiche, and magnetic disks have shared, each in turn, the distinction of being the most appropriate medium for archiving large amounts of information. For those in the business of compiling, maintaining, and indexing large stores of information, optical discs are sure to be a boon, adding yet another option to their list. However, making the transition from one archival method to another is full of new considerations and production requirements. This discussion examines what one company experienced in its efforts to keep up with the new storage technologies, tracking the progression from microfiche to CD ROM.

539

Historical Perspective

In 1974, Micromedex, Inc., of Denver, in conjunction with the University of Colorado Health Sciences Center, Denver General Hospital, the Rocky Mountain Poison Center, and the Rocky Mountain Drug Consultation Center, began producing and publishing medical information systems on computer-generated microfiche. These systems were designed for health care professionals to provide referenced and evaluated medical information, including:

○ Identifying characteristics of potentially toxic products and substances

○ Toxicology treatment protocols

○ Tablet and capsule identification

○ Clinical drug information

○ Diagnostics and therapeutics

Through the years, an editorial board of 350 physicians, pharmacists, and clinical toxicologists has updated the system every 90 days. Occasionally, this updating cycle, along with the large size, extensive indexing, and cross referencing of the databases, made the use of microfiche complex and unwieldy, especially in the emergency rooms, poison centers, and other hospital settings where access time is often a critical factor. With the increasing use of computers in hospitals, Micromedex began investigating, in 1979, delivery of a computerized version of its medical data.

A careful analysis of the online/timeshare method of delivery reveals that most available host/telephone hookup systems aren't effective. For one thing, the information is often bibliographic and therefore not useful to the physician, pharmacist, or nurse looking for quick answers to medical questions. Additionally, the complex access and retrieval methods, not to mention the sluggish response time, often leave much to be desired, especially for the computer-naive end users working under pressure to obtain the information. Also, high connection costs dissuade the user from "playing" with the system to learn its intricacies. And a poor royalty structure discourages the database publisher from offering databases via established online services; phone-line access was deemed unacceptable.

In 1983, Micromedex and MacNeal Memorial Hospital in Berwyn, Illinois, began developing an application for the IBM mainframe systems (with DOS, PCS/ADS, MVS, MVS-XR) using magnetic media. (This sort of approach is appropriate for hospitals with mainframe computers which have a commitment to providing clinical data for the entire hospital.) At the same time, they began to develop the software necessary for a personal computer application during the same year.

By early 1984, Micromedex began working with Reference Technology, Inc., of Boulder, Colorado, to define the system requirements for delivery of the PC version of the database on an optical laser disc. Several considerations were crucial: (1) the application had to be easy enough for the computer illiterate, (2) the system would be installed by nontechnical personnel and had to be straightforward, (3) access time had to be appropriate for critical-care use, and (4) the databases needed to be easily distributed because they would be updated and republished quarterly. Another early objective of the system was to deliver database access to a large number of hospital users for a flat cost.

The application software has been designed for use by medical personnel unfamiliar with computers.

A system was defined around the Reference Technology Series 2000 DataDrive and a proprietary file server from NCR Corporation. To create the optical disc, the database was ported directly from the Eagle disk drive through an IBM PC XT to 9-track tape, also attached to the XT. Reference Technology's Tridec™ Premastering System was used to encode the digital data into NTSC analog format for mastering by 3M onto a 12-inch Laservision™ format disc. Reference Technology supplied PC-DOS system drivers that provided complete application software transparency, making the application an immediate technical success.

The database organization remained unchanged from the hard disk version that was based on a program product intended for relatively small PC-based files. Extrapolating the B-tree organization of this database management system to a 400-megabyte database resulted in 30 to 50 disc accesses for each logical request. This caused less than optimal response times.

Another early objective of the system was to deliver database access to a large number of hospital users for a flat cost.

Initial reaction of the focus market was disappointing. By the time all this high-powered equipment was assembled and delivered through an equally high-powered channel of distribution, the cost was entirely out of line with the replacement of single-subscription microfiche installations. The desired configuration was 1 to 3 users, not 10 to 15 as expected. The application awaited further technological developments to lower the costs.

Also during 1984, Micromedex began exploring another system configuration from LaserData of Cambridge, Massachusetts. This system had a highly streamlined database management of its own design, providing the value-added service of data organization and access capabilities tailored for the optical disc and a less expensive system in the one- to three-user range. The LaserData system used commercially available constant angular velocity (CAV) videodisc players, with the TRIO-110 custom controller/analog decoder that provided 800 megabytes of digital data, 30 minutes of motion video, 70 hours of compressed digital audio, sound-over-still video, and 52,000 still frames of video, in any combination. Still, the market resistance remained high because of the skepticism about the 12-inch videodisc as a true personal computer peripheral, price considerations, and enthusiastic publicity about the coming CD ROM delivery method.

In 1985, Reference Technology introduced a CD ROM-based product. They had created several value-added software packages, including STA/F FILE, STA/F KEY, and a PC-DOS installable device driver for their D-2000 drives, which were now available in CD ROM format. STA/F FILE is highly optimized to the read-only environment, allowing single access file opens to discs with more than 14,000 separate files. It also enables portability across various operating systems. STA/F KEY, a keyed access technique, provides a high-performance ISAM-like method (indexed sequential access method) for very large read-only databases.

541

In July 1985, following tests of the Reference Technology CD ROM Data Drive, the Computerized Clinical Information System of Micromedex became the first medical database to utilize CD ROM technology with personal computers.

542

Read-only optical media is an ideal delivery system. Installation and distribution are simple. A single disc is mailed to the user and easily mounted in the player. After the disc is mastered, it is mass-duplicated at the factory. Other advantages of the optical disc are that it is nonmodifiable and nonerasable. The market acceptance of CD ROM has been high because of the lower costs and ease of use.

Creating the Database and Application Software

In the design phase of these kinds of applications, the clinically oriented medical databases are written and updated by the editorial staff and then entered into the IBM-4331-2 mainframe computer by data entry staff. When it comes time to prepare the data so that it is in the correct format for storage on the disc, the text must be scripted into formatted documents. Concurrently, the locations of terms that have been targeted for indexing are emitted. These terms are then processed against a synonym database. Eventually, all access and cross-referencing capabilities are moved to tapes, which are then shipped to be premastered. Reference Technology scans all the data to ensure conformance to specs, generates index files (containing 300,000 STA/F KEY records), builds a STA/F FILE directory for all files, and assembles these pieces into the appropriate sequence to drive the CD mastering equipment. All of this is written to tape, which is sent to 3M for mastering and duplication into compact discs. The data is republished quarterly.

The application software has been designed for use by medical personnel unfamiliar with computers. The data relationships are implemented as a hierarchical tree. The search process consists of entering a topic and successively qualifying it until a singular reference is resolved, at which time data are displayed. Depending on how broad a topic is entered, an immediate data hit may occur, or possibly up to seven qualifications may be necessary to obtain the desired data. A menu-driven approach has been used, requiring one keystroke to move forward or backward through the tree-search process. Screens and function keys are standard throughout the system, with all available options always being displayed on the screen.

Summary

The selection of the proper delivery media, whether microfilm, online, or optical disc, depends on an analysis of the system requirements, the data-processing expertise, and the cost constraints. The Computerized Clinical Information System of Micromedex is available on computer-generated microfiche, mainframe tapes, and digital optical discs for use on IBM XT-compatible computers.

543

Product Descriptions

The Poisindex® database is a complete single-source emergency poison identification and management information system. It provides comprehensive product or compound ingredient data and formula information. Information is gathered directly from pharmaceutical, commercial, chemical, paint, grocery, hardware, cosmetic, and OTC industries. All products are listed separately under each appropriate commercial brand or trade name, generic name, manufacturer, slang term, abbreviation, and common misspelling. Products are also identified as "no longer manufactured" and "product now called." Botanical and zoological items are listed by common and scientific names.

. . . making the transition from one archival method to another is full of new considerations and production requirements.

The Poisindex system contains complete management protocols, emphasizing specific signs and symptoms, and step-by-step treatment for toxicology problems secondary to ingestion, absorption, or inhalation of any of the substances listed.

The Emergindex® database is an emergency and critical-care medical information system that consists of three major sections. Clinical Reviews are designed to present data pertinent to the practice of acute-care medicine in the daily clinical setting for both diagnostic and therapeutic purposes. Detailed compartmentalized information concerning clinical presentation, laboratory and radiologic analysis, differential diagnoses, pharmacologic and nonpharmacologic therapeutics, and appropriate disposition is presented. Differential Reviews contain detailed etiologies for specific symptom complaints, common physical signs, and laboratory findings pertaining to an emergency-medicine or critical-care topic. Clinical Abstracts consist of an ongoing review of the world's medical literature, specifically oriented to emergency and critical-care medicine. This section allows a computerized literature search of over 10,000 abstracts. The abstracts, which are presented in a structured format, can be used for continuing education or research.

The Drugdex® database is a referenced drug information system designed to help solve the problems of delivering up-to-date, unbiased, critically evaluated drug information to pharmacists, physicians, and others who prescribe, order, dispense, or administer medication. The Drugdex system can also be used effectively for medical education, to assist with Pharmacy and Therapeutics (P&T) Committee decisions, and for drug therapy in-service programs.

STA/F FILE is highly optimized to the read-only environment, allowing single access file opens to discs with more than 14,000 separate files.

The Drugdex system consists of two major sections. Drug Evaluations present data in a standardized outline format relevant to the use of drugs in the clinical setting. Dosing, pharmacokinetics, contraindications, precautions, adverse reactions, teratogenic effects in pregnancy, drug interactions, IV incompatibilities, clinical applications, therapeutic indications, comparative efficacy, and patient instructions are included. The system provides information of FDA-approved and investigational drugs plus OTC and non-U.S. preparations. Drug Consults offer patient-related referenced consultations answering questions regarding disease states, use of drugs, and specific drug therapy problems. These consultations are generated from major drug information centers and clinical pharmacology services throughout the United States and Canada.

The Identidex® database is a tablet and capsule identification system. It uses manufacturer imprint codes as the primary identification source. Secondarily included are color and physical description. The Identidex system contains over 23,000 entries on U.S. and foreign preparations, generic drugs, look-alike drugs, and slang street terms.

The Pediatric CPR Dosing section of the Computerized Clinical Information System™ calculates CPR drug doses for pediatric patients in response to entry of weight or age.

The Acetaminophen and Salicylate Toxicity Nomograms of the CCIS interpret plasma levels of the drug measured in a patient and indicate whether the level is potentially toxic. Entry of the time since ingestion and the plasma level of the drug is required. Notations are included for proper treatment and prognosis.

About the Authors

Micromedex, Inc., of Denver, Colorado, a medical publishing company, developed and produced the Computerized Clinical Information System (CCIS), which consists of information on clinical toxicology (Poisindex), pharmacology (Drugdex), diagnostics and therapeutics (Emergindex), tablet and capsule identification (Identidex), and calculations to assist medical professionals in drug dosing and in predicting toxicity.

544

The Lawyer's Edge: CD ROM

by Mike Befeler

The combination of CD ROM storage devices and user-friendly text retrieval software running on a personal computer has opened up a new realm of information retrieval for the legal and accounting fields. And it couldn't happen to a more appropriate group.

Attorneys and tax accountants must review a tremendous amount of reference material that may be relevant to their clients' legal or tax needs. Clients naturally expect a thorough and effective representation of their interests. With increasing competition in the legal field, the responsiveness and cost-effectiveness of an attorney or tax accountant directly affects the client's decision of where to take future legal and tax business. Equipped with an entire electronic library at their fingertips, attorneys and tax accountants are sure to find it easier to track down and review the material, and in so doing, improve their ability to efficiently serve their clients.

A Well-Suited Profession

Attorneys have been trained for years to use impressive libraries of printed material: volumes of court decisions, statutes, digests, law reviews, loose-leaf services, citations, legal encyclopedias, treatises, and law journals. In the past decade, online database systems such as LEXIS and Westlaw have been used to supplement the printed material. Law school graduates typically have had experience using one or more of the online services, and as they enter their professional careers, they tend to look for computer-assisted tools.

Once they have subscribed to the database, they can use it 24 hours a day, if they choose, for a fixed, budgetable cost.

The online services offer the tremendous advantage of being able to perform sophisticated searches from selection criteria defined by the user against very large databases containing the text of court cases and other reference information. Attorneys must be able to reference the most current information available, since the law is constantly changing as new precedents are set; and online services are particularly effective at providing information that has recently been updated.

Unfortunately, online services are not used as much as they should be for two main reasons: Many prospective users are untrained or may even fear using a computer system; and more importantly, since most online services charge by the amount of connect time, there is a concern that an expensive "taxi meter" is always running.

546

The concept of putting a large database on an optical disc, distributing this disc to the user, and allowing the user to search to his or her heart's content on a personal computer without the meter running is clearly an appealing alternative. As such, it warrants close attention by both publishers of legal and tax information and the subscribers to this information.

Applications

CD ROM is an ideal medium for many legal applications. Here are just a few examples.

Tax

There is a tremendous amount of information published in the tax field that must be referenced by a tax attorney or accountant. Both the current information and the historical base of information must be used. This includes court decisions relative to tax matters, the Internal Revenue Code (Title 26 of the United States Code), IRS regulations, IRS general counsel memorandums, and IRS Private Letter Rulings. This historical base can be published very effectively on CD ROM.

Statutes

In addition to selecting portions of statutes to be combined with other information in a field such as tax, the federal code in its entirety or individual state statutes can be published on CD ROM.

Case Histories

Likewise, specific types of court cases can be grouped by subject area or in historical sequence by court jurisdiction (Supreme Court, U.S. Circuit and District Courts, or state courts).

Legal Forms

A tremendous number of different forms are required for such diverse actions as starting a new corporation or filing a tax return. These forms could be stored on a CD ROM, be retrieved by form type, and used with a word processing package to produce a complete document.

Patents/Trademarks

Information about patents and trademarks can be stored on CD ROM and accessed by text retrieval software. Of additional value is the capability to store digitized images of patent drawings with the text.

Value of Read-Only Optical Storage

For certain applications, such as those just described, read-only optical storage systems have a number of significant advantages over other storage systems.

Large Storage Capacity

Each CD ROM can store 550 million bytes of information. Storing information for full text search requires inverting the data (building an index for every word in the text) and typically requires a storage overhead of an additional 35 to 40 percent above the database size to contain the index. Consequently, close to 400 million bytes of uncompressed raw text can be stored with fully inverted indexes on one CD ROM. This equates to 200,000 pages of typed text, or approximatly 100 volumes of legal books, that could be found in a legal library. Rather than requiring the shelf space for 100 volumes in a crowded law firm, one disc can be kept in a desk drawer.

Good Archival Medium

Read-only optical disc storage lends itself very well to storing historical data. Case histories, previous tax rulings, and published articles must be kept in their original form and not adulterated. Clearly, new information is always becoming available, but the historical base must be retained in its original form for reference. Optical disc as a publishing medium retains the integrity of the original information.

Supplemental Updates

Discs can be added yearly, quarterly, or monthly, allowing new information to be published along with the previous historical base.

Increased User Control

Finally, read-only optical disc systems offer the user significant control at the workstation. By distributing a legal library on disc directly to the law firm, the attorney, paralegal, legal secretary, or legal librarian can each sit down at a personal computer to access the information. With menu-driven software, the user can fill in the blanks to make a request to search for any section of law that contains, for example, the word *patent* or *trademark*.

Freedom to Really Use the Information

Read-only optical disc systems also offer a very intriguing advantage that becomes apparent only after professionals have had a chance to sit down at a personal computer and experiment with a full text query against a CD ROM database.

There are two inherent psychological barriers to using online database services. One is the fear factor. Many attorneys, particularly those who graduated from law school more than 15 years ago, either don't like or actually fear using computer systems. The image of connecting a terminal to a computer somewhere and doing something that "breaks" the system is a concern to many potential users. The other factor is the tension associated with the concern that the meter is running and that charges are building by the second as the inexperienced user fumbles with the keyboard trying to formulate or retype a query. Too many times a neophyte user tries the system, has problems, becomes concerned about the cost, and never tries it again.

By contrast, read-only disc systems allow users to experiment because the whole system is under their control. Once they have subscribed to the database, they can use it 24 hours a day, if they choose, for a fixed, budgetable cost. There is no concern about a connect charge meter running. One lawyer stated that after years of tension trying to use online services, he was able to relax for the first time with his CD ROM tax database and really use it.

Hybrid Systems

Like any other technology, read-only optical disc systems have their limitations. CD ROM databases require time to publish, just like a book. The data must be prepared, indexes added, files structured, error correction codes added, a master produced, a mold or stamper made, replicas stamped out, replicas quality-assured, and finally replicas distributed to the user. This cycle is not responsive to a tax lawyer or accountant who wants to know what rulings were issued yesterday.

An emerging solution to this deficiency is the use of a hybrid system, in which technologies are combined so that the best characteristics of each can be applied to provide an improved information delivery system. Since online systems are ideal for accessing very current information but expensive for large historical searches, and since CD ROM is very effective for large historical databases distributed locally but not adequate for current information, a hybrid setup combining a CD ROM system and an online service can be an ideal match. Given the appropriate software, a user could instigate a search from a personal computer that would access the locally stored CD ROM for historical information and concurrently access a remote online service for the most up-to-date information.

549

Another hybrid solution combines distributed read-only optical disc with distributed magnetic media. The advantage of huge storage on CD ROM can be combined with the smaller capacity but quicker delivery of a floppy disk or cartridge disk update. (Reference Technology does this in its DataDrive™ Plus system using an IOMEGA™ removable magnetic disk cartridge.) As an example, historical tax databases can be distributed quarterly on CD ROM, with weekly updates distributed on the cartridge. Queries can be directed against both portions of the database to facilitate a full response.

Search Software

To take advantage of new CD ROM hardware capabilities, new software is needed as well. Along with the text database on CD ROM, the attorney or tax accountant needs the ability to easily search for needed reference information.

Many menu-driven systems (such as Reference Technology's STA/F Text software) provide the type of search capabilities needed by nontechnical users. In such systems the user simply fills in a series of blanks to formulate a query based on words, phrases, or prefixes of words found in the documents.

Searches can be made through documents that contain:

○ All the terms defined (connecting the terms together with AND)

○ Any one or more of the terms defined (connecting the terms with OR)

○ Terms in proximity to each other

The CD ROM disc is searched using an index to all the words contained in all documents in the database, and a response comes back to the user in seconds indicating the number of documents meeting the selection criteria. The user can review a list of the documents or proceed to view the documents themselves, in which the selection criteria are highlighted.

Equipped with an entire electronic library at their fingertips, attorneys and tax accountants are sure to find it easier to track down and review the material.

Searches can be continually refined to narrow the search to the appropriate documents, and the results can be printed if desired. The attorney who is not comfortable with computers can request that a search be made by a paralegal and can receive the printed results to read at his or her desk.

Some legal database users already proficient with front-end query capabilities of systems such as LEXIS might prefer that a front end be tailored to a particular command language and format. Some of the commercially available search programs have this feature (including STA/F Text).

Conclusion

The arrival of practical CD ROM information delivery systems combined with user-friendly search and retrieval software running on a personal computer offers a significant opportunity to the legal and tax professions for an effective means of obtaining needed reference information. It also offers an opportunity to the publishers of legal and tax information to deliver their information in a new and beneficial way.

About the Author

As director of market development for Reference Technology Inc. (RTI), Michael Befeler is responsible for market analysis, business planning, new market development, product introduction planning, and pricing. Before joining RTI he was business program manager for Storage Technology Corporation's optical storage products and held marketing and product planning positions with IBM. He received his B.S. degree in mathematics from Stanford University and his M.B.A. from UCLA.

Reference Technology Inc.
1832 North 55th Street
Boulder, CO 80301
(303) 449-4157

Geographic Applications

Maps, Optical Discs, and Vehicle Navigation

by Donald F. Cooke

Cartographers have stored and manipulated maps in computer-readable form for about a quarter of a century. In the past five years, largely due to advances in personal computers and business graphics, the hardware for encoding, manipulating, and displaying maps has matured. Map storage, the last obstacle to broad use of mapping, seems well served by optical disc technology, and more specifically by CD ROM. An incredible amount of digital map information can fit on a CD ROM disc. The next half-decade will see CD ROM-based mapping applications both in vehicles and on desktops.

553

Maps

Map storage, the last obstacle to broad use of mapping, seems well served by optical disc technology, and more specifically by CD ROM.

We use three types of maps in our everyday lives. Most often we use road and street maps to plan a vacation trip or to find a destination while driving. We see maps in newspapers and magazines showing election results by state or the route of the president's trip abroad. If we buy a piece of property, we see a detailed map showing the size and shape of the parcel, with adjoining property owners identified.

We can characterize these maps by scale and amount of detail. They're really quite different: the election map shows only state boundaries, the street map includes a line for each street, and the property map shows the width of the street as well as details about sidewalks and driveways. It would be inappropriate to show streets on the election map; we don't need parcel boundaries shown to get us from Disneyland to Knott's Berry Farm.

In the past quarter of a century, cartographers have developed ways to use computers to store and maintain maps. Virtually every utility company and city/county agency that maintains parcel-level maps has a map automation project in some stage of planning or operation. The boundaries of every state, county, city, town, zip code, and census tract have been computerized and are available as marketplace commodities. The Census Bureau and Geological Survey have "digitized" most of the streets in the country; my company sells improved versions of these computerized maps for computerized vehicle dispatching, routing, and navigation systems.

There are lots of other kinds of maps, of course, and they also are being computerized. For example, digital maps currently guide cruise missiles, and soon robot vehicles, to their targets; but this discussion is limited to civilian applications.

554

Maps: Pictures or Databases?

In grade school, we all memorized the definition of a map. Mine went like this: "A map is a graphical representation of a portion of the earth's surface."

Of course, times have changed since then. We've seen robot surveyors on the moon and many of the planets. It does not surprise us at all that the moon is better mapped than the earth was less than a century ago.

But there's been a more subtle and more significant change in addition to extending mapping beyond the earth's surface. Research in map encoding technology is leading cartographers to rethink the definition of a map. Today, the operational definition has probably evolved to something like: "A map is a database describing the topological and/or metrical relationships between objects in space."

As this new consciousness grows among cartographers, we see two distinct technologies developing. One treats a map as a picture, a diagram, a "graphical representation." The other treats a map as a database more like raw payroll data than the familiar form we're used to seeing.

Neither treatment of a map is right or wrong. Each method has strengths and weaknesses. However, these characteristics do determine whether treatment of a map as a picture or a database is appropriate in a given application.

This discussion concentrates on the database method of computerizing maps for two reasons. One, the author's experience is concentrated in this area; and two, this approach fits well with CD ROM characteristics, to suggest a family of products with a high probability of broad consumer acceptance.

Map Encoding

There are lots of ways to encode a map for computer storage. The pioneering days are behind us and there's no longer an excuse for random experimentation, given the body of information laid down by White, Corbett,

... a car

navigation

computer could be a

general device

available also for

entertaining

children or for

business use,

especially if linked

to an office

computer through a

mobile cellular

telephone.

Chrisman, and others. Fundamentally, they state that one must identify the elementary objects in the map, then apply the appropriate tools of mathematics and computer science, in that order. This boils down to recognizing that our state boundary maps consist of the lines that bound the states, the points where the lines meet, and the areas enclosed by the lines. We relate these by topology: what touches what; how the objects are connected. Finally we apply metrics: determine where the corner points are; define the wiggles of the Ohio River between Kentucky and Indiana. Once we're done with the mathematics, we observe the characteristics of the computer system that is to manipulate the digital map, and we organize the point, line, and area databases appropriately.

I used state boundaries as an example, but the process works equally well for street or parcel maps, which also consist of points, lines, and areas.

How big is a map in database form? Geographic Data Technology (GDT) sells a major set of boundary maps covering all states, counties, cities, towns, census tracts, and zip codes. Collectively this is a 140-megabyte database in ASCII character form. The map fits on four reels of computer tape at 1600 bpi. With trivial compression, consisting of eliminating blank spaces and converting numbers to binary representation, the size can be cut in half. With extreme compression, the size could be reduced to 12 megabytes.

Clearly there would be no problem distributing this boundary map, which describes in detail the shapes of 120,000 polygons, on an optical disc. In fact, National Decision Systems (NDS) and Criterion Corporation put this database, together with an immense array of census and marketing data, on the market in 1985 for use with a Reference Technology Classix Datadrive.

Although the NDS/Criterion offering is revolutionizing access to census data, the potential market for this kind of map is limited to market researchers and data analysts. A bigger revolution will begin—within a year—with the publication of digitally encoded street maps on CD ROM.

CD ROM street maps have static and mobile uses, just as paper maps do. The most intriguing application is in vehicle navigation systems.

Vehicle Navigation Appliances

Honda has sold a navigation appliance in Japan for three years, and ETAK, of Sunnyvale, California, is marketing its Navigator product. Virtually every automobile manufacturer has built both engineering prototypes and concept cars with navigation features.

Two functions define a vehicle navigation appliance: it must be able to locate the vehicle on the ground and it must be able to display the location in a familiar and useful form. Equipment now on the market provides these functions, which satisfy gadget buffs and commercial fleet operations. However, to reach a broad consumer market a VNA must also provide useful and entertaining information related to the location of the car or the desired destination.

This functional definition of a VNA requires six hardware subsystems for implementation:

1. A location device

2. A computer

3. An output facility

4. An input facility

5. Map storage

6. Storage for "other" information

Location Devices

Three location techniques seem promising for locating land vehicles: loran, satellite, and dead reckoning. Although "electronic signposts" serve to monitor buses along fixed routes, they are dismissed for supporting a broad consumer market because of the cost of the infrastructure required to work nationwide.

Loran.   A loran set receives coordinated radio signals from three fixed ground stations. It measures the time differences in the arrival of the signals. The time differences serve as coordinates, which can be looked up on special maps with time-difference coordinate overlays or converted to latitude and longitude.

About 250,000 ships and boats have loran sets, costing between $700 and $2500, for navigation. Loran transmitters cover not only the coastal and offshore waters but also the Great Lakes and the majority of the continental land area. Loran sets adapted for general aviation use are being well received; some units have thousands of locations of airports and navigation aids stored internally for recall and use by the pilot.

Loran manufacturers are also investigating land vehicle installations as another market. Loran accuracy is affected by a seasonal temperature-related drift and more drastically by local electrical disturbances. On land, the best-case accuracy will discriminate between most adjacent street intersections; use of a locally broadcast differential signal reportedly improves accuracy to 15 feet.

Satellite. Two proposed satellite systems may soon be able to support vehicle navigation: Geostar and the Navstar Global Positioning System (GPS). Geostar is a private venture which would have to charge users a fee for system access. Geostar has demonstrated its concept with simulated satellites on mountaintops. In addition to the location function, Geostar offers a communication channel, which opens up possibilities of message forwarding outside of cellular telephone coverage.

Research in map encoding technology is leading cartographers to rethink the definition of a map.

On the other hand, GPS/Navstar is a Defense Department system planned for operational deployment between 1986 and 1988. The mature system will consist of 21 satellites; 6 satellites are currently available for testing. GPS is really two systems: a highly accurate military one with coded signals unusable by civilians; and a civilian channel, which will be deliberately degraded, for national security reasons, to yield a location accuracy that is marginal for land vehicle location. Ironically, it appears possible to determine and broadcast a differential correction signal, or even generate a "pseudolite" that would look to a GPS receiver like another satellite, to further increase accuracy. Either of these corrections would make GPS adequate for VNA use.

Dead reckoning. Dead reckoning (DR) is a "position keeping" rather than "position finding" technology; a DR device keeps track of how far and in what direction a vehicle has gone to compute location relative to a known starting point. Dead reckoning hardware can be quite simple and inexpensive: an odometer and a heading indicator. Heading can be sensed by a magnetic compass, a differential odometer, or and inertial sensor. A combination of compass and differential odometer is used by most current systems.

Simple open-loop DR yields a position measurement that degrades, because of errors in distance and heading readings, as the vehicle moves. At least five firms have overcome this deficiency by map correlation/matching or closed-loop DR. In closed-loop DR the navigation computer compares sensed evidence of distinct turns with bends or intersections on a digital map. The computer chooses the most probable turn point and updates the vehicle's location, eliminating accumulated errors. But even closed-loop DR can get lost and require reinitializing if turns that allow position updating are too far apart; otherwise, closed-loop DR yields excellent accuracy.

Computer

Computing functions in a VNA include retrieving and displaying the appropriate map, updating the car's location on the display, managing queries from the operator, searching the directory of destinations, and supporting the DR function, if used, including map correlation in the closed-loop case. Other navigation-related functions might include calculation of a shortest path and voice synthesis of directions. These requirements are typical of today's home and business computers; a car navigation computer could be a general device available also for entertaining children or for business use, especially if linked to an office computer through a mobile cellular telephone.

Output Facility

The next half-decade will see CD ROM-based mapping applications both in vehicles and on desktops.

The VNA output facility must have a screen to display maps and to present various directories of streets and destinations. The 1985 Buick Riviera has an optional touchscreen CRT; other cars, such as recent Corvettes, have full-color LCD instrument displays. Another appealing output device would be a voice-synthesis unit to read directions, instructions, or descriptive text to the driver while the car is moving.

Input Facility

The VNA user must be able to request a function, specify a destination, or search through information stored in the system. A touchscreen or several function buttons around the display screen should suffice.

Map Storage

Navigation systems to date have used three different methods of map storage: photographic, digital image, and digitally encoded.

Photographic. Honda's Gyrocator uses photographic map storage. The user must slip a transparent map over the display CRT and register the overlay with the initial location of the vehicle. Given the power and flexibility realized by digitally encoded maps, it's doubtful that this technology will go much further.

Digital image.   The most publicized concept car, Chrysler's Stealth, uses videodisc images of paper maps in its "CLASS" (Chrysler Laser Atlas Satellite System). Others use videotape to achieve a similar effect. Chrysler reports having over 13,000 maps stored on its demonstration disc, covering the United States at several scale levels to permit zooming.

Digitally encoded.   A digitally encoded map is a data file describing the street network by connectivity and coordinates, augmented by street and city names and address ranges. This flexible and compact recording form supports many functions: DR map correlation, map display, specification of origin for DR reckoning, and selection of destination by street address or intersection. The digitally encoded map provides the most flexibility in windowing and zooming and can support shortest-path route-finding computations.

All three of these options presume that the map is stored on board the car, although Boeing's FLAIR (Fleet Location and Information Reporting) system was supporting closed-loop DR for 200 cars with central computing and map storage eight years ago. ETAK stores maps on audio cassette, taking advantage of a familiar medium and an inexpensive read mechanism. But this has two disadvantages: limited storage capacity and sequential access. Current "floppy" disks have less capacity than cassettes, and their virtue of random access is offset by a fivefold cost disadvantage for the hardware unit.

A panacea for map storage in vehicle navigation systems appears to be the compact disc used as a read-only memory for digital data. CD audio players are on the market for automotive music systems; only a modification to the error detection and correction circuitry is needed for data storage. Philips, a promulgator of the CD standard, is proposing automotive CD players wired for both in-car entertainment and information. Each CD ROM disc holds 550 million bytes of information, equivalent to over 100 ETAK cassettes.

Storage of "Other" Information

Only the CD ROM, or another laser disc like Chrysler's, holds the possibility of storing much information beyond the basic map. The point to establish here is that one CD ROM disc can store a complete digital map of every street in New England plus additional information equivalent to 300 unabridged copies of *Moby Dick*.

Virtually every automobile manufacturer has built both engineering prototypes and concept cars with navigation features.

Hardware Summary

An attractive vehicle navigation unit would require the computing power of a 256K IBM personal computer. It would share a CD player with the entertainment system, so the user would have access to both maps and music. ETAK's success with DR adds to the economic attractiveness of this location method, although a trouble-free system of the future might include a GPS or Geostar receiver for initializing, perhaps as an extra-cost option.

Mapping Considerations

Although it is easy to build digital map images by scanning existing paper maps at various scales, image storage is inferior to digital encoding for vehicle navigation for three reasons: Image maps do not support closed-loop DR; zooming and panning are relatively inflexible; and they require a separate index for looking up addresses of destinations. Note that the latter index is practically equivalent to the full content of a digitally encoded map.

An ideal digitally encoded map would have all streets represented with accurate and visually pleasing coordinates, and sufficient house-number and intersection information indexed to permit lookup of a precise street address or a street intersection. Additional useful information includes flagging one-way streets and turn restrictions and identifying highways and major arteries. These additions would permit highlighting of expressways on the map display and improve performance of route-finding algorithms.

This basic map information, judiciously compressed, amounts to 120 to 150 bytes per street. Since 60 percent of the U.S. population lives on about one million streets represented in the Census Bureau's GBF/DIME files (the basis for proprietary digital maps owned by GDT and ETAK), a simple extrapolation, allowing for rural streets that wiggle more than their urban counterparts, yields a nationwide digital map that will fit on one CD ROM disc.

Although it's possible to fit all the country on one CD ROM disc, it would make more sense to publish regional or state discs supplemented with a wealth of information targeted for specific markets. The business edition, for example, would contain a list of all companies in the region indexed by both industrial classification and geographic location. The family edition would have data about restaurants, tourist attractions, shopping centers, stores, and museums. The great capacity of CD ROM would permit an expansion of additional information well beyond the state birds and insects depicted on conventional highway maps.

Desktop Applications

A CD ROM street map doesn't have to be in a car in order to be useful. Availability of inexpensive CD ROM players that can be plugged into a personal computer will open up many new applications. To get an idea of the range of industries that will benefit from automated desktop street maps, consider:

Although it's possible to fit all the country on one CD ROM disc, it would make more sense to publish regional or state discs supplemented with a wealth of information targeted for specific markets.

○ Automated dispatching of taxicabs by pre-encoded geographic zones, reducing the possibility of favoritism on the part of the dispatcher

○ Assignment and sequencing of service calls by plumbers and repair personnel

○ Evaluating market and competition potential for 24-hour teller and bank branch sites

○ Routing delivery and pickup vehicles

○ Sales territory alignment and sales call planning

○ Modeling postal carrier routes for zip code and carrier route realignment

○ Evaluating performance of systems for home delivery of prepared food, redesignating assignment zones to conform with delivery performance

○ Inserting new customers into solid-waste pickup service routes, considering time and capacity constraints

○ Market penetration and trade area analysis

None of these are new applications. GDT is currently supporting most of these functions. However, the users are characterized as mainframe owners for the most part; they need the computer infrastructure capable of handling large volumes of data sent to them on several reels of industry-standard computer tape.

CD ROM's potential as an inexpensive medium for distribution of large digital maps overcomes the last hardware barrier to widespread digital map use. We need good software—a "spatial Spreadsheet"—to make tailoring a geographic system as accessible as creating a cash-flow system on Lotus 1-2-3.

562

CD ROM remains an enigma, a solution looking for a problem.

In conclusion, the market for read/write optical discs is evident as the next step in the evolution of online random access storage following Winchester disks. The market for write-once discs can be developed, at least for inexpensive off-line data backup. However, CD ROM remains an enigma, a solution looking for a problem. There has to be a use for this device beyond an online *Encyclopaedia Britannica*.

About the Author

Donald Cooke was a member of the Census Use Study team that developed the DIME method of map encoding in 1967. He was a founder of Urban Data Processing, Inc., a company that sells geographic data analysis services and software to commercial clients. Since 1980 his present company has served as an author and publisher of digital maps supporting thematic data display, vehicle routing, and in-car navigation. His publications include a series of technical comic books written for the Census Bureau. He is a member of ACSM, URISA, and NCGA.

Donald F. Cooke, Chairman
Geographic Data Technology, Inc.
13 Dartmouth College Highway
Lyme, New Hampshire 03768
(603) 795-2183

Cartographic Databases

by Stanley K. Honey
and Marvin S. White

CD ROM is an ideal storage medium for digital maps. Data volumes are very large, and random access is required for many applications. Etak has developed a digital map database which is used in conjunction with a vehicle navigation system. This database can be licensed for use in other applications. With CD ROM storage, the variety and depth of such applications is expected to expand dramatically.

The Etak digital street map database currently includes the San Francisco Bay Area, southern California, Detroit, Chicago, and the Eastern Seaboard from Boston through New York and Baltimore through Washington D.C. It will soon include Houston, Dallas-Ft. Worth, Atlanta, Seattle, and Miami, and within a year every metropolitan area in the United States.

Accuracy and Contents

Every map feature in Etak's digital map database is located by latitude-longitude coordinates to within 40 feet of its true location as determined by survey, but more importantly, within 20 feet of its location relative to other nearby features. Errors and omissions occur, and maps are always partially out of date because building is continuous. But Etak's digital map requirements specify that 98 percent of the coordinates are within the stated limits and 95 percent of the street network connections are correct.

Having detailed map features located accurately is insufficient for a digital map to be useful; other data is necessary as well. Streets must be prioritized according to travel characteristics: limited access, highway, arterial, collector, local street, ramp, and so on. Numeric addresses must be stored at every intersection to allow destinations to be found by matching street addresses entered by the user. Other types of information must be included, such as city names, zip codes, SMSAs, census tracts, elevation, and even information about the local magnetic field.

Topology

For a digital map covering a large area to be useful, more is required than merely coordinates, street names, classifications, and addresses. The final requirement is really the first requirement; it is at the core of any digital map database, and failure to provide it is the cause of many failures of automated mapping applications. This requirement is topology. A digital map must be able to provide answers to the questions a person viewing a paper map could easily answer, such as, "What cities are adjacent to Menlo Park?" To do this, it must explicitly contain a complete topological description of the map.

The central idea of topology, which is a branch of mathematics, is the *neighborhood.* In the neighborhood of a downtown intersection are the incident streets and the adjacent city blocks; in the neighborhood of a street segment are the endpoints (intersections or cul de sacs) and blocks on both sides; and in the neighborhood of a city block are the bounding streets or waterways, intersections, and adjacent city blocks. This is all information immediately grasped by geometric intuition without explicit statement (when viewing a paper map), but this information is required in exact and complete detail for automated use.

DIME Data Interchange Format

Etak's map database contains all this data in a format that includes topological relationships. This is the familiar (to digital map aficionados) DIME (Dual Incidence Matrix Encoded) format. Every record in a DIME file represents a line segment on the map and contains data about the bounding endpoints and the cobounding areas left and right. The topological name for a point is 0-cell, line is 1-cell, and area is 2-cell.

Nongeometric data is associated with the appropriate cells. For example, a city consists of many 2-cells and those 2-cells carry the city code. Likewise, a street is a chain of 1-cells and those 1-cells carry the street name. And 0-cells carry address information. For a detailed description of how the data is represented in Etak's DIME files, consult the File Specifications section at the end of this article.

Vehicle Navigation Considerations

Any database application has performance requirements in addition to data content requirements, but vehicle navigation is more demanding than most. The onboard computer must be able to find destinations quickly, maintain a map cache in DRAM that covers the vehicle's current location and its neighborhood, update that map for changes in position as the vehicle moves at highway speeds, and display that map in great detail in the immediate vicinity and decreasing detail as one views more distant regions. Topology is essential in efficiently performing these tasks.

Etak has developed a database structure that, like the DIME structure, maintains topological information but is specially designed for efficiency in the navigation application. While this structure is essential for the real-time requirements of vehicle navigation, its specialization and complexity put it beyond the scope of this discussion.

565

CD ROM and Vehicle Navigation

Having detailed map features located accurately is insufficient for a digital map to be useful; other data is necessary as well.

The present Etak Navigator™ uses a high-speed tape drive that has been specially designed to perform in the environmental rigors of the automobile. While tape storage allows the Navigator to be produced now, and offers useful map coverage per tape, we are eagerly looking forward to the improvements that CD ROM promises to provide. These improvements include faster data transfer and access to 100 times the amount of data. The CD ROM-based navigator will operate more quickly, particularly in destination finding, but the truly dramatic difference will be due to the two orders of magnitude increase in data capacity.

CD ROMs will permit coverage of entire states or regions of the country on a single Etakmap™. Indeed, we could squeeze the whole U.S. street map onto a single CD ROM. But there are many other more promising uses of the space, such as online geographically linked Yellow Pages, tourist information, roadside services, and motel and restaurant guides.

The geographic Yellow Pages is a fascinating example. A driver so equipped could find all the nearby hardware stores and select one based on proximity, operating hours, or other information retrieved from the CD. The automobile could become a fabulous information center, and considering its linkage to geography and mobility, a fabulously useful one.

Digital Maps Outside the Vehicle

Since maps are necessary to navigation, Etak has focused its attention on in-vehicle uses of maps, but useful applications of the same digital map database in the office and home abound. With a standard CD ROM reader attached as a peripheral to your personal computer, it won't be necessary to trudge out to your car to scan the Yellow Pages or review a map.

Etak's digital map database is unique in positional accuracy and broad coverage. By the end of 1986 every major U.S. city will be digitized with the relative accuracy of a car length. The database highlights major streets and highways and shows every local street and ramp. This, combined with relatively complete address data, presents an extremely useful general-purpose map database. We expect a significant part of our business will be licensing the digital map database for myriad uses beyond navigation.

Consider, for example, the services a travel agent could provide, armed with a digital map of all the major metropolitan areas combined with hotel and motel locations. The agent could call up a plot on a graphics monitor showing the location of your appointment and its environs. The display could also show hotels or rental car offices in the area and permit immediate selection. The agent could even print a map highlighting the important locations on a simple dot-matrix printer.

Out-of-plant facilities management, such as maintaining utility company equipment, is an exploding applications area for digital maps. The kernel of an information system for utilities is the so called land-base, a digital map. The building of such a land base is the major expense, major cause of delay, and the cause of many failures in the implementation of facilities management systems. The availability of Etak's digital map database eliminates these difficulties. The continuing availability in future years of Etak's map database with updated information removes a burden that utility companies were forced to bear just to do their jobs.

Automatic vehicle monitoring of emergency service fleets, public transportation, and private service and delivery fleets is becoming cost-effective. Whether navigation is performed by augmented dead reckoning (à la Etak), Loran-C, or GPS (Global Positioning System), a digital map with automated address matching is essential to efficient use.

Geographically based information systems in many areas can benefit from the map database. For example, a large daily newspaper is using Etak's map database to build a computer system for home and business delivery, routing of trucks, market penetration analysis, locally targeted advertising, and billing.

Etak's Vehicle Navigation System

As mentioned earlier, the Etak digital map database was developed to support vehicle navigation. As an example of one novel use of digital maps, the Etak Navigator will be described. Central to the Navigator is a graphic display which continuously shows a vehicle's position on a map of the surrounding area. An arrowhead symbol in the center of the display represents the position of the vehicle and points toward the top of the map, indicating the direction the vehicle is heading. As the vehicle is driven, the map rotates and shifts about the arrowhead, in order to keep the area that is geographically "in front of" the car at the top of the map. Different-size streets are represented by lines of varying brightness, with streets and key landmarks labeled.

566

Any database application has performance requirements in addition to data content requirements, but vehicle navigation is more demanding than most.

The operator can change the map's scale. As the display scale is increased or decreased, features and labels appear and disappear in an orderly fashion according to their priority. At the most detailed scale, even the smallest streets are displayed and labeled.

The driver selects destinations by entering the street address and scrolling through an index to choose the street name. Alternately, a destination can be entered by selecting two intersecting streets. The Navigator then displays a map on which both the car and the destination are shown. The direction and distance to the destination are continuously indicated, which helps orient the driver if the scale of the map display is changed so that the destination is no longer shown on the screen.

Hardware

The Etak navigation system is packaged in three major parts: a processor, a cassette tape drive, and a display. The processor can be mounted in the trunk or other accessible location. The tape drive is small enough to mount under the dashboard or in the glove compartment. Access to the tape drive is required only to change cassettes. The display, which uses vector graphics for high resolution, is mounted on a flexible stalk near the dashboard.

In addition, a solid-state compass and two wheel sensors are required. The compass is approximately half the size of an audio cassette and mounts either inside the vehicle's roof or on the rear window. Sensors are installed on two nondriven wheels.

Specially manufactured cassettes, similar to audio cassettes, are used for map data and program storage. The primary advantages of this approach are 3.5-megabyte storage capacity, low media cost, low drive cost, tolerance to the automotive environment, tolerable access time, and present availability. Each map cassette covers an area comparable to that covered by two typical paper street maps. For example, one cassette allows navigation on any street throughout one third of the San Francisco Bay Area. Highways over an extended area are also included on each cassette.

Navigation

Dead reckoning.   Dead reckoning (DR) is the ancient technique of advancing a known position from measurements of courses and distances traveled. The Navigator uses dead reckoning, with wheel sensors to measure distance, and differential wheel sensors and compass to measure heading. The nondriven wheels are sensed rather than the driven wheels, which are more subject to errors during high-speed driving or driving in conditions of poor traction. An adaptive filter combines relative turn

568

information from the differential wheel sensors with absolute heading information from the compass. This signal processing allows effects of magnetic anomalies and wheel skids to be ignored. As with any DR system, errors in position accumulate proportionally to the distance traveled and proportionally to the inaccuracy of the sensors.

Augmented dead reckoning.   The Navigator takes advantage of the fact that automobile drivers tend to drive on roads if there are roads nearby. By matching the vehicle's track to the digital map, the Navigator eliminates the accumulated error that results from dead reckoning.

The Navigator uses other parameters to make decisions to update the road network stored on the map. These parameters include the connectivity of the road network and analysis of ambiguous update options. The key to system performance is proper updating. The algorithm uses information available in the map to make certain of update corrections.

The central idea of topology, which is a branch of mathematics, is the neighborhood.

Self-calibration.   The Navigator additionally uses the comparisons between the map and the DR track to continually improve the calibration of both the wheel and compass sensors. For example, if the DR track generally is "long" compared to the map, the wheel calibration will be corrected.

Display

The display is adaptively configured by an algorithm designed to select only the information that the driver is likely to need and to present it in a form which is readable at a glance.

Limited complexity.   The driver is able to change the scale of the map display, thereby adjusting the area shown. As the scale of the map is changed, road priority information encoded in the map database is used to select the roads to be displayed, and still keep the display complexity limited.

Selective labels.   Only the streets most likely to be of interest to the driver are labeled. These include cross streets ahead, high-priority streets ahead, the street being driven, and streets near a selected destination. Labels are always written near-upright and at a constant size, regardless of map scale.

Heading up presentation.   The *heading up* display orientation causes the display to correspond to the drivers orientation and therefore align with what is seen out the window. This allows the driver to quickly grasp information sought from the map display.

Conclusion

In order to produce vehicle navigation products, Etak has developed a nationwide digital map. While this digital map has already been licensed in other applications, CD ROMs may allow a far greater range of digital map applications to be developed for both office and home. In particular, CD ROMs allow large databases such as the described digital map to become available to personal computers.

The storage capacity and high speed (relative to tape) of CD ROMs makes them attractive for use in vehicle navigation. New applications are easily offered to owners of Etak Navigators because programs are stored on the map media along with the digital map and other data. This technique will become even more powerful with the greater storage capacity of CD ROMs. We are convinced that many important applications will be invented, and to encourage innovation, Etak will gladly discuss ways to help developers of digital map-related products for Navigators, or for other applications in the car, office, or home.

File Specifications

Record Contents

Each record includes the following data:

Data Item	Description
class	classification (local street, major road, etc.)
name	feature name (street name, highway name, etc.)
from–x	longitude + − ddd.dddd
from–y	latitude + − ddd.dddd
to–x	longitude + − ddd.dddd
to–y	latitude + − ddd.dddd
left–fradd	left from address
left–toadd	left to address
left–geography	geographic codes (city, etc)
right–fradd	right from address
right—toadd	right to address
right–geography	geographic codes (city, etc)
shape–n	count of following shape points

A *shape record* is the same size as a DIME record but contains shape point coordinates and reference to the corresponding DIME record. As many shape records as necessary follow a DIME record.

Data Item	Description
shape x 1	x coordinate for 1st shape pt
shape y 1	y coordinate for 1st shape pt
shape x 2	x coordinate for 2nd shape pt
shape y 2	y coordinate for 2nd shape pt
. . .	
shape x n	x coordinate for nth shape pt
shape y n	y coordinate for nth shape pt

Record Classification

In the table below, the first column of class codes contains the most common codes, which apply to fully verified data. The second column contains corresponding codes for data that has not yet been verified.

Class	Description
1 A	Interstate highway or equivalent
2 B	Major highway (limited access or partly limited access)
3 C	Access road (providing access to limited access highways) or minor highway
4 D	Arterial or collector
5 E	Local street
6 F	Unpaved
8	Railroad
9	Ramps (provides access from class 3 to class 2 and 1)
S	Shoreline
P	Political boundary
Q	High-speed ramps
N	Incomplete feature; coordinates are not correct but street name and address are presumed correct.

Feature classes indicate the type of feature or class of road. The classifications are meant to correspond to differences in driving and may vary in exact meaning from locality to locality. Classes 1 and 2 provide the pathways to travel across town. Class 3 connects the local net to the highway net, usually via ramps.

Geography Fields

The geography fields contain the following data:

city	place (city) code
zip	zip (postal) code
smsa	Standard Metropolitan Statistical Area
tract	census tract
block	census block

About the Authors

Stanley Honey is a founder of Etak and the inventor of the navigational algorithm on which the Navigator is based. In May 1983, Mr. Honey started work on this project and assembled the engineering group. He had spent the previous five years as a research engineer at SRI International. There, he was principal investigator and leader of programs that produced innovations in ultraprecise radio navigation, underwater optical instrumentation, over-the-horizon radar, spectrum surveillance systems, radio-frequency circuit design, and digital signal processing.

Mr. Honey's expertise in navigation is not limited to its engineering aspects. He is well known as a world-class navigator in offshore yacht racing. He navigated and won two Transpac races, the Southern Ocean Racing Conference, and the Bermuda Race, and navigated the highest-scoring American boat in the 1981 Admiral's Cup. Mr. Honey built navigational computers that were instrumental in serveral of these victories.

Mr. Honey has a master's degree in electrical engineering from Stanford University and has a bachelor's degree with a distinction in engineering and applied science from Yale University. While at Yale, he earned the Lamphier Prize for "proficiency in electrical engineering and initiative in research."

Marvin White came to Etak from the U.S. Census Bureau, where he was a research scientist on the Applied Mathematics Research Staff. Mr. White was a principal designer of the digital map database system, now used by the Census Bureau in its large-scale digital mapping program (the DIME system). As an expert in automated cartography, topology, and graph theory, he established the foundation for automated mapping and geoprocessing.

Mr. White was the principal researcher in several projects that resulted in advances in multivariate data storage and retrieval, record linkage, and interactive graphics. He provided direction and advice to federal, state, and local government agencies and to private producers of geographic products. Mr. White is the author of 20 professional papers on digital mapping.

Mr. White received his bachelor's degree in physics with high honors at the University of Illinois in 1969, and has done graduate work in physics at the University of Los Angeles.

Etak Inc.
1455 Adams Drive
Menlo Park, CA 94025
(415) 328-3825

Archive and Research Applications

Putting the Smithsonian on Disc

by Walter Boyne

All research centers, particularly libraries and museums, are in the midst of three crises of epic proportions. The first crisis is the fact that much of the documentation of the past, on paper, film, or microfilm, is in the slow but inevitable process of self-destruction. The second is that there is an explosion of new material being generated at a rate that threatens to stifle not only the capability to store it but interest in storing it as well. Finally, costs of handling material have grown so high that we can no longer afford hundreds of separate "rice bowls," each nurturing the needs of a particular institution.

Much of the documentation of the past, on paper, film, or microfilm, is in the slow but inevitable process of self-destruction.

Nowhere were the crises more evident than at the National Air and Space Museum (NASM), which had an additional difficulty because no genuinely systematic approach to acquiring data had been used in the past.

Countering all this bad news, of course, is modern technology, which offers the hope of solving some or all of the problems. At NASM we were faced with the certainty of fixed budgets, limited space, burgeoning material, and the need to provide service to other similar museums. We were somewhat conversant with current technology and had been following the individual developments in the field, yet our first approach to actively combat the crises was philosophical.

In a series of conversations, we established to our own satisfaction the following ideas:

○ It was necessary to begin, even though the optimum solution might not exist; we had to gain some experience in what did exist so that we would be aware of the potential of what might come along.

○ We needed to have an ultimate goal, one that might be considered impossible to achieve—grandiose, even—but something to fix our eyes upon, not for next year but perhaps for the next century. We decided that we needed a system which would permit us to acquire all of the air- and space-related archival material in the world, to have this material easily accessible and retrievable, to be able to index it automatically, and finally, to be able to transmit it to any other institution wanting it, all on an economically viable basis. We admit that this may never be achieved, but it is a worthy goal to work toward. And it has obvious implications for other similar organizations.

576

**It does not matter
who creates the
means for us to
reach our dreams, as
long as they are
reached.**

○ We needed a system that could be used by others, which meant that it had to be inexpensive and available. This, in turn, dictated that it not be a closed system but instead could make use of off-the-shelf material wherever possible. We also needed a system which would induce others to cooperate with us in the acquisition and dissemination of the material by demonstrating that they, too, could have access to all the material. By becoming the central archival point we would simultaneously make all other cooperating archival points also "central."

○ In essence, we wished to devise a system that could be used not only by major research centers but by every school system, library, and private researcher in the country.

For the first step in this program, we wished to have a system which would permit college students with relatively little training on the equipment to copy entire archives for transmittal to NASM. At NASM, the material would be transferred to digital discs and also, as time permitted, be indexed by a knowledgeable curator. We then wished to make the material available to anyone who needed it, either by a duplicate tape or disc or transmittal by telephone.

Our initial success has been greater than we might have anticipated; even our breadboard model of the System for Digital Display worked quite well. Now we are in the process of developing it further, bringing in new elements of technology almost monthly. Far from having exhausted the possibilities implicit in the basic concept, we now believe that our original goals may have been relatively modest and that continued development will permit an expansion of our hopes. In practical terms, the first production system has proved itself, and a number of government agencies and firms, both foreign and domestic, are in the process of acquiring and using the system.

At times during the process we were bothered by the thought that from somewhere a Walkman-type equivalent of what we were attempting would emerge, something that would do what we are trying to do better and at lower cost. Upon reflection we decided that nothing would suit us better, that it does not matter who creates the means for us to reach our dreams, as long as they are reached. No Walkman has appeared as yet, and we'll continue working. But as long as our goals are reached, either with equipment we develop or with the ideas of others, we feel that the current triple crisis can be overcome.

About the Author

Walter Boyne is director of the National Air and Space Museum, Smithsonian Institution.

Isocrates: Greek Literature on CD ROM

by Paul Kahn

In the summer of 1985 a group at the Institute for Research in Information and Scholarship (IRIS) at Brown University began to assemble the pieces that would become the Isocrates computing environment for Classical Greek scholarship. The project was undertaken in collaboration with Professor Gregory Crane of Harvard University and with the permission and cooperation of Professor Theodore Brunner, director of the *Thesaurus Linguae Graecae* (TLG) based at the University of California, Irvine. We wanted to make available to scholars at Brown the TLG database of Greek texts, which consists of approximately 250 megabytes of sequential ASCII files, representing the full text of all authors writing in Greek prior to A.D. 700. This includes all the Classical Greek poets, dramatists, philosophers, historians, and medical writers; and later religious writings such as the New Testament.

577

Isocrates, whom we chose as the namesake for the project, was a fourth-century B.C. Athenian educator, a contemporary of Plato, whose work is included in the TLG texts. Isocrates, the system, is composed of a number of hardware and software modules: an experimental workstation computer system, a database on CD ROM, a prototype CD ROM player, a full-text retrieval and display system, and a document preparation system customized for working in both Greek and English. At the outset we defined three major goals for the project:

○ Demonstrate the use of an interactive application for accessing a large database on a CD ROM within the workstation computing environment

○ Create a productivity tool by tightly integrating the search and display application with a publication-quality document preparation application

○ Test the current theories concerning file systems for the CD ROM by using a large full-text application in a real-world setting

578

The Initial Retrieval and Display System

A full-text retrieval system designed for accessing the TLG texts, developed by the Harvard Classics Computer Project, served as our starting point. This software generated an inverted index of approximately 100 megabytes; it contained pointers into the TLG texts that indicated the location and author of each term. A suite of programs, designed along the lines of the UNIX "software tools" model, then allows the user to search this index for the occurrence of a string or a list of strings in the works of an author or a list of authors. Once a hit is found in the index, the software allows the user to display the result in various forms. The user can display a list of the works in which the search term is found, the line in Greek containing the term, or the entire passage of the original Greek text. These programs were designed for a standard UNIX command interface, with the usual abbreviated command names, optional switches, and redirection of output and input with filters and pipes.

The Harvard index and search software, originally designed on a VAX running 4.2BSD, is portable to many other versions of UNIX now in circulation. The display software was designed to be adaptable to any display or printing device capable of supporting a full Classical Greek character set. In adapting this for Isocrates, we added two forms of screen display and two forms of printer support to the list of supported devices.

Text Display and Printing

Isocrates requires that Greek and English text be displayed on the console of the experimental workstation and printed on an associated xerographic-type-printer. The original output-device independent design of the Harvard retrieval software allowed us to adapt that code to this environment with a minimum of changes. The search display and the document preparation display were treated as two different output devices. When displaying Greek text as the result of a search, the display fonts on the workstation are controlled entirely by the system software. Once we had developed a set of Greek character bit maps and installed them in a font accessible by the system software, we developed a table which translated the TLG Greek coding into the appropriate escape sequences to display these characters on the screen.

Within the document preparation system for the workstation, both the screen display and printer fonts are independent of the system software and are controlled entirely by the application itself. For this application we developed a matching set of 10- and 12-point screen and printer fonts, since these are the two point sizes in which scholars most often work.

Within the document preparation system for the workstation, both the screen display and printer fonts are independent of the system software and are controlled entirely by the application itself.

A translation table for this format was then developed and installed in the retrieval software. This allows the user to save in a file on the local magnetic disk, in the format understood by the document preparation system, any Greek text found by the search software.

While we expect the experimental workstation to be used primarily as a single-user machine, it is capable of supporting a limited number of terminals or personal computers acting as terminals. The Classics Department at Brown already has several Apple Macintosh computers, and the Macintosh is the most commonly available machine among students and graduate students here. It can even display a Greek font, thanks to a program called GreekKeys, developed by SMK. The Mac was available to our user community and was clearly capable of meeting their needs for a "Greek" terminal while Isocrates was under development.

The Compact Disc File System

Before we could create the CD ROM we had to decide on the file format we would use for recording the data. None of the commercial formats available in the fall of 1985 addressed two fundamental issues:

○ How to make the format of the data on the CD ROM completely independent of any particular machine hardware and operating system

○ How to make it compatible with CD DRAW (direct read after write) technology

While the Isocrates environment would be designed to run initially on a particular workstation running a particular version of the UNIX operating system, we wanted to create the CD ROM in a format that would be usable from other kinds of machines and operating systems as well. We also were hopeful that some form of CD DRAW hardware would soon be available and would open up new possibilities for creating and customizing large databases from a workstation. We felt that much could be learned by working with a file system that tried to address these important issues.

Through the sharing of information across the various networks that connect academic researchers we heard of a project, addressing just these concerns, that was going on at the Advanced Media Laboratory at M.I.T. Simson Garfinkel, an M.I.T. undergraduate under the direction of Professor Walter Bender, had developed a file system for CDs which had been tested with DOS and UNIX operating systems and was designed to

580

accommodate direct recording of data using DRAW technology as well. Known as the Compact Disk File System (CDFS), it was made available to us in source code. Unlike all the commercial CD ROM file structures, CDFS assumed that it did have to account for where data might be written to the compact disc. Therefore the directory and file list was designed to be dynamic. We wanted to use this file format for recording the CD so that the disc could be read not only by the UNIX application we were designing but also by a DOS application on a smaller machine, and at some later point (i.e., when CD DRAW technology is available) integrate a writable user workspace with the static texts on the disc. This would allow users to create their own annotated versions of the texts directly on the CD itself.

A device driver had to be developed for the workstation to read data from a prototype CD ROM player. We are fortunate at IRIS to have a number of researchers who have been involved in the development of experimental hardware and software and are familiar with the internals of UNIX. Once the device driver was created, the CDFS was used to make the data on the CD ROM appear as a parallel file system to be called by the search and display application running from the workstation's local hard disk.

Extending the Scholar's Tools

To meet our goal of extending the tools currently available to Classics scholars we wanted to address two major areas: enhancement to the user interface for the casual as well as the sophisticated user, and integration with a document preparation system of sufficient quality for the preparation of scholarly books and articles mixing the Roman and Greek writing systems.

The target user community for this kind of application at Brown is a researcher with special knowledge in the field which the database addresses but no special knowledge about computer databases themselves. In this case we are trying to serve teachers and students of Classical Greek texts who would have only occasional use for the database itself. Such texts are used regularly by scholars in the fields of Classics and Classical archaeology, and are of potential interest to scholars in history, philosophy, linguistics, religious studies, and comparative literature. Brown's plan for the eventual widespread deployment of workstations makes the assumption that all faculty and research staff will have access to a workstation within their department. Plans also call for the establishment of an infrastructure of local departmental computer coordinators to provide training and support to users within each academic department or unit. Given this context we wanted to make the application simple to use and easy to support.

So to begin with we did not assume that all users would be familiar with the syntax of the command language of the UNIX shell. We expected that the typical use for the search and display software would be to respond to a specific research query. Such a query might be posed infrequently by a faculty member or graduate student. We wanted a user interface that would anticipate the most common types of queries and prompt the user through the system. We also wanted to make it as easy as possible for a casual user to "browse" through the electronic copy of the Greek text on the screen. Professor Crane provided a prototype version of the system driven entirely by a simple menu interface. As there was no windowing system or user interface toolbox to work with on the workstation, we chose to extend and refine the menu system already begun. Our efforts were put into making this interface as simple and consistent as possible.

581

A typical use of the TLG database might be to identify how a word was used by a particular author or authors. By searching for all occurrences of a word in the works of a particular author, the user can quickly generate a list of all works containing various forms of the word and follow that list to browse through relevant passages. With the computer such an analysis is quick and exact. With the ability to display and/or print any relevant passage, the researcher is not left with a cryptic list of references to follow through a large stack of printed volumes. Isocrates can analyze, identify, and print the desired texts.

We want to substitute the Isocrates environment for a typewriter surrounded by a stack of books marked with slips of paper referring to cross references scribbled on index cards spread across a desk.

Another anticipated use of the database is to identify and extract passages of Greek texts to illustrate scholarly writing. It is for this purpose that a tight integration between the search software and a document preparation system is essential. We see this application of the TLG texts as the one with the most potential for freeing the scholar's creativity. We want to substitute the Isocrates environment for a typewriter surrounded by a stack of books marked with slips of paper referring to cross references scribbled on index cards spread across a desk. The Greek texts will all be stored on the CD ROM. The relevant passages will be located by the Isocrates search software, which can store commonly used references in local files. The passages themselves will be extracted and stored as documents that will appear on the document preparation system desktop display. The process of identifying a passage of Greek text, extracting that text into a file on the local disk, and integrating that text into a document has been made as easy as possible. We hope that this ease of use will make it possible for the researcher to access the TLG texts as part of their writing process.

On the workstation itself, the search and display menu and the document preparation system desktop can be running in parallel, though only one can display on the console at a time. A researcher is free to switch between the search and display and the document preparation applications at the touch of a key. The writer can then follow a thought in a draft by browsing the text. If a relevant passage appears, it is defined by pointing at the top and bottom of the text with the cursor and saving a copy of this text in the document preparation format.

One of the greatest strengths of the document preparation system we chose to work with is its open architecture. Any document can be saved as a file consisting of only standard printable ASCII characters, coded in a published markup format. It is a simple matter, then, to translate into this format any TLG Greek text as it is read from the CD ROM. When the writer switches back to the document preparation application, this text appears as a document icon on the desktop. "Opening" this icon automatically loads the marked-up ASCII file into a WYSIWYG format so that the writer can see how the Greek text will appear on the page. The Greek text can then be printed directly or "cut and pasted" into another document.

Conclusion

By basing Isocrates on a CD ROM we are able to deliver to the individual scholar what had previously been considered a massive amount of data available only on a large computer system. We have indexed this data in the manner most useful to the scholarly user and provided an interface to that index which makes the location and display of text both quick and simple. We have tightly integrated the location and display of the text with the ability to move that text off the static data repository of the CD ROM into the dynamic workspace of a document preparation application. It is basic to Isocrates that the full text be thought of as not only displayable text but also usable text, capable of being integrated into current writing with no special effort on the writer's part. It is also basic to Isocrates that documents created be of publication quality. The users of Isocrates not only have the entire corpus of Greek literature at their disposal, they also have all the tools needed to mix the Greek and English languages as they compose the actual page image of their book.

We have integrated a foreign language which uses a non-Roman writing system with a publication-quality document preparation system.

We recognize that a database of Classical Greek texts is of specialized and limited interest, but we expect the principles illustrated by this project to have very general application. There are many other databases, currently filling hundreds of megabytes of hard disk space, which would be appropriate candidates for migration to CD ROM. While in this case we have integrated a foreign language which uses a non-Roman writing system with a publication-quality document preparation system, the same method can be used to integrate a vector graphics database with a document preparation system capable of displaying and editing both text and vector graphic objects. Once a system capable of dealing with text and raster graphics is available, the same principles can be applied. When the CD DRAW technology becomes available, then such systems can be adapted to allow for user workspace on the optical disc itself. The development of such systems, making use of large databases stored on compact disk of one kind or another, will bring powerful and affordable new productivity tools to universities in the years to come.

About the Author

Paul Kahn received a B.A. in English literature from Kenyon College in 1971, and in the past fifteen years has studied a variety of subjects including anthropology, computer science, and Chinese language. He is the author of *The Secret History of the Mongols* (North Point Press, 1984) and several volumes of poetry. He served as a consultant in text processing systems with the Office of the University Publisher and the Office for Information Technology at Harvard University, and as applications specialist in charge of new communications software at Atex, Inc. He joined IRIS in the spring of 1985 and is the manager of the Isocrates project.

Researchers at Brown's Institute for Research in Information and Scholarship (IRIS) have been pursuing developments in the areas of workstation computing, networking software, enhancements to the UNIX operating system, the impact of computer technology on the university environment, and new forms of educational software since the institute's inception in 1983. Research is currently supported by grants from the IBM Corporation and the Annenberg Foundation/Corporation for Public

584

Broadcasting. Interest in distributed workstation computing and the manipulation of large databases led researchers at IRIS to begin experimenting with CD ROM technology in the summer of 1985. As part of a major equipment grant from IBM, IRIS will be deploying new workstation computers to the Brown faculty and research staff over the next several years. The development of the Isocrates system for use by the Classics Department, and with it the integration of a prototype CD ROM device, is meant to add vast new possibilities for local online storage to these workstations, and with it the potential for sharing large databases across local area networks.

Institute for Research in Information and Scholarship (IRIS)
Brown University, Box 1946
Providence RI 02912
(401) 863-2001

RESOURCES

Contributors

We owe special thanks to the people listed here. All of them contributed to *The New Papyrus*, either by writing an article or by answering our questions and giving us advice. We couldn't have done it without them.

588

Mr. Allen Adkins
Optical Media Services
P.O. Box 2107
Aptos, CA 95001

Ms. Connie Bailey
3M
3M Center Building
223-5N-01
St. Paul, MN 55144

Ms. D'Ellen Bardes
Alltech Communications, Inc.
Grandin House
2101 Grandin Road
Cincinnati, OH 45208

Mr. Bob Barnes
Drexler Technology Corp.
2557 Charleston Road
Mountain View, CA 94043

Mr. Ron Barney
VideoTools
445 Calle Serra
Aptos, CA 95003

Mr. Mike Befeler
Reference Technology Inc.
1832 N. 55th Street
Boulder, CO 80301

Mr. David Bowman
1815 Province Road
Pt. Roberts, WA 98281

Mr. Alan Boyd
OWL International
Plaza Center
10900 N.E. 8th Street
Bellevue, WA 98004

Mr. Walter Boyne
Smithsonian Institution, NASM
7th and Independence Ave. S.W.
Washington, DC 20560

Mr. Rush Brandis
Washington State Library
State Library Bldg. AJ-11
Olympia, WA 98504

Mr. Joel Bressler
825 Van Ness Avenue, #407
San Francisco, CA 94109

Mr. Bryan Brewer
Earth View Inc.
Star Route
Ashford, WA 98304

Mr. Peter Brown
Computing Laboratory
The University
Canterbury
Kent, England, CT2 7NF

Mr. Henry Burgess
Microsoft Corporation
10700 Northup Way
Bellevue, WA 98004

Ms. Matilda Butler
Knowledge Access Inc.
2685 Marine Way
Suite 1305
Mountain View, CA 94043

Mr. Marc Canter
Macro Mind
1028 West Wolfram
Chicago, IL 60657

Mr. Robert Carr
Forefront Development Center
Ashton-Tate
150 Iowa
Sunnyvale, CA 94086

Mr. Bill Casey
Advanced Storage Concepts
9660 Hillcroft, Suite 325
Houston. TX 77096

Dr. Joseph Clark
NTIS, Room 30R
5285 Port Royal Road
Springfield, VA 22161

Dr. Gregory Colvin
Reference Technology, Inc.
1832 N. 55th Street
Boulder, CO 80301

Mr. Peter Cook
Grolier Electronic Publishing, Inc.
95 Madison Avenue
New York, NY 10016

Mr. Donald F. Cooke
Geographic Data Technology, Inc.
13 Dartmouth College Highway
Lyme, NH 03768

Mr. Steve D'Anolfo
Activenture
P.O. Box 51125
Pacific Grove, CA 93950

Mr. Rodney Daynes
Rodney Daynes Interactive Assoc.
5763 Beaumont Avenue
La Jolla, CA 92037

Mr. Dave Ditmars
Battelle Software Products
505 King Avenue
Columbus, OH 43201

Mr. Richard Doherty
CMP Publications, Inc.
3864 Bayberry Lane
Seaford, NY 11783

Mr. Chris Doner
Advanced Analysis
344 Westline Drive
Suite C-121
Alameda, CA 94501

Mr. John Dove
Dove Electronics
413 Ridgewood Drive
Rome, NY 13440

Ms. Terri Duer
Brodart Library Automation
500 Arch Street
Williamsport, PA 17705

Mr. Jerry Fand
Reference Technology Inc.
1832 N. 55th Street
Boulder, CO 80301

Mr. Walter Finch
NTIS, Room 30R
5285 Port Royal Road
Springfield, VA 22161

Mr. Edward A. Fox
Virginia Technical University
Department of Computer Science
562 McBride Hall
Blacksburg, VA 24061

Mr. Ray Fox
Learning Technology Institute
50 Culpepper Street
Warrenton, VA 22186

Ms. Jean Freedman
National Bureau of Standards
Systems Components Division
Technology 225, Room A216
Gaithersburg, MD 20899

Mr. John Gale
Information Workstation Group
501 Queen Street
Alexandria, VA 22314

Mr. Jock Gill
Computer Access Corp.
26 Brighton Street
Suite 324
Belmont, MA 02178

Ms. Lois Grannick
American Psychological Assoc.
1400 N. Uhle Street
Arlington, VA 22201

Mr. Mason Grigsby
Acctex Information Systems
131 Steuart Street, Suite 600
San Francisco, CA 94105

Mr. Andrew Hardwick
Reference Technology, Inc.
1832 N. 55th Street
Boulder, CO 80301

Ms. Linda Helgerson
CD Data Report
Langley Publications
Suite 115-324
1350 Beverly Road
McLean, VA 22101

Mr. Martin Hensel
Entree Corporation
P.O. Box 135
Wellesley Hills, MA 02181

Mr. Mark Heyer
Mark Heyer Associates
62 Mason Street
Greenwich, MA 06830

Ms. Diane Hoffman
Disclosure
5161 River Road
Bethesda, MD 20816

Mr. Paul Hoffman
Palo Alto Research Group
1020 Corporation Way
Palo Alto, CA 94303

Mr. David Hon
Ixion Inc.
1335 N. Northlake Way
Seattle, WA 98103

Mr. Stanley K. Honey
ETAK Inc.
1455 Adams Drive
Menlo Park, CA 94025

Mr. Stan Huntting
Reference Technology Inc.
1832 N. 55th Street
Boulder, CO 80301

Mr. Paul Kahn
Brown University
Box 1946
Providence, RI 02912

Mr. Philippe Kahn
Borland International
4585 Scotts Valley Drive
Scotts Valley, CA 95066

Mr. Robert Kerr
Alexandria Institute
2070 Chain Bridge Road
Suite 500
Vienna, VA 22180

Dr. Stephen T. Kerr
College of Education
University of Washington
Seattle, WA 98195

Dr. Chris King
Planar Systems
1400 N.W. Compton Drive
Beaverton, OR 97005

Ms. Nancy Kuchta
Micromedex, Inc.
660 Bannock Street
Suite 350
Denver, CO 80204-4506

Mr. Dennis Kulvicki
Academic Microbroadcasting
  Educational Network
P.O. Box 1247
Dickinson, TX 77539

Mr. George Langworthy
College Systems Integration
6025 Martway, #111
Mission, KS 66202

Mr. Leonard Laub
Vision Three, Inc.
2110 Hercules Drive
Los Angeles, CA 90046

Mr. Tony Lavender
Reference Technology Inc.
1832 N. 55th Street
Boulder, CO 80301

Ms. Jan Lewis
Palo Alto Research Group
1020 Corporation Way
Palo Alto, CA 94303

Mr. Howard Lipson
Reference Technology, Inc.
1832 N. 55th Street
Boulder, CO 80301

Mr. Tom Lopez
Microsoft Corporation
10700 Northup Way
Bellevue, WA 98004

Mr. Gerald Lowell
Library of Congress
Cataloging Distribution Service
Washington, DC 20541

Mr. James P. McNaul
Data Copy
1215 Terrabella Avenue
Mountain View, CA 94043

Mr. Brian Martin
The Library Corporation
P.O. Box 40035
Washington, DC 20016

Mr. Chris Mayne
Reference Technology, Inc.
1832 N. 55th Street
Boulder, CO 80301

Ms. Nancy Melin
Meckler Publishing
42 Grandview Drive
Mt. Kisco, NY 10549

Mr. Fred Meyer
Video Tools
445 Calle Serra
Aptos, CA 95003

Mr. Rick Meyer
DIALOG Information Services, Inc.
3460 Hillview Avenue
Palo Alto, CA 94304

Ms. Kim Miklofsky
626 N. Tejon Street
Suite 2
Colorado Springs, CO 80903

Mr. David C. Miller
DCM Associates
Post Drawer 605
Benicia, CA 94510

Mr. Rockley L. Miller
The Videodisc Monitor
P.O. Box 26
Falls Church, VA 22046

Mr. Robert Moes
N.A. Philips
100 East 42nd Street
New York, NY 10017

Ms. Mary Ann O'Connor
Compact Discoveries
1050 South Federal Highway
Delray Beach, FL 33444

Dr. Gabriel D. Ofiesh
Communications & Training Systems
    International
4031 27th Road North
Arlington, VA 22207

Mr. Bob Ogden
10085 S. Pinedale Drive
P.O. Box 1037
Conifer, CO 80433

Mr. Hernan Otano
Smithsonian Institution, NASM
7th & Independence Ave. S.W.
Washington, DC 20560

Dr. William Paisley
Knowledge Access Inc.
2685 Marine Way
Suite 1305
Mountain View, CA 94043

Mr. John Perkins
70 Willow Circle
Carey, IL 60013

Mr. Larry Press
Small Systems Group
Box 5429
Santa Monica, CA 90405

Mr. Michael Prounis
Arthur Andersen & Company
1345 Avenue of the Americas
7th Floor
New York, NY 10105

Mr. Leonard S. Rann
Micromedix
660 Bannock Street
Suite 350
Denver, CO 80204-4506

Mr. Raleigh Roark
Microsoft Corporation
10700 Northup Way
Bellevue, WA 98004

Mr. Barry Richman
Advanced Media Publishing
148 Stonewall Road
Berkeley, CA 94705

Ms. Carol Risher
Assoc. of American Publishers
2005 Massachusetts Avenue N.W.
Washington, DC 20036

Mr. David Roscetti
Arthur Andersen & Company
1345 Avenue of the Americas
7th Floor
New York, NY 10105

Ms. Stephanie Rosenbaum
Tec-Ed
P.O. Box 1905
Ann Arbor, MI 48106

Mr. Edward Rothchild
Rothchild Consultants
P.O. Box 14817
San Francisco, CA 94114-0817

Mr. David Roux
DATEXT
444 Washington Street
Woburn, MA 01801

Ms. Jane Ryland
Reference Technology, Inc.
1832 N. 55th Street
Boulder, CO 80301

592

Mr. Jim Sanders
AIRS
335 Paint Branch Drive
College Park, MD 20742

Mr. Edward Schmid
Digital Equipment Corporation
333 South Street
Shrewsbury, MA 01545

Ms. Julie Schwerin
Infotech
P.O. Box 593
Pittsfield, VT 05762

Mr. Kenneth Shain
GEOVISION
303 Technology Park
Suite 135
Norcross, GA 30092

Mr. Chris Sherman

Ms. Sue Simone
DiscoVision Associates
2183 Fairview Road
Suite 211
Costa Mesa, CA 92627

Mr. Truett Lee Smith
Talus Corp.
985 University Avenue
Suite 29
Los Gatos, CA 95030

Mr. James Solomon
MicroTrends, Inc.
650 Woodfield Drive
Suite 730
Schaumburg, IL 60195

Ms. Frances Spigai
Knowledge Access Inc.
2685 Marine Way
Suite 1305
Mountain View, CA 94043

Ms. Betty Steiger
Alexandria Institute
2070 Chain Bridge Road
Suite 500
Vienna, VA 22180

Ms. Robin Tygh
Borland International
4585 Scotts Valley Drive
Scotts Valley, CA 95066

Dr. Dennis Walters
P.O. Box 1905
Tec-Ed
Ann Arbor, MI 48106

Mr. Carl Warren
Mini-Microsystems Magazine
2041 Business Center Drive
Suite 109
Irvine, CA 92715

Mr. Marvin S. White
ETAK Inc.
1455 Adams Drive
Menlo Park, CA 94025

Ms. Pat Wimberly
Information Handling Services
15-T Inverness Way East
Englewood, CO 80150

Mr. Frank Withrow
U.S. Department of Education
Office of Educational Research and
    Improvement
400 Maryland Avenue S.W.
711-H Brown Building
Washington, DC 20202

Mr. Toby Woll
Computer Access Corp.
24 Brighton Street
Suite 324
Belmont, MA 02178

Mr. Richard Young
Nissei Sangyo America, Ltd
1701 Golf Road
Rolling Meadows, IL 60008

Mr. Bill Zoellick
TMS
110 West 3rd Street
P.O. Box 1358
Stillwater, OK 74076

CD ROM Resources

Listed below are the companies and individuals we made contact with in some manner while compiling this book. The code or codes to the right of each company indicate its classification according to the categories shown in the following table:

BP	Book publisher
C	Consultant
DB	Database
DP	Data preparation
DR	Disc replication
E	Education
H	Hardware
J	Journal
M	Media
O	Organization (trade or professional)
OP	Optical publisher
S	Software

3M
3M Center Building
223-5N-01
St. Paul, MN 55144
(612) 733-5211
(612) 736-4723   DR

Optical Recording Project
420 North Bernardo Avenue
Mountain View, CA 94043
(415) 969-5200DR

**Academic Microbroadcasting
   Educational Network**
P.O. Box 1247
Dickinson, TX 77539
(713) 534-4982   OP,O,DP

Acctex Information Systems
131 Steuart Street, Suite 600
San Francisco, CA 94105
(415) 543-4290   M

Activenture
P.O. Box 51125
Pacific Grove, CA 93950
(408) 375-2638   OP,DP

Adaptec Inc.
580 Cottonwood Drive
Milpitas, CA 95035
(408) 946-8600   C

Adaptive Data Systems Inc.
126 Pioneer Place
Pomona, CA 91768
(714) 594-5858   H

Adcomp, Inc.
44 Rogers Road
Haverhill, MA 01830
(617) 374-1002   C

Advanced Analysis
344 Westline Drive
Suite C-121
Alameda, CA 94501
(415)865-7531   S

Advanced Interactive Video
88 E. Broad St, Suite 1240
Columbus, OH 43215
(614) 464-2777   M

Advanced Micro Devices Inc.
901 Thompson Place
P.O. Box 3453, Mail Stop 140
Sunnyvale, CA 94086
(408) 732-2400   H

Advanced Storage Concepts
9660 Hillcroft, Suite 325
Houston, TX 77096
(713) 729-6388   H

Advanced Technology Libraries
701 Westchester
White Plains, NY 10604
(914) 941-2020

Agenda Technology
20 Park Plaza, #455
Boston, MA 02116
(617) 542-7440

AIRS Inc.
335 Paint Branch Drive
College Park, MD 20742
(301) 454-2022   S

Alcatel-Thomson Gigadisc
La Boursidiere-R.N. 186-B.P. 140
92350 Le Plessis
Robinson, France

18 Depot Street
Franklin, MA 02038
(617) 528-8890   H

ALDE Publishing
1050 Connecticut Ave. NW
Suite 300
Washington, DC 20036
(202) 966-7192   OP,BP

Alexandria Institute
2070 Chain Bridge Road
Suite 500
Vienna, VA 22180
(703) 883-0838   O

Allied Amphenol Products
4300 Commerce Court
Lisle, IL 60532
(312) 983-3500   H

Alltech Communications, Inc.
Grandin House
2101 Grandin Road
Cincinnati, OH 45208
(513) 871-7767   C

Amcodyne Inc.
1301 South Sunset Street
Longmont, CO 80501
(303) 772-2601   H

American Federation of Information
Processing
1899 Preston White Drive
Reston, VA 22091
(703) 558-3600
(703) 620-8926   O

American Psychological Assoc.
1400 North Uhle Street
Arlington, VA 22201
(703) 247-7814   OP,DP,BP

AMIGOS Bibliographic Services
11300 North Central Expressway
Suite 301
Dallas, TX 75243
(214) 750-6130   DB

Ampex
401 Broadway
Redwood City, CA 94063
(415) 367-2011   H

Ampro Computers Inc.
67 East Evelyn Avenue
Mountain View, CA 94041
(415) 962-0230   H

Apple Computer, Inc.
20525 Mariani Avenue
Cupertino, CA 95014
(408) 996-1010   H

Aquidneck Data Corp.
936 West Main Road
Middletown, RI 02840
(401) 847-7260   H

Archive Corp.
3540 Cadillac Avenue
Costa Mesa, CA 92626
(714) 641-0279   H

Arthur Andersen & Co.
1345 Avenue of the Americas
7th Floor
New York, NY 10105
(212) 708-4459   OP

Aspen Systems Corp.
1600 Research Blvd.
Rockville, MD 20850
(301) 251-5185

Assoc. for Information & Image
Management
1100 Wayne Avenue
Silver Spring, MD 20910
(301) 587-8202   O

Assoc. of American Publishers
2005 Massachusetts Ave. NW
Washington, DC 20036
(202) 232-3335   O

AT&T
2002 Wellesley Blvd.
Indianapolis, IN 46219
(317) 352-6124   H,OP

ATA Corporation
1260 West Bayaud Avenue
Denver, CO 80223
(303) 722-7704   H,OP

Atari
1265 Borregas Avenue
P.O. Box 61657
Sunnyvale, CA 94086
(408) 745-2500   H,OP

Audio Engineering Society
60 E. 42nd Street, Room 2520
New York, NY 10065
(212) 661-8528   O

AV Video
Montage Publishing Inc.
25550 Hawthorne Blvd, Suite 314
Torrance, CA 90505
(213) 373-9993   BP

Banyan Systems Inc.
135 Flanders Road
Westboro, MA 01581
(617) 366-6681   H

Baseline Corp.
1800 30th Street
Suite 314
Boulder, CO 80301
(303) 444-6993   H

Battelle Software Products
505 King Avenue
Columbus, OH 43201
(614) 424-7387   S,OP

Bear River Associates
1600 Oxford Street
Berkeley, CA 94709
(415) 644-1738   C

Bell Northern Research
P.O. Box 3511
Station C
Ottawa, Canada K1Y4H7
(613) 726-2260   RD

Bibliographical Center for Research
1777 South Bellaire, Suite 425
Denver, CO 80222
(303) 691-0550   O,OP,DB

Borland International
4585 Scotts Valley Drive
Scotts Valley, CA 95066
(408) 438-8400   S

Britton Lee Inc.
14600 Winchester Blvd.
Los Gatos, CA 95030
(408) 378-7000   H

Brodart Library Automation
500 Arch Street
Williamsport, PA 17705
(717) 326-2461   OP,DB

Broderbund Software
17 Paul Drive
San Rafael, CA 94903
(415) 479-1170   S

BRS
1200 Route 7
Latham, NY 12110
(518) 783-1161
(800) 833-4707   DB,OP

Bull Peripherals Corp.
766 San Aleso Avenue
Sunnyvale, CA 94086
(408) 745-0855   H

Business Trend Analysts
2171 Jericho Turnpike
Commack, NY 11725
(516) 462-5454   C

Cambridge Scientific Abstracts
5161 River Road
Bethesda, MD 20816
(301) 951-7810   OP,BP

Canon, Inc.
3191-T Red Hill Avenue
Costa Mesa, CA 92626
(714) 556-4700   H

CAPCON
702 H Street, NW
Suite 401
Washington, DC 20001
(202) 628-9644

Carrollton Press Inc.
1611 N. Kent Street
Arlington, VA 22209
(800) 363-3008   OP,BP

CCSI
16 Crow Canyon Court
San Ramon, CA 94583
(415) 820-5050   H

CD Data Report
1350 Beverly Road
Suite 115-324
McLean, VA 22101
(703) 243-2400
(703) 237-0682   BP

Charles River Data Systems
983 Concord Street
Framingham, MA 01572
(617) 626-1000   C

Cherokee Data Systems
2334 Broadway, Suite 206
Boulder, CO 80302
(303) 449-8850   H

Chorus Data Systems
P.O. Box 370
6 Continental Blvd
Merrimack, NH 03054
(603) 424-2900   H,S

CIE Systems
2515 McCabe Way
Irvine, CA 92713-6579
(714) 660-1800   H

Cinram Laboratories, Inc.
P.O. Box 4985
Irvine, CA 92716
(714) 854-2400   H

Cipher Data Products Inc.
P.O. Box 85170
San Diego, CA 92138
(619) 578-9100   H

ComDisc
3264 Motor Avenue
Los Angeles, CA 90034
(213) 836-4358   DR

Communications & Training
  Systems International
4031 27th Road North
Arlington, VA 22207
(703) 525-7471   C

Communications Trends, Inc.
2 East Avenue
Larchmont, NY 10538
(914) 833-060   C

Compact Discoveries
1050 South Federal Highway
Delray Beach, FL 33444
(305) 243-1453   OP,C

Compass Inc.
358 South Fairview Avenue
Goleta, CA 93117
(805) 683-6777   H

CompuCard
5025 Arlington Center Blvd
Suite 480
Columbus, OH 43220

Computel, Inc.
716 Adair Avenue
Zanesville, OH 43701
(614) 454-0191   H

Computer Access Corporation
26 Brighton Street
Suite 324
Belmont, MA 02178
(617) 484-2412   S

Computer Systems Management
1300 Wilson Blvd, Suite 100
Arlington, VA 22209
(703) 525-8585   H

Congressional Records
P.O. Box 848
Cambridge, MA 02142
(617) 740-1463   S,OP

Control Data Corp.
8100 34th Avenue South
Minneapolis, MN   H,S

Cosmos Inc.
19530 Pacific Highway South
Seattle, WA 98188
(206) 842-9942   S

Council on Library Resources
1785 Massachusetts Ave., NW
Washington, DC 20036
(202) 483-7474   O

CPT Corporation
8100 Mitchell Road
Minneapolis, MN 55440
(612) 937-8000

CTA Company Ltd
523 West 6th Street
Suite 361
Los Angeles, CA 90014
(213) 626-4731   H

Cuadra Associates
2001 Wilshire Blvd, Suite 305
Santa Monica, CA 90403
(213) 829-9972   S,BP

Cygnet Systems, Inc.
601 West California Avenue
Sunnyvale, CA 94086
(408) 773-0770   H

Daisar Corp.
3300 Mitchell Lane
Suite 320
Boulder, CO 80301
(303) 443-4634   H

Data 77 Ltd
130 West 20th Street
New York, NY 10011   H

Data Copy
1215 Terrabella Avenue
Mountain View, CA 94043
(415) 965-7900   H,S

Data General Corp.
4400 Computer Drive
Westboro, MA 01580
(617) 366-8911   H

Data Technology Corp.
2775 Northwestern Parkway
Santa Clara, CA 95051
(408) 496-0434   H

Datapoint Corp.
9725 Datapoint Drive
San Antonio, TX 78284
(512) 699-7000   H

DATATEK
818 NW 63rd Street
Oklahoma City, OK 73116
(405) 843-7323   OP

Datext
444 Washington Street
Woburn, MA 01801
(617) 938-6667   OP

DBS Films, Inc.
3 Great Valley Parkway East
Malvern, PA 19355
(215) 296-5850   OP

DCM Associates
Post Drawer 42145
San Francisco, CA 94142
(707) 746-6728   C

Del Mar Group, Inc.
731 S. Pacific Coast Highway, 2P
Solana Beach, CA 92075
(619) 259-0444   OP

Denon America
27 Law Drive
Fairfield, NJ 07006
(201) 935-5300
(201) 575-7810   H

DEST Corp.
1201 Cadillac Court
Milpitas, CA 95035
(408) 946-7100   H

DIALOG Information Services, Inc.
3460 Hillview Avenue
Palo Alto, CA 94304
(415) 858-3776   DB,OP

Digital Audio Disc Corp.
1800 N. Fruitridge Avenue
Terre Haute, IN 47804
(812) 466-6821   DR

Digital Audio Disc Laboratories
1860 Heather Court
Beverly Hills, CA 90210
(213) 276-5334   DP

Digital Equipment Corp.
333 South Street (SHR)
Shrewsbury, MA 01545
(617) 841-3776   H

146 Main Street
Maynard, MA 01754
(617) 897-5111   H

Digital Images Inc.
P.O. Box 17229
Washington, DC 20041
(703) 241-1180   DR

Digital Library Systems
1010 Rockville Parkway
Suite 405
Rockville, MD 20852
(301) 294-9380

Digital United
282 Cabrini Blvd
6th Floor
New York, NY 10040
(212) 923-1202   DP

Disclosure
5161 River Road
Bethesda, MD 20816
(800) 638-8076
(301) 951-1413   OP,S,DP

DiscoVision Assoc.
2183 Fairview Road
Suite 211
Costa Mesa, CA 92627
(714) 957-3000   H

Disk Latis
756-G Lakefield Road
Westlake Village, CA 91361
(805) 895-0825   H

Distributed Processing Technology
132 Candace Drive
P.O. Box 1864
Maitland, FL 32751
(305) 830-5522

Dove Electronics
413 Ridgewood Drive
Rome, NY 13440
(315) 336-5048   C

Dow Jones & Company, Inc.
420 Lexington Avenue
14th Floor
New York, NY 10170
(212) 285-5000   DB

Drexler Technology Corp.
2557 Charleston Road
Mountain View, CA 94043
(415) 969-7277   H

Droidworks
P.O. Box CS 8180
San Rafael, CA 94912
(415) 485-5000   OP,S,H

Dynamics Research Corp.
60 Concord Street
Wilmington, MA 01887
(617) 658-6100   RD,C

Earth View Inc.
Star Route
Ashford, WA 98304
(206) 569-2261   DP

Eastman Kodak Co.
Rochester, NY 14650
(716) 477-4749   M

EDR Media
3592 Lee Road
Shaker Heights, OH 44120
(216) 751-7300   OP

Edudisc
3501 Amanda
Nashville, TN 37215
(615) 269-9508   S

Elbit USA
400 West Cummings Park
Suite 2850
Woburn, MA 01801
(617) 938-3737   H

Electronic Arts
2755 Campus Drive
San Mateo, CA 94403
(415) 571-7171   S

Electronic Engineering Times
CMP Publications, Inc.
3864 Bayberry Lane
Seaford, NY 11783
(516) 679-8168   BP

Electronic Processor Inc.
1265 West Dartmouth
Englewood, CO 80110
(303) 761-8540   H

Elsevier Science Publishing
52 Vanderbilt Avenue
New York, NY 10017
(212) 916-1265   OP

Emulex Corp.
Emulex/Persist
3545 Harbor Blvd
Costa Mesa, CA 92626
(714) 662-5600   H

Encyclopedia Britannica
310 South Michigan Avenue
Chicago, IL 60604
(312) 347-7000   BP

ENDL Consulting
14426 Black Walnut Court
Saratoga, CA 95070
(408) 867-6630   C

**ERIC Processing and Reference
  Facility**
4833 Rugby Avenue, Suite 301
Bethesda, MD 20814
(202) 287-5137   DB,OP

ETAK Inc.
1455 Adams Drive
Menlo Park, CA 94025
(408) 328-3825   OP,H

Expert Systems Engineering
1459 227th SE
Issaquah, WA 98027
(206) 392-1295   RD

F. W. Faxon Co.
15 Southwest Park
Westwood, MA 02090
(617) 329-3350   OP

FileNet Corp.
3530 Hyland Avenue
Costa Mesa, CA 92626
(714) 966-2344   H,S

Filetek Inc.
6100 Executive Blvd
Rockville, MD 20852
(301) 984-1542   H

Finder Information Tools Inc.
1430 West Peachtree Street
Suite 611
Atlanta, GA 30309
(404) 872-3488   S

Force Computers Inc.
727 University Avenue
Los Gatos, CA 95030
(408) 354-3410   H

Freeman Associates
311 East Carillo Street
Santa Barbara, CA 93101
(805) 963-3853   O

Fujitsu America Inc.
3055 Orchard Drive
San Jose, CA 95134
(408) 946-8777   H

Fulcrum Technologies Inc.
331 Cooper Street
Ottawa, Canada K2P0G5
(613) 053-4939   H

Geographic Data Technology, Inc.
13 Dartmouth College Highway
Lyme, NH 03768
(603) 795-2183   OP

GEOVISION, Inc.
303 Technology Park
Suite 135
Norcross, GA 30092
(404) 448-8224   OP

Grolier Electronic Publishing
95 Madison Avenue
New York, NY 10016
(212) 696-9750   OP

Group L
481 Carlisle Drive
Herndon, VA 22070
(703) 471-0030

Health Management Systems, Inc.
502 Washington Avenue, Suite 777
Baltimore, MD 21204
(301) 494-4800   S

Hewlett-Packard
700 71st Avenue
Greeley, CO 80634
(303) 350-4000   H,S,OP

1819 Page Mill Road
Palo Alto, CA 94304
(415) 857-4758   H,S,OP

Highlighted Data
P.O. Box 17229
Washington, DC 20041
(703) 241-1180

Hitachi Sales Corp. of America
1200 Wall Street West
Lyndhurst, NJ 07071
(201) 935-5300   H

401 West Artesia Blvd.
Compton, CA 90020
(213) 537-8383   H

Houghton Mifflin
93 Chestnut Street
Spencer, MA 01562
(617) 725-5028   BP

IBM
10401 Fernwood
Bethesda, MD 20817
(301) 564-2724   H

IBM Research Division
Department K67-282
5600 Cottle Road
San Jose, CA 95193
(408) 256-4944   RD

ICCE
Special Interest Group/Videodisc
University of Oregon
1787 Agate Street
Eugene, OR 97403
(503) 686-4414   O

Image Concepts
P.O. Box 211
West Boyleston, MA 01583
(617) 835-3273   S

Image Peripherals, Inc.
42 Nagog Park
Acton, MA 01720
(617) 263-4005   H

Imagitex
77 Northeastern Blvd.
Nashua, NH 03062
(603) 889-6600   H

IMLAC
150 A Street
Needham, MA 02194
(617) 449-0708   H

In-Four
885 North San Antonio Road
Los Altos, CA 94220
(415) 948-1064   S

Inacom International
4380 South Syracuse Street
Suite 600
Denver, CO 80237
(303) 694-4200   OP

Index Technology Corp.
5 Cambridge Center
Cambridge, MA 02142
(617) 491-7380

Info/DOC
P.O. Box 17109
Dulles International Airport
Washington, DC 20041
(703) 979-5363   DB

InfoCorp
20833 Stevens Creek Blvd.
Cupertino, CA 95014
(408) 973-1010   S

Informatics General Corp.
6011 Executive Blvd.
Rockville, MD 20852
(301) 770-3000

Information Access Co.
11 Davis Drive
Belmont, CA 94002
(800) 227-8431

Information Arts
P.O. Box 1032
Carmel, CA 93924
(408) 659-5135   BP

Information Handling Services
15-T Inverness Way East
Englewood, CO 80150
(303) 790-0600   OP

Information Industry Assoc.
316 Pennsylvania Ave. SE
Suite 400
Washington, DC 20003
(202) 544-1969   O

Information Storage Inc.
2768 Janitell Road
Colorado Springs, CO 80906
(303) 579-0460   H,S

Information Today
143 Old Marlton Pike
Medford, NJ 08055
(609) 654-6266   BP

Information Workstation Group
501 Queen Street
Alexandria, VA 22314
(703) 548-0363   C

InfoTech
P.O. Box 593
Pittsfield, VT 05762
(802) 746-8504   BP

Ingram Book Company
347 Reedwood Drive
Nashville, TN 37217
(800) 251-5902   OP,BP

Inmagic
238 Broadway
Cambridge, MA 02138
(617) 661-8124   S

Innovative Data Technology
5340 Eastgate Mall
San Diego, CA 92121
(619) 587-0555   H

Institute for Graphic Communication
375 Commonwealth Avenue
Boston, MA 02115
(617) 267-9425   O

Institute for Scientific Information
3501 Market Street
University City Science Center
Philadelpha, PA 19104
(215) 386-0100   OP,RD

601

602

Integrated Automation Inc
1301 Harbor Bay Parkway
Alameda, CA 94501

Integrated Solutions Inc.
2240 Lundy Avenue
San Jose, CA 95131
(408) 943-1902   H

Intelligent Optics Corp.
238 Main Street
Hackensack, NJ 07601
(201) 488-8819   H,S

Interac Coorporation
6301 DeSoto Avenue
Wooodland Hills, CA 91367
(818) 888-8498   H,S

Interactive Technologies Corp.
5900 Wilshire Blvd.
Suite 2710
Los Angeles, CA 90036
(213) 937-4050   DP

Interactive Video Systems
180 North LaSalle
Suite 1902
Chicago, IL 60601
(312) 327-7550   H

Interface Group
300 First Avenue
Needham, MA 02194
(617) 449-6600   O

International Communications
   Industries Assn.
3150 Spring Street
Fairfax, VA 22031
(703) 273-7200   O

International Computaprint Corp.
475-T Virginia Drive
Fort Washington, PA 19034
(215) 641-6000   OP

International Interactive
   Communications Society
2410 Charleston Road
Mountain View, CA 94043-1683
(415) 922-0214   O

International Standard Information
   Systems
150 A Street
New England Industrial Center
Needham, MA 02194   OP

International Thompson
   Information Inc.
1611 North Kent Street
Suite 910
Arlington, VA 22209
(703) 525-5940

Interwest Applied Research, Inc.
Box 8189
University Station
Portland, OR 97027
(503) 223-3396   RD

Introl Corp.
5132 Oliver Avenue South
Minneapolis, MN 55419
(612) 929-3688   H

ITVA
6311 North O'Connor Road
Irving, TX 75039
(214) 869 1112   O

IXION
1335 N. Northlake Way
Seattle, WA 98103
(206) 547-8801   DP

JVW Electronics
111 East Chestnut Street
Suite 48G
Chicago, IL 60611
(312) 266-1089   H

KNM Inc.
6118 Swansea Street
Bethesda, MD 20817
(301) 365-0354

Knowledge Access Inc.
2685 Marine Way, Suite 1305
Mountain View, CA 94043
(415) 969-0606   BP

Knowledge Engineering, Inc.
758 South 400 East
Orem, UT 84058
(801) 224-7978   C

Knowledge Industry Publications
701 Westchester Avenue
White Plains, NY 10604
(914) 328-9157   BP

Konan Corporation
4720 South Ash Avenue
Tempe, AZ 85282
(602) 345-1300   H

Krauss-Maffei Corp.
3629 West 30th Street South
P.O. Box 9104
Wichita, KN 67277
(316) 945-5251   H

Kurzweil Computer Products, Inc.
185 Albany Street
Cambridge, MA 02139
(617) 864-4700   H

LaBudde Engineering Corp.
650 Hampshire Road
Suite 200
Westlake Village, CA 91361
(805) 497-4777   RD

Lancore Technologies Inc.
31324 Via Colinas
Westlake Village, CA 91361
(818) 991-5100   H

Laser Computer Corp.
3808 Rosecrans Street
San Diego, CA 92110
(619) 569-281   H

Laser Licensing Technologies
4720 West Montrose
Chicago, IL 60641
(312) 327-7550   C

LaserData
One Kendall Square
Building 200
Cambridge, MA 02139
(617) 494-4900   DP

LaserDrive Ltd
1101 Space Park Drive
Santa Clara, CA 95054
(408) 727-8576   H

Lasertrack Corp.
6235-B Lookout Road
Boulder, CO 80301
(303) 530-2711   H

LaserVideo Inc.
One East Wacker Drive
Chicago, IL 60601
(312) 467-6755   DR

1120 Cosby Way
Anaheim, CA 92806
(714) 630-6700   DR

Lazersoft
300 NE 97th Street
Suite D
Seattle, WA 98115
(206) 526-9928   OP

Learning Technology Institute
50 Culpepper Street
Warrenton, VA 22186
(703) 347-0055   E

Library and Information Technology
   Assoc.
113 Bailey/Howe Library
University of Vermont
Burlington, VT 05482
(802) 656-2020   O

The Library Corp.
P.O. Box 40035
Washington, DC 20016
(800) 624-0559   OP

Library High Technology
Pierian Press
P.O. Box 1808
Ann Arbor, MI 48106
(313) 434-5530   BP

Library of Congress
Washington, DC 20540
(202) 287-5664   OP BP

LINK Resources
215 Park Avenue South
New York, NY 10003
(212) 473-5600   BP

Macro Mind
1028 West Wolfram
Chicago, IL 60657
(312) 327-5821   DP

MAD Intelligent Systems
2950 Zanker Road
San Jose, CA 95134
(408) 943-1711   H

604

Materials Research Society
9800 McKnight Road
Suite 327
Pittsburgh, PA 15237
(412) 367-3003   O

Matsushita Technology Center
1 Panasonic Way
Secaucus, NJ 07094
(201) 348-7768   H

Maxtor Corp.
150 River Oaks Parkway
San Jose, CA 95134
(408) 942-1700   H

McDonnell Douglas Electronics Co.
P.O. Box 426
St. Charles, MO 63302
(314) 925-6351   DR

McGraw-Hill
1221 Avenue of the Americas
New York, NY 10020
(212) 512-4890
(212) 512-2090   BP

Mead Data Central
9393 Springboro Pike
Dayton, OH 45401
(513) 865-6889   DB, OP

2730 Sand Hill Road
Menlo Park, CA 94025
(415) 854-9440   DB, OP

Meckler Publishing
42 Grandview Drive
Mt. Kisco, NY 10549
(914) 666-3394   J

Memorex
San Tomas at Central Expressway
Santa Clara, CA 95052
(408) 987-1000   H

Methode Electronics Inc.
Data Mate Division
7444 West Wilson Avenue
Chicago, IL 60656
(312) 867-9600   H

Micromedex, Inc
2750 Santa Shoshone Street
Englewood, CO 80110
(800) 525-908   OP

Micromint Inc.
25 Terrace Drive
Vernon, CT 06066
(203) 871-6170   H

Microsoft Corporation
16011 N.E. 36th
Box 97017
Redmond, WA 98073-9717
(206) 882-8080   BP, S, OP

MicroTrends, Inc.
650 Woodfield Drive
Suite 730
Schaumburg, IL 60195
(312) 310-8852   S, OP

Milton Eisenhower Library
The John Hopkins University
Baltimore, MD 21218
(301) 338-8325   RD

Mini-Microsystems Magazine
2041 Business Center Drive
Suite 109
Irvine, CA 92715
(714) 851-9422   J

Mizar Inc.
302 Chester Street
St. Paul, MN 55107
(612) 224-8941   H

Mobay Chemical Corporation
Mobay Road
Pittsburg, PA 15205
(412) 777-2495

Modern Memory
225 Clifton, #106
Oakland, CA 94618
(408) 447-6591

Moody's Investor Services
99 Church Street
New York, NY 10007
(212) 553-0870   DB

Mouse Systems
2600 San Tomas
Santa Clara, CA 95051   H

N. A. Philips
100 East 42nd Street
New York, NY 10017
(212) 697-3600   H

N. A. Philips Corp.
Philips Subsystems and Peripherals
    Div.
100 East 42nd Street
New York, NY 10017
(212) 850-5125   H

National Bureau of Standards
Systems Components Division
Technology 225, Room A216
Gaithersburg, MD 20899
(301) 921-3723   O

National Decision Systems
8618 Westwood Center Drive
Vienna, VA 22180
(703) 883-8900   OP

539 Encinitas Blvd
Encinitas, CA 92024
(619) 942-7000   OP

National Library of Medicine
National Institutes of Health
Bethesda, MD 20209
(301) 469-1936   OP

National Memory Systems Corp.
355-T Earhart Way
Livermore, CA   H

National Planning Data Corp.
P.O. Box 610
Ithaca, NY 14851
(607) 273-8200

National Semiconductor Corp.
2900 Semiconductor Drive
Santa Clara, CA 95051
(408) 721-5000   H

NCR Corp.
1700 South Patterson Blvd.
Dayton, OH 45479
(513) 445-5000   H

Microelectronics Division
1635 Aeroplaza Drive
Colorado Springs, CO 80916
(303) 595-5795   H

NEC America, Inc.
8 Old Sod Farm Road
Melville, NY 11747
(516) 753-7000   H

1701 Golf Road
Rolling Meadows, IL 60008
(312) 981-8989   H

2909 Oregon Court Road
Unit B-3
Torrance, CA 90503
(213) 328-9700H

NEC Corp.
1414 Massachusetts Avenue
Foxboro, MA 01719
(617) 264-8438   H

New Media Graphics Corp.
279 Cambridge Street
Burlington, MA 01803
(617) 272-8844   H

Newport Systems Ltd
137 Lafayette Road
Hampton Falls, NH 03844
(603) 926-7800   OP

Newsbank
58 Pine Street
New Canaan, CT 06840
(203) 966-1100   DB, OP

NewsNet
945 Haverford Road
Bryn Mawr, PA 19010
(215) 527-8030   DB

NISO
National Bureau of Standards
Administration 101/Library E-106
Gaithersburg, MD 20899
(301) 921-3241   O

Nissei Sangyo America Inc.
150 East 52nd Street
New York, NY 10022
(212) 755-2900   H

NLM
Blister Hill Center
8600 Rockville Pike
Bethesda, MD 20209   OP

NTIS
5285 Port Royal Road
Springfield, VA 22161
(703) 487-4805   OP,BP

OCLC, Inc.
6565 Frantz Road
Dublin, OH 43017
(614) 764-6063
(614) 764-6076   OP

OMTI
Scientific MicroSystems
339 Bernardo Avenue
Mountain View, CA 94043
(415) 964-5700

Online Computer Systems
20251 Century Blvd.
Germantown, MD 20874
(301) 428-3700   C

Optical Communications Corp.
950 Norwood Road
Silver Spring, MD 20904
(301) 924-2800   H

Optical Disc Corp.
17517-H Fabrica Way
Cerritos, CA 90701
(714) 522-2370

Optical Media Services
P.O. Box 2107
Aptos, CA 95001
(408) 662-1772   DP

Optical Memory News
Rothchild Consultants
P.O. Box 14817
San Francisco, CA 94114-081
(415) 621-6620   J

Optical Recording Project
3M Center 223-5S
St. Paul, MN 55144   DR

Optical Society of America
1816 Jefferson Place NW
Washington, DC 20036
(202) 223-8130   O

Optical Storage International
P.O. Box 58063
Santa Clara, CA 95052
(408) 496-3236   H

Optimem Inc.
435 Oakmead Parkway
Sunnyvale, CA 94086
(408) 737-7373   H

Optotech
700 Wooten Road
Suite 109
Colorado Springs, CO 80915
(303) 570-7500   H

Pacific Electro Data
26732 Carretas Drive
Mission Viejo, CA 92691
(714) 770-3244   H

Padgett Nelson Industries
3684 Hedgewood Drive
Winter Park, FL 32792
(305) 678-6776   H

Palo Alto Research Group
1020 Corporation Way
Palo Alto, CA 94303
(415) 493-1191   RD

Panasonic
1 Panasonic Way
Secaucus, NJ 07094
(201) 392-4602   H

PATH
885 North San Antonio Road
Los Altos, CA 94220
(415) 948-1064

Pearlsoft
Box 638
Willsonville, OR 97070   S

PEP Engineering
390 N. Oak Avenue
Carlsbad, CA 92008
(619) 434-6023   H

PEP Modular Computers Inc.
600 North Bell Avenue
Carnegie, PA 15106
(412) 279-6661   H

Perceptronics
1911 North Fort Meyer
Arlington, VA 22209
(703) 525-0184   OP,H,S

Perkin-Elmer Corp.
2 Crescent Place
Oceanport, NJ 07757
(800) 631-2154   H

Pertec Computer Corp.
17112 Armstrong Avenue
Irvine, CA 92714
(714) 660-0488   H

Pertec Peripheral Corp.
9600 Irondale Avenue
Chatsworth, CA 91311
(818) 717-3445   H

Philips Information Systems, Inc.
15301 Dallas Parkway
Suite 300 LB 35
Dallas, TX 75248
(214) 980-2000   H

Philips Laboratories
345 Scarborough Road
Briarcliff Manor, NY 10510   H

Phillips Subsystems & Peripherals
    Inc.
1111 Northshore Drive
Knoxville, TN 37919
(615) 558-5110   H

Pioneer Video, Inc.
5150 East Pacific Coast Highway
Suite 300
Long Beach, CA 90804
(213) 498-0300   H

Planar Systems
1400 NW Compton Drive
Beaverton, OR 97005
(503) 629-2006   H

Plasman Data Systems
23938 Craftsman Road
Calabasas, CA 91302
(818) 704-5967   H

Point 4 Data Corp.
2569 McCabe Way
Irvine, CA 92714
(714) 863-111   H

Polaroid Corp.
565 Technology Square
Cambridge, MA 02139
(800) 225-2770   H

Priam Corp.
20 West Montague Expressway
San Jose, CA 95134-2085
(408) 946-4600   H

Pullman Assoc.
Business Synergistics International
P.O. Box 331
West Boylston, MA 01583
(617) 835-4803   C

Quantum Corp.
1804 McCarthy Blvd.
Milpitas, CA 95035
(408) 262-1100   H

R. R. Bowker Co.
205 East 42nd Street
New York, NY 10017
(212) 916-1727
(212) 916-1812   BP,OP

Rancho Technology
10238 Monte Vista
Rancho Cucamonga, CA 91701
(714) 987-3966   H

Rand McNally-Infomap, Inc.
8255 North Central Park
Skokie, IL 60076
(312) 673-9100   S,OP

Random House, Inc.
201 East 50th Street
New York, NY 10022
(212) 572-2271   BP

Raytel Systems Corp.
1299 Parkmoor Avenue
San Jose, CA 95126
(408) 297-6900   OP

Recognition Equipment, Inc.
P.O. Box 660204
Dallas, TX 75266-0204
(214) 579-6000   H

Record Group
3300 Warner Blvd.
Burbank, CA 91510
(818) 953-3211   OP

608

Reed Telepublishing
3303 Edenvale Road
Fairfax, VA 22031
(703) 385-3578   BP

Reference Technology Inc.
1832 North 55th Street
Boulder, CO 80301
(303) 449-4157   S,H

Resources Library Group, Inc.
Jordan Quadrangle
Stanford, CA 94305
(415) 328-0920

RMG Consultants, Inc.
P.O. Box 7279
Silver Springs, MD 20907
(301) 585-2299   C

Rosscomp Corp.
1695 MacArthur
Costa Mesa, CA 92626
(714) 540-9393   H

Rothchild Consultants
P.O. Box 14817
San Francisco, CA 94114
(415) 621-6620   C

Joan Rubin Associates
1640 San Pablo Avenue
Suite C
Berkeley, CA 94702
(415) 527-7037   OP

SETS
7660 Pinemont
Orlando, FL 32819
(305) 352-1533   E

San Francisco Examiner
110 5th Street
San Francisco, CA 94103   BP

Sanyo Electric
1200 W. Artesia Blvd.
Compton, CA 90220
(213) 537-5830   H

Science & Communciations Inc.
352A University Avenue
Westwood, MA 02090
(617) 461-0200   H

Scientific Micro Systems Inc.
339 North Bernardo
Mountain View, CA 94043
(415) 964-5700   H

SCOS Management
18138 Bancroft Avenue
Monte Sereno, CA 95030
(408) 741-0445   H

Seagate Technology
920 Disc Drive
Scotts Valley, CA 95066
(408) 438-6550   H

Sharp
10-T Sharp Plaza
Paramus, NJ 07652
(201) 265-5600   H

Shugart Corp.
475 Oakmead Parkway
Sunnyvale, CA 94086
(408) 733-0100   H

Sigen Corp.
1800 Wyatt Drive
Suite 7
Santa Clara, CA 95054
(408) 988-2527   H

Signetics Corp.
811 East Arques Avenue
P.O. Box 3409
Sunnyvale, CA 94088-3409
(408) 739-7700   H

Silver Platter
37 Walnut Street
Wellesley Hills, MA 02181
(617) 239-0306   OP,DP

Simon & Schuster
Electronic Publishing Group
1230 Avenue of the Americas
New York, NY 10020
(212) 245-6400   BP

Smithsonian Institution NASM
7th & Independence Ave. SW
Washington, DC 20560
(202) 357-1300   OP

**Society for Applied Learning
    Technology**
50 Culpepper Street
Warrenton, VA 22186
(703) 347-0055   O

Society of Photo-optical &
    Instrumentation Engineers
P.O. Box 10
Bellingham, WA 98227-0010
(206) 676-3290   O

Software Publishers Assoc.
111 19th St. NW, Suite 1200
Washington, DC 20036
(202) 452-1600   O

Sony
1359 Old Oakland Road
San Jose, CA 95112
(408) 280-0111   H

1 Sony Drive
Park Ridge, NJ 07656
(201) 930-6104
(201) 930-6106   H

Spectra Image
540 North Hollywood Way
Burbank, CA 91505
(818) 842-1111   S

Sperry Corp.
P.O. Box 4648
Clearwater, FL 33518
(813) 577-1900   H

P.O. Box 500
Mail Station B-200
Blue Bell, PA 19424
(215) 542-4011   H

SRI International
333 Ravenswood Avenue
Menlo Park, CA 94025
(415) 326-6200   RD

Storage Technology Corp.
2270 South 88th Street
Louisville, CO 80027
(303) 673-5151   H

Sun Microsystems
2550 Garcia Avenue
Mountain View, CA 94043
(415) 960-7359   H

Sysgen Inc.
47853 Warm Springs Blvd.
Fremont, CA 94539
(415) 490-6770   H

System Planning Corp.
1500 Wilson Blvd.
Suite 1300
Arlington, VA 22209-2454
(703) 558-3604

Talus Corp.
985 University Avenue
Suite 29
Los Gatos, CA 95030
(408) 354-5322   H,S

Tandberg Data Inc.
Data Storage Division
1590 South Sinclair
Anaheim, CA 92806
(714) 978-6771   H

TD Systems Inc.
24 Payton Street
Lowell, MA 01853
(617) 937-9465   H

TDI Systems, Inc.
620 Hungerford Drive
Suite 33
Rockville, MD 20850
(301) 340-3700   H

Tec-Ed
P.O. Box 1905
Ann Arbor, MI 48106
(313) 995-1010   BP,C,DP

Technics
One Panasonic Way
Secaucus, NJ 07094
(201) 348-7130   H

Tecmar
6225 Cochran Road
Solon, OH 44139
(216) 349-0600   H

Texas Instruments
P.O. Box 2909
Austin, TX 78769   H

Thompson Publishing Group
1725 K Street, Suite 200
Washington, DC 20006
(202) 872-1766   BP

610

Thorn EMI Technology Inc.
8601 Dunwoody Place
Atlanta, GA 30338
(404) 587-0017   H

Time Management Systems, Inc.
110 West Third Street
P.O. Box 1358
Stillwater, OK 74076
(405) 377-0880   S

Times-Mirror
Mirror Systems-Optical Research
    Division
2067 Massachusetts Avenue
Cambridge, MA 02140
(617) 661-0777   OP

Toshiba America
2900 Macarthur Blvd.
Northbrook, IL 60062
(312) 564-5140   H

Information Systems Division
2441 Michelle Drive
Tustin, CA 92680
(714) 730-5000   H

3910 Freedom Circle
Suite 103
Santa Clara, CA 95054
(408) 727-3939H

Triad Systems
P.O. Box 91779
Sunnyvale, CA 94088

Trintex
123 Main Street
White Plains, NY 10601
(914) 993-2466

U.S. Department of Education
Office of Educational Research and
    Improvement
400 Maryland Avenue SW
711-H Brown Bldg.
Washington, DC 20202   RD

UMI Electronic Publishing
University Microfilms International
300 North Zeeb Road
Ann Arbor, MI 48106
(313) 761-4700   OP

University of Illinois
Coordinated Science Lab
1101 West Springfield Avenue
Urbana, IL 61801
(217) 333-1074   RD

University of Illinois
252 Engineering Research Lab
103 South Mathews Avenue
Urbana, IL 61801   RD

University of Michigan
Computing Center
1075 Beal
Ann Arbor, MI 48109
(313) 763-4885   RD

USGS National Center
Mailstop 526
12201 Sunrise Valley Drive
Reston, VA 22092
(703) 860-6201   DB,OP

UTLAS Corp.
1611 North Kent Street
Arlington, VA 22209
(703) 525-5940   OP

VCM Systems Inc.
427 Sixth Avenue SE
P.O. Box 2789
Cedar Rapids, Iowa 52406
(319) 364-6959   OP

Verbatim
323 Soquel Way
Sunnyvale, CA 94086
(408) 245-4400   M

Vermont Research Corp.
Precision Park
North Springfield, VT 05156
(802) 886-2256   H

Video and Optical Disk
11 Ferry Lane West
Westport, CT 06880
(203) 226-6967   J

Video Computing
P.O. Box 3415
Indialantic, FL 32903
(305) 768-2778   J

VideoTools
445 Calle Serra
Aptos, CA 95003
(408) 476-5858   DP

Videodisc Monitor
Future Systems Inc.
P.O. Box 26
Falls Church, VA 22046
(703) 241-1799   J

Virginia Polytech Institute
Department of Computer Science
Blacksburg, VA 24061
(703) 961-5113
(703) 961-6931   RD

Visage, Inc.
12 Michigan Drive
Natwick, MA 01760
(617) 665-1503   H

Vision Three, Inc.
2110 Hercules Drive
Los Angeles, CA 90046
(213) 650-1683   C

Wang Laboratories
1 Industrial Avenue
MS 1307B
Lowell, MA 01851
(800) 225-9264   H

Wangtek
41 West Moreland Road
Simi Valley, CA 93065
(805) 583-5255   H

Wayne Green Publishing, Inc.
WGE Center
Peterborough, NH 03458-1194
(603) 924-9261   BP

West Publishing
P.O. Box 64526
St. Paul, MN 55164
(612) 228-2738   BP

Western Digital
2445 McCabe Way
Irvine, CA 92714
(714) 863-0102   H

Wicat Systems
Training Systems Division
1875 South State Street
P.O. Box 539
Orem, UT 84057
(801) 224-6400   S

Wilson Cambridge Company
450 University Avenue
Bronx, NY 10452
(212) 558-8400   BP

1 Elliot Square
Cambridge, MA 02238
(617) 492-0800   BP

Wilson Learning Corp.
2009 Pacheco Street
Sante Fe, NM 87505
(505) 471-6500   OP, E

Wolfdata
187 Billerca Road
Chelmsford, MA 01824   H

World Book Encyclopedia
510 Merchandise Mart Plaza
Chicago, IL 60654
(312) 245-2997   BP

Xebec
7650 McCallum Blvd.
Suite 2102
Dallas, TX 75252
(214) 437-5105   H

2055 Gateway Place
Suite 600
San Jose, CA 95110
(408) 287-2700   H

432 Lakeside Drive
Sunnyvale, CA 94086
(408) 263-4100H

Xerox
P.O. Box 1600
Stamford, CT 06904
(203) 321-8711   H

Xiphias
13470 Washington Blvd.
Suite 203
Marina Del Rey, CA
(213) 821-0074   S,DP

Zenith Data Systems
1900 North Austin Avenue
Chicago, IL 60639   H

ZetaCo
6850 Shady Oak Road
Eden Prarie, MN 55344
(612) 941-9480   H

Ziff-Davis
1 Park Ave
New York, NY 10016
(212) 503-3500   BP

ZyLAB
233 East Erie Street
Chicago, IL 60611
(312) 642-2201   S

INDEX

About the Editors

Steve Lambert's fascination with personal computers has led him to investigate many of their practical uses. He explored online information services in *Online: A Guide to America's Leading Information Services* and taught BASIC programming techniques in *Creative Programming in Microsoft Basic*. He wrote about Microsoft Chart in *Presentation Graphics for the Apple Macintosh* and *Presentation Graphics for the IBM PC*. In addition, Steve has contributed articles to *High Technology*, *Computing for Business/Interface Age*, *Macworld*, and *PC World* magazines.

Suzanne Ropiequet started her career at Tektronix and later became one of the first employees of Dilithium Press, an early microcomputer book publisher. In addition, she has conducted classes in applications training, written technical documentation, and has been a designer and consultant in the field of interactive video technology. Suzanne is the editor of the best-selling book *The Peter Norton Programmer's Guide to the IBM PC* and is the founder of the Northwest chapter of the International Interactive Communications Society, which specializes in optical disc technology.

The manuscript for this book was prepared for Microsoft Press in electronic form using Microsoft Word.

Cover design by Ted Mader

Interior text design by The NBBJ Group

Illustrations by Paul Ackerman, Jane Bennett, and Nick Gregoric

Text composition by Microsoft Press in Stempel Garamond with display in Futura and Univers, using the CCI 400 composition system and Mergenthaler Linotron 202 digital phototypesetter.

Other Titles from Microsoft Press

Running MS-DOS 2nd edition.
Microsoft's guide to getting the most out of its standard operating system
Van Wolverton $21.95

The Peter Norton Programmer's Guide to the IBM PC
The ultimate reference guide to the *entire* family of IBM
personal computers   *Peter Norton* $19.95

Word Processing Power with Microsoft Word
Professional writing on your IBM PC   *Peter Rinearson* $16.95

Getting Started with Microsoft Word
A step-by-step guide to word processing   *Janet Rampa* $16.95

Managing Your Business with Multiplan
How to use Microsoft's award-winning electronic spreadsheet
on your IBM PC   *Ruth Witkin* $17.95

The Apple Macintosh Book 2nd edition.
Cary Lu $19.95

Excel in Business
Number-crunching power on the Apple Macintosh
Douglas Cobb $22.95

The Printed Word
Professional word processing with Microsoft Word
on the Apple Macintosh   *David A. Kater, Richard L. Kater* $17.95

Microsoft Macinations
An introduction to Microsoft BASIC for the Apple Macintosh
The Waite Group, Mitchell Waite, Robert Lafore, Ira Lansing $19.95

AppleWorks
Boosting your business with integrated software
Charles Rubin $16.95

Command Performance: Lotus 1-2-3
The Microsoft desktop dictionary and cross-reference guide
Eddie Adamis $24.95

Online
A guide to America's leading information services
Steve Lambert $19.95

Available wherever fine books are sold.